Company and Industry Cases
in Strategy and Policy

**The Irwin Series in Management and
The Behavioral Sciences
L.L. Cummings and E. Kirby Warren**

Consulting Editors

Company and Industry Cases in Strategy and Policy

John A. Pearce II
University of South Carolina

Richard B. Robinson, Jr.
University of South Carolina

Larry D. Alexander
Virginia Polytechnic Institute and
State University

1986

IRWIN

Homewood, Illinois, 60430

©Richard D. Irwin, Inc., 1986

ISBN 0-256-03558-X

Library of Congress Catalog Card No. 85-82002

Printed in the United States of America

3 4 5 6 7 8 9 0 ML 3 2 1 0 9 8 7

We dedicate this book
with love and appreciation
to our parents:

Mary Frances and Jack Pearce
Mattie and Braden Robinson

Preface

The inherent strength of a case book is that it offers an extraordinarily high degree of flexibility in the study of business management in terms of the number, nature, and variety of strategic situations that can be investigated. *Company and Industry Cases in Strategy and Policy* was designed and written to maximize this advantage.

The case method is widely accepted as the best approach for helping students to acquire competence in the areas of strategic management and business policy. However, it is clear that case studies must elucidate and reinforce the teaching objectives of the instructor in order to maximize the benefits of the course.

Thus, in contrast to books that commit the professor and students to a single perspective on both conceptual materials and business practices, this book allows a professor the opportunity to specify the course pedagogy. In this way the course can best reflect the unique talents, needs, and interests of both the instructor and the class. Among other advantages, this approach allows a wide variety of case method options to be considered:

—*Company and Industry Cases in Strategy and Policy* can be used in combination with any conceptual materials of the instructor's choosing: a text, special readings, journals, articles, newspapers and magazines, or other handout materials chosen by the instructor.

—It can be paired with other instructional methods, including computer simulations and experimental exercises.

—It can be used alone to maximize the advantages of the traditional case-study method.

Company and Industry Cases in Strategy and Policy offers additional flexibility because of its unique packaging of 29 business cases around eight industry notes. Thus, users of the book have the options of studying industries, businesses, or for maximum benefit, businesses within industries. Further, because four companies can be studied in two-part sets (cases A and B), students have the opportunity to experience both the developmental problems in strategy implementation and the need for continuous environmental and competitive assessments.

The greatest strength of this book is in its case studies, and for these we are very grateful to 17 professors who graciously contributed their cases:

Sexton Adams, North Texas State University
Shelia A. Adams, Arizona State University
Stephen E. Barndt, Pacific Lutheran University
M. Edgar Barrett, Southern Methodist University
Richard F. Beltramini, Arizona State University
Mary Pat Cormack, Southern Methodist University
Beth B. Freeman, Portland State University
Robert R. Gardner, Southern Methodist University
Adelaide Griffin, Texas Women's University
James R. Lang, University of Kentucky
Patricia McDougall, Georgia State University
Timothy Mescon, University of Miami
Leslie W. Rue, Georgia State University
Steven A. Sinclair, Virginia Tech
Neil H. Snyder, University of Virginia
Barbara Spencer, Clemson University
Tom Van Dyke, University of South Carolina

We also wish to thank three authors who joined with us as collaborators in case development. Gratefully, we acknowledge the exceptional work of doctoral students J. Kay Keels and Frank Winfrey of the University of South Carolina and Jerry Fox of Virginia Tech.

Complementing the cases are three appendixes that will help students to perfect their skills in strategy analysis. "The Guide to Industry Analysis" (Appendix A) was authored by Michael E. Porter of Harvard University as an article in the *Harvard Business Review*. "The Guide to Financial Analysis" (Appendix B) was written by Elizabeth Gatewood of the University of Georgia. "The Guide to Information Sources for Use in Strategy and Policy Analysis" (Appendix C) was provided by Jugoslav S. Milutinovich of Temple University and was based on his recent article in *Business Horizons*.

Finally, we wish to express our appreciation to several individuals whose assistance and support enabled the timely completion of this book. Our special thanks are due Dean James F. Kane, Associate Dean James G. Hilton, Program Director Joseph C. Ullman and secretary Kathleen M. Fine, all of the College of Business Administration at the Univeristy of South Carolina, and Robert Litschert, Chairman of the Virginia Tech Management Department.

Jack Pearce
Richard Robinson
Larry Alexander

Contents

Guide to Strategy and Policy Case Analysis

The Case Method

The case approach to strategic management offers you an exciting new educational experience for several reasons. First, instead of learning only theory, the case-oriented course focuses your attention on what a firm should do in an actual business situation. Second, the case method forces you to think and to use your analytical skills. For example, what are the specific issues facing A&P grocery stores? Which alternative grand strategy should Eastern Air Lines follow? Or, what additional actions should NCNB Corporation take to implement its move into Florida banking? Third, the case course is exciting because it more actively involves you, the student. In addition to delivering lectures, your professor will lead the class in a variety of case discussions. Fourth, this course lets you apply concepts that you have already learned in other business courses. This might involve the four P's of marketing in one case, financial ratio analysis and projections in another case, and changes in the management organizational structure in still another case. Finally, this case-oriented course will let you apply concepts that your professor will present from the rapidly developing strategic management field. Thus, there are a number of reasons why case analysis can be an interesting and challenging course format.

The cases included in this book are written accounts of actual situations facing a variety of firms in different industries. Please keep in mind that

This material was prepared by Larry D. Alexander, John A. Pearce II, and Richard B. Robinson, Jr. and copyrighted by Larry D. Alexander, Virginia Polytechnic Institute and State University, Blacksburg, Virginia. Copyright © 1986.

these cases have not been written to illustrate either effective or ineffective handling of business situations. Rather, they provide you with the opportunity to analyze what actual businesses might do to manage different strategic issues. Thus, the cases usually include a variety of qualitative and quantitative data in the text portion and accompanying exhibits. Some of the information is clearly important, while other information may not be so important. Keep in mind that the case method is highly situational, rather than general. The lessons that can be learned from analyzing one firm facing a specific set of circumstances cannot necessarily be applied automatically to another firm facing a different set of circumstances.

The cases in this book have been grouped into six industry sets. Each set contains an industry note plus cases on three different firms in that industry. The industry note will provide you with an understanding of the overall industry, its historical development, its major segments, issues and trends that confront the industry, and strategies utilized by major firms. In addition, cases have been provided on three individual firms within that specific industry. At times, your professor will ask that you read only a case on a specific firm, and other times he or she will ask that you also read the accompanying industry note. Studying and analyzing more than one firm and its industry will help you gain rich insights into the strategic management process. We hope that you will enjoy this unique approach to analyzing cases in your strategic management course.

Preparing for Class

Since this capstone course emphasizes a new learning mode, namely analyzing business case studies, you will have to prepare for class somewhat differently. In a typical lecture, if you do not prepare, you can still learn by attending and listening to the professor's lecture. Not so in this strategic management case-oriented course. If you come to class without having read the case, you will derive little benefit from the case discussion. The following ideas are suggested to help you effectively prepare for cases that will be assigned throughout the course.

1. *Start Early in Preparing Each Case.* You need to get started early on each case for several reasons. First of all, many of these cases are quite long and take time to read. Second, since many strategic management cases involve multiple issues, it helps if you can give yourself some time to think about the case after reading it. Furthermore, the initial ideas you consider to help the firm address the strategic issue may not be as appropriate as the ones you later develop after giving the case some thought.

2. *Read the Case More Than Once.* Since strategic management cases contain broad issues that typically involve complex, multifaceted

organizational decision making, you are urged to read each case at least twice. The first reading will give you a good overview of what is going on with the firm and the issue it is confronting. The second reading, however, will help you to fine tune your understanding of the case and to comprehend more fully information you may have quickly read over before.

3. *Focus on the Case's Strategic Issue.* As you read the case, always be on the lookout for the key issue on which the case focuses. Sometimes, it is stated by the case writer in the case's introduction. Or, it might be buried among other not so important issues, facts, opinions, and symptoms in the case. There, your task will be first to identify the root issue that the firm faces and then to make recommendations to address it.

4. *Study the Exhibits.* You should analyze the financial statements, study organization charts, look at pictures of the firm's products, etc. that may be found in the exhibits. In sum, view exhibits as an integral part of each case which often contain valuable information.

5. *Put Yourself in the Proper Time Frame.* One important rule in case analysis is to put yourself back to the year when the case ends. If the case ends in 1984, then that year becomes the present year for the purpose of analyzing the firm and its industry. While it is all right to do outside reading on the firm and its industry, confine it to material written before the case ends. Do not do outside reading on the firm written after the case ended unless your professor directs you to do otherwise. Your professor wants to see what analysis and recommendations you can develop rather than to assess the firm's actual strategic moves since the case ended.

6. *Apply Business Course Concepts to the Case.* Although analyzing cases may seem theory free, it is not. Thus, try to identify theories from your other business courses that can be applied to the case at hand. Think back to your marketing, finance, production, and economics courses, among others, that might help you analyze each case. In addition, try to apply strategic management concepts that your professor will present throughout the course. By doing so, you will improve the quality of your case analyses.

Participating in Class

The strategic management course typically relies heavily on a discussion format. To make this class discussion format succeed, both your professor and you need to perform specific roles. Let's first consider your professor's role and then your own roles.

Your Professor's Role

1. *Lead the Discussion.* Your professor's role is to lead the discussion of the various cases you will analyze. The professor will work to stimulate the class as a whole to share their insights and observations about the case. Since your professor is trying to facilitate the class's discussion of the case, don't expect your professor to respond to every comment you make. He or she is trying to get other students to share that responsibility.

2. *Keep the Class on the Issue.* Since strategic management cases often involve multiple strategic issues, it is easy for class discussions to bounce back and forth from one issue to the next. At times, your professor may want to focus the class's attention on one specific issue before going on to some other issue. Your professor may even ask you to hold your comment on some new issue until closure has been reached on some earlier one. The request does not mean your point is unimportant, only that you should wait a while to present it.

3. *Play the Devil's Advocate.* At times, your professor may play the devil's advocate by offering alternative positions to the ones that you and other students are taking. He or she is not being argumentative nor attempting to be more devil than advocate; rather, he or she is usually testing you, exposing alternative viewpoints, sometimes to see how sure you are of your position. Don't back down, but rather offer support and reasons for the point you are making.

4. *Drawing Students into the Discussion.* The professor does this in various ways. First, he or she will call on volunteers. Second, your professor will call on students who do not have their hands up (even if others do), in an effort to get different students involved.

5. *Help Students Understand Strategic Management Concepts.* At times, your professor will lecture on strategic management concepts. He or she may first lecture on some strategic management concept and then ask you to read and analyze one or more cases that illustrate it. In other instances, your professor may first have you struggle with one or more cases, then lecture on a strategic management concept that can be applied to those cases.

6. *Be a Jack-of-all-Trades.* Perhaps your professor's most difficult task is being a jack-of-all-trades. While you are majoring in one specific business administration discipline, say finance, your professor is trying to understand general administrative issues and all the functional areas, marketing, accounting, production, human resources, and finance. This is no easy task, especially

since your professor is trying to keep up with the rapidly expanding body of literature in the strategic management field.

Your Role as a Student

This case-oriented capstone course also requires students to take on new and challenging roles. You cannot sit back passively. Some of your roles are as follows:

1. *Attend Class Regularly.* Since class participation is often given more weight in this course than in other courses, you need to come to class to do well.

2. *Come to Class Prepared.* There are real incentives for coming to class with a good understanding of the case to be discussed. First, it will enable you to appreciate more fully the class discussion. Second, it will help you avoid being called on by your professor when you are unprepared. Finally, third, it will enable you to take an active role in the class and to be a part of the enjoyable exchange of ideas.

3. *Enter into the Class Discussion.* If you come to class regularly and prepare for each case, it will make entering the class discussion of these cases much easier. Start early in the term to participate in the class discussions. Raise your hand when you have something to say. If your professor calls on somebody else who says the same thing, raise it again as soon as you have something to say on another issue. Almost all professors consciously try to recognize students with their hands up who have participated less often for that case. Participate by doing any of the following: (1) address the question your professor is raising, (2) build on some idea that some other student has made, (3) tactfully disagree with your professor or some other student, or (4) simply ask a question.

4. *Participate an Appropriate Amount.* You should strive to be an active contributor in your class's discussion of cases. Be a balanced contributor, however, and avoid either extreme. Avoid being the quiet student that never raises his or her hand, even though you have prepared for class. At the same time, avoid participating too much. If you continually dominate the discussion, other students may become resentful and stop listening to you, even when you have good ideas to offer.

5. *Look at the Big Picture.* Unlike functional courses in marketing, finance, human resources, and production management, this course concerns the top management of the firm. That is why this field is becoming increasingly known as strategic management, since it

focuses on the issues that general managers face. As you analyze the various cases, force yourself to look beyond just the issues that relate to a specific functional area to the larger ones facing the overall firm.

6. *Stay on the Topic.* In discussing cases in class, you need to listen carefully to what your professor and other students are saying. This will help you avoid making a statement that someone else made just a few minutes earlier. Conversely, if a new issue has just been raised, avoid changing the topic instantly to something else. If you don't have anything to say about that present topic, wait a while before calling the class's attention to some other issue that you feel is important.

7. *Have Your Case in Class.* Please be sure to bring your textbook with you to every class and have it open to the case being discussed. This is a good practice for several reasons. Your professor may refer to material on a specific page or ask your opinion on some exhibit material. At other times, your professor may read a short passage from the case and ask you to comment on it. Finally, your professor may ask the class to help him clarify a case fact. In any event, if you have your case out, you'll be able to refer to material quickly or to refresh yourself with notes you put in the margin of the pages.

Conducting the Strategic Analysis for a Firm

We recommend that you conduct a strategic analysis for the cases you analyze. This three-phased analysis, however, will vary depending on the actual case being analyzed and the specific assignment that your professor will give you. The three phases of this analysis are as follows:

1. Analyzing the industry.
2. Evaluating the firm's corporate level strategy.
3. Analyzing the firm's SBU strategies.

Analyzing the Industry

Analyzing an industry is a complex, yet important phase of the strategic analysis. Competition within an industry is influenced greatly by the various competitive weapons that each firm utilizes. Competition is also influenced by the suppliers and buyers to the firms in the industry. Understanding competition thus involves looking backward toward the firms' sources of supply and forward in the distribution channels to the buyers of the industry's products. Competition within an industry is also influenced by the industry success factors, which are those things a firm must do well in that industry to be successful. Finally, competition in an industry is influenced by substitute products being offered by other industries, which may have lower or higher price performance payoffs.

Some key questions to consider when analyzing the industry are as follows:

1. What are the industry success factors that firms must satisfy to compete well in that specific industry?
2. What are the different segments in the industry, and how much is each segment growing?
3. What stage of the product life cycle is the industry in, and how has this stage affected competition?
4. Who are the major suppliers to the industry, and how much power do they have relative to the firms in the industry they supply?
5. Who are the major buyers of the industry's products, and what do they value when making purchasing decisions?
6. To what extent do suppliers and buyers pose a threat to integrate forward or backward vertically into the industry?
7. How do substitute products from this and other industries compare on their price/performance trade-off?
8. What developing technological breakthroughs in other industries may adversely impact on the industry in coming years?
9. To what extent are foreign competitors occupying a dominant position in the industry?
10. What legislative or regulatory changes are threatening the industry, and how might they change the nature of competition within the industry?
11. What impact do economic recessions and inflation have on the industry?
12. What industry trends may cause the industry to change in the coming years?

Although the above list is not meant to be exhaustive, it should help you get started in doing an industry analysis. The important point to stress is that a firm's strategy should be developed and implemented with a thorough analysis of the industry in which it competes.

Corporate Level Strategy

A second phase of strategic analysis involves evaluating the firm's corporate level strategy. This is top management's overall game plan for running the corporation. For firms that compete within only one industry, the corporate level strategy may be the same as the SBU (Strategic Business Unit) strategy level. For multidivisional firms that compete in more than one industry, however, the corporate level strategy is usually different from the SBU level. In the latter case, the corporate level strategy is determined by a few people at the corporate level and within each SBU. Corporate strategists must first decide the overall purpose, corporate mission, and long-term objectives of the firm. With this in mind, top management then decides which industry segments to compete in and what game plan to pursue in each.

You should consider asking a number of questions as you analyze a firm's corporate level strategy. While the list that follows is not exhaustive, it should get you started understanding a firm's corporate level strategy.

Company Mission

1. What is the company mission, which describes the product, market, and technological areas of emphasis for the business?
2. What are the values and philosophy of the corporate top management, and how are they reflected in its mission statement or creed?
3. Are competitive pressures impacting on the firm that might necessitate changing its company mission?

Company Profile

1. What are the corporation's various SBUs and how well is each one performing?
2. What are the distinctive competencies, or strengths, of the corporation as a whole?
3. How has the corporation performed financially in recent years?
4. Which SBUs have been identified as resource generators?
5. What are common weaknesses that the corporation currently has in a number of its SBUs?
6. How do the corporation's SBUs stack up against key competitors in the various industries in which they compete?

Strategic Choice

1. What long-term objectives have been established for the corporation as a whole?
2. What is the current corporate grand strategy (e.g., concentration, diversification, vertical integration) which serves as the basis for the firm's competitive posture?

3. What acquisitions, divestitures, joint ventures, or vertical integration competitive moves would enhance the corporation's overall position?

4. How should financial resources be allocated among the various SBUs?

5. Which SBUs are most consistent with the corporation's mission and its long-term objectives?

6. What key threats and trends from the task and remote environment are affecting each SBU?

Operationalizing and Institutionalizing the Strategy

1. What are the basic strategic guidelines that the corporate level has established for each SBU?

2. How have key corporate policies and procedures been communicated to each SBU?

3. What sort of formal business plan is each SBU required to submit to corporate top management?

4. Does the corporation have the right managers in the right job at the SBU level to carry out corporate strategic decisions?

Control and Evaluation of Corporate Level Strategy

1. What quantitative and qualitative measures are used to evaluate each SBU's performance?

2. What rewards and penalties are being used to motivate key SBU managers to carry out the agreed upon SBU formulated strategy?

3. Is the desired synergy between the SBUs working out as intended?

4. Are interim objectives being met?

Strategic Business Level Strategy

The third and final phase of the strategic analysis is the analysis of individual strategic business units. These SBUs are sometimes referred to as divisions in a multidivisional firm. Some SBUs are separate companies, whereas other SBUs are divisions within the same corporation. A SBU vice president or general manager, who often heads them, reports to either a group vice president, who manages several clustered SBUs, or directly to the chief executive officer at the corporate level. Still, SBU vice presidents and general managers have tremendous power to shape the overall SBU strategy, as well as the supporting functional area strategies.

Some key questions to ask in evaluating the strategy for a specific SBU are the following:

SBU Mission

1. What is the specific mission for the SBU?
2. What present threats and trends might necessitate a change in the SBU's mission?
3. How could the SBU's mission be changed to address these environmental changes?

SBU Profile

1. What are the major strengths and weaknesses found within the SBU and its functional departments?
2. What is the basic strategy the SBU uses to compete within its industry, and how effective has it been?
3. Is the present strategy really capitalizing on its major strengths, or distinctive competencies?
4. Where do the SBU's products/services fall within the product life cycle?
5. How does each of the SBU's products and/or services stack up against its competitors' similar offerings?
6. What changes have been made in the SBU's strategy in recent years, and how effective have the results been?

Strategic Choice

1. Which strategy offers the desired risk level and best uses the SBU's key resource strengths to exploit environmental opportunities?
2. Is the chosen strategy within the SBU's realistic capacity to support it?
3. Are the choices compatible with the corporate level mission and long-term objectives?
4. Does the SBU possess the financial and human resources to implement new strategic decisions?
5. What SBU long-term objectives is the strategy intended to achieve?

Supporting Functional Strategies

1. What supporting roles must functional areas play to achieve the SBU's strategy?
2. How should financial and human resources be allocated between these functional areas?

3. What mechanisms should be installed to insure that the SBU's functional departments cooperate toward common goals?

4. What policies and procedures need to be established to help support new SBU strategy moves?

Written Assignments

You may be given a number of written case assignments in the strategic management course. These written analyses are a very essential part of this course; in fact, they are typically given more weight than exams and quizzes. While your professor will give you the specific format to follow in writing a case analysis, there are a number of helpful generalizations for you to remember.

1. *Analyze, Don't Just Rehash the Facts.* In preparing your report, avoid a long introduction that merely repeats what has happened in the case. Instead, start by analyzing the issue the case focuses on, and logically lead up to your recommendations.

2. *Write Deductively.* Writing deductively involves putting the topic sentence at the beginning of the paragraph. This helps the busy reader by making the main point first and then by supporting it with facts, elaboration, or whatever is needed to make your point. After the topic sentence, include only sentences that directly relate to the topic sentence.

3. *Use Item Labels as You Write.* Use item labels as you write to help the reader understand what you are writing about. If you are explaining a major strength of the firm, use the label "strength" in that sentence so your professor will know that you view it as a strength. Similarly use words such as weakness, opportunity, threat, alternative, or recommendation as labels so it will be clear that is what you are discussing in that paragraph. In addition, consider numbering some paragraphs to make your main supporting points for your topic sentence stand out.

4. *Identify Alternatives.* Keep your presentation in the proper strategic management sequence by first identifying several good alternatives, evaluating them, and then recommending the best one.

5. *Develop Specific, Reasonable Recommendations.* Strategic management professors usually want you to develop specific recommendations. Avoid recommendations that are so vague as to be meaningless or trite. Rather, develop specific recommendations that are clearly explained and well defended. It is important for you to appreciate that there are many, potentially right answers to the questions presented by the cases you will be analyzing. Your professor does not have one right answer for any of the questions.

Rather, your professor is most concerned about the support and reason-ing you can provide for your recommendation. Here is where you can sell your idea by using case facts to build a strong argument, by relat-ing your recommendation back to strategic management concepts that your professor will provide. For example, show how your recommenda-tion builds on the company's strengths, relates to its overall corporate mission, exploits relevant product/market opportunities, or minimizes company weaknesses and environmental threats.

6. *Address Implementation Considerations.* Your recommendation is more likely to be evaluated favorably when you can suggest how it might actually be implemented. Address some of the specific actions or steps that will be needed to achieve what you are proposing. For example, identify who should head up the strategic decision; how the organizational structure should be changed; specific rewards and penalties to motivate employees to implement something new; specific key tasks that will need to be addressed, among others.

7. *State Your Assumptions.* Cases, like real-world decision making, involve incomplete information. As a result, decisions are often based on incomplete information. Clearly state any reasonable assumptions you have to make in analyzing the case. This will help your professor to appreciate the perspective you take in your case analysis.

Oral Presentations

Your professor may also ask that you make an oral presentation on a specific case being studied in this casebook. Oral case presentations are usually done by a group of students, each covering one aspect of the overall case. If you are asked to make a class presentation, consider the following recommendations:

1. *Talk in Your Own Words.* Instead of memorizing your presentation, prepare for it by having a brief outline of key points you want to make. Then, mentally rehearse the speech or practice it orally by yourself.

2. *Help Your Audience Remember the Important Points.* State your key points clearly and provide reinforcing examples for each.

3. *Use Visual Aids to Clarify Your Point.* A good visual aid may greatly improve understanding of your presentation. It might be a one page typewritten summary of the main points your team is making. This could also be put on the blackboard in large, neat printing so students in the back of the class can read it. It could also be a graph, chart, or exhibit put on large poster board.

4. *Handle Questions in an Appropriate Manner.* During and after your presentation, you will probably be asked questions by other members of your class. During the formal phase of your presentation, try to address only points of clarification. Postpone any questions that require an answer of more than a few words until the question-and-answer period at the end of your formal presentation.

Working in a Group

Many professors require students to work in teams when analyzing cases. They feel that since strategic decisions are usually addressed by a group of key managers, you should similarly work as a student group to address issues that various cases will present. If your professor assigns group work, you should strive to be an effective member, realizing that your own performance is tied to the overall performance of your group.

Several suggestions are presented here to help you become an effective team member.

1. *Divide the Workload Equitably.* This is sometimes a difficult task because you do not know how much is involved with various tasks. One suggestion is to assign primary responsibility to different group members for different tasks. If there are three distinct parts of the case to be analyzed, then it might be appropriate to make a different person responsible for each part. All students should read and analyze the complete case, but different people can be made responsible for each major aspect of the analysis. The assigned student would also be the logical person to draft that portion of a written report or to present it orally in class.

2. *Talk with Other Team Members when You Have Problems.* Your team should first strive to resolve any problems among yourselves. Openly discuss such issues as (1) some members not doing their fair share of work, and (2) other members always insisting that their viewpoint be in the final report. Avoid the temptation of going to your professor and asking for a resolution.

3. *Develop Your Main Ideas as a Team.* A group case analysis is meant to be the combined effort of your student group. The whole group should go over each part of your analysis, even if individual members were afterward asked to write up separate sections. Don't fall into a tempting trap of having the marketing major address all of the marketing issues, the finance major all of the financial issues, etc. That will hinder your group's case analysis by having only one student make the decisions in a specific area. Furthermore, this strategic management course is trying to develop

your ability to look at the big picture facing top management, which involves your need as an individual to develop an ability to integrate all of the functional areas.

4. *Establish Regular Meeting Times.* Meeting outside of class is almost always a requirement of analyzing cases as a team. As soon as your group is formed, identify common free times during the week for your group to meet. Then hold these times open by scheduling other activities around them. Arrive at your meetings on time, begin on time, and have an ending time for that meeting. Several shorter meetings will accomplish a lot more than one or two marathon sessions right before a major case is due.

Conclusion

The case approach to learning about strategic management offers great opportunities for acquiring practical business skills because it provides the most realistic preview of how strategic decision making and strategic action actually occur.

The megatask of developing and assessing strategic alternatives requires the active involvement of many and diverse organizational managers, just as case analysis will demand a generalist perspective from students. As in business practice, success in this strategic management case course will depend on teamwork, careful preparation, creativity, objectivity and critical thought, multiple but well-integrated perspectives, and systematic decision making.

case 1 Note on the Brewing Industry

Historical Perspective

1   Lager beer was introduced in the United States by the German immigrants in the 1840s. By 1850, 430 small local brewers produced 750,000 barrels of beer annually. The number of such independent brewers increased steadily until the introduction of 20th-century technologies, including artificial refrigeration, mechanized bottling, and pasteurization. These new technologies allowed brewers to ship warm beer and to store it for long periods of time, thus providing the first opportunities for national distribution of what had previously been only a local product.

2   Repeal of Prohibition in 1933 catapulted the modern brewing industry into existence with the appearance or reappearance of some 750 brewing companies. Each company was independent, and no one company developed any early dominance in the market.

3   Following World War II, there was a structural transformation of the industry. Competitive pressures lowered margins, forcing expansion of operations to increase sales. Expanding firms began national advertising and national distribution. Economies of scale soon began to force large numbers of small brewers out of business. By 1970, only 92 of the 750 brewers originally opened were in production. By late 1983, this number was reduced to only 42 operations in an industry that had become dominated by two giants, Anheuser-Busch and Miller, trailed by a shrinking number of national producers.

This industry note was prepared by John A. Pearce II and Richard B. Robinson, Jr., both of the University of South Carolina.

4   In the early 1960s, the top 10 breweries produced approximately half of the beer consumed in the United States. The other half was produced by independents, which relied on local loyalty. An 8-firm concentration ratio, which accounted for 21 percent of all beer sales in the United States in 1947, grew to 63 percent in 1977, before leaping to 95 percent in 1983. Each of these firms also held substantial markets in other countries. For example, Miller High Life, Miller Brewing's most popular label, was produced and distributed in Canada by Carling O'Keefe and had become that country's third largest selling beer with approximately 10 percent of Canada's total beer market. Perhaps even more important to the nature of competition was the fact that more than half of total domestic sales was produced by Anheuser-Busch (33 percent) and Miller (21 percent).

5   In 1983, beer sales were up less than 1 percent over 1982—the result of a sluggish economy and lower beer prices. Domestic brewers actually suffered a slight profit decline, the first in 25 years, although Anheuser-Busch and G. Heileman Brewing Company posted significant volume gains among domestic brewers. Imported beers sold 5.7 million barrels in the United States in 1983.

6   In the face of increasing competition, many of the remaining rival firms are expected to merge or look for acquisitions to maintain their viability as industry participants. For example, Stroh acquired Schlitz after the Justice Department barred Heileman from acquiring the troubled Schlitz in late 1981 on the grounds it would produce too heavy a concentration in the Midwest. Heileman has been the most effective challenger for Anheuser-Busch on a regional basis, using a strategy of acquiring and reviving local brands, keeping production costs low, and employing aggressive (some say "cutthroat") marketing techniques. Its strategy has been to revitalize the acquired regional brands, gradually introduce other Heileman brands to the region, and then saturate the new market with highly promoted products. Heileman's base is the Midwest, and a Schlitz acquisition would have provided plants in the West, South, and Southeast—markets that Anheuser-Busch has targeted as its major sources of future growth. Reacting to the Justice Department's decision, an Anheuser-Busch spokesman said, "Stroh-Schlitz is a lesser competitive threat than Heileman-Schlitz." Russell Cleary, Heileman chairman, offered a different opinion: "We are the only company Anheuser-Busch does not do well against. The prospect of our entry into the South scared them." Unfortunately for Heileman, the Justice Department also rejected a Heileman bid for Pabst, while clearing the way for an Olympia-Pabst merger.

7   As Anheuser-Busch and Miller bring their fight into local and regional markets, a widely recognized industry analyst argues that there is no room in the industry for brewers of under 20 million barrels per year, because of the economies of scale needed to compete in production and marketing.

8   The top U.S. brewers and their 1982 sales and market share are as follows:

No. 1—Anheuser-Busch, Inc. (59.1 million barrels/32.0 percent).
No. 2—Miller Brewing Co. (39.3 million barrels/21.3 percent).
No. 3—Stroh Brewing Co. (22.9 million barrels/12.4 percent).
No. 4—G. Heileman Brewing Co. (14.5 million barrels/7.9 percent).
No. 5—Pabst Brewing Co. (12.3 million barrels/6.7 percent).
No. 6—Adolph Coors Co. (11.9 million barrels/6.5 percent).
No. 7—Olympia Brewing Co. (5.2 million barrels/2.8 percent).
No. 8—Genesee Brewing Co. (3.4 million barrels/1.8 percent).
No. 9—Falstaff/General Brewing Co. (3.2 million barrels/1.7 percent).
No. 10—C. Schmidt & Sons (3.2 million barrels/1.7 percent).

Industry-Life-Cycle Stage

9   The brewing industry's moderate 1 percent growth rate in 1983 was evidence of its position in the maturity stage of the life cycle. When compared to the 4 percent average annual growth of the 1970s, it appeared that the periods of product growth had passed for the brewing industry. Its maturity was further characterized by a large, saturated market and brand-conscious buyers, despite a relatively standard product. There was, however, increasing market segmentation in the industry with the introduction of new products in an effort to extend the life cycle and broaden product lines. Price and advertising competition was intense as the major brands battled for market share.

Suppliers

10   Suppliers of the brewing industry ranged from high-technology computer and genetic technology companies to financial institutions and farmers. They were so many in number and so diverse in the worth, quantity, and scarcity of their products that no one supplier enjoyed any significant power over the industry. A partial list of the major suppliers included producers of grain and farm products, aluminum, glass, plastics, cans, coolers, flowers, extracts, machinery and equipment, sweeteners, trucks, and computers.

11   The power of suppliers was also limited by the high degree of product standardization that characterized the industry. Beer was packaged in seven ounce, twelve ounce, sixteen ounce, and thirty-two ounce cans or bottles, all with essentially the same shape. Bottles of beer were almost always brown, and labeling procedures were not substantially different. Machinery and equipment needed to produce and distribute beer were the same throughout the industry. This standardization allowed the industry to avoid most switching costs.

12   Through diversification, partial vertical integration, and nearly explosive growth and profitability, Anheuser-Busch and Miller were approaching

monopolistic proportions. Because of their vast size and resources, the two major producers held further threats of backward integration over their suppliers and, through this potential threat, controlled supplier prices for the entire industry.

13   One major exception to the low-power supplier pattern involved the providers of enzymes and genetic technology that were used to shorten the fermenting process from nine to three days. The obvious value of these products in the savings of both time and money were vital to the production process, and the small number of producers allowed them some influence over the decisions of brewers.

Buyers

14   There are two distinct groups in the buying chain for the malt beverage industry: wholesalers or distributors who purchased directly from the breweries, and consumers.

15   American breweries had become increasingly concentrated during the decades of the 1960s and 1970s. This concentration affected their distribution channels. Between 1948 and 1958 the total number of alcoholic beverage distributors grew from 6,954 to 7,689. These figures include beer, wine, and distilled-spirits distributors as shown in Exhibit 1. However, since 1958 these numbers steadily declined to 6,523, a smaller number than existed in 1948.

16   Wholesalers who distributed beer labels with decreasing market shares found themselves with increasing cost ratios. Their strategic response was often to sell out to a larger distributor, usually one with a major brand. The resulting effect was a further concentration in the number of wholesalers.

Exhibit 1

Multiple alcoholic beverage wholesalers 1963–1982

Year	Beer Only	Wine & Spirits Only	Beer, Wine & Spirits	Total
1982	3,441	862	1,110	6,523
1981	3,561	888	1,078	6,601
1980	3,693	900	1,020	6,633
1977	3,998	866	838	6,540
1972	4,347	984	767	6,865
1967	4,773	1,007	699	7,178
1963	5,126	1,039	662	7,489
1958	8,020	1,869	—	7,689
1954	6,004	1,562	—	7,566
1948	5,401	1,553	—	6,954

Source: Beverage Industry and Beverage Marketing Corp., January 28, 1983.

Another trend was the combination of beer, wine, and spirits distributorships. A beer wholesaler, for example, with a label experiencing decreasing market share, might acquire the distributorship of a wine label that was experiencing increasing sales. Although wine sales were not near the total sales volume of beer, they were increasing in a pattern exactly opposite that of beer, as indicated in Exhibit 2.

17   The industry trend toward fewer and larger wholesale operations was expected to continue through 1990; then it was projected that one half of all distributors would have sales volumes in excess of $5 million; one fourth, more than $10 million; and almost 10 percent, more than $25 million in sales (see Exhibit 3).

18   A decreasing number of distributors, each with growing volume purchases, would yield greater buying power. Although there would still be a large degree of interdependence between breweries and distributors because of the distribution of one brewer's labels, the group gaining power in this scenario was clearly the distributors and not the brewers. It seemed apparent that in the late 1980s and beyond, brewers' strategic decisions would be influenced by the power exerted from wholesalers and distributors, resulting from the changes in market share of the labels.

Beer Drinkers' Profile

19   Half of the beer consumed in the United States in 1983 was accounted for by those aged from eighteen to thirty-four. As indicated by Exhibit 4, this group, which expanded between 1960 and 1980, will contract during the 1980–2000 period. It was estimated that 30 percent of all beer was consumed by the 18- to 24-year-old group, which will decrease in size by 75 percent in the period from 1980 to 1990.

20   The shrinking size of the major consuming group appeared to be compounded by the growing number of states enacting legislation to make the minimum drinking age 21 rather than 18 as it has been in the past. There were 12 states in 1975 with the 21-year-old requirement, which represented 27 percent of the total market. That figure had grown to 16 states and 40 percent of the market by 1981. The social and political views in the United States in 1983 were leaning toward increasing the minimum age to 21, and more states were expected to increase the minimum age, thus further shrinking the major beer drinking group and the demand for the product.

Threat of New Entrants

21   The most substantial threat to the American brewing industry came from imported beers. This was true despite the fact that these beers were substantially more expensive than domestic beer because of the additional costs, including import taxes, transshipment problems, intermediate buy-

Exhibit 2

U.S liquid consumption trends: 1970–1982

	1970	1971	1972	1973	1974	1975	1976	1977	1978	1979	1980	1981	1982
Soft Drinks	27.0	28.6	30.1	31.5	31.4	31.0	33.7	35.9	37.1	38.1	38.8	39.5	40.1
Coffee	35.7	35.3	35.2	35.1	33.8	33.0	29.4	28.0	27.0	27.7	26.8	26.7	26.4
Beer	18.5	19.2	19.7	20.5	21.3	21.6	21.8	22.5	23.1	23.8	24.3	24.6	24.4
Milk	23.1	23.0	23.1	22.7	22.0	22.3	22.1	21.9	21.6	21.4	20.9	20.6	20.5
Juices	5.2	5.7	6.1	6.1	6.2	6.9	6.9	6.9	6.6	6.7	6.9	6.7	6.6
Tea	5.5	5.8	6.3	6.3	6.2	6.2	6.4	5.9	6.7	6.6	6.6	6.5	6.3
Powdered Drinks	NA	NA	NA	NA	NA	4.8	5.5	5.9	6.2	6.0	6.0	6.0	6.0
Wine	1.3	1.5	1.6	1.7	1.7	1.7	1.7	1.8	2.1	2.2	2.3	2.3	2.3
Bottled Water	NA	1.1	NA	NA	NA	1.2	1.2	1.3	1.4	1.5	1.6	1.9	2.2
Distilled Spirits	1.8	1.9	1.9	1.9	2.0	2.0	2.0	2.0	2.0	2.0	2.0	2.0	1.9
Subtotal	118.1	122.1	123.6	125.8	124.6	130.7	130.7	133.1	133.7	136.0	136.2	137.0	136.7
Inputed Water Consumption	64.4	60.4	58.9	57.6	56.9	51.8	51.8	49.4	48.8	46.5	46.3	45.5	45.8
Total	182.5	182.5	182.5	182.5	182.5	182.5	182.5	182.5	182.5	182.5	182.5	182.5	182.5

Source: USDA; DSI; USBA; ABWA; LBKL Research estimates, John Maxwell, Beverage Industry, May 20, 1983, p. 39.

Exhibit 3

Projected beer wholesaler establishments ranked by sales size (1981-1990)

Sales Range	1981	1990	Change		1990 Cum. % of total
			Amount	*%*	
$50 Million or more	7	50	43	614.3	1.3
$25 to 50 Million	42	300	258	614.3	9.3
$10 to 25 Million	286	500	214	74.8	22.6
$5 to 10 Million	473	1,000	527	114.2	49.3
$3 to 5 Million	689	1,100	411	59.2	78.6
$2 to 3 Million	1,113	550	-(563)	-(50.6)	93.3
Under $2 Million	2,027	250	-(1,777)	-(87.7)	100.0
Total	4,637	3,750	-(887)	-(19.1)	

Source: Beverage Marketing Corporation, Beverage Industry, January 28

ers, and extended distribution channels. Although imported beer only accounted for a small portion of total beer sales in the United States (3 percent by volume and 5.2 percent in dollars in 1983), it was a growing segment of the sluggish beer industry.

22   From 1975 to 1980, imports expanded at an average annual rate of 22 percent, while the industry as a whole expanded at approximately 4 percent annually. Import beers are expected to continue as the fastest growing segment of the beer industry—pegged at between 5 and 10 percent by industry analysts—culminating with a projected 5.6 percent market share (dollars) and annual sales of 12 million barrels. Overall industry growth is projected to run at 1.7 percent annually through the remainder of the 1980s.

23   Through 1982, the heaviest import consumption centered in the nation's largest metropolitan or regional markets (New York, Chicago, Florida, and California). In 1982, one in every four imported beers was consumed by a New Yorker. This is attributable to the fact that distribution is much easier, and volume is concentrated in large urban areas. Imports, moreover, are primarily consumed in restaurants and other food-service institutions—two thirds of all imports are consumed "on premises" according to 1982 industry figures. For domestic beer it is just the opposite—two thirds is purchased for home consumptior.. So imports have grown to date primarily in urban centers with high restaurant concentrations.

24   For example, Van Munching Incorporated of New York, which marketed Heineken, the leading brand of imported beer, reported a 17.6 percent increase in sales for 1982, to cap a trend on increasing sales for the imported brands.

25   Exhibit 5 shows that for 1982, Heineken from the Netherlands held the largest share of the import market with 38.4 percent. Three Canadian

Exhibit 4

Age distribution of the U.S. population with emphasis on the major beer consumption group (18–34 years old)

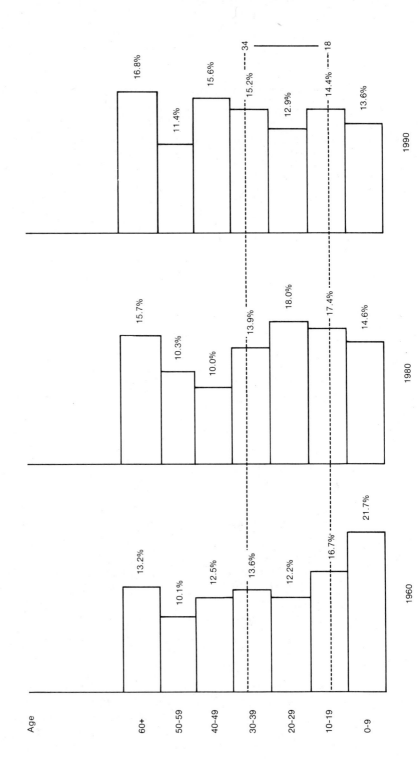

Exhibit 5

The top 10 imported beers (1982 figures)

Brands (country)	Case sales (millions)	% of import market
1. Heineken (Netherlands)	30.5	38.4
2. Molson (Canada)	14.2	17.8
3. Beck's (Germany)	6.2	7.8
4. Moosehead (Canada)	4.9	6.2
5. Labatt's (Canada)	4.2	5.3
6. Dos Equis (Mexico)	2.8	3.5
7. St. Pauli Girl (Germany)	2.0	2.6
8. Carta Blanca (Mexico)	1.9	2.4
9. Guiness-Harp (Ireland)	1.8	2.3
10. Tecate (Mexico)	1.2	1.5
— All others	8.7	12.2
Total Imports	79.4	100.0

Total U.S. sales: 2.5 billion cases.

brands, number two Molson, number four Moosehead, and number five Labatt's held a total of 29.3 percent of the import market. Beck's beer from Germany held the number 3 position in market share, and, coupled with St. Pauli Girl, German imports took 10.4 percent of the American import market. Mexico had two labels in the top 10 for 7.4 percent, and Ireland held one label with 2.3 percent of the import market.

26   The threat of imported beers making further advances in American market share was real. For example, Labatt's introduced a light beer in four U.S. cities in 1982. Labatt's Light was available in 28 states in 1983 and was to be distributed nationally by 1987.

Rivalry Among Existing Firms

27   Rivalry among existing firms could be evaluated on the basis of three types of segmentation: by price, by geography, and by content.

Segmentation by Price

28   Using price as the segmenting factor, brewing industry products fell into three major categories: (1) low-cost, (2) premium, and (3) imports, which were discussed earlier.

29   The recession of the early 1980s caused many brand-name beer drinkers to abandon their favorite brand in favor of less expensive, low-cost beers. The American public thus discovered a secret that was known by all brew masters but never admitted openly. That discovery was simply that "beer

is beer," and the major differences in the products were in how they were perceived. Widely recognized in the brewing industry was the fact that under test conditions consumers were unable to distinguish between brands.

30   Early recognition of this change in consumer-buying behavior by the Stroh and G. Heileman brewers resulted in increases in their market shares at the expense of Anheuser-Busch and Miller. Thus, the market share for smaller breweries was increased to the detriment of larger ones, representing a major reversal of the trends indicated for the previous 20 years, as illustrated by Exhibit 6.

31   G. Heileman purchased a dozen small breweries and began an intense marketing campaign of the lower-cost local labels. With 35 brands as of late 1983, including 6 purchased from retrenching Pabst, G. Heileman believed that it had a "taste" to suit everyone. Acquisitions include Lone Star in Texas, Red White and Blue in the Southeast, and Henry Weinhard in California. This strategic position allowed G. Heileman to sell a beer that locals were familiar with, and possibly loyal to, at a bargain price. Heileman subsequently moved from number 31 in market share percentage in 1982 to number 4 in late 1983.

32   Stroh acquired the well-known, low-cost labels of Schaefer, Schlitz, and Old Milwaukee and concentrated its marketing efforts in the largest beer markets, including Texas and California. Schaefer made strong advances in the major markets, and the bargain brand, Old Milwaukee, attained the status of a top-10 label for the first time in 1982. This brand boasted a 17 percent sales increase in 1983, thus becoming the industry leader in the low-cost market.

33   Number 2 Miller responded to the competitions' low-cost labels by introducing Meister Brau with a national advertising campaign launched during the last game of the 1982 World Series and specifically targeted to attack number 1 Anheuser-Busch. "Meister Brau tastes as good as Bud at a better price" was the claim of Miller Brewing Company. In contrast, Anheuser-Busch believed that the economic recovery would eventually bring its buyers back to the premium beers, and thus decided not to retaliate with a low-balling strategy, even though they possessed a low-end Busch label distributed principally in the East.

Segmentation by Geographic Region

34   Historically, the U.S. beer market was segmented geographically with emphasis on distinct regional markets due to the high cost of shipment.

35   As shown in Exhibit 7, from 1971 through 1983, the beer market in the United States increased by 40 percent to approximately 50 million, 32 gallon barrels. The fastest growing geographic region was the South Atlantic states with a 21 percent increase in consumption followed by the West South Central with an 18 percent increase and the Pacific Coast with a 17 percent gain. The largest percentage sales increases occurred in the Sun Belt.

Exhibit 6

Brewers' production (in millions of barrels)

	Year-end capacity												
	1971	1972	1973	1974	1975	1976	1977	1978	1979	1980	1981	1982	1983E
Anheuser-Busch	24.3	26.6	29.9	34.1	35.2	29.1	36.6	41.6	46.2	50.2	54.5	59.0	65.0
Miller	5.1	5.4	6.9	9.1	12.9	18.4	24.2	31.3	35.8	37.2	40.3	39.9	44.0
Stroh	26.0	28.6	31.5	32.8	34.3	35.1	32.9	29.8	26.4	24.8	23.4	23.3	30.0
Heileman	9.4	9.9	10.5	9.5	10.0	9.6	10.6	10.5	11.3	13.3	14.0	14.5	17.0
Pabst	11.8	12.5	13.1	14.3	15.7	17.0	16.0	15.4	15.1	15.1	13.5	12.5	17.5
Coors	8.5	9.8	10.9	12.3	11.9	13.5	12.8	12.6	12.9	13.8	13.3	12.0	15.0
Olympia	4.2	4.4	4.7	5.3	6.6	7.3	6.8	6.7	6.0	6.1	5.7	5.2	9.0
Genesee	1.6	1.7	1.9	2.1	2.4	2.5	2.8	3.0	3.4	3.6	3.6	3.4	4.0
Schmidt	3.2	3.2	3.5	3.5	3.3	3.5	3.5	3.8	3.8	3.6	3.2	3.2	4.3
General	5.1	6.2	6.0	5.8	6.1	4.2	4.2	3.5	3.0	2.6	2.1	1.8	8.8
Pittsburgh	1.0	0.8	0.9	0.9	0.9	0.8	0.7	0.6	0.7	1.0	0.9	1.0	1.2
All Others	29.7	24.8	20.5	17.9	11.2	11.2	8.1	6.5	9.9	5.2	4.7	3.6	5.1
Subtotal	129.9	133.9	140.3	147.6	150.5	152.2	159.2	165.3	170.7	176.5	179.2	179.4	220.9
Less tax-free exports and military	2.5	2.1	1.8	2.1	1.9	1.8	2.3	2.6	2.6	3.1	2.5	2.4	2.7
Subtotal	127.4	131.8	138.5	146.5	148.6	150.4	156.9	162.7	168.1	173.4	176.7	177.0	218.2
Imports	0.9	0.9	1.1	1.4	1.7	2.4	2.5	3.5	4.4	4.6	5.2	5.7	6.0
Consumption Total	128.3	132.7	139.6	146.9	150.3	152.8	157.1	165.7	172.5	178.0	181.9	182.7	224.2

Source: Beverage Industry and John Maxwell.

Exhibit 7

Changes in beer consumption by region 1971–1983

	Barrels	Share (%)
Northeast	2	4
Mid-Atlantic	4	8
East Northcentral	6	12
West Northcentral	4	8
South Atlantic	11	21
East Southcentral	2	3
West Southcentral	9	18
Mountain	4	9
Pacific	9	17
U.S. Total	51	100

Changes in wine and spirits consumption by region in 1971–1973

	Spirits	Wine	Net
Northeast	4%	65%	61%
Mid-Atlantic	-2	29	31
East Northcentral	3	40	37
West Northcentral	10	59	49
South Atlantic	17	64	47
East Southcentral	26	74	48
West Southcentral	55	58	3
Mountain	43	86	43
Pacific	16	54	38
U.S. Average	14	52	38

U.S. alcoholic beverage consumption

	Beer	Wine	Spirits
Total (Billions of Gallons)	5.65	.50	.45
Per Capita (Gallons)	34.00	2.99	2.70
Per Day (Ounces)	12.00	1.00	.90

Segmenting by Content

36   Beginning in the 1950s, the market for beer dollars was segmented in two other ways: (1) by caloric content and (2) by alcohol content.

37   The surge of sales for low-calorie beers appeared as a result of a more health-conscious America and paralleled the diet segment of the soft-drink industry, which approached 15 percent of the market. A conscious attempt on the part of the consumer to be more aware of the food and beverages that were consumed was evident. Thus the light beer labels showed increases at the expense of other labels.

38   In 1975, Miller Brewing Company began production of what would shortly become the largest selling light beer, Miller Lite, and by 1983 was the third largest selling label overall, behind only Budweiser and Miller High Life.

Market share for all light beers increased from 13.8 percent in 1981 to approximately 18 percent in 1983 and was projected to continue an upward trend.

39   The innovative introduction of a light beer by Miller was not seen as a major threat by the competition. Neither were the seven-ounce bottle and domestically produced Lowenbrau, despite its 25 percent price advantage over Michelob, the leading domestic premium beer.

40   America's premium and low-cost beers traditionally contained a 4 percent alcohol content. Although many low-alcohol-content labels had been introduced by small breweries, the first major brewery to market this formula was Carling O'Keefe, which introduced a low-alcohol label in Canada in 1982. Canadian beer traditionally carried a high-alcohol content (5%); however, this new label with 2.5 percent alcohol was well accepted, as evidenced by its 5 percent share of the Canadian market as of 1983. Following the lead of Carling O'Keefe, Anheuser-Busch successfully introduced L.A. (for low alcohol) with a 2 percent alcohol formula in the United States.

Substitutes

41   Although any type of consumable liquid could serve as a substitute for beer, only a few liquids actually competed directly for the same dollars. These close substitutes included soft drinks, wine, and distilled spirits. The largest seller by volume was soft drinks with 40.1 gallons consumed per person in the United States in 1982, an increase of 0.6 gallons over the previous year and the only category of liquids to show an increase with the exception of bottled and tap water. The increase came at the expense of coffee, beer, milk, juice, tea, and distilled spirits, all of which showed per capita decreases in consumption during the same period. Beer retained its traditional fourth place, ranking in total consumption behind water, soft drinks, and coffee.

Industry Problems

42   Nationally, the United States Brewers' Association ranked alcohol abuse as the single most distressing problem facing the industry. During the first four years of the 1980s, 32 states introduced and passed legislation designed to toughen their drinking and driving laws. Organizations like M.A.D.D. and S.A.D.D. (Mothers and Students Against Drunk Driving, respectively) became increasingly vocal and powerful.

43   Transshipping was ranked as the second greatest problem as brewers became international suppliers, followed closely by the concern over the negative effects of excise taxes and mandatory deposit laws. Of this group, excise taxes were probably the first that would call for attention. In 1982 alone, state legislatures considered 19 bills introduced to raise excise taxes

on beer and 22 bills proposed to earmark increased revenues for specific purposes such as alcohol rehabilitation or prison reform.

44   To combat what the United States Brewing Association saw as unfair and unjust legislation, they retained the services of Touche Ross to compile figures on the economic impact of the brewing industry on a state-by-state basis. The information included the number of employees, wages, salaries and benefits, dollars spent in packaging, and taxes paid for both brewers and wholesalers. This data was used by industry lobbyists to demonstrate the economic importance of the industry.

45   Another industry-wide problem was overcapacity, estimated to be 180 million barrels in 1983. The annualized growth rate for beer consumption was projected at only 1.7 percent through 1990, yet 75 percent of all brewers planned to make capital investments in 1984 according to a study produced by the Informetrics National Research Center. Of these brewers, 71 percent said they would spend more than they did in 1983, and 29 percent indicated plans to spend more than one million dollars on new equipment. Fifty-three percent had plans for new lines. Meanwhile, Pabst and Schlitz produced at approximately 70 percent of capacity, and Miller delayed its 1983 opening of an 8-million-barrel production plant in Ohio. Nevertheless, Anheuser-Busch planned a 27 percent increase in capacity by 1987.

case **2** # The Adolph Coors Company: The Decision to Expand Nationally

Introduction

1   Since its inception, Coors has been very profitable and has grown by emphasizing a single, premium brand of beer. It was the only major brewer located in the Rocky Mountains with one large production facility located in Golden, Colorado. While it had expanded into other states and was the sixth largest brewer in 1982, it was still a regional brewer.

2   In the 1980s, Coors faced increasingly stronger competition from two national brewers, Anheuser-Busch and Miller. Given the slow industry growth rate for beer sales in recent years, some industry analysts felt that an industry shakeup would occur. Regional brewers would be the most susceptible to going bankrupt or being acquired during such a consolidation. While Coors had been strong up through the 1970s, could it remain successful as just a regional brewer in the 1980s? Thus, two distinct strategic alternatives presented themselves to the Coors family, who held tight control of the firm. Should the firm remain as a regional brewer or go nationwide in the production and marketing of beer?

This case was prepared by Jeffrey M. Miner of IBM and Larry D. Alexander of Virginia Polytechnic Institute and State University.   © 1985 by Jeffrey M. Miner and Larry D. Alexander.

History

3   Adolph Herman Joseph Coors, a German immigrant, and Jacob Schueler, a Denver businessman, began brewing in an old tannery in the Clear Creek Valley of Golden, Colorado, in 1873. They called it the Golden Brewery. Coors was attracted to the area because of the numerous springs flowing from the Rocky Mountains. In 1880, Coors bought out Schueler and renamed the successful venture Coors Golden Brewery.

4   The company thrived until prohibition; then it survived by selling near beer and malted milk. It also developed several manufacturing operations for producing cement and porcelain during that same period. While Coors did well, most breweries did not. From 1910 to 1933, the number of breweries was cut in half from 1,568 to 750.

5   After prohibition, Coors company experienced phenomenal growth. Still, it remained a regional brewery that produced only one type of beer from a single brewery. Its beer was sold in 11 western states in 1970, with California being its largest market. By 1970, this regional brewer had become the nation's fourth largest brewer.

6   Coors beer began to develop a mystique in the early 1970s, perhaps because it was the only beer brewed with pure Rocky Mountain spring water. Many people thought it was of higher quality than other beers. It conveyed environmental purity and a western image, which were in vogue at that time. Also, the high price that Easterners had to pay to get the beer added to its mystique. The movie "Smokey and the Bandit" illustrated the degree to which some people would go to get Coors beer, and celebrities, such as Paul Newman and Clint Eastwood, regularly drank Coors beer on movie sets. Even President Jerry Ford carried the beer on board Air Force One.

7   Coors, the market leader in 9 of the 11 states it served, including California, then turned to geographical expansion. The company began selling beer in Texas and other nearby states, where it quickly gained market share. Its 1975 sales of $520 million represented a $270 million increase over 1971. Operating margin was 28 percent in 1975, the highest in the industry, and profit per barrel averaged almost $9, almost twice that of the industry leader, Anheuser-Busch. As a Coors marketing vice president put it at that time, "You could have sold Coors beer in Glad bags."[1]

8   But the tremendous success of Coors did not last; it started to lose market share for several reasons. First, Coors suffered from a negative public image. A brewery worker's union strike in 1977 led to a boycott of Coors beer by numerous AFL-CIO unions. Second, Joe Coors' ultraconservative philosophy alienated a number of minorities, including women, blacks, Hispanics, and gays. Third, Coors failed to realize that the industry was changing. Miller Brewing, which was acquired by Philip Morris in 1970, was the first to recognize that beer drinkers were not a single market, but

rather a number of differentiated segments. Whereas Anheuser-Busch used price and lower costs to compete with Schlitz in the 1960s, Miller shifted that emphasis towards heavy advertising and promotion and development of new products to appeal to these segments in the 1970s. This new strategy helped Miller jump from eighth at the start of the decade to second by 1977.

9   Unfortunately, Coors ignored the signs for quite a while, continued with its production orientation, and brewed only one beer, Coors Premium. Conversely, Coors' advertising expenditures were the lowest in the industry. In 1977, they were only about $.25 per barrel compared to an industry average of over $1.00. A marketing battle ensued as Miller attempted to unseat Anheuser-Busch from the number one spot, and Coors suffered from it.

10   Coors' loss in market share was most dramatic in California, its traditional stronghold. Its share dropped from 40 percent in the mid-1970s to under 20 percent by 1982. The loss for Coors was a gain for Anheuser-Busch, which then controlled about 47 percent of that market. Coors also lost its market share to Miller in Texas, which was another former stronghold. Overall, Coors dropped from the fourth place brewer in the early 1970s to sixth place in 1982. Volume was 13.5 million barrels in 1976, a 9.1 percent market share, and earnings were $76 million on sales of $594 million. In 1982, however, volume dropped to 11.9 million barrels, which represented only a 6.6 percent share, while earnings were only $40 million on sales of $915 million.

Management

11   Adolph Coors Company had sustained itself for over 100 years as a family owned and managed business. The Coors family had a pervasive influence over all aspects of company operations. Since 1970 the top spot had actually been shared by two brothers, William and Joseph Coors. Their late brother, Adolph Coors III, would have been chief executive had he not been killed in 1960. Adolph Coors II retained control of the company until he died in 1970, when control passed on to Bill and Joe. In the early 1980s, Joe's two oldest sons, Jeff and Peter, were added to the management team, supposedly to provide a transition between the two generations of management.

12   Bill Coors, age 66, was the elder of the two brothers, and his official position was Chairman and Chief Executive Officer. He handled the technical side of the business and had a reputation for being a genius in the brewing industry. Joe Coors, age 65, was the President and Chief Operating Officer and oversaw the financial and administrative functions. In reality, each brother acted in any capacity they wanted, and there were no formal lines of authority. Their apparent lack of rivalry amazed outsiders. Both men were lean, tall, rugged Westerners who were very open

and personal with employees. In fact, each was referred to as Bill and Joe by all employees, rather than by their famous last name.

13 The brothers devoted themselves to brewing the finest quality beer that they could. Bill and Joe did not put much faith in that mystique bit. They genuinely believed they simply made a better product, and that was why it sold so well. Bill was well respected for his technical know-how and was Chairman of the United States Brewers Association. The brothers had shunned the public eye in the past; however, the company's more recent unfavorable public image forced them to be more open with the public. Joe, a longtime conservative, was very outspoken and his views tended to alienate a number of minority groups.

14 The brothers realized that, in the new competitive brewing industry of the 1980s, maintaining market share and survival were key goals. This was one reason that they decided to infuse fresh thinking in the management team when they brought Jeff and Peter into top management in 1982.

15 Peter Coors, age 36, and Jeff, age 38, were named division presidents in 1982 when an expanded four-man office of the presidency was created. They both had engineering degrees from Cornell. Peter also had an M.B.A. degree and was involved in the sales and marketing aspect of the company. He initiated the company's first market research in the early 1970s, which his father disapproved of at the time. However, since he realized that the low-calorie beer-market segment was growing rapidly, he proved instrumental in developing Coors Light. Both Joe and Bill opposed this move at first. Peter was heir apparent to the presidency and more easily handled the pressures of being a public figure. Jeff oversaw research and development operations and was a one-man research team in the early 1970s. By the early 1980s, that department had grown significantly in size and importance. Jeff also headed up all new product development efforts at Coors in the 1980s.

16 Both were responsible for shifting the emphasis towards advertising, price competition, and new product development. These actions probably helped the company to survive. The pair disagreed with each other and also with Bill and Joe, but the differences tended to be constructive.

Production

17 Coors was considered a maverick among brewers because its brewing process defied industry norms. However, the company was highly regarded in the industry as a quality and technologically superior brewer. With Coors' single brewery, which had a 20-million-barrel capacity, uniformity and quality were easier to maintain. The drawbacks, however, were that transportation costs were quite high and that there were significant logistics problems in producing and packaging different kinds of beer in the same brewery.

18   All raw materials and finished products were constantly monitored for uniformity and quality. Coors used the highest quality ingredients possible. The water was pure Rocky Mountain spring water from over forty springs located on the brewery grounds. Rarely was water in its pure form suitable for brewing, but no chemical alterations of this water were necessary. Coors supplied its own special barley seed, Moravian III, to contract farmers in the West. Coors bought its hops from growers in Washington and Idaho and imported two types from Germany. Coors also had its own malt house to insure proper aging of the barley. Rice, grown for Coors in California and Arkansas, was used to give the beer its light body. A computer was used extensively to monitor many steps in the brewing operation, and flavor checks were performed regularly at each step. In addition, trained personnel routinely evaluated the quality of all ingredients and the final product.

19   Coors' brewing process was unique because it was entirely natural. No artificial ingredients were used. Since all biochemical processes were allowed to occur naturally, Coors had one of the longest brewing processes in the industry; it took an average of 68 days to brew and package the beer. Coors Light took even longer to produce because extra time had to be allowed for enzymes to dissolve the sugars.

20   In keeping with its natural brewing philosophy, Coors approached the problem of germ control in a unique way—the beer was not pasteurized. In 1959, company scientists discovered a better way, which involved a series of filters combined with controlled conditions. The conditions under which the filling process was performed were so germ free that they were likened to those in a sterile operating room.

21   Coors' filling process was designed to keep the beer cold at all times. This was supposed to enhance the flavor since heat was thought to take away some of the beer's body and flavor. Packaging was a completely computerized operation to maintain Coors' goals of uniformity and quality. The computer told the forklift drivers which pallets to pick up and where to put them. Because of this system, Coors did not require a warehouse. Beer that came off the line was sent almost immediately to trucks and railcars for distribution.

22   Coors was trying to minimize pollution caused by its packaging materials. The company was the founder and leader of aluminum can recycling. In 1979, 80 percent of its aluminum cans used in packaging were recycled. Coors paid out over $33 million for them. The major source for these cans were the recycling centers located at Coors' distributorships. Also, 50 can banks, which were reverse vending machines for aluminum cans, were being test marketed. This approach helped to make recycling more convenient for consumers. This program also enabled the company to be less dependent on the aluminum market. Recycling was not only cost effective for the company, it also provided consumers with supplemental income.

23   Brewery wastes were always a problem, but Coors had developed a method to transform much of this waste into animal feed. An average of 4 million gallons of industrial wastes were processed daily at Coors. The company was a leader in the efficient use of waste water, yielding only 3.5 barrels of it per barrel of beer, compared to 8 for most brewers.

24   Coors was also committed to energy conservation. The company began converting to coal in 1976 and by 1980 was virtually 100 percent coal dependent. This move was relatively risk free since Coors sat in the middle of America's most plentiful coal supply. Also, recycling saved about 95 percent of the energy required to produce new aluminum from bauxite.

25   Clearly, Coors was the most energy efficient brewer in America, with the lowest Btus (British thermal units) per barrel ratio in the industry. Its engineering capabilities enabled the company to become nearly energy self-sufficient while maintaining rigid pollution control standards. For example, Coors had been able to remove 99.5 percent of the pollutants caused by burning coal.

Marketing

26   In the 1980s, Coors' marketing capabilities were improving, but it still did not compare to what many of its major competitors were doing. Still, it had come a long way since the mid-1970s when the company brewed only one product, did no market research, and spent next to nothing on advertising. By the early 1980s, Coors was trying to remedy this through extensive advertising, promotion, and development of new products to cater to different segments of the beer-drinking population.

27   Coors switched its emphasis from producing one beer of superior quality to producing several products of superior quality. Until 1978, Coors Premium was the only beer that the company produced. Management felt that this was a superior beer, and they simply did not need another brand. Coors Premium was considered to be a rich and light-bodied beer, containing 138 calories per twelve ounces. This beer, the fourth bestselling brand of beer in the nation, was still the staple for the company. The company sold 8.4 million barrels of Premium in 1982, but this was down some 19 percent from 1981, mainly due to increased competition and the recession. By 1983, however, Coors also marketed several other brands of beer to different market segments.

28   Coors Light was introduced in 1978 in response to the fast-growing light beer segment. The company had earlier insisted that Coors Premium was light enough, but later realized the importance of developing a new product for this important growth segment. Coors Light contained 105 calories per twelve ounces. In an effort to provide a light beer with quality taste, Coors spent a great deal of time developing this product. Not surprising, it also used all natural ingredients. The brand's sales grew substantially after its introduction, but remained far behind the leader, Lite beer from Miller. The

company sold 3.2 million barrels of Coors Light in 1982, an increase of 2.1 million over 1980. However, many analysts felt that this growth had been at the expense of Coors Premium, which was another reason for Premium's sales decline.

29   In 1983, Coors started test marketing a new premium brew called Golden Lager 1873 because the company recognized that both Coors Premium and Light appealed generally to the same type of beer drinkers. Company research showed that many drinkers wanted a heartier-tasting beer. Coors hoped that Golden Lager would compete effectively with the national leaders in this category, Anheuser-Busch's Budweiser and Miller's High Life. The company tried to add credibility to the brand by linking it with its Rocky Mountain heritage. Initially, it was being tested in selected cities in the South and West. Coors also hoped that the new beer would help fill the brewery's excess capacity.

30   Coors had also tried to appeal to the growing import and super-premium beer-drinking segment. George Killian's Irish Red Ale from France had been sold to Coors, which began testing the product in 1980. Successful results prompted a market-wide rollout in 1982. The company claimed that high initial sales indicated that the product had already developed a strong following.

31   Earlier in 1980, Coors began testing its first super-premium brand, Herman Joseph's 1868. It was very rich and full bodied, due to a longer brewing and aging cycle. Coors hoped that the beer would be able to compete with Anheuser-Busch's Michelob, the leader in that segment. In 1982, the beer was still being tested in six states, but it had not yet been very successful. As a result, Herman Joseph's was periodically reformulated, repackaged, and readvertised, but it had never topped 100,000 barrels in annual sales.

32   In an industry as competitive as brewing, it was important for Coors to generate a strong following for its products. Advertising and promotional skills were a great concern, probably because the firm had grown complacent in its century of operation. Fortunately, Coors management realized that it could no longer rely on its product's mystique to cure marketing problems. Since 1975, advertising expenditures increased dramatically, as shown in Exhibit 1. But, because Coors made frequent ad theme changes over the succeeding few years, it had a branding identity problem.

33   To complement its own marketing department, Coors also enlisted the aid of two top advertising agencies. Advertising for Coors Premium emphasized its purity, freshness, and superiority. The campaign was supported by in-store point-of-purchase displays, which cost much less than television and were probably fairly effective. On television, Coors depicted its beer being drunk in traditional beer-drinking settings, such as bars and parties, and the ads targeted those who drank three or four beers at a time. Coors Light had an energetic new campaign to attract more

Exhibit 1

Coors advertising expenditures (1975–1983)

Year	Expenditure (in millions)
1975	$ 1.2
1976	2.0
1977	15.5
1978	33.5
1979	46.4
1980	66.8
1981	85.8
1982	88.1
1983	over 88.1

From *Adolph Coors Company: 1980 Annual Report* and *Adolph Coors Company: 1982 Annual Report.* Also see Robert F. Hartley's "Coors—We Are Immune to Competition," in his *Management Mistakes* (Columbus, Ohio: Grid Publishing Co., 1983), pp. 139–153.

consumers in the low calorie segment. It focused on its unsurpassed taste in informal, active settings.

34   Coors used outdoor billboards as a secondary medium, which was not standard for the industry. Billboards were used to depict the image of the snow-covered Rockies. This medium was used mainly for Coors Premium. While Coors used radio advertising to a rather limited extent, it was being used more extensively in the 1980s for Coors Light.

35   In 1982, there was an increase in advertising and promotional efforts directed at the young adult segment, which, while declining in absolute numbers, was usually the stronghold of brand loyalty. Campaigns to improve Coors product awareness among blacks and Hispanics, who accounted for a significant proportion of the target market, had been initiated. Corporate messages aimed at these groups tried to persuade them to give the company a chance to dispel its negative image, which still lingered on. Coors felt, however, that its new, open, straightforward public relations efforts would help win these consumers over to its side.

36   Perhaps the most important way in which brewers advertised their products was through sports promotions, especially on television. Coors focused on both participative and spectator sports events, selecting these events on the basis of a sports activity study performed by the company. Its recent sports emphasis had been on motor sports and cycling. In 1980, many Coors distributors registered sizeable sales increases before, during, and after various Coors-sponsored sporting events. Sports promotion also helped Coors gain valuable national exposure. However, Coors and other smaller brewers had some difficulty finding available spots on nationally

televised sports, due to exclusive arrangements that Anheuser-Busch and Miller had established with the networks.

37   Coors had over 350 distributors in its marketing territory. These distributors usually had to be large because Coors insisted that its products be refrigerated during distribution. This required both the company and its distributors to undertake added expenses and pains to keep the beer cold so that the flavor of the beer was preserved until it got to retailers. All beer was shipped from Coors in insulated railcars or refrigerated trucks. Distributors in turn were required to keep the beer refrigerated in their warehouses. Coors thus usually only took on veteran wholesalers who could make the necessary investments in refrigeration and insulation. The beer was placed in special vaults and kept at a constant 35 degrees. Because of this requirement, distributors had to pay an additional $100,000 or more each year just to keep Coors beer cold.

38   Retailers were encouraged to keep Coors beer refrigerated at all times, but because of increased promotions, there were often floor displays at room temperature. The company claimed that it would not harm Coors beer or cause it to lose its flavor faster than any other beer on the market. To further insure that flavor was preserved, the distributors were required to rotate retailer stocks every 60 days. This 60-day-rotation rule was the strictest in the industry.

39   The distributors also played a vital role in marketing the product. They set up point-of-purchase displays in retail outlets, prepared local advertising, and developed customer relations. In order to maintain better relations with its distributors, Coors established its own television network, Second Century, in 1980. Stories were periodically done on different wholesalers. Distributors had to purchase the equipment to view the films, but over 90 percent had already done so. Brewery employees also viewed what the distributors were doing on this network.

40   The company also owned six of its own distributorships, not to compete with the independent wholesalers, but to give Coors' management firsthand knowledge of actual conditions in the field. It also enabled the company to analyze local and regional consumer patterns, train management in marketing and sales, and test new programs before they were introduced elsewhere.

41   Approximately 78 percent of Coors' products were shipped by rail. The remaining 22 percent were shipped by truck. Of this, 14 percent went by common carrier or trucks owned by Coors distributors, and 8 percent went by the Coors Transportation Company. This wholly-owned subsidiary had grown in the last couple of years from 1980 when only 3 percent of Coors' products used it. The company was formed in 1971 to provide hauling flexibility. It operated 132 temperature-controlled trailers and 52 tractors. Each truck traveled about 215,000 miles a year. The purpose was to reach distributors who did not have rail service, to handle emergency loads, and to haul to areas where profitable backhauls were available. Backhauls

usually brought food products into the Denver area. The company was also formed as a reaction to rising railroad rates.

42   The advantage of having this flexibility was exemplified in 1980, when Coors was entering Arkansas. Thousands of extra cases were needed because demand had been underestimated. It could have turned into embarrassing shortages just when the company was trying to establish itself in a new territory. Fortunately, it turned into extra sales because of quick, backup trucking by Coors' trucks.

43   Coors had recently begun a two-pronged approach to gain market share. One way was to expand further into the East, and the other was to reverse share losses in its traditional 20-state territory, most notably in California and Texas. Neither way promised to be an easy task. The effort would mean head-to-head competition with leaders Anheuser-Busch and Miller and would require huge marketing expenditures. Coors had been trying to meet advertising expenditures, but aggressive marketing was still a relatively new experience for Coors.

44   In 1983, Coors' biggest expansion campaign yet was undertaken to enter the Southeast market. This region was considered to be a growth area by many brewers. It appeared that the mystique was still alive in the Southeast, where there had been strong initial customer acceptance of Coors Premium and Light. Initial sales were going well in 1983 for both brands in this region. While competition in this area was intense, Coors had selected large distributors who were well established in their markets to help implement this effort.

45   This expansion was also supported by heavy advertising on radio and television, which stressed that Coors could finally be purchased in the region. With that expansion, Coors marketed its products in 26 states and the District of Columbia. However, the good news was tempered by two factors. First, some analysts feared that the sales in the Southeast perhaps increased so very rapidly because of the novelty factor. Thus, they suggested that more time would be needed to determine if Coors' success would be maintained. Second, Coors' transportation costs to the Southeast were very high. One estimate was that the cost of shipping from Golden, Colorado to the Southeast was $7 to $8 per barrel, compared to an industry average of $3 per barrel.

46   Coors had purchased land options for the possible erection of another brewery in Virginia or Tennessee. However, there were no plans to begin building any time soon. If the company were to acquire or build another plant, a marketing problem could arise, since Coors's identity was associated with pure Rocky Mountain spring water. Jeff Coors remarked, "Now... you can make good water out of anything. We haven't crossed the hurdle of what impact we'd suffer if we dropped the Rocky Mountain water theme. But you never know. We might produce an entirely different beer for the East."[2] However, one analyst suggested that the delaying of the plant would only allow the competition time to solidify their hold even further in Eastern and Southeastern markets.

Finance

47   Coors had always been strong financially. Exhibits 2 and 3 show the consolidated balance sheets and consolidated income statements for the years 1980 through 1982. The company went public in 1975, only because it needed to raise money to pay inheritance taxes on the estate of Adolph Coors II. These public shares were traded over the counter, and there were some 9,000 shareholders by 1983. However, this public stock was class B non-voting, so outsiders did not have a say in management decisions. The Coors family owned 35 percent of the class B shares and 100 percent of the 1.26 million shares of class A voting stock. Thus, the family controlled their stock so much so that no other firm would be able to acquire it unless management allowed it. That didn't appear very likely, given the history of this maverick brewery.

48   Another aspect of Coors' financial approach was the company's refusal to borrow money. This was a family tradition that dated back to the company's beginnings. Coors' capital structure consisted almost entirely of common stock. Also, since the company did not plan to issue any more stock, all future expansion would have to be financed through internally generated cash. Its normal cash balance was around $70 million, but Coors planned to increase this. Although lack of debt was a sign of financial strength, this avoidance of debt financing altogether sometimes caused the company to bypass attractive opportunities. One was the addition of an Eastern plant, which the company agreed was necessary to offset huge transportation costs of shipping to Eastern markets. Another example concerns Coors's can manufacturing facility, which developed the technical process for making the two-piece aluminum can; the company sold the process to Continental Can Company and American Can Company because Coors would have had to borrow money to begin production.

Research and Development

49   Coors was often considered to be the most technically advanced brewery in the world. The company had Colorado's single largest engineering crew for any private-sector firm. R&D was concerned with developing new products, brewing techniques, and packaging techniques. Coors had developed technical superiority in ceramics and aluminum cans. There was an extensive barley R&D program, which had genetically developed Coors' own special variety called Moravian III. Yeast cells, used in the brewing process, were specifically selected for testing to develop new and better strains to upgrade the quality of its beer. Farmers wanted a higher yield for their crops, and Coors wanted reliable sources of supply, so much of the company's research dealt with counseling farmers on how to get higher yields while maintaining Coors' standards. The company also did

---

Exhibit 2

Adolph Coors Company—consolidated balance sheets

	12/28/80	12/27/81	12/26/82
		(in thousands)	
ASSETS			
Cash	$ 87,883	$ 76,614	$ 71,251
Accounts/Notes Receivable	57,930	66,667	64,909
Inventories	149,504	115,677	118,658
Prepaid Expenses	28,856	34,282	34,614
Income Tax Prepayments	6,036	2,215	4,236
Total Current Assets	330,209	295,455	293,668
Properties, Net	556,419	652,090	702,769
Excess of Cost Over Net	2,649	2,567	3,029
Other Assets	5,108	6,272	8,448
Total Assets	$894,385	$956,384	$1,007,914
LIABILITIES AND EQUITY			
Accounts Payable	$ 48,923	$ 40,033	$ 45,601
Salaries, Vacation	25,677	27,488	25,543
Taxes (not income)	19,872	18,494	17,252
Income Taxes	3,427	9,922	2,789
Accrued Expenses	18,195	21,577	28,820
Total Current Liabilities	116,094	117,514	120,005
Deferred Income Taxes	60,149	75,968	95,097
Other Long-Term Liabilities	6,042	9,335	9,600
Capital Stock:			
Class A Common, Voting	1,260	1,260	1,260
Class B Common, Non-Voting	11,000	11,000	11,000
Total	12,260	12,260	12,260
Paid-In Capital	2,011	2,011	2,011
Retained Earnings	724,284	765,751	795,396
Total	738,555	780,022	809,667
Less Treasury Shares	26,455	26,455	26,455
Total Equity	712,100	753,567	783,212
Total Liabilities and Equity	$894,385	$956,384	$1,007,914

From *Adolph Coors Company: 1982 Annual Report,* pp. 12-13.

50 the company a chance to dispel its negative image, whicl still lingered on. Coors felt, however, that its new, open, straightforward public relations efforts would help win these consumers over it its side.

Exhibit 3

Adolph Coors Company—consolidated income statements

	12/26/80	12/27/81	12/26/82
		(in thousands)	
Sales	$1,012,198	$1,060,345	$1,032,297
Less: Excise Taxes	133,301	130,429	117,039
Net Sales	887,897	929,916	915,258
Costs and Expenses:			
Cost of Goods Sold	629,758	659,623	659,033
Marketing, G&A	146,293	181,348	185,076
Research & Development	14,256	16,848	15,230
Total	790,307	857,819	859,339
Operating Income	97,590	72,097	55,919
Other:			
Interest Income	(16,514)	(13,788)	(10,411)
Interest Expense	1,563	1,601	2,480
Miscellaneous	6,764	4,651	(1,298)
Total	(8,187)	(7,536)	(9,229)
Income Before Taxes	105,777	79,633	65,148
Income Taxes	40,800	27,663	25,000
Net Income	64,977	51,970	40,148
Beginning Retained Earnings	668,939	724,284	765,751
	733,916	776,254	805,899
Cash Dividends	9,632	10,503	10,503
Ending Retained Earnings	$724,284	$765,751	$795,396

From *Adolph Coors Company: 1982 Annual Report*, p. 10.

the can was hard to open, and consumers often cut their fingers in the process.

51   Jeff Coors, who was responsible for R&D, became the first American in a quarter century to present a technical paper at the European Brewing Convention in 1979. R&D was a relatively minor part of the company's operations before Jeff became involved in the early 1970s. While many advancements in the industry occurred in the 1960s and 1970s, Jeff did not see any major technical breakthroughs on the horizon in the 1980s. Research appeared to have taken a distant back seat to marketing;

however, Coors remained committed to R&D. Bill Coors' credo was, "If technology exists, use it. If it doesn't, develop it..."[3]

Human Resources

52   Coors employed about 8,600 people in 1983, down some 850 from just 1981. Company officials blamed the layoffs on the recession, which reduced industry demand. Coors tried to develop its own personnel so they could later be promoted from within. This required extensive educational and training programs. The company's television network, Second Century, had also been used to produce in-house training programs.

53   Coors was committed to equal employment opportunity and supported an active affirmative action program. Minority employment agencies were used to recruit minorities, which represented 13.4 percent of the work force in 1979. Coors also had an employee opportunity training program which hired ex-convicts, disabled veterans, and the disadvantaged, and trained them for responsible positions within the firm.

54   An average salary for a Coors production worker was $20,000 a year, and Coors offered fringe benefits totalling an additional $5,800 per employee per year. Clearly, these wages and benefits were considerably higher than the average for Golden, Colorado, a city of approximately 11,000 people.

55   Coors' management maintained that business should operate as a free enterprise; thus, the company was philosophically opposed to unions. Unfortunately, Coors' brewery workers were unionized and represented a large proportion of the work force. They went out on strike in 1977. The issue was not money but the forcing of employees to take lie detector tests. A boycott of the company's products ensued, but Coors management stood its ground, replaced many of the striking workers, and rehired those who wanted to return.

56   In 1978, Coors' brewery workers voted out the union and the boycott's effect diminished. In 1982, "60 Minutes" did a story on Coors to try to uncover human rights violations. The show, often noted for its exposés, found no such violations which somewhat helped to ease Coors' negative image. As of 1983, Coors was still operating without a union.

57   Coors was very concerned about employee health and well-being. In 1982, the American Center for Occupational Health, a Coors subsidiary, continued to be committed to safer working conditions. The company provided health care tests and services to Coors' employees and other businesses, and it was currently completing the development of a light-weight, compact health-testing machine.

58   Coors opened a wellness center on its brewery property in 1981. All employees, retirees, spouses, and dependents were allowed to use the facility, which contained a track, trampolines, weight sets, stationary bicycles, and other equipment. The center also sponsored programs in physi-

cal fitness, nutrition, stress management, weight control, stopping smoking, and alcohol education. The staff was comprised of experts in each field. Thus far, it had been very successful. Bill Coors was not worried whether the center could be cost justified if it promoted health and happiness. Coors also funded participation in various sports for a number of employees, and many were sent to survival training courses. In sum, management regarded physical fitness as very important.

Coors' Vertical Integration and Diversification Efforts

59   In keeping with Coors' philosophy of independence in all aspects of operations, it became the most vertically integrated firm in the industry. Exhibit 4 shows a map of Coors' operations throughout the U.S. Coors had attempted to control its raw materials supply by having contract farmers grow its barley and rice and maintaining its own malt house. Coors also had its own supply of packaging materials. It owned a can manufacturing plant, which was the largest single such plant in the industry, a glass manufacturing plant, and a paper mill. Coors Energy Company owned a coal mine, 249 natural gas and oil wells, and it leased rights to 330,000 acres. Coors owned its own truck fleet and waste treatment facility, and company engineers designed and constructed most of its own machinery and equipment. This was all very important for cost control, stability, and independence from supplier price hikes and shortages. Clearly, Coors believed in vertical integration, both forwards and backwards.

60   Coors had also diversified into companies not directly related to brewing, though they complemented the primary product. Coors Porcelain Company was one of the world's foremost suppliers of technical ceramics, mainly for the computer industry and energy firms. The company was trying to decide whether to compete in the $1-billion-a-year dental-restoration industry. Coors Food Products Company did well in 1982, acquiring a snack food company that made potato chips. The Coors subsidiary also packaged rice and competed in the rice flour and cereal markets. They were experimenting with bread products made from brewer's grain 28, a high protein by-product of the brewing process. The sale of variety breads was growing by 15 percent yearly. They also made cocomost, a cocoa substitute derived from brewer's yeast.

Coors' Competition

61   Since Miller Brewing's effect on the industry was already discussed earlier, only Anheuser-Busch, Stroh, and Heileman are profiled here. While

Exhibit 4

Map of Coors operations

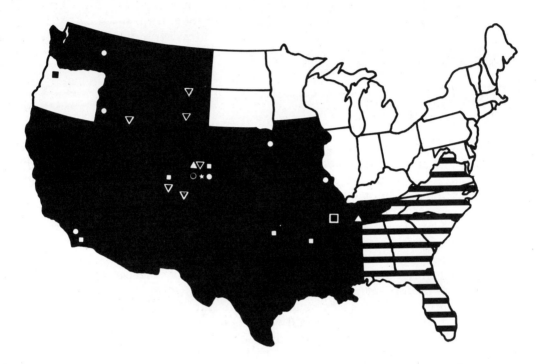

■ **Coors 1982 Marketing Territory**	▤ **1983 Expansion**	★ **Main Offices**
▪ **Ceramic Manufacturing Plants**	Alabama	Golden, Colorado
Benton, Arkansas	Florida	Largest single brewery
El Cajon, California	Georgia	and aluminum can
Golden, Colorado	North Carolina	manufacturing plant
Grand Junction, Colorado	South Carolina	in the United States
Hillsboro, Oregon	Eastern Tennessee	
Norman, Oklahoma	Virginia	● **Company-owned Distributorships**
	District of Columbia	Boise, Idaho
Foreign operations not shown		Denver, Colorado
Singapore	▽ **Grain Elevators**	Omaha, Nebraska
Glenrothes, Scotland	Burley, Idaho	Spokane, Washington
Rio Claro, Brazil	Delta, Colorado	St. Louis, Missouri
	Huntley, Montana	Tustin, California
	Longmont, Colorado	
□ **Rice Mill**	Monte Vista, Colorado	◎ **Glass Bottle Manufacturing Plant**
Weiner, Arkansas	Worland, Wyoming	Wheat Ridge, Colorado
	▲ **Paper Converting Plants**	
	Boulder, Colorado	
	Lawrenceburg, Tennessee	

From *Adolph Coors Company: 1982 Annual Report,* p. 26.

Anheuser-Busch was the industry's giant, these two, second-tier brewers were similar to Coors in size but followed different strategies. Exhibit 5 contains a list of the top six brewers and their major products in order of volume sold. Then, Exhibit 6 shows the top brewers' market shares for 1979 through 1982. Finally, Exhibit 7 shows the top ten domestic beer brands, along with their 1982 market shares.

Anheuser-Busch

62   Anheuser-Busch was the number one brewer in the U.S. ever since it took over that spot from Schlitz in the late 1950s. The giant lumbered along until the 1970s, when Miller's efforts to knock it out of its top position caused August Busch III, the company's chief strategist to rethink his game plan. In large part, he began to copy Miller's methods. He determined

---

Exhibit 5

Top 6 brewers and their major brands (1982)

1. ANHEUSER-BUSCH	4. HEILEMAN
Budweiser	Old Style
Michelob	Schmidt's
Busch	Blatz
Michelob Light	Black Label
Bud Light	Colt 45 Malt Liquor
Natural Light	Old Style Light
	Blatz Light
	Black Label Light
2. MILLER	5. PABST
High Life	Pabst
Lite	Red, White & Blue
Lowenbrau	Olde English Malt
	Blitz
	Pabst Light
	Jacob Best
	Andeker
3. STROH/SCHLITZ	6. COORS
Old Milwaukee	Coors Premium
Stroh's	Coors Light
Schlitz	George Killian's Ale
Schaefer	Herman Joseph's 1868
Schlitz Malt Liquor	
Old Milwaukee Light	
Stroh Light	
Goebel	
Schlitz Light	
Erlanger	

From Paul Mullins, "Brewing Industry Has Flat Growth in '82," *Beverage Industry,* January 28, 1983, p. 31.

Exhibit 6

Brewers' estimated market shares

Brewer	1979	1980	1981	1982E
Anheuser-Busch	26.8%	28.2%	30.0%	32.3%
Miller	20.8	20.9	22.2	21.8
Stroh/Schlitz	15.3	13.9	12.9	12.8
Heileman	6.6	7.5	7.7	7.9
Pabst	8.8	8.5	7.4	6.8
Coors	7.5	7.8	7.3	6.6
Olympia	3.5	3.4	3.1	2.8
Genessee	2.0	2.0	2.0	1.9
Schmidt	2.2	2.0	1.6	1.8
General	1.7	1.4	1.2	1.0
Pittsburgh	0.4	0.6	0.5	0.5
Others	4.4	3.8	4.1	3.8

From Paul Mullins, "Brewing Industry Has Flat Growth in '82," *Beverage Industry,* January 28, 1983, p. 34.

Exhibit 7

Top 10 beer brands in 1982

Brand	Market share (percent)	Volume (mil. barrels)
Budweiser	22.0	40.0
Miller High Life	11.0	20.0
Lite from Miller	9.6	17.5
Coors Premium	4.6	8.4
Michelob	4.6	8.3
Pabst	4.5	8.1
Old Milwaukee	3.1	5.7
Stroh's	3.0	5.6
Old Style	3.0	5.5
Schlitz	2.6	4.7

From "Many Top Brews Give Ground to Other Brands," *Beverage World,* April 1983, p. 33.

that Miller's success was a direct function of heavy advertising in sports media, product diversification, and a switch in emphasis to the beer-drinking young-adult segment. This strategy change occurred in 1977, and was often viewed as the turning point in the industry. From then on, Anheuser-Busch steadily pulled away from Miller. It was the best performing brewer in 1982, with a market share of 32.7 percent. Its 59.1 million barrels sold topped Miller's by almost 20 million.

63   By 1983, the firm was pursuing a total marketing effort, continuing to focus on the young-adult segment with a well-balanced line of quality beers. The Budweiser brand, by far the nation's bestselling beer and leader in the premium segment, represented an amazing 40.7 million of total barrels sold. Michelob was the leader in the super-premium segment. While Miller controlled 60 percent of the light beer segment with its bestselling Lite, Anheuser-Busch had set its sights on taking over that market. It marketed three light beers with different tastes, prices, and images, and controlled 28 percent of the segment. Budweiser Light, introduced in 1982, had become the second bestselling light beer already. This brewing giant also had its sights on international expansion. Budweiser was already the bestselling import in Japan, and it was also strong in Canada.

64   The firm was the nation's biggest sponsor of sporting events. It had the 22nd largest advertising budget among all U.S. firms, and it far outdistanced all competitors in television advertising. Furthermore, Anheuser-Busch was locked into many exclusive contracts, as was Miller. The company's operating efficiency was outstanding, and it boasted the highest profit per barrel in the industry. It had the best distribution system in the industry, and its plants were located strategically throughout the U.S. It was committed to new capacity increases, especially in Los Angeles. Like Coors, the company had vertically integrated to better control raw material supplies and costs. The firm's growth was expected to continue, and recent capacity expansions had increased pressure to capture more market share. Some industry observers felt that Anheuser-Busch might control 40 percent of the market by 1990.

Stroh Brewing Company

65   Stroh saw merger as the only way to survive against the two industry giants. The company acquired Schlitz in 1982, which had been suffering vast market declines. The merger put Stroh in the third spot in the brewing industry. Management was quite strong, and had done a good job with its Stroh brand. However, the company had put itself at a disadvantage because it had leveraged itself so heavily with debt. Key problems for Stroh's were how successfully to integrate its acquisitions into the company and how to reverse the sales decline of its Schlitz brand.

66   Stroh was not advertising the Schlitz brand very much in 1983, although there were plans to step it up in the near future. The company appeared to be using cash flow from the brand to finance marketing expenditures for its bestselling brand, Old Milwaukee. It was being promoted with heavy television advertising and cents-off coupons, which were fairly new to this industry. Many analysts attributed the success of Old Milwaukee, a popular-priced brand, to the 1981-1983 recession.

G. Heileman Brewing Company

67   Heileman, like Coors, had been very successful as a regional brewer. It was targeted for markets in the Midwest and Northwest, but was presently the fourth largest brewer in the U.S. The company had increased barrelage dramatically over the past few years, from 4.5 million barrels in 1975 to 14.9 million in 1982. It was the only major brewer, except Anheuser-Busch, to register a sales gain in 1982.

68   In 1982, Heileman took a big step towards long-term viability by acquiring Pabst and its 49 percent share of Olympia. However, due to objections raised by the Department of Justice, a new Pabst entity was spun off to the remaining Olympia shareholders. Heileman strongly believed that continued consolidation of second-tier and small brewers needed to take place to compete more effectively. As a side note, 7 of the top 11 brewers were involved in acquisitions or attempted acquisitions in 1982.

69   Heileman also had very good management. The company was unusually adept at being able to market more than three dozen regional beers, of which Old Style was the best selling. It also had a very good cost structure, which was quite competitive with that of Anheuser-Busch. To remain competitive, Heileman knew it had to expand into new markets. But having regional products might have helped the company to target some of its products to local market conditions.

70   There were two potential problems for Heileman. First, it served only the popular-priced market segment. This was one of the reasons that the company did so well in the face of a recession. Lack of brand loyalty may be in Heileman's favor, however, if people continued to trade down from higher priced brands. Second, Heileman tried to remain well under Anheuser-Busch's prices; unfortunately, the industry giant had not raised prices in Heileman's market for about two years. If an increase did not come shortly, profit margin pressures might reduce Heileman's profitability.

Legal/Political Issues

71   A number of legal and political issues faced the brewing industry in the 1980s. First, the vast number of traffic deaths related to alcohol had increased dramatically. There had been a number of bills introduced in the U.S. congress to raise the legal drinking age nationally to 21, and such bills were gaining increasing support. Raising the age would cause a decrease in beer sales. Perhaps substitutes, such as near beer, would crop up. Also, a number of consumer groups were asking the Consumer Protection Agency to look into the advertising practices of brewers. They claimed that brewers were encouraging the consumption of alcohol by highly vulnerable younger groups, which brought about heavy drinkers.

72   The company even started distributing counter cards and posters to bars throughout its marketing area with a message from E.T., the extra-terrestrial. E.T. advised, "If you go beyond your limit, please don't drive. Phone home." Coors had a long-standing policy against alcohol abuse. They sponsored alcohol awareness classes at its wellness center, and supported many organizations that dealt with alcohol abuse.

73   Another major issue was the threat of mandatory deposits for bottles and cans. This would increase the price of beer and decrease customer convenience, possibly affecting demand. The difficulties in handling, shipping and selling beer under this law were well known, as 18 percent of the beer sold in the U.S. in the early 1980s was covered by such laws. The law's rationale was to cut down on litter along the roadside, in the city, or out in the country. However, recycling might be an alternative means to accomplish this. Coors had a vigorous program for recycling both bottles and cans.

74   A third issue was excise taxes. Various state legislatures currently had bills to raise the excise tax on beer. There had also been some activity at the federal level. A number of groups had advocated taxing all alcoholic beverages by their alcohol content, which would result in drastically higher taxes on malt beverages. This, too, would result in increased prices for the consumer.

Produce/Market Opportunities

75   Under market penetration, Coors could more heavily advertise its products on television. Radio might also be a promising medium for beer advertising. One survey revealed that beer drinkers spent only about 33 percent of their media time watching television, while 47 percent of their time was spent listening to radio, which was less expensive for advertisers.[4] Another method could be increased price competition through such means as price cuts, cents-off coupons, and rebates. Coupons might attract more women who presently did not buy much beer. Finally, Coors could merge with other brewers, which could help it penetrate existing markets with a wider selection of products.

76   Under market development, Coors could continue to expand nationally. This could be done by expanding its own facilities or by acquiring another brewery to give it additional capacity. A list of the top 40 breweries in the U.S. is shown in Exhibit 8. Expansion abroad might also be a viable alternative, especially since Anheuser-Busch was doing well in Japan. Clearly, this later option would require additional plants to make it feasible.

77   Under product development, Coors could develop near beer or other nonalcoholic beverages in response to a raising of the mandatory drinking age. Near beer was one product that helped Coors survive during

Exhibit 8

Top 40 U.S. commercial brewers

		1983 sales, 31 gallon barrels	Gain or loss in percent over 1982	
1.	Anheuser-Busch, Inc.	60,500,000	2.4	St. Louis, MO
2.	Miller Brewing Co.	37,500,000	-4.6	Milwaukee, WI
3.	The Stroh Brewery Co.	24,300,000	6.1	Detroit, MI
4.	G. Heileman Brewing Co.	17,549,000	20.9	LaCrosse, WI
5.	Adolph Coors Co.	13,719,000	15.1	Golden, CO
6.	Pabst Brewing Co.	12,804,000	***	Milwaukee, WI
7.	Genesee Brewing Co.	3,200,000	-5.9	Rochester, NY
8.	Christian Schmidt & Sons	3,150,000	0.0	Philadelphia, PA
9.	Falstaff Brewing Co.	2,704,884	-15.1	Vancouver, WA
10.	Pittsburgh Brewing Co.	1,000,000*	1.0	Pittsburgh, PA
11.	Latrobe Brewing Co.	700,000*	0.0	Latrobe, PA
12.	Champale Products Corp.	450,000*	4.7	Trenton, NJ
13.	Hudepohl Brewing Co.	400,000*	0.0	Cincinnati, OH
14.	The F.X. Matt Brewing Co.	400,000*	0.0	Utica, NY
15.	Eastern Brewing Co.	350,000*	0.0	Hammonton, NJ
16.	The Schoenling Brewing Co.	315,000*	5.0	Cincinnati, OH
17.	Joseph Huber Brewing Co.	272,000	-1.1	Monroe, WI
18.	The Lion Inc. - Gibbons	230,000	0.0	Wilkes-Barre, PA
19.	D.G. Yuengling & Son	143,000	0.0	Pittsburgh, PA
20.	Jones Brewing Co.	122,000	-2.9	Smithton, PA
21.	Dixie Brewing Co., Inc.	113,000	-24.7	New Orleans, LA
22.	Jacob Leinenkugel Brewing	67,000	-1.5	Chippewa Falls, WI
23.	Fred Koch Brewery	60,000	-7.7	Dunkirk, NY
24.	Stevens Point Brewery	48,900	0.8	Stevens Point, WI
25.	Cold Spring Brewing Co.	40,000*	0.0	Cold Spring, MN
26.	Spoetzl Brewery, Inc.	36,000	-3.0	Shiner, TX
27.	August Schell Brewing Co.	35,000	0.0	New Vim, MN
28.	Straub Brewery, Inc.	35,000	0.0	St. Mary's, PA
29.	Anchor Steam Brewery Co.	33,500	16.6	San Francisco, CA
30.	Walter Brewing Co.	26,800	-3.9	Eau Claire, WI
31.	Dubuque Star Brewing	5,400**	-75.3	Dubuque, IA
32.	Old New York Beer Co.	3,629*	—	New York, NY
33.	Geyer Brothers	3,500	-12.5	Frankenmuth, MI
34.	Redhook Ale Co.	3,000	—	Seattle, WA
35.	William S. Newman Brewing	2,800	12.0	Albany, NY
36.	River City Brewing Co.	2,500	108.3	Sacramento, CA
37.	Sierra Nevada	2,200	25.7	Chico, CA
38.	Yakima Brewing	1,400	—	Yakima, WA
39.	Boulder Brewing Co.	500	25.0	Longmont, CO
40.	Thousand Oaks Brewing	232*	—	Berkerly, AZ

*Estimate.
**Less than a full year's production.
***Due to Pabst-Olympia merger, 1983 figures are not comparable to 1982.
From *MBA Blue Book, 1984,* pp. 6, 8, 10, 168.

prohibition. It could also sell bottled spring water. Coors could also develop plastic containers for beer products, which would be a response to the threat of mandatory deposits and a way to lower transportation costs with lighter plastic containers. Another alternative would be to develop a beer product for the popular-priced segment in order to have a more complete line of products. Coors could also import a name brand to compete more effectively in that segment. Coors' engineers could do consulting jobs for area firms. Finally, Coors Porcelain Company could accelerate its plans to get into the lucrative billion-dollar-a-year dental-restoration market.

78   Finally, under diversification, Coors could consider other glass products, such as test tubes. Also, the company could get into other areas related to the beverage industry, such as soft drinks or distilled spirits.

The Future

79   The Coors family remained confident of their firm's success in the future. Bill and Joe Coors felt their firm had survived because of the superior quality of its product. But, would Coors' quality and its Rocky Mountain mystique be enough to survive a changing industrial structure?

80   It appeared that slow growth would continue to plague the U.S. brewing industry. This meant that any significant increase in sales by one brewer would be at the expense of other competitors. In addition, increased concentration among brewers—via acquisitions, mergers, and bankruptcies—would continue, and it was predicted that the top three firms could have up to 80 percent of the market by 1990.[5] As a result, a major strategic decision faced Coors management in the mid 1980s. Could Coors remain a regional brewer and be successful? If so, what would it need to do differently as a regional brewer to compete against the national breweries and other regional firms? Conversely, should Coors go into nationwide production and distribution? These two clear strategic alternatives presented themselves to the Coors family members in top management.

81   Over the years, Coors had increased its territory to 26 states and Washington, D.C. It had announced that it would add Alaska and Hawaii by the end of 1983, and move into Maryland in early 1984. But would this be enough to compete against the two national giants, Anheuser-Busch and Miller? Could one production facility serve a nationwide distribution, or would Coors have to operate additional breweries? Which alternative—remain regional or go nationwide—that Coors management would select remained undetermined as 1983 came to a close.

Notes

1. "A Test for the Coors Dynasty," *Business Week,* May 8, 1978, p. 69.
2. Bob Lederer, "Can Coors Survive Its Image?" *Beverage World,* April 1979, p. 49.

3. Bob Lederer, "Coal Power," *Beverage World,* September 1978, p. 58.

4. "Industry News," *Beverage Industry,* April 10, 1983, p. 58.

5. Michael C. Bellas, "Beer Wholesaler Sales Concentration: Implications for the 80's and Beyond," *Beverage Industry,* January 28, 1983, p. 30.

Joseph Schlitz Brewing Company: Retrenchment Reconsidered

1 In early May 1981, Frank Sellinger, Vice Chairman and Chief Executive Officer of Joseph Schlitz Brewing Company, heads the management team for a struggling company in a highly competitive industry. Schlitz, once the number-one brewer in the United States, slipped to fourth place at the end of 1980, behind Anheuser-Busch (A-B), Miller, and Pabst. Massive advertising expenditures, technological changes, strengthened quality controls and fiscal belt-tightening have not yet resulted in the turnaround which will return the company to its once proud position.

Background and History

2 Joseph Schlitz Brewing Company was incorporated in Wisconsin in 1924, growing out of a company established in Milwaukee in 1849 by August Krug. Joseph Schlitz took over at Krug's death in 1856. At Schlitz's death in 1875, the company was willed to August Krug's four nephews, the Uihleins, with the stipulation that the name remain unchanged. At the end of 1980, the Uihlein family retained an estimated 60 to 75 percent of the stock of the company. Joseph Schlitz Breweries were headed by a Uihlein

This condensed case was prepared by Sexton Adams of North Texas State University and Adelaide Griffin of Texas Women's University, with the assistance of M. Felton, S. Taudman, R. Neiman, and P. Norton. Copyright © 1981 by Sexton Adams and Adelaide Griffin.

for four generations, until 1976, when Chairman Robert Uihlein died of leukemia at the age of sixty. Daniel McKeithan, present Chairman, was previously married to a Uihlein and served as a director of the company. The family had such respect for his abilities that they made him Chairman after Robert Uihlein's death, despite the fact that his marriage with a Uihlein had ended and there were other Uihleins available to take over the position. Today Schlitz is one of the largest U.S. corporations still under family control.

3   The Joseph Schlitz Brewing Company has grown from a one-brand, single-plant brewery to a six-brand, multi-plant company. The product line includes *Schlitz* (a premium beer), *Schlitz Lifht, Old Milwaukee* (popularly priced), *Old Milwaukee Light, Schlitz Malt Liquor,* and *Erlanger* (a super-premium beer). In addition to their six brands, Schlitz operates five aluminum-can manufacturing plants through its container division. Other subsidiaries of the company include Geyser Peak Winery, a wholly-owned subsidiary in Geyserville, California, acquired in 1972, which produces and sells twelve different wines under the brand labels *Voltaire* and *Summit;* and Murphy Products Company in Burlington, Wisconsin, a wholly-owned subsidiary acquired in 1971, which processes and markets animal feeds and feed concentrates from by-products of brewery grains. C & D Foods, a subsidiary of Murphy Products Company, grows and processes ducklings, which are sold to food wholesalers and major food chains. Schlitz has investments in two Spanish breweries (La Cruz del Campo and Henninger Espanola) that do not contribute significantly to Schlitz's operations.

Organization and Management

4   Schlitz's organization structure, as of May 1, 1981, is shown in Exhibit 1; further detail on the organization of the marketing and operations departments is shown in Exhibit 2. The container division, as well as the wholly-owned subsidiaries, report directly to the president, as do the areas of finance, sales, government and legal, purchasing and materials services, and general counsel. The average age of all Schlitz officers as of March 1, 1980, was fifty. Schlitz has attempted to strengthen management over the past several years by recruiting marketing executives from the beverage industry. As mentioned previously, the Uihlein family owns a significant portion of the stock in Schlitz, and the family continues to be involved in the operations of the company. A former president of Schlitz, Roy C. Satchell, says he left the company because he would never feel free to run it "... There were not many family members in management, but the family did influence the company behind the scenes."[1]

5   Current problems facing Schlitz began in 1976, when competition from Miller was affecting the entire brewing industry due to the large amount of funds Philip Morris could invest. The expansion of plant capacity at

Exhibit 1

Schlitz organization chart

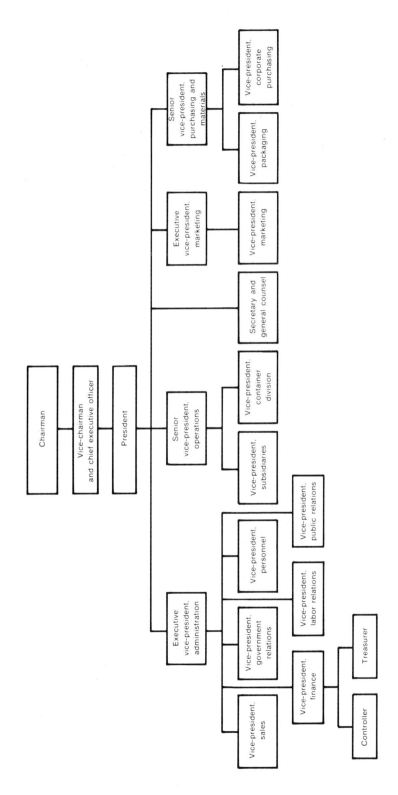

Source: Joseph Schlitz Brewing Company Annual Reports, 1977-1980.

Exhibit 2

Marketing department and operations department

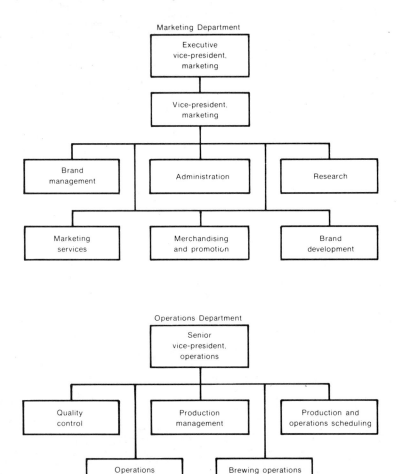

Schlitz was completed at the same time sales began dropping. A change in the brewing process resulted in a loss of a large number of loyal Schlitz-brand drinkers. Management at this time had a cloud of indictments alleging improper payments to distributors. Constant feuding among the two-hundred-plus descendents of Uihleins perpetually diverted top executives from more important things. After Frank J. Sellinger joined the company in 1977, Schlitz mounted an aggressive internal campaign to increase efficiency and spur new product development. The end result was an increase in 1980 profits and vigorous activity with new products such as *Erlanger,* an all-barley malt beer, and *Old Milwaukee Light* beer. Publicity releases from Schlitz characterize Sellinger as follows:

> In his forty-four years in the brewing industry, Frank J. Sellinger has become one of the most knowledgeable figures in the industry. There is no major part of the beer business with which he is not personally familiar.
>
> Today, at age sixty-six, Frank J. Sellinger could be in sunny retirement. Instead, he's battling with gusto in the much publicized beer wars and, as Chief Executive Officer of Joseph Schlitz Brewing Company, is a pivotal member of the new management team that is leading the firm out of the trenches and into the attack.[2]

Production

6   In the mid-1970s, Schlitz phased in a more efficient brewing process, which saved money, but customers did not like the new beer. Schlitz completed this conversion after eight years of research and a large capital investment. This change, known as "Accurate Balanced Fermentation," keeps the yeast in active suspension for the exact time necessary to complete fermentation. Seeking to cut costs, Schlitz also put in more corn syrup and less barley malt, the relatively expensive ingredient commonly used to give beer its flavor and body. To get uniform quality and taste from each brewery, Sellinger imposed strong central controls. The tasting department now gets daily samples from each plant, and quality control has improved by having test control personnel report directly to Milwaukee and also by giving them final say over what leaves the plant.

Marketing

7   In 1977, Schlitz was marketing four of the nine American beers in national distribution, more than any other brewer. Since that time, Schlitz's two major brands, premium-priced *Schlitz* and popular-priced *Old Milwaukee,* have both lost market share. (Market share in Texas dropped 4 percent in 1979, and the gain went to A-B and Miller.) *Schlitz Light,* introduced in 1975, has continually fallen below sales expectations, despite reformulations and repackaging to improve its image. In 1980, Schlitz entered the fast growing and highly profitable super-premium category with *Erlanger* to compete with earlier introductions by A-B *(Michelob)* and by Miller *(Lowenbrau). Erlanger* was introduced to test markets in 1979, and in only one year expanded nationally. This is an impressive statistic for any product, but *Erlanger* has a long way to go to catch up. Schlitz also test marketed another light beer, *Tribute,* later renamed *Old Milwaukee Light,*

and its expansion to full nationwide distribution is planned by the summer of 1981.

8   Schlitz leads the industry in the malt liquor market with their *Schlitz Bull* brand. This malt liquor represents 3 percent of the total beer market, and, according to company executives, aggressive advertising has been responsible for its success. Schlitz's strength in each region of the U.S. is indicated in Exhibit 3.

9   Due to the importance of marketing in the beer industry, advertising is very critical. According to Schlitz representatives, Schlitz conducts major segmentation studies on a periodic basis to determine how to properly position brands in the marketplace. These studies identify need segments of beer drinkers, identifying those with physiological needs and those with psychological needs. Schlitz also conducts a major consumer tracing study each year to determine to whom commercials should be targeted from a media standpoint. The study aids in developing the demographic profile of the target drinker, as well as in identifying those bought by different demographic groups. This information allows Schlitz to determine the target groups to reach via different media, such as television, radio, print, and outdoor advertising.

10   The current advertising agencies that handle the Schlitz account include: J. Walter Thompson (Chicago) for the *Schlitz* and *Erlanger* brands; Della Fermina, Travisano, and Partners (New York) for *Schlitz*

Exhibit 3

Schlitz barrelage by region (millions)

	1974	1975	1976	1977	1978	1979	1980	1981E	1984E
New England	2.3	2.2	2.1	1.7	1.2	0.9	0.7	0.6	0.3
Mid-Atlantic	1.3	1.2	1.7	1.7	1.5	1.0	0.8	0.7	0.4
Total Northeast	3.6	3.4	3.8	3.4	2.7	1.9	1.5	1.3	0.7
East North Central	3.2	3.1	2.9	2.5	2.1	1.7	1.4	1.2	0.9
West North Central	1.9	2.0	2.0	1.7	1.4	1.2	1.0	0.8	0.5
Total North Central	5.1	5.1	4.9	4.2	3.4	2.9	2.4	2.0	1.4
South Atlantic	5.0	5.1	5.5	4.8	4.7	4.2	3.9	3.6	2.7
East South Central	2.3	2.3	2.3	1.9	1.4	1.0	0.9	0.8	0.6
West South Central	4.8	5.0	4.8	5.1	4.7	4.3	3.9	3.5	2.8
Total South	12.1	12.4	12.6	11.8	10.8	9.5	8.7	7.9	6.1
Mountain	0.7	0.8	0.9	0.9	0.9	0.8	0.7	0.6	0.5
Pacific	1.2	1.6	2.0	1.8	1.8	1.7	1.6	1.5	1.2
Total West	1.9	2.4	2.9	2.7	2.7	2.5	2.3	2.1	1.7
Total all regions	22.7	23.3	24.2	22.1	19.6	16.8	14.9	13.3	9.9

Source: U.S. Brewer's Association, Beer Marketer's Insights, Inc., and Sanford C. Bernstein & Company.
Note: Discrepancies due to rounding.
E = Estimated.

Light; Benton and Bowles (New York) for *Schlitz Malt Liquor;* B.B.D. & O. International (New York) for *Old Milwaukee.*

11   *Schlitz* premium beer accounts for over 60 percent of Schlitz's sales. Schlitz's famous advertising campaign for premium, "Go for the Gusto," was very successful for many years. In 1977, *Schlitz* advertising began to lose its edge. To revive themselves, Schlitz brought out a series of formidable beer drinkers who responded to a suggestion that they abandon *Schlitz* for another beer. The beer drinker would glower into the camera and demand, "You want to take away my gusto?" The commercials did not receive a good reception from most viewers and were dropped in the fall of 1977, when they were replaced by the traditional "gusto" commercials.

12   The *Schlitz* premium marketing program initiated in August 1979 featured strenuous activities and people who reached for the gusto. This was the so-called "Go for it" campaign. Packaging for *Schlitz* premium was also changed to a tapered "classic" bottle, emphasizing slim lines and a gold foil label. The beer was distributed to bars and restaurants of primary importance.

13   In 1980, the trend in beer advertising was toward using presidents of the brewing companies for television commercials. Since March 1979, when Pittsburgh Brewing introduced the first, three breweries have used their presidents to promote their beer. They are Pittsburgh Brewing Company, F. X. Matt Brewing Company, and Schlitz. Pittsburgh and Matt are both regional brewers, and the president concept has been highly successful for them. Schlitz feels the president concept has improved sales, but no conclusive figures are available. All have received positive responses from wholesalers, an important group in the beer industry. Schlitz currently plans to film another commercial with Frank Sellinger, the Chief Executive Officer, who has appeared in two previous commercials.

14   Also during 1980, Schlitz initiated the taste test during National Football League playoff games. The *1980 Schlitz Annual Report* states, "More than one hundred million Americans watched the Super Bowl (1981) which included the fifth of Schlitz beer's Great American Beer Tests. In these unique live television commercials, beer drinkers compared the taste of Schlitz and their regular brand of beer—with impressive results for Schlitz."[3] Participants identified themselves as a competing brand drinker. The highest percentage of drinkers selecting their regular beer brand in the taste test was 54 percent (Budweiser). Schlitz has also placed in the top three in several regional taste tests conducted by various news media. Several points should be clarified to avoid any misleading interpretation. Most American beers, unlike most European brands, are subtly flavored, and a trained palate is required to distinguish among beers. Probably no more than one person in one hundred has such a palate. In addition, one former Schlitz marketing executive has expressed doubts that the tests will prompt anyone to try Schlitz. The beer's reputation is so bad, he contends, that many people are actually ashamed to be seen drinking it. He suggests

that no matter how favorable the results may seem, television viewers will automatically reject them.

15   The Great American Beer Tests represent Schlitz's continued strategy of heavy television advertising for sports events. In 1980, Schlitz estimated that commercials during network sports were seen seven times per month in 91 percent of American households.

16   The remaining brands brewed by Schlitz have their own advertising campaign tailored to reflect the particular advantage of each and its own packaging strategy. *Old Milwaukee* beer is second in sales volume for Schlitz. Its advertising strategy includes point of sale advertising, and radio and television commercials that enforce the name via the following: "Whenever you think of the town of Milwaukee, you think of beer—and *Old Milwaukee* tastes as great as its name."

17   *Schlitz Malt Liquor,* the largest selling malt liquor in the U.S. and third largest volume seller for Schlitz, utilizes an advertising campaign centered around the famous *Schlitz Malt Liquor* bull. *Erlanger,* the super premium beer that went national in April 1980, features advertisements emphasizing the unique bottle and the slogan, "Taste the Moment."

18   *Old Milwaukee Light,* introduced in August 1980, debuted with the slogan, "We got the taste of light right." The *Old Milwaukee Light* advertising campaign in the first quarter of 1981 featured a discount in price of *Old Milwaukee Light* and *Old Milwaukee,* introduced by the slogans "The price of great taste just went down" and "It doesn't get any better than this."

19   Schlitz has not been able to match the major brewers in advertising dollars; however, in 1981-82, Schlitz executives announced that they will strive to develop advertising that is more cost effective than that of its competition. On a per barrel basis, however, Schlitz leads the industry. Frank Sellinger summarized Schlitz's advertising opportunities as follows:

> The brewing industry has become a marketing battleground with the continuing barrage of advertising. It must confuse the consumer. Sometimes I'm not sure if people know whether they're buying a good beer or clever advertisement. We're trying to cut through that confusion with a simple message: we brew superior beer; try it and judge for yourself.[4]

Litigation

20   Legal battles have continually plagued Schlitz. A six-year-old antitrust lawsuit filed by the Pearl Brewing Company of San Antonio, Texas, and seven of its independent wholesalers was finally settled in 1977 with Schlitz agreeing to pay Pearl $2.6 million. Following a three-year federal grand jury investigation, assisted by the ATF and IRS, Schlitz was indicted on March 15, 1978, on three counts of felony tax fraud, one misdemeanor charge of conspiracy, and seven hundred individual

misdemeanor counts allegedly in violation of the Federal Alcohol Administration Act (FAAA). These charges stemmed from questionable marketing practices, including the furnishing of products, equipment, services, and possible cash payments by Schlitz to retail accounts to induce the purchase of Schlitz products. Settlement was reached in November 1978; all but one count, including the felony tax fraud counts, was dismissed. Schlitz, although not admitting any wrongdoing, agreed to pay $761,000 and to refrain from questionable marketing practices in the future.

21   A civil suit by the Securities and Exchange Commission (SEC) alleged violations of the antifraud, proxy, and reporting provisions of federal securities law, particularly in regard to the company's domestic marketing practices and relationship with Spanish brewing investments designed to evade Spanish tax and exchange control laws. The suit was settled in 1978. Schlitz, again without admitting or denying any of the allegations, consented to:

1. A permanent injunction prohibiting future violations

2. The appointment of a Special Review Person by the SEC to review Schlitz's procedures followed in its internal investigation, accounting and bookkeeping practices in the Export Marketing Division, disclosures, and to make recommendations regarding past and future disclosures

3. The establishment of an Audit Committee of the Board of Directors, comprised of three outside directors, to review the company's financial controls and accounting procedures

22   The United States Court of Appeals Seventh Circuit in 1979 upheld the dismissal of claims filed by the Miller Brewing Company against Schlitz in 1975. Miller alleged trademark infringement in the way Schlitz used the term "light" in distributing *Schlitz Light* beer. The court reaffirmed an earlier determination that the words "light" and "lite" may not be exclusively appropriated by Miller as a trademark. The appeals court remanded for trial Miller's claim against Schlitz for unfair competition.

23   Various other allegations and suits (criminal and civil) against Schlitz have occurred in the antitrust areas of price fixing, monopoly practices, and illegal trade promotions. These allegations have been resolved with no material erosion of Schlitz's position.

Finance

24   After nearly three decades of growth, Schlitz sales began falling in the late seventies. Beginning with the end of 1978, the company logged five straight quarters of red ink. As of December 31, 1980, four straight quarters of profits had been reported; however, barrel shipments were down. Despite

reported profits, the company faces a challenge in turning around sales of the *Schlitz* brand (see Exhibits 4-8).

25   Earning from operations were $30.1 million in 1980, compared to a $77 million loss in 1979, and earnings of $36.0 million in 1978. Sales dollars in

---

Exhibit 4

Schlitz—Consolidated balance sheets December 31, 1980 and 1979 (dollars in thousands except per-share data)

	1980	*1979*
Assets		
Current assets:		
Cash	$ 8,097	$ 10,661
Marketable securities, at lower of cost or market	134,525	30,525
Accounts receivable, less reserves of $913 in 1980 and $891 in 1979	31,049	25,011
Receivable from sale of assets	30,000	30,000
Refundable income taxes	—	24,292
Inventories, at lower of cost or market	54,571	55,491
Prepaid expenses	3,756	5,501
Total current assets	261,998	181,481
Investments and other assets:		
Notes receivable and other noncurrent assets	38,621	63,028
Investments	14,514	16,407
Land and equipment held for sale	6,710	6,711
	59,845	86,146
Plant and equipment at cost	663,176	661,305
Less—Accumulated depreciation and unamortized investment tax credit	346,056	319,783
Total investments and other assets	317,120	341,522
	$638,963	$609,149
Liabilities		
Current liabilities:		
Notes payable	$ 920	$ 2,084
Accounts payable	49,833	47,393
Accrued liabilities	39,790	44,495
Federal and state income taxes	10,284	157
Total current liabilities	100,827	94,129
Long-term debt	119,767	131,032
Deferred income taxes	92,834	85,439
Shareholders' investment:		
Common stock, par value $2.50 per share, authorized 30,000,000 shares, issued 29,373,654 shares	73,434	73,434
Capital in excess of par value	2,921	2,921
Retained earnings	255,808	228,822
	332,163	305,177
Less—Cost of 310,672 shares of treasury stock	6,628	6,628
	325,535	298,549
Total shareholders' investment	$638,963	$609,149

Exhibit 5

Schlitz—Statements of consolidated earnings (loss) for the years ended December 31, 1980, 1979, and 1978 (dollars in thousands except per-share data)

	1980	1979	1978
Sales	$1,027,743	$1,042,583	$1,083,272
Less—Excise taxes	131,076	148,427	172,431
Net sales	896,667	894,156	910,841
Cost and expenses:			
Cost of goods sold	721,278	746,415	729,854
Marketing, administrative, and general expenses	145,304	155,439	144,939
	866,582	901,854	874,793
Earnings (loss) from operations	30,085	(7,698)	36,048
Other income (expense):			
Interest and dividend income	21,796	4,485	3,311
Interest expense	(11,508)	(12,784)	(15,359)
Gain on repurchase of debentures	4,153	1,175	114
Gain (loss) on disposal of assets	596	(86,076)	(3,045)
Miscellaneous, net	734	54	(299)
	15,771	(93,146)	(15,278)
Earnings (loss) before income taxes	45,856	(100,844)	20,770
Provision for income taxes	18,870	(50,199)	8,809
Net earnings (loss)	$ 26,986	$ (50,645)	$ 11,961
Net earnings (loss) per share	$.93	$(1.74)	$.41

Schlitz—Statements of consolidated retained earnings and capital in excess of par value for the years ended December 31, 1980, 1979, and 1978 (dollars in thousands except per-share data)

	Retained earnings	Capital in excess of par value
Balance, December 31, 1977	$286,978	$2,921
Net earnings, 1978	11,961	—
Cash dividends declared, $.47 per share	(13,660)	—
Balance, December 31, 1978	285,279	2,921
Net loss, 1979	(50,645)	—
Cash dividends declared, $.20 per share	(5,812)	—
Balance, December 31, 1979	228,822	2,921
Net earnings, 1980	26,986	—
Balance, December 31, 1980	$255,808	$2,921

1980 increased slightly from $894 million in 1979 to $897 million in 1980. Sales of cans and lids to outside parties amounted to $78.9 million in 1980, $76.5 million in 1979, and $36.9 million in 1978. Factors in the company's

Exhibit 6

Schlitz—Five-year financial summary (amounts in thousands except per-share data)

	1980	1979	1978	1977	1976
Sales including excise taxes	$1,027,743	$1,042,583	$1,083,272	$1,134,079	$1,214,662
Net sales	896,667	894,156	910,841	937,424	999,996
Earnings (loss) from operations	30,085	(7,698)	36,048	60,855	112,645
Net earnings (loss)	26,986	(50,645)	11,961	19,765	49,947
Depreciation of plant and equipment	34,445	44,516	45,946	41,127	35,685
Working capital provided from operations	63,307	41,638	68,179	85,423	101,178
Capital expenditures	9,778	11,426	14,461	35,670	111,234
Total assets	638,963	609,149	691,935	726,762	737,843
Net working capital	161,171	87,352	40,254	47,694	36,070
Current ratio	2.6 to 1	1.9 to 1	1.4 to 1	1.6 to 1	1.4 to 1
Plant and equipment, net	317,120	341,522	526,596	564,620	585,785
Long-term debt	119,767	131,032	140,362	196,506	223,195
Long-term debt to total capital ratio	26.9%	30.5%	28.3%	35.5%	38.5%
Average number of shares outstanding	29,063	29,063	29,063	29,063	29,063
Per-share data					
Net earnings (loss)	$.93	$(1.74)	$.41	$.68	$1.72
Dividends	—	.20	.47	.68	.68
Shareholders' investment	11.20	10.27	12.22	12.27	12.27
Barrels of beer sold	14,954	16,804	19,580	22,130	24,162
Brewery capacity in barrels	25,600	31,000	31,400	29,500	27,000

Schlitz—Price range of common stock

	1980		1979	
	High	Low	High	Low
First quarter	$9\frac{1}{4}$	5	$12\frac{3}{8}$	$9\frac{7}{8}$
Second quarter	$8\frac{1}{4}$	$6\frac{1}{4}$	$13\frac{3}{8}$	9
Third quarter	$9\frac{1}{8}$	7	$12\frac{1}{8}$	$9\frac{1}{8}$
Fourth quarter	$9\frac{7}{8}$	$7\frac{1}{4}$	$13\frac{3}{8}$	$7\frac{7}{8}$

Stock listed—New York Stock Exchange. As of February 13, 1981, there were 17,622 holders of record of Schlitz common shares.

1980 earnings performance included higher beer selling prices, lower production costs, and higher interest income.

26   The success of Schlitz's cost-cutting efforts was due to cutbacks of personnel over the past four years, a gradual decrease in expenditures in the capital improvements program, and discontinuation of a quarterly divi-

Exhibit 7

Cash flow, 1976–1981E (millions)

	1976	*1977*	*1978*	*1979*	*1980*	*1981E*
Internal sources						
Net income	$ 49.9	$ 19.8	$ 12.0	$(50.6)	$ 30.0	$ 30.0
Depreciation	31.9	36.4	41.1	39.5	33.0	30.0
Deferred tax	19.1	20.9	14.1	(23.4)	3.0	5.0
Other (mostly ITC)	15.8	3.5	—	—	—	—
Total	$116.7	$ 80.6	$ 67.2	$ 34.5	$ 66.0	$ 65.0
Internal uses						
Dividends	$ 19.8	$ 19.8	$ 13.7	$ 5.8	—	—
Capital expenditures, net	110.1	24.5	9.5	(95.2)[b]	11.0	12.0
Debt repayment	34.5	26.7	70.8	9.3	12.0	10.0
Other	(5.8)	(2.0)	(4.7)	(1.6)	—	—
Increase in working capital[a]	(2.4)	19.1	(12.0)	32.6	10.0	5.0
Total	$156.2	$ 88.1	$ 77.3	$ 49.1	$ 33.0	$ 27.0
Net internal cash	$ (39.5)	$ (7.5)	$(10.1)	$ 14.6	$ 33.0	$ 38.0
External sources						
Equity, net	—	—	—	—	—	—
Debt	$ 45.0	—	$ 14.6	—	—	—
Other[c]	—	—	—	—	$ 40.0	$ 30.0
Total	$ 45.0	—	$ 14.6	—	$ 40.0	$ 30.0
Net change in cash	$ 5.5	—	$ 4.5	$ 14.5	$ 73.0	$ 68.0
Yearend cash	29.5	22.1	26.6	41.2	114.2	182.0

[a]Excludes cash and equivalents.
[b]Largely the disposal of the Syracuse Brewery.
[c]Receivable from sale of brewery.
Source: Emanuel Goldman, "The Brewing Industry," *Research Bernstein,* 1980.

dend since the third quarter of 1979. Over the period 1977–81, staff have been cut by 20 percent. Beer selling prices increased approximately 10 percent in 1980. Lower production costs and higher interest income were related to the closing of the Syracuse brewery, sold in February 1980.

27   At the time of the sale of the Syracuse brewery, A-B agreed to the sale for $100 million, payable in three installments over a two-year period. The $30 million payable in January 1981 has been received, and the last payment of $35,714,000 plus interest is due January, 1982.

28   Plant and equipment are carried at cost and include expenditures for improvements to existing facilities, as well as expenditures for new facilities. Plant and equipment as of December 31, 1980 and 1979, are shown in Exhibit 9.

Conclusion

29   Schlitz feels they are operating in a capital-intensive business where inflation and price changes can hit particularly hard. Schlitz has

Exhibit 8

Selected operating results, 1976–1981E (millions)

	1976	1977	1978	1979	1980	1981E
Barrels sold	24.16	22.13	19.58	16.80	14.70	13.20
Sales	$1,214.7	$1,134.1	$1,083.3	$1,042.6	$1,040.0	$1,030.0
Net sales	$1,000.0	$ 937.4	$ 910.8	$ 894.2	$ 910.0	$ 910.0
Cost of goods sold	755.7	726.4	723.2	740.2	740.0	730.0
Marketing, general and administrative expense	131.6	150.1	151.6	161.6	135.0	150.0
Earnings from operations	$ 112.7	$ 60.9	$ 36.0	$ (7.7)	$ 35.0	$ 30.0
Interest and other expense, net	16.0	25.8	15.3	93.1[a]	(15.0)	22.0
Pretax income	$ 96.7	$ 35.0	$ 20.8	$ (100.8)	$ 53.0	$ 52.0
Tax rate	48.4%	43.6%	42.4%	—	42.0%	43.0%
Net income	$ 49.9	$ 19.8	$ 12.0	$ (50.6)	$ 30.7	$ 29.6
Net per share	$ 1.72	$ 0.68	$ 0.41	$ (1.74)	$ 1.05	$ 1.00
Per barrel						
Sales	$ 50.27	$ 51.25	$ 55.33	$ 62.04	$ 70.74	$ 78.03
Net sales	$ 41.39	$ 42.36	$ 46.52	$ 53.21	$ 61.90	$ 68.94
Cost of goods sold	31.28	32.82	36.94	44.05	50.34	55.30
Marketing, general and administrative expense	5.45	6.78	7.74	9.62	9.18	11.36
Earnings from operations	$ 4.66	$ 2.75	$ 1.84	$ (0.46)	$ 2.38	$ 2.27
Interest and other expense	0.66	1.17	0.78	5.54	(1.02)	(1.67)
Pretax income	$ 4.00	$ 1.58	$ 1.06	$ (6.00)	$ 3.60	$ 3.94
Net income	$ 2.06	$ 0.89	$ 0.61	$ (3.01)	$ 2.09	$ 2.24

[a]Loss on sale of Syracuse brewery.
Source: Emanuel Goldman, "The Brewing Industry," *Research Bernstein,* 1980.

identified two keys to its planned future growth: demographic factors and the ability to develop new markets. The company feels that with the right combination of marketing strategies and new products, per capita beer consumption should increase. According to Daniel McKeithan, Schlitz will continue to make major commitments in all areas of marketing support, especially advertising designed to generate positive images for new and established brands. Frank Sellinger states,

> I think that this opportunity to run Schlitz is probably the biggest thing I've ever done. I knew the problems when I came here three years ago. I felt then...and I continue to feel—that I can help correct them.[5]

Exhibit 9

Plant and equipment analysis[a]

Plant and equipment	1980	1979
Land	$ 8,754	$ 9,007
Building	114,782	114,177
Machinery and equipment	463,516	459,032
Cooperage and pallets	42,977	44,932
Construction in progress	3,147	4,157
	663,176	661,305
Accumulated depreciation	(334,431)	(305,420)
Unamortized investment tax credit	(11,625)	(14,363)
Total	$ 317,120	$341,522

[a]Provision for depreciation was calculated using the "straight-line method."
Source: Joseph Schlitz Brewing Company, *1980 Annual Report,* p. 14.

30   Massive advertising expenditures, additions to the product line of *Erlanger* and *Old Milwaukee Light,* and continued reduction of plant capacity have not to date solved the continued plunge of Schlitz in the brewing industry. A final decision on Sellinger's success remains to be seen.

Notes

1. Charles G. Burck, "Putting Schlitz Back on the Track," *Fortune,* April 24, 1978, p. 46.
2. Publicity Release—Frank J. Sellinger, Joseph Schlitz Brewing Company, (Milwaukee, Wisconsin: n.p., 1981).
3. *1980 Schlitz Annual Report* (Milwaukee, Wisconsin, 1981), inside cover, p. 4.
4. Publicity Release—Frank J. Sellinger, Joseph Schlitz Brewing Company.
5. Stanley Ginsberg, "Is the Gusto Forever Gone?" *Forbes,* December 8, 1980, p. 34.

Anheuser-Busch Companies, Inc. (A): The Miller Challenge

Background of the Firm

1   In 1852, George Schneider opened the Bavarian Brewery on the south side of St. Louis, Missouri. Five years later, the brewery faced insolvency. In 1857, it was sold to competitors who renamed it Hammer and Urban. The new owners launched an expansion program with the help of a loan from Eberhard Anheuser, a successful soap manufacturer at the time. By 1860, the brewery had faltered once again, and Anheuser assumed control. Four years later, his son-in-law, Adolphus Busch, joined the brewery as a salesman. Later Adolphus became a partner and finally president of the company. Busch was the driving force behind the company's success, and in 1879, the company name was changed to Anheuser-Busch Brewing Association.

2   An important reason for the brewery's success was Adolphus Busch's innovative attempt to establish and maintain a national beer market. In 1877, he launched the industry's first fleet of refrigerated freight cars. He also pioneered the application of a new pasteurization process. Busch's talents were not limited to technology alone; he concurrently developed merchandising techniques to complement his technological innovations. By 1901, annual sales had surpassed the million-barrel mark for the first time.

This case was prepared by Douglas J. Workman, Neil H. Snyder, Rich Bonaventura, John Cary, Scott McMasters, and Karen Cook of the McIntire School of Commerce of the University of Virginia.

3   August A. Busch succeeded his father as president of Anheuser-Busch in 1913. With the advent of Prohibition, he was forced to harness the company's expertise and energies into new directions (corn products, bakers' yeast, ice cream, commercial refrigeration units, truck bodies, and nonalcoholic beverages). These efforts kept the company from collapsing during the dry era. With the passage of the 21st Amendment, Anheuser-Busch was back in the beer business. To celebrate, a team of Clydesdale horses was acquired in 1933—the Budweiser Clydesdales.

4   In 1946, August A. Busch, Jr., became president and chief executive officer. During his tenure, the company's beer operation flourished. Eight breweries were constructed, and annual sales increased from 3 million barrels in 1946 to more than 34 million in 1974. The corporation also diversified extensively, adding family entertainment centers, real estate, can manufacturing, transportation, and a major league baseball franchise.

5   August A. Busch III was elected president in 1974 and chief executive officer the following year, making him the fifth Busch to serve in that capacity. Thus far under his direction, Anheuser-Busch has accomplished the following: opened its 10th brewery; introduced Michelob Light, Anheuser-Busch Natural Light, and Würzburger Hofbräu; opened a new Busch Gardens theme park; launched the largest brewery expansion project in the company's history; vertically integrated into new can manufacturing and malt production facilities; and diversified into container recovery, soft drinks, and snack foods.

The Industry and Competition

6   Ninety percent of Anheuser-Busch's sales come from their beer products. (Generically, the term *beer* refers to any beverage brewed from a farinaceous grain.) The type of beer consumed in America today originated in the 1840s with the introduction of lager beer. Lager beer is bottom fermented (meaning yeast settles to the bottom during fermentation). The beer is then aged (or lagered) to mellow, resulting in a lighter, more-effervescent potation. Prior to 1840, Americans' tastes closely resembled British tastes (that is, heavily oriented toward ale, porter, and stout). The influx of German immigrants in the 1840s initially increased the importance of lager beer because of the influence of German tastes and brewing skills.

7   By 1850, there were 430 brewers in the United States producing a total of 750,000 barrels per year, and by the end of the decade, there were 1,269 brewers producing over 1 million barrels per year. At that time, brewers served relatively small local areas. In the latter half of the 19th century, several significant technological advances were adapted to the beer industry, including artificial refrigeration, mechanized bottling equipment, and pasteurization. The latter innovation enabled brewers to ship warm beer and store it for a longer period of time without refermentation. With devel-

opments in transportation technology, the 20th century saw the rise of the national brewer. The combined impact of these technological advances resulted in greater emphasis on marketing as the primary instrument of competition.

8   The modern era of the brewing industry begins with the end of World War II. Prior to that time, only a few brewers sold beer nationally, and they primarily operated out of a single plant. To offset additional transportation costs not incurred by local or even regional brewers, the national firms advertised their beers as being of premium quality and charged a premium price. This structural change in the industry (from predominantly local or regional to national producers) after World War II has resulted in a steady decline in the number of brewers and plants and an increase in the market concentration of the large national brewers. Exhibit 1 shows the number of breweries and brewery firms for 1946–1976. Exhibit 2 shows concentration ratios for 1935–1977.

9   In the period following World War II, annual beer sales hit a record high in 1947 and then declined and stagnated until 1959. Exhibit 3 shows per-capita demand trends in total beer, packaged beer, and draft beer for this period.

10   Many analysts blamed the lack of growth in demand upon demographic factors. According to *Brewers Almanac 1976* (p. 82), past industry surveys have shown that persons in the 21–44 age group account for about 69 percent of beer consumption. Since this age group exhibited little growth during 1948–1959, population demographics offer a good explanation for stagnated demand during this period. However, other factors must be introduced to account for post-'59 growth, because beer sales grew more than twice as fast as the number of people in this age group.

Economies of Scale

11   A major reason for the growth of national firms is the economies of scale obtained in their plant operations. Economies of scale in plant size enable brewers to obtain the lowest possible unit cost. According to Dr. Kenneth G. Elzinga of the University of Virginia (an authority on the brewing industry), the minimum efficient size (MES) plant capacity for the brewing industry is 1.25 million barrels per year. Cost savings accrue from water-processing equipment, sewage facilities, refrigeration equipment, management, laboratories, and custodial cost reductions. Scale economies from most of these sources continue to plant capacities of 10 million barrels per year, but beyond the size of 4.5 million barrels, cost savings are negligible. Exhibit 4 shows one method used to estimate the extent of economies of scale: the survivor test.

12   Economies of scale played a central role in the restructuring of the brewing industry that led to the demise of hundreds of breweries between 1945 and 1970. Moreover, according to Charles F. Keithahn of the Bureau

Exhibit 1

Number of breweries and brewery firms: 1946–1976

Year	Plant	Firms
1946	471	
1947	465	404
1948	466	
1949	440	
1950	407	
1951	386	
1952	357	
1953	329	
1954	310	263
1955	292	
1956	281	
1957	264	
1958	252	211
1959	244	
1960	229	
1961	229	
1962	220	
1963	211	171
1964	190	
1965	179	
1966	170	
1967	154	125
1968	149	
1969	146	
1970	137	
1971	134	
1972	131	108
1973	114	
1974 (June)	108	
1976	94	49

Source: For the years 1946–74: *Brewing Industry Survey* (New York: Research Company of America, 1973, 1974); 1947–72 (for number of firms): U.S. Bureau of the Census, *Census of Manufactures;* and 1976: *Brewers Digest Brewery Directory, 1977.*

of Economics of the Federal Trade Commission, an analysis based solely on economies of scale would indicate a decline in firm concentration over the 1970s (in a world in which all plants are of minimum efficient size but no larger). Exhibit 5 shows the minimum market share a firm with a MES plant would need for survival.

The Effects of Mergers on Industry Concentration

13   Leonard Weiss of the University of Wisconsin at Madison developed a means of delineating the impact of mergers on an industry's structure.

Exhibit 2

National beer sales concentration ratios: 1935–1977 (percent)

Year	Four firm	Eight firm
1935	11	17
1947	21	30
1954	27	41
1958	28	44
1963	34	52
1966	39	56
1967	40	59
1970	46	64
1972	52	70
1973	54	70
1974	58	74
1975	59	78
1976	59	80
1977	63	83

Source: For the years 1935–72: U.S. Bureau of the Census, *Census of Manufactures* (based on value of shipments, establishment basis); 1973: based on share of total sales of U.S. brewers in *Brewing Industry Survey* (New York: Research Company of America, 1974); 1974–75: based on sales data in *Advertising Age,* November 3, 1975, and December 27, 1976; and 1976–77: based on sales data in *Modern Brewery Age,* February 14, 1977, and February 13, 1978, by permission.

Using his methodology, Dr. Elzinga found that mergers accounted for a negligible amount of the concentration occurring in the brewing industry. In fact, concentration trends in the brewing industry are rather unique in that most of the increased concentration was brought about by internal expansion rather than by merger or acquisition. Strict enforcement of the antitrust laws by the Justice Department (DOJ) is the reason mergers have accounted for such a small share of the increase in concentration. But the DOJ, through its rigid enforcement of the antitrust laws, may have promoted the end result it was seeking to prevent—increased national concentration. With the elimination of the merger route, the national brewers were forced to expand internally. They built large new breweries, which were more efficient than the older, smaller ones. If mergers had been permitted, the national firms might have acquired old, small breweries and might have grown more slowly than they actually did.

The Effect of Advertising

14   Forced to expand internally in a capital-intensive industry (it costs between $25 and $45 for each additional barrel of capacity), the national firms sought to ensure a steady demand for their products. The need for larger

Exhibit 3

Analysis of per capita beer demand in the United States, 1935–1963

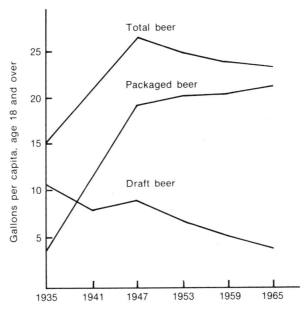

Source: John G. Keane (Ph.D. diss., University of Pittsburgh).

Exhibit 4

Surviving breweries by capacity: 1959–1973

Listed capacity (thousands of barrels)	1959	1961	1963	1965	1967	1969	1971	1973
0–25	11	9	8	7	3	3	2	2
26–100	57	51	46	44	33	23	19	11
101–250	51	44	39	30	26	23	19	11
251–500	40	37	33	24	18	14	14	10
501–750	14	15	13	12	13	15	12	5
751–1,000	16	19	20	20	22	20	20	15
1,001–1,500	14	14	12	13	15	13	13	13
1,501–2,000	4	5	5	3	3	8	8	7
2,001–3,000	5	6	6	7	5	6	9	9
3,001–4,000	3	3	4	5	5	3	3	3
4,001+	2	2	3	3	4	7	7	11

Source: Compiled from plant capacity figures listed in the *Modern Brewery Age Book* (Stamford, Conn.: Modern Brewery Age Publishing Co., various years), and from industry trade sources. These figures do not include plants listed only on a company-consolidated basis (in the case of multiplant firms) or single-plant firms not reporting capacity in the *Blue Book.* Most plants list their capacity.

Exhibit 5

Economies of plant scale expressed as a percentage of total industry production for 1970, 1975, 1980

	Production (millions of barrels)	MES plant as a percent of production
1970	134.7	.9%
1975	150.3	.8
1980 (estimated)..................	176.8	.7

Source: Dr. Willard Mueller, from testimony before the Subcommittee on Antitrust and Monopoly of the Committee of the Judiciary, United States Senate, 95th Congress, 2d sess. (1978).

markets resulting from increased capacity coincided with the development of television, which led to an increase in the firm's desired level of product identification. Advertising, particularly television spots, became the key to product differentiation in an industry where studies have shown that, under test conditions, beer drinkers cannot distinguish between brands. Exhibit 6 shows comparative advertising expenditures for 10 brewers. Exhibit 7 shows relative advertising effectiveness.

Exhibit 6

Barrelage sold, measured media advertising expenditures, and advertising expenditures per barrel, 10 leading brewers, 1972–1977

	Philip Morris-Miller			Anheuser-Busch		
Year	Barrels (000)	Advertising* ($000)	A/B†	Barrels (000)	Advertising* ($000)	A/B†
1977	24,410	$42,473	$1.74	36,640	$44,984	$1.23
1976	18,232	29,117	1.60	29,051	25,772	.89
1975	12,862	20,894	1.62	35,200	19,237	.55
1974	9,066	12,140	1.34	34,100	12,359	.36
1973	6,919	10,002	1.45	29,887	12,936	.43
1972	5,353	8,400	1.57	26,522	14,808	.56

	Schlitz			Pabst		
Year	Barrels (000)	Advertising* ($000)	A/B†	Barrels (000)	Advertising* ($000)	A/B†
1977	22,130	$40,830	$1.85	16,300	$10,843	$ .67
1976	24,162	33,756	1.40	17,037	9,112	.53
1975	23,279	23,173	1.00	15,700	9,007	.57
1974	22,661	17,977	.79	14,297	7,711	.54
1973	21,343	16.615	.78	13,128	6,422	.49
1972	18,906	17,782	.94	12,600	6.142	.49

Exhibit 6 (concluded)

Year	Coors Barrels (000)	Coors Advertising* ($000)	Coors A/B†	Olympia (Hamm 1975) Barrels (000)	Olympia (Hamm 1975) Advertising* ($000)	Olympia (Hamm 1975) A/B†
1977	12,824	$ 3,966	$ .25	6,831	$ 8,470	$1.24
1976	13,665	1,626	.12	6,370	5,430	.85
1975	11,950	1,093	.09	5,770	5,555	.96
1974	12,400	801	.06	4,300	2,764	.64
1973	10,950	699	.06	3,636	2,323	.64
1972	9,785	1,332	.14	3,330	2,491	.75

Year	Heileman (Grain Belt 1975) Barrels (000)	Heileman (Grain Belt 1975) Advertising* ($000)	Heileman (Grain Belt 1975) A/B†	Stroh Barrels (000)	Stroh Advertising* ($000)	Stroh A/B†
1977	6,245	$ 4,636	$ .74	6,114	$ 7,212	$1.18
1976	5,210	3.616	.69	5,765	5,017	.87
1975	4,535	2,864	.63	5,133	3,950	.77
1974	4,300	2,329	.54	4,364	3,477	.80
1973	4,420	2,243	.51	4,645	3,145	.68
1972	3,675	2,260	.61	4,231	3,567	.84

Year	Schaefer Barrels (000)	Schaefer Advertising* ($000)	Schaefer A/B†	C. Schmidt Barrels (000)	C. Schmidt Advertising* ($000)	C. Schmidt A/B†
1977	4,700	$ 4,219	$ .90	3,571	$ 3.912	$1.10
1976	5,300	2,516	.47	3,450	2,703	.78
1975	5,881	2,637	.45	3,330	2,269	.68
1974	5,712	2,308	.40	3,490	3,035	.87
1973	5,500	2,438	.44	3,520	2,916	.83
1972	5,530	2,994	.54	3,194	2,104	.66

*Advertising expenditures in six measured media as reported in *Leading National Advertisers,* various issues.
†Advertising per barrel.
Source: Company sales for 1970–77 from *Advertising Age,* various issues.

15   In the last decade, a new rivalry has developed among major national brewers (this time at the instigation of Miller Brewing Company). In 1970, Philip Morris completed an acquisition of Miller, and according to Dr. Willard F. Mueller of the University of Wisconsin, Philip Morris's multiproduct and multinational operations in highly concentrated industries enabled it to engage in cross-subsidization of its brewing subsidiary. This capacity, coupled with the relatedness of the marketing function between Philip Morris and Miller, provided a powerful vehicle for industry restructuring. Miller adopted aggressive market segmentation and expansion strategies, thus increasing its capacity fivefold between 1970 and 1977. According to Dr. Mueller, a doubling of 1977 capacity was planned by 1981. Exhibit 8 shows comparative financial data on Philip Morris and the rest of the leading brewers.

Exhibit 7

Relative media advertising effectiveness by beer brand, 1975–1978

	Media advertising expense ($ million)	Total barrels (millions)	Advertising expense per barrel	Barrel change 1978 versus 1974	Advertising expense per incremental million barrels
Premium category					
Budweiser	$71.5	100.2	$ .71	1.1	$65.00
Miller High Life	60.5	61.3	.99	13.5	4.48
Schlitz	70.4	59.3	1.18	(5.2)	n.a.
Light category					
Lite	63.8	22.9	2.79	8.4	7.60
Anheuser-Busch					
Natural Light	24.0	3.8	6.32	2.3	10.43
Michelob Light	6.5	0.9	7.22	0.9	7.22
Schlitz Light	30.3	3.6	8.42	0.7	43.29
Super premium category					
Michelob	35.9	23.0	1.56	4.3	8.35
Lowenbrau	29.4	1.7	17.29	1.2	24.50

n.a. = Not available.
Source: C. James Walker III, *Competition in the U.S. Brewing Industry: A Basic Analysis* (New York: Shearson Hayden Stone, September 26, 1979).

Exhibit 8

Assets, sales, net profit, net income on stockholders' investment, and total advertising expenditures, 1977 ($ millions)

Company	Assets	Sales	Net profit	Total profit on equity	Total advertising
Philip Morris (Miller)	$4,048	$3,849*	$335	19.8%	$277
Anheuser-Busch	1,404	1,838	92	13.5	79
Joseph Schlitz	727	937	20	5.5	55
Pabst Brewing	396	583	22	8.1	27
Adolph Coors	692	593	68	12.2	12‡
Total 2d to 5th	3,219	3.951	202	9.8†	176
Philip Morris as a percent of 2d to 5th	126%	97%	166%	202%	157%

*Excludes U.S. and foreign excise taxes.
†Unweighted average.
‡Estimate.
Source: "500 Largest Industrials," *Fortune,* May 1977; advertising data reported in individual company Security and Exchange Commission's Form 10-K reports for 1977.

16   In 1975, Miller found a successful method for promoting a low-calorie beer, Lite, which they had purchased from Meister Brau, Inc., of Chicago in 1972. They spent heavily, around $6 per barrel, to introduce it nationwide. However, Lite's success was not wholly attributable to heavy advertising. Low-calorie beers were promoted in the past with a notable lack of success. Through marketing research, Miller discovered that a significant portion of the beer market is comprised of young and middle-aged men who are sports fans with dreams of athletic prowess. In advertising Lite, Miller relied predominantly on retired athletes renowned for their speed and agility. The message was that one could drink a lot of Lite and still be fast, not that one should drink Lite to keep from getting fat.

17   By 1975, Schlitz and, to some extent, Anheuser-Busch began to increase their own advertising expenditures and made plans to enter the low-calorie beer market. This was done not only as a response to Miller's aggressiveness but also because of a general lack of growth in demand in the face of increasing industry capacity. By 1978, 9 of the 10 largest brewers had light brands on the market. Exhibits 9 through 11 show brand shipment breakdowns for the 3 major brewers.

18   Currently, the only company with the financial resources to battle Miller and its multinational conglomerate backer is Anheuser-Busch, the industry leader, and Anheuser-Busch responded aggressively to Miller's program. In 1977, Anheuser-Busch surpassed Miller and Schlitz in advertising expenditures by spending over $44 million.

19   Exhibit 12 shows market share performance for the top five brewers and all others in the 1974–1978 period.

20   Clearly, Anheuser-Busch's and Miller's growth have been at the expense of the regional brewers and the faltering national brewers (Schlitz and Pabst). C. James Walker III, an industry analyst for Shearson Hayden Stone, Inc., estimates only 2.7 percent per year industry growth for the

---

Exhibit 9

Estimated Anheuser-Busch brand breakdown: 1974–1978; shipments in barrels (millions)

	1978	*1977*	*1976*	*1975*	*1974*
Budweiser	27.5	25.4	21.1	26.2	26.4
Michelob	7.4	6.4	5.0	4.2	3.1
Michelob Light	0.9	—	—	—	—
Busch	3.5	3.3	3.0	4.8	4.6
Natural	2.3	1.5	—	—	—
Total	41.6	36.6	29.1	35.2	34.1

Source: C. James Walker III, *Competition in the U.S. Brewing Industry: A Basic Analysis* (New York: Shearson Hayden Stone, September 26, 1979).

Exhibit 10

Estimated Miller brewing brand breakdown: 1974–1978; shipments in barrels (millions)

	1978	1977	1976	1975	1974
High Life	21.3	17.3	13.5	9.2	7.8
Lite	8.8	6.4	4.6	3.1	0.4
Lowenbrau	1.2	0.5	0.1	0.0	—
Other	0.0	0.0	0.2	0.5	0.9
Total	31.3	24.2	18.4	12.8	9.1

Source: C. James Walker III, *Competition in the U.S. Brewing Industry: A Basic Analysis* (New York: Shearson Hayden Stone, September 26, 1979).

Exhibit 11

Estimated Schlitz brewing brand breakdown: 1974–1978; shipments in barrels (millions)

	1978	1977	1976	1975	1974
Schlitz	12.7	14.3	15.9	16.8	17.9
Old Milwaukee	4.3	4.9	5.5	5.2	3.9
Schlitz Light	0.7	1.3	1.4	0.2	—
Malt Liquor	1.7	1.4	1.3	1.0	0.8
Primo	0.2	0.2	0.1	0.1	0.1
Total	19.6	22.1	24.2	23.3	22.7

Source: C. James Walker III, *Competition in the U.S. Brewing Industry: A Basic Analysis* (New York: Shearson Hayden Stone, September 26, 1979).

early 1980s. The capital-intensive nature of the industry, coupled with huge advertising outlays, make it very unlikely that any firm will be able to challenge the two leaders. To quote August Busch III, "This business is now a two-horse race."

Organization of Anheuser-Busch

21   Effective October 1, 1979, Anheuser-Busch, Inc. became a wholly owned subsidiary of a new holding company, Anheuser-Busch Companies, Inc., and the outstanding shares of Anheuser-Busch, Inc. were exchanged for an

Exhibit 12

Market share performance

1978

	Barrel shipments (millions)	Market share	Barrel increment (millions)	Percent increase (decrease)
Anheuser	41.6	25.1%	5.0	13.7%
Miller	31.3	18.9	7.1	29.3
Schlitz	19.6	11.8	(2.5)	(11.3)
Pabst	15.4	9.3	(0.6)	(3.8)
Coors	12.6	7.6	(0.2)	(1.6)
Top 5	120.5	72.7	8.8	7.9
All others	41.7	25.2	(3.5)	(7.7)
U.S. industry	162.2	97.9	5.3	3.4
Imports	3.45	2.1	0.8	30.8
All beer	165.6	100.0	6.1	3.8

1977

	Barrel shipments (millions)	Market share	Barrel increment (millions)	Percent increase (decrease)
Anheuser	36.6	22.9%	7.5	25.8%
Miller	24.2	15.2	5.8	31.5
Schlitz	22.1	13.9	(2.1)	(8.7)
Pabst	16.0	10.0	(1.0)	(5.9)
Coors	12.8	8.0	(0.7)	(5.2)
Top 5	111.7	70.0	9.5	9.3
All others	45.2	28.3	(3.0)	(6.2)
U.S. industry	156.9	98.4	6.5	4.4
Imports	2.6	1.6	0.2	8.3
All beer	159.5	100.0	6.7	4.5

1976

	Barrel shipments (millions)	Market share	Barrel increment (millions)	Percent increase (decrease)
Anheuser	29.1	19.0%	(6.1)	(17.3)%
Miller	18.4	12.0	5.6	43.8
Schlitz	24.2	15.8	0.9	3.9
Pabst	17.0	11.1	1.3	8.3
Coors	13.5	8.8	1.6	13.4
Top 5	102.2	66.9	3.3	3.3
All others	48.2	31.5	(1.5)	(3.0)
U.S. industry	150.4	98.4	1.8	1.2
Imports	2.4	1.6	0.7	41.2
All beer	152.8	100.0	2.5	1.7

1975

	Barrel shipments (millions)	Market share	Barrel increment (millions)	Percent increase (decrease)
Anheuser	35.2	23.4%	1.1	3.2%
Miller	12.8	8.5	3.7	40.7
Schlitz	23.3	15.5	0.6	2.6
Pabst	15.7	10.4	1.4	9.8
Coors	11.9	7.9	(0.4)	(3.3)
Top 5	98.9	65.8	6.4	6.9
All others	49.7	33.1	(3.3)	(6.2)
U.S. industry	148.6	98.9	3.1	2.1
Imports	1.7	1.1	0.3	21.4
All beer	150.3	100.0	3.4	2.3

Exhibit 12 (concluded)

	1974		1974-1978		
	Barrel shipments (millions)	Market share	Increased barrel shipments (millions)	Market share point change	Compounded annual shipment growth
Anheuser	34.1	23.2%	7.5	+ 1.9	5.1%
Miller	9.1	6.2	22.2	+12.7	36.2
Schlitz	22.7	15.4	(3.1)	− 3.6	(3.3)
Pabst	14.3	9.7	1.1	− 0.4	1.9
Coors	12.3	8.4	0.3	− 0.8	0.4
Top 5	92.5	63.0	28.0	+ 9.7	6.8
All others	53.0	36.0	11.3	−10.8	(4.9)
U.S. industry	145.5	99.0	16.7	− 1.1	2.7
Imports	1.4	1.0	2.0	+ 1.1	24.9
All beer	146.9	100.0	18.7	0.0	3.1

Source: C. James Walker III, *Competition in the U.S. Brewing Industry: A Basic Analysis* (New York: Shearson Hayden Stone, September 26, 1979).

equal number of shares of the holding company. Concerning this change, August A. Busch III said,

> The holding company's name and structure will more clearly communicate the increasingly diversified nature of our business, thereby reflecting not only our position of leadership in the brewing industry but also our substantial activities in yeast and specialty corn products, family entertainment, transportation, can manufacturing, real estate, and other businesses. The new structure will also provide management with increased organizational and operational flexibility.
>
> Each of our businesses can eventually be operated as separate companies under Anheuser-Busch Companies, Inc., with responsibilities divided among management personnel.
>
> This reorganization will help facilitate our long-range plan to not only continue to grow in production and sales of beer but also to continue to expand and diversify into other areas which offer significant opportunities for growth.

22   Additionally, Busch announced that Fred L. Kuhlmann, executive vice president, had been elected vice chairman of the board of Anheuser-Busch Companies, Inc., and that Dennis P. Long had been elected president and chief operating officer of Anheuser-Busch, Inc., a subsidiary of the holding company. Long has overall responsibility for the conduct of the company's beer business, and he reports to Busch. (Busch is chairman and chief executive officer of Anheuser-Busch, Inc.)

23   Also, Long was elected a member of the corporate office of Anheuser-Busch Companies, Inc. Three individuals comprise the corporate office. They are Busch, Kuhlmann, and Long. Kuhlmann and Long consult with Busch on major corporate matters and assist him in implementing corporate policy.

24   Busch announced that the operating executives of two other divisions and subsidiaries have been named presidents of their respective operating units. W. Robert Harrington was named president of Industrial Products, and W. Randolph Baker was named president of Busch Gardens.

Key Executives*

25   August A. Busch III was born June 16, 1937, and attended public and private schools in St. Louis, the University of Arizona, and the Siebel Institute of Technology, a school for brewers in Chicago. Chairman of the board and president of Anheuser-Busch Companies, Inc., he began his career with the company in 1957 in the St. Louis Malt House. Since that time, he has worked in practically every department of both the brewing and operations divisions. In 1962, he moved into marketing, working in the field with

---

*The information presented in this section was obtained from the corporate headquarters of Anheuser-Busch Companies, Inc.

wholesalers, as well as in company-owned branches in all areas of the country. Returning to St. Louis, he was promoted to assistant sales manager for regional brands; later he was named sales manager for regional brands where he was responsible for the marketing of Busch throughout the product's marketing area.

26   Busch was named a member of the company's board of directors and appointed vice president for marketing operations in 1963. He became general manager in July 1965, executive vice president and general manager in April 1971, president in February 1974, chief executive officer in May 1975, and chairman of the board in April 1977.

27   Fred L. Kuhlmann, a native of St. Louis, is vice chairman of the board of directors and executive vice president of Anheuser-Busch Companies, Inc. He joined Anheuser-Busch, Inc. in August 1967 as general counsel and was elected a vice president in January 1971, senior vice president for administration and services and member of the board of directors in February 1974, and executive vice president for administration in June 1977. He was elected to his present position in October 1979.

28   Kuhlmann received his A.B. degree from Washington University in St. Louis and his LL.B. from that institution's school of law. He also has an LL.M. degree from Columbia University School of Law in New York. He has been active in a number of business and civic groups and serves as a director of the St. Louis National Baseball Club, Inc., and Manufacturers Railway Company. He is also a director of Boatmen's National Bank of St. Louis, Civic Center Redevelopment Corporation, and St. Louis Regional Commerce and Growth Association.

29   Dennis P. Long, 44, president of Anheuser-Busch, Inc., attended Washington University in St. Louis, Missouri. He has extensive experience spanning more than 25 years at Anheuser-Busch in both brewing and non-brewing areas. After serving as national price administrator in beer marketing from 1960 to 1964, he was promoted to assistant to the vice president of beer marketing operations and worked in the field with the nationwide beer wholesaler network, as well as with the company-owned branch distribution centers. He was promoted to assistant to the vice president and general manger in 1965.

30   In 1972, Long was elected group vice president responsible for the Busch Gardens and industrial products division and Busch Properties, Inc. Under his leadership, the industrial products division became the nation's leading producer of bakers' yeast; the division's sales of both yeast and corn products and profitability increased to record proportions. He also headed the transition of Busch Gardens from beer promotional facilities to a separate profit center. Since then, a new Busch Gardens has been opened in Williamsburg, Virginia, and that division also operates profitably. Since he took charge of Busch Properties, Inc., the real estate subsidiary has gone further into residential and resort development, in addition to the commercial-industrial field, and the performance of Busch Properties has improved markedly.

31   In June 1977, Long became vice president and general manager of the beer division, and since that time, has embarked upon a strong effort to increase beer sales volume and profitability. His efforts include new and expanded marketing efforts, increased productivity in brewing and packaging, and a strong cost control and cost reduction effort.

Products Offered by Anheuser-Busch

32   Over the past five years, Anheuser-Busch's beer division has accounted for approximately 90 percent of consolidated net sales. It produces Budweiser, Michelob, Busch, Michelob Light, Classic Dark, and Anheuser-Busch Natural Light. The remaining 10 percent of the consolidated net sales come from family entertainment (Busch Gardens Division), can manufacturing, container recycling, transportation services (St. Louis Refrigerator Car Company and Manufacturers Railway Company), major league baseball (St. Louis Cardinals), real estate development (Busch Properties, Inc.), and the manufacture and sale of corn products, brewer's yeast, and bakers' yeast (industrial products division). Anheuser-Busch is the nation's leading producer of bakers' yeast with a market share of well over 40 percent. Exhibit 13 presents data by product line.

33   During 1978, Anheuser-Busch made significant progress in redefining its diversification objectives as a means of building for the future. A corporate policy was established to concentrate initially on developing new food and beverage products that are compatible with the existing capabilities and, where possible, on distributing these products through the company's existing wholesaler network. The company is presently working on developing a line of snack foods, reportedly called Eagle Snacks, which would also be compatible with existing production and distribution facilities.

Exhibit 13

Revenue generated by product class (in thousands of dollars)

	1978	*1977*	*1976*	*1975*	*1974*
Consolidated sales...........	$2,701,611	$2,231,230	$1,752,998	$2,036,687	$1,791,863
Federal and state beer taxes..................	441,978	393,182	311,852	391,708	378,772
Consolidated net sales.......	$2,259,633	$1,838,048	$1,441,146	$1,644,979	$1,413,091
Beer division	2,056,754	1,691,004	1,282,620	1,480,481	1,271,782
Percent of consolidated net sales	91%	92%	89%	90%	90%
Other divisions*.............	$ 202,879	$ 147,044	$ 158,526	$ 164,498	$ 141,309
Percent of consolidated net sales..................	9%	8%	11%	10%	10%

*All other divisions include: industrial products division, Busch Gardens division, Busch Properties, Inc., transportation, and the St. Louis Cardinals.
Source: Anheuser-Busch Company, Inc., annual reports, 1974–1978.

34   The company began test marketing Würzburger Hofbräu beer in the United States early in 1979. This full-bodied, premium, German beer will be brewed in Wurzburg, West Germany, and shipped in large insulated barrels to the United States where it will be bottled by Anheuser-Busch and distributed through the company's wholesaler network.

35   Anheuser-Busch has a new installation in St. Louis, Missouri, which annually produces 1.8 million pounds of autolyzed yeast extract, a flavoring agent for processed foods. As the only producer of the extract in the United States with its own captive supply of brewer's yeast, Anheuser-Busch entered this new venture with a decided competitive advantage.

36   Anheuser-Busch's well-known family of quality beers includes products in every market segment. Budweiser has been brewed and sold for more than 100 years. Premium Bud, available in bottles, cans, and on draught nationwide, is the company's principal product and the largest selling beer in the world. Michelob was developed in 1896 as a "draught beer for connoisseurs." Superpremium Michelob is sold nationally in bottles, cans, and on draught.

37   With a greater percentage of the population entering the weight-conscious 25–39-year-old range, Anheuser-Busch has introduced Michelob Light. It has 20 percent fewer calories than regular Michelob, and when introduced in 1978, it was the first superpremium light beer. In order to capitalize on this by transferring the consumer appeal for Michelob to Michelob Light, Anheuser-Busch communicates "the heritage of Michelob and the taste of Michelob Light" in its advertising. Michelob Light is available nationwide in cans, bottles, and on draught. Anheuser-Busch also offers Natural Light for weight-conscious beer drinkers.

38   Busch Bavarian beer was introduced in 1955 as a low-priced beer in direct competition with subpremium regional beers. In April 1978, a smoother, sweeter, and lighter Busch beer was successfully test marketed in New England as a premium-priced brand to capitalize on anticipated growth of the premium segment of the market in future years. In 1979, with new package graphics and advertising, premium Busch was introduced in areas where the company previously marketed Busch Bavarian.

39   Anheuser-Busch's expanding corporate programs of vertical integration into can manufacturing and barley malting play an important role in overall beer division activities and profitability. The company's various vertically integrated enterprises provide an added advantage in controlling the cost and supply of containers and ingredients. Vertical integration helps to reduce cost pressures in brewing operations and to ensure continuity and quality of supply.

40   Metal Container Corporation, a wholly owned subsidiary of Anheuser-Busch Companies, produces two-piece aluminum beer cans at facilities in Florida, Ohio, and Missouri. Container Recovery Corporation, another wholly owned subsidiary of Anheuser-Busch Companies, operates container recovery facilities in Ohio and New Hampshire, which are actively involved in collecting and recycling aluminum cans.

41   The company's materials-acquisition division is responsible for purchasing all agricultural commodities, packaging materials, supplies, and fuel. Its objective is to increase stability and flexibility in the procurement of commodities and materials. This division investigates alternative methods of supply, analyzes vertical-integration opportunities available, and monitors the supply and cost of all commodities purchased by the company.

42   Anheuser-Busch processes barley into brewer's malt at plants in Manitowoc, Wisconsin (total capacity of 8.5 million bushels annually), and Moorhead, Minnesota (annual capacity of 6.4 million bushels). These two malt production facilities provide the company with the capability to self-manufacture approximately one third of its malt requirements.

43   The industrial products division produces corn syrup and starch for numerous food applications, including the processing of canned frozen foods and the manufacture of ice cream and candy. Additionally, the division markets starch and resin products used in the manufacture of paper, corrugated containers, and textiles. The company's corn processing plant in Lafayette, Indiana, currently has a grind capacity of 11 billion bushels of corn yearly.

44   The company's brewer's yeast food plant in Jacksonville, Florida, has a yearly capacity of 3 million pounds. The debitterized brewer's yeast is sold to health food manufacturers for use in a variety of nutritional supplements. Busch Entertainment Corporation, the company's family entertainment subsidiary, operates theme parks in Florida and Virginia. Unique blends of natural beauty and family entertainment activities and attractions are featured in both locations. Busch Properties, Inc., is the company's real-estate development subsidiary. It is currently involved in the development of both residential and commercial properties at sites in Virginia and Ohio. St. Louis Refrigerator Car Company, Manufacturers' Railway Company, and five other companies compose Anheuser-Busch's transportation subsidiaries. They provide commercial repair, rebuilding, maintenance, and inspection of railroad cars, terminal railroad switching services, and truck cartage and warehousing services.

Marketing

45   Anheuser-Busch has a coast-to-coast network of 11 breweries, which are selectively situated in major population and beer-consumption regions. Once the beers leave the breweries, distribution to the consumer becomes the responsibility of 959 wholesale distribution operations and 11 company-owned beer branches, which provide the company with its own profit centers within the distribution system. The beer branches perform sales, merchandising, and delivery services in their respective areas of primary responsibility. The company's beer branches are located in Sylmar and Riverside, California; Denver, Colorado; Chicago, Illinois; Louisville, Kentucky; New Orleans, Louisiana; Cambridge, Massachusetts; Kansas City, Missouri; Newark, New Jersey; Tulsa, Oklahoma; and Washington, D.C.

46   The beer industry has always been a highly competitive industry. Success depends on volume, and sales by the nation's top five brewers account for an estimated 70 percent of the total market. There is intense competition between the industry leaders. According to *Value Line,* it was expected that by 1980, the top five brewers would account for approximately 80 percent of the market.

47   Competitive pressures have led Anheuser-Busch to take an aggressive stance in its marketing strategy. It is the country's largest brewer in terms of barrel sales per year and the 34th largest national advertiser. The 1978 annual report of Anheuser-Busch said their marketing efforts were "the most extensive and aggressive in company history," stressing product and packaging innovations, brand identity, and off-premise merchandising. The company entered the 1980s with new packaging innovations and new marketing programs. The aggressive packaging is aimed at further market segmentation and penetration. Presently, the company sells more than 80 basic packages.

48   Anheuser-Busch's advertisements have traditionally been aimed at communicating the quality of the company's beer products, which appeal to virtually every taste and price range. Television advertisements and sports sponsorships continue to be the major focal point for marketing the company's beer brands. Television advertisements focus on prime-time programming and sports. To increase its presence on college campuses, Anheuser-Busch utilizes a unique marketing team of 400 student representatives at major colleges and universities across the country.

49   Anheuser-Busch has enlarged its marketing staff in the beer division. A field sales task force has been established to provide immediate and concentrated assistance in markets needing a sales boost. The national accounts sales department was created to provide better marketing coordination and communication between the company's sales staff and large national chain accounts such as grocery stores, convenience stores, fast-food outlets, hotels, motels, liquor chains, and athletic stadiums. The marketing services department coordinates and expands activities in the areas of sales promotion, merchandising, special markets, point-of-sale, and incentive programs.

Production Facilities

50   Reviewing the production facilities utilized by Anheuser-Busch provides insight into the growth pattern of the organization. Devotion to investment in plant capacity has been extensive in the past decade, and the future capital expenditure program allows for future expansion and modernization of facilities (annual report, 1978).

51   The largest subsidiary of Anheuser-Busch Companies is the beer production sector. Exhibit 14 is a listing of the geographically dispersed breweries with their corresponding annual capacity in millions of barrels and dates of first shipments.

52   As can be seen from this exhibit, many of the beer production facilities are quite new. Plants in St. Louis and Newark have undergone extensive modernization programs to upgrade older plants and equipment and ensure consistent quality regardless of brewery location. In 1980, Anheuser-Busch purchased a brewery formerly owned and operated by Schlitz. The seller was forced to close the plant because of declining sales due to competitive pressures.

53   Commitments to plant expansion have been extensive in the past few years. For example, capital expenditures will approach $2 billion for the five years ending 1983, with 93 percent for beer-related activities, according to industry analyst Robert S. Weinberg. Expansion is currently being undertaken at several of the 11 breweries. At the Los Angeles plant, the largest expansion project, capacity is being increased by more than 6 million barrels. Capacity in Williamsburg, Virginia, is being increased   threefold.

54   Plant expansion in the areas of can manufacturing and industrial products manufacturing is being conducted at rapid rates. Vertical integration into can manufacturing and malt production is requiring substantial increases in plant investment. Can-production facilities were completed in Jacksonville, Florida, in 1974; in Columbus, Ohio, in 1977; and in Arnold, Missouri, in 1980. Nearly 40 percent of cans used were provided internally by 1980. In addition, two can-recycling facilities are currently in production.

Exhibit 14

Production facility locations and capacities

	Millions of barrels	*Beginning of shipment*
St. Louis, Missouri	11.6	1880
Los Angeles, California	10.0	1954
Newark, New Jersey	4.7	1951
Tampa, Florida	2.2	1959
Houston, Texas	2.6	1966
Columbus, Ohio	6.2	1968
Jacksonville, Florida	6.5	1969
Merrimack, New Hampshire	2.8	1970
Williamsburg, Virginia	7.5	1972
Fairfield, California	3.5	1976
Baldwinsville, New York	6.0	1982

Source: Anheuser-Busch annual reports.

Research and Development

55   According to the 1978 Securities and Exchange Commission's Form 10-K report, Anheuser-Busch

> does not consider to be material the dollar amounts expended by it during the last two fiscal years on research activities relating to the development of new products or services or the improvement of existing products or services. In addition, the company does not consider the number of employees engaged full time in such research activities to be material.

56   The company is, however, extensively involved in research and development. R&D funds are currently being used to develop new food and beverage products which are consistent with the company's production and distribution capabilities. The organization has a corn products research group which recently developed a number of new and very profitable modified food starches. In addition to these, Anheuser-Busch's research on possible new beer products helped to place Michelob Light and Anheuser-Busch Natural Light beers on the market.

57   Along with research on new and profitable products, the company is striving to cut packaging costs by doing research in the production of aluminum. Anheuser-Busch paid $6 million in 1978 to a major international aluminum company, Swiss Aluminum, Ltd., for access and participation rights in this company's ongoing research in the development of certain new technologies in aluminum casting. This area should greatly reduce costs in the future.

58   Besides product and container research, Anheuser-Busch's R&D departments are studying matters of social concern. The reasons for this type of research are that the company can remain active in its social responsibility as a public corporation and also strengthen its influence in reducing government regulations and thus avoid possible costly restrictions to its operations. Research to determine the causes of alcoholism and develop effective treatment and prevention programs, in co-operation with the United States Brewers Association, is one example of the company's effort here. Other examples relate to environmental matters. In an independent effort toward developing and utilizing alternative energy systems, other than scarce natural gas and oil, Anheuser-Busch is researching solar energy. In 1978, the company installed a new pilot project at its Jacksonville, Florida, brewery. At this plant, solar energy is being tested in pasteurizing bottled beers. In addition, the company is developing new land application programs aimed at soil enrichment and energy conservation. Under these programs, rich soil nutrients are taken from the breweries' liquid wastes and used to grow various crops, primarily sod, grass, and grains.

Money Matters at Anheuser-Busch

59   Exhibits 15, 16, 17, and 18 contain relevant financial data on Anheuser-Busch.

60   In his letter to the shareholders in the 1978 annual report, August A. Busch III discussed Anheuser-Busch's expansion and diversification plans. He wrote:

> We continue to commit substantial resources to provide the capacity necessary to support our planned sales growth and to maintain our industry leadership. Future growth and profitability also depend, however, on our willingness to commit funds and energies to the development of new products and new areas of business activity.
>
> For a number of years, we have been investing considerable sums of money and a great deal of effort in the area of vertical integration of our beer business...new can and malt plants and, more recently, in exploring the possibility of producing our own aluminum sheet used in the manufacture of cans. These activities have proved to be successful in controlling costs, and we will continue to pay close attention to vertical integration.
>
> We are also exploring opportunities to diversify into other business ventures which are not beer related. We can do this either through acquisitions or through internal development of new products. At the present time, we are emphasizing a program aimed at maximizing use of existing capabilities. We are in the process of developing internally a line of soft drinks and other consumer products which can be distributed through our wholesale network. We recognize from the outset that we may not achieve success in every one of

---

Exhibit 15

Per share data ($)

	Year-end December 31									
	1978	*1977*	*1976*	*1975*	*1974*	*1973*	*1972*	*1971*	*1970*	*1969*
Book value	16.71	15.07	13.72	13.17	11.93	11.11	10.25	9.20	8.02	7.03
Earnings*	2.46	2.04	1.23	1.88	1.42	1.46	1.70	1.60	1.40	1.01
Dividends	0.82	0.71	0.68	0.64	0.06	0.60	0.58	0.53	$0.42\frac{1}{2}$	0.40
Payout ratio	33%	35%	55%	34%	42%	41%	34%	33%	30%	39%
Prices—High	$27\frac{3}{4}$	$25\frac{1}{4}$	$38\frac{5}{8}$	$39\frac{5}{8}$	38	55	69	$57\frac{1}{2}$	$39\frac{5}{8}$	$36\frac{7}{8}$
Low	$17\frac{1}{2}$	$18\frac{3}{4}$	$20\frac{3}{4}$	$24\frac{1}{2}$	21	$28\frac{5}{8}$	51	37	$27\frac{1}{8}$	$28\frac{1}{2}$
Price-earnings ratio	11–7	12–9	31–17	21–13	27–15	38–20	41–30	36–23	28–19	36–28

Data as originally reported. Adjusted for stock dividends of 100 percent April 1971.
*Before results of discontinued operations of—0.09 in 1972.
Source: Standard OTC Stock Reports 46, no. 125, sec. 5 (October 31, 1979). Copyright © 1979 Standard & Poor's Corporation. All rights reserved.

Exhibit 16

Income data ($ millions)

Year ended December 31	Revenues	Operating income	Percent operating income of revenues	Capital expenditures	Depreciation	Interest expense	Net before taxes	Effective tax rate	Net income	Percent net income of revenues
1978	2,260	288	12.8%	229	66.0	28.9	206	46.0%	111	4.9%
1977	1,838	246	13.4	157	61.2	26.7	170	45.9	92	5.0
1976	1,441	181	12.6	199	53.1	26.9	103	46.4	55	3.8
1975	1,645	226	13.8	155	51.1	22.6	165	48.7	85	5.2
1974	1,413	164	11.6	126	45.0	11.9	122	47.3	64	4.5
1973	1,110	162	14.6	92	41.1	5.3	126	48.1	66	5.9
1972*	978	184	18.8	84	39.0	6.0	147	48.0	76	7.8
1971	902	170	18.9	73	35.0	6.6	136	47.3	72	7.9
1970	793	155	19.5	65	33.8	7.1	121	48.2	63	7.9
1969	667	122	18.2	71	30.1	7.4	93	51.2	45	6.8

*Before results of discontinued operations of —0.09 in 1972.
Source: Standard OTC Stock Reports 46, no. 125, sec. 5 (October 31, 1979). Copyright © 1979 Standard & Poor's Corporation. All rights reserved.

Exhibit 17

Balance sheet data ($ million)

| December 31 | Cash | Current | | Ratio | Total assets | Return on assets | Long-term debt | Common equity | Total capital | Percent long-term debt of capital | Return on equity |
		Assets	Liabilities								
1978	196	492	255	1.9	1,648	7.3%	427	754	1,393	30.7%	15.5%
1977	154	400	212	1.9	1,404	6.9	337	680	1,191	28.3	14.0
1976	135	347	167	2.1	1,268	4.5	341	618	1,101	30.9	9.1
1975	224	420	161	2.6	1,202	7.9	342	594	1,041	32.9	15.0
1974	89	252	113	2.2	931	7.5	193	538	818	23.6	12.3
1973	60	176	100	1.8	765	9.0	93	501	666	14.0	13.6
1972*	69	166	81	2.0	698	11.3	99	462	617	16.1	17.4
1971	69	163	75	2.2	654	11.3	117	414	579	20.1	18.5
1970	61	158	78	2.0	605	10.8	128	358	527	24.3	18.6
1969	45	142	65	2.2	550	8.4	135	314	485	27.8	15.1

*Before results of discontinued operations of—0.09 in 1972.
Source: *Standard OTC Stock Reports* 46, no. 125, sec. 5 (October 31, 1979). Copyright © 1979 Standard & Poor's Corporation. All rights reserved.

Exhibit 18

Ten-year financial summary (thousands of dollars, except per share and statistical data)

Consolidated summary of operations	1978	1979	1976
Barrels sold	41,610	36,640	29,051
Sales	$2,701,611	$2,231,230	$1,752,998
Less federal and state beer taxes	441,978	393,182	311,852
Net sales	2,259,633	1,838,048	1,441,146
Cost of products sold	1,762,410	1,462,801	1,175,055
Gross profits	497,223	375,247	266,091
Less marketing, administrative, and research expenses	274,961	190,470	137,797
Operating income	222,262	184,777	128,294
Interest income	11,693	7,724	10,304
Interest expense	(28,894)	(26,708)	(26,941)
Other income net	751	4,193	1,748
Loss on partial closing of Los Angeles Busch Gardens (1)			10,020
Income before income taxes	205,812	169,986	103,385
Income taxes	94,772	78,041	47,952
Income before extraordinary item	111,040	91,945	55,433
Extraordinary item (2)			
Net income	$ 111,040	$ 91,945	$ 55,433
Per share (3) income before extraordinary item	2.46	2.04	1.23
Net income	2.46	2.04	1.23
Cash dividends paid	37,013	32,036	30,646
Per share (3)	.82	.71	.68
Dividend payout ratio	33.3%	34.8%	55.3%
Average number of shares outstanding (3)	45,138	45,115	45,068
Book value per share	16.71	15.07	13.72
Balance sheet information:			
Working capital	236,396	188,069	194,814
Current ratio	1.9	1.9	2.2
Plant and equipment, net	1,109,243	951,965	857,073
Long-term debt	427,250	337,492	340,737
Debt to debt plus total equity	34.5%	31.7%	34.0%
Deferred income taxes	153,080	125,221	99,119
Deferred investment tax credit	58,053	48,371	43,174
Shareholders' equity	754,423	680,396	618,429
Return on shareholders' equity	15.1%	14.2%	9.2%
Other information:			
Capital expenditures	228,727	156,745	198,735
Depreciation	66,032	61,163	53,105
Total payroll cost	421,806	338,933	271,403
Effective tax rate	46.0%	45.9%	46.4%

Notes to 10-year financial summary:
(1) In December 1976, the company decided to close a portion of the Los Angeles Busch Gardens and convert the remainder to a sales promotion facility. Closing a portion of the Gardens resulted in a nonoperating charge of $10,020,000 (before reduction for income tax benefits of approximately $5 million). This nonoperating charge, which reduced earnings per share by 11 cents, has been reported in accordance with *Accounting Principles Board Opinion No. 39*, which was effective September 30, 1973.

Exhibit 18 (concluded)

1975	1974	1973	1972	1971	1970	1969
35,196	34,097	29,887	26,522	24,309	22,202	18,712
$2,036,687	$1,791,863	$1,442,720	$1,273,093	$1,173,476	$1,036,272	$871,904
391,708	378,772	333,013	295,593	271,023	243,495	205,295
1,644,979	1,413,091	1,109,707	977,500	902,453	792,777	666,609
1,343,784	1,187,816	875,361	724,728	658,886	579,372	490,932
301,195	225,275	234,346	252,782	243,567	213,405	175,677
126,053	106,653	112,928	108,008	108,087	92,660	84,113
175,142	118,622	121,418	144,774	135,480	120,745	91,564
10,944	9,925	4,818	3,299	3,102	3,715	3,604
(22,602)	(11,851)	(5,288)	(6,041)	(6,597)	(7,104)	(7,401)
1,816	4,840	5,287	4,855	4,065	3,420	5,171
165,300	121,536	126,235	146,887	136,050	120,776	92,938
80,577	57,517	60,658	70,487	64,412	58,227	47,627
84,723	64,019	65,577	76,400	71,638	62,549	45,311
			4,093			
$ 84,723	$ 64,019	$ 65,577	$ 72,307	$ 71,638	$ 62,549	$ 45,311
1.88	1.42	1.46	1.70	1.60	1.40	1.02
1.88	1.42	1.46	1.61	1.60	1.40	1.02
28,843	27,041	27,037	26,109	23,784	18,991	17,843
.64	.60	.60	.58	.53	.425	.40
34.0%	42.3%	41.1%	36.0%	33.1%	30.4%	39.2%
45,068	45,068	45,063	45,020	44,887	44,686	44,616
13.17	11.93	11.11	10.25	9.20	8.02	7.03
268,099	145,107	82,352	88,711	92,447	85,102	80,963
2.7	2.3	1.8	2.1	2.2	2.1	2.3
724,914	622,876	541,236	491,671	453,647	416,660	387,422
342,167	193,240	93,414	99,107	116,571	128,080	134,925
35.6%	25.7%	15.3%	17.2%	21.4%	25.6%	29.2%
80,748	66,264	54,281	41,456	34,103	27,274	23,212
24,293	21,157	17,225	14,370	14,276	13,563	12,577
393,642	537,762	500,784	461,980	413,974	358,476	314,121
15.0%	12.3%	13.6%	16.5%	18.6%	18.6%	15.1%
155,436	126,463	91,801	84,217	73,214	65,069	66,396
51,089	45,042	41,059	38,970	34,948	33,795	30,063
268,306	244,437	221,049	190,517	176,196	156,576	133,872
48.7%	47.3%	48.1%	48.0%	47.3%	48.2%	51.2%

(2) In December 1972, the company decided to close a portion of the Houston Busch Gardens and convert the remainder to a sales promotion facility. Closing a portion of the Gardens resulted in an extraordinary aftertax charge against 1972 earnings of $4,093,000, or 9 cents per share, net of applicable income tax benefits of $4,006,000.
(3) Per share statistics have been adjusted to give effect to the two-for-one stock split in 1971.
Source: Anheuser-Busch Companies annual reports, 1969–1978.

these new ventures. However, the financial risks are relatively small, and the potential rewards are considerable.

61   C. James Walker III, an industry analyst, predicted a 1981 shipment level of 55 million barrels, indicating a 9.2-million-barrel growth in the 1979–1981 period. This is comparable to that achieved in 1977–1979. However, without the presence of a visible new major category similar to "Light" in size, Walker doubts that growth in the 1980s can match the expansion of the late 1970s. According to Walker, new brands such as Würzburger and Busch Premium seem unlikely to garner the growth that Natural Light and Michelob Light may attain. Exhibit 19 shows Walker's estimate for 1981, which would make Anheuser-Busch fall 6 percent shy of its goal of 98 percent capacity utilization.

62   Busch, on the other hand, was more optimistic. He wrote:

> In anticipation of what we can expect to encounter in the marketplace, we have developed strong and aggressive marketing and promotion programs to enhance our position as industry leader. We will be introducing more new products and new packages to keep Anheuser-Busch in the forefront of market segmentation. And we will be intensifying our emphasis on the quality of our products.

Exhibit 19

Estimated volume by brewer 1978 and 1981

	1978		1981*		1978–1981	
	Barrel shipments (millions)	Market share	Barrel shipments (millions)	Market share	Barrel increment (millions)	Compounded annual rate of growth
Anheuser-Busch	41.6	25.1%	51.5	28.7%	+ 9.9	7.4%
Miller	31.3	18.9	44.9	25.0	+13.6	12.6
Schlitz	19.6	11.8	17.2	9.6	- 2.4	(3.8)
Pabst	15.4	9.3	14.7	8.2	- 0.7	(1.2)
Coors †	12.6	7.6	17.2	9.6	+ 4.6	11.1
Top 5	120.5	72.8	145.5	81.1	+25.0	6.6
All others ‡	41.7	25.2	28.4	15.8	- 13.3	(9.7)
U.S. industry	162.2	97.9	173.9	97.0	+11.7	2.3%
Imports	3.4	2.1	5.4	3.0	+ 2.0	16.5
All beer	165.6	100.0	179.3	100.0%	+13.7	2.7%

*Estimated.

† Coors was in a 16-state market in 1978 and an estimated 19-state market in 1981 (additions: Arkansas, Louisiana, and Minnesota).

‡ In 1981, the operations of Blitz-Weinhard are included with Pabst; in 1978, about 600,000 barrels of Blitz are in the all-other group.

Source: C. James Walker III, *Competition in the U.S. Brewing Industry: A Basic Analysis* (New York: Shearson Hayden Stone, September 26, 1979).

Competitive pressures will demand the most dedicated and creative efforts that we can muster, but we are confident that with our strong sales momentum, our quality products, our great wholesaler family, and the team effort of our employees, we will have another successful year and will continue to build a solid corporate foundation for future growth and profits.

case 5 Anheuser-Busch (B): Saying "Bud" Doesn't Say It All

1 1982 represented a banner year for Anheuser-Busch Companies, Inc. The company savored both the best financial performance in its history and the World Series victory of its St. Louis Cardinals. Anheuser-Busch successfully weathered its competitive duel with Miller Brewing Company to maintain its position as the "King of Beers," and it enhanced its dominant market position through the successful introduction of Budweiser Light in 1982 and its entry into several international markets. During 1982, the company aggressively pursued its diversification strategy into consumer products by acquiring Campbell Taggart, Inc., the second-largest manufacturer of fresh-baked goods in the United States. Commenting about the acquisition in a letter to stockholders, August A. Busch III, chairman of the board and president of Anheuser-Busch Companies, Inc., stated:

> Anheuser-Busch Companies decided that its first major acquisition should have a relatively low down-side risk, while at the same time providing up-side growth potential. Campbell Taggart met that objective. The combination of Campbell Taggart with Anheuser-Busch Companies will allow us to capitalize on our strengths within our organization and benefit from synergies between the business operations of the two companies.

2 Campbell Taggart represented Anheuser-Busch's first major externally generated diversification effort. Prior to this acquisition, Anheuser-Busch had concentrated on internally generated diversification efforts in the 1977-1982 period. By 1982, Anheuser-Busch was still solidly a beer brewer with over 90 percent of its total revenue coming from the sale of beer.

The Brewing Industry

3   The brewing industry in the United States was populated by hundreds of small local and regional brewers prior to the 20th century. Following World War II, there was a structural transformation of the industry. The pressure for national advertising and national distribution at low-shipping costs combined with increased price competition necessitated increased size and geographic dispersion in order to remain competitive. As economies of scale became a major key to success in brewing, large national brewers increased their market share while the attrition rate among small competitors skyrocketed. By 1970, the number of breweries had dropped from over 300 to just 92 American breweries. The 8-firm concentration ratio increased from 21 percent in 1947 to 63 percent in 1977.[1] Only 43 brewers remained in business in 1982. Ten of these brewers accounted for 95 percent of all beer sold, Anheuser-Busch and Miller controlling 56 percent of the market (see Exhibit 1). Analysts expect the trend toward industry concentration to continue and predict the two giant brewers, Anheuser-Busch and Miller, will grab an estimated 70 percent of the market by 1990.

4   In the face of increasing competition, many of the remaining rival firms are expected to merge or look for acquisitions to maintain their viability as industry participants. For example, Stroh acquired Schlitz after the Justice Department barred Heileman from acquiring the troubled Schlitz in late 1981 on the grounds it would produce too heavy a concentration in the Midwest. Heileman has been the most effective challenger for Anheuser-Busch on a regional basis, using a strategy of acquiring and reviving local brands, keeping production costs low, and employing aggressive (some say "cutthroat") marketing techniques. Its strategy has been to revitalize the acquired regional brands, gradually introduce other Heileman brands to the region, and then saturate the new market with highly promoted products. Heileman's base is the Midwest, and a Schlitz acquisition would have provided plants in the West, South, and Southeast—markets Anheuser-Busch has targeted as its major sources of future growth. Reacting to the Justice Department's decision, an Anheuser-Busch spokesman said, "Stroh-Schlitz is a lesser competitive threat than Heileman-Schlitz." Russell Cleary, Heileman chairman, offered a different opinion: "We are the only company Anheuser-Busch does not do well against. The prospect of our entry into the South scared them." Unfortunately for Heileman, the Justice Department also rejected a Heileman bid for Pabst while clearing the way for an Olympia-Pabst merger.

5   As Anheuser-Busch and Miller bring their fight into local and regional markets, a widely recognized industry analyst argues that there is no room in the industry for brewers of under 20 million barrels because of the economies of scale needed to compete in production and marketing.

---

[1]Concentration ratio refers to the percent of total industry sales accounted for by one or several firms. In this case, the sales of 8 firms represent 63 percent of total beer sales in the United States.

Exhibit 1

The brewing industry

The 10 largest brewers in 1977

How they had changed by the end of 1981

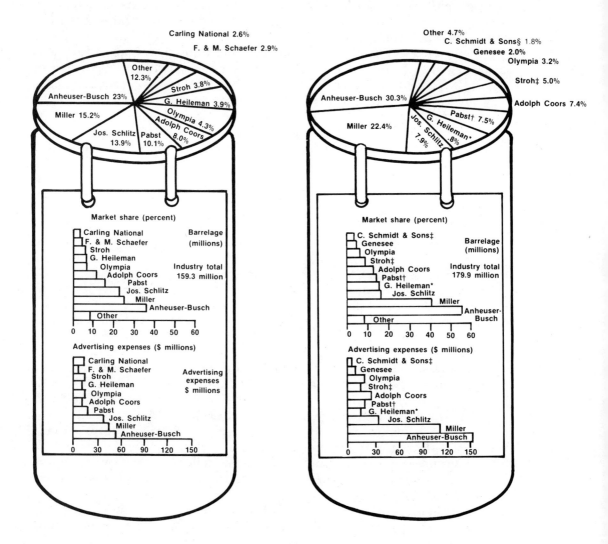

*Includes acquisition of Falls City, Carling National, Rainier.
†Includes acquisition of Blitz-Weinhard Co.
‡Includes acquisition of F. & M. Schaefer.
§Includes acquisition of Henry F. Ortieb Brewing.
Source: Business Week, July 12, 1982, p. 51.

6   In 1982, beer sales were up less than 1 percent over 1981—the result of a sluggish economy and lower beer prices. Domestic brewers actually suffered a slight profit decline, the first in 25 years, although Anheuser-Busch and G. Heileman Brewing Company posted significant volume gains among domestic brewers. Imported beers sold 5.7 million barrels in the United States in 1982, a 10 percent increase from 1981. Representing 3 percent of the market by volume, imports (because of their higher prices) accounted for approximately 5 percent of total 1982 retail dollars for beer sales in the United States.

7   From 1975 to 1980, imports expanded at an average annual rate of 22 percent, while the industry as a whole expanded at approximately 4 percent annually. Import beers are expected to continue as the fastest-growing segment of the beer industry—pegged at between 5 and 10 percent by industry analysts—culminating with a projected 5.6 percent market share (dollars) and annual sales of 12 million barrels. Overall industry growth is projected to run at 1.7 percent annually through the remainder of the 1980s.

8   Through 1982, the heaviest import consumption centered in the nation's largest metropolitan or regional markets (New York, Florida, Chicago, and California). In 1982, one in every four imported beers was consumed by a New Yorker.

9   Distribution is much easier and volume is concentrated in large urban areas. Imports, moreover, are primarily consumed in restaurants and other food-service institutions—two thirds of all imports are consumed "on premises" according to 1982 industry figures. For domestic beers, it's just the opposite—two thirds are purchased for home consumption. So imports have grown to date primarily in urban centers with high restaurant concentrations.

10   Three fourths of the import volume comes from two countries—the Netherlands (Heineken) and Canada (Molson, Moosehead, and Labatt's). Germany and Mexico supply the next-largest group of import offerings.

11   Several factors that should have a major impact on the beer industry are summarized below.

The 20 percent expansion of the adult population in the 1970s will trickle to half that rate in the 1980s. The 18-34-year-old group, which accounts for more than half of all beer consumed, will increase by less than 2 percent by 1990. The 18-24-year-old group, historically the most important single beer-consuming group (approximately 29 to 30 percent), will decline in size by 1990 to three fourths its 1980 size (see Exhibit 2).

Fueling the contraction of demand in the 18-to-24 age group is a push by many states to raise their legal drinking ages—6 states in 1982, 12 in 1983, and 25 with such legislation in the 1984-85 agenda—to 20 or 21 years.

Exhibit 2

Age distribution of the U.S. population

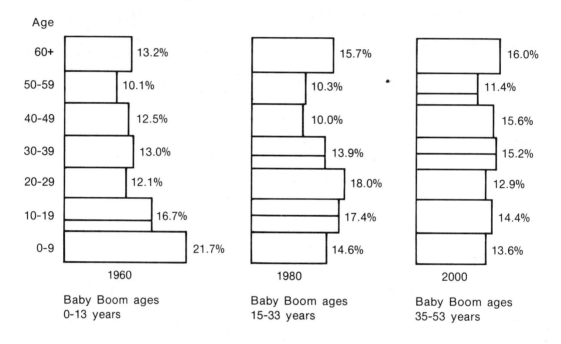

Age

	1960	1980	2000
60+	13.2%	15.7%	16.0%
50-59	10.1%	10.3%	11.4%
40-49	12.5%	10.0%	15.6%
30-39	13.0%	13.9%	15.2%
20-29	12.1%	18.0%	12.9%
10-19	16.7%	17.4%	14.4%
0-9	21.7%	14.6%	13.6%

1960	1980	2000
Baby Boom ages 0-13 years	Baby Boom ages 15-33 years	Baby Boom ages 35-53 years

State and federal governments are increasing attempts to raise excise taxes on alcoholic beverages. Relatedly, trends in some states are to require the use of expensive, market-disrupting packaging like returnable bottles and nonpenetrable packaging because of the Tylenol poisoning experience.

Social and legislative concern with the problems of alcoholism is growing. Thirty-two states passed increasingly stringent drinking-and-driving penalties between 1980 and 1984. Powerful organizations such as MADD (Mothers against Drunk Drivers) have become vocal and prominent in the 1980s.

Overcapacity (estimated to be 181 million barrels in 1983) looms heavily over the industry. Volume projections for industry growth noted earlier project a 1.7 percent annualized growth rate in beer consumption through 1990. Yet several brewers, most notably Pabst and Schlitz, are producing at approximately 70 percent of capacity in 1984. Anheuser-Busch is scheduled to complete a $2 billion, 27 percent increase in capacity by 1987. This would boost its current 63-million-barrel capacity to over 80 million barrels. On the other hand, Miller indefinitely delayed (in 1984) opening a new, 8-million-barrel plant in Ohio that was ready to produce at the end of 1983. The top U.S. brewers and their 1982 sales and market share are as follows:

No. 1—Anheuser-Busch, Inc. (59.1 million/barrels/32.0 percent).
No. 2—Miller Brewing Co. (39.3 million barrels/21.3 percent).
No. 3—Stroh Brewing Co. (22.9 million barrels/12.4 percent).
No. 4—G. Heileman Brewing Co. (14.5 million barrels/7.9 percent).
No. 5—Pabst Brewing Co. (12.3 million barrels/6.7 percent).
No. 6—Adolph Coors Co. (11.9 million barrels/6.5 percent).
No. 7—Olympia Brewing Co. (5.2 million barrels/2.8 percent).
No. 8—Genesee Brewing Co. (3.4 million barrels/1.8 percent).
No. 9—Falstaff/General Brewing Co. (3.2 million barrels/1.7 percent).
No. 10—C. Schmidt & Sons (3.2 million barrels/1.7 percent).

The region population growth rates are highest in the South. At the same time, the rate of growth is dropping in the areas as shown in Exhibit 3.

Anheuser-Busch Brewery

12   Founded in 1852 on the south side of St. Louis, Missouri, Anheuser-Busch has enjoyed a position of preeminence in the brewing industry since the late 19th century. Under the leadership of successive generations of the Busch family, the company has continued to maintain the dominant position in the U.S. brewing industry.

13   Anheuser-Busch's primary business has always been brewing with the brief exception of their successful diversification into the production of bakers' yeast during Prohibition. Today, Busch Industrial Products produces 50 percent of all the bakers' yeast sold in the United States.

14   For 30 years following World War II, Anheuser-Busch concentrated on building a dominant position in the brewing industry. Between 1946 and 1974, the company increased its brewery capacity from 3 million barrels to 34 million barrels annually. It was also during this time that Anheuser-Busch diversified on a limited basis. When August A. Busch III was elected CEO in 1975, the corporation had limited interests in real estate, family entertainment centers, can manufacturing, transportation, and a major-league baseball franchise—the St. Louis Cardinals. However, revenue from these nonbrewing interests comprised less than 10 percent of total corporate receipts.

15   Despite Anheuser-Busch's previous success and its position as the market-share leader in the brewing industry, the mid-1970s represented a critical juncture in the company's history. A formerly lackluster Miller Brewing Co., acquired by Philip Morris Incorporated in 1970, rose from 7th place to the No. 2 market-share position in the brewing industry by 1977. Miller created a virtual revolution in the brewing industry through the

Exhibit 3

Population growth by region

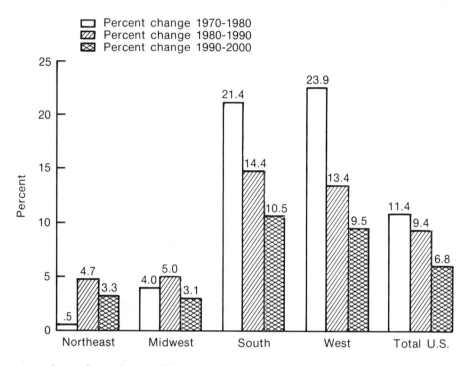

□ Percent change 1970-1980
▨ Percent change 1980-1990
▩ Percent change 1990-2000

Source: Census Bureau, 1981.

introduction of sophisticated marketing techniques. As a subsidiary of Philip Morris, Miller Brewing was transformed into an aggressive effective marketing firm through its ability to draw on both the marketing and financial resources of its parent company. Miller's successful strategy included market segmentation, innovative promotion and advertising, and improved production efficiency. Miller was not content with its No. 2 position, however. Its announced goal by 1976 was to wrest the No. 1 position from Anheuser-Busch.

16   Initially, Anheuser ignored Miller's challenge and was caught off guard by Miller's huge success in the low-calorie segment of the beer market in 1976. Concurrently, Anheuser-Busch was hit with a devastating 95-day labor strike in 1976. These factors precipitated the company's worst financial performance since the Depression. The firm's inability to meet deliveries during the strike left its traditionally powerful marketing network in a shambles and its executives unable to meet the Miller challenge. Indus-

try analyst Donald Rice reflected the view of many industry observers when he stated: "A lot of people thought Miller would end up on top."

17   Faced with this formidable challenge, August C. Busch III (the fifth-generation Busch to lead Anheuser) initiated a massive reorganization designed to transform the lumbering giant into an efficient and effective modern brewery. He totally revamped the corporation's strategy in his efforts to fend off Miller's attack and regain the market share Anheuser-Busch lost during the 95-day strike.

18   In order to overhaul the company's marketing strategy, Busch recruited experienced executives from major marketing-oriented firms, such as Procter & Gamble and General Mills. Management teams composed of merchandising, advertising, and planning specialists were established both to spearhead an aggressive new marketing posture and determine where Miller had made its most damaging inroads. To increase sales and re-establish its traditionally strong relationship with its wholesalers, Anheuser-Busch developed extensive training seminars for its wholesalers in 1980.

19   The training program emphasizes such topics as financial management, warehousing, and aggressive marketing—operating topics designed to support and shore up Anheuser-Busch's extensive wholesaler network. The company further helped its network by developing a computerized shelf-space management program for retailers that audits sales, margins, and turnover by brand, package, and promotion. This system also facilitates Anheuser-Busch's monitoring of wholesaler performance and marketing activity (account-call frequency, weekly and monthly sales, and so forth). This detailed attention is critical, says CEO Busch, "because much of this decade's fight will be waged at the wholesale and field level."

20   Promotional emphasis has been considered a key component of Anheuser-Busch's overall strategy. The company almost doubled its media advertising budget between 1976 and 1981 to over $145 million. It allocated approximately $45 million in 1982 to support one brand—Budweiser Light. It has chosen to dominate sponsorship of sporting events—98 professional and 310 collegiate sports events in 1982 versus 12 and 7, respectively, in 1976. Anheuser-Busch has also emphasized market segmentation by expanding from three brands in 1976 to eight in 1982—Busch and Natural Light in the popular price range; Bud and Bud Light in premium; and Michelob, Michelob Light, Michelob Dark, and Würzburger (an import) in superpremium.

21   Historically, Anheuser-Busch had always operated at very high capacity levels, and it was not unheard of for sales to exceed capacity during the peak selling season in the summer months. It was critical, therefore, that the company seriously consider increasing its production capabilities to meet the volume increases expected from its aggressive marketing thrust. Otherwise, it might stimulate demand and encourage a distribution network it couldn't support. Confronted with this risky, capital-intensive deci-

sion, Busch decided to undertake an extensive program of expansion and modernization of Anheuser-Busch's beer-production facilities. Capacity was increased by 60 percent in five years (1976-1981) at a total cost of $1.8 billion. To further enhance operating efficiency and lower production costs (one of the key ingredients for long-term success in the increasingly competitive brewing industry), Anheuser-Busch vertically integrated into can, labeling, and malt production (see Exhibit 4).

22   The final leg of Anheuser-Busch's strategy was to upgrade and expand its distribution system by employing more personnel and building a network of modern refrigerated warehouses (see Exhibit 5). This tactic not only improved delivery but also enhanced the maintenance of product quality from production to delivery.

23   By 1982, Budweiser was recognized by most industry observers as having the best distribution system in the country.

24   In 1980, Emanuel Goldman, a respected brewing-industry analyst, predicted that Miller wouldn't be able to overtake Anheuser-Busch's top market share, even with the 95-day strike because, "Anheuser has taken the right marketing steps." Goldman's prediction proved to be based on insight. By 1982, Anheuser-Busch had not only halted Miller's attack but had solidified its once precarious No. 1 ranking by garnering a 32.0 percent market share in the $10.5 billion beer industry. This represented an 8.5 percent increase in sales volume over 1981 and translated into a record high 19.8-million-barrel margin over Miller. Miller's market share was 21.3 percent in 1982, down from its 22.3 percent in 1981. "We are working hard to stay humble," insisted Chairman Busch in commenting on Anheuser-Busch's victory.

Strategic Management at Anheuser-Busch

25   In 1982, *Dun's Business Month* selected Anheuser-Busch Companies, Inc., as one of the five best-managed companies of the year. In making the selection, the editor stated, "excellent management is more than an ability to make money in difficult times. It is the mark of companies smartly led, prudently financed, and sure of their direction. This year's winners had all that and something else—a carefully worked strategy to wrest greater market shares from their competitors."

26   Anheuser-Busch is managed on three basic principles as set forth by Chairman Busch: planning, teamwork, and communications. The 10-member Policy Committee, composed of senior executives from every major function within the organization, is involved in all decisions on strategies, planning, policies, and other major issues concerning the company. Busch claims that the high level of teamwork and open communications on the Policy Committee have been the catalyst for Anheuser-Busch's outstanding performance. The committee approves and reviews each subsidiary's an-

nual budget and also formulates a five-year plan of company goals and strategy. Busch believes this detailed, continuous planning process has created a predictable climate in which to operate. In fact, according to Busch, the company's beer production in 1982 was within 300,000 barrels of the amount planned for seven years ago. (See Exhibits 6 and 7.)

27   Commenting on future strategic priorities, CEO Busch said in 1982:

> The company's primary objective is well-planned and well-managed growth. In addition to continued volume and profit increases in the beer and beer-related businesses, Anheuser-Busch Companies is pursuing its strategy through diversification, vertical integration activities, and the internal development of new business areas, which have constituted the major diversification thrust in the past.

Diversification Strategy

28   As the premier beer producer in the world, what do you do for an encore? Jerry E. Ritter, vice president-finance and treasurer, acknowledged in 1980 that "beer earnings and share growth may slow as we approach our long-term 40 percent market share goal." Anheuser-Busch is planning for the future, he said "by getting our feet wet in new business areas, not massive diversification efforts." The company has coined the term *learning probe* to describe its incremental approach to diversification.

29   Hoping to trade on its established strength in producing and marketing packaged beverages, the company extended its first learning probe into the soft-drink industry. Root 66 root beer was test marketed in five major cities in 1979. After two years of testing in the industry dominated by Coca-Cola and Pepsi, President Busch remarked, "We've learned it's a competitive jungle out there, just like us and Miller in the brewing industry." On October 7, 1981, Anheuser-Busch quietly announced it was suspending further test marketing of Root 66.

30   A second learning probe for Anheuser-Busch has been the addition of salted snack foods called "Eagle" snacks. Initially the superpremium snack line was sold through on-premise outlets in market testing. The company's powerful distribution system of 950 beer wholesalers, which has fleets of trucks and established relationships with bars, restaurants, and supermarkets was deemed a key strength for entry into this market. The size of the salted-snack market was more than $6.5 billion at the retail level—unit volume growth was over 6 percent in 1981.

31   Frito-Lay, a PepsiCo division, which dominates in salted snack foods, claims 35 percent of the potato chip market. Otherwise, the salted-snack market is very fragmented. Supermarkets account for about 60 percent of salted-snack sales, and convenience stores represent another 9 percent of sales.

32   Eagle snacks sales have been encouraging in $\frac{1}{2}$-ounce bags and $1\frac{3}{4}$-ounce tins—primarily in airport lounges, in Amtrak train bars, and on

Exhibit 4

Anheuser-Busch's vertical integration

Busch Agricultural Resources, Inc.

Busch Agricultural Resources processes barley into brewer's malt at plants in Wisconsin and Minnesota. These plants, with a combined annual capacity of more than 15 million bushels, provide Anheuser-Busch, Inc. with a dependable supply of high-quality malt. During 1981, they supplied the company's brewing operations with approximately 28 percent of its malt requirements. In addition, the subsidiary operates rice-handling and storage facilities in Arkansas and Missouri in connection with its rice acquisition program. A rice milling facility is under construction in Arkansas.

Metal Label Corporation

Metal Label Corporation was formed in 1979 to extend the company's capabilities into the production of beer labels and other printed materials. Metal Label formed a partnership with Illochroma International, S.A., an integrated metalizing and printing firm based in Brussels, Belgium. This joint venture is known as International Label Company.

    Clarksville, Tennessee: International Label Company constructed the first fully integrated paper metalizing and printing plant in the United States. The 100,000-square-foot plant began some phases of production in late 1980.

Metal Container Corporation

Metal Container Corporation, the company's can manufacturing subsidiary, is a significant factor both in company brewing operations and the U.S. can industry. During 1981, Metal Container produced 3.6 billion cans, providing approximately 40 percent of Anheuser-Busch, Inc.'s total can requirements and representing more than 10 percent of all the beer cans produced in the United States.

Brewery Production

Anheuser-Busch, Inc.'s strategically located network of 11 operating breweries provides the company with the most extensive production network in the world.

    The company's operating breweries provide a combined estimated shipping capacity of 60 million barrels, equivalent to 827 million cases of beer. By the mid-80s, the company plans to expand its brewing capacity to more than 70 million barrels.

Brewing Facilities (year established)

St. Louis, Missouri (1870): In 1946, annual shipping capacity of approximately 13.0 million barrels.
Newark, New Jersey (1951): Shipping capacity of approximately 5 million barrels.
Los Angeles, California (1954): An expansion, the largest in company history, was complete in early 1982. It nearly tripled the brewery's capacity to approximately 10.5 million barrels.
Tampa, Florida (1959): Approximate annual shipping capacity of 1.8 million barrels.
Houston, Texas (1966): Shipping capacity of approximately 3.7 million barrels.
Columbus, Ohio (1968): Shipping capacity of 6.3 million barrels.
Jacksonville, Florida (1969): Annual shipping capacity of approximately 6.7 million barrels.
Merrimack, New Hampshire (1970): Approximate shipping capacity of 2.8 million barrels.
Williamsburg, Virginia (1972): A major expansion project, completed in 1980, increased the plant's shipping capacity to 8.3 million barrels.
Fairfield, California (1976): Annual shipping capacity of approximately 3.9 million barrels.

Exhibit 4 (concluded)

Baldwinsville, New York (1980): The company purchased the former Jos. Schlitz Brewing Co. Capacity of approximately 6 million barrels.

Beer Distribution System

Once Anheuser-Busch, Inc.'s beers leave the breweries, distribution to the consumer becomes the responsibility of its more than 960 independent beer wholesalers and 16 company-owned wholesale operations. Together, they provide the company with the most extensive and effective beer distribution system in the brewing industry.

St. Louis Refrigerator Car Company

St. Louis Refrigerator Car Company, one of the company's transportation subsidiaries, has been in existence since 1878. This operation provides commercial repair, rebuilding, maintenance, and inspection of railroad cars at facilities in Missouri, Illinois, and Texas. In addition, St. Louis Refrigerator Car operates a fleet of 900 specially insulated and cushioned railroad cars, used exclusively for the transportation of Anheuser-Busch, Inc.'s beer products, and a 17,000-ton molasses terminal on the Mississippi River, to receive barge shipments of molasses for the St. Louis yeast plant.

Manufacturers Railway Company

Manufacturers Railway Company, the company's other transportation subsidiary, provides terminal rail switching services to industries in St. Louis, Missouri, over its 42 miles of company-owned and operated rail track. In addition, Manufacturers operates a fleet of 50 hopper cars and 270 general service box cars utilized by the company and outside firms. Manufacturers' four trucking subsidiaries, utilizing a fleet of 200 specially designed trailers, furnish cartage and warehousing service at six Anheuser-Busch, Inc. brewery locations— Fairfield, California; St. Louis, Missouri; Houston, Texas; Williamsburg, Virginia; Newark, New Jersey; and Merrimack, New Hampshire. The subsidiary will also serve the Baldwinsville, New York, brewery when it opens.

Busch Creative Services Corporation

Busch Creative Services, the company's multimedia and creative design subsidiary, was formed in early 1980 to produce a variety of multimedia, print, videotape, film, and other corporate and marketing communications materials and programs. The subsidiary is a full-service business and marketing communications company, selling its products and creative services to both Anheuser-Busch and clients outside the company. New services include theatrical services, consisting of stage and scenic design, lighting design, special effects, live entertainment, and theme party production.

Container Recovery Corporation

Container Recovery Corporation, the company's can reclamation and recycling subsidiary, was established in 1978. The creation of the subsidiary reflects growing corporate concerns for reducing litter, reclaiming vital raw materials and conserving energy while, at the same time, providing a positive alternative to mandatory deposit legislation and reducing container costs for Anheuser-Busch, Inc.

To meet these goals, Container Recovery functions in two different ways—by collecting aluminum cans for recycling at the consumer level and by operating container recycling process plants in Ohio, New Hampshire, and Florida. This program, operating in 35 states by the end of 1981, collected more than 100 million pounds of scrap aluminum during 1981.

Source: Anheuser-Busch Fact Book, 1982.

Exhibit 5

Major operations

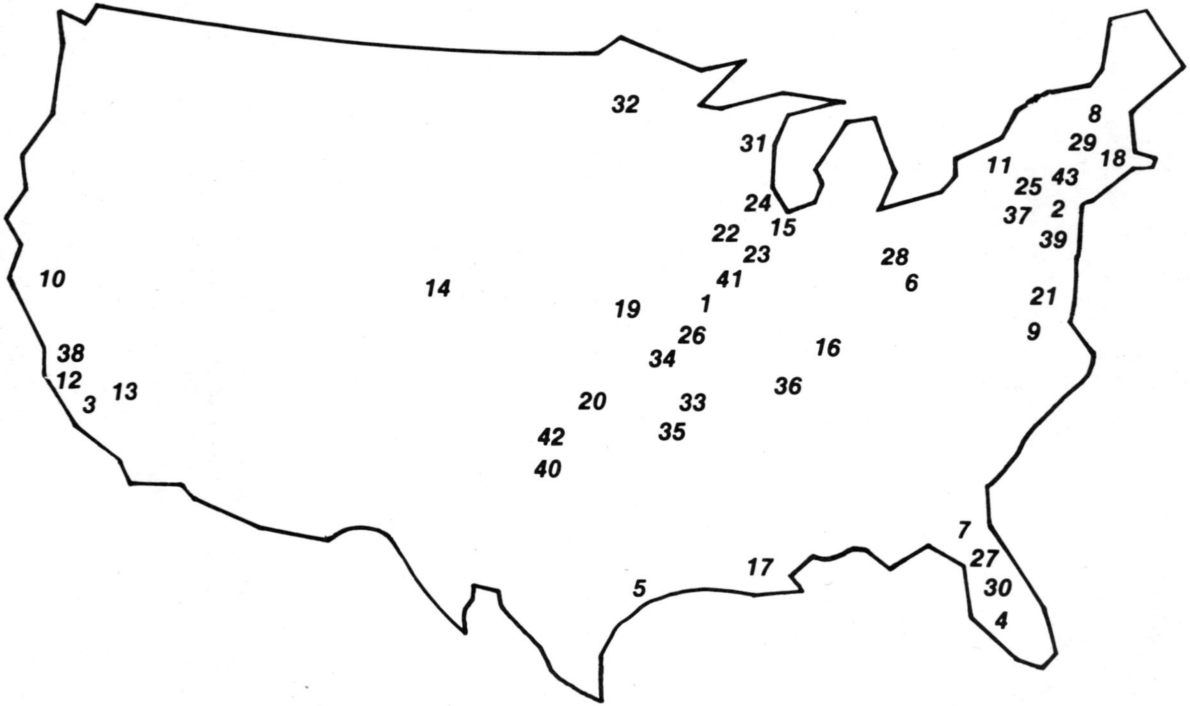

Corporate offices:
1. St. Louis

Breweries:
1. St. Louis
2. Newark
3. Los Angeles
4. Tampa
5. Houston
6. Columbus
7. Jacksonville
8. Merrimack
9. Williamsburg
10. Fairfield
11. Baldwinsville

Wholesale operations:
12. Sylmar
13. Riverside
14. Denver
15. Chicago (2)
16. Louisville
17. New Orleans
18. Boston
19. Kansas City
2. Newark
20. Tulsa
21. Washington, D.C.
22. Addison
23. Joliet
24. Waukegan
25. Liverpool

Can/lid manufacturing:
7. Jacksonville
6. Columbus
26. Arnold
27. Gainesville

Container recycling/processing:
28. Marion
29. Nashua
30. Cocoa

Malt production:
31. Manitowoc
32. Moorhead

Rice storage:
33. Jonesboro
34. Springfield
35. Brinkley

Label production:
36. Clarksville

Yeast production:
1. St. Louis
37. Old Bridge
38. Bakersfield

Family entertainment:
4. Tampa
9. Williamsburg
39. Langhome
40. Dallas/Fort Worth

Real estate development:
9. Williamsburg
6. Columbus
10. Fairfield

Rail car repair:
1. St. Louis
41. Wood River
42. Saginaw

Transportation services:
10. Fairfield
1. St. Louis
5. Houston
9. Williamsburg
43. Saratoga Springs, N.Y.

Baseball:
1. St. Louis

Tourist attractions:
1. St. Louis
8. Merrimack
4. Tampa
6. Columbus
7. Jacksonville
9. Williamsburg

Source: *Anheuser-Busch Fact Book*, 1982.

Exhibit 6

Anheuser-Busch Companies, Inc., and subsidiaries—1978–83 financial summary—operations (millions, except per share data)

	1982	1981	1980	1979	1978
Barrels sold	59.1	54.5	50.2	46.2	41.6
Sales	$5,185.7	$4,409.6	$3,822.4	$3,263.7	$2,701.6
Federal and state beer taxes	609.1	562.4	527.0	487.8	442.0
Net sales	4,576.6	3,847.2	3,295.4	2,775.9	2,259.6
Cost of products sold	3,331.7	2,975.5	2,553.9	2,172.1	1,762.4
Gross profit	1,244.9	871.7	741.5	603.8	497.2
Marketing, administrative, and research expenses	752.0	515.0	428.6	356.7	274.9
Operating income	492.9	356.7	312.9	247.1	222.3
Interest expense	(89.2)	(89.6)	(75.6)	(40.3)	(28.9)
Interest capitalized	41.2	64.1	41.7	—	—
Interest income	17.0	6.2	2.4	8.4	11.7
Other income (expense), net	(8.1)	(12.2)	(9.9)	5.4	.7
Gain on sale of Lafayette plant	20.4	—	—	—	—
Income before income taxes	474.2	325.2	271.5	220.6	205.8
Income taxes	186.9	107.8	99.7	76.3	94.8
Net income	$ 287.3	$ 217.4	$ 171.8	$ 144.3	$ 111.0
Per share—net income	$ 5.97	$ 4.79	$ 3.80	$ 3.19	$ 2.46
Per share—fully diluted	$ 5.88	$ 4.61	$ 3.80	$ 4.34	$ 2.46
Cash dividends paid	$ 65.80	$ 51.20	$ 44.80	$ 40.70	$ 37.00
Per share	$ 1.38	$ 1.13	$ .99	$ .90	$ .82
Average number of shares outstanding (millions)	48.10	45.40	45.20	45.20	45.10

Notes to consolidated financial statements:
The following summarizes the company's business segment information for 1982. Segment information is not presented for 1981 and 1980, because the company's beer operations represented dominant industry segment.

	Beer and beer-related	Food products	Other diversified operations	Eliminations	Consolidated
Net sales	$4,488.1	$282.8	$145.1	$339.4	$4,576.6
Operating income	464.1	23.5	5.3		492.9
Identifiable assets	2,758.1	779.3	365.4		3,902.8
Depreciation and amortization expense	110.8	8.8	14.0		133.6
Capital expenditures	310.1	23.4	22.3		355.8

several airlines. These lines carry sizable profit margins.[2] But competing with Frito-Lay at retail outlets is much more difficult. Frito-Lay has a substantial delivery system bolstered by its Pepsi network, and a steady

---

[2]The Eagle line has over 11 products, including honey-roasted peanuts, lattice-style potato chips, tortilla chips with nacho cheese flavor, and pretzels.

Exhibit 7

Anheuser-Busch Companies, Inc., and subsidiaries—1978–1983 financial summary— balance sheet and other information (millions, except per share and statistical data)

	1982	*1981*	*1980*	*1979*	*1978*
Balance sheet information:					
Working capital	$ 45.8	$ 45.9	$ 26.3	$ 88.1	$ 223.7
Current ratio	1.1	1.1	1.1	1.3	1.8
Plant and equipment, net	$2,988.9	$2,257.6	$1,947.4	$1,461.8	$1,109.2
Long-term debt.................	$ 969.0	$ 817.3	$ 743.8	$ 507.9	$ 427.3
Total debt to total debt					
plus equity	35.4%(1)	42.4%	43.4%	36.0%	36.4%
Deferred income taxes..........	$ 455.1	$ 357.7	$ 261.6	$ 193.8	$ 146.9
Common stock and other					
shareholders' equity	$1,526.6	$1,206.8	$1,031.4	$ 904.3	$ 747.9
Return on shareholders'					
equity	19.9%	19.3%	17.8%	16.9%(2)	15.6%
Total assets	$3,902.8	$2,875.2	$2,449.7	$1,926.0	$1,648.0
Other information:					
Capital expenditures	$ 355.8	$ 421.3	$ 590.0	$ 432.3	$ 228.7
Depreciation and					
amortization	133.6	108.7	99.4	75.4	66.0
Total payroll cost	853.3	686.7	594.1	529.1	421.8
Effective tax rate	39.4%	33.1%	36.7%	34.6%	46.0%
Pro forma information assuming					
retroactive application of the					
flowthrough method of ac-					
counting for the investment					
tax credit (3):					
Net income (4)	$ 287.3	$ 217.4	$ 171.8	$ 144.3	$ 121.9
Net income per share (4)					
Primary	5.97	4.79	3.80	3.19	2.70
Fully diluted	5.88	4.61	3.80	3.19	2.70
Common stock and other					
shareholders' equity	1,526.6	1,206.8	1,031.4	904.3	800.1
Return on shareholders'					
equity	19.9%	19.3%	17.8%	16.9%	16.1%
Book value per share	$ 31.61	$ 26.57	$ 22.83	$ 19.98	$ 17.72
Effective tax rate	39.4%	33.1%	36.7%	34.6%	40.8%

Notes to 10-year financial summary—balance sheet and other information:

(1) This percentage has been calculated by including redeemable preferred stock as part of equity because it is convertible into common stock and is trading primarily on its equity characteristics.

(2) This percentage has been adjusted to reflect the change in the method of accounting for the investment tax credit in 1979 but excludes the cumulative effect.

(3) Effective January 1, 1979, the company adopted the flowthrough method of accounting for the investment tax credit. In prior years, the company followed the practice of adding investment tax credit to income over the productive lives of the assets generating such credit, rather than adding it in the year in which the assets were placed in service. Accordingly, such benefits deferred in prior years are being added to income in the current year.

(4) Includes the capitalization of interest effective January 1, 1980, that relates to the capital cost of acquiring certain fixed assets.

stream of new products, resulting in fast turnover—a considerable entice- ment for retailers. And other big snack companies, such as the recently merged Standard Brands and Nabisco, Inc., have invested substantial resources without visible inroads into Frito-Lay's turf.

33   Anheuser-Busch's third major diversification arena is its entertainment division. The company has operated Busch Gardens in Tampa, Florida, since 1959. The 300-acre African theme park has consistently been one of the most popular family attractions in Florida with approximately 3 million visitors each year. In 1975, the Old Country was opened in Williamsburg, Virginia. This 17th-century European theme park occupies 360 acres and entertains approximately 2 million guests annually.

34   Building on its expertise developed through the operation of these parks, Anheuser-Busch established a joint venture with Children's Television Workshop, the creator of "Sesame Street" educational television programs. In the summer of 1980, the result of this collaboration was unveiled with the opening of the first Sesame Place park just north of Philadelphia. This innovative entertainment concept features contemporary entertainment for families, including science exhibits, computer games, and outdoor play elements instead of the traditional theme-park concept. The primary advantage of this new approach to family entertainment is its relative cost advantage: The parks require only a small fraction of land compared to the theme parks (15 acres in Philadelphia), and elaborate amusement rides are not included. A 30.3 acre Sesame Place was opened in Dallas/Ft. Worth in the summer of 1982.

35   In 1982, Anheuser-Busch Entertainment Corporation played host to 6.3 million guests, but profits were down from previous years. Company representatives considered the decline a temporal one caused by a sluggish economy.

36   Anheuser-Busch plans to continue expansion of its entertainment division in order to benefit from the demographic changes predicted for the 1980s. The company believes the theme parks and Sesame Place parks have a relatively strong appeal among the adult and preteen segments of the population. These segments are expected to be among the fastest-growing age groups for the remainder of the decade.

International Expansion

37   The final probe in Anheuser-Busch's diversification strategy, one requiring less capital than the others, was international expansion. Industry experts were not optimistic about Anheuser-Busch's prospects as an international brewer. Foreign protective tariffs and laws would make exported beers or brews produced in an Anheuser-Busch plant overseas prohibitively expensive to consumers. "Besides," remarked one beer marketing expert, "what makes them think foreigners crave American beer?"

38   Despite the experts' pessimism, Anheuser-Busch entered the Canadian market in 1980, aligning itself with John LaBatt, Ltd., the second-largest brewer in that country. Although most foreign beers tend to be heavier than American brews, market research by the company indicated Budweiser could be sold on its own merits, one of which was that it was well

known to Canadians. In retrospect, one competitor said, "They've got to have stressed the overflow of U.S. television advertising (into Canadian markets) in their planning." By 1981, Budweiser was pulling close to 7 percent of the market in Ontario, surpassing even the most optimistic predictions of their marketing executives.

39   In discussing Anheuser-Busch's interest in international diversification, industry analysts maintain that the company's preeminent market position in the United States allows and even compels it to diversify abroad. Andrew Melvick, an analyst at Drexel Burnham Lambert, Inc., noted, "They're running out of space here; it's as simple as that."

40   As the first American brewer to enter the world beer market, Anheuser-Busch is positioning itself in a market four times larger than the U.S. market. The company's strategy for market entry has been to enter into licensing agreements with foreign brewers, allowing the company to circumvent import and tariff regulations to keep the price of their product within a feasible range and utilize the existing distribution system of its overseas affiliates. Exhibit 8 lists the current foreign markets and licenses for Anheuser-Busch products. Other licensing arrangements are pending with several Third World countries, Sweden, and the People's Republic of China.

Campbell Taggart, Inc.

41   In October 1982, Anheuser-Busch made its first major diversification away from beer with the acquisition of Campbell Taggart, Inc., the nation's

---

Exhibit 8

Anheuser-Busch around the world

Market	Licensee	Date introduced	Name of product
Canada	Labatt's Ltd.	June 1980	Budweiser
France	SEB (BSN sub.)	March 1982	Busch
Japan	Suntory, Ltd.	1984 (1980 import)	Budweiser
Israel....................	General Brewing	1984	Name not determined

Import market	Product
Japan...	Budweiser
Trust territories (including Guam)..............	Budweiser, Budweiser Light, Michelob, Michelob Light, Natural Light
American Samoa...............................	Budweiser, Budweiser Light, Michelob, Michelob Light, Natural Light
England	Budweiser
Chile..	Budweiser
Sweden	Budweiser
New Zealand..................................	Budweiser

Source: "Anheuser-Busch Goes Flat in Europe but Scores in Canada, Japan," *Advertising Age,* February 14, 1983, p. 12–13.

second-largest bakery firm. This represented a significant strategic shift for Anheuser-Busch, as all its previous diversification efforts had focused on internally generated new products.

42   Anheuser-Busch paid $36 each for about half of Campbell Taggart's 15 million shares and converted the rest into a new Anheuser-Busch convertible preferred stock. Including the assigned redemption value, the acquisition cost Anheuser-Busch approximately $570 million.

43   Wall Street's initial reaction to the merger of the two premier companies in their fields was mixed. Although both are considered the low-cost producers in their industries, the profit margins for Campbell Taggart are only about 3.6 percent compared to the 5.6 percent margin Anheuser-Busch gets from beer, and the acquisition was expected to dilute 1983 earnings. However, some industry analysts deemed the acquisition a "tremendous fit." Emanuel Goldman of Sanford C. Bernstein & Co. stated "this makes sense." As the nation's largest yeast supplier, Anheuser-Busch "knows Campbell Taggart and the baking industry extremely well, and they are well positioned to handle a major acquisition."

44   Several of Campbell Taggart's strengths may have attracted Anheuser-Busch. The bakery company has invested heavily in the last five years (approximately $50 million annually) to maintain modern plants and equipment and has a strong distribution system, particularly in the healthy Sun Belt market. This strength may aid Anheuser-Busch in marketing its new Eagle line of snack foods.

45   In 1981, Campbell Taggart's net income was $41.7 million ($2.50 per share) on sales of $1.26 billion, while Anheuser-Busch earnings per share were $4.79 on net income of $217.4 million. The Dallas-based Campbell Taggart has been averaging a 17 percent return on equity for the past five years—the same as Anheuser-Busch.

46   The baking industry is fragmented and highly competitive. Campbell Taggart's strategy has been market segmentation and product diversification while avoiding entry into the more highly competitive and saturated New York and Chicago markets. The company offers a wide array of baked products under such labels as Rainbow, Earth Grains, and Honey Grain in addition to refrigerated dough products, frozen foods, refrigerated salad dressings, snack dips and toppings, and prepared sandwiches for retail and food-service customers.

47   The future of the food-processing industry is promising. The cost of raw materials has leveled off, and growth is expected in the 12- to 14-percent range in the near future. Higher rates of growth are expected for expensive products due to changing consumer tastes. The rising number of women in the work force is also expected to produce a positive impact on industry sales.

48   Industry analysts now claim that Anheuser-Busch may have struck a bargain in their purchase of Campbell Taggart, because they paid only a 15 percent premium over the market price. From the standpoint of An-

heuser-Busch's goal of diversification, this acquisition will decrease their level of dependence on beer alone. Corporate earnings from nonbeer operations were expected to rise from 10 percent to 20 percent by the end of 1983 as a result of the acquisition.

Future Directions

49   Anheuser-Busch plans to continue looking for growth opportunities beyond its primary line of business, the domestic beer market. American's beer consumption is expected to decline as the population ages, and Anheuser-Busch is planning to expand its diversification efforts through further acquisitions and internal expansion. Although the company's international beer operations and snack-food line are still a "drop in the barrel," Busch believes their growth potential is greater than that for domestic beer sales.

50   Anheuser-Busch's primary objective is well-planned and well-managed growth. Its strategy for achieving this goal is to make other sizable acquisitions while continuing to excel in its primary line of business—beer. President Busch has stressed that Anheuser-Busch will continue to search for acquisitions in recession-resistant segments of the consumer products area that are based on a sound business strategy and fit the corporation's standards for quality products and services.

case **6** **Note on the Financial Services Industry**

Industry Definition

1   It could be claimed that the financial services industry traces its beginnings to the invention of money in ancient times. However, the industry's all-encompassing label, "financial services," is relatively new. The name has evolved in direct market response to consumer demand for more comprehensive servicing of financial needs. Clearly, consumers are becoming less and less interested in drawing fine historical product lines among those institutions with which they transact their financial business. In keeping with a growing demand for time-saving convenience and comprehensive one-step supermarket-type service, members of various financial institutions have responded by offering customers a wider range of traditional financial services, as well as innovative new packages. The lines of demarcation between traditional industries such as banking, insurance, and real estate are rapidly disappearing.

2   A working definition of the financial services industry is that group of institutions that provides four categories of service:

1. obtaining funds for those who wish to invest them—includes underwriting, investment banking services, brokerage services, and the provision of loans;

2. providing income-earning outlets for those with funds to lend or invest—includes deposit services, brokerage activities, money market funds, mutual funds, life insurance, and pension funds;

This note was prepared by J. Kay Keels and John A. Pearce II of the University of South Carolina.

3. payments services—includes traditional payments services as well as credit cards, bill-paying services, and cash management services;

4. advice on the best way to get the services needed in the first three categories.

This definition clearly emphasizes the importance of focusing on customer needs as opposed to individual products, product lines, or specialized institutions.

3   The list of institutions that could legitimately be members of the financial services industry is lengthy. As a general categorization, these institutions can be divided into one of two classifications—banks and nonbanks. While membership in the bank category is fairly obvious, participants in the nonbank group include insurance companies, mutual savings banks, finance companies, investment companies, real estate investment trusts (REITs), savings and loan associations (S&Ls), pension funds, and credit unions. In light of the dynamism of the current financial environment, the line of demarcation between banks and nonbanks is rapidly growing less clear.

Banks

4   The banking system in the United States has been called a dual system for two reasons. First, banks are categorized as either state or national banks depending upon their charter. Second, banks are classified by their association with the Federal Reserve System (the Fed) as either members or nonmembers.

5   In the case of distinction by charter, "dual" is a misnomer for the system because there are actually fifty different banking systems for state-chartered banks. One of the major differentiating factors among state systems deals with the establishment of bank branches. Some states allow no branches at all while some states permit branching statewide. A related and very sensitive issue in the banking community has been the prohibition nationwide of any interstate branching.

6   Membership in the Fed is another characteristic which separates banks. All federally chartered banks were required to join the Federal Reserve System when it was established in 1913. State banks were permitted to join if they wished to do so. Recently, the number of member banks has declined as state banks have exercised their option to withdraw, and national banks have circumvented the membership requirement by applying for state charters. In 1980, of the 14,600 commercial banks in the U.S., 4,600 were nationally chartered, and therefore Fed members; and of the remaining 10,000, which are state chartered, only about one-tenth are members of the Fed.

Nonbank Financial Institutions

7   Since the end of World War II, nonbank financial institutions have grown in number, in resources, and in importance to the financial community. Figure 1 depicts growth rates of various nonbank financial institutions from the post-war period into the early 1970's. By the end of 1973, nonbank financial institutions collectively held 24 percent more assets than commercial banks. The two largest holders of these assets were S&Ls and life insurance companies. Although such institutions as insurance companies, and savings and loan associations are commonly familiar to most consumers, many nonbank financial institutions are less well known. Eight of the more important types of nonbank financial institutions are described below:[1]

Figure 1

Average annual growth rates of major nonbank financial institutions, 1945–1973

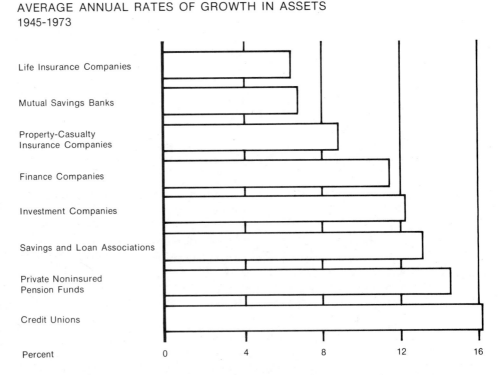

AVERAGE ANNUAL RATES OF GROWTH IN ASSETS
1945-1973

Source: Harless, Doris E., *Nonbank Financial Institutions.* (Federal Reserve Bank of Richmond, October 1975), p. 8.

8   *Insurance companies* can be divided into two major categories: life insurance companies and property-casualty insurance companies. The first life insurance company was begun well over two centuries ago and was called "The Corporation for Relief of Poor and Distressed Presbyterian Ministers and of the Poor and Distressed Widows and Children of Presbyterian Ministers." Today some of the largest corporations in the U.S. are life insurance companies, and Americans hold over $1 trillion worth of life insurance. The huge policy reserves (excess of premiums charged over benefits paid) accumulated by these life insurance companies make them legitimate members of the financial services industry in at least two ways. First, the reserves are invested by the insurance firms, and these investment earnings are used to reduce the premiums a policyholder pays. In this way, the earnings on reserves act as a kind of interest-earning savings account. Second, with such tremendous sums of money to invest, life insurance companies become big lenders principally in the form of domestic corporate bonds and mortagages.

9   As is also true with life insurance companies, property-casualty insurance companies are primarily guided in their investment decisions by the major goal of safety of principal, followed closely by income maximization and liquidity requirements. Life insurance policies must always eventually pay in full whereas property-casualty companies only pay on a fraction of their policies. Further, payment requirements are much more predictable for life insurance companies than for property-casualty firms. For these two reasons, investment patterns for the two types of companies differ, property-casualty companies investing much more heavily in bonds and common stocks.

10   The first *mutual savings bank* was established in Scotland in 1810, but the idea spread quickly, and in less than a decade 2 savings banks had been founded in the U.S. The majority of these institutions, which numbered nearly 500 in 1973, is still concentrated in a five-state area in New England and the Middle Atlantic region. The primary purpose of mutual savings banks is to invest collectively the savings of small investors. All mutual savings banks are state-chartered, state-supervised, non-stock, deposit institutions. Earnings from investments are credited to investors accounts as interest. Mutual savings banks are restricted by most states in their investment and lending activities to an approved list of securities and loans.

11   Once considered to be only a small step up from the neighborhood "loan shark," *finance companies* are now beginning to take their place as full-fledged members of the financial services industry. In the past, these companies were identified primarily by their lending practices—direct or indirect lending or the purchasing of accounts receivable—and by their particular customer groups' needs, for such services as sales financing, consumer financing, or commercial financing. However, as is characteris-

tic of the entire industry, services are becoming much more diversified and the lines of demarcation increasingly blurred.

12   *Investment companies* primarily serve small investors by pooling their collective funds and investing those funds in a wide variety of securities. The types of portfolios managed by investment companies vary a great deal, some investing principally in stocks; some, in bonds; and some companies maintaining a "balanced" portfolio of common stock, preferred stock, and bonds.

13   *Real estate investment trusts* (REITs) allow individuals and institutions an opportunity to hold interest in real property and mortgages. Funds from the REITs share sales are pooled and used to make mortgage loans and to acquire property. Earnings consist mostly of interest on loans or rent from owned property. REITs are publicly held, and shareholders are generally small individual investors.

14   The concept of a *savings and loan (S&L) association* was born in 1831 when a group of citizens met at an inn and drew up articles for the first co-operative home-financing society in the United States, the Oxford Provident Building Association of Philadelphia County. Each member of the association contributed some savings, and when his name was drawn from a hat, he could borrow money to buy a home. Today, besides being lending institutions, S&Ls serve nonborrowing customers with a variety of savings options, including the interest-bearing "NOW" accounts, in which savers are allowed to write negotiable orders of withdrawal (NOW), instruments that are functionally the same as checks. The granting of the right to S&Ls to offer personal checking services brought the S&Ls into closer competition with banks, another example of the diversification occurring within the financial services industry.

15   *Pension funds* are established primarily to pay retirement benefits. The two major types of pension funds are public, the largest of which are government pension plans, and private. Private pensions funds are either insured or noninsured. Noninsured pension funds are usually separate financial entities, whereas insured ones are not. Two main services of funds for private, noninsured pension funds are employer contributions and investment income. Pension-fund investment practices have leaned heavily toward common-stock portfolios.

16   Every *credit union* requires four essential features: (1) a group of people, (2) a common interest, (3) pooled savings, and (4) loans to each other. It is a co-operative self-help thrift and loan society composed of individuals bound together by some common tie. Credit unions under state or federal charter, are member-owned, member-operated, and member-controlled. Purchased ownership shares resemble savings accounts, and dividends are paid to members from loan and investment income. Loan privileges are extended to members only.

Historical Overview of
Financial Institutions

17 The course of regulation of the nation's financial institutions appropriately traces out the history and evolution of today's financial services industry (see Figure 2). Financial regulation can be separated into three eras: chartered banking, free banking, and cartel banking, and each of these regimes has sought to balance three objectives. The first objective, structure, is concerned with the degree of competitiveness in the industry; the second, safety, deals with the risk associated with liabilities; and the third, stability, addresses the effect of the financial system on the development and stability of the economy as a whole. In each era these three elements have been balanced in a way that reflects the relative strength of the various groups affected by financial regulation.

18 The chartered banking era began late in the 18th century and lasted through 1837. Structure was the prime concern during this period, and much of the controversy centered around who should charter banks— federal or state governments. Since both governments claimed the right, the result was the aforementioned dual banking system in which both state and federal governments issued bank charters. At first only two banks were federally chartered: the First (1791-1811) and Second (1811-1836) Banks of the United States. Because the federally chartered banks wielded so much power, they aroused intense opposition from their state-chartered counterparts. Each of the national banks was established to help the government manage its finances and promote the nation's economic growth and development. A number of particular advantages accrued to the national banks because, not only did they hold the federal government's deposit account, but they could also circulate their own notes as legal tender, and perhaps most importantly, they had a nationwide system of branches. However, the federal charters were issued for only twenty-year periods, and because each of the early national banks came to symbolize corporate power, monopoly and privilege, political corruption, and social inequality, neither charter was renewed after the initial twenty years. After the demise of the First Bank, Congress reconsidered and chartered the Second Bank only because of its need to manage the nation's finances after the War of 1812. Andrew Jackson championed the defeat of the Second Bank as a political issue. The prohibition against nationwide banking is a legacy from this era that remains today.

19 Even during these early days in U.S. banking history, the need for a securities market was recognized. Shortly after George Washington took office in 1789, the U.S. government issued stocks to finance the debt incurred in fighting the Revolutionary War. New York City merchants and auctioneers began to deal in these as well as some bank shares. In 1792, the

Figure 2

Summary of events and legislation shaping the financial services industry

Date	Event	Impact
1760	The Corporation for Relief of Poor and Distressed Presbyterian Ministers…	first life insurance company in the U.S.
1791–1811	First Bank of the United States	first federally chartered bank
1792	Brokers for the Purchase and Sale of Public Stock	laid foundation for NYSE
1816–1836	Second Bank of the United States	federally chartered to aid in organizing debt from War of 1812
1816	The Provident Institution for Savings in the Town of Boston; The Philadelphia Saving Fund Society	nation's first two savings banks
1817	Constitution of the New York Stock and Exchange Board	first formal constitution of NYSE
1829	Safety Fund Act	first insurance of bank liabilities
1830	Introduction of railroad stocks to Wall Street	opened new era of American finance
1831	Oxford Provident Building; Association of Philadelphia County	first cooperative home-financing society in the U.S.; forerunner of S&Ls
1837	Panic of 1837	financial disaster brought on by land speculation
1863	The name "New York Stock Exchange" officially adopted	
1868	NYSE memberships first made saleable	
1869	Black Friday	panic caused by gold speculation
1871	NYSE call market replaced by continuous auction market	
1875	American Express retirement fund	nation's first noninsured retirement fund
1891	Sherman Act	against monopolies and combinations in restraint of trade
1907	Panic of 1907	spurred lobbying for lender-of-last-resort
1909	Credit union founded by Alphonse Desjardins	first U.S. credit union
1913	Federal Reserve Act	created Federal Reserve to control federally chartered banks
1927	McFadden Act	gave national banks the right to establish branches
1929–1933	Great Depression	bankruptcies, bank closings, widespread economic hardship
1933	Banking Act of 1933 (Glass-Steagall Act)	separated commercial and investment banking
1933	Securities Act of 1933	required full disclosure of information to stock purchasers
1934	Securities Exchange Act of 1934	required registration of brokers and dealers handling securities; created SEC
1940	Investment Company Act of 1940	protected shareholders of investment companies

Figure 2 (concluded)

Date	Event	Impact
1945	McCarran-Ferguson Act	delegated regulation and taxation of casualty-property insurance companies to state authorities
1956	Bank Holding Company Act	brought all bank holding companies under supervision of Federal Reserve
1958	Welfare and Pension Plans Disclosure Act	regulated disclosure of information and financial condition
1960	Introduction of negotiable certificate of deposit (C/D)	allowed banks to compete openly for corporate funds
1960	Amendments to Internal Revenue Code	granted tax-exempt status to REITs
1966	Interest Rate Adjustment Act	established interest-rate ceilings for S&Ls
1969	Consumer Credit Protection Act	federal regulation of consumer lending
1970	Investment Company Amendments Act of 1970	established new standards for management fees and mutual fund sales charges
1973	Bill passed by Connecticut General Assembly	paved way for S&Ls to offer checking services with demand deposits
1974	Employee Retirement Income Security Act of 1974	pension reform legislation
1980	Depository Institutions Deregulation and Monetary Control Act	provided for the phase-out of Regulation Q

forerunner of the New York Stock Exchange was founded as twenty-four members drew up an agreement for "Brokers for the Purchase and Sale of Public Stock" under a tree on Wall Street. After the War of 1812, the nation began its westward expansion, and money flowed into Wall Street from all over the country. As trading in securities became an integral part of the nation's financial activities, the first formal Constitution of the New York Stock and Exchange Board was drawn up in 1817.

20   The second era, of free banking, began after the Panic of 1837. Unbridled speculation in land and securities led to the Panic, and some of the nation's strongest banks, financial houses, and business enterprises did not survive. During the free banking period, the issue of safety was concerned with banks' backing their outstanding notes with collateral. Reliance on the gold standard was supposed to ensure stability; however, after the Panic of 1907 a lender-of-last-resort, the Federal Reserve, was created. Structure was designed to promote efficiency. Charter requirements were reduced to a minimum; thus entry was essentially free. The Federal Reserve was designed to be a banker's bank, and implicitly the Act that created it assumed that the Federal Reserve would continue to maintain the gold standard. However, the United States emerged from World War I as a major economic power, and the responsibility of operating a world-

dollar standard fell to the Federal Reserve. The creators of the Federal Reserve had never envisioned such power, nor was the Fed prepared to deal with this responsibility. Between 1929 and 1933 the nation's money supply fell by 33 percent, producing the Great Depression and bringing to a close the free banking era.

21   At the beginning of the cartel banking era, the prime concern was for the safety and stability of each bank. The appropriate solution according to regulations was to limit the amount of risk and competition to which any bank could be exposed. The Banking Act of 1933, also known as the Glass-Steagall Act, was supposed to be such a safety measure. For the first time in banking history, the industry was divided into commercial and investment banking segments, each type to be regulated by a separate body. The Securities and Exchange Commission (SEC), created by the Securities Act of 1933 and the Securities Exchange Act of 1934, was to regulate investment banking. Further segmentation occurred as the Bank Holding Company Act of 1956 brought all holding companies under the supervision of the Federal Reserve Board. Amendments to this act in 1970 further restricted banks to prevent them from entering other areas of financial business. The Banking Act of 1935, along with all the other legislation, further solidified the cartel-like nature of the industry. New bank charters were granted, subject to a test of demonstrated need. The 14,000 banks that survived the Great Depression were indeed a protected cartel.

22   Since the New Deal legislation began the cartel era, the industry has contined to be a cartel, but one that has become increasingly weaker. One of the first weakening agents was the negotiable certificate of deposit (C/D), which was introduced in 1960 to allow commercial banks to compete more effectively for corporate funds that were being lost to securities markets, due to rising interest rates. Banks were suddenly thrust into the business of liability management.

23   Liquidity crunches resulted in The Interest Rate Adjustment Act of 1966, allowing ceilings on time-deposit interest rates. This act allowed thrift institutions to pay higher rates than commercial banks.

24   Yet another threat appeared in 1979 as interest rates once again soared above the Regulation Q ceilings. The newest competition for consumer deposits came in the form of the money-market mutual fund. Many banks and especially thrifts were hit hard by this new competition. The result was the Depository Institutions Deregulation and Monetary Control Act of 1980, which called for the gradual phasing out of the Regulation Q ceilings. By late, 1982, free and open price competition for deposits was virtually a fact.

Porter's Five Industry Forces

25   The five major forces which drive competition in the financial services industry and which shape the nature of the industry are shown in Figure 3.

Figure 3

Forces driving financial services industry competition

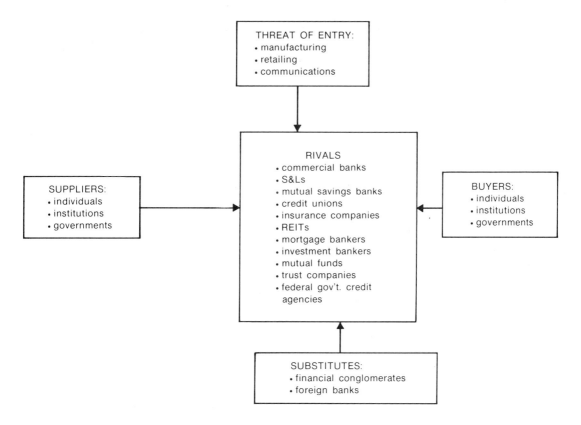

To analyze the financial services industry each of these five forces will be examined.

The Threat of Entry

26   The possible entry of new participants into an industry can be determined by a unique set of factors that determines the significance of threats of entry into a particular industry. At least six factors affect who provides financial services and how they are provided. Consideration of these factors would affect entry decisions by potential competitors. The six factors are: (1) characteristics of services offered and the demand for them, (2) relative importance of the customer's price versus nonprice considerations, (3) risk, (4) economies of joint production and distribution, (5) regulations, and (6) federal government participation.[2]

27   One important characteristic of financial services that determines production and distribution is the place where the service falls on the continuum between mass-produced services and unique, tailored services. Automobile loans are an example of a mass-procuced service. By contrast, a uniquely tailored service would be the private placement of a debt issue. To those institutions offering services at the mass-production end of the continuum advantages of an economies-of-scale barrier would exist. At the tailored-service end of the continuum, barriers associated with product differentiation would be present.

28   One increasingly important nonprice consideration in the financial services industry is convenience. Institutions have sought to sell convenience through such tactics as longer hours, credit cards, bill-paying services, and automatic tellers. A second important nonprice consideration is advice, a selling point used extensively in life insurance companies, brokerage and investment banking firms, and bank trust departments. Other nonprice tradeoffs are liquidity and insurance against loss. The specialized nature of advice leads to a product-differentiation barrier while the growing importance of convenience is related to the switching cost barrier.

29   There are four types of risk that could affect who offers financial services: (1) interest rate risk, (2) default risk, (3) liquidity risk, and (4) portfolio risk. Interest-rate risk arises because of the fluctuation of the general interest-rate level, and the mismatch of maturity dates of assets and liabilities. Default risk is the risk that a loan will not be repaid. Liquidity risk refers to the risk that an institution will not be able to produce sufficient cash to meet its obligations at a specified time. Portfolio risk is concerned with the uncertainty of the rate of return on a managed portfolio. A potential entrant's attitude toward risk could suggest a sizeable entry barrier in terms of capital requirements.

30   The joint economies of production and distribution factors result from the growing demand among customers to have more financial services sold together. This trend toward the consolidation of larger and larger packages of financial services suggests at once several barriers to entry available to those firms capable of offering multiple services as well as serious substitute threats to more traditional single-service firms. (Substitutes will be addressed more fully in a later section.) In addition to economies of scale, some non-scale cost advantages include proprietary product technology and the experience curve, since many potential entrants are in businesses outside the realm of traditional financial services. Favorable locations might also prove to be a barrier since traditional industry participants, like insurance, real estate, and finance companies, often have nationwide networks of offices. Joint economies of product and distribution could lead to entry barriers created by more favorable access to distribution channels. Finally, these joint economies certainly suggest the possibility of entry barriers posed by capital requirements.

31   The final two service-affecting factors of regulations and federal government participation are directly related to the government policy entry barrier. Three types of regulatory restrictions that significantly affect the financial services industry are: (1) rate restrictions, (2) powers restrictions, and (3) locational restrictions. Rate restrictions include those placed on rates charged to users of funds, as well as those paid to providers of funds. Powers restrictions involve the limitation of services that can be offered. Locational restrictions refer to those affecting such banking practices as branching and interstate banking. Other regulatory considerations include capital and reserve requirements and disclosure statements. By its very imposing size and by the broad range of its financial activities, the federal government has a profound effect on the structure of the financial services industry. Not only is it a regulator, but also a customer and a supplier to the industry, as well as an industry participant.

32   The primary mode of entry into the financial services industry recently has been by acquisition. Citing such reasons as synergy, entry into fast-growth glamour markets, or sources of steady cash flow to balance seasonal swings, many retailing and industrial firms have scrambled to get into financial services. Figure 4 illustrates the diversity of participants that had entered the industry by the early 1980s.

Rivalry

33   The intensity of rivalry in an industry is the result of at least eight interacting factors:[3] (1) numerous or equally balanced competitors, (2) slow industry growth, (3) high fixed or storage costs, (4) lack of differentiation or switching costs, (5) capacity augmented in large increments, (6) diverse competitors, (7) high strategic stakes, and (8) high exit barriers. Several of these factors are clearly at work in the financial services industry although some of these factors become difficult to track because industry participants seem to be rapidly changing. When acquisitions such as those noted in the previous section change the nature of an industry's participants, rivalry is naturally affected.

34   The presence of numerous or equally balanced competitors suggests the notion that a firm should "only pick on someone its own size." Within the financial services industry, participants are certainly numerous. The banking segment alone has over 14,000 members. To examine the "equally balanced" part of this factor, perhaps the industry's "elite" could serve as an example. In its 1984 second-quarter report on the performance of the nation's top 900 corporations, *Business Week* listed 74 members of the financial services industry, or 8 percent of all firms listed (see Figure 5). By virtue of such national prominence, the entire list might be considered "equally balanced" on a very crude national scale. This list, however, yields to even finer gradations of competitive groupings. Using 1984 second-quarter sales as rankings, half the list (37 firms) falls into a $100 million to

Figure 4

New entrants into the financial services industry

Company	Company acquired	Industry	Year acquired	Purchase price (millions of dollars)
American Can	Voyager Group	Insurance	1983	$ 45
	PennCorp Financial	Insurance	1983	295
	Transport Life	Insurance	1982	152
	Associated Madison	Insurance	1981	127
Ashland Oil	Integon	Insurance	1981	238
BAT Industries	Eagle Star	Insurance	1984	1,300
Crown Central	Continental Amer. Life	Insurance	1980	32
Ethyl	First Colony	Insurance	1982	270
General Electric	Employers Reinsurance	Insurance	1984	1,075
National Steel	United Financial	Thrift	1980	241
RCA	CIT Financial Corp.	Consumer finance	1980	1,500
St. Regis	Colonial Penn	Insurance	1984*	590
	Dependable Insurance	Insurance	1983	46
	Drum Financial	Insurance	1981	51
Sears Roebuck	Coldwell Banker	Real estate	1981	202
	Dean Witter	Brokerage	1981	610
Xerox	Van Kampen Merritt	Investment banking	1984	150
	Crum & Forster	Insurance	1982	1,600

*Acquisition pending.
Source: *Business Week,* August 20, 1984, p. 54

$400 million category, while the other half is at $500 million and above. Even further, firms that reported sales over the billion-dollar mark numbered 17, the top 6 of which represented a span of over $3 billion in sales to less than $7 billion. It appears that industry participants at various size levels face numerous equally strong competitors.

35   Slow industry growth has also been listed as a contributor to intensified rivalry. As illustrated in Figure 6, the diversified financial and the commercial banking sectors ranked near the bottom in service sector growth, being far out-stripped by the retailing, diversified service, and transportation sectors in the decade from 1973 to 1983. In slow growth environments, rivalry is intensified because market share can only be increased by stealing it from one's competitors.

36   The pattern of acquisitions both from outside (see Figure 4) and from inside (see Figure 7) the financial services industry suggests that augmentation of capacity in large increments and diversity of competitors may be two more factors contributing to rivalry in the industry. The size and reputation of some of the firms listed among recent acquisitions gives credence to the large incremental capacity addition argument. Figure 4 documents the growing diversity among competitors in the financial services industry. Rivalry is heightened due to the uncertainty among industry incumbents as to how a retailer like Sears or a manufacturer like American Can will compete.

37   When competition for the consumer's dollar increases, the effort to attract the consumer's attention usually intensifies. The seriousness of such effort is often gauged in terms of advertising expenditures. Figure 8 shows that the top 10 financial service advertisers spent over $56 million in the first half of 1983 on advertising. With so many name changes, mergers, and acquisitions, advertising for name recognition has become increasingly important. The meandering bull, people listening, and earning money the "old-fashioned way" have come to be readily associated with Merrill Lynch, E.F. Hutton, and Smith Barney, respectively. Observers seemed to think that the two-pronged marketing battle to maintain traditional strongholds while concurrently scrambling for new opportunities would continue to be a volatile one for some time in the financial services industry.

Substitute Products

38   A rash of innovative new products arising from industry participants posed a threat to some of the traditional financial services. As was noted earlier, banks began issuing C/Ds in the 1960s, thrifts were allowed to open NOW accounts in the 1970s, and the idea of a cash management account (CMA) was introduced by Merrill Lynch in the early 1980s. Even the brokerage business was not exempt, as was demonstrated by the rise of discount brokers in the 1970s.

39   Three environmental shocks tended to affect the financial system and led to product innovations: (1) changes in technology, (2) changes in demand, and (3) changes in public regulation. Technological demands on the financial services industry had intensified, particularly in the 1980s. Figure 9 illustrates the dynamic growth in computerization in the industry for the early 1980s. National electronic networks made it apparent that, as the last shackles of banking regulation were shed, many of the financial industry giants would be poised and ready to enter into nationwide banking. Further, changing demands, especially for increased convenience and the bundling of financial services, would continue to challenge the industry to create more innovative services.

40   The threat of substitutes is not confined just to current industry participants, however. Given the nature of acquisitions in the industry, precedent

Figure 5

Top financial services industry competitors

5 BANKS & BANK HOLDING COMPANIES

COMPANY	SALES 2nd quarter 1984 $ mil.	SALES Change from 1983 %	SALES 6 months 1984 $ mil.	SALES Change from 1983 %	PROFITS 2nd quarter 1984 $ mil.	PROFITS Change from 1983 %	PROFITS 6 months 1984 $ mil.	PROFITS Change from 1983 %	MARGINS 2nd quarter 1984 %	MARGINS 2nd quarter 1983 %	PROFITS Return on common equity 12 months ending 6-30	PROFITS Price-earnings ratio 7-31	PROFITS 12 months' earnings per share
Allied Bancshares	269.4	40	504.5	33	29.6	14	57.5	13	11.0	13.5	20.5	8	2.69
Banc One	253.7	46	481.8	50	29.6	38	51.6	43	10.5	11.1	16.1	8	2.73
Bank of Boston	798.8	29	1472.3	18	30.9	-1	55.8	-18	3.9	5.0	11.7	5	6.51
Bank of New England	198.0	37	381.4	31	10.8	23	20.2	2	5.5	6.1	13.6	6	7.67
Bank of New York	401.6	24	761.1	16	26.3	20	52.1	20	6.5	6.7	14.8	4	6.11
BankAmerica	3537.4	10	6920.6	6	109.6	-23	210.7	-20	3.1	4.4	5.9	9	1.76
Bankers Trust New York	1178.2	22	2232.6	17	72.0	11	146.0	16	6.1	6.7	14.8	5	8.85
Barnett Banks of Florida	329.7	36	621.9	35	25.3	25	49.3	29	7.7	8.3	17.8	7	5.01
CBT	175.9	34	344.3	30	10.4	11	20.4	8	5.9	7.2	12.9	6	4.61
Chase Manhattan	2329.4	13	4567.0	10	90.2	-14	192.7	-9	3.9	5.1	11.2	4	10.30
Chemical New York	1480.2	27	2766.5	17	76.8	10	158.1	12	5.2	6.0	13.6	4	6.28
Citicorp	4989.0	22	9716.0	19	206.0	-2	429.0	-2	4.1	5.2	14.6	5	6.28
Citizens & Southern Georgia	203.6	23	391.5	17	18.0	31	32.9	26	8.8	8.3	16.1	7	2.10
Comerica	246.6	36	475.1	30	14.9	18	27.2	13	6.0	6.9	11.0	6	4.40
Continental Illinois	993.0	-9	2213.0	0	-1158.0	NM	-1129.0	NM	NM	2.9	-63.1	NM	-27.29
CoreStates Financial	266.2	19	510.4	30	26.9	15	50.6	25	10.1	10.5	16.7	6	5.68
Crocker National	660.6	5	1321.7	4	6.1	-60	-114.7	NM	0.9	2.4	-14.7	NM	-7.77
First Atlanta	182.7	39	344.2	34	14.5	15	28.6	16	7.9	9.6	17.7	6	3.12
First Bank System	574.1	22	1114.4	22	32.5	3	64.2	3	5.7	6.8	11.9	6	4.09
First Chicago	1104.6	25	2098.8	18	53.0	23	102.7	19	4.8	4.9	10.6	5	4.00
First City Bancorporation of Texas	470.4	20	901.6	14	25.6	-3	48.9	-16	5.4	6.7	3.0	18	0.86
First Interstate Bancorp	1207.3	16	2357.2	13	67.5	11	131.2	10	5.6	5.8	12.2	6	5.86
First National State Bancorp	266.4	31	518.9	30	20.9	31	39.5	26	7.9	7.9	11.5	5	7.14
First Union	206.0	36	395.0	25	20.4	72	38.5	31	9.9	7.9	16.1	7	3.84
Harris Bankcorp	246.6	31	471.1	26	9.4	4	17.1	-5	3.8	4.8	7.4	18	4.56
InterFirst	598.3	21	1173.9	16	13.4	-58	23.0	-67	2.2	6.4	-20.1	NM	-3.26
Irving Bank	534.2	20	1029.7	14	26.3	10	53.0	11	4.9	5.3	11.6	5	5.12
Manufacturers Hanover	2011.6	27	3753.0	18	73.7	-8	157.7	-3	3.7	5.1	11.0	3	7.61
Marine Midland Banks	664.1	29	1283.1	24	26.4	12	49.0	4	4.0	4.6	9.6	4	4.86
Mellon National	762.7	20	1434.1	26	39.4	-20	72.5	-17	5.2	7.7	11.1	6	6.18
Mercantile Texas	343.6	33	656.7	27	24.3	-8	48.0	-6	7.1	10.3	13.8	5	3.76
Michigan National	209.9	11	414.1	11	5.2	NM	9.5	86	2.5	NM	-0.6	NM	-0.18

Figure 5 (continued)

COMPANY	SALES 2nd quarter 1984 $ mil.	Change from 1983 %	SALES 6 months 1984 $ mil.	Change from 1983 %	2nd quarter 1984 $ mil.	Change from 1983 %	6 months 1984 $ mil.	Change from 1983 %	MARGINS 2nd quarter 1984 %	MARGINS 2nd quarter 1983 %	PROFITS Return on common equity 12 months ending 6-30	Price-earnings ratio 7-31	12 months' earnings per share
Midlantic Banks	174.7	55	337.2	50	15.6	43	29.7	41	8.9	9.7	15.8	6	3.96
Morgan (J.P.)	1551.7	9	3093.4	7	103.7	-10	249.7	7	6.7	8.1	14.0	6	10.81
NBD Bancorp	327.0	19	642.4	16	22.3	10	42.9	8	6.8	7.4	10.3	6	7.10
National City	178.7	12	349.3	8	14.3	35	27.8	27	8.0	6.7	12.3	6	4.76
NCNB	417.1	40	777.8	30	29.1	31	57.3	23	7.0	7.4	13.7	6	3.81
Northern Trust	185.9	12	360.7	8	5.7	19	11.3	15	3.1	2.9	5.5	15	3.93
Norwest	675.7	19	1306.2	17	32.4	-5	66.2	-5	4.8	6.0	10.1	6	3.81
PNC Financial	374.9	24	710.8	20	34.1	13	64.5	16	9.1	10.0	14.3	6	5.92
Rainier Bancorporation	203.5	21	388.7	17	15.2	38	28.5	32	7.5	6.5	12.9	7	5.57
Republic New York	261.0	10	508.3	4	24.3	15	47.1	17	9.3	9.0	14.5	6	5.50
Republic Bank	532.2	28	1017.2	24	32.3	-15	62.0	-19	6.1	9.2	11.3	6	4.00
Security Pacific	1231.1	16	2387.2	15	68.6	6	136.6	8	5.6	6.1	14.8	5	7.45
Southeast Banking	252.9	19	490.7	18	16.2	15	32.6	16	6.4	6.6	10.8	8	3.09
Southwest Bancshares	214.3	21	417.0	18	13.3	NM	26.3	187	6.2	NM	10.7	6	2.88
Sovran Financial	222.9	11	435.9	9	19.7	8	37.9	10	8.8	9.0	15.6	7	4.18
Sun Banks	257.8	79	505.2	79	17.7	57	36.9	63	6.9	7.8	11.2	8	3.27
Texas Commerce Bancshares	510.5	28	980.6	23	46.4	5	92.2	3	9.1	11.1	16.4	7	5.57
U.S. Bancorp	189.8	18	360.0	13	14.6	5	27.4	1	7.7	8.7	10.5	7	2.94
Valley National	237.7	18	459.7	16	15.1	34	28.3	23	6.4	5.6	11.3	7	3.03
Wachovia	224.5	21	442.2	16	23.7	16	48.1	13	10.6	11.0	17.6	8	5.59
Wells Fargo	842.3	15	1630.2	12	40.9	1	80.9	8	4.9	5.6	12.3	6	6.18
INDUSTRY COMPOSITE	36759.9	19	71228.0	16	680.2	-63	2427.7	-34	1.9	5.9	8.8	7	4.29
21 NONBANK FINANCIAL													
Aetna Life & Casualty	3838.2	6	7475.8	2	48.7	-27	67.7	-63	1.3	1.8	4.6	16	1.87
Alexander & Alexander Services	131.8	-8	268.5	-6	1.0	-84	9.6	-27	0.8	4.4	-2.6	NM	-0.27
American Express	3153.0	28	6049.0	27	139.0	-28	255.0	-28	4.4	7.9	10.2	14	1.95
CNA Financial	888.0	11	1767.5	10	18.3	-58	47.1	-41	2.1	5.5	8.5	11	2.25
Chubb	508.2	23	956.2	20	14.5	-41	27.5	-44	2.9	5.9	8.2	12	3.39
Farmers Group	222.7	14	437.6	15	41.7	20	78.9	19	18.7	17.8	16.1	8	4.44
Hutton (E.F.) Group	591.5	3	1185.4	10	-7.8	NM	5.3	-94	NM	7.8	5.7	20	1.34
Kemper Corp.	594.9	0	1179.0	8	-3.8	NM	-4.9	NM	NM	2.9	NA	17	1.73
Lincoln National	1046.7	11	2096.5	13	40.3	-3	82.8	15	3.9	4.4	11.2	7	4.07
March & McLennan	268.8	13	548.0	11	29.0	14	0.7	-99	10.8	10.7	8.0	47	0.92
Merrill Lynch	1358.3	-13	2747.6	-8	-32.8	NM	-14.2	NM	NM	7.2	-1.2	NM	-0.25
Paine Webber Group (3)	377.3	-9	760.7	-3	-4.0	NM	1.1	-98	NM	5.8	6.7	20	1.35

Figure 5 (concluded)

COMPANY	SALES				PROFITS				MARGINS		Return on common equity 12 months ending 6-30	Price-earnings ratio 7-31	12 months' earnings per share
	2nd quarter 1984 $ mil.	Change from 1983 %	6 months 1984 $ mil.	Change from 1983 %	2nd quarter 1984 $ mil.	Change from 1983 %	6 months 1984 $ mil.	Change from 1983 %	2nd quarter 1984 %	2nd quarter 1983 %			
Phibro-Salomon	6927.0	-13	13576.0	-3	103.0	-10	223.0	-3	1.5	1.4	19.7	8	3.25
SAFECO	485.7**	15	927.8	11	20.4	-25	53.2	-8	4.2	6.4	12.3	8	3.45
St. Paul	634.3	11	1262.0	12	-40.9	NM	-31.9	NM	NM	7.0	0.8	81	0.49
Student Loan Marketing Assn.	296.6	38	561.4	41	24.2	49	45.8	61	8.2	7.6	24.5	16	1.64
Transamerica	1367.1	12	2603.2	12	53.7	9	115.5	11	3.9	4.1	11.5	7	3.28
Travelers	3368.3	13	6580.8	9	76.6	-3	145.0	-7	2.3	2.7	10.8	7	3.96
U.S. Leasing International	90.6**	24	180.1	23	7.4	5	14.9	1	8.1	9.6	13.8	7	4.04
USF&G	670.8	14	1310.6	13	32.5	-20	57.9	-31	4.8	6.9	12.4	8	2.63
USLIFE	238.3	12	452.5	11	17.4	-4	31.8	-3	7.3	8.5	9.6	7	3.57
INDUSTRY COMPOSITE	27058.1	3	52926.1	6	578.5	-44	1211.8	-42	2.1	3.9	9.3	16	2.37

Source: Business Week, August 20, 1984, p. 81.

Figure 6

Financial services industry growth

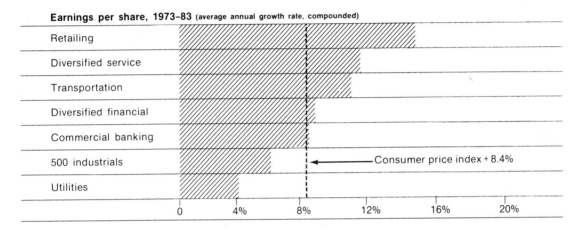

Earnings per share, 1973–83 (average annual growth rate, compounded)

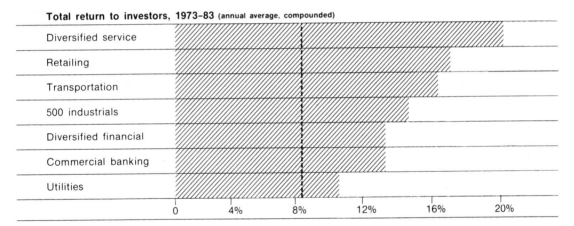

Total return to investors, 1973–83 (annual average, compounded)

The ten-year record: service vs. smokestacks

Only the utilities lagged behind the 500 industrials in boosting earnings per share from 1973 to 1983. But the industrials beat three Service 500 sectors in total return to investors—stock price appreciation plus dividends. Life insurers were excluded because their accounting methods are unique.

Source: Fortune, June 11, 1984, p. 155.

had been set for some powerful new entrants into the industry. Already financial institutions had begun to redefine themselves as information and communications companies. It easily followed that communications companies might begin to redefine their self-images as consumer companies.

Figure 7

Acquisitions in the financial services industry

Firm	Acquired by	Date
Loeb Rhoades	Shearson	1979
Blythe Eastman Dillon	Paine Webber	1979
Bache	Prudential	1981
Salomon Brothers	Phibro	1981
Shearson	American Express	1981
Dean Witter	Sears	1982

Source: Fortune, December 18, 1981, p. 58.

Figure 8

Top financial services firms' advertisement spending

Bankers and brokers spend the ad bucks
Top 10 financial services advertisers, Jan.-June, 1983

Company	Total	Magazines	Newspaper supplements	$(000) Network TV	Spot TV	Network radio	Spot radio	Outdoor
1. BankAmerica Corp.	9,640.3	2,412.6	—	305.8	2,625.7	—	3,684.0	612.2
2. Merrill Lynch & Co.	7,698.6	2,268.7	61.2	4,258.7	766.3	—	343.7	—
3. Citicorp	6,757.0	1,051.1	47.0	1,823.6	3,623.0	—	207.6	4.7
4. Prudential-Bache Securities	5,848.8	2,670.1	—	984.8	2,193.9	—	—	—
5. First Jersey Securities	5,595.0	823.4	—	1,134.2	2,298.5	—	1,338.9	—
6. First Interstate Bancorp	5,124.7	819.6	—	762.4	3,095.7	—	286.1	160.9
7. E.F. Hutton Group	4,938.9	2,258.6	77.6	1,853.8	131.7	259.2	358.0	—
8. Great Western Savings & Loan	4,299.5	201.7	—	—	2,844.2	—	1,253.6	—
9. Manufacturers Hanover Corp.	3,661.4	1,796.4	61.2	—	1,402.4	—	400.2	1.2
10. Smith Barney Harris Upham & Co.	3,042.0	73.7	—	2,855.1	—	—	113.2	—
Total	56,606.2	14,375.9	247.0	13,978.4	18,981.4	259.2	7,985.3	779.0

Note: Includes banks, brokerage houses, savings & loan associations, mutual fund groups, credit unions. Does not include newspaper or direct mail expenditures.
Sources: Leading National Advertisers, Radio Advertising Bureau.

Source: Advertising Age, February 13, 1984, p. M-11.

The door was opened for an AT&T or an IBM as potential suppliers of financial services.

41   The threat of substitute services existed not just on a national basis but on an international scale as well. Until the passage of the International

Figure 9

Industry EDP equipment costs growth

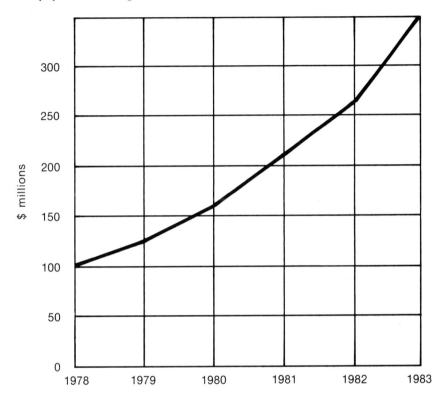

Source: Financial World, January 31, 1983, p. 66.

Banking Act of 1978, foreign banks were virtually unrestricted in the establishment of full-fledged banks in this country. By 1979, there were over 300 foreign bank entities operating in the United States.

Buyers

42   Customers of the financial services industry can be basically separated into three groups: (1) individuals, (2) institutions, and (3) governments. The consumers of the 1980s were more affluent, more sophisticated, more interest-rate sensitive, and were less loyal to specific institutions than in the past. Although a number of circumstances might contribute to the bargaining power of buyers, only two seem particularly relevant to financial service customers: (1) price sensitivity and (2) availability of full information.

Fluctuating interest rates and rising inflation contribute to financial customers' price sensitivity. Buyer power is enhanced because financial services customers demand more from every dollar they invest. The trend toward increased advertising among financial service industry participants served to make consumers more sophisticated and better informed.

Suppliers

43 There are basically two categories of resources for the financial services industry: funds and personnel. Funds are not only the industry's input but are also its output. All of the statements made above about the industry's customers pertain equally to the industry's suppliers for, in many cases, they are the same. However, supplier power tends to be a mirror image of buyer power. Two contributors to supplier power deserve mention: (1) lack of substitutes and (2) the importance of the product as an input. Since there are no substitutes for funds, and since funds are the industry's only input, suppliers of funds do wield some power.

44 The second basic resource in the financial services industry is its personnel. Although the following statements were made with respect to banking in particular, they easily apply to all segments of the industry.

45 "Quite simply, people are *everything* in banking....People are the principal competitive weapon a bank has...A bank is not strong by virtue of its buildings, machines, name, or money. Pure and simple, it is its people that count— for everything....Banking...is almost always a personal service— people-to-people business. Whether we sell our service, get our price, or develop a quality product, is totally dependent on people. Our people often *are* the service we sell. They are selling themselves and their ability to provide services."[4]

The Future of the Financial Services Industry

46 Much has been written and there has been much speculation as to the shape of the financial services industry in the future. There are at least eight major environmental determinants that could play a role in the industry's future: (1) consumer demand and preference, (2) technological developments, (3) regulatory uncertainty, (4) new institutional arrangements, (5) increase in competition, (6) increasing global orientation, (7) increasing diversity of products, and (8) increased volatility of economic events. Since consumers, regulations, new institutional arrangements, and increased competition have been treated elsewhere, the following brief discussion notes the remaining four factors.

47 Electronic technology already plays a key role in the industry, and the progression of more sophisticated links between data processing and communications hints at future possibilities that almost defy imagination.

Some major forces sure to play a part include satellites, digital communications, and the home computer.

48   As is true of many other industries, the orientation in financial services is becoming increasingly global. This globalism can be attributed to technology, growing per capita wealth, and economic volatility. Electronic impulses and satellite transmissions are oblivious to national boundaries. It seems almost unnatural to confine financial activities to one country any more. Many products, such as the American Express and Visa cards and travelers checks, have indeed already become universal.

49   The increasing diversity of products has led to the "supermarket" approach to financial services as evidenced by such giants as Sears. In the early 1980s, the typical affluent American household dealt with about 20 different financial vendors and purchased nearly 40 different products and services.

50   Volatility of economic events has become an expected norm. Changing interest rates, fluctuations in the money supply, the consumer price index, and variations in the gross national product have made the nation, institutions, and consumers very information-sensitive.

51   Those financial services institutions that thrive and prosper beyond the 1990s and into the twenty-first century will likely have found ways to deal effectively with these environmental elements. By that time, these same forces may well have drastically changed the players in the game.

Notes

1. Doris E. Harless, *Nonbank Financial Institutions* (Federal Reserve Bank of Richmond, October 1975).
2. P. Michael Laub, "Banks and Financial Services," in *The Future of the Financial Services Industry* (Conference Proceedings, Federal Reserve Bank of Atlanta, June 3–4, 1981), pp. 62–76.
3. Michael E. Porter, *Competitive Strategy* (New York: Free Press, 1980).
4. Elbert V. Bowden, *Revolution in Banking* (Richmond, Vir.: Robert F. Dame, 1980).

Appendix: Largest Financial Industry Participants

Exhibit 1

The 100 largest commercial banking companies ranked by assets

Rank 1983	1982	Company
1	1	Citicorp (New York)
2	2	BankAmerica Corp. (San Francisco)
3	3	Chase Manhattan Corp. (New York)
4	4	Manufacturers Hanover Corp. (New York)
5	5	J.P. Morgan & Co. (New York)
6	6	Chemical New York Corp.
7	8	First Interstate Bancorp. (Los Angeles)
8	7	Continental Illinois Corp. (Chicago)
9	10	Security Pacific Corp. (Los Angeles)
10	9	Bankers Trust New York Corp.
11	11	First Chicago Corp.
12	13	Wells Fargo & Co. (San Francisco)
13	15	Mellon National Corp. (Pittsburgh)
14	12	Crocker National Corp. (San Francisco)
15	16	Marine Midland Banks (Buffalo)
16	14	InterFirst Corp. (Dallas)
17	22	First Bank System (Minneapolis)
18	20	Norwest Corp. (Minneapolis)
19	18	Bank of Boston Corp.
20	19	Texas Commerce Bancshares (Houston)
21	21	RepublicBank Corp. (Dallas)
22	17	Irving Bank Corp. (New York)
23	23	First City Bancorp. of Texas (Houston)

Exhibit 1 (continued)

Rank		Company
1983	*1982*	
24	25	NBD Bancorp. (Detroit)
25	26	NCNB Corp. (Charlotte, N.C.)
26	24	Bank of New York Co.
27	31	PNC Financial Corp. (Pittsburgh)
28	27	Mercantile Texas Corp. (Dallas)
29	29	Republic New York Corp.
30	37	Barnett Banks of Florida (Jacksonville)
31	62	Sun Banks (Orlando, Fla.)
32	34	Southeast Banking Corp. (Miami)
33	30	European American Bancorp. (New York)
34	43	CoreStates Financial Corp. (Philadelphia)
35	33	Comerica (Detroit)
36	35	Valley National Corp. (Phoenix)
37	38	Southwest Bancshares (Houston)
38	32	Union Bank (Los Angeles)
39	46	Allied Bancshares (Houston)
40	39	Wachovic Corp. (Winston-Salem, N.C.)
41	41	National Westminster Bank USA (New York)
42	36	Harris Bankcorp. (Chicago)
43	61	Banc One Corp. (Columbus, Ohio)
44	81	Sovran Financial Corp. (Norfolk, Va.)
45	47	Citizens & Southern Georgia Corp. (Atlanta)
46	42	Michigan National Corp. (Bloomfield Hills)
47	45	First Union Corp. (Charlotte, N.C.)
48	40	National City Corp. (Cleveland)
49	50	U.S. Bancorp. (Portland, Ore.)
50	44	Northern Trust Corp. (Chicago)
51	63	First National State Bancorp. (Newark)
52	72	Midlantic Banks (Edison, N.J.)

Exhibit 1 (continued)

Rank		Company
1983	*1982*	
53	48	Rainier Bancorp. (Seattle)
54	58	CBT Corp. (Hartford)
55	49	BancOhio Corp. (Columbus)
56	55	Manufacturers National Corp. (Detroit)
57	59	Bank of New England Corp. (Boston)
58	51	AmeriTrust Corp. (Cleveland)
59	71	First Atlanta Corp.
60	54	Shawmut Corp. (Boston)
61	60	Maryland National Corp. (Baltimore)
62	76	Fidelcor (Philadelphia)
63	52	Mercantile Bancorp. (St. Louis)
64	56	Huntington Bancshares (Columbus, Ohio)
65	64	United Virginia Bankshares (Richmond)
66	67	Texas American Bancshares (Fort Worth)
67	57	Centerre Bancorp. (St. Louis)
68	86	Norstar Bancorp. (Albany, N.Y.)
69	53	First Pennsylvania Corp. (Philadelphia)
70	65	First Wisconsin Corp. (Milwaukee)
71	68	First Security Corp. (Salt Lake City)
72	70	Trust Company of Georgia (Atlanta)
73	84	Riggs National Corp. (Washington, D.C.)
74	75	Hartford National Corp.
75	85	BayBanks (Boston)
76	92	First Tennessee National Corp. (Memphis)
77	74	Bank of Tokyo Trust (New York)
78	73	California First Bank (San Francisco)
79	79	Society Corp. (Cleveland)
80	80	Lincoln First Banks (Rochester, N.Y.)
81	83	First of America Bank Corp. (Kalamazoo, Mich.)
82	78	State Street Boston Corp.
83	87	United Banks of Colorado (Denver)
84	82	BanCal Tri-State Corp. (San Francisco)
85	93	Bank of Virginia Co. (Richmond)

Exhibit 1 (concluded)

Rank 1983	1982	Company
86	99	Dominion Bankshares (Roanoke, Va.)
87	90	Fidelity Union Bancorp. (Newark)
88	●	First American Bankshares (Washington, D.C.)
89	●	Meridian Bancorp. (Reading, Pa.)
90	●	Third National Corp. (Nashville)
91	91	American Security Corp. (Washington, D.C.)
92	●	Old Kent Financial Corp. (Grand Rapids, Mich.)
93	89	First Maryland Bancorp. (Baltimore)
94	97	AmSouth Bancorp. (Birmingham, Ala.)
95	98	United Jersey Banks (Princeton)
96	88	Florida National Banks of Florida (Jacksonville)
97	●	Boatmen's Bancshares (St. Louis)
98	●	First American Corp. (Nashville)
99	●	Key Banks (Albany, N.Y.)
100	94	Commerce Bancshares (Kansas City, Mo.)

Source: Fortune, June 11, 1984, pp. 176–78.

Exhibit 2

The 100 largest diversified financial companies ranked by assets

Rank 1983	1982	Company
1	1	Federal National Mortgage Assoc. (Washington, D.C.)
2	2	Aetna Life & Casualty (Hartford)
3	4	American Express (New York)
4	3	CIGNA (Philadelphia)
5	5	Travelers Corp. (Hartford)
6	6	Merrill Lynch & Co. (New York)
7	21	Financial Corp. of America (Los Angeles)
8	7	First Boston (New York)
9	8	H.F. Ahmanson (Los Angeles)
10	10	Great Western Financial (Beverly Hills, Calif.)

Exhibit 2 (continued)

Rank 1983	1982	Company
11	9	American General Corp. (Houston)
12	●	CalFed (Los Angeles)
13	18	E.F. Hutton Group (New York)
14	12	Loews (New York)
15	13	Lincoln National (Fort Wayne, Ind.)
16	11	Transamerica (San Francisco)
17	16	American International Group (New York)
18	17	Continental (New York)
19	●	Student Loan Marketing Assoc. (Washington, D.C.)
20	20	First Nationwide Financial (San Francisco)
21	19	Golden West Financial (Oakland, Calif.)
22	●	First Federal of Michigan (Detroit)
23	34	Paine Webber (New York)
24	22	Walter E. Heller International (Chicago)
25	23	Kemper (Long Grove, Ill.)
26	●	Home Federal Sav. & Loan Assoc. (San Diego)
27	31	City Federal Sav. & Loan Assoc. (Elizabeth, N.J.)
28	24	Beneficial (Wilmington, Del.)
29	27	Imperial Corp. of America (San Diego)
30	29	Gibraltar Financial Corp. of Calif. (Beverly Hills)
31	●	Fleet Financial Group (Providence)
32	26	St. Paul Companies. (Minn.)
33	25	Donaldson Lufkin & Jenrette (New York)
34	30	General Re Corp. (Greenwich, Conn.)
35	28	U. S. Fidelity & Guaranty (Baltimore)
36	36	Capital Holding (Louisville)
37	35	American Financial (Cincinnati)
38	●	Carteret Sav. & Loan Assoc. (Morristown, N.J.)
39	37	Gibraltar Savings Association (Houston)
40	39	Chubb (Warren, N.J.)
41	●	Florida Federal Sav. & Loan Assoc. (St. Petersburg)
42	52	United Financial Group (Houston)
43	40	Reliance Group Holdings (New York)

Exhibit 2 (continued)

Rank 1983	1982	Company
44	43	SAFECO (Seattle)
45	42	Torchmark (Birmingham, Ala.)
46	●	First Federal Sav. & Loan Assoc. of Arizona (Phoenix)
47	46	American Savings & Loan Assoc. of Florida (Miami)
48	44	Western Savings & Loan Assoc. (Phoenix)
49	●	Farm & Home Savings Assoc. (Nevada, Mo.)
50	45	Combined International (Northbrook, Ill.)
51	50	Financial Corp. of Santa Barbara (Calif.)
52	48	TRANSOHIO Financial (Cleveland)
53	49	Guarantee Financial Corp. of Calif. (Fresno)
54	●	Valley Federal Sav. & Loan Assoc. (Van Nuys, Calif.)
55	47	American Savings & Loan Assoc. (Salt Lake City)
56	55	Citadel Holding (Glendale, Calif.)
57	54	Farmers Group (Los Angeles)
58	51	Broadview Financial (Cleveland)
59	88	Beverly Hills Savings & Loan Assoc. (Calif.)
60	65	Freedom Savings & Loan Assoc. (Tampa, Fla.)
61	59	Downey Savings & Loan Assoc. (Costa Mesa, Calif.)
62	●	Great Lakes Fed. Sav. & Loan Assoc. (Ann Arbor, Mich.)
63	60	GEICO (Washington, D.C.)
64	63	Mercury Sav. & Loan Assoc. (Huntington Beach, Calif.)
65	●	Dallas Federal Savings & Loan Assoc.
66	58	Ohio Casualty (Hamilton)
67	62	First Columbia Financial (Englewood, Calif.)
68	68	Far West Financial (Newport Beach, Calif.)
69	66	Citizens Savings Financial (Miami)
70	67	Sooner Federal Savings & Loan Assoc. (Tulsa)
71	74	Monarch Capital (Springfield, Mass.)
72	97	Homestead Financial (Burlingame, Calif.)
73	76	Texas Federal Financial (Dallas)
74	61	Alexander & Alexander Services (New York)
75	●	Fortune Fed. Sav. & Loan Assoc. (Clearwater, Fla.)
76	64	Orbanco Financial Services (Portland, Ore.)

Exhibit 2 (concluded)

Rank 1983	1982	Company
77	71	American Family (Columbus, Ga.)
78	●	United First Fed. Sav. & Loan Assoc. (Sarasota, Fla.)
79	●	Bell National Corp. (San Mateo, Calif.)
80	70	Old Republic International (Chicago)
81	69	First Savings Assoc. of Wisconsin (Milwaukee)
82	75	Buckeye Financial (Columbus, Ohio)
83	●	Metropolitan Fed. Sav. & Loan Assoc. of Fargo (N.D.)
84	72	Hanover Insurance (Worcester, Mass.)
85	73	Colonial Penn Group (Philadelphia)
86	●	First Southern Fed. Sav. & Loan Assoc. (Mobile, Ala.)
87	86	First Lincoln Financial (Monterey Park, Calif.)
88	●	Home Federal Savings & Loan Assoc. (Tucson)
89	●	Coast Federal Sav. & Loan Assoc. (Sarasota, Fla.)
90	89	United States Leasing International (San Francisco)
91	79	Nevada Savings & Loan Association (Las Vegas)
92	56	Southland Financial (Irving, Tex.)
93	82	Mission Insurance Group (Los Angeles)
94	81	First Western Financial (Las Vegas)
95	91	Lomas & Nettleton Financial (Dallas)
96	77	Frank B. Hall & Co. (Briarcliff Manor, N.Y.)
97	87	Fremont General (Los Angeles)
98	●	Security Capital (New York)
99	84	Liberty (Greenville, S.C.)
100	92	Nafco Financial Group (Naples, Fla.)

Source: Fortune, June 11, 1984, pp. 180–82.

Exhibit 3

The 50 largest life insurance companies ranked by assets

Rank 1983	1982	Company
1	1	Prudential (Newark)

Exhibit 3 (continued)

Rank 1983	1982	Company
2	2	Metropolitan (New York)
3	3	Equitable Life Assurance (New York)
4	4	Aetna Life (Hartford)
5	5	New York Life
6	6	John Hancock Mutual (Boston)
7	7	Travelers (Hartford)
8	8	Connecticut General Life (Bloomfield)
9	9	Teachers Insurance & Annuity (New York)
10	10	Northwestern Mutual (Milwaukee)
11	11	Massachusetts Mutual (Springfield)
12	12	Bankers Life (Des Moines)
13	13	Mutual of New York
14	14	New England Mutual (Boston, Mass.)
15	15	Mutual Benefit (Newark)
16	16	Connecticut Mutual (Hartford)
17	18	State Farm Life (Bloomington, Ill.)
18	17	Lincoln National Life (Fort Wayne, Ind.)
19	20	Continental Assurance (Chicago)
20	19	Penn Mutual (Philadelphia)
21	23	Nationwide Life (Columbus, Ohio)
22	21	Phoenix Mutual (Hartford)
23	25	National Life & Accident (Nashville)
24	22	Western & Southern Life (Cincinnati)
25	33	Variable Annuity Life (Houston)
26	31	IDS Life (Minneapolis)
27	36	Executive Life (Beverly Hills, Calif.)
28	24	Pacific Mutual (Newport Beach, Calif.)
29	34	Aetna Life & Annuity (Hartford)
30	27	American National (Galveston, Tex.)
31	28	State Mutual of America (Worcester, Mass.)
32	29	Franklin Life (Springfield, Ill.)
33	32	Transamerica Occidental Life (Los Angeles)
34	30	National Life (Montpelier, Vt.)

Exhibit 3 (concluded)

Rank 1983	1982	Company
35	35	Union Mutual (Portland, Me.)
36	38	Minnesota Mutual Life (St. Paul)
37	39	Guardian of America (New York)
38	37	General American Life (St. Louis)
39	26	National Investors Pension (Little Rock)
40	●	Capitol Life (Denver)
41	44	Northwestern National (Minneapolis)
42	40	United of Omaha Life
43	42	Home Life (New York)
44	43	Provident Life & Accident (Chattanooga, Tenn.)
45	41	Provident Mutual (Philadelphia)
46	47	Charter Security Life (Chatham, N.J.)
47	50	Kemper Investors Life (Chicago)
48	●	National Health & Welfare Mutual (New York)
49	46	Liberty National (Birmingham, Ala.)
50	48	American United Life (Indianapolis)

Source: Fortune, June 11, 1984, p. 184.

case **7** **The American Express Company: New Games, New Rules, New Strategies**

1   By the middle of 1981, the finance-related and insurance industries were in periods of rapid change and turmoil. Each industry was facing problems resulting from general economic conditions and intensified competition. The basis for competition was changing as companies left traditional and historic roles, new and powerful entrants threatened, and technological innovation was obvious everywhere. As an active participant in these industries, American Express was also experiencing a year of transition and challenge. James D. Robinson III, the chief executive officer, offered his view of the future:

> By 1990 you'll have a stockbroker in California, a banker in New York, an insurance agency in Maryland and a realtor jetting between Chicago and Boston. All your purchases will be on the American Express Card, of course. And within the decade you'll have the option of banking by mail or by cable television.[1]

The challenge for American Express is to chart a course to this vision.

Credit Card Industry

2   The first credit cards in the United States were issued in the 1920s by oil companies as a means of promoting brand loyalty and providing a billing convenience for traveling customers. Use of cards was expanded slightly

James R. Lang, "The American Express Company" case, from Robert A. Comerford and Dennis W. Callaghan, *Strategic Management: Text, Tools, and Cases for Business Policy* (Boston: Kent Publishing Company, 1985), pp. 823-43. © 1984 by James R. Lang. Reprinted by permission of Kent Publishing Company, a division of Wadsworth, Inc.

during the 1930s when department stores issued cards to their charge account customers and major oil companies developed reciprocal billing arrangements. This relatively limited use of cards was abruptly changed in the early 1950s when the credit card industry was born with the formation of Diners Club. Diners Club began in February 1950 with twenty-two restaurants and 200 card holders. After a first-year loss of $158,730, Diners Club earned a $61,222 profit in its second year and then continually expanded the scope of its operations during the 1950s. American Express entered the industry in 1958 and took over industry leadership in 1959 by acquiring two smaller competitors. Carte Blanche became industry competitive in 1959 when Hilton Hotels added establishments outside of the Hilton chain to its credit card system.

3   Banks entered the industry in the late 1950s when the first bank credit card was issued by Franklin National Bank. Through the 1960s the bank cards grew through the offering of cards to a wider segment of the population and allowing their use for goods and services beyond travel and entertainment.

4   By 1980 there were over 600 million credit cards in circulation in the United States and it was estimated that there would be a billion cards worldwide by 1985. Americans are by far the greatest users of credit cards, holding about 82 percent of all cards. As of 1978 U.S. consumers held an average of 5.2 cards and business persons an average of 11.3 cards each. Of the 1979 total installment borrowing of $300 billion in the United States, about $100 billion was through credit cards.

5   In spite of their early entry in the industry, travel and entertainment (T&E) cards have not maintained a significant share in terms of number of cards in circulation. In 1980 T&E accounted for one half of the cards in existence. Sears Roebuck was the single largest issuer: in 1978 Sears, alone, had 47 million cards in circulation. The proportion of retailers' cards has been on the decline, however, as smaller retailers are being absorbed by conglomerates that tend to favor the use of bank credit cards. In 1979 there were about 115 million bank cards in circulation, and that number is expected to increase to 255 million by 1985. Oil companies maintained about 22 percent of the cards outstanding in 1980, and all other types (airlines, etc.) had about 3 percent.

Bank Cards

6   In 1980 banks held about 22 percent of the number of cards outstanding, but were by far the most aggressive segment of the industry. Traditionally the bank cards have been differentiated from T&E cards by extending a line of credit to the cardholder; T&E cards demand payment on request each month. Young families, families with children, and families headed by those without a college degree are most likely to use the credit feature of cards, whereas others use the cards primarily to facilitate transactions. In

the mid- to late-1970s the use of the credit feature grew rapidly. In 1978, for instance, there was $23 billion of credit outstanding on bank cards, which was a 33 percent increase over the previous year. By the late 1970s, interest charges provided 70 percent of the bank's credit card earnings, which was far greater than the percentages received from merchant discounts (about 2 percent of the amount purchased) and fees. Recently, however, the costs of financing receivables have increased markedly, and many banks have begun to charge annual fees of $10 to $15 or transactions fees to offset these costs. Transaction fees are typically 12 cents per transaction. In 1980 about one half of all bank card holders paid either annual or transaction fees. In 1979 there were practically none. In other moves to combat higher financing costs, some banks have been moving their operations to states that allow higher than the standard 18 percent interest rate.

7   In spite of these changes to improve position, most banks lost money on their credit card operations in late 1979 and 1980. More and more customers were paying off their accounts within the interest-free grace period. In 1980 the banks seemed to suffer no significant drop in business because of the institution of fees, but the proportion of billings incurring no interest approached 50 percent. This payoff phenomenon has led many banks to conclude that they are not selling credit so much as convenience or "transfer of value." On the basis of this conclusion, banks are considering offering other transfer-of-value instruments such as debit cards[2] and travelers' checks as potential services. For instance, bank cards have teamed up with Western Union's emergency money order service to allow callers to wire up to $300 to any of 8,100 offices in the United States and to have the amount charged to their credit cards. It is generally felt that if consumers should continue to decrease their amounts of credit card debt, the competition will intensify and bank cards will move more aggressively into travelers' checks and other segments of the travel and entertainment segment. In fact surveys already show that more consumers are using bank cards than are using T&E cards for restaurant checks and hotel bills. As of 1978, Visa and MasterCard claimed 2.5 million outlets accepting cards; Diners Club 400,000; American Express 350,000; and Carte Blanche 250,000.

8   The two strongest competitors among bank cards are Visa and Master-Card. While Visa has recently overtaken MasterCard as the leader in worldwide volume and number of holders, MasterCard still retains an edge in the United States. Both provide debit cards and are venturing into the travelers' check business.

9   Visa changed its name from Bank Americard in 1977 in order to shed its national identity with its political connotations and to project more of a worldwide image. The number of Visa card holders increased dramatically during the late 1970s, with over 70 million by 1979. The volume of Visa transactions also has increased rapidly (91 percent in the 1977–1979 period), primarily from retail stores and restaurants.

10   Visa presents increasingly formidable competition in the credit card

industry, displaying corporate agility that fostered innovations such as the debit card (800,000 accounts in 1980), the trendy name, and strong initiatives in foreign markets. Although Visa's management sees travelers' checks as a regression into paper processing (which runs counter to its electronic processing strength), the company has aggressively entered the travelers' check market. Depending upon cooperation with Barclay's (presently fourth largest issuer of travelers' checks), Visa's business has been growing at a 15 percent annual rate. In 1980 Visa had 8 percent of the U.S. market and was expecting a 40 percent share by 1985. As of 1980 about 90 percent of the checks processed were, in fact, Barclay's. The largest bank to build Visa travelers' checks sales from scratch is First National Bank of Chicago. As of 1980 that bank had sold $50 million in checks. Visa's plan for the travelers' check business is to allow participating banks to place their own names on the checks. Visa hopes this approach will lure banks who have been selling American Express checks.

11   MasterCard, with its 65 million worldwide card holders in 1979, has been fighting the Visa challenge with larger advertising outlays (40 percent increase in 1979), a name change from Master Charge to MasterCard, debit cards, and a delayed venture into travelers' checks. The travelers' check delay was caused by a legal roadblock set up by Citibank, a member of the MasterCard system, which already held 12 percent of the world travelers' check market. Along with Visa, the MasterCard system is large enough and integrated enough to provide economies-of-scale advantages in authorization and interchange procedures.

Travel and Entertainment Cards

12   In 1978 it was estimated that $385 billion was spent on domestic and international travel and that by 1988 the amount spent will be $755 billion. American Express is by far the largest T&E card company, with 11.9 million card holders in 1980. The American Express card is held by more than half of the country's families who earn more than $25,000 annually. The company engages in heavy advertising campaigns and frequently cosponsors ads with hotels and restaurants that accept the card.

13   Diners Club intensified its marketing efforts in the late 1970s with large increases in marketing budgets. In 1979 Diners Club claimed 2.5 million card holders, with about 60 percent of the holders residing outside of the United States. Carte Blanche, with 800,000 holders in 1979, serves the affluent, has snob appeal, and turned down 75 percent of its 40,000 monthly applicants in 1978. Acquired from AVCO by Citicorp in 1979, Carte Blanche was generally thought to be in need of new marketing emphasis in order to survive.

14   In contrast to bank cards, which credit merchants' accounts on the same day an invoice is received, merchants who handle T&E cards generally must wait several days for payment. The T&E cards also charge a higher

discount to the merchants, typically 3.5 to 4 percent of the price of purchase. American Express, for instance, offers retailers the option of being paid one to thirty days after receipt, with the discount rates correspondingly lower as the period is extended.

Travelers' Checks

15   Closely related to the T&E credit card segment is the travelers' check industry. Started in 1891 by American Express, which maintains 60 percent of the market, the major competitors are Bank of America, Citibank, Barclay's, and Thomas Cook. In 1978, 735 million travelers' checks were sold at a value of $25 billion. The five major U.S. and British issuers earned an estimated total of $239 million. In the five-year period 1974–1979, the industry sales grew 120 percent, and by 1979 worldwide sales had reached $30 billion.

16   Most income on travelers' checks is made not on the nominal fee charged (usually 1 percent of face value), but on the "float"—that is, on checks that are purchased and paid for, but not yet cashed. The average float period for travelers' checks is about two months. The companies can then invest this cash for two months until the checks are cashed. American Express, for instance, had about $2.3 billion in travelers' check float in 1979. Thus industry experts indicate that it is unlikely that a company can be profitable in travelers' checks with an annual volume of less than $2 billion.

Property/Casualty Insurance Industry

17   In contrast to the concentration of the credit card industry, the property/casualty (p-c) insurance industry has a large number of competitors with 200 companies that have written over $40 million in premiums in 1980. Many, but not all, of the leading p-c companies are also leaders in life insurance (see Exhibit 1). Even within the p-c segment, not all companies offer full lines of p-c insurance services. The importance of the various insurance lines in the p-c segment is shown in Exhibit 2.

18   A historical characteristic of the insurance business is the "underwriting cycle." The cycle affects profitability of insurance companies through the relationship between premium pricing and claims costs. At the peak of the cycle, competition is intense and prices are forced to a low level. When claims begin to come in at a level higher than provided for in the reserves, losses occur. At this point there is a shakeout of sorts, with some companies dropping from the competition in their less profitable segments and the remaining companies raising their premiums.

19   The overall industry growth rate has slowed from 10.7 percent in 1980. This slowing of premium growth rate is indicative of another trough in the underwriting cycle and stiff price competition. In 1980 the top 100 compa-

nies averaged an underwriting loss of 3.53 percent of earned premiums (after dividends to policy holders). This loss totaled $2.8 billion for the industry. The forecasts for 1981 indicate that it could be even more competitive, with worse results than in 1980. Most insurance companies have been able to offset underwriting losses with investment income. *Best's* reported, however, that 5 of the top 100 firms were not, in fact, able to offset underwriting losses in 1980. Some industry experts predicted that this pressure,

Exhibit 1

Leading property/casualty companies and groups (1980 net premiums written in thousands)

	Rank	Total p-c cos. premiums	Life ins. premiums	Total premium volume	Rank	Percent increase 1 Yr.	Percent increase 5 Yr. compound
State Farm	1	8,011,787	551,365	8,563,152	3	10.83	19.10
Allstate	2	5,270,426	240,300	5,515,454	6	9.89	12.27
Aetna Life and Casualty	3	4,558,426	3,939,761	10,294,080	1	3.72	16.05
Travelers	4	2,888,253	2,526,244	7,128,640	4	9.05	5.64
Liberty Mutual	5	2,867,423	39,677	2,911,727	10	4.29	18.47
Continental Insurance	6	2,822,595	44,886	2,883,049	11	6.25	7.61
Harford Fire	7	2,661,964	301,050	3,217,105	9	4.73	9.83
Farmers Insurance	8	2,552,756	133,413	2,719,557	13	7.32	20.69
INA	9	2,550,211	458,050	3,349,209	8	6.08	9.20
Fireman's Fund	10	2,350,283	75,354	2,525,217	17	2.43	12.94
U.S. Fidelity and Guaranty	11	2,043,653	48,008	2,093,985	20	2.63	16.40
Nationwide	12	1,951,339	574,703	2,590,320	15	10.95	18.21
Kemper	13	1,689,683	363,964	2,053,740	21	5.48	12.55
Home Insurance	14	1,689,386	45,964	1,814,049	22	4.04	14.26
Crum and Forster	15	1,620,970	—	1,620,970	25	2.38	13.07
St. Paul	16	1,520,073	96,832	1,682,636	23	9.00	14.18
CNA	17	1,418,916	413,262	2,469,170	18	8.61	16.20
American International	18	1,374,564	203,950	1,632,035	24	10.34	24.82
Chubb	19	1,142,373	88,380	1,281,117	27	6.21	9.31
Commercial Union	20	1,115,897	20,939	1,137,437	28	15.19	8.58
Prudential of America	21	1,023,892	5,847,490	9,681,087	2	11.82	28.79
Connecticut General	22	1,011,796	629,059	2,872,063	12	-1.76	10.88
Royal Insurance	23	957,059	8,890	956,949	35	3.27	7.55
American Financial	24	898,823	177,897	1,079,999	29	9.64	4.82
Reliance	25	875,799	107,299	1,036,609	30	-3.67	10.48

Source: Adapted from *Best's Review: Property/Casualty Insurance Edition,* June 1981.

following the 1973-1975 trough by only five years, may force weaker firms into insolvency.

20   The use of investment income to offset underwriting losses has kept the industry profitable, exhibiting a strong capital surplus (see Exhibit 3) in spite of the downturn in the cycle. The increasing dependence of companies on investment income is shown dramatically in Exhibit 4 and may have permanently changed the nature of the insurance business. Some analysts feel that the ability to depend on investment income will delay the normal

Exhibit 2

Property/casualty insurance industry premium distribution by line

	Total premiums[a]	% of total	Gain in premiums[a]	Loss Ratio[b]			
				1980	1979	1978	1977
Fire	2,887,770	3.0	-19,425	56.1	51.6	47.5	51.0
Allied lines	1,673,619	1.7	44,043	69.1	67.9	57.1	46.6
Farm owners' multiperil	594,335	0.6	60,316	76.5	61.4	60.3	61.0
Homeowners' multiperil	10,012,854	10.4	982,901	67.1	61.5	53.5	53.1
Commercial multiperil	7,663,589	7.9	320,269	55.4	52.9	44.4	42.9
Earthquake	53,558	0.1	11,934	5.0	1.8	1.9	.9
Ocean marine	1,015,670	1.1	74,631	87.9	82.5	66.1	60.8
Inland marine	2,744,061	2.8	383,791	68.9	58.1	51.6	49.1
Group A&H	1,853,362	1.9	143,767	80.8	76.4	77.5	78.2
All other A&H	655,389	0.7	1,704	64.2	62.5	62.4	60.2
Worker's compensation	15,743,510	16.3	1,411,445	70.4	75.3	77.9	74.1
Total misc. liability	9,408,956	9.7	-148,140	60.9	55.4	50.6	40.4
Medical malpractice	1,491,403	1.5	85,412	82.6	75.3	60.6	41.8
Other liability	7,917,553	8.2	-233,552	57.1	51.6	48.7	40.1
Private passenger auto liability	18,564,090	19.2	1,188,824	67.6	66.4	64.7	63.4
No fault	2,170,962	2.2	116,823	78.3	74.0	76.7	78.3
Other liability	16,393,128	17.0	1,072,001	66.2	65.4	63.1	61.5
Commercial auto liability	4,936,684	5.1	136,871	69.0	66.4	61.7	57.9
No fault	154,251	0.2	-9,769	71.1	62.7	60.3	64.9
Other liability	4,782,433	4.9	146,640	68.9	66.5	61.7	57.7
Private passenger auto physical damage	13,188,141	13.6	1,161,405	64.9	68.7	65.2	61.6
Commercial auto physical damage	2,726,160	2.8	112,358	59.4	59.6	55.4	53.2
Aircraft	389,376	0.4	71,892	82.3	78.6	101.0	63.3
Fidelity	399,686	0.4	18,517	48.1	44.8	55.2	56.0
Surety	1,000,732	1.0	98,180	46.1	33.2	43.5	36.3
Glass	31,666	0.0	-972	54.1	50.6	47.8	46.6
Burglary and theft	125,653	0.1	-1,831	37.3	36.6	25.8	26.4
Boiler and machinery	377,519	0.4	8,908	49.4	40.4	31.9	31.7
Credit	79,229	0.1	8,840	56.7	35.1	37.9	38.7
Miscellaneous	584,253	0.6	-54,299	54.3	85.2	46.7	46.2
Totals	96,709,863	100.0	6,015,930	65.5	64.3	60.8	57.7

[a]In dollars, 000 omitted.
[b]Loss ratio = Losses incurred (Premiums earned – Dividends).
Source: Adapted from *Best's Review: Property/Casualty Insurance Edition,* July 1981.

Exhibit 3

Summary of five-year industry results

Year	Premiums written, $ billion	Rate of increase, percent	Pre-tax underwriting profits,[a] $ billion	Capital gains, $ billion	Surplus, $ billion
1976	60.4	21.9	-2.2	2.0	24.6
1977	72.4	19.8	1.1	-0.8	29.3
1978	81.6	12.8	1.3	0.5	35.2
1979	90.1	10.3	-1.3	2.3	42.8
1980	96.3	6.9	-3.4	4.8	52.3
5 Years	400.8	14.3	-4.5		

[a] After dividends.
Source: Best's Review: Property/Casualty Edition, September 1981.

Exhibit 4

Underwriting and investment income growth trends

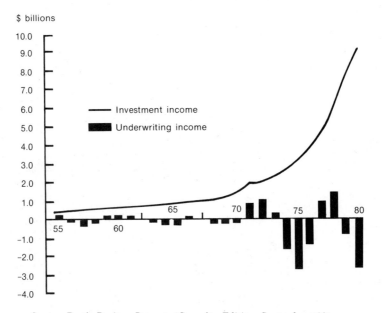

Source: Best's Review: Property/Casualty Edition, September 1981.

shakeout of unprofitable lines and companies and will prolong the present trough much longer than usual.

21   Given the prospect of extended competitive pricing, attention to cost reduction may be one of the keys to survival. The current trends in the industry are summarized in *Best's* as follows:

1. As product and service distinctiveness becomes more difficult to maintain, insurance is taking on the aspects of a commodity game where low-cost producers are winners.

2. Competitive pricing is assuming growing importance.
   - Competition from major new entrants is forcing insurers to offer a competitive price.
   - Independent agencies are undergoing structural changes that are increasing price competition.
   - Customers are becoming more price conscious as insurance costs rise.

3. As competition increases among all types of insurers, companies are seeking new revenue avenues such as fee-based administration, loss control, and claim services.

4. Since price increases and premium growth are not keeping up with inflation, primarily because of competition, companies with uncompetitive expense ratios[3] may pay a substantial penalty for their inefficiency.[4]

22   Among the suggestions provided for increasing expense ratios are the following:

1. Programs to increase productivity.
2. Investment in automated systems.
3. Delegation of expense management responsibilities to branches.
4. Building expense accountability into the reward systems.

American Express Company

23   American Express was founded in 1850 and boasts of 114 years of uninterrupted profitability. The chairman of the board and chief executive officer is James D. Robinson III, who succeeded Harold L. Clark in 1977. In the 17 years of Clark's tenure, American Express revenues grew from $77 million to $3.4 billion in 1977. Clark ran the company with a very personal style of management that minimized bureaucratic controls and allowed a great deal of latitude to the division heads. He also recognized the importance of good relationships with banks to the success of American Express's business and used these contacts to build the business. When he left the company, four of the six largest banks were represented on the American Express board of directors.

24 Robinson, who has been at American Express since 1970, has indicated that "Our prime objective is to provide, directly with banks, the widest variety of consumer financial services available from any single source." The transition from Clark to Robinson was orderly and gradual, with Clark maintaining active company involvement for some time after the official transfer of duties in 1977. Although Clark and Robinson are both conservative in financial matters, differences in their management styles have become apparent. American Express has evolved into a more highly structured organization. Along with Roger Morely (who succeeded him as president), Robinson implemented a rigorous system of planning and control, which included not only annual plans, but also divisional level monthly forecasts. Morley was replaced as president in 1979 by Alva Way, formerly the chief financial officer at General Electric. Among the qualities in Way that were found attractive by Robinson were his abilities in strategic planning, data processing, and communications. Observers feel that all of this organizational emphasis has paid off in the form of significant improvements in the coordination among the divisions within the past few years.

25 A major part of American Express's growth has been through acquisition. In 1968 American Express acquired Fireman's Fund Insurance, the nation's ninth largest property-liability insurer. In 1972 the company bought a 25 percent interest in Donaldson, Lufkin and Jenrett, but sold the interest in 1975 at a $23 million loss. Within Robinson's first three years, American Express attempted to make four acquisitions: Walt Disney Productions, Book-of-the-Month Club, Philadelphia Life Insurance, and McGraw-Hill. The company's recent acquisitions are listed in Exhibit 5, the most significant and most recent being the merger with Shearson Loeb Rhoades.

26 As of early 1981, American Express was organized into four major business areas: Travel Services Group, Warner Amex Cable Services, Inter-

---

Exhibit 5

Acquisitions of American Express

Acquisition	*Date*
American Express Direct Response	April 1979
Warner Amex Cable Communications (joint venture)	December 1979
First Data Resources	January 1980
Southern Guaranty Insurance Company	September 1980
Food and Wine magazine	September 1980
Mitchell Beazley, Ltd.	November 1980
WATS Marketing of America	December 1980
Interstate Group of Insurance Companies	December 1980
New England Bank Card Association	March 1981
Shearson Loeb Rhoades	Awaiting approval

Source: Moody's Bank and Finance Manual, Vol. 2.

national Banking Services, and Insurance Services. The company had assets of $19.7 billion, 44,000 employees, 1,000 travel offices, and 77 international banking and investment offices. Total revenues for 1980 were $5.5 billion with a net income of $376 million. In 1980 dividends were increased from $0.45 to $0.50 per share, the sixth increase in five years. The consolidated financial statements are shown in Exhibit 6, and contributions of the various segments are summarized in Exhibit 7. The scope of the company's international operations is shown in Exhibit 8.

Exhibit 6

American Express Company consolidated income statement (millions)

	1980	*1979*	*1978*	*1977*	*1976*
Revenues					
Commissions and fees	1,522	1,130	912	738	643
Interest and dividends	1,264	1,007	759	580	496
Property—liability and life					
insurance premiums	2,589	2,450	2,341	2,080	1,771
Other	129	80	64	48	48
Total	5,504	4,667	4,076	3,446	2,948
Expenses					
Provisions for losses:					
Insurance	1,545	1,482	1,393	1,255	1,142
Banking, credit, financial					
paper, other	214	161	127	108	100
Salaries and employee benefits	833	685	578	472	421
Interest	870	572	368	249	208
Commissions and brokerage	403	371	355	311	275
Occupancy and equipment	247	187	141	125	105
Advertising and promotion	187	140	127	84	66
Taxes other than income taxes	145	133	120	101	85
Telephone, telegraph, postage	117	93	83	74	63
Financial paper, forms, and					
other printed matter	82	65	51	45	35
Claims adjustment service	78	102	116	130	90
Other	362	285	234	188	162
Total	5,083	4,276	3,693	3,142	2,752
Pretax Income	421	391	383	304	196
Income tax provision	45	46	69	52	17
Net Operating Income	376	345	314	252	179
Gains on Sale of Investment					
Securities	—	—	—	10	15
Net Income	376	345	314	262	194
Net Income per Share	$5.27	$4.83	$4.39	$3.65	$2.70

Exhibit 6 (continued)

	1980	*1979*	*1978*	*1977*	*1976*
Assets					
Cash	1,069	1,051	844	674	542
Time Deposits	1,084	976	891	858	821
Investment Securities (Cost):					
U.S. government	750	519	435	459	429
State and municipal	4,070	4,104	3,808	3,167	2,458
Other bonds and obligations	1,200	1,044	735	720	710
Preferred stocks	57	52	48	48	43
Total[a]	6,077	5,719	5,026	4,388	3,640
Investment Securities (Lower of Cost or Market)					
Preferred stocks	67	83	99	111	95
Common stocks	99	83	72	66	56
Total[b]	166	166	171	177	151
Investment Securities (Market)					
Preferred stocks	63	57	50	49	45
Common stocks	783	652	563	507	506
Total[c]	846	709	613	556	551
Accounts Receivable and Accrued Interest, Less Reserves: 1980, $287; 1979, $213; 1978, $171; 1977, $146; 1976, $125	4,887	3,597	2,705	2,164	1,754
Loans and Discounts, Less Reserves: 1980, $89; 1979, $82; 1978, $75; 1977, $60; 1976, $52	3,690	3,369	3,320	2,571	2,073
Land, Building, and Equipment (cost); less depreciation	448	347	285	263	239
Prepaid Policy Acquisition Expenses	271	244	206	153	130
Other Assets	1,171	930	637	542	467
	19,709	17,108	14,698	12,346	10,368
Liabilities					
Customers' deposits and credits held by subsidiaries	5,087	4,749	4,192	3,755	3,024
Travelers' checks outstanding	2,542	2,343	2,105	1,859	1,716
Money orders and drafts outstanding	212	289	324	175	140
Accounts payable	1,020	889	785	593	471
Reserves for:					
Property—liability losses and expenses	2,589	2,364	2,057	1,723	1,363
Unearned premiums	1,008	974	875	792	673
Life and disability policies	259	227	184	147	130
Short-term debt	2,302	1,595	1,117	776	555
Long-term debt	1,099	689	479	330	304
Deferred income taxes	161	135	108	117	117
Other	1,244	996	852	711	621
Total Liabilities	17,523	15,250	13,078	10,978	9,114
Preferred Stock	24	25	27	28	30
Common stock (100,000,000 shares authorized, $0.60 par value; 71,274,306 outstanding in 1980)	43	43	43	43	43
Capital surplus	208	204	202	200	201

Exhibit 6 (concluded)

	1980	*1979*	*1978*	*1977*	*1976*
Net unrealized security gains	208	115	87	78	116
Retained earnings	1,703	1,471	1,261	1,019	864
Total Common Share- holders' Equity	2,162	1,833	1,593	1,340	1,224
	19,709	17,108	14,698	12,346	10,368

[a] Market: 1980, $4,612; 1979, $5,070; 1978, $4,686; 1977, $4,396; 1976, $3,612.
[b] Cost: 1980, $191; 1979, $192; 1978, $188; 1977, $188; 1976, $167.
[c] Cost: 1980, $ 531; 1979, $523; 1978, $471; 1977, $433; 1976, $370.
Source: Annual Reports.

Travel Services Group

27   The Travel Services Group includes the Card Division, Travelers' Cheque Division, Travel Division, Communications Division, and the Financial Institutions Services Division. Revenues for the group increased 34 percent from 1979 to $1.7 billion in 1980, and net income rose 17 percent to $177 million, which is 47 percent of the company's total earnings.

28   The Card Division provides corporate and personal credit card services to 11.9 million card holders. The familiar "green card" is marketed not as a credit card implying a line of credit, but as a convenience device. As such, payment in full is required on demand, with the exception of certain tour plans and airplane tickets that can be financed over an extended period. There are approximately 6.5 million personal green card holders who pay an annual fee of $35. About 1.5 million customers hold the "gold cards" at an annual fee of $50. In addition to the charge features, the gold card allows members to finance purchases and to obtain cash through a line of credit that American Express has established with 1,800 participating banks.

29   The American Express cards are issued in twenty-three currencies and are honored by 438,000 establishments world-wide. The company has been attempting to build the number of establishments and about 50,000 new establishments were added during 1980. In expanding beyond the traditional emphasis on food, lodging, and travel, a new emphasis has been placed on recruiting prestigious retail and department stores that are likely to provide a high average purchase value.

30   A major cost of the card business is the financing of card receivables. American Express sells its receivables to Credco, a wholly owned subsidiary. Credco then finances them through commercial paper, equity capital, lines of credit, and long-term debt. In 1980 Credco purchased $19.2 billion of receivables, up from $14.6 billion in 1979. The weighted average interest cost of all Credco financing rose from 8.48 percent in 1978 to 15.7 percent

Exhibit 7

American Express Company industry segments 1980 (millions)

	Travel-related services	International banking services	Insurance services	Other and corporate	Adjustments and eliminations	Consolidated
Revenues	$1,661	$ 930	$2,914	$ 35	$ (36)	$ 5,504
Pretax income before general corporate expenses	236	67	215	16	—	534
General corporate expenses	—	—	—	(113)	—	(113)
Pretax income	236	67	215	(97)	—	421
Net income	177	41	210	(52)	-376	
Assets	$6,877	$6,926	$5,846	$469	$(409)	$19,709

Insurance services comprised of

	Commercial lines	Personal lines	Investment income	Other	Total	Total insurance services
Revenues	$1,788	$626	$282	$218	$2,696	$2,914
Pretax income	$ (37)	$(39)	$277	$ 14	$ 201	$ 215

Source: Annual Report.

Exhibit 8

American Express Company geographic operations 1980 (millions)

	United States	Europe	Asia/ Pacific	All other	Adjustments and eliminations	Consoli- dated
Revenues	$ 3,953	$ 700	$ 281	$ 604	$ (34)	$ 5,504
Pretax before general corporate expenses	435	21	15	63	—	534
General corporate expenses	(113)	—	—	—	—	(113)
Pretax income	322	21	15	63	—	421
Assets	11,718	3,704	1,774	2,603	(528)	19,271
Corporate assets						438
Total assets						$19,709

Source: Annual Report.

during the first two months of 1980. These increased financing costs have led American Express to tighten its collection policies by reducing the grace period and increasing the finance charge.

31   American Express cards have achieved a high degree of market penetration in the United States. It is estimated that about 50 percent of the families with incomes greater than $25,000 have the card, as do 64 percent of those with incomes greater than $50,000, and 71 percent with incomes over $75,000. Growth rates in membership have averaged 11 percent over the last three years. A major contribution to the growth rate has come from countries outside of the United States, where the growth rates have been of the order of 25 percent. The number of card holders outside of the United States was 2.7 million in 1980.

32   The charge card volume has increased at annual rates of 26 percent (1978), 29 percent (1979), and 32 percent (1980). This positive trend in the face of government controls on credit spending during the period has reinforced management's view that the card is used by consumers as a convenience rather than a credit device. Customers also seem to be attracted to the country club style of itemizing the bills (a feature not provided by bank cards), the absence of charge limits, check-cashing privileges, and the snob appeal of the card.

33   American Express travelers' checks are sold through 105,000 outlets worldwide, including banks, travel agents, and credit unions. Although check buyers are charged a fee of 1 percent of the check's face value, the issuing banks retain about two thirds of that fee. The primary source of travelers' check revenues for American Express is from the "float," or cash, the company controls from checks that have not yet been cashed. This float is invested by American Express in tax-free securities and

provided a significant amount of the company's total revenues in 1980. The average period that the checks are outstanding is two months. An advertising campaign begun in 1979, featuring actor Karl Malden, appealed to consumers to hold unused checks for emergencies—an attempt to extend the float period. The dollar value of the travelers' checks outstanding at year end has increased from $1.72 billion in 1976 to $2.5 billion in 1980.

34   Increasing competitive pressure is being felt in the travelers' check industry and the growth rate of American Express checks has been slowing over the last three years. Many banks, which sell the majority of the checks, are now selling their own checks under Visa or MasterCard trademarks. American Express plans to combat this competitive pressure through increased service and through new international initiatives. In 1981 the company began construction of a $35 million operations center near Salt Lake City, Utah. It is anticipated that the center will enhance the company's ability to provide cost-effective servicing of travelers' checks. American Express also now owns 34 percent of Société Français du Chéque de Voyage, which began issuing French franc travelers' checks in 1980. American Express has converted all of its French franc business to the new checks.

35   The Travel Division offers retail and wholesale (tours) travel services worldwide through 1,000 offices in 126 countries. Services include trip planning, reservations, ticketing, and other incidental services. Revenues for the division are earned through commissions from carriers, hotels, and so on, and through fees from customers for incidental services.

36   American Express reported major changes in the Travel Division in 1980, including a restructuring of the organization to decentralize along geographic lines. It is anticipated that this move will provide greater flexibility to respond to localized customer needs and opportunities. The company also has been redesigning its tour packages to achieve greater consumer affordability and to eliminate low-revenue programs. A major automation step was taken in 1980 with the implementation of a computerized Travel Information Processing System (TRIPS). TRIPS eventually will become an integrated worldwide information and reservation system.

37   The financial performance of the Travel Division has varied over the years: the period 1973–1976 being weak. A stronger revenue showing was reported for 1977, although it is not clear whether the division was profitable. In 1979 and 1980, the division reported losses, in spite of increased revenues during 1980. The company explained that part of the problem in 1980 has been attributable to slackened demand for tours, lower margins on discount ticket purchasing, and the costs of restructuring the division.

38   The Communications Division was formed in January 1980, and has responsibility for American Express Publishing Corporation, Merchandise Sales, American Express Direct Response (ADR), and Mitchell Beazley, Ltd., a London-based international publishing house.

39   The division has taken over publication of *Food and Wine* magazine and has published *Travel and Leisure* magazine (circulation 925,000) since 1970. A growing emphasis in the division is on direct-mail marketing through Merchandise Sales (revenues increased by 70 percent in 1980), supported by the computer services of ADR. Direct Response also supplies direct-mail marketing services to outside businesses and to other American Express divisions.

40   The Financial Institutions Services Division was formed in 1980 to consolidate operations relating to the financial community. Within the division is First Data Resources, Inc., a recently acquired provider of data and telephone marketing services to financial institutions and merchandisers. Also included are the Money Order Division and Payment Systems, Inc., which provides information and research in payment systems and electronic funds transfer.

Warner Amex Cable Services

41   In 1979 American Express paid $175 million for one-half interest in Warner Cable Company, which was owned by Warner Communications. The joint venture includes the subsidiaries, Warner Amex Cable Communications, Inc., and Warner Amex Satellite Entertainment Company. American Express sees the cable systems as the technical hardware link for the financial supermarket of the future they expect to build around the television screen.

42   Warner Cable Company owns and operates 141 cable television systems with 736,000 subscribers in twenty-seven states. Among the most recent awards are major franchises in Pittsburgh, Dallas, and Cincinnati, and in areas surrounding St. Louis, Boston, Chicago, and Akron. These awards provide the potential for entering 1.1 million households.

43   Most Warner Amex systems have twelve to thirty channels; however, new systems will provide many more channels. The company has a head start on its competition in two-way cable systems with a system called Qube. Warner Amex spent $20 million to develop the Qube system, and it is presently operating in Columbus and Cincinnati, Ohio. Although the talk-back feature of Qube is now used primarily for entertainment purposes, such as voting on boxing matches, answering viewer polls, and calling plays for football games, the two-way link is critical for potential home-selling, burglar alarm, and financial transaction uses. The Qube system is now offering a retrieval service for business analysis and money management information. A twenty-four-hour security system was recently added to the Columbus system and is servicing 2,500 households and businesses.

44   Warner Amex Satellite Entertainment Company (WASEC) operates five satellite transponders, which receive television signals and transmit them

over the entire country. The entertainment company has two major services: "The Movie Channel" and "Nickelodeon." "The Movie Channel" offers twenty-four hours of feature films, and "Nickelodeon" provides varied programming for children and young adults. The company is planning a joint venture with ABC Video Enterprises, Inc., called the Alpha Repertory Television Service, which will furnish programming devoted to the performing and visual arts. Firm plans also have been made to offer "The Music Channel," which will provide continuous popular music with complementary visual material.

45   Although a significant amount of risk exists in the cable video industry in that franchises must be awarded by local governments, Warner Amex has proved an effective competitor. In 1980 Warner Amex won 1.1 million of the 1.6 million households up for bids in the United States. The company anticipates a need for significant financing to support future expansion efforts. In 1980 it received a $250 million line of credit from a group of banks, but additional capital will be needed in 1981 from external sources, and from the parent companies, where appropriate.

Insurance Services

46   Fireman's Fund Insurance was founded in 1863 and was acquired by American Express in 1968. Fireman's Fund provides a broad range of insurance services, including commercial and personal property liability insurance, life insurance, and annuities. Policies are sold in the United States through 11,000 independent agents and brokers. The company also operates overseas through AFIA World Wide Insurance, a consortium of U.S. insurance companies. The Fireman's Fund commercial insurance lines include property, general liability, multiple peril, and worker's compensation, and the personal lines include homeowner's and automobile insurance. Life insurance is offered through Fireman's Fund American Life Insurance Company (FFAL), which sells a full portfolio of life insurance products, including ordinary and term life insurance, annuities, group term life insurance, and group accident and health insurance. FFAL also underwrites the supplemental life insurance offered to American Express card holders.

47   Firemen's Fund was caught in the insurance underwriting cycle in 1974 when earnings dropped by 17 percent. Even then the drop was softened since the company was able to call upon $9 million from a "catastrophe reserve" built up during more profitable years. This practice of banking earnings has since been ordered abolished for the entire industry by the Financial Accounting Standards Board, since it was considered to be misleading to investors.

48   Following the 1974 experience, American Express decided to institute policies to avoid the cycle. It vowed to price more aggressively when

premium rates are rising and not to write unprofitable policies by cutting prices when competition stiffens.

49   Feeling the competitive pressures of the most recent trough in the underwriting cycle, the growth rate in premiums written has been declining as the company has attempted to concentrate on more profitable business in underwriting and investment. In 1980, $2.4 billion in premiums were written, which is a 2.5 percent increase. The increase in 1979 was 4.5 percent and in 1978 the increase was 9.1 percent.

50   Fireman's Fund gross revenues for 1980 were $2.9 billion, which is a 7.2 percent increase over 1979. A significant contribution to the increase in revenues has been from specialized products in rural markets, commercial group packages, and reinsurance. The company has suffered underwriting losses for the past three years because of higher claims costs that were not offset by premium revenues. The underwriting losses were $76 million in 1980, $53 million in 1979, and $13 million in 1978. According to *Best's,* Fireman's Fund ranked fifty-third in the industry in underwriting performance with a loss ratio of 58.1. These losses were offset by investment income, which increased by 21 percent in 1980. Fireman's Fund is attempting to remedy the losses through rate increases, increased deductibles, and shorter terms so that premiums can be adjusted more frequently.

51   The underwriting expense ratio has been increasing over the last three years, from 30.8 percent in 1978 to 33.3 percent in 1980. This increase has been attributed to slower premium growth and long-term development spending. The company has been increasing the number of branch offices, automating its network of offices, and developing a program of standardization of field office procedures.

International Banking Services

52   American Express International Banking Company (AEIBC) accounts for 17 percent of American Express's total revenues, 35 percent of the company's total assets, and 11 percent of the net income. AEIBC operates eighty-three offices in thirty-four countries, providing commercial banking services, investment banking, wholesale banking, equipment finance, and financial advisory services. It also offers consumer banking service in certain locations, including contracted services on overseas U.S. military bases. The bank does not provide services in the United States except as incidental to its foreign operations. AEIBC is also an active dealer in foreign exchange markets; these activities contributed $35 million in revenues in 1980.

53   Income from interest increased 21 percent to $197 million in 1980, and commission fee revenues increased 14 percent to $100 million. The latter increase reflects an emphasis on the expansion of nonasset-related sources of revenues. In 1980 operating costs rose 19 percent, primarily as a result of inflation and automation of the banking network.

The Shearson Merger

54   In April 1981 American Express and Shearson Loeb Rhoades, Inc., announced that they had reached agreement on a merger. The terms were 1.3 American Express shares for each Shearson share. At the time of the merger, Shearson brought into American Express 11,000 employess and $8 billion in assets, mostly in money-market funds. The company reported $653 million in revenues in 1980 and had an estimated 500,000 customers.

55   The level of revenues in 1980 put Shearson in the number two position in the brokerage industry and is largely the product of eight acquisitions in the ten years since Shearson went public. Shearson's acquisitions were usually of "old line" brokerage houses that were having financial difficulty. To make the acquisitions work, Shearson cut out levels of management, consolidated and automated the "back office" operations into a strong network, and added new services. The consolidated financial statements for the company are shown in Exhibit 9.

56   Under the terms of the merger, Sanford I. (Sandy) Weill will remain in charge of Shearson and will head American Express's executive committee, while Robinson will become chairman of the merged entity. After the transaction Weill will personally own an estimated .6 percent of American Express stock. Weill has built a reputation of competence along with his building of Shearson, and has demonstrated a willingness and an ability for making fast decisions.

57   The merger is seen by many as giving strong impetus to a trend in the financial industry of many of the leading brokerage companies looking for capital inputs to remain competitive on a national scale. The competitive surge appears to be aimed at providing consolidated "one-stop" financial services. Several securities dealers who have survived a tight decade and are showing profitable years now appear attractive to the large insurance and other financial firms.

58   The trend in these acquisitions may have been triggered by Merrill Lynch, Pierce, Fenner & Smith, which is the industry's primary brokerage house and has considerable capital ($1 billion) strength of its own. In 1977 Merrill Lynch broke with tradition and created a cash management account that allows customers to access cash in the account and money funds and also provides a line of credit. All this can be accomplished through special Visa cards or through Merrill Lynch checks. This move proved attractive to customers and was difficult for the smaller companies to match.

59   In March 1981 Prudential Insurance merged with Bache Group, Inc. Through the merger it is expected that Prudential can provide not only the financial stability to remain competitive and to ride out the fiscal variability that is a problem in the brokerage business, but also to provide marketing and promotional support as well as new services to the Bache customers.

Exhibit 9

Shearson Loeb Rhoades, Inc. consolidated income statement (thousands)

	1980[a]	*1979*[a]	*1978*[a]
Revenues			
Commissions	327,497	188,744	136,732
Principal transactions	82,038	17,427	16,299
Interest	128,961	56,293	36,674
Investment banking	57,203	23,900	23,339
Mortgage banking	28,455	6,008	—
Other	28,312	11,658	8,181
Total	652,466	304,030	221,225
Expenses			
Employee compensation	310,065	152,802	113,078
Floor broker commissions	26,703	16,785	12,658
Interest	57,407	21,178	18,037
Other operating expenses	142,653	73,180	57,591
Total	536,828	263,945	201,364
Income Before Distribution	115,638	40,085	19,861
Distribution to Profits Participation	10,669	—	—
Pretax Income	104,969	40,085	19,861
Income Taxes	49,162	20,010	9,857
Net Income	55,805	20,075	10,004
Net Income per Share	$6.99	$3.78	$2.11
Dividends per Share	$.40	$.34	$.27
Assets			
Cash	52,768	15,372	7,110
Segregated cash and treasury bills	316,739	167,085	123,226
Securities on deposit	52,514	9,853	13,963
Receivables from customers	966,759	547,677	485,588
Receivables from brokers	461,126	135,360	88,676
Mortgages and construction loans	69,481	92,146	—
Other receivables	17,651	7,164	7,176
Spot commodities owned	—	—	254
Securities owned (market)	248,769	127,586	122,960
Secured demand notes	716	7,394	7,394
Exchange membership	5,175	2,883	2,874
Investments in affiliates	3,203	—	—
Securities purchased	1,849	9,630	184,927
Purchased mortgage contracts	6,778	7,197	—
Deferred income taxes	5,610	—	—
Office equipment, etc.	22,011	12,197	8,286
Excess acquisition cost	14,559	4,647	4,245
Differed expenses and other assets	21,983	8,358	3,433
Total	2,267,691	1,154,549	1,060,114
Liabilities			
Bank loans	212,668	154,377	149,393
Payables to brokers	557,752	154,743	109,556
Payables to customers	607,497	292,992	196,189
Accrued liabilities, etc.	341,465	255,874	168,355
Securities sold[b]	166,260	127,683	115,583
Repurchased securities sold	43,517	1,966	211,565
Deferred income tax	—	662	749
Term notes	26,503	17,826	7,513

Exhibit 9 (concluded)

	1980a	*1979a*	*1978a*
Subordinate debt	137,671	61,233	32,994
Secured demand obligation	—	7,394	7,394
Contributions of profit participation agreement	30,113	—	—
Preferred stock	175	1,482	2,026
Common stock	661	527	487
Paid in capital	50,665	29,639	26,259
Retained earnings	96,295	51,713	33,546
Reacquired stock	(3,561)	(3,562)	(1,496)
Total	2,267,691	1,154,549	1,060,114

[a] Year ended June 30.
[b] Securities sold, but not yet purchased.
Source: Annual Reports; *Moody's Bank and Finance Manual.*

60   The American Express/Shearson merger announcement has caused considerable concern for banks, which see a new kind of financial institution that can offer a broad range of services that banks are not allowed to sell. Banks are presently prohibited from selling securities by the Glass-Steagall Act of 1933. Their reaction has been in several directions. Larger banks have been lobbying to have the government restrictions on themselves lifted so that they can enter the competitive field, but others have been attempting to block formation of such strong competition. The Independent Bankers Association has written to the Justice Department asking that the American Express/Shearson merger be delayed pending investigation of the deal's "potential anticompetitive effects." The strength of the overall opposition to the merger is difficult to assess without the support of the larger banks. But given the present political trends toward less government involvement, it is unlikely that the merger will be disapproved.

Notes

1. Thomas O'Donnell, "The Tube, The Card, The Ticker, and Jim Robinson," *Forbes,* May 25, 1981.
2. Debit cards operate similarly to credit cards except that when the bank is notified of a sale, it immediately deducts the amount from an account balance that the consumer maintains with the bank, much in the same manner as a bank deducts money from a checking account.
3. Expense ratio = Operating costs/Premiums earned.
4. William F. Kinder, "A Look at the Leaders: Has the Game Changed?" *Best's Review: Property/Casualty Insurance Edition 82* (September 1981), p. 132.

case **8** # NCNB Corporation Moves into Florida

Introduction

1   NCNB Corporation was the leading multi-bank holding company in the southeastern region of the United States. In 1982, it was the 26th largest bank holding company in the U.S. and its consolidated assets totaled $8,434,954,000. While the corporation was started in 1969, by the end of 1982 it had 526 offices located in North Carolina, ten other states, the United Kingdom, Australia, Brazil, Hong Kong, South Africa, and the Cayman Islands. The various banking and financial services NCNB offered included general banking, merchant banking, consumer finance, corporate finance, leasing, trust, investment management, discount brokerage services, and international banking.

2   In 1982, NCNB expanded its banking operations into the lucrative Florida market through the acquisition of four banks. After all four acquisitions had received Federal Reserve Board (Fed) approval, NCNB was faced with a fundamental issue concerning these Florida banks. How should NCNB best manage these acquisitions? Should the banks be permitted to operate pretty much as they had in the past? Since these banks were attractive enough to have been acquired by NCNB, perhaps each should be left to operate autonomously. Conversely, should the Florida acquisitions be reined in and required to follow overall NCNB corporate goals, operating policy and procedures, and become an integral part of the NCNB family? Thus, NCNB corporate management was faced with de-

This case was written by Karen O'Quinn Brooks of NCNB Corporation and Larry D. Alexander of Virginia Polytechnic Institute and State University. Copyright © 1985 by Karen O'Quinn Brooks and Larry D. Alexander.

ciding which of these approaches, or a mixture of both, was the best way to manage its first banks located outside North Carolina.

The Banking Industry

3   The 14,500 banks operating throughout the United States were classified into one of three basic types. One type was money center banks, such as Chase Manhattan Corporation and Manufacturers Hanover Corporation, which operated both in the United States and throughout the world providing a wide variety of international lending and corporate services. A second type was regional banks, like NCNB and Wacovia Corporation (a major competitor of NCNB in North Carolina), which were major forces in particular regions of one or several states. Regional banks usually moved into other states by acquiring existing financial institutions, usually not banks. The third and final type was country banks. They were unit banks (single branch banks) or small branch chains, which offered much more limited financial services to a very small geographical area.

Industry Trends

4   Historically, banking was a conservative industry, highly regulated by federal and state laws aimed at keeping banks solvent and assuring them of a steady income. However, economic and technological changes, especially since the mid-1970s, brought about major changes in the banking industry. For example, rising interest rates threatened banks by causing bank deposits to be shifted to brokerage houses and money market mutual funds, which were not limited by interest ceilings. One technological change stemmed from the rapidly expanding network of automated tellers and bank-owned computers. These networks enabled them to offer their products and services to much greater geographical regions, thus intensifying competition.

5   While regional and country banks made up the vast majority of banks in the United States, this did not provide them with safety in numbers. With the increasing move towards interstate banking in recent years, the money center banks posed a significant threat. If they are permitted to enter other states in the future, their sheer size and financial strength could result in a competitive shakeout, which could cause some regional and numerous country banks to be acquired or go bankrupt. Some regional banks hoped to prepare themselves for interstate banking by first expanding their presence in a wider geographical area. NCNB hoped that its move into Florida, and perhaps into other states in the future, would help turn itself into a leading money-center bank when true interstate banking became legal.

6   Many industry observers felt that banks would no longer be able to improve their profitability by obtaining low-interest deposits and making

high interest loans. Low interest deposits were disappearing as the U.S. Congress continued to deregulate banking by removing interest-rate ceilings on deposit accounts. For example, the gradual deregulation of the banking industry resulted in the introduction of new money market deposit accounts in 1982. These new accounts paid market interest rates, were federally insured, and competed directly with money-market mutual funds.

7   In the 1980s, an increasing number of substitute products and services competed against money center, regional, and country banks. Some 4,500 savings and loans offered many of the same services as banks. Work-related credit unions often provided low interest loans to employees who used their jobs as collateral. Nonbanking institutions, such as Merrill Lynch, also had begun offering other close substitute products like its equity access loan, which competed with traditional loans from banks and savings and loan companies. Even Sears, Roebuck and Company was becoming an accepted place where people could invest their money.

8   Banks remained divided over whether these various industry trends, taken as a whole, represented threats or opportunities. The largest banks were pushing for laws to let them compete head-on with the regional and country banks, as well as other financial institutions. These banks were clearly pushing for true interstate banking. On the other hand, most smaller banks opposed interstate banking and wanted to keep the existing legal restrictions intact. Thus, many larger banks viewed these changes as opportunities whereas most smaller bankers saw them as threats.

NCNB Corporation History

9   NCNB Corporation was incorporated on July 5, 1968 as a bank holding company. Initially, this was done to acquire control of North Carolina National Bank. That bank had been originally chartered in 1933 as Security National Bank, which later merged with Depositors National Bank of Durham in 1959. The name North Carolina National Bank was adopted in 1960 with the merger of American Commercial Bank in Charlotte. From 1960 through 1967, North Carolina National Bank merged or acquired nine additional banks in North Carolina.

10   North Carolina National Bank was acquired by American Security National Bank, a wholly owned subsidiary of NCNB Corporation, on November 4, 1968. American Security National Bank immediately changed its name to North Carolina National Bank. The bank then came under the control of NCNB Corporation and remained its principal subsidiary, contributing 92.6% of the corporation's total earnings in 1981.

11   NCNB Corporation formed three other subsidiaries during 1968. Amcon, Inc. was formed in November and later merged with American Commercial Agency, Inc. NCNB Properties, Inc., another wholly owned subsidiary, was also established that same month. NCNB Mortgage Corpora-

tion was establised in December. Then, during mid-1969, Stephenson Finance Company, Inc. was acquired, which was later renamed Transouth Financial Corporation, an NCNB subsidiary.

12   NCNB Corporation pursued a number of acquisitions during the 1970s. They included, among others:

1. In 1970, Factors, Inc., which provided various financial services, for stock.

2. In 1972, C. Douglas Wilson and Company, a mortgage banker, for stock.

3. In 1972, Trust Company of Florida, for stock.

4. In 1974, Blanchard and Calhoun Mortgage Company, for stock.

5. In 1975, MAR, Inc., which handled foreclosed properties, for stock.

NCNB's Corporate Plan for the 1980s

13   By the close of the 1970s, NCNB faced intense competition in North Carolina, and future growth there was expected to be modest. To cope with this problem, NCNB developed an overall strategic plan to position itself better in the banking and diversified financial services industry.

14   In 1979, NCNB developed a three-phase strategic plan for the 1980s to support two goals. One goal was to continue as the dominant financial institution in the Southeast. The other goal was to become a significant competitor among the world's major money center Banks. This corporate plan for the 1980s called for NCNB to do the following:

Phase 1. Improve the corporation's capital position, managerial depth, and technical expertise.

Phase 2. Expand the geographic coverage of the corporation to achieve economies of scale and offer innovative products to a broader market.

Phase 3. Achieve profitable internal growth by managing products, pricing, and markets for increased market share.[1]

15   This three-phase corporate plan helped unify corporate management's strategy and that of NCNB's various strategic business units.

16   NCNB's corporate level marketing, financial, human resources, and management strategies are discussed briefly in the following sections.

Marketing Strategy—An Emphasis on Innovation

17   NCNB Corporation had a history of pursuing innovative products and services. During the 1970s, NCNB was the first North Carolina bank to install 24-hour automatic teller machines (ATMs). It was also the first to

introduce a deposit access card called Checkmate. In addition, NCNB began to offer unique bank services to its customers with high savings balances.

18   More recently in 1982, NCNB introduced several new products that may change the way NCNB and its customers do business in the future. The introduction of its money-market account was the most significant step in new product development. This allowed NCNB to offer high yielding, liquid deposit instruments to compete with the money-market funds offered by nondepository institutions. That same year, NCNB joined the Plus System, a 26 bank network of automated teller operators throughout the country. This system allowed NCNB's customers to have access to most of the same services offered by NCNB's ATMs as they traveled throughout the country.

19   NCNB also established two new subsidiaries during 1982. A discount brokerage subsidiary was set up to handle security sales and purchases for bank customers. The second subsidiary, NCNB Futures Corporation, was created to trade in financial futures.

20   Domestically, NCNB did everything possible to further penetrate existing markets. It had even established an industrial development department to encourage companies, headquartered elsewhere, to open plants and offices in NCNB communities. This department had already helped Miller Brewing Company, Measurements Group, Inc., Union Carbide, and Verbatim Corporation to open facilities in cities where NCNB's banks operated.

21   In addition to its domestic operations, NCNB had already moved into six foreign countries. NCNB offered a wide variety of international banking services including some of the best import/export financing programs available anywhere. NCNB wanted to penetrate further in foreign countries where it already had operations and to move into additional foreign countries throughout the 1980s.

Financial Strategy

22   The time period from the mid-1960s through 1981 can be divided into three distinct financial periods for NCNB. The first period was rapid growth which continued through the early 1970s. In fact, NCNB's sales grew so fast that it was rated one of the premier bank growth stocks. The second period, from the early 1970s until 1979, focused on recovering from loan losses. These losses caused a sharp decline in NCNB's earnings, particularly in 1974. The price of its stock dropped from a high of 42 in 1973 to a low of 7 in 1974. From 1974 to 1979, NCNB concentrated on cleaning up problem loans, second-home financing, and mobile-home lending. The third period, which started in 1979, involved building capital equity.

23   The early 1980s brought about conflicting results for NCNB. Earnings improved slightly in the first half of 1980. Then, they became somewhat

depressed through mid-1981. This was caused by NCNB's extending the maturity dates on many of its overseas loans in 1980. It took this action to avoid foreclosing on foreign businesses that would have been forced to default on repaying high-interest loans during a severe, recessionary period. Since then, quarterly earnings rebounded strongly due to sustained improvement in the net interest margin.

24   Exhibit 1 shows NCNB Corporation's consolidated balance sheet summary from 1977 through 1982. NCNB Corporation and its subsidiaries' total assets for 1982 were $8,434,954,000, which excluded the Florida acquisitions. This was almost double the 1977 total of $4,804,556,000. When the approximate $2,800,000 assets from the Florida acquisitions were added, plus some other assets, NCNB's 1982 total assets became $11,559,531,000. Exhibit 2 then shows NCNB's consolidated earnings summary for the same six year period. Net income for 1982 was $76,140,000, which represented a 274% increase over its 1977 total of $27,771,000.

25   A key part of Phase 1, improving the corporation's capital position, was accomplished in 1980 and 1981. Shareholder's equity of $240,543,000 in 1977 increased by $102,862,000 in 1980, but then rapidly increased by another $136,262,000 to $479,667,000 in 1982.

26   NCNB felt that it was important to accelerate the growth of equity to provide an expanded base for asset growth. Common stock issued in December of 1980 provided $12,000,000 of additional capital. Later, an exchange of shares for debentures in October of 1981 increased equity by $29,000,000. From 1980 through 1982, sales of shares through the dividend reinvestment program and employee stock plans brought in $12,000,000. Retained earnings contributed $136,000,000 during this time, and mergers brought an additional $36,000,000.

27   The company's dominant financial strategy for 1983 and beyond involved concentrating on building equity through earnings retention while maintaining its dividend policy. Thus, NCNB's watchword for the 1980s was asset/liability management. The goal of NCNB's asset/liability management committee was to maximize net interest margin and net interest income under prudent levels of risk.

Human Resources Strategy

28   NCNB strengthened its managerial depth and technical expertise, as a part of Phase 1, in an attempt to improve the quality of its 7,784 overall work force. In addition, NCNB greatly expanded its college recruitment program starting in the late 1970s. For 1983, NCNB was planning to hire 144 college graduates, of which 40% to 50% would have M.B.A. degrees.

29   President McColl described the kind of people he wanted to work for the organization.

"I put a high priority on attracting people who not only are smart and energetic, but can also relate to people, can talk to people, and can sell our company. If we get the people who have those qualities, we'll give them two important kinds of training—technical and leadership."[2]

30   NCNB's philosophy concerning its employees stressed that pay increases and promotions should be based on individual performance instead of automatically occurring after a set length of time. Each individual was encouraged to gain a broad range of experience and to assume responsibility for his or her own development at NCNB.

Management Strategy

31   Another key area of Phase I involved improving the corporation's managerial depth and technical expertise. NCNB emphasized a variety of in-house training and management development programs at all levels of management. In turn, this helped its employees develop a strong personal commitment to NCNB. The focus at the executive level was using strategic planning for continued success in the challenging banking environment of the future.

32   Members of NCNB's executive management had been with NCNB an average of 15 years, with some having over 30 years experience in banking. In spite of their extensive experience, NCNB's top management had been described as wild and woolly innovators, unafraid to tread where the more fainthearted money men might falter.[3] This attitude helped explain NCNB's aggressive move into Florida.

33   Thomas Storrs, Chairman and Chief Executive Officer, explained NCNB's move into Florida this way.

"The Southeast needs a strong bank organization—one that competes with money center banks—if it is to continue to grow and prosper. We believe we are developing that organization."[4]

34   NCNB's President, Hugh McColl, while supporting Storrs's acquisitions, viewed NCNB's future differently. He remarked, "The major acquisition phase is over. We have achieved the size needed to be a meaningful force in interstate banking. Now our emphasis is going to be on profitability."[5] While McColl was President, he also was slated to become NCNB's next Chairman when Storrs retired in August of 1983.

NCNB Moves into Florida

35   NCNB was clearly a leading force in the state of North Carolina. NCNB had 22.6% of the North Carolina consumer deposit market as of late 1982 when it ranked second. Wachovia was the state leader with a 31.1% market

Exhibit 1

NCNB Corporation and Subsidiaries
Consolidated Six-Year Balance Sheet Summary
(Average Amounts in Thousands of Dollars)

	1982	*1981*	*1980*	*1979*
Assets				
Cash and due from banks	$ 656,355	$ 818,957	$ 801,536	$ 815,597
Time deposits placed	895,156	965,618	953,748	678,338
Investment securities:				
Taxable	803,403	559,053	620,424	539,854
Tax-exempt	306,344	325,784	324,496	292,535
Total investment securities	1,109,747	884,837	944,920	832,389
Trading account securities	57,690	60,943	32,036	77,915
Federal funds sold and securities purchased under agreements to resell	364,405	395,687	307,437	277,363
Loans and leases—net of unearned income:				
Commercial loans	2,260,940	1,868,404	1,544,783	1,295,348
Commercial leases	150,779	110,446	80,744	60,431
Total commercial loans and leases	2,411,719	1,978,850	1,625,527	1,355,779
Consumer loans	1,181,498	1,100,794	1,000,379	933,146
Mortgage loans	267,020	236,220	266,739	272,741
Construction loans	205,736	144,379	136,734	145,543
Foreign loans and leases	581,618	507,510	269,327	147,437
Other loans	28,368	30,741	23,738	35,276
Total loans and leases—net of unearned income	4,675,959	3,998,494	3,322,444	2,889,922
Less: Allowance for loan and lease losses	(54,582)	(46,905)	(37,671)	(34,010)
Net loans and leases	4,621,377	3,951,589	3,284,773	2,855,912
Real estate acquired through foreclosure	17,969	22,095	26,191	31,107
Premises, equipment and lease rights—net	135,088	104,116	98,811	95,505
Other assets	577,167	474,246	416,058	285,146
	$8,434,954	$7,678,088	$6,865,510	$5,949,272
Liabilities				
Demand deposits:				
Net	$ 682,383	$ 649,350	$ 744,793	$ 766,074
Float, reserves and deposits in other financial institutions	557,932	749,140	753,261	736,217
Total demand deposits	1,240,315	1,398,490	1,498,054	1,502,291
Consumer savings and other time deposits	1,155,218	925,687	872,179	957,113
Consumer money market certificates	969,639	709,080	437,193	144,788
Certificates of deposit and other time deposits of $100,000 or more	1,007,035	897,397	738,837	709,351
Other domestic time deposits	26,737	26,268	39,901	65,623
Total domestic savings and time deposits	3,158,629	2,558,432	2,088,110	1,876,875
Foreign time deposits	1,326,152	1,346,402	1,171,550	766,243
Total savings and time deposits	4,484,781	3,904,834	3,259,660	2,643,118
Total deposits	5,725,096	5,303,324	4,757,714	4,145,409

Exhibit 1 (continued)

	1978	1977	One-Year Increase (Decrease) 1981/82	Five-Year Compound Growth (Reduction) Rate 1977/82
Assets				
Cash and due from banks	$ 757,909	$ 761,168	(19.9)%	(2.9)%
Time deposits placed......................	459,195	348,242	(7.3)	20.8
Investment securities:				
Taxable...................................	390,346	337,192	43.7	19.0
Tax-exempt	295,537	313,147	(6.0)	(.4)
Total investment securities.............	685,883	650,339	25.4	11.3
Trading account securities	78,329	56,912	(5.3)	.3
Federal funds sold and securities purchased under agreements to resell	230,298	239,824	(7.9)	8.7
Loans and leases—net of unearned income:				
Commercial loans........................	1,249,092	1,179,889	21.0	13.9
Commercial leases	40,311	29,049	36.5	39.0
Total commercial loans and leases......	1,289,403	1,208,938	21.9	14.8
Consumer loans..........................	805,255	688,003	6.4	11.4
Mortgage loans	270,506	263,999	13.0	.2
Construction loans	133,845	130,444	42.5	9.5
Foreign loans and leases.................	143,515	162,983	14.6	29.0
Other loans	23,570	19,967	(7.7)	7.3
Total loans and leases—net of unearned income..............................	2,666,094	2,474,334	16.9	13.6
Less: Allowance for loan and lease losses.	(30,131)	(29,455)	16.4	13.1
Net loans and leases....................	2,635,963	2,444,879	16.9	13.6
Real estate acquired through foreclosure	48,321	53,192	(18.7)	(19.5)
Premises, equipment and lease rights—net ..	94,580	104,181	29.7	5.3
Other assets	181,324	145,819	22.0	31.7
	$5,171,802	$4,804,556	9.9	11.9
Liabilities				
Demand Deposits:				
Net	$ 783,659	$ 737,113	5.1	(1.5)
Float, reserves and deposits in other financial institutions....................	720,020	725,388	(25.5)	(5.1)
Total demand deposits	1,503,679	1,462,501	(11.3)	(3.2)
Consumer savings and other time deposits..	966,315	929,661	24.8	4.4
Consumer money market certificates	13,357		36.7	
Certificates of deposit and other time deposits of $100,000 or more	534,921	451,721	12.2	17.4
Other domestic time deposits...............	78,818	72,860	1.8	(18.2)
Total domestic savings and time deposits	1,593,411	1,454,242	23.5	16.8
Foreign time deposits	584,826	483,473	(1.5)	22.4
Total savings and time deposits	2,178,237	1,937,715	14.9	18.3
Total deposits........................	3,681,916	3,400,216	8.0	11.0

Exhibit 1 (continued)

NCNB Corporation and Subsidiaries
Consolidated Six-Year Balance Sheet Summary
(Average Amounts in Thousands of Dollars)

	1982	1981	1980	1979
Borrowed funds:				
Federal funds purchased and securities				
sold under agreements to repurchase.....	1,042,758	868,211	754,603	586,813
Banks....................................	685	1,885	11,656	3,343
Commercial paper........................	170,713	205,200	140,976	154,927
Other notes payable	277,529	269,769	237,338	215,113
Total borrowed funds	1,491,685	1,345,065	1,144,573	960,196
Other liabilities	554,524	452,296	417,807	326,114
Capital leases.............................	26,043	28,046	29,715	31,320
Long-term debt............................	157,939	147,445	172,296	184,506
Total liabilities........................	7,955,287	7,276,176	6,522,105	5,647,545
Shareholders' Equity	479,667	401,912	343,405	301,727
	$8,434,954	$7,678,088	$6,865,510	$5,949,272

From *NCNB Corporation Annual Report 1982*, pp. 52-53.

Exhibit 1 (concluded)

	1978	1977	One-Year Increase (Decrease) 1981/82	Five-Year Compound Growth (Reduction) Rate 1977/82
Borrowed funds:				
Federal funds purchased and securities sold under agreements to repurchase.....	485,575	510,422	20.1	15.4
Banks....................................	14,947	73,274	(63.7)	(60.7)
Commercial paper........................	135,563	89,315	(16.8)	13.8
Other notes payable	161,323	118,881	2.9	18.5
Total borrowed funds	797,408	791,892	10.9	13.5
Other liabilities	206,230	148,030	22.6	30.2
Capital leases.............................	31,686	33,136	(7.1)	(4.7)
Long-term debt............................	189,833	190,739	7.1	(3.7)
Total liabilities........................	4,907,073	4,564,013	9.3	11.8
Shareholders' Equity	264,729	240,543	19.3	14.8
	$5,171,802	$4,804,556	9.9	11.9

From *NCNB Corporation Annual Report 1982*, pp. 52-53.

Exhibit 2

NCNB Corporation and Subsidiaries
Consolidated Six-Year Earnings Summary
(Dollars in Thousands Except Per Share Data)

	1982	1981	1980	1979
Income from Earning Assets				
Interest and fees on loans and leases:				
Commercial loans	$328,092	$318,786	$220,356	$163,228
Commercial leases	23,859	16,942	11,769	8,362
Total	351,951	335,728	232,125	171,590
Consumer loans	192,494	167,465	138,443	124,428
Mortgage loans	30,964	24,759	27,473	27,512
Construction loans	31,832	25,606	20,426	19,369
Foreign loans and leases	85,636	82,800	38,230	18,487
Other loans	2,379	2,087	1,979	3,356
Total	695,256	638,445	458,676	364,742
Interest and dividends on investment securities:				
U. S. Treasury	58,353	29,656	31,640	30,819
Other U. S. Government agencies and corporations	20,607	22,499	24,190	16,668
Other	9,966	5,904	6,013	3,210
Total taxable	88,926	58,059	61,843	50,697
States and political subdivisions (exempt from federal income taxes)	17,934	17,776	17,364	14,711
Total	106,860	75,835	79,207	65,408
Interest on time deposits placed	128,406	160,228	122,175	78,936
Interest on federal funds sold and securities purchased under agreements to resell	45,642	66,067	42,872	31,181
Interest on trading account securities	6,631	7,816	3,258	7,563
Other interest income	1,280	409		
Total income from earning assets	984,075	948,800	706,188	547,830
Interest Expense				
Savings deposits	46,973	37,956	33,303	33,880
Time deposits	280,639	243,626	160,575	110,984
Total domestic savings and time deposits	327,612	281,582	193,878	144,864
Foreign time deposits	177,524	218,215	164,710	86,659
Total savings and time deposits	505,136	499,797	358,588	231,523
Federal funds purchased and securities sold under agreements to repurchase	119,263	137,440	92,815	64,018
Commercial paper	21,419	34,762	18,780	17,634
Other notes payable	31,980	35,987	27,781	22,134
Total borrowed funds	172,662	208,189	139,376	103,786
Capital leases	2,747	3,144	2,638	2,743
Long-term debt	15,870	12,247	14,106	14,981
Total interest expense	696,415	723,377	514,708	353,033
Net interest income	287,660	225,423	191,480	194,797
Provision for Loan and Lease Losses	30,723	21,544	22,290	17,749
Net credit income	256,937	203,879	169,190	177,048
Other Operating Income	88,771	81,589	84,085	56,166
Other Operating Expenses	243,091	208,356	182,871	160,095

Exhibit 2 (continued)

	1978	1977	One-Year Increase (Decrease) 1981/82	Five-Year Compound Growth (Reduction) Rate 1977/82
Income from Earning Assets				
Interest and fees on loans and leases:				
Commercial loans.........................	$122,734	$ 95,818	2.9%	27.9%
Commercial leases	5,707	4,958	40.8	36.9
Total.................................	128,441	100,776	4.8	28.4
Consumer loans..........................	104,011	89,632	14.9	16.5
Mortgage loans	25,030	23,036	25.1	6.1
Construction loans	14,259	10,016	24.3	26.0
Foreign loans and leases.................	13,862	12,768	3.4	46.3
Other loans	1,591	766	14.0	25.4
Total	287,194	236,994	8.9	24.0
Interest and dividends on investment securities:				
U. S. Treasury	14,123	11,122	96.8	39.3
Other U. S. Government agencies and corporations...........................	11,541	7,100	(8.4)	23.8
Other	2,932	4,005	68.8	20.0
Total taxable	28,596	22,227	53.2	32.0
States and political subdivisions (exempt from federal income taxes)	14,188	14,908	.9	3.8
Total.................................	42,784	37,135	40.9	23.5
Interest on time deposits placed............	36,594	21,438	(19.9)	43.0
Interest on federal funds sold and securities purchased under agreements to resell	18,913	13,584	(30.9)	27.4
Interest on trading account securities	5,537	3,071	(15.2)	16.6
Other interest income			213.0	
Total income from earning assets	391,022	312,222	3.7	25.8
Interest Expense				
Savings deposits	32,745	31,268	23.8	8.5
Time deposits	66,738	48,757	15.2	41.9
Total domestic savings and time deposits	99,483	80,025	16.3	32.6
Foreign time deposits	46,431	29,938	(18.6)	42.8
Total savings and time deposits	145,914	109,963	1.1	35.7
Federal funds purchased and securities sold under agreements to repurchase............	37,478	27,389	(13.2)	34.2
Commercial paper..........................	10,850	5,082	(38.4)	33.3
Other notes payable	14,443	11,826	(11.1)	22.0
Total borrowed funds	62,771	44,297	(17.1)	31.3
Capital leases..............................	2,769	2,762	(12.6)	(.1)
Long-term debt.............................	15,345	15,339	29.6	.7
Total interest expense...................	226,799	172,361	(3.7)	32.2
Net interest income	164,223	139,861	27.6	15.5
Provision for Loan and Lease Losses...	15,893	14,186	42.6	16.7
Net credit income	148,330	125,675	26.0	15.4
Other Operating Income	49,731	42,221	8.8	16.0
Other Operating Expenses	140,708	130,396	16.7	13.3

Exhibit 2 (continued)

NCNB Corporation and Subsidiaries
Consolidated Six-Year Earnings Summary
(Dollars in Thousands Except Per Share Data)

	1982	*1981*	*1980*	*1979*
Earnings				
Income before income taxes, securities losses and extraordinary items	102,617	77,112	70,404	73,119
Income tax expense	25,615	14,268	18,897	24,478
Income before securities losses and extraordinary items	77,002	62,844	51,507	48,641
Securities losses—net........................	862	4,733	265	814
Extraordinary items—net		11,509	146	2,966
Net income	$76,140	$ 69,620	$ 51,388	$ 50,793
Per Share				
Income before securities losses and extraordinary items	$ 3.22	$ 2.78	$ 2.41	$ 2.30
Securities losses—net........................	.04	.21	.01	.04
Extraordinary items—net		.51	.01	.15
Net income	$ 3.18	$ 3.08	$ 2.41	$ 2.41
Cash dividends paid	$ .91	$ .82	$ .76	$ .62
Average shares outstanding................	23,964,155	22,682,708	21,350,546	21,189,716

From *NCNB Corporation Annual Report 1982*, pp. 54-55.

share, and First Union was third with a 20.0% share.[6] Because future growth prospects seemed limited in North Carolina, NCNB felt that it could be more successful by entering higher growth markets in other states. Unfortunately, all states seemed to prohibit outsiders from acquiring banks inside their states.

36   A top management task force was assembled at NCNB's corporate head-quarters in 1980. This task force included Frank Gentry, Joe Martin from corporate affairs, Paul Polking from legal affairs, and Winston Pool, Vice President of Marketing. Its task was to identify potential ways that this bank holding company could grow. After various meetings, this group generated a list of some 20 to 30 possible growth alternatives. They also reviewed a separate, demographic study of 16 states, which identified Florida and Texas as the two states with the highest growth rates. However, this looked discouraging since all states prohibited banks or bank holding companies from acquiring commercial banks (or starting up new banks) in other states.

Exhibit 2 (concluded)

	1978	1977	One-Year Increase (Decrease) 1981/82	Five-Year Compound Growth (Reduction) Rate 1977/82
Earnings				
Income before income taxes, securities losses and extraordinary items	57,353	37,500	33.1	22.3
Income tax expense	18,670	10,486	79.5	19.6
Income before securities losses and extraordinary items	38,683	27,014	22.5	23.3
Securities losses—net........................	506	196	(81.8)	34.5
Extraordinary items—net	1,594	953		
Net income	$39,771	$ 27,771	9.4	22.4
Per Share				
Income before securities losses and extraordinary items	$ 1.48	$ 1.29	15.8	20.1
Securities losses—net........................	.02	.01	(81.0)	32.0
Extraordinary items—net	.08	.05		
Net income	$ 1.90	$ 1.33	3.2	19.0
Cash dividends paid	$ .58	$ .52	11.0	11.8
Average shares outstanding.................	21,075,541	21,010,160	5.6	2.7

37   One possible alternative NCNB had identified was to set up industrial banks in other states. An industrial bank was pretty much the same as a household finance company. It operated by gathering time deposits and made consumer loans and paid interest. It was prohibited from offering checking accounts, did not have demand deposits, and was not FDIC (Federal Deposit Insurance Corporation) insured.

38   Paul Polking, Assistant Legal Counsel for NCNB, was asked to research the various state laws to determine if this less desirable financial institution would even be permitted. Polking later hand carried a legal opinion back to Frank Gentry, which stated that he believed it would be legal for NCNB to establish an industrial bank in Florida. Attorney Polking based his opinion on the fact that NCNB had acquired the Trust Company of Florida in October of 1972, three months before Florida passed a law prohibiting any banks or bank holding companies in other states from owning Florida banks. Thus, Polking believed that NCNB could be grandfathered into Florida because it already had established a presence there

with its trust company.

39   Polking added, however, a most stunning comment. He told Gentry that by using the same grandfather-clause reasoning, it looked as if NCNB could also establish a commercial bank. That is, if it held up to probable legal challenges from opponents in Florida wanting to prevent outsiders from entering their lucrative market. This more attractive option of opening a bank had been disregarded earlier by NCNB because of the general prohibition of interstate banking.

40   Gentry and Polking met soon with Tom Storrs, NCNB Chairman of the Board, to discuss the option of moving into Florida. Interestingly, some NCNB executives had even questioned over the years why NCNB was keeping Trust Company of Florida. Coincidentally, it was Storrs who squelched that idea and flatly stated that he wanted to hold on to it. Storrs was obviously pleased with the news that Polking and Gentry provided him that NCNB's earlier acquisition might prove to be the key to opening the doors to Florida.

41   Subsequently, NCNB top management met on a number of occasions to decide how to move into Florida. Some shared Polking's opinion that NCNB could legally move into that sunshine state. Other NCNB officials were more pessimistic and felt that NCNB could not legally acquire a bank there. One point was agreed upon; if NCNB did expand into Florida, it should be through acquisition rather than trying to start up a new bank itself. Despite differences over the likelihood of its success, most top management felt that NCNB should continue forward to determine if it could move into the lucrative Florida market.

42   NCNB finally decided that it would be best to test the Florida law by trying to acquire a small, inexpensive bank. NCNB wanted to make sure that any proposed bank acquisition would be a pure case, one which minimized a number of other issues that might lead to an unfavorable ruling. Thus, it established three criteria that any acquisition would have to satisfy. First, NCNB wanted any proposed acquisition to be in a county of Florida where its Trust Company of Florida or its Atlantic Discount Company of Jacksonville (a subsidiary of NCNB's Transouth Financial Corporation) did not operate. That would help eliminate any anti-competitive issues from clouding the legal question. Second, any acquisition candidate needed to be a national, rather than a state bank. That would prevent having additional state laws brought into consideration when the Federal Reserve ruled on the application. Third, the ownership of any potential bank would need to be tightly held. That way, it would be easier for NCNB to acquire control of the bank. If a proposed acquisition met these three criteria, NCNB's management felt that its chances for Federal Reserve approval would be greatly enhanced. Thus, a pure case would hopefully be decided on the merits of the grandfathering clause and would hopefully avoid any contaminating issues.

43   NCNB discreetly approached an investment banker in Florida with the various criteria that any acquisition candidates would have to satisfy. Per instructions, the investment banker kept NCNB's name confidential as it tried to identify potential acquisition candidates. The investment banker soon provided NCNB with a list of half a dozen small banks that fulfilled its three criteria.

44   The second bank contacted by NCNB representatives was the First National Bank of Lake City, Florida. This single branch had assets of $21,600,000. NCNB offered a very high figure of $3,900,000 for the bank sight unseen simply to test the law with a national bank, with closely held stock, and located in a county where no other NCNB financial institution operated.

45   On June 11, 1981, Chairman Tom Storrs publicly announced that NCNB would try to acquire First National Bank of Lake City. NCNB waited until after the Florida State legislature had ended its session before making this public announcement. This prevented the legislature from introducing legislation to revise the Florida statute, unless it called a special session to prevent NCNB from entering its state.

46   In Storrs' announcement, he didn't explain why NCNB expected the Federal Reserve Bank in Richmond, Virginia to approve the petition. This left many industry observers speculating how NCNB would be able to make such an acquisition, since interstate banking was still outlawed. Storrs only noted that NCNB was proceeding on its lawyers' advice and that NCNB believed its position was sound. Storrs did note, however, that the move represented an extension of NCNB's existing operations in Florida.

47   The Federal Reserve commented on the proposed acquisition the very next day. Floyd Boston, an enforcement official for the Federal Reserve Bank of Richmond, noted that if the Lake City acquisition was approved, it would mean that NCNB could expand further in Florida with other acquisitions. Obviously, this was exactly what NCNB management hoped to hear for a final outcome.

48   NCNB did not wait for a ruling by the Fed to go after other acquisitions. On Sunday, June 21, 1981, NCNB announced that it wanted to acquire Florida National Banks of Florida, Inc. It was the fourth largest bank holding company in the state with total assets of $2,500,000,000. NCNB officials also noted that C. A. Cavendes Sociedad Financiera of Caracas, Vensuela, which controlled $32 \frac{1}{2}\%$ of Florida National's stock, had agreed to vote for a merger. NCNB offered $210,000,000 for this bank holding company, which owned 25 banks with 88 combined offices in the state. Stockholders of Florida National Banks would receive NCNB preferred stock worth $28 for each share of Florida National, which closed two days earlier at $19.68. In addition, $45,000,000 would be put in an escrow fund to be established for Cavendes to draw income on between the time the

merger agreement was signed and the time it is closed. Finally, NCNB would invest $20,000,000 in the Cavendes-controlled South American bank. Like the earlier Lake City announcement, NCNB officials did not explain why they hoped their application to enter banking in another state would be approved by the Federal Reserve.

49   There was lots of discussion in the banking community over NCNB's two proposed acquisitions. Some bank analysts quickly speculated that NCNB was probably going to argue that its 1972 acquisition of the Florida Trust Company grandfathered it into Florida for future acquisitions. One industry observer even speculated that NCNB might try to argue that its Florida Trust Company already qualified as a commercial bank under Florida laws.

50   Later in June, NCNB formally submitted its application to the Federal Reserve to acquire the Lake City bank. Unfortunately, it had to wait quite some time for a final ruling by the Federal Reserve.

51   On June 27, 1981, 45-year-old NCNB Vice Chairman, Hugh McColl, commented on how NCNB had prepared for its move into Florida. McColl, who was talking from NCNB's temporary command post at the Holiday Inn in Jacksonville, noted:

> "It was planned as sophisticatedly as you would plan an invasion....We put our logistics in place, put together a team of lawyers and negotiators...lined up pilots and airplanes, telephones, and telexes. We had a scheme of everything that would have to be done. We built a battle plan. Everyone had assignments, and we've been carrying them out constantly....We believe you must grow if you are going to survive. You either go forward or get overrun. All of us think that way."[7]

52   NCNB withdrew its offer to acquire the Florida National Banks of Florida on July 10, 1981. This action was not surprising, given that three days earlier, Florida National Banks flatly stated that it would not consider the $210,000,000 offer from NCNB until after the Federal Reserve or a court ruled that NCNB's efforts were legal to move into Florida. In retracting NCNB's earlier offer, Tom Storrs noted:

> "It's just good business that when you make an offer and the recipient doesn't consider it, you withdraw it. There are a lot of other banks in Florida. We will continue to look at the banking structure of the state."

He further added that NCNB was willing to acquire banks as large as Barnett Banks of Florida, which was the state's second largest holding company with $4,400,000,000 in assets. Storrs observed:

> "Barnett is a great bank. The top management there includes some very good friends of mine. I certainly wouldn't rule this out."[8]

53   The Florida Bankers Association and two competitors of the First National Bank of Lake City urged the Federal Reserve to reject NCNB's application. The Bankers Association contended that the grandfather

clause was never intended for acquisitions by out-of-state bank holding companies. Lloyd Boston of the Federal Reserve Board in Richmond responded to this challenge by stating: "The board is required to consider the meaning and applicability of state law. So the board will be looking at Florida statutes and trying to determine if they do make it permissible for NCNB...to acquire banks and/or trust companies in Florida."[9]

54   NCNB responded by filing a response to the Florida Bankers Association challenge with the Federal Reserve. Its response even included a statement from former Florida Representative Robert Hartnett, who was the main sponsor of the legislation and chairman of the Banking and Finance Subcommittee of the Florida House from 1968 through 1974. Hartnett said in his statement that he was concerned with "protecting the rights and future opportunities of those non-Florida banking organizations, which already had acquired banks or trust companies in Florida."[10]

55   On December 9, 1981, the Federal Reserve Board in Richmond finally ruled in favor of NCNB's application to acquire the First National Bank in Lake City. In making its decision, the Fed noted that NCNB would consider reducing the bank's service charges and making credit insurance available at lower rates. The Fed also noted that NCNB intended to offer new or improved services and to open branches, which should provide widespread access to all these services. Thus, the Federal Reserve felt that acquisition was clearly in the public interest. More importantly, the Federal Reserve concluded:

> "NCNB may, in accordance with Florida law, acquire, retain, or own all the assets of, or control over, any Florida bank or trust company."[11]

56   NCNB spokesman, attorney Paul Polking, who discovered the legal loophole, responded as the company spokesman this time. He observed:

> "We have several options. When we acquire First National Bank of Lake City, we have the authority to establish branches of that bank in other communities. We could also acquire other banks or bank holding companies in the state."[12]

57   Florida officials responded in different ways. Many bankers were very disappointed with the ruling. Sun Bank's Senter Fitt noted, "When NCNB is in Florida, it is here with all its assets. It is here as the largest holding company in Florida."[13] Some other bankers reacted more strongly and called for action. For example, Charles Rice, President of Jacksonville-based Barnett Banks, publicly stated that he hoped that the NCNB ruling would spur the Florida legislature to pass reciprocal banking legislation. The legislation he envisioned would require states whose banks wanted to enter Florida to grant similar privileges to Florida banks in their home states.

58   Even with the Federal Reserve approval, NCNB still had to wait 30 additional days before it could acquire 82% of the stock for almost $4,000,000.

This one-month delay was to give time for the Justice Department to review the decision on antitrust grounds. Since NCNB had no other operation in the county where Lake City operated, the 30-day period passed uneventfully. Finally, in early January of 1982, NCNB had finally moved into Florida banking through an acquisition of a bank it had never even personally visited before offering an inflated purchase price. Still, NCNB had used that small bank successfully to test the Florida statutes and get the green light to acquire larger, more important Florida banks in the future.

59   While this legal loophole applied to only Florida, Florida was the best possible state for NCNB to enter in the southeastern region of the U.S. Compared to North Carolina, the Florida marketplace was less developed, yet substantially larger. The Florida bank deposit base ranked 9th nationwide with $43,800,000,000 in domestic bank deposits, while North Carolina finished in 21st place with only $19,800,000,000 in deposits. Florida also had twice as many corporations located in middle-sized markets. In 1982, some 4,353 such companies were identified in Florida, compared to only 2,142 in North Carolina.

60   Florida was an attractive market for other reasons. Its population was growing quickly, its income base was stable, the business climate was favorable, and tourists regularly visited the state. Furthermore, Florida's economy was expected to lead the nation's recovery from the recession that started in late 1980.

61   In the remainder of 1982, NCNB sought out and got approval from the Federal Reserve to acquire three other Florida banks, with combined assets of $2,779,000,000. On September 3rd, NCNB Corporation consummated its acquisition of Gulfstream Banks, Inc. in Boca Raton. NCNB paid $91,000,000 cash for Gulfstream which had total assets of $787,000,000.

62   Gulfstream was a full service national bank and a member of the F.D.I.C. Its 21 branches were located in Broward, Palm Beach, and Dade counties. Its banks provided checking, loan, savings, and other time deposits for its individual and commercial customers. Gulfstream also had 24 hour ATMs in 12 locations, issued Visa and MasterCard credit cards, offered various trust services, offered a money-market account, sold securities and funds to finance loans, purchased investment securities for its customers, and traded in foreign currencies to realize profits for its own account.

63   On December 31, 1982, NCNB consummated its acquisition of Exchange Bancorporation of Tampa. Exchange operated 51 offices in 11 counties and had assets of $1,622,270,000. This largest of the acquisitions was purchased for $134,000,000 cash.

64   Like Gulfstream, Exchange Bancorporation also offered a wide range of banking services. It provided checking, loan, savings, and other time deposits at 44 of its branches. It also had a money-market account, a direct payroll deposit system for its customers, 24 hour ATM service at 38 locations, issued name credit cards, and provided trust services. In addition, it

was a dealer in governmental and municipal bonds and was an underwriter for state and municipal bonds. Finally, it had various foreign services, which included borrowing funds in overseas markets and engaging in foreign currency exchange trading to meet the needs of its customers and itself.

65 The fourth Florida acquisition was also finalized in December. It involved Peoples Downtown National Bank in Miami, a single branch bank with only $9,000,000 in assets, which was purchased for $6,000,000.

66 NCNB's earlier successful building of its equity capital position allowed the corporation to enter phase two of its plan for the 1980s, the geographical expansion of the corporation. NCNB paid $225,000,000 alone to acquire its two major Florida acquisitions, Gulfstream Banks, Inc. and Exchange Bancorporation of Tampa. Though these funds were obtained from a variety of sources at an after-tax cost of slightly more than 6%, they did not dilute NCNB's 1982 earnings. Exhibit 3 shows the various sources used for these Florida acquisitions, which included short-term debt, long-term debt, new equity, and the use of existing corporate resources.

67 The Florida acquisitions combined with North Carolina gave NCNB a market that ranked sixth in size in the entire country. This tripled NCNB's potential market for deposits, retail customers, and business firms. NCNB

Exhibit 3

**NCNB Corporation Financing Program
($ in millions)**

	Cash Purchase Price	Net Aftertax Annual Interest Cost
A. Original Issue Discount Debentures	$ 38.0	$ 2.2
B. 14½% Notes, due 1992	83.5	6.8
C. Special Dividend, North Carolina National Bank	25.0*	1.7
D. Refund of 1981 Federal Income Taxes	10.0	---
E. Tax Benefits from Sale of Acquired Assets with Tax Bases in Excess of Market Values	21.0	---
F. Sale of Parent Company Liquid Assets	20.0	1.4
G. Utilization of Uncommitted Parent Company Equity	22.5*	1.6
	$220.0	$13.7
Aftertax Cost of Funds		6.2%
Pretax Cost of Funds		11.5%

*Prime of 13% used.

Source: The First Boston Research Corporation, 1982

estimated that it had gained access to over 30% of the total banking market of the 12 southeastern states, as compared to only 10% to 12% represented by North Carolina. Due to its size, NCNB could legally lend $100,000,000 to a single corporate customer. This was more than either of the leading Florida banks could lend. Barnett could lend $88,500,000 and Southeast $65,000,000 to $70,000,000. Both NCNB and Wall Street were optimistic about NCNB's future after these acquisitions. Thomas Storrs, Chairman, was confident that NCNB would become larger in Florida than in its home state. Salomon Brothers, a leading investment banking company, supported Storrs' optimism by recommending the purchase of NCNB's stock and raising its forecasted five-year-earnings growth rate from 13% to 15%.

Consolidation of Operations

68   NCNB's four acquisitions offered different products and services, were of different sizes, and had varying degrees of managerial talent. They also differed in the geographical areas that they covered in Florida, as Exhibit 4 shows. The first acquisition was no more than a one-branch country bank that had cost only a few million to purchase. Similarly, the fourth Florida acquisition, Peoples Downtown National Bank of Miami, was done basically to obtain a charter to operate in that county. Peoples had been stripped of its depositors and its management was not going to stay on after the acquisition was finalized. Still, Peoples was acquired for a very good reason. If NCNB had tried to start up its own bank from scratch, Florida law would have required it to operate in one county for two years before being permitted to expand into other counties.

69   The second and third acquisitions were a different story. Gulfstream Banks, Inc. in Boca Raton was acquired for close to a $100,000,000 and had 21 branches. Management was asked to stay on, including Gulfstream's President, Les Nell. Similarly, Exchange Bancorporation of Tampa was purchased for even more money and Don Buchanan, its C.E.O., stayed on as well.

70   NCNB wanted to improve the efficiency of its Florida operations as soon as the four acquisitions had been finalized. Clearly, NCNB wanted to do everything possible to increase its presence in Florida and to successfully compete against Barnett Banks, Flagship Banks, Inc., and Southeast Banking Corporation, its three strongest competitors in Florida.

71   As 1982 came to a close, a fundamental issue faced NCNB's corporate management. What should it do with these four Florida banks and how should they operate? How much autonomy should each bank be provided? Should they continue to follow the policies and procedures they had independently established before the takeover? Should NCNB require them to follow uniform procedures handed down by corporate headquarters in Charlotte, North Carolina? Should their names be changed to indicate

Exhibit 4

Tarheel Bankers Stake the Market

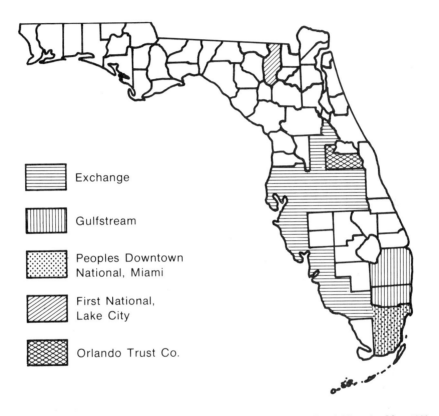

Exchange

Gulfstream

Peoples Downtown
National, Miami

First National,
Lake City

Orlando Trust Co.

Source: NCNB Corporation Annual Report 1982 and *Florida Trend Magazine,*May 1983.

they were under the NCNB holding company? How should these four
Florida banks, as shown in Exhibit 5, be organized along with NCNB's
other major operating units? What human resource programs might be
needed to make the Florida bank employees feel a part of the friendly
neighborhood bank? These and many other questions were beginning to
surface as NCNB corporate management considered the best course of
action to take to consolidate its Florida acquisitions and to start developing
its new base of operation.

Exhibit 5

**NCNB Corporation
Office Directory**

NCNB Corporation
Charlotte, N. C. 28255
704/374-5000

**Exchange Bank & Trust
Company of Florida N.A.**
600 North Florida Avenue
Tampa, Fla. 33602
813/224-5151

**First National Bank of Lake
City**
201 North Marion Street
Lake City, Fla. 32055
904/752-2524

NCNB Financial Services Inc.
P. O. Box 30533
Charlotte, N. C. 28230
704/374-5876

NCNB Leasing Corporation
Charlotte, N. C. 28255
704/374-5269

**NCNB National Bank of
Florida**
150 East Palmetto Park Road
Boca Raton, Fla. 33432
305/393-5100

**NCNB National Bank of
North Carolina**
Charlotte, N. C. 28255
704/374-5000

Representative Offices
Suite 1705
375 Park Avenue
New York, N. Y. 10152
212/935-8303

Suite 4060, First National Plaza
70 West Madison Street
Chicago, Ill. 60602
312/372-0742

Suite 1535, CNA Tower
255 South Orange Avenue
Orlando, Fla. 32801
305/423-0828

**TranSouth Financial
Corporation**
518 South Irby Street
P. O. Box F471
Florence, S. C. 29501
803/662-9341

Trust Company of Florida
200 East Robinson Street
P. O. Box 2951
Orlando, Fla. 32802
305/841-6000

INTERNATIONAL:

Carolina Bank Limited
14 Austin Friars
London EC2N 2EH, England
01-628-4821

NCNB Overseas Corporation
Charlotte, N. C. 28255
704/374-5212

**NCNB International Banking
Corporation**
44 Wall Street
P. O. Box 536
Wall Street Station
New York, N. Y. 10005
212/943-6300

NCNB (Asia) Limited
35th Floor, New World Tower
16-18 Queens Road Central
Hong Kong, B. C. C.
5-220192

NCNB Spedley Australia Ltd.
68 Pitt Street
Sydney, Australia 2001
22-33-7076

**NCNB National Bank
Branches**
14 Austin Friars
London EC2N 2EH, England
01-588-9133

35th Floor, New World Tower
16-18 Queens Road Central
Hong Kong, B. C. C.
5-220192

Representative Offices
68 Pitt Street
G. P. O. Box 3951
Sydney, Australia 2001
22-33-7076

Edificio Olivetti
Avenida Paulista 453
Sao Paulo, Brazil
11-251-3473

16th Floor, Nedfin Place
Corner Simmonds and Kerk
Streets
Johannesburg, South Africa
2001
11-834-7911

From *NCNB Corporation Annual Report 1982,* and *Florida Trend Magazine,* May 1983.

Notes

1. *1982: Meeting the Challenge of Growth* (Charlotte, North Carolina: NCNB Corporation, 1982).
2. *The Challenge of Our Future Could be Part of Your Success,* (Charlotte, North Carolina: NCNB Corporation, 1982).
3. "NCNB Defies Convention, Keeps Breaking Ground, *The Tampa Tribune,* May 29, 1982, p. A1.
4. "N. C. Bank Shines in Florida," *USA Today,* October 6, 1982.
5. Ibid.
6. Thomas H. Hanley, et al. *NCNB Corporation: The Sunshine Bank* (New York: Salomon Brothers Inc., February 3, 1983).
7. Dick Stilley. "NCNB Takes its Aggressive Style into Florida," *Charlotte Observer,* June 28, 1981, p. A1.
8. Dick Stilley. "NCNB Withdraws Bank Offer," *Charlotte Observer,* July 11, 1981, p. 1A.
9. Dick Stilley. "Former Legislator Supports NCNB in Florida Deal," *Charlotte Observer,* September 18, 1981, p. 8B.
10. Ibid.
11. Dick Stilley. "Fed's Ruling Frees NCNB to Expand Florida Interests," *Charlotte Observer,* December 11, 1981, p. 7C.
12. Ibid.
13. Dick Stilley, "NCNB Bidding for Regional Dominance," *Charlotte Observer,* December 13, 1981, p. 8C.

Merrill Lynch & Co. (A): The Movement toward Full Financial Service

1   In 1978, Merrill Lynch & Co., Inc., was a leading financial services company. Through its subsidiaries, Merrill Lynch offered a broad range of services that were tailored to the varying financial and investment needs of individuals, corporations, institutions, and governments. While Merrill Lynch strived to expand its position as leader in the securities business, in recent years it had also expanded beyond that industry to fulfill its commitment better to serve the financial needs of its customers. Merrill Lynch was considering the "Cash Management Account" to give customers full financial service and to help offset the cyclical nature of their commissions earnings. The Cash Management Account would represent a further move into the banking industry by providing bill-paying, record-keeping, checking, and credit-transactions services.

Historical Background

2   Charles Merrill began the firm of Charles E. Merrill & Co. in January 1914. Initially, the firm occupied a space sublet from Eastman, Dillon, but by May 1914, had moved to 7 Wall Street. In July of that year, Merrill persuaded Edmund Calvert Lynch to join him in a co-partnership agreement, and the firm became known as Merrill Lynch & Co. The new firm followed through on Merrill's and Lynch's personal philosophy for success: there are many potential investors, beyond the elite, that Merrill Lynch could

---

This case was prepared by John A. Pearce II of the University of South Carolina.

cater to. These small investors represented a segment which the old brokerage houses had ignored.

3   During the early years, Merrill and Lynch emphasized the importance of developing their clients' trust of the partners as financial advisors. Merrill Lynch's first newspaper ads, inviting the public to invest in stocks and bonds, were also designed for maximum credibility. One of the first Merrill Lynch ads was a full-page spread in a newspaper, running eight columns of small type, explaining the fundamentals of stocks and bonds. The Merrill Lynch monthly investment plan was one of the first marketing campaigns on Wall Street to appeal directly to the small investor, and the firm was also one of the first proponents on Wall Street of lower commission rates.

4   Merrill Lynch & Co.'s first big deal, completed in 1915, was an offering of McCrory Stores. Through the 1920s, Merrill Lynch introduced the invesing public to some up-and-coming retail enterprises, including J.C. Penney, National Tea, Western Auto Supply, First National Stores, People's Drug, and a couple of retailers that would become today's Winn-Dixie.

5   Merrill Lynch also played a major role in bringing several industrial companies to market. Many of these were in areas not then accepted by the financial establishment, such as automobiles, movies, and oil. As the Great Depression began in the late 1920s, Charles Merrill foresaw a prolonged period of suffering for Wall Street, and he decided to retrench and withdraw from the retail commission business and concentrate on investment banking. He sold the firm's retail business and branches to E. A. Pierce and Co. in early 1930, thus transferring many of Merrill Lynch's employees to Pierce. At the time, Pierce was the nation's largest wire house with extensive branch networks connected by private telegraph wires.

6   E. A. Pierce and Company survived the Depression. The return on partners' capital was small, however, and with the 10-year partnership agreement due to run out at the end of 1939, there was growing doubt that enough partners were willing to renew.

7   At this time Winthrop Hiram Smith, who ran Pierce's Chicago office, was extremely concerned whether the E. A. Pierce and Co. partnership would be renewed. Smith, who had previously been employed by Merrill, approached Merrill about resuming work with him, bringing together Merrill Lynch and E. A. Pierce.

8   Merrill knew that brokerage firms were experiencing a slump in activity. There was a large amount of distrust, disinterest, and misunderstanding of the financial markets, and stockbrokers were widely regarded as dishonest. In 1936, Merrill met Ted Braun, a leading public relations expert who had done several studies on public attitude. One of Braun's studies outlined what people wanted in a securities firm. Merrill used this study as the organizational blueprint for a new company which would cater to a mass of investors and would be guided by the principles of scientific management. The new firm was ready for business on April 1, 1940, as Merrill

9   Lynch, E. A. Pierce & Cassatt. Cassatt was the long-establised Philadelphia firm of Cassatt and Co., which had been sold to E. A. Pierce in 1935.

9   The new company made itself known to the public through attention-drawing advertisements, with the initial announcement stating Merrill's policy. Referred to as the "Ten Commandments," the first stated: "The interests of our customers MUST come first."

10   By 1941, Merrill Lynch wanted not to be known merely as the nation's largest wire house, but also wanted acceptance of itself and Wall Street as essential public institutions. Its new policies and ideas caused a large response nationwide. More than 12,000 new accounts were opened before the end of 1940, which is impressive considering total customers at year-end totaled only 50,000. Then, completely unprecedented, Merrill Lynch published an annual report. This move was even more surprising, for it showed a loss of $309,000 for the nine months the company operated in 1940. Since 1941, however, the company has been profitable each year.

11   In August 1941, there was a major addition to Merrill Lynch, and the firm became known as Merrill Lynch, Pierce, Fenner & Beane. Fenner was the founder of Fenner and Solari, which teamed with Alpheus C. Beane, Sr., in 1905. Fenner and Beane had been a large cotton house and had developed a large network of branch offices specializing in commodity futures. Fenner and Beane, upon deciding to handle its own stock business, became the second-largest wire house behind Pierce. The merger of Fenner and Beane with Merrill greatly strengthened Merrill's commodities trading.

12   Merrill Lynch continued to be innovative, and in 1945, they initiated the first training program for brokers. Merrill and Smith felt that training their own young executives would enable them to make a broker's career more inviting and would therefore attract top-flight candidates. Since the first training school class in 1945, Merrill Lynch has graduated more than 20,300 account executives from its program.

13   In addition to educating his employees, Charles Merrill believed strongly in educating the public. He wanted to show people how to become investors, to teach them to invest intelligently, and to supply them with data and analysis of specific investments. Merrill's long-time advertising director, Lou Hengel, put out a series of famous educational ads and pamphlets. In addition, Hengel wrote the best seller, *How to Buy Stocks,* which had more than 4 million copies in print.

14   Charles Merrill also emphasized the importance of providing meaningful research information to all investors. In further serving investors, Merrill made certain that their business was properly processed. This was known as the backstage function. To help in the proper processing of business, Merrill brought in an administrator, Michael W. McCarthy, who had previously worked with Merrill. McCarthy worked to establish procedures and installed the machines, systems, and people needed for Merrill Lynch to continue progressing. The progress McCarthy achieved since the mid-1940s is well illustrated by the following incident. In 1947, the U.S.

Department of Justice filed antitrust charges against 17 major investment-banking firms, but Merrill Lynch was not even mentioned in these cases.

15   Upon Charles Merrill's death in 1956, McCarthy was appointed as the new managing partner. Alpheus C. Beane, Jr., son of the late cofounder of Fenner and Beane, decided to withdraw from the firm because of his disapproval of McCarthy, and so in early 1958, the company became Merrill, Lynch, Pierce, Fenner & Smith.

16   Not until 1953, did the New York Stock Exchange permit brokers to incorporate. Five years later, in 1958, only 51 (mostly small) of 655 brokerage firms had done so. The 119 partners of Merrill Lynch were planning to become incorporated, again showing Merrill's leadership in the industry, for at that time, they were already the world's largest brokerage firm (see Exhibit 1). Merrill Lynch's reason for incorporating in January 1959 was "to assure continuity of the firm because each partner cannot add to his capital in the firm until after individual income taxes are paid; and because each is liable for the debts or lawsuits of others, the threat of a capital drain is always present."[1]

17   After much early success, Merrill Lynch continued to remain at the top by actively pursuing new ideas. In 1964, Merrill Lynch acquired the business of C. J. Devine, a leading government securities dealer, forming the base of Merrill Lynch Government Securities, Inc. "We the People" or "The Thundering Herd," as Merrill Lynch was called, continued expansion through further acquisitions. In 1968, Merrill Lynch entered real estate financing by acquiring Hubbard, Westervelt, and Mottelay. Through this acquisition, Merrill Lynch became a major dealer in Ginnie Maes and helped develop such financing innovations as mortgage-backed pass-throughs.

18   A major development took place in 1968 when Donald Regan became president of Merrill Lynch. He became chief executive officer in 1971. With Regan in power, the company grew a great deal. Some of his innovations included putting internally trained financial managers at the top and putting the "business getters," who traditionally filled the top positions in partnerships, farther down the corporate structure. This arrangement was a radical innovation on Wall Street. He also increased computer capacity to upgrade the firm's efficiency and instituted a diversification program.

19   In 1969, Merrill Lynch changed its strategy from seeking small clients to trying to attract large accounts. This change in strategy was made possible by the acquisition of Lionel D. Edie & Co., a large investment management and consulting firm.

20   At that time, while Merrill Lynch continued their expansion, many Wall Street firms were entering a disastrous era. Other firms overextended, resulting in their losing track of the trades they made, the whereabouts of the certificates they represented, and the status of their customers' ac-

---

[1]"The Herd, Inc.," *Business Week,* October 4, 1958, p. 30.

Exhibit 1

1959 brokerage and underwriting standings

Fifteen biggest brokers—gross income ($ millions)		Fifteen leading underwriters—corporate underwritings managed or co-managed ($ millions)	
1. Merrill Lynch	$136.0	First Boston	$1,042
2. Bache	38.0	Morgan Stanley	965
3. Francis I. du Pont	38.0	Lehman	880
4. E. F. Hutton	30.0	Blyth	868
5. Paine, Webber, Jackson & Curtis	29.1	White, Weld	833
6. Dean Witter	*	Merrill Lynch	815
7. Walston	27.2	Kuhn, Loeb	696
8. Goodbody	24.8	Halsey, Stuart	650
9. Shearson, Hammill	24.0	Eastman Dillon	456
10. Loeb, Rhoades	23.0	Stone & Webster	388
11. Harris, Upham	22.0	Goldman, Sachs	366
12. Reynolds	21.6	Dillon, Read	363
13. Hayden, Stone	21.5	Smith, Barney	358
14. Eastman, Dillon, Union Securities	*	Kidder, Peabody	275
15. Thomson & McKinnon	18.0	Harriman Ripley	245

*Gross income figure not available.
Source: "The Biggest Broker in the World," Fortune, August 1960, p. 98.

counts. Many Wall Street firms were unable to meet their obligations and subsequently collapsed, taking their customers' accounts with them. In 1970, the New York Stock Exchange requested Merrill Lynch to take over the fifth-largest retail broker, Goodbody & Co., which was sinking fast. This was a high-risk job for Merrill Lynch even though there were some reimbursement, provisions from the total New York Stock Exchange community. The Wall Street crisis that forced Merrill Lynch to take over Goodbody threw Merrill Lynch's long-range plans for greater involvement in the financial services industry off schedule. Merrill Lynch, however, was able to set up important underpinnings of a sound diversification effort by establishing a holding company. This holding company, known as Merrill Lynch & Co., had Merrill Lynch, Pierce, Fenner & Smith as the principal subsidiary. Under this new format, Merrill Lynch, which had already expanded into such areas as government securities, real estate, financing, and economic consulting, diversified farther into specialty insurance, relocation services, and asset management.

21   Throughout the 1970s, Merrill Lynch campaigned for a national market system. Merrill Lynch managers felt that the national market system would greatly help their business. If another brokerage firm handled the other side of the transaction, Merrill Lynch wanted that member of the industry to handle the transaction efficiently, thereby making Merrill Lynch more efficient.

22   In 1974, Merrill Lynch acquired Family Life Insurance, a Seattle-based company that specialized in mortgage-protection insurance for home-owners. Also during that year, Merrill Lynch added AMIC, which offered mortgage-default insurance to the institutions that issue mortgages. Merrill Lynch had also become the top-ranked U.S. investment banking house internationally by 1974.

23   In early 1977, Merrill Lynch acquired a company that became Merrill Lynch Relocation Management. This subsidiary, which contracted corporations to help their employees who needed to transfer, also provided Merrill Lynch with the executive expertise to form Merrill Lynch Realty Associates. In June 1977, Merrill Lynch launched a national weekly stock option guide, *Options Alert,* representing a major entry into the publishing business for Merrill Lynch. It was the result of Merrill Lynch's corporate planning unit, which had been established in May 1975 to further the firm's continuing diversification program into areas not subjected to the market's cyclical nature.

The Managerial Philosophy of Merrill Lynch

24   To gain and keep its competitive advantage in the financial services field, Merrill Lynch had developed a unique managerial personality for a brokerage house.

The Merrill Lynch Concept of Management

25   Merrill Lynch worked toward financial diversification through the process of management by objectives, a process rarely attempted on Wall Street. The process involved setting specific long-term and short-term goals—in a continuous succession of one-year, three-year, and five-year plans—for every operating unit and every executive in the company. Also, management by objectives meant having a periodic critical review to see that each unit and manager was on target.

26   Merrill Lynch first brought its strategic planning to life in 1973. The company had until then been product-sales oriented. It had only a few products and services that it sold. The new plan called for Merrill Lynch to be market oriented, that is, organized around the needs of potential customers. These customers fell into four groups: individuals, corporations, institutions, and governments.

Concentration in Financial Services

27   By going public in 1971, Merrill Lynch acquired enough capital to under-

take a wide range of new ventures. Company officials continually stressed, however, that all diversification efforts would be within the realm of financial services. Merrill Lynch's size gave it the opportunity to try out a variety of new businesses at once. It learned these businesses and either expanded or divested them. It had the ability to experiment, and a single failure did not pose as grave a problem for them as it would have for some smaller firms. For example, Merrill Lynch's move from a broker-oriented

Exhibit 2

Merrill Lynch's fast-branching family tree

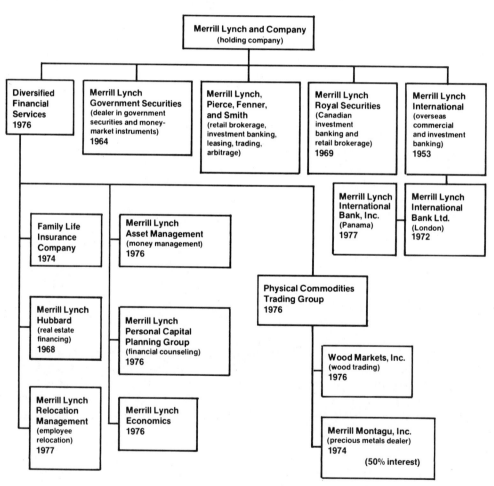

Dates represent years when units were acquired or established by Merrill Lynch.
Source: "Merrill Lynch: The Bull in Banking's Shop," *Business Week*, August 8, 1977, p. 51.

28 stock exchange system to one of dealer markets, in which brokers trade with customers from their own inventories, made capital a vital factor. Merrill Lynch was divided into five separate units, as shown in Exhibit 2. These units were (1) the Merrill Lynch, Pierce, Fenner, & Smith brokerage unit; (2) Merrill Lynch International; (3) Merrill Lynch Government Securities; (4) Merrill Lynch Royal Securities (a Canadian subsidiary); and (5) Merrill Lynch Diversified Financial Services.

Services Offered by Merrill Lynch

29 Merrill Lynch offered many services, including corporate securities trading, options and commodity futures, equity trading and arbitrage, and investment banking.

Corporate Securities Trading

30 According to the 1977 Form 10-K of Merrill Lynch, the major source of the revenues of Merrill Lynch, Pierce, Fenner & Smith (MLPF&S) was from commissions earned as broker, or agent, for its customers in the purchase or sale of common and preferred stocks. MLPF&S had traditionally emphasized its services to individual investors, but in recent years, the institutional investor had taken on greater importance. On May 1, 1975, fixed minimum commission rates for brokerage transactions were eliminated by the Securities and Exchange Commission. It became the policy of MLPF&S to negotiate commissions for accounts that were actively traded, including both individual and institutional accounts. Under the MLPF&S Sharebuilder Plan, which involved mass processing of orders, individual customers received discounts on commission rates on transactions of $5,000 or more.

31 Securities transactions made by MLPF&S were executed on either a cash or margin basis. Under the margin transactions, MLPF&S extended credit to customers based on the market value of the securities in the customer's account. To finance customers' margin account borrowings, MLPF&S used its own capital, bank borrowings, and borrowings provided by free credit balances in customer accounts.

Options and Commodity Futures

32 MLPF&S was licensed to buy and sell options on the Chicago Board Options Exchange, the American Stock Exchange, and in the over-the counter market. MLPF&S bought and also wrote options for its customers.

33 MLPF&S was a dealer and broker in the purchase and sale of futures contracts in substantially all commodities and held memberships on all

major commodity exchanges in the United States and Canada. Since substantially all buying of commodity futures was done on margin, the required margin was significantly lower than that required of common-stock customers. Commodity trading was a high-risk, speculative business, and MLPF&S was exposed to a large amount of financial risk due to the market volatility of commodities.

Equity Trading and Arbitrage

34   MLPF&S regularly made a market in approximately 650 domestic common stocks and more than 100 foreign securities. Its market-making activities were conducted with other dealers in the interdealer market and in the retail market. As part of its trading activities, MSPF&S engaged in both riskless and risk arbitrage. Whereas riskless arbitrage typically involved the simultaneous purchase and sale of securities, risk arbitrage depended upon ability to assess rapidly certain market conditions. At Merrill Lynch, all positions were liquidated as soon as possible, and positions in arbitrage were not taken without an analysis of the security's marketability. Merrill Lynch also made a market in municipal obligations and corporate fixed-income securities.

Investment Banking and Research

35   MLPF&S was a major investment banking firm that was active in every aspect of investment banking in a principal, agency, or advisory capacity. They underwrote the sale of securities themselves or arranged for a private placement with investors. They also provided a broad range of financial and advisory services for clients, including mergers and acquisitions, mortgage and lease financing, and advice on specific financing problems.

36   To provide its customers with current information on investments and securities markets, MLPF&S maintained Wall Street's largest securities research division, which performed technical market analysis as well as fundamental analysis of fixed-income securities and analysis of the municipal and corporate bond markets. MLPF&S had a computer-based opinion retrieval system that published current information and research opinions on approximately 1,400 foreign and domestic corporations.

Other Activities

37   MLPF&S sold shares of 191 income, growth, and money market funds, 13 of which were advised by Merrill Lynch Asset Management, Inc. In the money market area, MLPF&S also sponsored municipal investment trust funds, corporate income funds, and government securities income funds.

These were all closed-end unit investment trusts that were registered under the Investment Company Act of 1940.

38   MLPF&S also provided transaction clearing services to broker-dealers on a basis which was fully disclosed to the broker-dealers' customers. While the original firm retained all sales functions, MLPF&S handled all settlement and credit aspects of the transaction.

Competition

39   All aspects of MLPF&S's financial services business were extremely competitive. MLPF&S was in direct competition with firms such as Dean Witter, Bache & Co., and E. F. Hutton. MLPF&S also competed for investment funds with banks, insurance companies, and mutual fund management companies. Since the elimination of fixed commissions on May 1, 1975, the security brokerage industry had become intensely competitive. In addition to commissions charged, MLPF&S also competed on the basis of its services to investors, both individual and institutional. The establishment of a national market system, which MLPF&S supported, was intended to provide investors with the benefits of competing market places. Many firms had merged on Wall Street, resulting in securities firms with strengthened financial resources. In turn, these firms provided increased competition to the MLPF&S network of financial services.

40   The life insurance business of Merrill Lynch was also highly competitive. Many companies, like Prudential and Metropolitan, were older and larger than Family Life and provided strong competition because of their strong financial base and large agency organization. However, Family Life did have an advantage, as it specialized in mortgage-cancellation life insurance.

41   Merrill Lynch's operations in the real estate area were divided into two parts: (1) employee relocation and (2) real estate financing, mortgage banking, and real estate management. There were approximately eight companies that provided employee relocation services, Merrill Lynch Relocation Management, Inc., and Homequity, Inc., being predominant in the industry. Of course, numerous organizations were involved in real estate and mortgage banking.

Regulation

42   The securities business of MLPF&S was regulated by several different agencies. Although the SEC provided the bulk of the regulations, the company was also regulated by the National Association of Securities Dealers, Inc., The securities industry was more highly regulated than

many other industries; and violations of applicable regulations could result in the suspension of broker licenses, fines, or suspension or expulsion of a firm, its officers, or employees.

43   As a brokerage firm registered with the SEC and as a NYSE firm, MLPF&S was subject to the Uniform Net Capital Rule, which was designed to measure the general financial integrity and liquidity of a broker dealer. Under this rule, MLPF&S was required to maintain "net capital" equal to 4 percent of the total dollar amount of customer related assets. Under NYSE rules, MLPF&S had to reduce its business if its net capital was less than 6 percent of its total customer-related assets. Compliance with these net capital rules tended to limit their operation, especially in underwriting and maintaining the securities inventory required for trading.

The Brokerage Industry in 1976

44   The after-tax earnings of all New York Stock exchange brokerage firms increased about 22 percent from 1975, to a total of about $508 million. The total revenues rose 18 percent to $6.9 billion. Profits for the 12 large publicly-held brokerage firms showed a 16 percent increase to $230 million and an 18 percent increase in revenues to $2.9 billion.

45   The trading volume also increased in 1976, the daily trading average up 14 percent to 21.2 million shares. The total dollar value of New York Stock Exchange share volume increased 16 percent to $152 billion.

46   Brokerage firms were depending less on securities commissions and more on other products and services. For the past several years, most of the leading firms had increased their diversification and strengthened their activities not dealing with security commissions. Firms were entering the insurance business, going into foreign brokerage operations, developing new services, and increasing marketing efforts. Investment banking, principal transactions, and commodity trading were being emphasized. Exhibit 3 summarizes some of the effects of diversification on brokerage firms' revenues. In 1976, revenues from securities commissions were about 46 percent of total revenues, as compared to 52 percent in 1975.

47   The number of brokerage firms had been decreasing since 1962 because of closings or mergers of member firms. In the 1970s, several large, respected institutional firms had closed or sought mergers because of the unprofitability of keeping large research staffs while the commission rates for the larger accounts had been cut back. Major moves in 1976 were the merger of William D. Witter into Drexel Bunham and the Reynolds Securities International acquisition of Baker, Weeks, and Co.

Exhibit 3

Diversification of the major brokers

	Merrill Lynch	E. F. Hutton	Bache Group★	Paine Webber
Brokerage commissions	39%	60%	53%	50%
Trading government, municipal, corporate, and money-market securities	23	10	9	17
Interests on margin balances and securities owned	21	13	17	18
Investment banking	10	14	17	13
Other business	6	3	4	2
Total 1976 revenues ($ millions)	$1,125	$315	$248	$225

*Year ended July 31.
Source: "Merrill Lynch: The Bull in Banking's Shop," *Business Week,* August 8, 1977, p. 52.

Expenses Increase

48 A major reason for increased expenses in 1976 was that many firms were building their capacity to handle larger volumes of transactions. The attempts to increase capacity had begun in 1975. Many major firms had been increasing their computer and communications capabilities in order to facilitate handling larger volumes of transactions and to put them in a better position to shift to a central market system.

49 Congress and the Securities and Exchange Commission were pushing for the development of a central market system, and this was likely to involve sophisticated electronic switching of orders between the various marketplaces and make the market a more efficient system. Firms with the most advanced computer and communications capabilities were projected to move into this market easily and with relatively low additional expense.

50 Another factor that increased expenses in 1976 was inflation. Inflation had remained at a level high enough to have a significant impact on costs. The percentage increases were especially high for postage and telephone services, two services that securities firms use very heavily.

Banks' Impact on the Brokerage Industry

51 Several banks had begun offering automatic investment services where particular stocks could be purchased on a monthly basis by the banks' checking-account customers. Banks were able to bunch orders together to take advantage of the lower commission rates available on large transac-

tions. In September 1976, Chemical Bank took brokerage services one step farther. It offered retail brokerage rates well below the rates that individuals could get at brokerage houses. Chemical Bank could offer the discount rates because the bank got large discounts itself by placing the orders through Pershing and Co., a New York Stock Exchange member firm. On all but the smallest of orders, the transaction fees from going through Chemical Bank were well below the prevailing retail commissions charged by brokers. Individuals making large or frequent trades would have quickly made up the $30 annual fee for access to Chemical's order desk. Chemical also offered safekeeping of the securities.

52   Chemical's plan was forecast to have a significant impact on the securities industry if it was profitable and if Congress did not act to keep them from continuing the plan. The Senate was investigating banks' securities activities and could possibly take action unfavorable to Chemical's service. The Securities Industry Association was also considering asking the Federal Reserve Board or state banking authorities to bar Chemical's brokerage activities. If Chemical could make profits on its brokerage service, and if the activities were not illegal, Chemical's lower rates would cause brokers to lower the rates they charged in order to remain competitive. Such actions would cut further into the profits of the brokerage industry.

The Brokerage Industry in 1977

53   The 12 large publicly held brokerage companies monitored by Standard & Poor's reported earnings of $60 million in the first half of 1977—down 54 percent from the record $130 million in 1976's first half. In the same period, total revenues declined only 2 percent from the first half of 1976.

54   Brokerage firms were relying less on securities commissions, although they remained the largest source of revenue, and more on diversified products and services. Firms were actively entering the insurance business, expanding foreign brokerage operations, developing new services, and intensifying marketing efforts. In the years 1972 through 1975, investment firms' securities commissions accounted for 52 percent of gross revenues. In 1976, they represented 46 percent, and in 1977, they were 44 percent of the total.

55   In May 1975, fixed commission rates were abandoned on all transactions, regardless of size. Rates did come down slightly but were expected to come under increased pressure for downward revision because of the proliferation of discount brokerage firms. The major area in which competition had driven rates down was in institutional transactions, whose rates had fallen 44 percent since April 1975. The impact of discounted commissions on revenues was reflected in the fact that while the dollar value of NYSE trades in 1977 declined 9.4 percent, commission revenues fell 17

percent. The problems of discounts were substantial for some firms. About one third of NYSE member firms lost money in 1977.

56   The decline in the number of brokerage firms continued in 1977. Since 1970, the number of NYSE member firms fell to 370 in 1977 from about 570. The expense of maintaining large research staffs and cutting commission rates had pared profits to the point that many firms had merged, cut back, diversified, or gone out of business. With the decline in the number of firms doing a public business, concentration in the securities industry was increasing. By 1977, the largest firms had 65 percent of the industry's capital, 56 percent of commission revenues, and 64 percent of total revenues.

57   Trading profits continued to grow and account for 20 percent of total revenues in 1977. Trading profits were derived from brokers' market-making activites and from interest and dividends on securities held for trading. Because this source of income depended on the value of financial assets, it was a more volatile source of earnings than commission revenues. Likewise, underwriting income was quite volatile, and this source of revenue fell 12 percent in 1977.

58   An increasingly important source of revenues, interest on margin borrowing, accounted for 10 percent of gross revenues in 1977, up from 8 percent in 1976. Such interest income was a relatively stable portion of earnings, tending to bolster profitability when other sources of earnings were down. In fact retail brokerage operations probably could not have been conducted profitably at 1977 rates were it not for margin lending.

59   In recent years, brokerage firms had noticed increased competition from banks. Several banks continued to offer automatic investment services, where certain stocks could be purchased monthly by checking-account customers. However, Chemical Bank, which had begun to offer brokerage services in 1976, dropped its program as unsuccessful. As of 1977, all bank brokerage services account for less than 1 percent of the total value of transactions on all stock exchanges. Bank expansion of brokerage services in the future was a genuine possibility, however, because of regulatory changes and access to customer's money.

Current Situation

60   Nineteen seventy-seven was a year of declining earnings and profits for Merrill Lynch. Markets were poor in each important area that the corporation served as broker or dealer. Total commission revenues from listed securities, options, over-the-counter, mutual funds and commodities were expected to drop from $442,947,000 to about $365 million—a decline of over 17 percent. Total principal transaction revenues were also down about 28 percent, falling from $261,285,000 to a projected $188 million. As a result of these declines, net income was expected to fall from $106 million in 1976 to about $44 million in 1977. Earnings had fallen to about $1.25 per share for

1977 as compared to $3.01 per share in 1976. (Statements of Merrill Lynch's financial position in December 1977 are presented in Appendixes A through E). These declines occurred in a year marked by the uncertainty among both large and small investors. Despite moderate but steady growth in GNP as well as improvement in other leading economic indicators, investors seemed to focus on the negatives.

61   The Federal Reserve had been periodically stepping into the markets to tighten the money supply. Short-term and intermediate-term interest rates were increasing. As a result, trading activities, especially in the fixed income markets, were especially hard hit. Stocks had declined in attractiveness for investment purposes, because with the high interest rates, it was possible to get a good return on an investment by buying six-month certificates. Investors increasingly turned to high-yielding bonds or to holding capital assets for future investment.

62   Merrill Lynch's problems were compounded by lower commission rates. A new era of competition caused by lower commission rates charged to large investors had begun about the middle of 1975. Merrill Lynch had become involved in the scheme of reduced commissions for larger investors in hopes of attracting the larger accounts. This aggressive approach substantially increased the capital committed to handling large transactions. Merrill Lynch's new policy was to offer discounts to meet those offered by their competitors in order to gain orders and market share, as long as the business attracted by the discounted commissions remained profitable. The policy was one of the major reasons for the increase of Merrill Lynch's share of public New York Stock Exchange volume, which was reversing the downtrend of 1975 and 1976.

63   Merrill Lynch experienced increases in revenues in its other traditional areas. The corporation had maintained its position as the leading manager of corporate underwritings and had increased its penetration of the fee-based corporate finance business. Merrill Lynch also ranked first in municipal financing for the third straight year. On an international scale, the American dollar had declined in value against other major currencies. The weakening dollar, in combination with the U.S. securities markets, weakened the confidence of foreign investors and lessened the attractiveness of American securities.

Commercial Banking Activities

64   With its huge asset base and network of branch offices, Merrill Lynch was in a position to move into activities normally associated with commercial banks. The 1933 Glass-Steagall Act mandated the separation of investment and commercial banks in the United States.

International Banking

65   The Glass-Steagall Act had no effect on foreign bank operations since they fell outside U.S. jurisdiction. Merrill Lynch, in fact, already operated commercial banks in London and Panama that took deposits and made loans to overseas corporations. The total capital in these banks reached $50 million during 1977. Such growth indicated that commercial banking activities would offer tremendous financial clout for a financial services firm.

66   Consistent with its strategy to provide a full range of financial services to its customers, Merrill Lynch International wanted to increase its consumer banking overseas. However, any expansion into international banking would put the firm in direct competition with U.S. banks, foreign subsidiaries, and such universal banks as Deutsche Bank and Union Bank of Switzerland.

Domestic Banking—the Cash Management Account

67   Merrill Lynch was considering a type of broker-bank plan that would integrate a wide variety of financial services and, hopefully, circumvent the restrictions of the Glass-Steagall Act. The proposed account, called a Cash Management Account (CMA), would offer a whole range of services, such as bill paying, record keeping, checking, and credit transactions. The idea for the CMA was recommended by SRI International. Merrill Lynch itself had spent one and a half years developing the conceptual, legal, and computer systems details.

68   The account would allow Merrill Lynch customers to deposit money in a Merrill Lynch money market fund and draw on those funds with either a check or a VISA card. Any unused balances in the customer's brokerage account would be transferred into the money fund once a week and would earn dividends daily. Additionally, those customers with stocks and bonds would also be able to borrow up to 50 percent of the value of those securities on deposit. This ability to borrow against securities would be, in essence, a direct line of credit as well as overdraft protection for checking purposes. Each Cash Management Account customer's securities, including the money market fund shares, would be protected up to $300,000 through the Securities Investor Protection Corporation and supplemental securities protection. The interest on margin loans would be in the range of 6 to 8 percent compared with the $6\frac{3}{4}$ percent prime rate at commercial banks. However, more pertinent to individuals, the CMA rates would be considerably lower than the 10 to 12 percent conventional automobile loans or the 12 to 18 percent rate on most bank card purchases. Borrowing would automatically be triggered only after all the investment funds had been utilized.

69   Merrill Lynch had contracted the services of City National Bank of Columbus, Ohio, to handle the processing of checks, credit card drafts, and record keeping. Merrill Lynch would effect payment for CMA holders, extend credit, and provide a consolidated account statement. Both Merrill Lynch and City National saw the system, in which all units would be linked electronically, as the first step in a nationwide system of electronic funds transfer.

70   Merrill Lynch considered its ability as a superior mass merchandiser to be a distinctive competency and an advantage for entering the highly competitive banking field. Also, its national network of offices would be of tremendous benefit in marketing the CMA. In advertising the CMA, Merrill Lynch considered a direct-mail and print campaign as most effective. If implemented, the CMA would first be tested in a few pilot cities around the country.

71   Internally, the firm appeared to have the administrative capability to handle a large volume of new inputs. Merrill Lynch's data entry operators had shown great flexibility and adaptability in handling new applications. There was also sufficient capacity available to handle new data with the present systems, as shown by the fact that Merrill Lynch processed work for other companies during its own low-volume periods and work gaps.

Legal Implications

72   There were a number of major legal problems that Merrill Lynch had been considering. The firm had its own and other lawyers working to make sure the new product would not transcend any legal boundaries, such as the Glass-Steagall Act. It had presented the idea to the Federal Reserve, the Justice Department, and selected members of Congress. The Fed said that the new account would not violate any of its rules, but warned that it would closely monitor the impact of this and any similar programs. The Justice Department neither approved nor disapproved the idea. Other anticipated implications were the almost certain outcries from bankers that Merrill Lynch became chartered and regulated by the Federal Reserve System.

73   For several years, the issue of separating investment and commercial banks had been blurred. The 1975 Securities Act directed a review of the Glass-Steagall Act. If brought to fruition, the CMA would surely add pressure to redefine or alter such legislation. Meanwhile, banks had been participating in activities that brokers consider to be Glass-Steagall infractions. Such activities included (1) financial advice to customers on long-term credits, mergers, and acquisitions, (2) certain kinds of term loans, and (3) lining up insurance or pension fund money for private placements. The Federal Reserve Board had fully endorsed banks' private placement activities. In response, the brokers' trade group (the Securities Industry Association) denounced the Fed's stand and urged Congress to solve the problem. Also, Congress had been debating the related issues of (1) whether to give interest-bearing checking-account privileges to nonbank

thrift institutions and (2) whether to allow interstate branching of banks.

74   In light of the banking brokerage confrontation, however, Merrill Lynch viewed the CMA move more as a threat to brokers than to large banks. Merrill Lynch was one of the very few brokerage houses large enough to invade the banking business. It had $632 million in capital; its next largest rival had only $167 million. However, while Merrill Lynch was huge in comparison to other brokers, it was small compared to the large money-center banks.

How Banking Activities Could Benefit Merrill Lynch

75   Along with Merrill Lynch's other attempts to diversify its financial products and services, the company's move into commercial banking would be an attempt to offset the decreasing profitability and the cyclicality of brokerage profits. In a way, all brokers were already in the banking business through the medium of margin credit. In August 1977, Merrill Lynch topped $2 billion in margin loans—a loan portfolio that only 30 commercial banks could match. These margin loans were very profitable; in fact, 10 percent of Merrill's 1976 revenues came from interest on margin balances.

76   Merrill Lynch had its eye on a much broader source of customers and money through international and CMA banking activities. The CMA would be a way to attract new accounts as well as to hold old accounts. The CMA would have a finely segmented target market—probably the young (ages 35 to 45) executive beginning to build a stock portfolio and used unsecured credit. These customers would add money to Merrill's cash reserves and would have been good present and future investing clients for Merrill's brokers.

77   Margin loans were more extensively used under the CMA concept. Merrill Lynch held billions of dollars of value in fully paid securities owned by customers, which represented billions in potential low-interest borrowing power. Through CMAs, funds that had previously been idle in brokerage accounts could be put to work in an interest-earning fund. The CMA would, in essence, allow margin credit for purchases other than additional securities.

78   The movement into banking would have other effects on Merrill Lynch. First, commercial banking opened up huge possibilities in diversified financial services. Second, the movement into banking could give Merrill Lynch a reputation for cleverness that it lacked. In spite of Merrill's size and scope, it had an image problem. To most observers, it appeared as a giant who had succeeded not through talent but simply because it was so big. The firm led in most investment fields, but it did not have the classy image of a Morgan Stanley or a First Boston or a Salomon Brothers. Merrill Lynch's movement into banking offered it an opportunity to do something unique. The firm would have the chance to prove its innovativeness and to establish a unique competitive advantage.

Other Areas of Interest

79   In its effort to become a leader in virtually all areas of financial services, Merrill Lynch was considering many alternatives. It would probably undertake all of them, but the consideration was how soon it would choose to do so. For example, a system of real estate offices throughout the country was on Merrill's forward schedule, assuming its current venture into the employee relocation business worked well. It could also decide to expand its Personal Capital Planning Group, which provided financial planning for people with $30,000 or more in income, beyond its three test offices into a national branch system. Alternatively, it could move immediately to expand and broaden the product lines of Family Life Insurance.

Criteria for Accepting a New Project

80   Whatever moves Merrill Lynch decided to make, they were to be the result of systematic planning. The company had repeatedly expressed the willingness to sacrifice the possibility of large immediate profits to avoid the probability of large future losses. Any new project had to offer $500,000 in aftertax earnings and to provide a 15 percent aftertax return on investment within a three-year period. Merrill Lynch, in all instances, sought to repeat the successful formula it had used in the past—start small, learn the language and problems of the business, groom it to fit into Merrill's system of controls, and then plow in capital and personnel to grow.

Appendix A

Merrill Lynch & Co.—Statement of changes in consolidated financial position years ended December 30, 1977, and December 31, 1976 (in thousands of dollars)

	1977	1976
Sources of funds:		
Funds from operations:		
Net earnings	$ 43,947	$ 106,608
Noncash charges—depreciation and amortization	19,862	15,584
Total funds provided by operations	63,809	122,192
Increase in borrowings:		
Securities sold under agreements to repurchase	572,819	282,142
Bank loans	168,437	679,756
Commercial paper	239,081	215,070
Borrowing agreements with institutions	78,800	—
Intermediate term loans	102,500	—
Total increase in borrowings	1,161,637	1,176,968
Increase in net payables to brokers and dealers	5,436	54,579
Proceeds from issuance and sale of stock	10,082	11,073
Other, net	(15,062)	95,178
Total sources of funds	$1,225,902	$1,459,990

Appendix A (concluded)

	1977	1976
Uses of funds:		
Increase (decrease) in financial assets:		
Net securities inventory	$ 451,462	$ 815,544
Securities purchased under agreement to resell	233,984	(68,566)
Customer receivables, net	383,988	587,811
Residential properties under contract	74,179	—
Total increase in financed assets	1,133,613	1,334,789
Increase in deferred insurance policy acquisition costs	15,780	11,815
Purchase of office equipment and installations, net of retirements	29,337	18,366
Treasury stock purchased	10,019	24,685
Cash dividends	30,215	28,341
Decrease in income tax liability	8,037	40,507
Increase (decrease) in cash and securities on deposit	(1,099)	1,487
Total uses of funds	$1,225,902	$1,459,990

Appendix B

Merrill Lynch & Co.—Statement of changes in consolidated shareholders' equity years ended December 30, 1977, and December 31, 1976 (in thousands of dollars)

	Common stock	Paid-in capital	Retained earnings	Treasury stock
Balance, December 26, 1975: 36,140,179 common shares issued and 571,904 shares in treasury	$48,187	$87,418	$440,330	$ (8,518)
Net earnings			106,608	
Cash dividends: Common stock, $80 per share			(28,341)	
Common stock sold to employees under stock option and stock purchase plans (587,235 shares held in treasury)		(233)		11,306
Treasury stock purchased (997,900 shares)				(24,685)
Balance, December 31, 1976:	48,187	$87,185	$518,597	(21,897)
Net earnings			43,947	
Cash dividends: Common stock, $.86 per share			(30,215)	
Common stock sold to employees under stock option and stock purchase plans (726,782 shares held in treasury)		(5,558)		15,640
Treasury stock purchased (521,900 shares)				(10,019)
Balance, December 30, 1977: (36,140,179 common shares issued and 777,687 shares in treasury)	48,187	81,627	532,329	(16,276)

Source: Merrill Lynch & Co., Inc., 1977 Annual Report, p. 10.

Appendix C

Merrill Lynch & Co.—Consolidated balance sheet December 30, 1977, and December 31, 1976 (in thousands of dollars)

	1977	*1976*
Assets		
Cash and securities on deposit:		
Cash (includes time deposits of $33,718 in 1977 and $54,582 in 1976)	$ 84,069	$ 88,406
Cash segregated in compliance with federal and other regulations	17,699	16,125
Securities on deposit in compliance with federal and other regulations, at market value	132,106	130,442
Total cash and securities on deposit	233,874	234,973
Receivables:		
Brokers and dealers	192,176	165,207
Customers (less allowance for doubtful accounts of $10,622 in 1977 and $13,528 in 1976)	2,908,989	2,363,833
Securities purchased under agreements to resell	1,156,477	932,493
Other	176,652	101,982
Total receivables	4,434,294	3,563,515
Securities inventory, at market value:		
Bankers' acceptances, certificates of deposit, and commercial paper	580,810	870,342
U.S. and Canadian governments	1,927,010	1,350,763
States and municipalities	210,891	135,318
Corporates	364,988	246,559
Total securities inventory	3,083,699	2,602,982
Other:		
Investment securities, principally bonds, at amortized cost (market value, $53,869 in 1977 and $41,837 in 1976)	55,524	41,653
Office equipment and installations (less accumulated depreciation and amortization of $57,444 in 1977 and $49,548 in 1976)	92,409	74,337
Residential properties under contract	74,179	—
Deferred properties policy acquisition costs	44,513	37,330
Other assets	76,107	60,797
Total other	342,732	214,117
Total assets	$8,094,599	$6,615,587

Appendix C (concluded)

	1977	*1976*
Liabilities and Shareholders' Equity		
Loans:		
Bank loans	$1,926,278	$1,757,841
Commercial paper	632,878	393,797
Borrowing agreements with institutions	78,800	—
Securities sold under agreements to repurchase	2,176,604	3,755,785
Intermediate-term loans	102,500	—
Total loans	4,917,060	3,755,423
Payables and accrued liabilities:		
Brokers and dealers	373,153	341,748
Customers	1,088,782	927,614
Drafts payable	238,022	206,976
Insurance policy benefits	33,456	30,268
Income taxes	53,811	61,848
Employee compensation and benefits	75,000	78,688
Other	214,256	156,013
Total payables and accrued liabilities	2,077,480	1,803,155
Commitments for securities sold but not yet purchased, at market value:		
U.S. and Canadian governments	317,894	341,421
Other	136,298	83,516
Total commitments	454,192	424,937
Shareholders' equity:		
Common stock, par value $1.33⅓ per share—authorized 60 million shares; issued 36,140,179 shares	48,187	48,187
Paid-in capital	81,627	87,185
Retained earnings	532,329	518,597
Total shareholders' equity	662,143	653,969
Less common stock in treasury, at cost—777,687 shares in 1977 and 982,569 shares in 1976	16,276	21,897
Total shareholders' equity less common stock	645,867	632,072
Total liabilities and shareholders' equity	$8,094,599	$6,615,587

Source: Merrill Lynch & Co., Inc., 1977 Annual Report, pp. 8, 9.

Appendix D

Merrill Lynch & Co.—Statement of consolidated earnings years ended December 30, 1977, and December 31, 1976 (in thousands of dollars except per-share amounts)

	1977 *(52 weeks)*	*1976* *(53 weeks)*
Revenues:		
Commissions	$ 366,138	$ 442,947
Interest	353,784	237,857
Principal transactions	188,464	261,285
Investment banking	120,091	115,295
Insurance	44,650	34,358
Other	51,089	33,187
Total revenues	1,124,216	1,124,929
Expenses:		
Employee compensation and benefits	436,079	431,029
Interest	312,769	202,703
Occupancy expense and equipment rental	70,375	64,459
Communications	60,516	54,684
Brokerage, clearing, and exchange fees	36,436	38,476
Advertising and market development	33,557	26,039
Office supplies and postage	24,268	21,953
Insurance policyholder benefits	15,532	14,517
Other operating expenses	63,402	64,616
Total expenses	1,052,934	918,476
Earnings before income taxes	71,282	206,453
Income taxes	27,335	99,845
Net earnings	$ 43,947	$ 106,608
Net earnings per common share	$ 1.25	$ 3.01

Source: Merrill Lynch & Co., Inc., 1977 Annual Report, p. 7.

Appendix E

Merrill Lynch & Co.—Five-year financial summary year ended last Friday in December 1973–1977 (in thousands of dollars, except per-share amounts)

	1977 (52 weeks)		1976 (53 weeks)		1975 (52 weeks)		1974 (52 weeks)		1973 (52 weeks)		Compound growth rate, percent (1973–77)
Revenues:											
Commissions:											
Listed securities	$ 257,037	22.8%	$ 319,882	28.5%	$ 313,827	32.1%	$ 236,052	29.5%	$ 273,498	36.0%	(1.5)%
Options	44,977	4.0	59,948	5.3	38,891	4.0	8,681	1.1	2,279	0.3	110.8
Over-the-counter securities	16,831	1.5	17,883	1.6	11,796	1.2	8,259	1.0	13,117	1.7	6.4
Mutual funds	2,610	0.2	2,185	0.2	2,848	0.3	4,556	0.6	25,012	3.3	(43.2)
Commodities	44,683	4.0	43,049	3.8	37,408	3.8	34,572	4.3	42,739	5.6	1.1
Total commission revenues	366,138	32.5	442,947	39.4	404,770	41.4	292,120	36.5	356,645	46.9	0.7
Interest:											
Margin balances	145,895	13.0	112,896	10.0	99,551	10.2	141,220	17.6	141,916	18.7	0.7
Securities owned and deposits	207,889	18.5	124,961	11.1	105,824	10.8	89,501	11.2	44,442	5.8	47.1
Total interest revenues	353,784	31.5	237,857	21.1	205,375	21.0	230,721	28.8	186,358	24.5	17.4%
Principal transactions:											
Government and agency											
securities	56,693	5.0	122,968	10.9	93,023	9.5	78,048	9.8	45,780	6.0	5.5
Municipal securities	21,075	1.9	29,428	2.6	23,638	2.4	14,961	1.9	11,666	1.5	15.9
Corporate securities	96,067	8.6	90,510	8.0	49,421	5.0	41,944	5.2	39,201	5.2	25.1
Money market securities	14,629	1.3	18,379	1.7	21,178	2.2	23,557	2.9	8,955	1.2	13.0
Total principal transaction revenues	188,464	16.8	261,285	23.2	187,260	19.1	158,510	19.8	105,602	13.9	15.6
Investment banking:											
Underwriting fees	47,366	4.2	39,298	3.5	44,583	4.5	23,738	3.0	22,741	3.0	20.1
Selling concessions	72,725	6.5	75,997	6.8	80,984	8.3	44,280	5.5	35,237	4.6	19.9
Total investment banking revenues	120,091	10.7	115,295	10.3	125,567	12.8	68,018	8.5	57,978	7.6	20.0
Insurance:											
Life	32,593	2.9	27,222	2.4	23,505	2.4	20,674	2.6	18,252	2.4	15.6
Accident and sickness	7,028	0.6	7,007	0.6	7,299	0.7	7,374	0.9	6,933	0.9	0.3
Other	5,029	0.5	59	—	31	—					—
Total insurance revenues	44,650	4.0	34,358	3.0	30,835	3.1	28,048	3.5	25,185	3.3	15.4
Other revenues	51,089	4.4	33,187	3.0	25,446	2.6	23,212	2.9	28,361	3.8	15.9
Total revenues	1,124,216	100.0	1,124,929	100.0	979,253	100.0	800,629	100.0	760,129	100.0	10.3

Appendix E (concluded)

	1977 (52 weeks)		1976 (53 weeks)		1975 (52 weeks)		1974 (52 weeks)		1973 (52 weeks)		Compound growth rate, percent (1973-77)
Expenses:											
Employee compensation and benefits	$ 436,079	41.4%	$ 431,029	46.9%	$ 370,170	47.3%	$ 308,430	42.3%	$ 312,572	45.4%	8.7%
Interest	312,769	29.7	202,703	22.1	158,585	20.3	194,029	26.6	148,553	21.6	20.5
Occupancy expense and equipment rental	70,375	6.7	64,459	7.0	60,828	7.8	57,980	7.0	55,840	8.1	5.9
Communications	60,516	5.7	54,684	6.0	45,694	5.8	41,491	5.7	41,418	6.0	9.9
Brokerage, clearing, and exchange fees	36,436	3.5	38,476	4.2	33,969	4.3	26,752	3.6	29,941	4.3	5.0
Advertising and market development	33,557	3.2	26,039	2.8	21,674	2.8	17,481	2.4	19,451	2.8	14.6
Office supplies and postage	24,268	2.3	21,953	2.4	17,799	2.3	15,730	2.2	14,251	2.1	14.2
Insurance policyholder benefits	15,532	1.5	14,517	1.6	13,927	1.8	12,916	1.8	11,434	1.7	8.0
Other operating expenses	63,402	6.0	64,616	7.0	59,575	7.5	54,419	7.5	55,020	8.0	3.6
Total expenses	1,052,934	100.0%	918,476	100.0%	782,221	100.0%	729,228	100.0%	688,480	100.0%	11.2
Earnings before income taxes	71,282		206,453		197,032		71,401		71,649		(0.1)
Income taxes	27,335		99,845		101,341		33,866		34,921		(5.9)
Net earnings	43,947		106,608		95,691		37,535		36,728		4.6
Preferred dividend requirement	—		—		5		202		202		—
Net earnings applicable to common stock	43,947		106,608		95,686		37,333		36,526		4.7
Average number of common shares outstanding	35,147,074		35,389,834		35,595,107		35,917,361		35,738,835		
Net earnings as a percent of revenues	3.9%		9.5%		9.8%		4.7%		4.8%		
Per common share data:											
Net earnings	$ 1.25		$ 3.01		$ 2.69		$ 1.04		$ 1.02		5.2
Cash dividends declared	.86		.80		.59		.56		.56		11.1
Shareholders' equity	18.26		17.98		15.95		13.92		13.45		7.9
Balance sheet data (at year-end):											
Total assets	$ 8,094,599		$ 6,615,587		$ 4,879,012		$ 4,124,554		$ 3,815,571		
Shareholders' equity	645,867		632,072		567,471		506,002		486,775		
Return on average shareholders' equity	6.9%		17.8%		17.8%		7.6%		7.7%		

Source: Merrill Lynch & Co., Inc., 1977, Annual Report, p. 6.

Merrill Lynch & Co. (B): Its Struggling Broker System

Introduction

1   Until 1940, Merrill Lynch was a midsized brokerage firm whose most noteworthy achievement was surviving the Depression. At that time, however, cofounder Charles E. Merrill became convinced that brokerage houses, which had catered to the elite, had ignored a huge potential market. Merrill thus renamed his stockbrokers "account executives" and built a vast system of retail branches to sell Wall Street to Main Street. The firm used its retail distribution muscle to leverage itself into the leadership position in institutional brokering, trading, and investment banking.

2   Merrill Lynch remained the leading brokerage firm on Wall Street through the 1970s. During that period, the firm evolved from a product-oriented partnership to a financial market-oriented diversified-services corporation. They also dealt successfully with extensive deregulation of the financial-services industry in the late 1970s and early 1980s.

3   The Merrill Lynch of 1984 emerged as a publicly owned, financial conglomerate with a market orientation targeted to four principal groups of customers: individuals, corporations, institutions, and governments.

An Industry of Dynamic Change

4   The development of the financial services industry was determined by a

This case was prepared by Frank L. Winfrey and John A. Pearce II of the University of South Carolina.

line of important deregulation milestones: the Federal Reserve Board's removal of interest-rate ceilings on banks' large certificates of deposit in 1970; the Securities and Exchange Commission's 1975 dictum to stop the fixing of brokerage commissions; the creation of six-month market-rate certificates of deposit for banks and thrifts in 1978; and landmark legislation in 1980 and 1982 that cleared the way for interest-bearing checking accounts nationwide and the removal of the remaining interest-rate ceilings on bank accounts. These deregulation milestones combined with product innovation, government economic policy, rapid inflation, and historically high interest rates to produce a turbulent industry environment.

5   With market positions no longer set by regulation and with savers free to choose from a selection of investments, the financial services industry rapidly took on the characteristics of an industry shaped by market forces.

6   The first such characteristic was consolidation of resources as companies tried to achieve economies of scale. Two methods used to achieve these economies were (1) merging with similar institutions (see Exhibit 1) and (2) developing new services suited to distribution through existing facilities. A striking example of consolidation was the 1981 acquisition of Dean Witter Reynolds by Sears, Roebuck & Company, which combined with Sears's Allstate and Coldwell Banker subsidiaries to make Sears a retail financial supermarket. The creative development of Universal Life insurance by E. F. Hutton Life in 1980 was an example of a new service suited to distribution through existing facilities, since the offices of E. F. Hutton stockbrokers performed the function.

7   Specialization through the unbundling of services was a second new characteristic of the industry. For example, discount brokers emerged after the "unfixing" of brokerage commissions in 1975. Discounters offered a no-frills transaction service without advice, or a broad product line, to their customers. By forgoing research services, discount brokers routinely underpriced their full-service competitors, such as Merrill Lynch, by as much as 70 percent of the normal commission. In 1983, discount firms accounted for about 15 percent of the share volume generated by individual investors.

8   A third characteristic was a profit squeeze in the financial-services industry. Heightened competition exerted strong pressure on profit margins that led to an increased emphasis on each company's productivity. An example of the pressure on profit margins was the trimming of staff research positions among merged firms. Typically, when firms with research staffs merged, the new organization promptly cut back the equivalent of one staff, thus reducing costs and improving profit margins.

9   The consulting firm McKinsey and Company reported that the financial-services companies most likely to survive the 1980s would be either relatively large firms (assets in excess of $1.5 billion) with plenty of excess capital or relatively small firms (assets of less then $800 million), which would be able to move quickly into specialized markets.

10   On May 1, 1975, the Securities and Exchange Commission "unfixed"

Exhibit 1
Mergers involving Wall Street firms, 1981-82

Acquired company	Acquiring company	Date	Price ($ millions)
Bache	Prudential	June 1981	376
Shearson Loeb Rhoades	American Express	June 1981	1,038
Salomon Brothers	Phibro	October 1981	554
Dean Witter Reynolds	Sears, Roebuck	December 1981	607
Foster and Marshall	Shearson/AmEx	March 1982	75
Loewi	Kemper	May 1982	64
Robinson-Humphrey	Shearson/AmEx	June 1982	77

Source: "The Morning after at Phibro-Salomon," *Fortune,* January 10, 1983, p. 76.

commission rates on stocks. Over the following nine years, the average commission paid by institutional customers declined by about 40 percent, which meant that firms in the industry had to attempt to extract maximum revenues from other parts of the business. The source of these revenues became the retail operations, which focused on the individual investors. The fervor to expand and to obtain retail business flourished in what became a highly competitive environment.

11   While the industry exhibited an increasing concentration of capital through merger activity, the capital devoted to the securities industry actually declined as many firms diversified to other interests, such as real estate, insurance, oil and gas investments, and employee-relocation services.

12   Survival for the major brokerage firms in the new environment seemed to require firms to be all things to all people. The traditional mandate to the brokers to sell stocks was supplanted by a new priority to capture assets. The idea was to get as much of the clients' funds as possible: the risk money, the savings money, the sheltered income, and the insurance premiums. Revenues from such nonequity products grew from about 15 percent to about 50 percent of firms' retail income from 1975 to 1984.

13   The retail broker was naturally the one elected to market the new products, and the broker was expected to introduce new products to existing and prospective clients. The strategy was intended to work to the advantage of the brokers whose income would not be exclusively tied to the Dow, given their involvement with a satchel of diversified products.

14   The trouble was that the product proliferation created too many products for the broker to understand expertly. To exacerbate the problem, there was an ever-widening array of options, commodities, financial futures, tax shelters, financial planning, life insurance, annuities, cash management accounts, and money market funds. Virtually every large brokerage house needed its own expensive and elaborate support system to help the increasingly less-authoritative brokers.

The New Face of the Competition

15 Merrill Lynch had long been the largest firm in the brokerage business in terms of assets, revenues, and range of activites. The financial-services industry transitions that occurred from 1975 through 1984 rapidly changed its pre-eminent position, making the firm one of the new pack (see Exhibits 2 and 3). The new entities Merrill Lynch faced matched its financial strength and scope of activity.

Sears, Roebuck & Company

16 In late 1981, Sears became a major force in the financial services industry. The giant retailer augmented its presence in insurance and consumer credit by acquiring Dean Witter Reynolds Organization Incorporated, the nation's fifth-largest investment firm, and Coldwell Banker and Company, the nation's largest real estate broker. These two firms added to Sears's already impressive stable of existing financial services—Allstate property, casualty, and life insurance; mortgage life insurance; 87 Allstate Savings and Loan Association branches in California (with $3 billion in assets);

Exhibit 2

How Merrill Lynch ranks against its rivals (as of December 31, 1982)

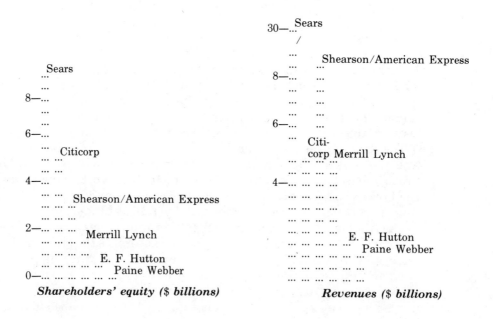

Source: "Merrill Lynch's Big Dilemma," *Business Week,* January 16, 1984, p. 62.

Exhibit 3

The score on the Big Five (as of September 30, 1981, $ millions)

	Shearson/ American Express	Citicorp	Merrill Lynch	Prudential-Bache	Sears/ Dean Witter
What they get:					
Revenues	$ 7,000	17,300	3,800	13,200	2,770
Net income	510	420	200	n/a	630
What they've got:					
Assets	23,700	121,700	15,700	67,500	32,700
What they do:					
Securities brokerage	**		**	**	**
Securities trading	**	**	**	**	**
Cash management services			**		**
Investment management	**	**	**	**	**
Commodities brokerage	**		**	**	**
Corporate underwriting					
United States	**		**	**	**
International	**	**	**	**	**
Commercial banking					
United States		**			
International	**	**	**		
Savings and loan operations					**
Small-loan offices		**			**
Credit cards, charge cards	**	**			**
Traveler's checks	**	**			
Foreign-exchange trading	**	**	**	**	**
Leasing	**	**	**	**	**
Data processing services	**	**	**	**	**
Property and casualty insurance	**			**	**
Life insurance, health insurance	**		**	**	**
Mortgage insurance					**
Mortgage banking	**	**	**		**
Real-estate development				**	**
Commercial real-estate brokerage			**		**
Residential real-estate brokerage			**		**
Executive-relocation services			**		**

n.a.—Not available.
Source: "The Fight for Financial Turf," *Fortune,* December 28, 1981, p. 57.

interest-bearing credit for some 25 million active users of Sears credit cards; automobile and boat installment loans; and commercial realty and store leasing.

17   The company's 831 retail stores, 2,388 catalog outlets, 1,950 stand-alone

Allstate Insurance sales offices, 348 Dean Witter offices, 87 savings and loan branches in California, and several hundred real estate locations clearly offered the Sears organization enormous competitive potential on a distributional basis.

18   Sears's in-house data base on consumer credit, by far the biggest of its kind, became the nucleus for a carefully targeted selling of home loans or financial products to prequalified Sears customers. The data base, data processing, and telecommunications capabilities of the company were also upgraded to provide a convenient nationwide electronic payment system capable of providing complete financial transaction services.

BankAmerica Corporation

19   BankAmerica Corporation skirted the Glass-Steagall and Bank Holding Company Acts which barred banks from markets and products that included mutual funds, insurance and securities underwriting, and brokerage services when it purchased Charles Schwab and Company, the country's largest discount brokerage firm. Because Schwab served only as an executor of orders and neither bought stock for its own account nor underwrote stock issues, BankAmerica was able to conform to the letter of the law. In acquiring Schwab, BankAmerica obtained a highly automated brokerage firm plus some 220,000 investors for its customer base. Beyond that, the acquisition offered a way for Bank of America, the nation's second-largest bank, to provide brokerage service to its 4 million customers.

20   In early 1984, Bank of America announced it would rent branch space to Capital Holdings Group of Louisville, Kentucky. Capital was an insurance holding company that planned to sell automobile, homeowner, and life insurance from the branch locations. A Bank of America spokesperson said the arrangement was designed to give the bank a head start in the race of commercial banks to expand into other financial services such as the insurance business.

Shearson/American Express

21   American Express's acquisition of Shearson Loeb Rhoades linked the Number 1 company in one financial field with the Number 2 company in another financial field. American Express was a unique financial house whose 113-year history had revolved around money transfers, travel services, card services, insurance, and international banking. Shearson was a brokerage house which had been developed through a series of acquisitions of old-line brokerages. The merger created an entity that could offer a plethora of financial-services packages from the combination of the American Express credit-card operations with 11 million cardholders, Shearson's money market fund and securities operations, Shearson's mortgage banking operations, Warner/Amex Cable and Satellite Communications subsidiaries, American Express Fireman's Fund insurance, and American

Express International Banking Corporation. Additionally, shortly after the merger, Shearson/American Express acquired the Boston Company, an investment management firm; Balcor, a packager of real estate investments; four regional securities brokerage firms; the Trade Development Bank of Geneva (one of Switzerland's five largest banks), an overseas banking firm catering to the owners of "flight capital" and other very wealthy individuals; and Investors Diversified Services of Minneapolis, a company that specialized in selling life insurance, annuities, and mutual funds to individuals, particularly middle class Americans. The Shearson/American Express strategy was to use the company's various sales forces to promote products manufactured by Shearson—Fireman's Fund, the International group, and the Travel Related Services group—to targeted individuals (see Exhibit 4).

22   Shearson/American Express made a distinct effort to change the image of its sales force to adapt to the new competitive environment. The firm renamed its 4,500 stockbrokers "financial consultants" and outfitted each of them with a private office.

23   In April 1984, Shearson/American Express agreed to acquire Lehman Brothers Kuhn Loeb Incorporated. The purchase was an expedient way for Shearson to strengthen two of its weakest lines—investment banking and trading, particularly in fixed-income and equity securities. The company was renamed Shearson Lehman/American Express.

Exhibit 4
Segments of the financial services retail market as determined by Shearson/American Express

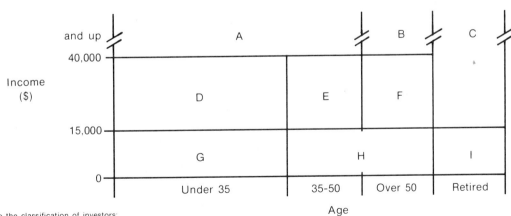

Key to the classification of investors:
  A—Up and comers.
  B—Affluent established.
  C—Affluent retired.
  D—Successful beginners.
  E—Mainstream family.

  F—Conservative core.
  G—Young survivors.*
  H—Older survivors.*
  I—Retired survivors.*
  *Denotes incomes below targeted levels.

Source: "Fire in the Belly at American Express," *Fortune,* November 28, 1983, p. 92.

Citicorp

24   Citibank expanded its activities into the retail securities industry when it began to offer discount-brokerage services at its 275 New York City branches. Some 600 of the nation's more than 14,500 banks offered discount brokerage services by early 1984. The Citibank discount-brokerage accounts were handled by Q&R Clearing Corporation, a unit of Quick and Reilly Incorporated, the New York discount-brokerage concern. Although Citibank had been offering such services as a part of its "personal asset account," Citibank's entrance into the brokerage business represented an expansion of financial-service activity by Citicorp, Citibank's parent.

25   As part of Citicorp's effort to develop a nationwide presence in the financial-services industry, the company purchased savings and loan associations in California, Illinois, and Florida, and developed industrial banks, which offered commercial-banking services except checking accounts and trust services, in some 22 states.

26   Citicorp, the nation's largest bank holding company, pushed the state of New York unsuccessfully for changes in state banking laws to allow it to sell insurance. However, Citicorp did achieve a position in the travel and entertainment segment of the financial-services industry with its acquisition of the Diners Club credit-card operations. In late 1983, Citicorp purchased a maximum allowable 29.9 percent share of the London stock-brokerage firm Vickers da Costa (Holdings) PLC and approximately 75 percent of Vickers's overseas operations, which included branches in Hong Kong, Singapore, Tokyo, and New York.

27   These services, combined with its traditional banking services, strongly positioned Citicorp as major entrant in the financial-services industry of the 1980s.

E. F. Hutton

28   In its 1982 annual survey of the 1,000 leading U.S. companies, *Forbes* magazine ranked E. F. Hutton first in the brokerage group in return on equity, first in return on capital, and first in per share earnings growth. According to Lipper Analytical Associates, E. F. Hutton had the highest production per retail account executive in the industry. Besides its retail brokerage operations, Hutton was also active in tax-sheltered investments, life insurance, annuities, investment-management programs, and Hutton Credit company, which specialized in Commercial paper. Still, E. F. Hutton chose to be viewed as one of the last basic securities business specialists. This was an image that Hutton management hoped would attract investors who felt stifled in the larger, less-entrepreneurial financial supermarkets.

29   E. F. Hutton was the first brokerage firm to enable its clients to access their account information electronically via personal computer or videotex. This "Huttonline" service allowed Hutton customers to tap into the CompuServe Network and retrieve any of their account information. The system

also provided a broker-client electronic mail link so that each could leave messages for the other in the system. This helped to leverage both the customers' and the brokers' time. The electronic system was seen as a major new way to hold down expenses and generate revenues.

Prudential/Bache

30   After the acquisition of Bache Halsey Stuart Shields by Prudential in 1981, the firm was renamed Prudential-Bache and reorganized into eight major operating groups structured around its various sales forces and lines of business. The firm offered more than 70 different investment products, including stocks, options, bonds, commodities, tax-favored investments, and insurance. A group of mutual funds was offered by the company through the investment management of Prudential, which represented a transfer of fund management resulting in a considerable savings to Prudential-Bache. The combination also produced several new investment products in areas such as real estate, options, and oil and gas investments, which were sold by both Prudential-Bache account executives and Prudential insurance agents licensed by the National Association of Securities Dealers.

31   Prudential, working through its Prudential Bank and Trust Company in Hapeville, Georgia, announced it would offer a credit card with a line of credit through one of the existing major credit-card networks.

Merrill Lynch

32   The 1983 earnings for Merrill Lynch rose more than 50 percent over the historically high levels of 1982 and 1981. However, this earnings pattern was threatened by competitive challenges resulting from the deregulated industry.

33   One of the essentials for competing in the new environment was a strong capital position. In 1972, Merrill Lynch's total stockholder equity was less than half a billion dollars, but by 1984, the company was above $2 billion. Merrill Lynch also continued to improve its return on equity in 1982 and 1983, though it lagged the industry average on this measure. Overall, it appeared that Merrill Lynch had the financial strength to compete on multiple fronts in the financial-services industry (see case appendixes).

34   Despite environmental transitions and increasingly direct competition from Sears, Roebuck & Company, Shearson/American Express, Prudential-Bache, Citicorp, and other formidable companies, Merrill Lynch moved deftly to innovate services and to defend and expand its markets. By 1984, it, too, had formed a state-chartered bank. Merrill Lynch formed the bank in New Jersey through a legal loophole in the federal definition of a bank by simply not offering a demand deposit service. The purpose of this new bank unit was to take consumer deposits, move into consumer lending, and offer unsecured lines of credit attached to VISA cards.

35   Merrill Lynch identified 38 products that affluent households purchased from 20 different financial-service vendors, such as lawyers, accountants, banks, finance companies, and real estate brokers. It then began packaging those services, creating total financial-care products such as the Cash Management Account (CMA).

36   The success of the Cash Management Account service was a star example of product innovation. The service went from 4,000 customers in 1978 to over 1 million customers in 1983. The significance of the product was magnified because it brought to Merrill Lynch a great many high-quality customers who had not previously done business with the firm.

37   Although Merrill Lynch's greatest strength was its retail system of 431 branch offices with 8,763 brokers, it had become a handicap as well. Because of its broad range of customer services, its compensation methods, and its full-service brokerage house culture, Merrill Lynch's approach remained very expensive at a time when discount brokering and other low-cost methods were gaining legitimacy and market share.

38   To counter the problem, Merrill Lynch began to convert its account executives into financial advisors. These advisors were seen as the hub of a network of salaried professionals and assistants specializing in insurance, lending, and tax matters. This new structure served a twofold purpose: (1) to upgrade, modernize, and reduce the labor intensiveness of internal communications and (2) to allow the company to gain control of the marketing and delivery function from its account executives. Customer communications and control of the client relationship were seen as a means for Merrill Lynch to gain the primary share of the profit derivable from a given product or service, thus permitting increased profitability for the firm.

The Potential for a Brokers' Mutiny

39   Merrill Lynch account executives shared four concerns with their counterparts in competing firms pertaining to the reorientation of the brokerage business:

40   An information overload developed as companies introduced new products and services. Brokers were expected to acquire a familiarity with the new products and new services in addition to their daily routine of 8 to 12 hours of selling, prospecting, environmental scanning, and transaction-related paperwork.

41   Many brokers maintained that their best clients resisted one-stop financial shopping, preferring instead to use specialists. Successful brokers did not want to dilute their image as brokers with their wealthy investor clients.

42   The new products and new services did not offer much, if any, return to the individual brokers. The commissions on selling insurance or annuities relative to selling equities did not warrant the effort and, thus, represented a significant opportunity cost to an individual broker. Some of the new

services, such as cash management accounts, did not even offer commissions, while requiring account executive time.

43   The increased pressure by management to sell the new products and new services made many brokers uneasy. Many felt that some of the new products ill-served certain investors. Those brokers recognized that the key to their long-run success rested in serving their clients well, not by pushing their firm's new products or services.

The Merrill Lynch Cash Management Account Financial Service

44   The Cash Management Account (CMA) financial service combined a brokerage account with other major financial services to simplify and organize most day-to-day money-transaction activities of participants. The CMA account was made available to investors who placed $20,000 or more in any combination of securities and cash in a Merrill Lynch brokerage account.

45   Idle cash in the securities account was invested automatically in shares of one of three no-load CMA money market funds (the CMA Money Fund, the CMA Government Securities Fund, or the CMA Tax-Exempt Fund), or the generated cash was deposited in an insured savings account. Dividends earned from any of the money funds were reinvested in the CMA account daily, and the interest on the savings account was compounded daily and credited monthly.

46   The CMA service provided investors with imprinted checks that could be used like bank checks to gain access to the assets in the account (both cash and securities). Additionally, a special VISA debit card issued through Bank One of Columbus provided the means to access a CMA account.

47   The program was set up so that a CMA account provided a line of credit backed by the assets in a hierarchy of cost of the asset, cash, money market funds, and then margin-loan (borrowing) power. These assets were accessible through either a VISA transaction or a CMA check.

48   The CMA program provided comprehensive monthly statements listing all transactions in the account chronologically. All securities transactions, money market fund earnings, interest on savings, and VISA and checking transactions were provided separately by category.

49   The innovative Merrill Lynch CMA account worried bankers and competing brokerage firms. The combination of a money fund with a debit card backed by a line of credit based on a customer's securities and funds on deposit proved to be an extremely popular product. Industry sources estimated that at least 6 million investors were prospective customers for these types of accounts, and it was reported that 1,000 new CMA accounts were being opened each day at Merrill Lynch. This phenomenal success prompted bankers and the other brokerage houses to start programs similar to the Merrill Lynch CMA account service.

50   Bache announced a similar product, the Bache Command Account, with

an added feature of automatic insurance coverage on the account holder through its parent, Prudential Insurance Company of America.

51   Shearson/American Express introduced a Financial Management Account (FMA), which required a $25,000 cash or securities minimum. Shearson's FMA provided an American Express Gold Card to its participants, and its monthly statement also provided a summary of net worth for the current month and on a year-to-date basis for the customer.

52   Dean Witter's so-called Triple-A program allowed customers to draw on their investment accounts using checks or debit cards with any idle funds automatically swept into high-yield money-market funds.

53   Citibank offered a "personal asset account" encompassing the same combination of money funds, credit, and range of banking and investment services as their competitors.

54   Paine Webber had only some 35,000 clients with its version of the CMA, the "Resource Management Account," in early 1984, but the average balance in its customers' accounts was nearly twice the $70,000 to $80,000 average in the Merrill Lynch accounts.

55   The CMA account marked a change in fundamental focus for Merrill Lynch as the firm made an effort to increase its large-volume retail business and reduce its exposure to low-profit customers. The president of Merrill Lynch's Individual Services unit announced that the firm no longer desired to seek small accounts for its account executives. Such accounts were to be handled in the future by a clerk operating in a client services department at each branch. This move was designed to cut the cost of servicing individuals.

56   In some parts of the country, as many as 25 percent of the Merrill Lynch stockbrokers switched to competitor firms every year due to the increased pressure from the firm to be more productive. In response to this turnover problem, Merrill Lynch began to use litigation to prevent its brokers from walking away with clients, or at least, to force them to pay back the $16,000 to $18,000 cost of their training. It was a particularly active litigant because it was trying to change the dynamics of the relationship among the firm, the broker, and the customers. It wanted its customers to think of themselves as Merrill Lynch customers rather than as clients of a particular account executive. This was a large part of the rationale for the initiation of the CMA service—to develop customers who would stay with Merrill Lynch even if their broker account executive moved to another brokerage firm.

Additional New Products

57   Sophisticated investors were chased by a pride of brokerage house felines in the 1980s: CATS, LIONS, and TIGERS. These were acronyms for a successful variety of zero-coupon Treasury certificates Merrill Lynch and other firms packaged for Individual Retirement Accounts (IRAs). Merrill Lynch also introduced a new stock fund tied to the performance of the Standard & Poors 500 Stock Index that proved to be very successful.

58   In late 1983, Merrill Lynch expanded its consumer lending activities by

the introduction of its Equity Access Account, a type of second mortgage which also proved to be very successful.

59   Merrill Lynch introduced the Capital Builder Account (CBA) in early 1984. The product was quickly dubbed the "Son of CMA," as it was basically a lower-priced and streamlined version of the CMA targeted at the more-modest investor, requiring a minimum investment of only $5,000, but it required customers to pay for each service above an allotted number of transactions.

Merrill Lynch Research

60   To provide professional, accurate, and timely research to its customers, Merrill Lynch assembled the largest research staff in the investment business. Merrill Lynch employed 94 equities analysts who covered 1,200 domestic firms, 200 foreign firms, and over 40 industries. Along with this vast breadth of coverage, the research staff was consistently rated as having the best analysts of the major brokerage firms.

61   Most of the men and women of Merrill Lynch's research division were finance-trained MBAs with operating experience from the industries they were assigned to cover. Merrill Lynch managed to attract and retain such talented analysts through a combination of factors: Merrill Lynch's prestigious research reputation, an attractive pay scale, extensive staff resources, and the computer-based opinion retrieval system (the QRQ System).

62   The Merrill Lynch QRQ System was an expanded equity data base which contained the detailed financial projections developed by the research analysts. This information was made available electronically to all branch offices at each account executive's desk. The data base contained current year, next year, and quarterly estimates of earnings; current and projected dividend rates; and the analysts' assessments of rates of growth in dividends and earnings projected five years into the future.

63   Besides providing fundamental equity analyses, Merrill Lynch's research effort employed 12 technical analysts who studied market data and produced technical market analyses, investment strategy advice, and fixed-income and government securities analyses.

The MRP Program
(A Personnel Development Program)

64   The Merrill Lynch Management Readiness Program (MRP) was designed to respond to the need to identify talented employees and to prepare them for management positions. The first step in the program involved a selection process in which several levels of management participated in choosing candidates for the program.

65   The second step, the participant's seminar and program kickoff, was a highly interactive event. The employees studied themselves and the or-

ganization and began action planning. Each participant left the seminar with established career goals and a development plan detailing skill and knowledge areas necessary to achieve the goals. The participant's managers were given tools to help them and their subordinates define development goals and activities for the six-month program.

66   High-level managers served as mentors and were given development activities with four assigned protégés. They met monthly with the protégés and used whatever information and instructional approach they preferred.

67   In the final phase of the MRP, participants wrote a profile, or self-statement, that documented their goals and skills. The profiles were then presented to a wide range of high-level managers throughout the company to acquaint them with the potential management candidates. In its first two years of operation, more than 83 employees experienced some type of positive job change such as a promotion or special assignment.

The Perspective of Merrill Lynch's Management

68   In addresses to the Los Angeles Society of Securities Analysts and to the Twin Cities Society of Securities Analysts, Roger E. Birk, then president of Merrill Lynch, and Donald T. Regan, then chairman and chief executive officer of Merrill Lynch, outlined management's view of the firm's strengths and basic corporate objectives.

69   The two senior officers listed six major strengths:

1. Merrill Lynch's leadership in diverse market areas.
2. The firm's top credit ratings and financial strength.
3. A strong sales force backed by sophisticated staff and equipment.
4. Merrill Lynch's ability and willingness to adapt to new customer needs and attempts to provide better services.
5. The leadership, vision, and experience of the senior management group (which was relatively young and thus well positioned to offer long-term continuity).
6. Merrill Lynch's strong but flexible management-by-objectives (MBO) planning system.

70   The president and chairman listed three basic objectives for the company: (1) to improve profitability on a long-term sustainable basis; (2) to soften the cyclicality of earnings—both within their established operating areas and through the addition of new services; and (3) to make each cyclical peak higher than the preceding peak.

Future Directions

71   In 1984, Merrill Lynch was attempting to automate the delivery of its

investment information. The firm bought a sizable interest in the cable television Financial News Network and had experimented with a two-way cable system that provided Merrill Lynch research through the Dow Jones News Retrieval System.

72   To expand its business information and business communications interests, Merrill Lynch announced that it planned to build a satellite communications center and office park on a 350-acre site on New York's Staten Island in conjunction with the Port Authority of New York and New Jersey.

73   In March 1984, Merrill Lynch announced a joint venture with International Business Machines Corporation (IBM) for the delivery of stock-quote and financial data to IBM desktop computers. The plan called for marketing the service to brokerage firms, banks, thrift institutions, real estate firms, and insurance companies. Merrill Lynch saw the financial information-services business as a means to cut its costs and generate revenue from existing operations such as its research and support units.

74   These attempts by Merrill Lynch to position itself as a technology leader in financial services were interpreted by analysts as strategies designed to reverse its recently eroding stature as the dominant force in the industry.

Appendix A

Merrill Lynch & Co.—Statements of consolidated earnings years ended December 30, 1983, December 31, 1982, and December 25, 1981 (in thousands of dollars except per share amounts)

	1983 (52 weeks)	1982 (53 weeks)	1981 (52 weeks)
Revenues:			
Commissions	$1,523,291	$1,132,898	$ 928,645
Interest	1,792,478	1,943,980	1,835,471
Principal transactions	675,527	656,212	427,879
Investment banking	746,638	595,515	359,881
Real estate	392,035	245,051	167,759
Insurance	116,371	116,471	116,313
Other	440,566	336,074	202,234
Total revenues	5,686,906	5,026,201	4,038,182
Expenses:			
Compensation and benefits	2,266,278	1,732,483	1,295,255
Interest	1,432,555	1,607,915	1,511,103
Occupancy and equipment rental	325,349	243,836	168,556
Communications	230,331	188,725	151,471
Advertising and market development	229,537	155,818	138,772
Brokerage, clearing, and exchange fees	143,824	121,645	93,578
Office supplies and postage	106,309	88,930	75,746
Insurance policyholder benefits	49,887	27,865	28,135
Other	356,514	303,739	242,151
Nonrecurring charges	153,500	—	—
Total expenses	5,294,084	4,470,956	3,704,767

Appendix A (concluded)

	1983 (52 weeks)	*1982* (53 weeks)	*1981* (52 weeks)
Earnings before income taxes	392,822	555,245	333,415
Income taxes	162,659	246,414	130,541
Net earnings	$ 230,163	$ 308,831	$ 202,874
Earnings per share:			
Primary	$ 2.68	$ 3.79	$ 2.57
Fully diluted	$ 2.59	$ 3.74	$ 2.57

Appendix B

Merrill Lynch & Co.—Consolidated balance sheets December 30, 1983, and December 31, 1982 (in thousands of dollars, except per share amounts)

	1983	*1982*
Assets		
Cash and securities on deposit:		
Cash	$ 223,353	$ 311,939
Interest earning deposits	577,302	584,229
Cash segregated and securities on deposit for regulatory purposes	358,179	363,661
Total cash and securities on deposit	1,158,834	1,259,829
Receivables:		
Brokers and dealers	600,137	734,015
Securities borrowed	876,703	464,665
Customers (less reserve for doubtful accounts of $73,920 in 1983 and $79,304 in 1982)	6,061,184	4,777,978
Loans (less reserve for doubtful accounts of $16,925 in 1983 and $11,250 in 1982)	887,732	615,397
Resale agreements	5,975,094	4,361,346
Other	1,298,755	967,811
Total receivables	15,699,604	11,921,212
Securities inventory, at market value:		
Money market instruments	2,192,726	1,545,781
Governments and agencies	2,450,424	2,058,036
Corporates	1,320,529	963,401
Municipals	864,404	804,264
Total securities inventory	6,828,083	5,371,482
Other assets:		
Investment securities	462,373	624,749

Appendix B (concluded)

	1983	1982
Property, leasehold improvements, and equipment (less accumulated depreciation and amortization of $180,722 in 1983 and $155,755 in 1982)	615,699	443,738
Equity advances for residential properties	372,957	412,363
Deferred insurance policy acquisition costs	99,269	87,953
Other	902,264	575,913
Total other assets	2,452,562	2,144,716
Total assets	$26,139,084	$20,697,239

Liabilities and Stockholders' Equity

	1983	1982
Liabilities:		
Short-term borrowings:		
Bank loans	$ 1,033,777	$ 501,738
Commercial paper	4,890,164	2,684,387
Repurchase agreements	7,609,198	6,237,890
Demand and time deposits	869,814	1,004,933
Securities loaned	593,386	800,601
Total short-term borrowings	14,996,339	11,229,549
Long-term borrowings	1,264,096	756,869
Total borrowings	16,260,435	11,986,418
Commitments for securities sold but not yet purchased, at market value:		
Governments and agencies	1,408,248	641,994
Corporates	536,934	585,572
Municipals	52,418	50,421
Total commitments for securities sold	1,997,600	1,277,987
Other liabilities:		
Brokers and dealers	394,777	541,576
Customers	3,168,070	3,123,700
Drafts	514,953	397,277
Insurance liabilities	129,537	84,937
Income taxes	143,275	295,594
Compensation and benefits	560,107	468,840
Other	1,082,311	1,088,028
Total other liabilities	5,993,030	5,999,952
Stockholders' equity:		
Common stock, par value $1.33⅓ per share; 200,000,000 shares authorized in 1983 and 1982; 89,970,834 shares issued in 1983, and 78,559,846 shares issued in 1982	119,960	104,746
Paid-in capital	419,551	112,191
Accumulated translation adjustment	(7,355)	(4,280)
Retained earnings	1,390,683	1,226,757
Total stockholders' equity	1,922,839	1,439,414
Less:		
Treasury stock, at cost; 442,089 shares in 1983 and 515,022 shares in 1982	9.314	6.532
Unamortized expense of restricted stock grants	25.506	—
Total	1,888,019	1,432,882
Total liabilities and stockholders' equity	$26,139,084	$20,697,239

Appendix C

Merrill Lynch & Co.—Statements of changes in consolidated financial position years ended December 30, 1983, December 31, 1982, and December 25, 1981 (in thousands of dollars)

	1983	1982	1981
Source of funds:			
Net earnings	$ 230,163	$ 308,831	$ 202,874
Cash dividends	(66,284)	(52,232)	(45,480)
Earnings retained	163,879	257,599	165,394
Non-cash charges:			
Nonrecurring charges	153,500	—	—
Other	237,652	168,465	161,513
Increase (decrease) in:			
Commitments for securities sold but not yet purchased	719,613	46,362	443,480
Brokers and dealers payable	(146,799)	258,360	(80,742)
Customers payable	44,370	648,272	161,510
Drafts payable	117,676	(253,163)	340,526
Income taxes	(152,319)	143,873	(114,814)
Compensation and benefits	91,267	195,092	46,237
Other liabilities	(5,717)	203,028	269,326
Other, net	(349,580)	(149,359)	(165,254)
Funds provided before financings	873,542	1,518,529	1,219,176
Increase (decrease) in financings:			
Short-term:			
Bank loans	532,039	(495,259)	(351,332)
Commercial paper	2,205,777	836,966	753,966
Repurchase agreements	1,371,308	324,605	2,765,822
Demand and time deposits	(135,119)	300,253	(37,159)
Securities loaned	(207,215)	259,323	(93,175)
	3,766,790	1,225,888	3,038,122
Long-term:			
Senior debt	623,910	102,733	134,701
Subordinated debt	(116,683)	152,395	—
Issuance of common stock	97,850	—	—
Sale of common stock under employee stock plans and conversion of convertible subordinated debentures, net of treasury stock and restricted stock grants	196,436	15,443	44,468
	801,513	270,571	179,169
Funds provided from financings	4,568,303	1,496,459	3,217,291
Total funds provided to increase assets	$5,441,845	$3,014,988	$4,436,467
Increase (decrease) in assets:			
Cash and securities on deposit	$ (100,995)	$ 247,052	$ (239,262)
Brokers and dealers receivable	(133,878)	395,838	(188,207)
Securities borrowed	412,038	235,157	93,287
Customers receivable	1,283,206	102,575	(95,562)
Loans receivable	272,335	269,679	(35,541)
Resale agreements	1,613,748	(66,980)	2,081,264
Securities inventory	1,456,601	1,158,716	2,155,794
Other, net	638,790	672,951	664,694
Increase in assets	$5,441,845	$3,014,988	$4,436,467

Appendix D

Merrill Lynch & Co.—Five-year financial summary year ended last Friday in December, 1979-1983 (in thousands of dollars except per share amounts)

	1983 (52 weeks)		1982 (53 weeks)		1981 (52 weeks)		1980 (52 weeks)		1979 (52 weeks)	
Revenues:										
Commissions:										
Listed securities	$ 852,920	15.0%	$ 650,385	12.9%	$ 554,512	13.7%	$ 630,876	20.9%	$ 421,887	20.6%
Options	166,712	2.9	167,487	3.3	125,564	3.1	141,960	4.7	80,023	3.9
Commodities	187,572	3.3	168,730	3.4	156,107	3.9	159,616	5.3	103,501	5.0
Over-the-counter securities	106,352	1.9	53,993	1.1	61,066	1.5	57,415	1.9	29,386	1.4
Mutual funds	126,730	2.2	46,595	.9	24,494	.6	22,309	.7	7,061	.4
Money market instruments	83,005	1.5	45,708	.9	6,902	.2	—	—	—	—
Total commissions	1,523,291	26.8	1,132,898	22.5	928,645	23.0	1,012,176	33.5	641,858	31.3
Interest:										
Margin loans	462,127	8.1	450,566	9.0	619,401	15.3	447,182	14.8	340,475	16.6
Securities owned and deposits	905,679	15.9	856,988	17.0	676,778	16.8	433,694	14.3	296,097	14.4
Resale agreements	424,672	7.5	636,426	12.7	539,292	13.3	249,999	8.3	178,177	8.7
Total interest	1,792,478	31.5	1,943,980	38.7	1,835,471	45.4	1,130,875	37.4	814,749	39.7
Principal transactions:										
Money market instruments	18,079	.3	23,163	.5	15,103	.4	12,263	.4	4,868	.2
Governments and agencies	45,710	.8	143,434	2.8	60,687	1.5	22,472	.7	17,387	.9
Corporates	399,430	7.0	289,308	5.8	223,285	5.5	210,205	7.0	174,136	8.5
Municipals	212,308	3.8	200,307	4.0	128,804	3.2	55,950	1.9	35,233	1.7
Total principal transactions	675,527	11.9	656,212	13.1	427,879	10.6	300,890	10.0	231,624	11.3
Investment banking:										
Underwriting and advisory fees	247,743	4.3	206,934	4.1	147,051	3.6	106,410	3.5	79,006	3.9
Selling concessions	498,895	8.8	388,581	7.7	212,830	5.3	172,768	5.7	83,647	4.1
Total investment banking	746,638	13.1	595,515	11.8	359,881	8.9	279,178	9.2	162,653	8.0
Real estate:										
Brokerage	272,980	4.8	160,397	3.2	100,555	2.5	39,940	1.3	8,586	.4
Relocation fees	64,951	1.1	56,863	1.1	45,209	1.1	28,729	1.0	28,758	1.4
Other	54,104	1.0	27,791	.6	21,995	.6	17,698	.6	15,679	.8
Total real estate	392,035	6.9	245,051	4.9	167,759	4.2	86,367	2.9	53,023	2.6
Insurance:										
Life	60,895	1.1	55,992	1.1	52,514	1.3	47,325	1.6	42,780	2.1
Annuities	46,975	.8	52,616	1.0	37,352	.9	13,426	.4	6,561	.3
Mortgage guaranty	—	—	—	—	20,251	.5	23,237	.8	20,867	1.0
Other	8,501	.1	7,863	.2	6,196	.2	6,507	.2	6,800	.3
Total insurance	116,371	2.0	116,471	2.3	116,313	2.9	90,495	3.0	77,008	3.7
Other	440,566	7.8	336,074	6.7	202,234	5.0	122,492	4.0	71,081	3.4
Total revenues	5,686,906	100.0	5,026,201	100.0	4,038,182	100.0	3,022,473	100.0	2,051,996	100.0

	1983 (52 weeks)		1982 (53 weeks)		1981 (52 weeks)		1980 (52 weeks)		1979 (52 weeks)	
Expenses:										
Compensation and benefits	2,266,278	39.8	1,732,483	34.5	1,295,255	32.1	1,079,283	35.7	736,728	35.9
Interest	1,432,555	25.2	1,607,915	32.0	1,511,103	37.4	879,002	29.1	638,498	31.1
Occupancy and equipment rental	325,349	5.7	243,836	4.8	168,556	4.2	123,817	4.1	100,671	4.9
Communications	230,331	4.1	188,725	3.8	151,471	3.7	113,610	3.8	90,025	4.4
Advertising and market development	229,537	4.0	155,818	3.1	138,772	3.4	101,185	3.3	60,006	2.9
Brokerage, clearing, and exchange fees	143,824	2.5	121,645	2.4	93,578	2.3	83,028	2.7	57,060	2.8
Office supplies and postage	106,309	1.9	88,930	1.8	75,746	1.9	53,752	1.8	40,014	2.0
Insurance policyholder benefits	49,887	.9	27,865	.6	28,135	.7	24,087	.8	19,554	1.0
Other	356,514	6.3	303,739	6.0	242,151	6.0	203,180	6.7	116,721	5.6
Nonrecurring charges	153,500	2.7	—	—	—	—	—	—	—	—
Total expenses	5,294,084	93.1	4,470,956	89.0	3,704,767	91.7	2,660,944	88.0	1,859,277	90.6
Earnings before income taxes	392,822	6.9	555,245	11.0	333,415	8.3	361,529	12.0	192,719	9.4
Income taxes	162,659	2.9	246,414	4.9	130,541	3.3	160,460	5.3	75,773	3.7
Net earnings	$ 230,163	4.0%	$ 308,831	6.1%	$ 202,874	5.0%	$ 201,069	6.7%	$ 116,946	5.7%
Earnings per share:										
Primary	$ 2.68		$ 3.79		$ 2.57		$ 2.72		$ 1.60	
Fully diluted	$ 2.69		$ 3.74		$ 2.57		$ 2.71		$ 1.60	
Average shares used in computing earnings per share:										
Primary	86,410,000		82,744,000		80,920,000		74,088,000		72,892,000	
Fully diluted	92,178,000		84,478,000		80,950,000		74,354,000		72,892,000	

Per share and share amounts have been restated to reflect the two-for-one common stock split that was distributed in June 1983.

case **11** # Note on the Deregulated Airline Industry

Focus

1 The U.S. airline industry can be segmented into three groups: major, national, and regional airlines. Major carriers are defined by the Civil Aeronautics Board (CAB) as those carriers with more than $1 billion in revenues annually. National carriers are airlines that have annual revenues of $75 million to $1 billion. Regional airlines are those with revenues less than $75 million annually.

2 In 1984, there were 11 major carriers in the United States, 16 national carriers, and over 260 regional or commuter airlines. Exhibit 1 presents a listing of major and national airlines.

3 Major airlines' operations can be broken down into international and national operations, but this industry note will deal only with national operations, since to include international factors would require the consideration of several additional complex issues such as exchange rate, political risk, and foreign governments' regulations.

4 Furthermore, only the passenger travel activity of the three groups will be considered. Other services offered by the carriers, such as airmail or air cargo, will not be discussed for two reasons. First, these other activities are not main generators of revenue, and second, there are other airlines which specialize in some of those services, and they have their own unique characteristics. Including an analysis of nonpassenger travel would not

---

This industry note was prepared by John A. Pearce II of the University of South Carolina.

Exhibit 1

Carrier grouping in 1984

*Major carriers**	
American Airlines	Republic Airlines
Continental Air Lines	Trans World
Delta Air Lines	United Airlines
Eastern Air Lines	USAir, Inc.
Northwest Airlines	Western Air Lines
Pan American World Airways	
National carriers	
Air California	Ozark Air Lines
Air Florida System	Pacific-Southwest
Alaska Airlines	Piedmont Aviation
Aloha Airlines	Southwest Airlines
Capitol International Airways	Texas Air Corporation
Flying Tiger	Transamerica
Frontier Airlines	Wien
Hawaiian Airlines	World Airways

*Braniff International was dropped from the list in 1983.

help in accomplishing the main purpose of this industry note, namely, to identify the broad framework of critical factors that have impacted the airline industry since deregulation.

5   Finally, data for the years 1979-1984 will be used to support the analysis, since these years reflect most, if not all, of the factors which affected the industry in its deregulation period.

Impact of Deregulation

The Pre-Deregulation Era

6   For 40 years, from 1938 until late 1978, all airline carriers were subject to CAB regulation, and four conditions characterized this pre-deregulation era:

1. Fares that were tightly controlled.
2. Competition that was restricted.
3. New service(s) that could be granted only if the carrier proved to the CAB that there was a public need.
4. Cost increases, such as in labor cost, that were passed by the carriers directly to the consumer.

7   As a result of these conditions, competition among the various carriers concentrated on services and schedule convenience. Furthermore, competition between national and regional carriers was minimal because regional airlines were largely feeder airlines to the larger national carriers, who would then provide the link that carried passengers to their final destinations.

The Deregulation Era

8   The passage of the Airline Deregulation Act in October 1978 set in motion a complete transformation of the U.S. airline industry. Among other changes, this act removed almost all market-entry barriers and fare control. Consequently, the industry became more susceptible to swings in the business cycle, leading the industry to a major shake-up, with various players and factors involved. The remainder of this industry note will provide detailed information regarding those players and factors. The discussion will be presented in a manner which highlights the considerations that were critical to the airline industry.

Political and Legal Factors

9   Before the Airline Deregulation Act, the U.S. airline industry was treated as other important public utilities—such as electric and telephone services. This meant total regulation of fares, of markets, and, consequently, of competition. However, the deregulation act enabled airlines not only to set their own fares, but it also allowed trunk carriers to eliminate services to marginally profitable markets. As a result, the route systems of all carriers were substantially restructured, and a number of new carriers entered the market. Specifically, prior to deregulation, the 11 major airlines shown in Exhibit 1, plus Braniff International, served 679 locations. At the end of 1981, these same carriers served 692 locations, but these locations represented the deletion of 132 cities and the addition of 145 others.

10   A company-specific illustration of the rerouting that took place involved Pan American World Airways. Between September 1980 and September 1982, its airlines operations lost over $906.9 million. Pan Am's stock went as low as $2.50 in 1982, bringing the company's market value to only $180 million—approximately the price of two new 747 airplanes. Edward Acker, the chairman of Pan Am, attributed the situation to several reasons, one of which was the disorganized, unprofitable domestic route system. Therefore, one of the first things he did when he took over the chairmanship in late 1981 was to rearrange Pan Am's dometic network to work mainly as a feeder system for the company's international flights from New York, Miami, Los Angeles, and San Francisco. By the second quarter of 1983, the

company was again generating profits. This example also illustrates how major and national airlines exited from many short-haul, lighter-density routes during the years from 1979 to 1983. The decreased competition of major airlines created some attractive growth potential for the various regional airlines, and in response, several regional carriers not only added routes but also expanded former routes and acquired larger, longer-range aircraft. Some even arranged with major airlines to provide reciprocal traffic feed and to share facilities such as reservation systems and ticketing. For instance, Dolphin Airlines, a two-year-old carrier, signed agreements with Ozark, Delta, Republic, Northwest, and American Airlines that included joint and add-on fares. Specifically, American Airlines agreed to take a passenger into a Dolphin hub city, and Dolphin would carry that passenger anywhere on its Florida network for $19.

11   However, the U.S. government retained control over other important aspects of the airline industry. For instance, the Federal Aviation Administration (FAA) monitored the safety of the airplanes and controlled air traffic. This power was enhanced as a consequence of the illegal strike by members of the Professional Air Traffic Controllers Organization (PATCO) in August 1981. As a result of the subsequent firing of the strikers, the FAA was designated to hire and train new controllers and to allocate slots to airlines because of reduced traffic in airports.

12   To a lesser extent, government regulations affected the industry through a subsidy program. The government paid a number of carriers to provide services for communities too small to support profitable operations. From June 30, 1980, to June 30, 1982, the government paid a total subsidy of $181.6 million. Of this amount, approximately 37 percent went to major airlines; 47 percent, to the national airlines; and 16 percent, to the regional airlines. Overall, subsidization accounted for 1 percent of the total revenue of all certified airlines.

Economic Factors

13   Bad economic conditions hurt the airline industry in many ways. For example, looking upstream in the industry, aircraft purchases represented multimilion-dollar capital outlays—amounts beyond airlines' cash capabilities. Attempts to enter money markets to borrow the necessary funds became extremely difficult and even unprofitable when interest rates were high. Delta Airlines can be a case study that reflects these problems. Until the end of 1981, Delta International was considered by many experts to be the world's most-profitable airline. But due to various factors, one of which was the general state of the economy, Delta's profits shrank from $146.5 million in 1981 to $20.8 million in 1982. Then, in its 1983 fiscal year, Delta reported a loss of $86.7 million, its first loss in 36 years. The 1980-1982 recession, combined with record-high interest rates, forced Delta to delay the delivery of its new Boeing 757s and 767s.

14   Delta was not the only airline hurt by the recession. Most major carriers, as well as nationals and regionals, experienced sharp reversals of their profit trends. For instance, TWA fell from a $25.6 million profit in 1982 to a $16.2 million loss in 1983, while Eastern's deficit grew from $3 million to $33.7 million during the same period. Only United and American Airlines generated profits. United went from a $4.4 million loss to a $109.9 million profit. American Airlines enjoyed a jump from $466,000 to $34.4 million in profits, largely attributable to the selling of tax credits. An even worse pattern could be shown if the national and the approximately 260 regional airlines were included in the analysis. With few exceptions, (for example, Southwest) the recession forced small carriers to remain in the red because of low traffic and high interest rates. This led to a total of $1.3 billion in operating loss in the years 1980-82 for all airlines combined, compared to an estimated profit of $200-$800 million in 1983.

15   When the U.S. economy started to improve, particularly in the second half of 1983, carriers began to realize some profits. For instance, the net income of Southwest Airlines for the first half of 1983 reached $13 million, up 30 percent over the same period in 1982. People Express showed a $4.2 million net profit in the second quarter of 1983, on top of an $3 million gain in the first quarter. Northwest Airlines, which had a net loss of $1.5 million in the last quarter of 1982, jumped to a $14.4 million net profit in the second quarter of 1983.

Price/Cost Structure

16   Profitability in the airline industry depended largely on a carrier's ability to control costs, particularly those for labor and fuel.

17   **1. Labor cost.** Employee wages and salaries were among the largest controllable expenses faced by the airlines, particularly the major ones. Wages grew steadily during the period of government regulation, but the carriers passed down most of their costs to consumers. After deregulation, however, the pass-through technique could not be used since passengers had the option of using cheaper competitors. In 1984, Air Line Pilots Association (ALPA) members earned about $69,000 a year for about 50 hours of flight per month, and mechanics earned an average of $30,000 a year, plus fringe benefits. In contrast, the new, small, nonunionized airlines could hire unemployed pilots to fly 70 hours a month for approximately $30,000 a year. In fact, labor cost represented 33 to 37 percent of the total operating costs of the major airlines in 1982. On the other hand, nonunionized national and regional carriers enjoyed a substantial advantage over the majors by keeping their labor costs in the 19- to 27-percent range (see Exhibit 2).

18   This cost differential was perhaps the main reason that small airlines were able to offer and sustain low fares for a long period of time. The new airlines utilized their cost savings to promote their low-fare strategies.

Exhibit 2

Labor costs as a share of total 1982 cost

Low-fare airlines

Muse Air	19%
People Express	20%
Southwest	27%

Major carriers

Continental	34%
Eastern	37%
Pan Am	34%
Republic	36%
TWA	35%
Western	34%

Adapted with modifications from: "Airlines in Turmoil," *Business Week,* October 10, 1983, p. 100.

People Express, for example, succeeded in generating more than $2 million in profits during the first nine months of 1982, while Pan Am, Eastern, and TWA were all in the red. The key to People's success was a cost base which averaged 5.3 cents per seat-mile, compared to an 11-cent average for major airline competitors. This advantage enabled People Express to offer a one-way ticket to Florida for only $69, thus luring passengers from Eastern, Delta, and others.

19   Another successful small airline was Southwest, which gained market share by controlling its costs while charging rock-bottom fares. Cost control at Southwest did not stop at labor costs. Its ticketing procedures were simplified, with 55 percent of its tickets sold through its cash registers, 15-18 percent through its vending machines, and the remaining 25 percent through travel agents. In contrast, travel agents sold 60 percent of Delta's

tickets and 50 percent of USAir's tickets, while charging a 10 percent commission. Such cost savings provided Southwest and other similar carriers an additional leverage against competition.

20   To compete with these nationals and regionals, larger carriers were pressed to cut labor costs, trim work rules, and increase workers' productivity. Republic Airlines, which lost $214 million from 1979 through 1981, bargained successfully for $73 million in 1982 temporary pay cuts and wage deferrals. In early 1983, Republic received an additional 15 percent pay cut for nine months, which translated to about $100 million in savings.

21   The threat of Pan Am's bankruptcy enabled it to obtain a 10 percent wage cut from its employees, saving approximately $110 million in 1983. In return, employees received stock-ownership and profit-sharing plans, which Pan Am's management counted on to boost employee morale as well as productivity. Pan Am also cut its work force by 5,000 workers down to a level of 25,000.

22   Western Airlines reached an agreement with its unionized labor in early 1983 to accept a 10 percent pay cut which translated to a $50 million savings. In exchange, the airline gave its workers 25 percent of the company stock. Even the financially strong United succeeded in persuading its pilots not only to defer two wage increases but also to increase their flying time 15 percent. In return, the company provided a lifetime no-layoff guarantee.

23   These examples have one particular common and unique feature—almost all the concessions were made in a relatively friendly and cooperative atmosphere. However, other airlines such as Continental Air Lines and, to a lesser extent, Eastern Airlines, took a confrontational approach. For example, despite an excellent route structure, strong marketing, and an efficient fleet, Eastern had serious liquidity problems resulting from high labor costs and an accelerated capital-spending program. As a result, Eastern's lenders disapproved the additional costs that would have been incurred from new contracts with IAM and the Transport Workers Union, which represented Eastern's flight attendants. The company then appealed to its workers, asking for a 15 percent pay cut to save $300 million through 1985. Eastern added that if the employees refused the proposed cut, the carrier would either go out of business—as happened to Braniff in 1982—or would face reorganization under Chapter 11 of the bankruptcy laws—as Continental had done only a few weeks prior. Pressures and threats from both sides made the disruption of Eastern's services imminent, influencing travel agents to avoid bookings on the airline. However, only hours before the planned strike was to have taken place, an agreement was reached. Basically, it called for wage cuts and the formation of a team of outside consultants who would study Eastern's books and records to see whether they supported the company's claims of near-insolvency.

24   Perhaps the most dramatic example of the confrontational approach

was provided by Continental Airlines. In 1982, the company asked for $90 million in permanent pay cuts and work-rule improvements from its pilots, and got them. Yet, Continental continued to lose money at a potentially disastrous rate. Five contributing factors were known:

1. Price wars that were ravaging the industry.
2. A weak economy and accompanying low traffic levels, particularly at Continental's main hub in Houston.
3. The competition from Continental's low-cost rivals, such as Muse Air, Southwest Airlines, and People Express. (Refer again to Exhibit 2.)
4. A poor marketing strategy.
5. Management instability.[1]

25   In combination, these factors led the company to report an $18 million loss in the second quarter of 1983, instead of an expected $10 million profit. Therefore, Continental asked its pilots and flight attendants to make up the difference. They declined. Consequently, on September 24, 1983, Continental asked for protection from its creditors under Chapter 11 of the Bankruptcy Code of 1978. An important aspect of this law was that it permitted the company to dismiss its union contracts. The financial impact was a 50 percent pay cut for pilots and flight attendants, shorter vacations, suspension of the pension plan, and tighter work rules designed to increase productivity. These cost savings enabled a redesign of Continental's marketing strategy. It offered a "price-slashed" fare of $99 between any two cities in the country. Continental claimed this fare would satisfy its cash needs if their planes could fill 40 percent of its seats. This meant the company had dropped its load factor from 65 to 40 percent, which enabled it to compete head-to-head against its low-cost rivals.

26   **2. Fuel Cost.** Fuel costs were the second most important element, after labor expenses, in the cost structure of the airline industry. Fuel costs for a single airline were as high as 34 percent of operating expenses, as was the case with Pan Am. This high percentage resulted from two facts: (1) Most jets used by major carriers were not fuel efficient, and (2) fuel cost was itself very high. For example, in 1981, Pan Am's fuel cost was $1.15 per gallon. Fortunately, however, by the end of 1982, the glut of oil in world markets, record high inventories, and reduced industry demand started fuel prices on a downward trend. In 1982, Pan Am's fuel costs had dropped to 95 cents per gallon. Exhibit 3 displays trends in fuel consumption and revenues and illustrates the downward trend of fuel consumption for the years 1975 through 1982.

27   In the area of fuel costs, regional carriers again enjoyed an important

---

[1]"Airlines in Turmoil," *Business Week,* October 10, 1983, pp. 98, 102.

Exhibit 3

Fuel consumption versus traffic for major carriers (monthly)

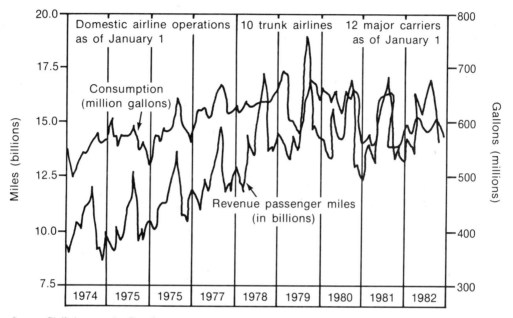

Source: Civil Aeronautics Board.

advantage over the major airlines. The cost of fuel per gallon was essentially the same for all airlines, but the use of fuel-efficient airplanes that seated from 8 to 50 passengers on economical runs of up to 250 miles proved to be a successful weapon in the small airlines' efforts for survival and market share.

28   The basic-niche strategy used by regionals usually involved providing services between major cities and airports that were underused or ignored. For example, Atlantic Express realized that people from New York's Long Island found it extremely time consuming to commute through New York's airports. Therefore, in January 1983, Atlantic inaugurated service from Republic Airport in Farmingdale to several major cities, including Boston, Syracuse, New York, and Albany. In March 1983, Atlantic Express's load factor—defined as the percentage of filled seats on a given flight—was only 10 percent. But by the end of July, its load factor reached 49 percent, its break-even point. For major carriers, a load factor of up to 60 percent was needed to break even because of higher fuel costs and less-fuel-efficient planes.

29   Perhaps an even more striking case was that of Waring Air. On December 1982, the company received certification from the FAA to begin business as a scheduled carrier. By the end of 1983, with only four, eight-seat planes, Waring had reached $770,000 in sales and a profit of $75,000. In most of its routes, only four passengers were required to reach the break-even point. However, no major airlines could obtain such results with their 90- to 150-seat aircraft.

30   In 1982, almost 20 million people flew with regionals whose aircrafts held fewer than 50 seats. In that same year, regional airlines served 817 airports in North America, compared to only 766 in 1981. In fact, about 65 percent of all airports in the United States were being serviced exclusively by regional carriers.

31   In response to such challenges, many major and national airlines tried to minimize the effects of their cost disadvantage. To reduce fuel costs, most large carriers decided to upgrade their fleets. Delta and Eastern Airlines, for example, retooled their fleets by purchasing Boeing 757s, the most-advanced and most-fuel-efficient jetliners in the world. Other national carriers, such as Southwest, emphasized the flexible, smaller, fuel-efficient Boeing 737-200, which became the world's best-selling airplane in 1980 and 1981, with orders of 106 and 129 planes, respectively.

32   As a result of such conservation steps, total fuel consumption for major airlines declined 8 percent in 1982, following an increase of 5 percent in 1981 and far larger jumps in the two preceding years, as shown in Exhibit 3.

33   An issue related to fuel costs concerned what economists call the substitution effect. They argue that the consumer is only willing to pay a certain price for a certain good or service. Once the price exceeds that level, the consumer will attempt to substitute a less-expensive product (for example, margarine for butter, vinyl for leather). The phenomenon also operated in the airlines industry. Since many airline passengers were tourists, there was a time/cost trade off involved in their decision to choose air travel over other methods of transportation. As fuel costs rose, the travel-time savings offered by air travel were increasingly offset by the dollar savings offered by substitute transportation modes. This specific condition seriously affected Delta Airlines. From June 1982 until June 1983, many of Delta's traditional Florida passengers chose to drive instead of fly. Since Florida travelers constituted 25 percent of Delta's passengers, the airline faced a serious problem. As a counterstrategy, Delta discounted approximately 90 percent of its Florida tickets, resulting in a very substantial decline in its 1982-1983 fiscal year profit margins.

Capacity Utilization

34   Idle capacity translates to lower income and eventually less profit or even loss. What made this issue especially complicated in the airline industry was that demand fluctuated around seasonal variations. For example,

traffic evaporated as schools opened, while business travel was at its heaviest from October through May.

35   From 1979 to 1984, capacity in the airline industry, as measured by available seat-miles, rose faster than traffic demand. As seen in Exhibit 4, the industry experienced a fairly stable load factor, while available seat-miles were constantly increasing. As a result, the average certified carrier was losing money. In addition, the rising capacity had an important implication for the industry's future, namely, that even modest increases in rates might further depress demand.

36   A widely used measure of an airline's ability to market its capacity effectively was the ratio between the carrier's share of total revenue passenger miles flown by its industry group and its share of domestic capacity—available seat-miles. A positive traffic/capacity relationship, meaning a greater share of traffic than capacity, indicated an above-average load factor and effective marketing of capacity. Exhibit 5 illustrates these relationships for the 11 major carriers in 1982. An important observation is that some of those carriers shown in Exhibit 5 had positive ratios and yet were losing money. The explanation was that it was not enough for airlines to utilize their available capacity. Rather, the prices they charged also had

Exhibit 4

Airline traffic statistics

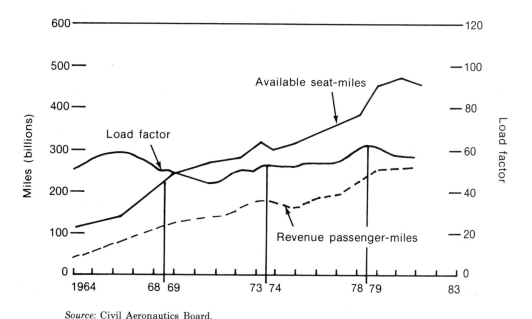

Source: Civil Aeronautics Board.

Exhibit 5

Airline market shares

Airline	Share of total revenue passenger-miles	Share of total available seat-miles
American	14.9%	13.8%
Continental	13.3	14.4
Delta	14.1	14.4
Eastern	4.8	5.1
Northwest	4.0	4.0
Pan Am	4.4	4.4
Republic	4.4	5.0
TWA.....................	9.3	8.9
United	19.9	19.1
USAir	3.1	3.1
Western.................	4.2	4.1

Source: Adapted with modification from: Thomas Canning, "Air Transportation: Current Analysis," *Standard & Poor's Industry Survey* (October 1983), p. A60.

to be high enough to cover operating costs. In many cases, sufficient margins were not achieved as a consequence of high labor costs, high fuel costs, and fare wars.

37   Another measure that reflected the underutilization of airlines' capacities was the post-1978 decline in the share of domestic traffic transported by the U.S. major carriers. For instance, in June 1982, the major carriers accounted for 87 percent of the revenue passenger-miles for all CAB-certified airlines. Before deregulation, however, those carriers accounted for 95 percent of the revenue passenger-miles. This shift illustrates the success of national and regional carriers in obtaining larger market shares and also partially explains the occurrence of fare wars.

Demographics and Psychographics

38   During the late 1970s and early 1980s, the Sun-Belt states of Florida, Texas, Arizona, and California experienced the nation's greatest population growth, enabling further penetration by carriers in these areas. In fact, between September 1978 and December 1981, the West and the South accounted for approximately 70 percent of the new stations added by both major and national airlines. This growth was more than twice that in the North Central and Northeast regions of the country during the same period. Houston, Orlando, Phoenix, Dallas/Fort Worth, and Las Vegas all showed substantial increases in the number of airlines and the number of flights serving their airports. Weekly departures from Orlando increased

over 50 percent, while flights from Phoenix rose about 60 percent. Airlines that were either creating new hubs at those cities or connecting those cities to their existing hubs were United, American, Southwest, Pacific Southwest, Delta, and Dolphin Airlines.

39   A psychographic-related effect on the airline industry was the preference organizations had for holding their conferences in warm cities, particularly during fall and winter seasons. Such high-margin travel combined with normal business travel to account for 50 percent of all passenger-miles, prompting many airlines to undertake aggressive strategies designed to increase their direct sales to associations and corporate meeting planners. The rationale for these actions were twofold. First, airlines sought to eliminate their excess capacity. Second, they wished to reduce the commissions they paid to travel agents and meeting planners. Travel agents, who sold more than 65 percent of domestic air tickets, charged a 10 percent commission on each ticket they sold. When airlines could save this commission, they could be more flexible in offering discounts directly to associations and corporations. The potential importance of these actions is suggested by the statistics in 1982 that showed that U.S. organizations held about 10,000 conventions and 707,000 company meetings.

40   Finally, demographic and psychographic information, such as birth and death rates, styles of living, and educational patterns, were crucial to the planning process of all airlines. Exhibit 6 presents an example of how one such variable, disposable personal income, could be used to improve carrier predictions of industry growth trends.

An Industry Overview of Competitive Strategies

41   The passage of the Airline Deregulation Act resulted in a massive restructuring of the industry. Increased competition and greater fare flexibility were some of the goals as well as the end results of the act. After historically controlling about 95 percent of the passenger travel business, major airlines experienced sharp (8 percent) declines in passenger-miles with accompanying declines in revenues and profits. New entrants enjoyed certain cost advantages over the major, well-established carriers attributable to the use of nonunion labor forces with much lower wage scales, greater flexibility in work rules, and more fuel-efficient aircraft that were much less expensive to operate.

42   Regional carriers also skillfully executed some innovative and well-planned strategies. For example, many relied on older airports, which offered ease of access because of their centralized locations. Regional airlines also attempted to select routes that did not put them in head-to-head competition with larger airlines. In fact, as discussed earlier, some regionals established co-operative agreements with major and national carriers,

Exhibit 6

Airline performance and disposable personal income

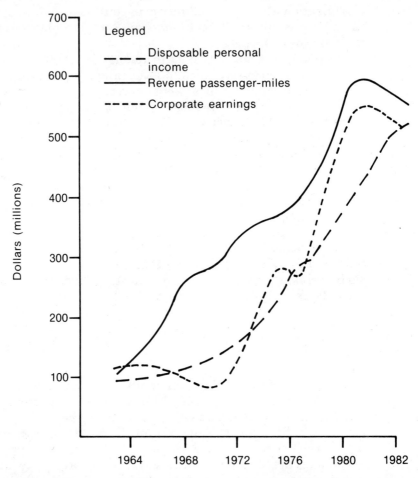

Legend

- – – Disposable personal income
- —— Revenue passenger-miles
- - - - - Corporate earnings

Source: Thomas Canning, "Air Transport: Current Analysis," *Standard & Poor's Industry Survey* (October 1983), p. A5.

such as working as feeders or by providing the last portions of trips for their passengers.

43   In many respects, the operating strategies of the national carriers were similar to those of the majors. Both emphasized hub areas where they had strong competitive positions as a basis for extending their operations to other profitable locations. Piedmont's grand strategy, for example, was to connect medium-sized cities in the Southeast with major cities in Florida,

the Southwest, and the West. Piedmont's success with the strategy resulted in a fivefold growth in net income between 1979 and 1983.

44   In contrast, the main strategy of the major airlines following deregulation was the establishment of hub operations. This requires designing feeder routes to bring passengers to a central hub, where they could be transferred to other flights of the same carrier. Some airlines, United and Delta among them, established multiple hubs to capture or keep bigger shares of strategically located airports or cities.

45   With the major carriers, however, differences existed in the way they responded to deregulation and the new competitive environment. One clear contrast can be seen in the experience of USAir and Braniff. USAir followed a conservative path by adding new stations gradually, by being very selective in its equipment purchases, and by stressing the suitability of its new planes to its primarily short-haul system. This well-planned growth raised the company's net income from $22 million in 1978 to $59.6 million in 1982.

46   In contrast, Braniff aggressively started 48 nonstop segments and entered 18 new cities in the United States after only two months of deregulation. As its financial position steadily deteriorated, Braniff took some desperate actions in 1981 and early 1982, trying to create turnaround momentum. Strategies included the sale of some of its fleet, the cancellation of new orders, the abandonment of unprofitable routes, and the restructuring of its debt with its creditors. Despite all of these actions, Braniff was forced to file for bankruptcy in May 1982. Following reorganization and after being acquired by Hyatt Corporation in Chicago, Braniff staged a downscaled comeback in early 1984.

Conclusion

47   As the first half-decade of the modern deregulated era drew to a close, several observations seemed relevant to strategic planning in the airline industry:

1. Demand was relatively and somewhat predictably seasonal.
2. Technological innovation offered increasing release from high fuel consumption. But new airplanes would require considerable capital expenditures.
3. With the industry life cycle in its maturity stage, the success of one airline seemed always to come at the expense of another.
4. Profitability depended largely on a carrier's ability to control costs, particularly those for labor and fuel.
5. Telecommunications technology increasingly threatened the industry as a substitute for business travel.

6. Mobility barriers were greatly diminished.

7. Low operating ratios, high contribution margins, and capital intensity all served as important, though partial, determinants of a carrier's profitability.

Recommended Reading

1. "Another Airline Price War Is In the Making." *Business Week,* October 3, 1983, pp. 46-47.
2. Dreyfack, Medeleine, "Airlines Battle for Survival." *Marketing & Media Decisions,* April 1983, pp. 119-26.
3. Farrell, Kevin. "New Airlines Go Regional," *Venture,* July 1983, p. 73.
4. Fenwick, Thomas. "Airlines." *U.S. Industrial Outlook,* 1983, pp. 44:6-44:8.
5. Kozicharow, Eugene, "Carriers Press to Cut Labor Costs." *Aviation Week & Space Technology,* August 29, 1983, pp. 29-31.
6. Ott, James, "Airlines Pursue Convention Market." *Aviation Week & Space Technology,* August 15, 1983, pp. 28, 29.
7. "Regional Carriers Facing Multiple Challenges," *Aviation Week & Space Technology,* January 17, 1983, pp. 28-29.

case **12** **Eastern Air Lines, Inc.: New Strategies for a New Environment**

Introduction

1 In 1983, Eastern Air Lines, Inc. was the third largest airline in the United States. With 37,500 employees and an extensive route system, Eastern boasted that it continued to be America's favorite way to fly. In fact, since 1980, more people flew on Eastern than on any other airline in the free world.

2 As Exhibit 1 shows, Eastern provided scheduled air transportation between the principal metropolitan areas of the northeastern and southeastern portions of the United States. Although Eastern's route system was predominantly North-South, it also serviced major cities in the West. In addition, Eastern provided air service between points in the United States and various parts of Central and South America.

3 Eastern operated in an oligopolistic industry. Actions taken by any one airline had to be taken in light of possible retaliation by other carriers serving the same routes. Since deregulation went into effect in 1978, significant upheaval had taken place in this industry. Surprisingly, many large, established airlines were having financial difficulties in this new setting while some new, lower-cost airlines were tasting success.

4 Eastern Air Lines, unfortunately, was one of the major airlines that was facing difficult times. In October of 1983, Eastern was on the brink of financial disaster. Despite its size and power, Eastern had recorded net

This case was prepared by M. Dwight Shelton and Larry D. Alexander of Virginia Polytechnic Institute & State University. Copyright © 1985 by M. Dwight Shelton and Larry D. Alexander.

Exhibit 1

Eastern route system

EASTERN

Eastern serves 128 cities in 22 countries throughout North and South America and in number of passengers is the largest airline in the free world.

From *Eastern Air Lines, Inc., 1982 Annual Report*, p. 31.

losses totalling approximately $287,100,000 since 1980 as shown in Exhibit 2. Some industry observers felt that Eastern might follow two other major U.S. airlines, Braniff International and Continental Airlines, into bankruptcy.

5   A key strategic issue facing Eastern and Borman in late 1983 was how to position the firm in a more competitive, deregulated industry. Did Eastern need to lower its cost structure significantly to be competitive? Could it focus on specific segments of the industry and be successful? Could it somehow differentiate itself to compete successfully against the no-frills airlines? Conversely, was the industry's future so bleak that Eastern should diversify into other industries with more promising sales and profit potential? At the same time, Eastern's day to day operating problems were so severe that short-term survival was becoming as important as its basic positioning in the industry.

The Airline Industry

Deregulation of the Airline Industry

6   President Jimmy Carter targeted deregulation of the airline industry as a top legislative priority shortly after assuming office in early 1977. President Carter appointed Alfred Kahn, an economist and expert on regulations, to head the Civil Aeronautics Board (C.A.B.). This agency had regulated commercial aviation for nearly forty years. Under Kahn's direction, the C.A.B. began easing airline regulatory controls in 1977. With the passage of the Airline Deregulation Act of 1978, the airline industry was

Exhibit 2

Eastern net income (loss)

Year/Period	Operating Income (Loss) in Millions			Net Income (Loss) in Millions		
1976	$ 96.7			$ 39.1		
1977	58.1			27.9		
		$326.6			$191.9	
1978	96.8			67.3		
1979	111.0			57.6		
1980	1.9			(17.4)		
1981	(49.9)	(66.8)		(65.9)	($158.2)	
			($123.1)			($287.1)
1982	(18.8)			(74.9)		
1/1/83-9/30/83	(56.3)			(128.9)		
Totals 1976 – 9/30/83	$239.5			($ 95.2)		

Source: Eastern Airlines, Inc., 1982 Annual Report, p. 20.

rapidly transformed. Before deregulation, competition had been on the basis of service and amenities other than price. After deregulation, however, there was full-scale competition on a host of factors, including price.

7 Deregulation changed the C.A.B.'s powers in a number of ways. From October 24, 1978 to December 31, 1981, the burden of proof required to deny new route applications shifted to those opposing the applications. Then, starting on January 1, 1982, the Board could no longer determine whether routes met the public convenience and necessity, only whether applying carriers were fit to operate on these routes. One year later on January 1, 1983, the C.A.B.'s domestic authority over fares expired. Until that time, a zone of reasonableness was to be enforced that was far more lenient than earlier price minimums that carriers could not go below. These price regulations were usually followed by all air carriers since they did not want to charge above the minimum price and lose customers. The act also eliminated the C.A.B.'s control over mergers and acquisitions, but carriers became subject to the same antitrust laws as other industries.

The Industry After Deregulation

8 The airline industry primarily transported passengers, cargo, and mail. During 1980 and 1981, passenger service accounted for approximately 84% of total air carrier revenues, cargo for 9%, mail for 2%, and other operations for the remaining 5%. In 1981, operating revenues were $37 billion; however, 1982 revenues declined for the first time in history.

9 The airline industry experienced major changes since deregulation. With artificial barriers to entry eliminated, the number and variety of airlines increased significantly. From 1976 to 1982, the increase in the number of airlines by carrier type was the following: 1 major carrier, 18 national carriers, 8 regional carriers, and 15 local carriers. In return, the increasing number of airlines reduced market concentration and the market power of the 10 or so major carriers.

10 New market entrants since deregulation were generally nonunionized, low-cost operations. They stressed high productivity and the ability of employees to perform a variety of jobs. This approach resulted in a lower-cost per-seat mile, the basis on which the new entrants successfully competed. Typically, they did not provide the same level of service as the older, established airlines.

11 Deregulation brought about significant changes to the industry. Significant route alterations occurred as airlines fought for the most profitable routes. While the airlines differed widely in their cost structure, the number one weapon they started using was price competition. While the fortunes of individual airlines varied greatly, the overall industry recorded major losses since 1980, and the trend was getting worse by mid-1983. Many industry analysts believed that this condition could not continue in the

long term. Airlines worried that a competitive shake out might occur that might force many airlines to go under.

12   In May of 1982, Braniff International Airlines filed for bankruptcy and ceased operations. Since then, it has continually discussed restarting operations; however, the earliest possible time would be sometime in 1984. In September of 1983, Continental Airlines declared bankruptcy and then restarted operations as a significantly smaller, lower-cost carrier. By late 1983, several other major carriers were on the verge of financial disaster.

13   While deregulation got its fair share of the blame for the industry's poor performance, other factors such as fare wars, excess capacity, and the economy also contributed to the losses. Regardless of the reason, it was generally conceded that the customers benefited at the expense of the airlines that were trying to maintain their market shares. Fares increased overall by 48% from 1978 to 1983; however, the Civil Aeronautics Board estimated that fares under regulation would have increased by 67%.[1]

Eastern's History

1928-1972

14   Eastern Air Lines, Inc., began operations on May 1, 1928 as a mail transport carrier on a New York to Miami route with several intermediate stops. Passenger service started on August 18, 1930, with various stops along the East Coast. Captain Eddie Rickenbacker, a famous World War I flier, joined Eastern as General Manager in 1935. During the next 28 years, he developed Eastern into one of the country's largest airlines. His overall plan was to join all viable eastern cities with the resort cities of the South. The impact of his approach was still easily seen in Eastern's route structure in the 1980's.

15   During 1961, Eastern launched its innovative air shuttle service between cities in the heavily traveled northeastern markets. This extremely successful service was unique since it guaranteed customers seats on a no-reservation basis. In fact, the Eastern air shuttle continued to dominate the northeastern business traveler market segment in the mid-1980s.

16   Eastern converted its entire fleet to jet-powered aircraft during the 1960s. Also at that time, Eastern began its commitment to be the first airline to use new improved aircraft. For example, Eastern was the first airline to place the wide-bodied Lockheed L-1011 into service in 1972.

1973-1975

17   In 1973, Eastern posted a staggering $51,700,000 loss, the largest in its history. Although the firm had generally recorded modest profits in prior

years, several factors combined to bring about Eastern's financial difficulties. First, its pilot productivity was one of the lowest in the industry.
This was due to fewer hours worked combined with high wages. Second, its
new L-1011's were experiencing significant operating difficulties. Third, it
faced significantly increased competition due to a merger between Delta
and Northeast Airlines. This allowed Delta, already Eastern's biggest
competitor, to enter many of Eastern's most profitable markets. Fourth,
Eastern responded poorly to a sluggish economy during those years. Finally, fifth, its management team was very large and used a disjointed management approach.

18   Operations improved in 1974 as Eastern's load factor, the percent of
seats occupied by paying customers, increased. Net income for 1974 was
$11,500,000; however, 1975 resulted in another record loss of $88,700,000.
Despite increased total traffic and revenue yield, load factors decreased as
capacity increased. Eastern continued to be an overstaffed airline with
excess capacity and a crushing debt load.

1976-1979

19   This period represented the best overall operating period in the company's
history. It was a dramatic turnaround over 1975. The four years from 1976
through 1979 were the most profitable years ever for Eastern as shown in
Exhibit 2.

20   Former astronaut Frank Borman, who joined Eastern as a vice president
in 1970, became president and chief executive officer in December of 1975.
Borman was generally credited with improving the fortunes of Eastern in
the late 1970s. He made and implemented several, key strategic decisions
that assisted Eastern's recovery. President Borman persuaded employees
to accept a 1976 wage freeze. He developed an innovative five-year variable
earnings program that diverted 3.5% of employees' earnings into corporate
investment. Its fleet of aircraft was restructured to improve operating
efficiency. He made Eastern shift its marketing emphasis to the business
traveler. Subsidiaries were disposed of that did not relate to air travel.
Significant cuts were made in top and middle management. Finally, he
took action to improve Eastern's customer service image, which had long
been quite poor by industry standards.

21   Perhaps the most significant change during the period was the new
image Eastern projected under Borman. Employee loyalty increased as did
customer service. Employees liked Borman and believed that he would be
able to lead them into a better future. During 1978 and 1979, the period of
early deregulation, Eastern's most vital operating statistics continued to
increase. New operating records were set as the company followed Borman's strategy of rapid growth.

1980-1982

22   Although 1976-79 represented prosperous years, these subsequent ones were filled with intense competition, labor problems, and increasing losses. Losses in 1980-82 totaled approximately $158,200,000. Although Eastern continued the strategies developed by Borman in the 1970s, external events largely beyond the company's control had a significant negative impact. While the economy faltered, costs increased significantly, especially for fuel. In fact, the increased fuel costs in 1980 and 1981 completely offset the economic gains the company had made by converting to more fuel-efficient aircraft.

23   The airline industry suffered during 1980-82 with operating-performance indicators down for most of the airlines. As Exhibit 3 indicates, several of Eastern's key financial and operating statistics declined. Although its revenues increased by $316,695,000 from 1980 to 1982, this was offset by the 4.7% decline in its load factor during that same period. Furthermore, the actual load factor failed to meet the breakeven load factor for each of the three years.

Exhibit 3

Key financial and operating statistics

	1982	1981	1980
Financial results:			
Revenues (000)	$ 3,769,237	$ 3,727,093	$ 3,452,542
Yield per revenue passenger mile	13.00 ¢	12.95 ¢	11.15 ¢
Net loss (000)	$ (74,927)	$ (65,877)	$ (17,358)
Per average share of common stock	$ (3.82)	$ (3.44)	$ (0.97)
Common stock and retained earnings (deficit) (000)	$ 255,274	$ 350,194	$ 435,456
Per common share outstanding	$ 9.87	$ 13.69	$ 17.21
Shares of common stock outstanding at year end	24,818,160	24,818,122	24,731,500
Operating results:			
Revenue passengers carried (000)	35,032	35,515	39,052
Revenue passenger miles (000)	26,140,147	26,107,611	28,227,015
Available seat miles (000)	46,143,756	46,789,684	46,028,393
Passenger load factor	56.65%	55.80%	61.33%
Breakeven load factor	58.76%	57.37%	62.23%
Number of employees at year end	39,200	37,700	40,000
Average flight length	579	580	563
Jet aircraft in fleet	268	278	275

From *Eastern Air Lines, Inc., 1982 Annual Report,* p. 1.

24   Eastern continued its strategy of rapid growth. After failing in an earlier bid to merge with National Airlines in 1979, Eastern entered into merger talks with Braniff International Airlines in 1980. Braniff's lucrative South American routes were viewed as a logical, important extension to the Eastern route system. Although the merger did not go through, Eastern still obtained the routes in 1982 for $30 million when Braniff declared bankruptcy.

1983

25   Eastern's financial problems continued to accelerate during 1983. The company lost $128,900,000 through September 30th, which almost equaled the combined losses for the previous three years. Concerns that Eastern might go bankrupt increased, and its lenders temporarily cut off additional funds to the company. Labor unrest increased significantly, and Borman lost credibility as he tried to balance contradictory goals of avoiding union strikes, appeasing lenders, and continuing cost-cutting efforts.

26   The U.S. economy improved as did Eastern's overall operating statistics during the first six months of 1983. However, renewed fare wars created a significant decline in the firm's revenue yield. This change resulted in a loss of approximately $84,000,000 in revenues during this time. The decline in yield was caused by the continual, intense price reductions that Eastern's competitors offered, particularly the new, low-cost airlines.

27   During this period, drawdowns were made on a $400 million line of credit in order to finance current operations. The increase in interest expense combined with debt repayments lowered the firm's cash reserves. So much so, that Eastern was forced in October to cancel the payments of dividends on its preferred stock.

28   In September of 1983, Borman asked "all employees to accept 15% wage cuts, effective November 1, and other concessions...as a last-ditch effort to save the airline."[2] He later threatened to close Eastern permanently or have it file for protection under the bankruptcy laws if the employees did not give in to his demands.

29   Eastern and its unions agreed to an independent audit of the firm's financial condition and also of its management strategies. Both sides agreed that the results of the audit would become the basis for joint actions to save the airline. In addition, management agreed to drop its threat of filing bankruptcy. In October of 1983, management remained optimistic that its position would be vindicated by the audit and that the unions would cooperate in taking the necessary actions to enable the company to survive.

Eastern's Functional Area Strategies

Marketing/Sales

30   The airline industry's product, or rather service, was a combination of items including the seat, various in-flight services, the route network, the airline fleet, and scheduling flexibility. The actual trip itself was a highly perishable service, since an empty seat on a flight could not be stored or recovered. In addition, airline service was often described as a commodity because it was difficult to achieve product differentiation.

31   Eastern's response to fare wars was to match competitors' restricted fares in order to maintain its market share. Restricted fares had various matters such as day of travel, length of stay, minimum time booked in advance, and scheduling requirements to satisfy. On the other hand, unrestricted fares were available to everyone without any such conditions. Since Eastern believed that unrestricted discount fares were destructive, it avoided initiating new rounds of price wars.

32   In general, Eastern planned to use some discounts to help increase the demand for discretionary travel, but wanted to maintain higher fare levels for business travelers. Eastern tried to structure discounts so they had modest but meaningful requirements, such as a seven day advance purchase. These inducements were offered in order to try to stimulate people to fly who otherwise would not.

33   The company also used its frequent traveler program to generate additional travel. This program provided business customers with travel incentives, usually over a specified period of time. It was designed to stimulate business traffic while building and retaining customer loyalty among those who regularly flew on commercial airlines by providing personal discretionary travel benefits.

34   Eastern also actively developed joint promotions that usually ran for a limited time. These programs tried to encourage price sensitive, discretionary travelers to fly by appealing to their needs for complementary products and services. Reduced prices (sometimes even free) were offered on services and products that Eastern and the cosponsoring company were promoting. Eastern estimated that its joint promotional program with Chevrolet, which cost very little, generated $70 million in revenues for Eastern. Furthermore, it was estimated that 75% of these travelers would not have traveled with Eastern without this program.

35   Coupons were used by Eastern on occasion to stimulate traffic on certain routes. Coupons were generally recognized as being very effective when the discount being offered was substantial. Generally, their cost was well

worth it when Eastern needed to protect its market share on a route.

36   Eastern also utilized a mileage-based fare program. This fare structure reduced the number of fare classifications and charges on a progressive rate determined by travel distance. Still, the longer the trip, the lower the cost per mile. Eastern's new fare program started gaining acceptance in the industry during 1983.

37   One major goal that Eastern had was to continue its leadership in the number of passengers boarded. This leadership was a major emphasis in Eastern's advertising campaigns. Eastern frequently used Frank Borman as the company spokesman on its television commercials. Borman's former celebrity status as an astronaut helped increase the public visibility and recognition of the airline.

38   The company emphasized travel agencies as the best method to distribute airline tickets. Eastern aggressively marketed its computerized reservation system, system one direct access (SODA), to travel agents. By early 1983, Eastern had placed its system with 1,275 travel agents, approximately 6% of all agencies. Since the company recognized the growing use of computerized reservation systems, it also joined American Airlines as a cohost on American's SABRE reservation system. That system was used by more travel agents than any reservation system in the industry.

Flight Operations

39   Eastern's flight operations in the 1980s were designed to achieve several key goals. One important goal was to improve its reputation as a punctual, reliable, no-nonsense airline. Eastern's customer service reputation had been very poor in years past and was still somewhat weak when Frank Borman became C.E.O. in 1975. Under Borman, however, many industry observers felt that Eastern's service reputation was improving. Unfortunately, Eastern's strongest competitor, Delta Airlines, had a long standing reputation for providing excellent service.

40   Route consolidation and expansion were two important dimensions of Eastern's flight operations. The company's approach was to continue expansion by adding routes that logically extended its existing route system. Eastern also consolidated routes through cooperative agreements with commuter airlines. These agreements generally required Eastern to provide reservation, customer, and other marketing services to the commuter airline. In return, the commuter airlines coordinated their efforts to route customers onto Eastern's flights. The company was also continuing its route expansion to Latin and South American markets, where there was significantly less competition.

41   Another goal for flight operations was Eastern's desire to have a very modern fleet of airplanes. More specifically, Eastern wanted to be the first airline to try new aircraft. This was pursued through its aggressive fleet

modernization program. By the end of 1983, Eastern had one of the most modern fleets in the industry.

42   While the first airline to launch new aircraft faced debugging problems, Eastern felt that it received an offsetting competitive advantage in the marketplace. For example, Eastern was the first airline to use the relatively fuel- and labor-efficient European Airbus. In another instance, Eastern even went to Boeing to discuss a proposed new B-757 jet in the late 1970s. Eastern wanted Boeing to develop an aircraft that would use new technology to reduce flying costs while increasing customer comfort. Not only did Boeing then build the 757; it did it to specifications that suited Eastern Air Lines.

43   Eastern's fleet composition clearly had changed rapidly in recent years. Exhibit 4 shows how Eastern's fleet stood, with its future deliveries, at the end of 1978 and 1982. The new B-757s and A-300 Airbuses were significantly lowering Eastern's operating costs. For example, the B-757s were replacing the B-727-225s. They used less jet fuel per flight hour and carried about 25% more passengers, 185 versus 149. Eastern's larger, older L-1011s were deployed on longer-haul flights, such as the South American routes, which required more in-flight customer service.

44   Eastern believed that modern ground facilities were just as important as a modern fleet. As such, Eastern had an ongoing program to improve its terminals. During 1982, major improvements were made at two North Carolina facilities at Charlotte and Greensboro.

45   Eastern had made various attempts to reduce its operational costs. Eastern continually emphasized productivity improvements in its negotiations with its unionized work force. In the early 1980s, it obtained a 6% increase in pilot flying hours and a 20% reduction in their vacation time. The fleet modernization program also helped lower operating costs. The B-757 required only a two-pilot crew versus three pilots for the aircraft that it replaced. Finally, Eastern was looking to its employees to suggest improvements in operations and quality. During 1981, Eastern established more than 100 quality circles throughout the company.

Finance/Accounting

46   Eastern's balance sheets and income statements are shown in Exhibits 5 and 6. For the year ending December 31, 1982, Eastern had total operating revenues of $3,769,237,000. Unfortunately, it had a net loss of $74,927,000 for that same year. In addition, earnings per share of common stock were -$3.82.

47   Debt had long been used by Eastern to finance its fleet and ground facilities modernization programs. This caused the firm to be one of the most highly leveraged airlines. As of June 30, 1983, Eastern's long-term debt was approximately $2 billion. This generated approximately $111

Exhibit 4a

Eastern fleet composition (as of December 31, 1982)

Aircraft type	Current fleet			On order	Scheduled deliveries (retirements)			On option
	Owned	Leased	Total		1983	1984	1985	
Four engine jets								
DC-8-61[1]	—	5	5	—	(4)	(1)	—	—
Three engine jets								
L-1011[2]	20	11	31	—	—	—	—	—
B-727-225	38	58	96	—	—	—	—	—
B-727-100	25	—	25	—	—	—	—	—
Two engine jets								
A300-B2/B4	23	7	30	4	4	—	—	5
A300-600	—	—	—	—	—	—	—	21
B-757	2	—	2	25	13	6	6	24
DC-9-51	4	17	21	—	—	—	—	—
DC-9-31	37	21	58	—	—	—	—	—
Total	149	119	268	29	13	5	6	50

[1]These aircraft are currently grounded following their return in December 1982 from the sublessee. The prime lease terminates in 1983 and 1984.
[2]Three of the owned aircraft are currently on lease to a foreign carrier.
From *Eastern Airlines, Inc., 1982 Annual Report*, p. 8.

Exhibit 4b

Eastern fleet composition (as of December 31, 1978)

Aircraft type	Current fleet			On order	Scheduled deliveries					On option
	Owned	Leased	Total		1979	1980	1981	1982	Beyond	
Four engine jets										
DC-8-61	—	5	5	—	—	—	—	—	—	—
Three engine jets										
L-1011	21	11	32	—	—	—	—	—	—	13
L-1011 (seasonal)	—	2	2	—	—	—	—	—	—	—
B-727-225	32	23	55	10	10	—	—	—	—	31
B-727-100	46	—	46	—	—	—	—	—	—	—
B-727-QC	21	3	24	—	—	—	—	—	—	—
Two engine jets										
A310	—	—	—	—	—	—	—	—	—	25
A300-B4	3	4	7	16	4	4	4	4	—	9
B-757-225	—	—	—	21	—	—	—	—	21	24
DC-9-51	4	13	17	—	—	—	—	—	—	—
DC-9-31	33	25	58	—	—	—	—	—	—	—
DC-9-14	—	9	9	—	—	—	—	—	—	—
Subtotal jets	160	95	255	47	14	4	4	4	21	102
Electra	2	—	2	—	—	—	—	—	—	—
Total	162	95	257	47	14	4	4	4	21	102

From *Eastern Air Lines, Inc., 1978 Annual Report*, p. 6.

Exhibit 5

Eastern Air Lines, Inc. balance sheets for 1981 and 1982 (all figures in thousands except share amounts)

			December 31	
			1982	*1981*
Assets				
Current assets:				
Cash..			$ 21,512	$ 14,795
Short-term investments, at cost, which approximates market			149,100	101,468
Accounts receivable, after allowance for doubtful accounts of $4,500 and $4,500			332,979	323,083
Materials and supplies, at average cost after valuation reserves of $32,368 and $36,767			180,803	184,742
Prepaid expenses and other current assets			28,407	19,509
Total current assets...			712,801	643,597
Investments and advances...			34,650	28,538
Property and equipment, at cost				

	Flight equipment	Other property and equipment	Leased property under capital leases			
1982	$2,080,085	$507,379	$1,251,748	....	3,839,212	
1981	$1,905,837	$461,793	$1,184,176	....		3,551,806
Accumulated depreciation and amortization:						
1982	$ 815,872	$241,484	$ 479,842	....	1,537,198	
1981	$ 808,387	$221,882	$ 403,956	....		1,434,225
					2,302,014	2,117,581
Advance payments for new equipment					116,958	119,938
					2,418,972	2,237,519

Deferred charges, net of amortization:				
Preoperating costs			9,589	7,976
Route acquisition and development costs			26,742	1,180
Other			22,133	15,709
			58,464	24,865
			$3,224,887	$2,934,519

million in net interest expense for the first half of 1983 alone.

48   Eastern continued to issue convertible debt and equity securities to raise funds to help finance equipment purchases. In 1980, the company issued 4,500,000 shares of preferred stock, which generated $106 million in new capital. In 1983, it issued additional preferred stock which raised an additional $47 million. From January 1, 1982 through June 30, 1983, the company also issued $63 million in equipment trust certificates. Eastern also used various federal tax laws, such as safe harbor leases, to finance a portion of the equipment purchases. For that same 18-month period, this

Exhibit 5 (continued)

	December 31	
	1982	**1981**
Liabilities, capital stock and retained earnings (deficit)		
Current liabilities:		
Notes payable within one year	$ 82,740	$ 76,650
Current obligations—capital leases	73,560	64,291
Accounts payable and accrued liabilities	459,426	442,985
Unearned transportation revenues	232,712	159,385
Total current liabilities	848,438	743,311
Long-term debt	1,053,567	815,868
Long-term obligations on capital leases	857,330	852,055
Deferred credits and other long-term liabilities	70,727	33,753
Redeemable preferred stock:		
$2.69 cumulative preferred stock—2,000,000 shares issued and outstanding (liquidation preference $50,000)	47,722	47,611
$3.20 cumulative preferred stock—4,500,000 shares issued and outstanding (liquidation preference $97,312)	91,829	91,727
	139,551	139,338
Common stock and retained earnings/(deficit)		
Common stock, par value of $1.00 per share		
Authorized—50,000,000 shares		
Issued—24,934,440 and 24,934,412 shares	24,934	24,934
Reserved—21,023,054 and 21,135,982 shares		
Capital in excess of par value	333,090	352,870
Earnings (deficit) retained for use in the business	(101,877)	(26,737)
	256,147	351,067
Less 116,280 and 116,290 shares held in Treasury, at cost	(873)	(873)
	255,274	350,194
	$3,224,887	$2,934,519

From *Eastern Air Lines, Inc., 1982 Annual Report*, pp. 12–13.

tactic provided about $85 million, with another $92 million anticipated in the second half of 1983.

49   In light of its financial results, cash position, and status with its creditors, short-term survival was a pressing problem for Eastern in 1983. Fortunately for Eastern, a company must declare bankruptcy only when it can no longer pay its bills, not merely because its financial statements show sizable losses. Eastern's cash equivalent assets in 1983 were at roughly the same level as in the prior two years.

50   Eastern's survival in the long run with its current financing structure was questionable. Its high-debt load brought about a high interest expense that represented an ongoing drain on its cash reserves. Eastern was drawing down on its $400 million line of credit in 1983. If this resource was exhausted, or withdrawn by lenders, securing additional financing might be a major challenge.

Exhibit 6

Eastern Air Lines, Inc., statement of operations and earnings (deficit) retained for use in the business (all amounts in thousands except per share amounts)

	1982	1981	1980
Operating revenues:			
Passenger	$3,406,009	$3,386,731	$3,151,798
Cargo	180,022	178,193	163,472
Incidental and other revenues	183,206	162,169	137,272
Total operating revenues	3,769,237	3,727,093	3,452,542
Operating expenses:			
Salaries, wages and benefits	1,386,257	1,347,486	1,274,211
Aircraft fuel	1,032,935	1,141,434	1,029,026
Aircraft maintenance materials and repairs	96,330	102,476	107,522
Rentals and landing fees	154,090	141,052	109,375
Passenger food and supplies	136,116	129,368	125,987
Commissions	220,467	195,475	158,345
Advertising and promotional	81,144	70,782	63,191
Depreciation and amortization	224,882	229,071	200,572
Other operating expenses	455,796	419,898	382,456
Total operating expenses	3,788,017	3,777,042	3,450,685
Operating profit (loss)	(18,780)	(49,949)	1,857
Non-operating income and (expense):			
Interest income	27,784	44,839	41,118
Interest expense (net of interest capitalized in the amounts of $18,320, $12,431 and $10,276)	(178,274)	(141,234)	(109,836)
Profit on sale of equipment	32,735	36,562	17,886
Gain on sale of tax benefits	51,279	29,825	—
Other, net	10,329	14,080	2,708
Total	(56,147)	(15,928)	(48,124)
Loss before income taxes and extraordinary item	(74,927)	(65,877)	(46,267)
(Reduction in) income taxes	—	—	(4,255)
Loss before extraordinary item	(74,927)	(65,877)	(42,012)
Extraordinary item—net of a provision in lieu of income taxes of $2,498	—	—	24,654
Net loss	(74,927)	(65,877)	(17,358)
Earnings (deficit) retained for use in the business:			
Balance at beginning of year	(26,737)	56,255	78,273
Gain (loss) on distribution of Treasury Stock to employees	—	77	(529)
Amortization of excess of redemption value of preferred stock over carrying value	(213)	(185)	(96)
Cash dividends—preferred stock, net of $19,780, $2,973, and zero charged to capital in excess of par value	—	(17,007)	(4,035)
Balance at end of year	$ (101,877)	$ (26,737)	$ 56,255
Earnings per common share:			
Loss before extraordinary item	$ (3.82)	$ (3.44)	$ (1.96)
Extraordinary item	—	—	.99
Net loss	$ (3.82)	$ (3.44)	$ (0.97)
Fully diluted earnings per common share:			
Loss before extraordinary item	*	*	*
Extraordinary item			
Net loss			

*Anti-dilutive.

From *Eastern Air Lines, Inc., 1982 Annual Report*, p. 14.

Human Resources/Labor Relations

51   A significant portion of Eastern's human resource management effort involved with powerful labor unions. Approximately 22,500 of its 37,500 employees were union members. Eastern's approach in negotiations was to present its earnings and financial situation openly to the unions and all its employees. It then asked employees to share in the financial burden through salary freezes, cuts, and/or wage-deferral plans. This approach had been employed continually since 1976. Overall, these tactics had worked well for Eastern. Its success was attributed to its employees' fear of losing their jobs and the employees' loyalty to Frank Borman.

52   Perhaps Eastern's best known wage tactic was its variable earnings program. This five-year program was developed in 1977 to assist the airline with its financing problems. Under the program, employees left 3.5% of their gross pay with the company. The money was retained for investment purposes and paid back to employees only if a 2% sales profit level was achieved.

53   During 1983, Eastern faced strike threats from two unions. Management talked tough to the unions but then settled before the strike deadline. Management settled before the contract expired because it did not believe the firm could survive a major strike, especially given its weak financial position. Still, the company obtained concessions from its pilots and non-union employees. They accepted a securities-for-pay program in lieu of wage increases for 1983 and 1984. Nonunion employees also participated in the program on a voluntary basis.

54   Eastern, like most other airlines except Delta, laid off employees during economic recessions to reduce labor costs. Surprisingly, Eastern even laid off 1,600 employees after a new union contract had been signed in 1983. Management furloughed these employees three hours after a new machinists' contract was approved to counter higher labor costs.

55   Eastern also provided extensive training, particularly for its pilots and maintenance workers. This training emphasized how to use and maintain its new aircraft, which arrived frequently.

Management/Leadership

56   Eastern's management relied heavily on a strong, well-known public figure for leadership. Frank Borman's image as a "no-smoking, no-drinking, no-nonsense boss" generated significant employee loyalty.[3] Known as the colonel, Borman was the key reason the company pursued its growth objective, which he had earlier formulated. Borman's image extended beyond the corporate headquarters. For example, Eastern's ability to obtain financing for fleet modernization had been partially credited to Borman's ability to generate confidence among its creditors.

57   His high-growth objective was backed up by several supporting strategies to help implement it. While many of them were discussed earlier, two additional strategies helped pursue the high-growth objective. One strategy was that Eastern might seek to merge with another airline in order to improve its market standing, equipment, and/or financial position. The other strategy was Eastern's decision to concentrate only on the airline business. In fact, restaurant and hotel subsidiaries acquired in earlier years were sold soon after Borman's appointment as C.E.O.

58   Eastern strategy to remain a large airline was confirmed by Borman in 1983. He noted, "We're not interested in becoming 75% smaller. What we're interested in doing is lowering our unit costs so that we can be successful in very difficult economic times."[4]

59   While Frank Borman was recognized as the strong leader that Eastern needed, his leadership was being questioned in the mid-1980s. Besides his loss of trust among rank and file unionized employees, his credibility as a manager was also on the line. In 1983, some of his key managers questioned Borman's ability to lead the firm out of its current crisis.

60   Responding to comments about his management and leadership abilities, Borman pointed to recent performance when Eastern's operating loss for the twelve months ending June 30, 1983 was $50.1 million as compared to rival Delta Airlines' $207.3 million loss. This was the best performance that Eastern ever had against Delta.

61   However, rumors circulated in October of 1983 that Borman might step down as the head of Eastern. When asked about the resignation rumors, Borman replied, "Why should I resign? I'm not going to resign. I have no intention of resigning. I don't know why everyone speculates on that. Look, this is not a management problem." He added, "I am not at all ashamed of our performance."[5]

Industry Structure

62   The airline industry was made up of three basic types of airlines. They were majors, nationals, and regionals, all of which existed on a continuum. Major airlines flew most domestic routes, and had annual revenues of at least $1 billion. Examples of major carriers included Eastern, American, Delta, and United.

63   National airlines comprised a wide variety of carriers that had annual revenues between $75 million and $1 billion. The national airlines operated similarly to major carriers. Since deregulation, they were able to enter long-haul routes that were almost exclusively served by the majors. Examples of this type of airline included Frontier, Ozark, and Southwest Airlines.

64   Regionals were the third type of airlines. Many of these new airlines were a direct result of the deregulation era. These airlines typically oper-

ated round-trip service between two or more points, unencumbered by the complex network of routes that full service airlines offered. The major attraction of these carriers was their low cost. Typically, their fares were 40% to 50% below full price fares. People's Express, Midway, and New York Airlines were typical examples of regional carriers.

Competitor Profiles

American Airlines

65   Although American Airlines was the second largest U.S. airline, it lost $20 million during 1982. It had a reputation as a first class, customer-oriented airline. American was led by Robert Crandall, a tough, aggressive president. Under Crandall, American had done the following: (1) strengthened existing hubs and built new ones, (2) significantly reduced its cost structure, (3) maintained personalized, full customer service, (4) abandoned unprofitable routes, which were primarily in the Northeast, and (5) marketed its product aggressively.[6]

66   American was a recognized leader in marketing. It pioneered the successful frequent flier program. In addition, its computerized reservation system, Sabre, led the market and was placed in approximately 39% of all U.S. travel agencies. Being first in these areas had given American significant marketing advantages.

67   American was a financially stable airline in comparison to most of the major carriers. Still, its debt and cost structures were relatively high. American's fleet was much older than the average airline, and it was uncertain if sufficient capital could be raised to modernize its fleet.

68   In 1983, American achieved major victories in its efforts to reduce its cost structure. It obtained cost-cutting contracts with its pilots, flight attendants, and machinist unions. American's management felt that these agreements would eventually reduce its cost-per-seat mile to 6.5¢. This rate would be comparable to the costs of the low-cost airlines.

69   American Airlines proposed a mileage-based fare program in 1983. Its various rate classifications were reduced to four basic fares plus a business traveler classification. American's new fare structure was designed to simplify its fare structures and to increase revenue yield. Several other airlines, including Eastern, had similar mileage-based fare programs. Even United Airlines was able to reduce substantially the number of different fares it offered when it adopted this format.

70   American's success in achieving cost reductions spurred it to announce planned route expansions. It even hoped to overtake United as the number one airline eventually.

Delta Airlines

71   Delta Airlines had consistently been the most profitable U.S. airline. Headquartered in its central hub in Atlanta, Delta's strength was in the Southeast. By 1983, however, its route structure covered almost all of the United States. From 1947 through mid-1982, Delta had never recorded a loss. From 1971 through 1980, Delta's earnings totaled $857 million, almost twice that of United Airlines, the world's largest airline.

72   Delta's success was attributed to a variety of factors. They included the following: (1) excellent long range planning and a willingness to adhere to these plans during lean times, (2) excellent wages and benefits plus a no-layoff policy, which kept it the least unionized major airline, (3) high employee productivity obtained by asking people to perform various jobs during the day, (4) a highly trained management team of generalists that used consensus decision making, (5) an efficient hub and spoke system, and (6) a low debt level. Delta had traditionally been Eastern's biggest rival, and, since deregulation, Eastern competed on about 80% of Delta's same routes.

73   Despite its strengths, even Delta had begun to encounter the full impact of deregulation and a sluggish economy. For the fiscal year ending June 30, 1983, Delta recorded a rare loss of $87 million. This set back caused Delta to reconsider some of its strategies for the future. It moved to reduce its cost structure by freezing nonunion workers' salaries for 1983-84, and requesting its union employees to do the same. Delta's salaries and fringe benefits' costs, which were 42% of total expenses, had gotten too big for even it to handle. This occurred despite its high employee productivity achieved by treating employees like family and shifting them around during the day when they were needed elsewhere.

74   Delta was trying to give more emphasis to marketing, an area that had long been regarded as a weak part of its operations. It adopted a much more aggressive pricing strategy of not being undersold in any market. In addition, Delta was making up for lost time in another area by developing and marketing its own automated reservation system. If Delta could significantly improve its marketing strategies, it would become an even stronger force to be contended with in the future.

Continental Airlines

75   In January of 1983, Continental Airlines was the eighth largest U.S. airline. With its central hub in Houston, it serviced a large portion of the United States and some foreign countries. However, the impact of deregulation coupled with a maturing industry had been very tough on Continental. From 1978 through the third quarter of 1983, Continental Airlines

posted losses totaling approximately $500 million.

76   Since his appointment as Continental's Chairman in 1980, Frank Lorenzo had been striving for wage concessions and other cost cuts. He hoped to convert Continental to a low-cost carrier. In a surprise move on September 24, 1983, however, Continental filed for bankruptcy under Chapter 11. Under the protection of the courts, Continental restarted operations with only one-half of its planes flying and one-third of its prior work force. Returning employees received significant pay cuts and changed work rules. Pilots were forced to accept 50% pay cuts, a 57% increase in flying time, and the loss of seniority and protective work rules. Continental management stated that these changes would allow it to reduce its cost structure by 25%, making it competitive with other airlines.

77   Although Continental was not technically out of cash on September 24th, company officials said that it would have ceased operations very soon without the bankruptcy action. However, some industry observers felt that the company's actions were designed to void its union contracts. Not surprisingly, Continental's unions went to court to try to reverse the bankruptcy filing. They charged that the filing was an improper use of the bankruptcy laws. However, they eventually lost out in their legal efforts; thus, Continental continued to operate with significantly lower costs.

78   The costs of the bankruptcy filing were high for Continental in terms of travel agent confidence, employee morale, and customer loyalty. In addition, the unions went on strike on October 1, 1983, an action that hampered Continental quite a bit.

79   Still, Continental survived the early restart-up period and continued to operate on a reduced scale. Lorenzo immediately stated that the new Continental would be at 80-90% of its previous flights by the spring of 1984. Its flights were operating at 67% capacity as of October 30, 1983 as compared to a pre-filing level of less than 50%. Lorenzo believed that Continental was ready to compete successfully in the deregulated environment as 1983 came to a close.

Piedmont Airlines

80   Piedmont Airlines, which started operations as an air freight carrier after World War II, later evolved under regulation into a regional airline serving several large cities on the east coast and in the midwest. In addition, Piedmont served numerous smaller communities with air transportation to and from larger airports.

81   Under deregulation, however, Piedmont had significantly expanded and became a national carrier in the early 1980s. Piedmont used secondary markets such as Charlotte, North Carolina, and Dayton, Ohio as hub cities. This reduced the likelihood of customers transferring to competing airlines to continue on to their destination city. In addition, it had entered new long-haul markets that were consistent with its existing route struc-

ture while eliminating some unprofitable, short commuter routes. These marketing strategies helped Piedmont achieve record earnings in 1981 of $33 million.

82   Piedmont had been profitable in every year since deregulation. Its total earnings during the 1978-82 period were about $96 million. Piedmont's successful performance was also partially attributed to (1) record performances in revenue passenger miles, the number of passengers boarded, and seating capacity, (2) a fuel-efficient fleet properly designed for its route system, and (3) high employee productivity, due in part to a high percentage of nonunion workers.

People's Express

83   People's Express was the role model of a new low-cost, no-frills airline. Started in only April of 1981, it began service between Newark, New Jersey and the surrounding cities. By the end of 1981, it was flying thirteen planes to ten outlying locations. Since its strategy of providing high frequency, low-cost service to New York had worked well, People's Express expanded operations to other regions and markets. The airline had such ambitious growth plans that it expected to operate 67 jets by 1985.

84   People's had achieved a cost-per-seat mile which was far below all of the major and regional airlines. People's achieved this low cost by cutting a variety of operating costs and providing few of the normal customer services. For example, reservations could be made by phone but tickets were only sold on the plane. Baggage was checked for $3 per bag, and no interline baggage transfer was available. In addition, only cold meals were served, and the customer had to pay extra for them. Finally, its employees were trained to handle many different tasks, which brought about high employee productivity.

85   People's routes covered many of the same markets serviced by Eastern. Thus, Eastern was forced to match fares with the acknowledged leading low-cost airline or lose substantial traffic. Obviously, Eastern found it difficult to compete successfully with People's Express on a price basis, particularly given its higher cost structure.

86   In 1983, People's Express operated at an annual rate of about 3.4 billion revenue passenger miles, which was only about 12% of Eastern's revenue passenger miles. However, People's load factors ran about 77% for the same year. Thus, People's had become a very serious threat to the other established airlines with competing East Coast routes.

Industry Practices and Problems

87   The impact of deregulation was apparent in current airline operations in various ways. However, other underlying problems existed which had a

major impact on the industry. Some of these strategic problems and issues are discussed below.

Economic Conditions

88   The economic environment clearly had a major impact on the airline industry's performance. Unfortunately, this factor was largely beyond the control of the airlines. Although the 1974-75 recession had a significant, negative effect on the industry, the recessionary impact increased significantly under deregulation. Exhibit 7 provides data on operating statistics during these two most recent recessionary periods, 1974-1975 and 1980-1982. During the later recession, airlines used various marketing tools and cost-cutting measures, chiefly wage concessions, to reduce the negative impact of the slumping economy.

Fare Wars/Pricing Strategies

89   A major reason that economic conditions had such a major impact on airlines was the price elasticity of demand. The airline industry had both elastic and inelastic demand segments. The discretionary portion of air travel, such as vacationers, had often been described as price elastic. In other words, a small change in the price of airline tickets could have a larger effect on the demand for tickets. The business traveler market segment was more price inelastic, in part because these customers were time

---

Exhibit 7

U.S. airline traffic—1974–1983 (all certificated carriers; scheduled service)

Year	Revenue passengers enplaned (000)	% Chg.	Revenue passenger kilometers (000,000)	% Chg.	Freight and express metric tons (000,000)	% Chg.
*1974	207,449	2.6	262,133	0.6	7,139	3.2
*1975	205,062	(1.2)	261,961	(0.1)	6,953	(2.5)
1976	223,313	8.9	287,992	9.9	7,408	6.5
1977	240,326	7.6	310,889	8.0	7,862	6.1
1978	274,716	14.3	364,891	17.6	8,414	7.0
1979	316,863	15.3	421,595	15.5	8,626	2.5
*1980	296,903	(6.3)	410,604	(2.6)	8,301	(3.8)
1981	285,720	(3.8)	400,250	(2.5)	8,200	(1.2)
1982	297,149	4.0	416,260	4.0	7,790	(5.0)
1983	309,035	4.0	432,910	4.0	8,063	3.5
Total 1974–1983 increase						
	101,586	49.0	170,777	65.2	924	12.9

*Recessionary period.
From "1983 Forecast: A Slow Turnaround Expected," *Air Transport World,* January 1983, p. 29.

sensitive. However, the degree of elasticity differed from one airline to another. For example, People's Express, a low cost, no-frills airline, found that its traffic was very elastic.

90   Airlines used various approaches to stimulate discretionary travel during weak economic times. Restricted discount fares, such as supersaver fares, were used to stimulate discretionary travel. This well-known discount fare required a seven-day advance purchase and at least one Saturday night layover. However, this fare discouraged business travelers from using it because (1) they did not want to stay over Saturday night and (2) they usually booked flights at the last moment.

91   Airline management teams lacked experience with pricing in a competitive environment. As a result, pricing strategies varied greatly. Industry observers often charged that airline management teams were not behaving rationally with respect to pricing. Fare wars were generally started by the use of unrestricted discount fares that were lower than the restricted discounts. This resulted in intense competition in specific markets where many airlines suffered losses. Once started, fare wars were perpetuated by the airlines' belief that fares must be matched in order to prevent a significant loss of market share.

92   Fare wars were also initiated by other factors. These included (a) financially troubled airlines pricing to generate cash flow, (b) the lower cost structure of new market entrants, and (c) excess industry capacity. Discount fares were so prevalent that by 1983, 80% of all fares were discounted at an average rate of 53% off of the stated fare.[7] Discounting became so severe that generally only the low-cost carrier made money on routes with fare wars, and even they sometimes did not cover all of their costs.

93   Fare wars caused significant damage because business traveler fares decreased significantly without generating much additional traffic in the business segment. This meant revenue yields declined, resulting in a corresponding decline in pretax profits.

Increasing Costs

94   Despite the carriers' desire to reduce their cost structures, cost reduction was not an easy task. Their costs were high because the airline industry was labor, energy, and capital intensive. For example, Eastern's percentages of total expenses for these three costs in 1982 were 36%, 27% and 5%, respectively. See Exhibit 8 which compares Eastern's 1982's expenses with 1978's. Fortunately, fuel costs, which were largely beyond the carriers' control, had stabilized in the early 1980s.

Employee Relations

95   The pressures to reduce costs, which included labor costs, caused considerable employee unrest and resistance. Airline employees were paid con-

Exhibit 8

Eastern expense and fuel costs analysis

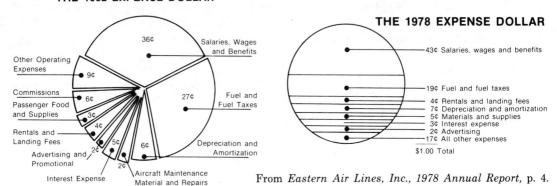

THE 1982 EXPENSE DOLLAR

- Salaries, Wages and Benefits 36¢
- Other Operating Expenses 9¢
- Commissions 6¢
- Passenger Food and Supplies 3¢
- Rentals and Landing Fees 4¢
- Advertising and Promotional 2¢
- Interest Expense 2¢
- Aircraft Maintenance Material and Repairs 5¢
- Depreciation and Amortization 6¢
- Fuel and Fuel Taxes 27¢

Payroll and fuel remain the major expense items.

From *Eastern Air Lines, Inc., 1982 Annual Report*, p. 3.

THE 1978 EXPENSE DOLLAR

- 43¢ Salaries, wages and benefits
- 19¢ Fuel and fuel taxes
- 4¢ Rentals and landing fees
- 7¢ Depreciation and amortization
- 5¢ Materials and supplies
- 3¢ Interest expense
- 2¢ Advertising
- 17¢ All other expenses
- $1.00 Total

From *Eastern Air Lines, Inc., 1978 Annual Report*, p. 4.

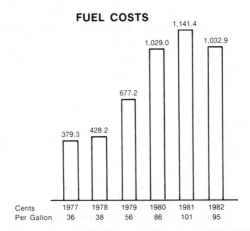

FUEL COSTS

	1977	1978	1979	1980	1981	1982
	379.3	428.2	677.2	1,029.0	1,141.4	1,032.9
Cents Per Gallon	36	38	56	86	101	95

Upward pressure on costs eased in 1982; consumption changed little in the years charted.

From *Eastern Air Lines, Inc., 1983 Annual Report*, p. 12.

siderably more than were most other professions. Their $42,000 average salary clearly attested to that fact. Since deregulation in 1978, airline employees were facing major salary and benefits setbacks. Their respective airlines felt that labor cost reductions would help them to be more competitive.

96   Union leaders, especially at the more militant machinists' union, were urging strikes and national walkouts to protest these pay concessions. Union employees, however, were divided as to how to respond. While they resented the pay cuts and charged that the airlines were wasting profits on fare wars, the employees often felt that they had to go along with the carriers' demands or lose their jobs. Clearly, the bankruptcies at Braniff and Continental had significantly strengthened management's position with its employees on wage and benefit issues.

Safety

97   Airline unions had consistently charged that the cost cutting procedures, such as increased pilot flying time and reduced maintenance and inspection procedures, had reduced the margin of safety for air travel to a dangerous level. F.A.A. spokesmen and some industry analysts believed that safety had actually increased, and that the unions were making these statements for political purposes. So far, there had not been any increased pattern of accidents since deregulation in 1978, or since Reagan broke the P.A.T.C.O. strike by hiring almost all new air traffic controllers.

Distribution Channels

98   Almost all tickets were currently sold by either travel agencies (65% of all sales), the airlines, or through corporate in-house travel departments. This latter group acted as a branch of a travel agency for a specific organization. While agents generally received a 10% commission, in-house operations often received 80-90% of a 3% commission paid to the agents. Although the airlines generally dislike the in-house operations, they had little power to curtail them. In fact, in-house operations were expected to flourish in the future with the possible development of corporate travel subsidiaries. The airline industry feared that corporations would eventually be able to use their power to obtain commissions (discounts) in excess of those currently provided to the travel agents.

99   Travel agencies may face possible competition from various retailing firms in the future. In December of 1982, the C.A.B. voted to permit the sale of airline tickets by anyone starting in 1985. This might mean that such retail giants as Sears, J.C. Penney's or K mart could begin selling airline tickets.

Computerization

100   Computerization had become a very important tool to the airlines, especially in the marketing areas. The airlines found that it was necessary to utilize effectively the promotional programs currently provided by the airlines.

101   Computerization had been most important in the development of automated reservation systems. These systems were marketed to travel agencies as a scheduling tool, and they became a necessity with the proliferation
of airline fares. A few airlines controlled most of the existing reservation
systems. The market shares for these reservation systems among all travel
agencies were 39% for American Airlines' Sabre system, 29% for United
Airlines' Apollo, 26% for Trans World Airlines' PARS I and II, 3% for
Tymshare, Inc.'s Mars Plus, and 13% for other systems collectively (e.g.,
Eastern, Delta).[8] These systems also became an important marketing tool
for the airline that developed them. All of these systems, with the exception
of Delta's, had a built-in bias to favor the developing airline in the way
flight data was displayed. The system also generated revenues for the
developer, who charged a fee per flight segment to other airlines who were
listed in the system as co-hosts and received second-best status. In addition,
the systems also provided valuable, confidential marketing information
for the host airline.

102   Airlines without such a computer system were at a competitive disadvantage, and many of them had complained to the government. As a
result, the Justice Department was reviewing the systems for anti-trust
violations, and the C.A.B. planned to remove the bias features in the
system in 1984. Several airlines without such systems were suggested
divestiture of the systems by their owners to neutral companies who could
compete with each other.

Possible Reregulation

103   The intensity of the fare wars and the inability of some carriers to compete
caused some airlines to ask for some form of reregulation. These proposals
stressed some form of price floors developed by the C.A.B. to prevent
destructive competition. Republic Airlines, at least three other airlines, and
some U.S. Congressmen were among those advocating reregulation. The
fate of deregulation and reregulation were dependent upon the well-being
of the major carriers. If several more of them folded, reregulation would
probably gain additional support. However, it should be noted that the
Reagan administration opposed any form of reregulation.

Repositioning Eastern after Deregulation

104   In order to compete successfully in a highly competitive, mature industry,
Eastern needs to find a strategy to position itself in the industry that it can
successfully defend. As of late 1983, Eastern had been unable to avoid the
adverse impact of competition. In fact, Eastern's key routes were those
which had the most highly discounted fares in the U.S. Furthermore, three

of its direct competitors—Delta, Piedmont, and People's Express—were among the strongest airlines in the industry.

A Low Cost Strategy

105   One basic alternative for Eastern would be to pursue a low-cost strategy. Eastern would have a long way to go to implement this strategy since its cost structure was still high compared to some of its major competitors. However, this strategy made a great deal of sense, especially since recent fare wars lowered operating margins. While Eastern might have a difficult time becoming "the" low-cost major airline, failure to further reduce costs could bring about bankruptcy.

106   Aggressive cost cutting efforts would be needed for Eastern to pursue a low-cost strategy. Its modern fleet of airplanes had already helped to reduce operating costs. The concessions that Borman had obtained from its employees had further reduced costs and improved employee productivity. Still, significant further measures would be needed to pursue this strategy actively.

107   Eastern might be able to achieve even greater cost-saving measures with its unionized and nonunionized workers. Other airlines had recently been successful. For example, in March and April of 1983, American Airlines achieved major cost-cutting contracts with its pilots, flight attendants, and machinist unions. If American achieved its hoped for cost reduction to 6.5¢ per seat mile, it would become very competitive with some of the best low-cost airlines. Perhaps, Eastern could be as successful as American Airlines hoped it would be with its cost-cutting efforts.

108   Another option for Eastern to use to lower its cost structure might be to declare bankruptcy as did Continental Airlines. If a bankruptcy filing was approved, Eastern could then, perhaps quickly, reorganize the airline. It could cut down on the number of its flights, trim back its work force, lower wages and benefits, and ask for more hours worked. Although this approach may seem drastic, it could be very effective if Eastern could win lawsuits that would inevitably be filed by its organized employees—lawsuits that would effect union busting.

109   A problem with this approach, however, was that it could possibly hurt both customer loyalty and employee morale. Also, many employees might feel that bankruptcy was declared just to void its union contracts. Therefore, all of these factors would have to be taken into consideration if this strategic option was to be implemented.

A Focus Strategy

110   Another basic alternative for Eastern would be to focus, or specialize, on satisfying specific customer segments in the industry. For example, with

most airlines fighting hard for coach passengers, one overlooked customer group might be the first-class traveler. The potential for Eastern's first-class service could be significant. First-class travel accounted for only 6.7% of all travel in the early 1980s, but it generated almost 10% of the total revenue. Furthermore, since Eastern's cost structure was high, this customer group might be a good one to focus on since they were less price conscious. Finally, expansion of first-class service might also provide Eastern with a competitive advantage over its competitors during good economic times when demand for first-class service grew.

111 Eastern might consider focusing on the business traveler or leisure traveler segments. For the business customer segment, numerous possibilities existed for expanding its frequent traveler program. In addition, enumerable joint promotions could be used with hotels, rental car agencies, restaurants, convention facilities, etc. to specialize on business travelers. For the leisure or discretionary traveler, lots of possibilities exist to help stimulate interest in air travel. Eastern might attract more discretionary travelers with cooperative agreements at major resorts, like its agreement with Disney World. Eastern might also emphasize joint promotions with such complementary services as free travelers' checks, reduced prices for city tours, a free night's lodging after so many paid nights, and so on.

112 The company could choose to develop an all-frills air service to capture a sizable portion of that market niche. Focusing on this segment would undoubtedly overlap with the first-class traveler segment and might produce some synergies. Air One and FirstAir were two examples of airlines that were trying to promote high-class, all-frills flights. Eastern might accomplish this by converting some of its older, wide-bodied L-1011s for all-frills, first-class flights. These planes could operate efficiently on long-haul routes (e.g., New York to Miami), since Eastern possessed the necessary route structure to support such a new service.

113 If Eastern does pursue a focus strategy, it could choose to focus on several segments of the industry at the same time. Furthermore, it could select segments to focus on that overlapped with one another. For example, all-frills flights could overlap with long-haul routes to South America and other vacation areas. Similarly, a focus on first-class customers might simultaneously be pursued with business travelers.

A Differentiation Strategy

114 A differentiation approach involves offering a product or service that is perceived industry-wide as being unique. For example, Eastern had long been recognized as a technological leader. They could key in on this fact and aggressively promote it in their advertising. Along the same lines, they could also promote the safety features found in their modern, sophisticated aircraft.

115   Eastern could also differentiate itself with its pre-flight and in-flight services. In its boarding areas, Eastern could have a wide screen TV tuned to one of the cable news networks. Free copies of *USA Today* and the *Wall Street Journal* could be handed out to passengers. On the flight, they could have in-flight movies as some other airlines do on transcontinental flights. Fashion shows, in-flight telephones, television sets, and personal computers could all be gimmicks Eastern could use to differentiate itself. Low-cost airlines would have a hard time trying to match such services and keep their low-cost emphasis.

116   In-flight seminars on video cassettes, which used headsets to access tape channels, could be another way to differentiate itself. Some topics for the leisure travelers might include investment strategies, tax preparation, inspirational speeches, self-improvement topics, and various do-it-yourself topics. For the business traveler, in-person talks or cassettes could be given on a variety of finance, marketing, and management topics. If Eastern did this, it might not only become the airline that business travelers use, but also the one where they received additional business training.

Diversification

117   Diversification into industries outside the airline business is another possibility for Eastern. Although Frank Borman so far has had Eastern concentrate on only the airline business, so far its profitability in that mature industry has been very poor. The reality may be that too many firms are competing in a cut-throat fashion in a mature industry with low-growth potential. As a result, perhaps Eastern needs to pursue higher profit potential opportunities elsewhere, while retaining only those airline routes which really make money.

118   Some diversification efforts might be into related businesses that are complementary to Eastern's operations. Starting up or acquiring a travel/ tour business is one such option which would complement its airline operations. Such a program could feed travelers to Eastern. It might also make Eastern more competitive with other major airlines that already provide such services.

119   Eastern could also go into services that its airline customers need after arriving at their destination. Many customers, especially business travelers, need a rental car to get around in the area. Thus, operating a rent-a-car business in selected, major cities Eastern serves might be a good opportunity to pursue. Similarly, Eastern could also provide limousine services to customers needing to go to hotels and/or business meetings. Eastern might also consider starting up its own hotel chain. For example, Trans World Airlines owns Hilton International Corp. a chain of hotels and encourages its airline customers to stay there. It might be possible for Eastern to develop a system so that when customers purchase their airline tickets, a

rental car and hotel reservations at Eastern facilities could also be made. These other businesses could be promoted through discounts and joint promotions.

120   Eastern could also start operating its own food service business. Most Airlines typically buy food for their flights from outside vendors instead of preparing the food themselves. Marriott Corporation is an example of a firm that provides such food services. Thus, if Eastern decides to enter into the hotel business, operating a food service chain would appear to be a logical extension of its operations.

Eastern's Future Direction

121   As Eastern prepares for the later 1980s and the coming 1990s, the basic strategy it selects will be critical. Lots of factors need to be considered in deciding how to position itself in the airline industry. Is it possible for Eastern to become a low-cost airline? Could it be successful by focusing on specific segments of the market? Are there ways for it to differentiate itself from other airlines which would really stimulate customer loyalty? Could a combination of strategies be creatively used?

122   Are the future prospects for the airline industry so bleak that Eastern should consider diversifying into other businesses? Should they somehow relate and be complementary to the airline industry? Should Eastern diversify into unrelated industries that look promising? These and other basic strategic options need to be addressed as Eastern tries to reposition itself for long-term profitability.

Notes

1. "U.S. Carrier Officials Oppose Regulation in Spite of Losses," *Aviation Week and Space Technology,* June 6, 1983, p. 51.
2. Margaret Loeb, "Outlook for Eastern Air Appears Brighter Despite $34.4 Million Net Loss for Quarter," *Wall Street Journal,* October 10, 1983, p. 5.
3. Robert E. Dallos and Barry Bearak, "Eastern's Beleaguered Borman," *The Charlotte Observer,* October 9, 1983, p. 20A.
4. Margaret Loeb and Thomas E. Ricks, "Future of Eastern Airlines Hinging on Chief's Credibility With Unions," *Wall Street Journal,* September 29, 1983, p. 33.
5. *Ibid.*
6. "American Rediscovers Itself," *Business Week,* August 23, 1982, pp. 66-78.
7. Eugene Kozicharrow, "Carriers Attempting to Reduce Capacity," *Aviation Week and Space Technology,* March 14, 1983, pp. 188-189.
8. Cindy Skrzycki, "Airline Flight That Affects Tickets You Buy," *U.S. News & World Report,* August 22, 1983, p. 53.

case **13** **Braniff International Corporation (A): False Signs of Success**

1   Braniff International Corporation, incorporated in 1930 as Braniff Airways, Inc., carried passengers, freight, and mail in the southwest corner of the United States. In 1965, Greatamerica Corporation assumed control of Braniff by purchasing 52 percent of its stock, and as part of a reorganization plan, Harding Lawrence was named president. Lawrence, a former executive vice president for Continental Airlines, utilized an unusual promotional campaign that exhibited panache in a relatively conservative industry. Some of the promotional tactics for the Dallas-based airine, designed to increase exposure outside the southwest United States were:

1. Establishing VIP lounges in all major airports so business passengers traveling with Braniff would have a special place to relax before, between, or after flights.
2. Hiring fashion designer Pucci to design several different uniforms for the stewardesses.
3. Painting Braniff planes with bright colors such as blue, orange, and green.

2   Coupled with an attempt to overcome a bad on-time record, these highly visible maneuvers were very successful in achieving national recognition

---

This case was prepared by Professors John A. Pearce II and Sandra J. Teel of the University of South Carolina.

for Braniff and in helping to increase Braniff's passenger-load factor.

3   Braniff experienced rapid growth until late 1969, when its military charter collapsed and the Justic Department cited Braniff for antitrust activities. The company took a number of measures to effect its recovery. Though financially unable to purchase large, wide-body airplanes (747s), Braniff took advantage of the benefits which planned fleet standardization could provide. Use of a narrow selection of planes allowed Braniff to reduce costs in several ways—pilots and maintenance crews were trained for only one type of airplane, and parts could be interchanged among planes.

4   Since the proportion of business travelers was greater for Braniff (70 percent) than for the industry (60 percent), Braniff focused its turnaround measures on the business traveler, increasing the number of cities served and the number of flights to each city. The average daily usage per plane exceeded the industry average by 0.9 hours, and the time between major maintenance overhauls that kept the plane on the ground for several days was lengthened. Thus Braniff, in an attempt to boost profits, opted to increase productivity of the planes rather than increase fares.

5   The turnaround measures were successful, and Lawrence was applauded as one of the most-competent chief executive officers in the airline industry.

6   Braniff's response to problems encountered in the mid-1970s was equally successful. From 1975 to 1976, fuel prices increased 30 percent, and labor costs increased 17 percent. During negotiations for a new union contract, Braniff traded arbitration on unresolved issues for a union agreement not to strike. Rather than pulling back, Braniff forged ahead through route expansion and diversification.

7   These diversifications were either a complement to the airline or a means to maximize its strengths. Braniff International Hotels, Inc., as a service to Braniff passengers, provided private housing and dining facilities in Braniff's headquarters at Dallas-Fort Worth (DFW) airport as well as a hotel and discotheque in Austin, Texas. Braniff Realty Company provided fueling and tie-down services at Love Field in Dallas and owned six aircraft, which it leased to Braniff.

8   To capitalize on existing strengths, Braniff Education Systems, Inc., (BES) was established. BES taught courses for the public on such topics as ticketing, reservations and sales, travel agency operations, and flight engineer training. The BIC Guardian Services, Inc., (BIC) was established shortly after airports increased security screening to prevent hijacking. BIC conducted security screening for several airports, including DFW.

9   In an attempt to improve productivity, interdepartmental competition was encouraged. Departments prepared progress reports that were first examined by management, then distributed to other departments for comparison. Fleet standardization continued as standard operating procedure for Braniff as did high-frequency flights. By the end of 1976, all parts of the Braniff operation were working well. Revenue per passenger-mile and the passenger load factor had increased over the previous year. Braniff was planning to expand its services to Europe. This expansion effort was

supported by a strong financial picture with ample cash and a net working capital of $14.3 million.

International Operations

10   Braniff extended its service to international markets, beginning with flights to Central and South America. As early as 1952, Braniff was flying to Mexico, Panama, and most countries in South America where Lima served as the hub of its operations. Despite the 1975 discovery of payoffs by Braniff to Latin America travel agents to influence tickets sales, Braniff continued to cultivate this market, because load factors in Central and South America were higher than domestic load factors. In 1977, prior to its entry into the European market, Braniff's load factor for international operations was 56.6 percent versus 47 percent for domestic operations.

11   In late 1977, Braniff's scope of international operations was broadened to include transatlantic service to London. The new service, scheduled to begin March 1, 1978, was to be a daily round-trip service from DFW to Gatwick, requiring 18 operating hours out of every 24 for the "great 747 pumpkin." Lawrence, renowned for his policies of frequent and nondiscriminating service and fares for the southwestern transatlantic passenger, proposed low promotional fares that would rival any East Coast passenger rate. Experience gained from service to Honolulu evidenced the benefit of long in-flight engine utilization which caused less engine wearout than more frequent takeoff utilization (at full throttle).

12   Before Braniff could commence the London flights, a conflict arose between the CAB and the British Civil Aviation Authority (BCAA) over the proposed DFW/London fare. While awaiting the eventual settlement of the fare dispute, Braniff was already planning and implementing its strategies for getting the new service underway. Briefly, some of its tactical moves were:

1. Arranging for an aircraft prior to final CAB approval.
2. Leasing as opposed to buying a ticket office in London.
3. Hiring and training British citizens as agents and clerks.
4. Delivering ticket stock to both British travel agents and wholesalers.
5. Training 10 extra 747 flight crews.

13   Braniff continued its expansion into European markets. In January 1979, it entered into an agreement with British Airways and Air France to provide a through service via Washington, D.C., to London and Paris. Braniff operated the Concorde from DFW to Washington, and the British and French airlines flew the transatlantic stretches. Under this arrangement, Braniff gained additional exposure to European markets through its inclusion in London and Paris airline traffic schedules.

14   In June 1979, Braniff further expanded its European connections by offering low-fare nonstop direct service from DFW and Boston to Paris, Frankfurt, Amsterdam, and Brussels. Further expansions in 1979 took Braniff to the Far Eastern market where it began service to Guam, Hong Kong, Korea, and Malaysia. Braniff anticipated adding Japan and the Philippines to round out its route structure.

Deregulation

15   Representing the first deregulation of an entire industry in decades, the Deregulation Act (October 24, 1978) was viewed as a possible precursor to anticipated relief for other "overregulated" U.S. industries. Under federal regulation, routes and fares had to be approved by the CAB, thereby limiting the factors of competition to such variables as scheduling and service. Deregulation was intended to return airlines to a market-controlled industry. According to the 1978 law, the CAB's authority over fares and rates would end by 1983, and by 1985, the agency itself would be abolished. In the years 1979 to 1981, each airline was permitted to claim one new route of its choice without the board's approval. At the same time, carriers were assured of more-speedy application and approval for new routes, acquisition of which required only a demonstration that a carrier was "fit, willing, and able" to serve the new route and that its operation would be consistent with, rather than required for, public convenience. Opposition to any new entry had to prove, at the very least, danger to the public welfare.

16   Although fares were still partially regulated in markets where an airline controlled less than 70 percent of the traffic, an airline could otherwise adjust its fare without CAB approval by:

1. A reduction of up to 70 percent from the standard industry fare.

2. An increase of up to 10 percent over the standard industry fare—the fare level in effect as of July 1, 1977, for each pair of points.

17   Unfortunately, the impact of deregulation was experienced during a rapid growth period for the airline industry. Cheaper fares and intense promotional campaigns had brought an increase in the number of routes available and the number of travelers. Simultaneously, spiraling fuel prices, recessionary trends, decreases in disposable income and, thus, in the number of vacation travelers, and other limiting factors caused unanticipated and mounting problems for the airline industry. Deregulation was thus tested during an economic downswing.

Industry Reponse to Deregulation

18   The industry reaction to deregulation was slow and somewhat cautious, holding back and reassessing, "enhancing and integrating," and strength-

ening existing route structures. The trunk lines seemed to be searching only for profits as a means for determining scheduling strategies. Retrenchment had been difficult. The choice was between a reduction in the size of the fleet or in the size of the jet in order to transport fewer passengers yet serve more locations and increase the frequency of service. At the same time, the commuter lines had great expansion opportunities. Some carriers leaned either aggressively or defensively toward acquisition or merger to bolster their positions.

19   The changes in pricing due to deregulation were hailed as particularly helpful to the struggling industry. Prices continued to increase, but more slowly under competition than under artificial regulation. The new policy was more responsive since it allowed for quicker adjustments both upward (to pass on fuel-price increases) or downward (to attract new customers through discounting). Services could be reduced or even eliminated more quickly, and equipment could be used more productively through the flexibility afforded by the act.

20   While the airline industry as a whole had assumed a rather conservative position in response to deregulation, Braniff had responded quite differently. Dubbed as "sprinting strategy," Braniff's aggressive route expansion was met with near disbelief by the other trunk carriers. In October 1978, Braniff picked up 89 dormant routes. In December, they applied for 59 more but were able to activate only 32 (due to a CAB-established 45-day limitation on activation). With the end-of-the-year push, Braniff added 16 new cities to its schedule before Christmas, increasing its route-miles by 35 percent and its available seat-miles by 11 percent. In mid-January, Braniff applied for approximately one third of the dormant routes and, for the period January 1, 1979, to February 25, 1979, offered one-third off discounts between new cities and other domestic points. On January 25, 1979, service was introduced for an additional 14 nonstop routes.

21   In conjunction with the route expansion, Braniff hired 627 pilots and undertook work on a $45 million expansion of its terminal facilities in the DFW airport. To be completed by 1988, the expansion was expected to increase simultaneous loading space accommodations from 24 to 47 aircraft.

Braniff's Operating Strategies

22   The deregulation strategy was based on Lawrence's faith in Braniff's flexibility, which he attributed to fleet standardization. Braniff's domestic fleet consisted almost exclusively of Boeing 727s—both the 727-100 series with a capacity of 100 passengers and the 727-200 series with a capacity of 130 passengers. The 727 had only three engines and substantial commonality of parts and subsystems between the 100 and 200 series. Lawrence's claim, even as early as 1972, was that fully allocated operating costs per mile for the DC-10 were double those for the 727-200. The 727 could be operated twice as often with more seats available.

23   Frequency rather than capacity was the key to Braniff's scheduling success. The size of the Boeing 727 permitted multistops without creating bottlenecks, and yet it was cost efficient, particularly for the low-density markets in which Braniff operated. Because it was efficient and suitable for smaller airports, the 727 could also be used to develop new markets.

24   Braniff subscribed to high fleet utilization. Figures for 1977 show Braniff operated its carriers an average of 8.3 hours per day versus the industry average of 7.4 hours per day.

25   As a result of fleet standardization, small spare parts inventory, lower training costs for crews, and high fleet utilization, Braniff experienced lower-than-average direct operating costs, which meant earning a profit with a smaller percentage of seats filled. The low break-even load factor enabled Braniff to maintain its additional routes with low load factors that were sufficient to cover the additional operating expenses.

26   Like Delta, Braniff had developed a good hub-and-spoke system for feeding its routes, particularly in DFW and Denver. With good feeders into the hubs, Braniff increased its opportunities for picking up new or extended routes out of the hubs. Braniff's choice of low-density routes provided yet another competitive advantage.

27   These operating strategies seemed to have placed Braniff in a sound position for expanding its routes. Its adopted strategies for dealing with the expansion also seemed technically sound. For example, Braniff curtailed its training of other airline crews in Dallas and began training only its own crews. It provided only light service to new routes and scheduled new flights for off-peak hours to prevent disruption of existing flights until it could assess demand. Further, until permanent set-ups could be justified, Braniff leased counter and gate space and negotiated service agreements in newly entered airports.

28   Braniff's expansion was rapid, but its moves were not irrevocable. Braniff chose to enter markets quickly, make temporary arrangements, assess the demand, and adjust scheduling accordingly.

Financial and Other Relevant Data

29   Braniff was attracted by the potential profits to be realized as a result of deregulation and the apparent growth of the airline industry. Industry earnings were a record high in 1978 but fell in 1979 because of the weakening economy and the increased costs of both fuel and other operations. Airline traffic continued to grow with the help of new routes and promotional fares which reduced the passenger yield (the average fare collected per passenger-mile), but traffic gains were offset by this drop in passenger yield and the rising costs of operations.

30   Domestic traffic was up by 15 percent for the trunk lines (major carriers) in the first four months of 1979, and international traffic was up 21 percent. During the same period, the locals (regionals) also achieved a 33 percent

gain in traffic. However, during the first quarter of 1979, the yield dropped 3.3 percent, and operating expenses increased 15.7 percent, resulting in an operating deficit of $13 million and an increase of only 12 percent in operating revenue. The net loss for the first quarter 1979 amounted to $603,000 for the industry. In 1978, the industry had recorded $9.8 million in net income for the same period.

31   During 1979, the U.S. economy was unstable and was predicted to worsen in 1980. Gross national product (GNP) increased by only 3.3 percent in 1979 compared to a 3.9 percent gain in 1978. Real disposable personal income registered only half of its 1978 gain in 1979—2.3 percent versus 4.6 percent. Paralleling these declines was a growth drop in revenue passenger-miles, up only 5.8 percent in 1979, a minor gain when compared to the 15.9 percent increase of 1978. As a result, the depressed economy had heightened price consciousness so greatly that fare reductions were perceived as the only means to achieve traffic gains.

32   Braniff experienced a net *loss* of $44,330,000 in 1979 as compared to a net *gain* of $45,230,000 in 1978. Factors contributing to the loss were rapid expansion, the price of jet fuel, the increase in labor and other operating costs, and the state of the economy. In 1979, Braniff substantially increased its operation as a result of the deregulation of the airlines. A comparison of the 1978 and 1979 balance sheets (see Exhibit 1) shows that total assets increased from $855 million to $1.13 billion, an increase of 32.7 percent, while total liabilities increased from $605 million to $936 million, an increase of 54.72 percent. In contrast, the equity of the firm decreased 26 percent. Braniff was constantly increasing the size of its fleet, the size of the work force, and the number of its facilities during the year. The sixth-largest airline in number of enplaned passengers, Braniff planned an increase in fleet second only to United, the largest airline.

33   Braniff did, however, achieve a significant gain in revenue and airline traffic, and revenues reached a record high of $1.2 billion. Operating revenues were up 38.5 percent from 1978, and airline passenger traffic in revenue passenger-miles increased 39.7 percent while available seat-miles also were up 33.7 percent. Domestic traffic increased 32.3 percent, and international traffic was up 6.1 percent. Exhibit 2 compares the fluctuations in airline traffic and the revenue per ton-mile of Braniff to its major competitors.

34   However, these gains in revenues and traffic were counteracted by the explosive increasing in operating expenses, especially the cost of jet fuel. The composition of Braniff's operating expenses is shown in Exhibit 3. Aircraft, fuel, oil, and taxes, along with labor costs, accounted for the bulk of expenses. Fuel alone increased 94.2 percent in 1979, and labor costs rose 34.2 percent. Braniff spent $409 million for fuel in 1979 in contrast to $210 million in 1978. The average price per gallon jumped from 40.2 cents to 78 cents. The increase in each operating expense can be seen in Exhibit 4, which compares the income statements for the years 1978-1979.

Exhibit 1

Braniff International Corporation and subsidiaries consolidated balance sheet, December 31, 1978, and 1979 (in thousands of dollars)

	1979	1978
Assets		
Current assets:		
Cash	$ 32,007	$ 6,607
Marketable securities	1,486	6,558
Net accounts receivable	105,987	88,929
Receivables from airport authorities	2,821	11,180
Inventory	37,772	26,072
Other current assets	7,788	2,173
Total current assets	187,861	141,519
Equipment purchase deposits	30,391	67,355
Property and equipment, net	863,429	612,189
Other assets:		
Deferred charges	32,798	15,930
Long-term prepayments	18,450	15,911
Long-term receivables and investments	1,792	2,261
Total assets	$1,134,721	$855,165
Liabilities		
Current liabilities:		
Notes payable and current maturities of long-term debt	$ 23,393	$ 14,112
Accounts payable	118,420	56,605
Current liabilities under capital leases	10,558	7,997
Unearned revenues	19,822	11,231
Dividends payable	1,023	1,820
Accrued compensation and retirement benefits	26,791	27,926
Accrued vacation pay	21,677	15,741
Other current liabilities	31,466	20,111
Total current liabilities	253,150	155,532
Long-term debt:		
Senior debt	507,912	320,985
Subordinated debt	70,286	27,692
Total long-term debt	578,198	348,677
Other noncurrent liabilities:		
Capital leases	87,047	49,393
Other	3,335	3,145
Total other noncurrent liabilities	90,382	52,538
Deferred credits:		
Deferred federal income taxes	10,312	46,280
Other	4,062	1,976
Total deferred credits	14,374	48,256
Preferred stock:		
Authorized, 5,000,000 shares of $1.00 par value; none outstanding		
Common shareholders' equity		
Common stock; authorized, 30,000,000 shares of $0.50 par value; issued and outstanding: 1979, 20,019,045; 1978, 20,018,671	10,010	10,009
Paid-in capital	46,785	46,783
Retained earnings	141,822	193,356
Total common shareholders' equity	198,617	250,151
Total liabilities	$1,134,721	$855,164

Source: Braniff International Corporation, 1979 Annual Report.

Exhibit 2

Selected airline traffic and freight statistics, 1977–1979 (in thousands of miles)

	Revenue-miles			Revenue passenger-miles			Total revenue ton-miles		
	1977	1978	1979	1977	1978	1979	1977	1978	1979
Domestic:									
American	21,418	22,447	23,751	1,748,014	1,921,089	2,210,871	231,775	247,424	270,728
Braniff	8,361	9,452	9,762	490,646	643,986	631,821	58,061	73,351	72,148
Continental	6,814	7,970	8,316	570,448	666,205	622,543	80,135	91,749	84,587
Delta	18,827	20,363	20,515	1,575,288	1,909,226	1,862,276	182,601	214,903	209,996
Eastern	19,766	20,527	21,803	1,388,892	1,657,241	1,924,288	154,973	184,612	211,685
Trans World	17,077	16,320	15,228	1,270,707	1,309,958	1,188,124	156,769	155,451	139,650
United	30,963	35,574	35,174	2,613,138	3,274,376	3,673,152	327,619	398,024	432,030
International:									
American	2,418	2,477	2,631	234,315	293,612	330,749	36,054	38,526	41,514
Braniff	1,747	1,961	1,934	151,214	170,778	188,302	18,338	20,141	21,729
Continental	239	423	740	11,641	27,811	68,471	1,492	3,714	14,229
Delta	338	502	338	34,806	51,997	47,129	4,248	5,825	5,706
Eastern	2,031	2,401	2,689	251,636	308,271	367,853	34,470	38,631	45,149
Pan Am	10,424	10,386	9,955	1,386,225	1,565,124	1,542,800	244,107	251,816	248,872
Trans World	4,567	4,569	3,731	546,125	614,540	564,657	84,526	85,140	76,069

Source: Aviation Week and Space Technology 108 (February 6, 1978), p. 41; 110 (February 5, 1979), p. 33; 112 (February 18, 1980), p. 37.

Exhibit 3

Operating expense comparison, Braniff International Corporation, 1978–1979

	Composition (percent)		Percent increases	
	1979	*1978*	*1979 versus 1978*	*1978 versus 1977*
Aircraft fuel, oil, and taxes	29.8%	23.8%	94.2%	26.7%
Salaries, wages, related taxes, and employee benefits	29.3	33.9	34.2	19.3
Depreciation and capital lease amortization	4.9	6.6	16.5	8.9
Operating leases and rentals	3.4	2.7	93.8	47.9
Landing fees	2.2	2.6	33.0	7.6
Outside services and repairs	9.3	8.2	75.2	32.5
Materials and supplies..............................	2.5	2.9	36.1	28.0
Traffic commissions	5.0	5.1	52.6	43.1
Passenger food service.............................	4.4	4.4	56.1	38.4
Advertising and promotion	1.4	2.0	6.4	17.0
Communications....................................	1.5	1.6	51.9	33.3
All other expenses	6.3	6.2	55.2	29.3
Total	100.0	100.0	55.3	24.4

Source: Braniff International Corporation, 1979 Annual Report.

35   Exhibit 5 shows the significant difference in fuel-price increases and the airline-fare increases. Although CAB granted fare increases in 1979, the increases lagged behind in dollar value and time. The industry experienced a loss of approximately $470 million as a result of the lag, more than $60 million (12.76 percent) of which was experienced by Braniff.

36   As of December 31, 1979, Braniff had 30 million shares of 50 cents par value of authorized common stock issued and outstanding. Earnings per share were –$2.21 for the year, with the price of the stock fluctuating from $14⅜ to $6¾, as shown in Exhibit 6. The price-earnings ratio of 1978 was 2.0, but because of the loss in 1979, it was not meaningful for 1979. Also, Braniff had 5 million shares of preferred stock with none outstanding.

Alternatives

37   Grumblings among the stockholders suggested that any action Braniff took to respond to third quarter 1979 losses would be closely inspected at the next stockholders' meeting. Meetings of top management to determine the course of action needed generated a wide variety of alternative viewpoints but coalesced around the following analysis.

38   Increases in fuel costs coupled with the sizable increase in routes were responsible for the strain on Braniff's budget. While it had no control over fuel costs, the number of routes could certainly be reduced. Obviously, the choice of routes to drop should depend on the route's profitability. Only

Exhibit 4

Braniff International Corporation and subsidiaries statement of consolidated income, for the periods ending December 31, 1978, and 1979 (in thousands of dollars except per share amounts)

	1979	*1978*
Operating revenues:		
Airline:		
Passenger	$1,200,329	$845,353
Express, freight, and mail	84,559	68,080
Charter	15,226	18,843
Transport related	28,213	24,789
Other	8,039	8,238
Nonairline subsidiaries	9,909	6,805
Total operating revenues	1,346,275	972,108
Operating expenses:		
Airline:		
Flying and ground operations	546,841	382,277
Aircraft fuel, oil, and taxes	409,635	210,883
Maintenance	131,691	88,853
Nonairline subsidiaries	3,271	2,992
Sales and advertising	158,659	108,737
Depreciation* and amortization, less amounts charged to other accounts	75,343	60,980
General and administrative	41,273	37,227
Total operating expenses	1,384,713	891,949
Operating income (loss)	(38,438)	80,159
Nonoperating expenses (income):		
Interest expense	55,919	34,201
Interest capitalized	(6,265)	(4,992)
Interest income	(3,809)	(3,129)
Other—net	(2,553)	(1,156)
Total nonoperating expenses	43,292	24,924
Income (loss) before income taxes	(81,730)	55,235
Provision (credit) for income taxes	(37,400)	10,005
Net income (loss)	$ (44,330)	$ 45,230
Earnings (loss) per common share	$(2.21)	$2.26
Weighted average number of common shares outstanding	20,019	20,016

*Depreciation was computed on the straight-line method.
Source: Braniff International Corporation, 1979 Annual Report.

months earlier, the Federal Aviation Authority (FAA) had proposed that Braniff be fined because of maintenance irregularities which the FAA attributed to rapid route expansion. Thus, another benefit of route reduction would be a return to standard maintenance of aircraft. Dropping some routes would also free aircraft that could then be sold to generate additional revenues to offset the increased fuel costs. This measure was seen as

Exhibit 5
Fuel price increases versus airline fare increases,
1979 domestic operations

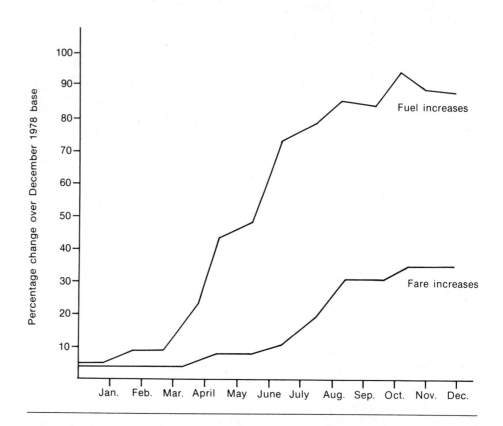

merely temporary since Braniff had no intention of halting its growth.

39   Braniff was reviewing its labor contracts in an attempt to secure an agreement for a wage cut. The exact size of the wage cut could only be determined through negotiations. However, as a sign of good faith, Lawrence offered to take double the wage cut other employees took.

40   A new promotional campaign was suggested as a measure for increasing the passenger load factor. An advertising campaign would focus on the services Braniff offered and on how their services differed from other airlines. Since their cash was already depleted, they planned to follow the lead of Pan Am and Continental to trade airline tickets for advertising time and space. Since advertising alone was seen as insufficient to overcome the problems, part of the promotional campaign was to be some type

Exhibit 6

Common stock data, Braniff International Corporation, 1970–1979

	Per share data						
					Price		
Year ending December 31	*Book value*	*Earnings*	*Dividends*	*Payout ratio*	*High*	*Low*	*P/E ratio*
1970	$ 4.14	$*d*0.13	$0.47 7/8	NM	10 2/3	5 7/7	NM
1971	4.60	0.49	Nil	Nil	16 1/2	7 6/8	34-16
1972	5.44	0.85	Nil	Nil	19 5/8	12 7/8	23-15
1973*	6.61	1.15	Nil	Nil	16 1/4	8 1/4	14-7
1974*	7.77	1.30	0.15	11%	12 1/2	4 1/2	10-3
1975	8.37	1.02	0.20	20	9 1/4	5	9-5
1976	9.47	1.31	0.23	17	14 1/4	8 3/4	11-7
1977	11.00	1.82	0.28 1/2	16	11 1/8	7 1/2	6-6
1978	12.50	2.26	0.34 1/2	16	18 5/8	8 7/8	8-4
1979	9.92	*d*2.21	0.36	NM	14 4/8	6 3/4	NM

Data as originally reported. Adjusted for stock divisions of 3 percent November 1972, 3 percent November 1971.
*Reflects accounting change.
Fully diluted: 0.81 in 1972, 0.43 in 1971.
NM = Not meaningful.
d = Deficit.
Source: Standard & Poor's Stock Reports: New York Stock Exchange, A-C, January 1981, vol. 47, no. 231 (New York: Standard & Poor's, December 1), sec. 6.

of discounted fare program. One suggestion was a 10 percent reduction in fare between certain cities, provided the traveler used Braniff for the entire trip.

41 Braniff also considered increasing its fares by the maximum allowed by the deregulation act. This would boost revenues since ticket sales constituted the bulk of Braniff's revenues.

42 Long-term debtholders had become increasingly uneasy over Braniff's plight and had stipulated that Braniff could not secure any other senior long-term debt. Besides postponement of the payment of long-term debt, Braniff's only other options appeared to be the sale of preferred stock and short-term debt. The company considered selling 3.75 million shares of preferred stock in an attempt to generate $75 million to retire debt and finance aircraft. Braniff also had a verbal commitment for a $100 million loan (short-term) at an interest rate of $1^1/_2$ percent above prime.

43 Braniff continued to have many strong points, most notably its Latin American operations. Therefore, a merger with another airline was being considered. It was hoped that a merger would bolster domestic and European lines. One company seen as highly probable for a merger was Eastern Airlines, but Eastern had also been experiencing problems. Chief Executive Frank Borman had been credited with an Eastern turnaround since 1975

even though he had been unable to reduce its debt load significantly. Other problems associated with an Eastern-Braniff merger were that (1) both companies had very high debt-to-equity ratios, (2) restraint of trade questions would arise since virtually all of Latin American travel was controlled by Eastern and Braniff, and (3) both airlines had agreed to very costly contracts for new airplane deliveries. Nonetheless, the strength of Braniff's Latin American operations coupled with Eastern's domestic strength suggested a potentially good merger.

44   It was crucial that Braniff have a positive response to its problems in the short run since it was highly unlikely stockholders would allow the losses to continue without demanding some reorganization of top management.

case **14** **Braniff (B):
The Fall and Rise
of an Airline**

"We have our costs under control...and our economic picture will vastly improve from here on out." (H. L. Lawrence, February 29, 1980)

"Braniff is a financially sound company. Braniff isn't in financial trouble. Braniff isn't in a financial hole." (H. L. Lawrence, August 21, 1980)

"Braniff is on the right course and should do well. (H. L. Lawrence, December 31, 1980)

Problems of a Billion-Dollar Airline

1   Braniff International Chairman Harding L. Lawrence had a goal: to make Braniff a billion-dollar airline. When the deregulation of the airline industry took effect in October 1978, Lawrence seized the opportunity to embark upon an ambitious growth strategy, and in just one year, Braniff expanded its passenger capacity by 37 percent to become the nation's sixth-largest airline. In that one year, 1979, Braniff was indeed the billion-dollar airline Lawrence had envisioned. Revenues rose by 65 percent from the beginning of the expansion to a total of $1.35 billion by year-end.

2   The expansion included the addition of 20 domestic destinations as well as service to Europe, Asia, and the Pacific. But such large-scale expansion proved costly for Braniff. Its operating expenses rose 55 percent in 1979, compared with an average industry rise of 21 percent, and to service all its new routes, it borrowed heavily to acquire additional aircraft. At 2.9, Braniff had one of the highest debt-to-equity ratios in the industry. Begin-

This case was prepared by John A. Pearce II and J. Kay Keels of the University of South Carolina.

ning with the third quarter of 1979, net losses were reported for four consecutive quarters.

3   Braniff had originally undertaken its expansion strategy to protect itself against its larger competitors, especially American Airlines. Braniff's management anticipated that under deregulation, its competitors would drastically reduce fares, a move that would drive smaller airlines out of business. Braniff felt that increased size would be its best means of survival if such fare wars occurred. However, much of the expansion was based on second-choice routes that either no other carrier wanted because of low traffic or because a particular airline already was firmly entrenched in those routes.

4   Braniff was not alone in facing financial strain. The entire airline industry encountered sharply rising fuel costs coupled with a general slowdown in airline traffic because of an economic recession. It was not surprising, then, that the increased competition and fare wars Braniff feared became a reality. However, because of its expansion, Braniff was more exposed to these hardships than most of the major carriers in the industry.

5   By late 1980, Braniff's finances were in serious trouble. Planned stock offerings had to be cancelled due to its failure to meet earnings requirements; it was blocked from using its bank line of credit; and some of its creditors had placed it on a cash-only status. Braniff's shortage of cash was becoming desperate, and drastic measures were required.

6   Braniff began by cutting capacity by eliminating several of its less profitable routes, and by October 1980, capacity had been slashed by nearly one third from a year earlier. The flashy Concorde service from Dallas to London and Paris, several of the Pacific flights, and a number of domestic flights were all gone.

7   One fund-raising tactic employed by Braniff was that of selling aircraft. During 1980, more than 20 jets were sold, including 15 727-200's to American Airlines and a 747 jumbo jet to an Argentine firm.

8   A second measure used to help ease the cash shortage was borrowing from banks, insurance companies, and suppliers. To obtain these loans, Braniff was forced to take the drastic step of offering its planes and equipment as collateral.

9   Although strapped for cash, to remain competitive, Braniff was forced to engage in drastic fare cutting, and in some domestic markets, the cuts exceeded 80 percent.

10   In the last quarter of 1980, Lawrence appealed to Braniff employees to help the company ease its financial problems by accepting a 10 percent pay cut. As a show of sincerity, he pledged to cut his own $300,000 per year salary by 20 percent if the deal was accepted. This time the Lawrence confidence backfired. On one hand, the chairman was assuring the press that Braniff's financial condition was solid, while on the other hand, he was appealing to Braniff's employees because the firm's financial position was tenuous. The unions representing Braniff's employees cited Lawrence's

duplicity as they rejected the pay-cut plan, even though some employees had already been laid off as a result of worsening financial conditions.

11   Merger talks were begun with Eastern Airlines late in 1980. Although a joint agreement might have helped pull the troubled Braniff through its financial troubles, Eastern itself was experiencing cash problems which ultimately ended the merger talks.

12   Overall, Lawrence's turnaround measures were viewed as too little too late. Under pressure from bankers and other lenders, Braniff's board solicited Lawrence's resignation on December 31, 1980.

13   On January 7, 1981, John J. Casey, formerly board vice chairman, was named president, chairman of the board, and chief executive officer. Among other problems, Casey inherited a long-term debt that had grown to over $600 million. Braniff's lenders took an active role in designing a new course for the airline by selecting a group of assistants for Casey who were known for their financial expertise.

14   Under Casey's direction, Braniff's operations were streamlined to emphasize three major areas: marketing—to plan to sell the product; operations—to produce and maintain the product; and finance—to analyze expenses and report on revenues. Management's immediate objectives were increased revenues and decreased expenses, and its initial strategies included reassigning resources to the most-profitable areas, eliminating nonprofitable operations, and selling additional aircraft.

15   Shortly after his election, Casey succeeded in rallying the company's employees to Braniff's cause. Effective March 1, 1981, all of the airlines unions approved an employee salary program whereby all employees' pay, including that of top management, was cut by 10 percent. These pay cuts were deemed voluntary contributions and were put into a special fund to help meet corporate cash requirements. Perhaps employees were convinced of Casey's commitment when he suspended his own $180,000 a year salary indefinitely.

16   However, a crisis arose simultaneously. Some $40 million in principal and interest on Braniff's long-term debt were due on March 1. Braniff sought a deferral until July 1, which its creditors reluctantly granted, contingent upon two factors: (1) the initiation of the employee salary program and (2) the company's development of a detailed operating plan for the remainder of the year.

17   To handle the debt-restructuring task, Casey brought in Howard P. Swanson as his top financial executive. Swanson was credited with having performed a similar task at Trans World Airlines.

18   Despite all these efforts, the question of Braniff's continued viability was raised by its auditors in the annual report issued at midyear 1981. Casey emphasized that the firm's continuation was at least partially dependent upon the continued deferral of debt payments.

19   Surprisingly, the deferral was again granted. This time Swanson was credited with convincing the airline's lenders to forgive interest payments

on debt outstanding until February 1982. The once-critical July 1 deadline passed, and Braniff was still operating.

Changes in Market Strategy

20   Just before the final quarter of 1981, Braniff moved to strengthen its management. Howard Putnam, president and CEO of Southwest Airlines, was named president and chief operating officer of Braniff. The contrast between Southwest and Braniff was dramatic. For the previous six quarters, Southwest had posted the industry's highest margin of operating profit, while Braniff was the industry's biggest loser. The announcement of Putnam's appointment was viewed as a positive sign. Observers felt Putnam would not have accepted the job had he not believed a Braniff turnaround was possible.

21   Putnam first moved to revamp completely Braniff's fare structure. The new marketing strategy, called Texas Class, featured discounted single-class air service for a single price. The number of different fares charged by Braniff nationwide dropped from 582 to just 15. Under the system, the new fares undercut regular coach fares by an average of 45 percent, and were to be available every day for every seat of every Braniff flight. Putnam referred to the strategy as "getting back to basics." Braniff had been transformed from a conventional trunk airline into one that more nearly resembled a commuter airline. The success of the strategy was dependent upon the success of the new fare system in generating additional passenger traffic. Braniff was relying on its convenience and simplicity to appeal to travel agents and the general public.

22   One undesired effect of the Texas Class fare structure was retaliation by Braniff's competitors. American Airlines, Braniff's chief competitor, announced it would immediately meet Braniff's fares on every competing route. Braniff's fare strategy was revolutionary and risky. If it worked, Braniff would have effected a complete change in the structure of air travel prices. No longer would there be discounts and other fancy pricing tactics—just prices, some high and some low.

23   As a further attempt to make its resources more productive, Braniff scheduled its planes to fly more hours every day. For example, late-night and early-morning departures were added to existing routes. In addition to their pay cuts, pilots agreed to fly 10 extra hours per month, half of them without pay. Layoffs continued to reduce the size of Braniff's work force.

24   As the February 1 deadline for debt payment approached, Braniff's only hope for survival was yet another extension. The company was broke, but it continued to operate. Although no major airline had ever failed, many observers questioned how much longer the carrier's creditors would support its operation since they held the liens on Braniff's planes.

25   The 37 creditors—22 banks, 15 insurance companies, and 2 suppliers—

had to be convinced one more time. Braniff sought to have its debt commitments extended to October 1, 1982, and again to be forgiven the $40 million in interest payments.

26 Braniff's competitors, especially its chief rival, American Airlines, would benefit directly from the company's bankruptcy, and American had retaliated immediately in the fare wars even though it meant substantial losses. However, American was large and strong enough to withstand such losses in the short term while it knew Braniff was not. Further, American had added several directly competing routes in an attempt to defeat Braniff's strategy. Now there was evidence that American was urging Braniff's creditors to withdraw their support.

27 There was little incentive, however, for the creditors to let the troubled carrier fail. If Braniff were forced into bankruptcy, creditors would be left with their collateral—dozens of 727 jets for which there was almost no market because of the recession-induced U.S. travel slump. The alternative was for lenders to accept some equity and forgive some of the total long- and short-term private debt that at this point had reached $733.2 million.

28 Throughout this period, Braniff continued its slimming and trimming tactics. Late in April 1982, the South American routes were leased to Eastern Airlines in a $30 million deal. Despite Braniff's precarious financial position, its officials were guardedly optimistic that the Eastern deal might lead the way toward generating sufficient revenues for survival.

29 Then, two weeks later, Braniff surprised the industry and some of its own executives. At midnight on May 12, 1982, Braniff suspended all flying operations. The reason for the abrupt cessation of service was not immediately clear, but it was suggested that one of Braniff's lenders had called in its portion of the debt. Braniff was one step away from bankruptcy.

30 Even as the announcement halting flights and telling workers to stay home were made, Braniff directors were meeting to decide whether to file under Chapter 11 or Chapter 7 of federal bankruptcy proceedings. Under Chapter 11, the company would be protected from its creditors while the court oversaw its reorganization plans. Chapter 7 would guide the liquidation of the company's assets.

31 A few hours later, Howard Putnam declared he had not taken the Braniff job in order to preside over its liquidation. Braniff was filing to reorganize under Chapter 11.

32 Bankruptcy experts were puzzled by the way Braniff had proceeded. Normally, a troubled firm will file under Chapter 11 in order to continue to operate while being protected from its creditors. Braniff, however, had first shut down its operations, then laid off its employees, and finally filed for reorganization. Despite the unorthodox procedure, Putnam insisted that the airline would resume operations—either under its own name or under someone else's as a consequence of a merger. Putnam explained that the decision to cease operations was made because Braniff was simply out of cash. The next day, May 13, 1982, would have been a scheduled payday for

Table 1

Balance sheet of Braniff International (system data; $ thousands)

	March 31, 1982	1981	1980	1979
Assets				
Current assets				
Cash and short-term investments	29,213	42,480	13,626	23,724
Notes and accounts receivable	141,342	150,923	176,670	136,664
Less: allowance for uncollectible accounts	7,960	7,462	5,894	4,825
Spare parts, supplies and other	40,825	47,333	48,925	49,895
Less: allowance for obsolescence	4,896	4,790	4,673	4,737
Total current assets	198,524	228,484	228,654	200,722
Investments and special funds	1,670	1,706	1,702	1,792
Operating property and equipment				
Flight equipment	757,916	733,232	863,325	952,553
Ground property, equipment and other	152,771	154,089	165,501	155,705
Less: allowance for depreciation	342,780	341,512	323,362	335,703
Owned property and equipment—net	567,907	585,809	705,464	772,556
Leased property under capital leases	111,212	114,670	151,100	152,757
Less: accumulated depreciation	45,910	47,230	71,643	68,081
Capital leases property—net	65,302	67,440	79,457	84,676
Equipment purchase deposits	9,397	9,397	13,724	30,391
Owned and leased property and equipment—net	642,606	662,646	798,645	887,623
Nonoperating property and equipment, owned and leased—net	38,731	38,731	219	284
Other assets	15,447	14,236	17,950	45,648
Total assets	896,978	945,803	1,047,170	1,136,069

Braniff employees, and Putnam indicated the company could not have met its payroll.

The Search for a Reorganization Plan

33   Braniff was allowed 120 days to file its reorganization plan with the courts. The firm's management quickly decided that its best hope lay in a joint venture. Throughout the remainder of 1982, Braniff engaged in merger talks with several airlines. As the filing deadline drew near, Braniff sought and obtained an extension on its filing date, and 1982 closed without a concrete decision.

34   Through the first quarter of 1983, Braniff's fate remained a question mark. Putnam negotiated with 16 airlines concerning the utilization of the company's aircraft, equipment, facilities, and personnel, but only Pacific Southwest Airlines presented a viable plan. Although major creditors and

Table 1 (continued)

	March 31, 1982	1981	1980	1979
Liabilities and Stockholders' Equity				
Current liabilities				
Current maturities of debt and notes payable	78,329	77,806	35,718	16,319
Current obligations under capital leases	4,307	4,428	10,217	10,543
Air traffic liabilities	79,685	95,911	87,727	38,634
Other	198,088	194,948	187,737	196,736
Total current liabilities	361,409	373,093	321,399	262,232
Noncurrent liabilities				
Long-term debt	395,118	401,731	444,602	480,311
Advances from associated companies				
Obligations under capital leases	70,430	71,782	79,473	86,918
Other	30,851	30,652	7,598	3,309
Total noncurrent liabilities	496,399	504,165	531,673	570,538
Deferred credits				
Deferred income taxes	2,755	2,755	2,849	10,240
Deferred investment tax credits				
Other	48,170	33,776	1,292	4,087
Total deferred credits	50,925	36,531	4,141	14,327
Stockholders' equity				
Preferred stock	121,483	119,330	110,000	80,000
Common stock	15	15	15	15
Subscribed and unissued				
Total capital stock	121,498	119,345	110,015	80,015
Additional capital invested	67,188	67,188	67,188	67,188
Total paid-in capital	188,686	186,533	177,203	147,203
Retained earnings				
Retained earnings	-200,441	-154,519	12,754	141,769
Net unrealized loss noncurrent market equity security				
Total stockholders' equity	-11,755	32,014	189,957	288,972
Less: treasury stock				
Stockholders' equity—net	-11,755	32,014	189,957	288,972
Total liabilities and stockholders' equity	896,978	945,803	1,047,170	1,136,069

the bankruptcy court approved the pact, it was rejected by a U.S. appeals court, thereby terminating the Braniff-PSA talks.

35   With its last hope of a joint venture seemingly gone, Braniff's management turned its attention toward a reorganization plan that stopped just short of full liquidation. Under the plan, due to be submitted in federal bankruptcy court on April 4, 1983, the firm would divest itself of all its assets related to flying and would form a small business that would provide ground service and contract maintenance for other carriers. Braniff offi-

cials continued to believe that a live company in any form was better for creditors than a dead one. In Braniff's favor, the court deadline was postponed until April 18 due to a crowded court calendar.

The Hyatt Alternative

36   In the meantime, Braniff began talks with Hyatt Corporation, the Chicago-based hotel chain. Hyatt offered an investment proposal in return for an interest-bearing note and a majority of the voting stock in the reorganized company. Under the Hyatt plan, Braniff would resume flight operations.

37   The talks with Hyatt encountered some major obstacles, most notably the disapproval of Howard Putnam who considered the plan to be under-funded. Even after the original offer was raised considerably, Putnam still opposed it. As the April 18 deadline for filing reorganization plans drew near, no agreement had been reached. Braniff filed its original ground service proposal but with the stipulation that revised plan could be filed that could include resumption of flight operations. Clearly the door was being left open for Hyatt to sweeten its offer. The talks continued.

38   Finally, in June 1983, Braniff and Hyatt agreed on a plan to put Braniff back in the air. Under the plan, Hyatt would ensure the new airline some $70 million in funding. In return, Hyatt would get 80 percent interest in the reorganized airline and more than $300 million in Braniff tax credits.

39   However, the agreement still faced numerous hurdles. First, there was an effort by American Airlines to squelch the deal. American knew Hyatt was having trouble convincing Braniff's creditors to accept its offer. So American attempted to sway the creditors by offering to buy Braniff's remaining fleet, thus effectively halting any plan that would put Braniff in the air again. Second, the environment was less than ideal for a new entrant into an industry already plagued by overcapacity and revenue-draining fare wars. Third, the immediate problem was to get Braniff's major creditors to agree to the proposal. Many of them were skeptical and feared they might end up as two-time losers. Finally, the proposal required the approval of the bankruptcy court.

40   The major obstacle turned out to be the secured creditor's objections to the lease offer made to them by Hyatt. As holders of the liens on Braniff's planes, the creditors felt they could realize a larger yield by selling the aircraft. For weeks, Hyatt's Jay Pritzker, a principal in the firm, mediated between Braniff's management and its creditors, trying to secure agreement from the lenders.

41   After much negotiation, an acceptable offer was tendered. The last major hurdle had been cleared. In September 1983, the Braniff reorganization plan was approved by a federal bankruptcy court, and the stage was finally set for Braniff to fly again.

Table 2

Income statement data on Braniff International showing revenues, expenses, and income ($ thousands)

	1981	*1980*	*1979*
Operating Revenues			
Transport scheduled			
Passenger, first class	12,518	40,334	50,002
Passenger, coach	202,622	250,657	257,146
Total passenger revenues	215,150	290,991	307,148
Freight	9,306	13,032	17,580
Air express	603	182	230
Excess baggage	1,751	2,204	6,780
Total property revenues	11,660	15,418	24,590
Priority U.S. mail	4,629	5,909	1,509
Nonpriority U.S. mail	73	136	38
Foreign mail	129	142	95
Total mail revenue	4,831	6,187	1,642
Other	1,013	1,154	779
Total scheduled revenues	232,644	313,750	334,159
Transport nonscheduled			
Charter, passenger	1,307	1,827	3,113
Charter, freight			
Total nonscheduled revenues	1,307	1,827	3,113
Total transport revenues	233,951	315,577	337,271
Transport-related			
Subsidy			
Other transport-related	7,885	7,892	7,177
Total transport-related revenues	7,885	7,892	7,117
Total operating revenues	241,836	323,469	344,448
Operating Expenses			
Flying operations	133,938	146,720	174,931
Maintenance	21,338	27,761	34,366
Passenger service	25,073	31,511	38,679
Aircraft and traffic servicing	48,065	58,009	63,852
Promotion and sales	39,896	50,789	44,690
General and administrative	12,869	15,974	10,479
Transport-related	4,415	5,156	4,195
Amortization of development and preoperation			
expenses, etc.	711	2,078	2,339
Depreciation, owned flight equipment	14,444	13,046	13,812
Depreciation, other than owned flight equipment	3,124	3,121	2,682
Amortization, capital leases	3,335	2,285	2,834
Total depreciation	21,614	20,530	21,667
Total operating expenses	307,208	356,450	392,859
Operating profit (loss)	−65,372	−32,981	−48,411

Table 2 (continued)

	1981	1980	1979
Nonoperating Profit (Loss)			
Interest expense on debt	-5,021	-16,164	-12,347
Interest expense on capital leases	-1,669	-1,933	-2,559
Total interest expense	-6,690	-18,097	-14,906
Capitalized interest		-3,190	2,344
Capital gains (losses) operational property	5,269	741	1,775
Other income (expenses)—net	-9,295	-19,526	811
Nonoperating income and expenses—net	-10,716	-40,072	-9,977
Net Income			
Net income (loss) before income taxes	-76,088	-73,053	-58,388
		-470	-12,012
Net income (loss) after income taxes	-76,088	-73,523	-46,376
Nonrecurring Items			
Income (loss) discontinued operations			
Extraordinary items income (loss)			
Accounting changes income (loss)			
Net income (loss) after nonrecurring items	-76,088	-73,523	-46,376

42   Hyatt's plan for Braniff was ambitious, but it held many advantages. From the beginning, the plan had the support of Braniff's unsecured creditors and its employees. Most of its unions granted positive cost advantages in wage contract renegotiations, and these concessions alone gave Braniff the chance to operate as one of the lowest-cost carriers in the industry. In addition, many Braniff workers volunteered to work without pay prior to the start-up date to get their jets back in the air. Some employees even came out of retirement to help.

43   Industry analysts believed Hyatt's toughest job would be to put together a capable management team. Though none of the top management of the "old Braniff" remained, good management was a Hyatt trademark. It had consistently been rated as one of the best-managed chains in the lodging industry. Perhaps Hyatt could bring from outside the industry what the airline lacked.

44   Braniff also had to win over doubting and somewhat disgruntled travelers and travel agents. When the airline had abruptly shut down in 1982, many of its passengers had been left stranded, holding worthless tickets. Competing airlines were reluctant to honor Braniff tickets since they knew they would be unable to collect from Braniff. Additionally, since travel agents sell more than 60 percent of all airline tickets, their acceptance was crucial.

45   Hyatt's strategy was aimed at getting travelers and agents to try the "new Braniff." Hyatt was confident their service was good enough to keep

customers once it had them. To attract customers, a joint promotional campaign with the March of Dimes was initiated whereby a 5 percent savings on the ticket price would be donated to the March of Dimes. To build goodwill among travel agents, Braniff held elaborate receptions in many of the cities it served and also gave agents free tickets. An additional aid to booking travelers came as part of a lawsuit settlement against Braniff's old rival, American Airlines. Braniff was awarded the right to placement in American's computerized reservations system.

46   The new Braniff that began flight operations on March 1, 1984, was a sleeker, slimmer edition of the former major carrier. There would be no overseas flights and no first-class service. Instead, Braniff divided its passengers into business-traveler and leisure-traveler segments. Counting heavily on the business traveler, Braniff offered its "business cabin" area as a special attraction.

47   The new airline initially employed some 2,200 people to handle its flight schedules to 19 cities. The 30 727 planes that remained in Braniff's fleet featured the standard red, white, blue, and silver exterior but had a plush new look inside.

48   Despite the tenuous condition of the industry that had not fully recovered, despite the many months of management failure and employee unrest, despite the doubts of creditors, despite the obstacles posed in trying to win over a skeptical public, and despite the stiff competition Braniff faced on every one of its planned routes, the new Braniff proudly rolled down the runway once again. The optimism that prevailed against all the odds was evident in Braniff's March 1984 public announcement:

The new Braniff
Only in America

This is the beginning of a modern American success story. Today, the first day of operation for the new Braniff, is proof to us that the system works.

We're not talking about business as usual here. The largest start-up in the history of aviation does not just happen. This is the result of twenty-two months of intensive work. Twenty-two months of searching for new solutions and new ideas. Twenty-two months of joint effort.

The new Braniff is a proud symbol for a new era of cooperation. The spirit of cooperation that exists between Braniff employees and our new management team is a signpost for the future.

We frankly admit that without the support, without the outstanding reasonableness of all Braniff people (who are now 65% more productive than their counterparts at other airlines), there would be no new Braniff.

We're confident that twelve months from today, our spirited service and redoubled efficiency will have earned and secured your continued patronage.

case **15** **Southwest Airlines:
Interstate Travel**

1 "It's been a hectic few months," reflected Camille Keith (Southwest Airlines' vice president of public relations), "but we're finally spreading love outside of Texas." While the urge to sit back and relax was very strong, she knew that the job of expanding air service to the three new markets had just begun. Was the introduction successfully launched? What did the new market customers think of Southwest? Was the advertising working?

2 Ms. Keith knew that marketing research held the answers to many of her questions, and that a thorough review of recent strategy was in order. Some information was already available, but some other would probably need to be collected. "Let's see where we stand," she commented to Tom Volz (Southwest's vice president of marketing and sales).

3 "Fine!" replied Mr. Volz, "Let's get together first thing tomorrow morning."

4 "Tomorrow's meeting means a long today," though Ms. Keith, as she began reviewing the background on the campaign planning. "Hold my calls and see if my other meeting this afternoon can be postponed," she called to her secretary.

The Company

5 Southwest Airlines began intrastate service in Texas on June 18, 1971, with three Boeing 737-200 aircraft, and a marketing strategy which highlighted several unique attributes:

This case was prepared by Richard F. Beltramini of Arizona State University.

1. Simplicity of operations (one type of aircraft, Dallas' Love Field headquarters, simplified passenger check-in and fare structure, and no food service)

2. High productivity (daily aircraft utilization of more than 11 hours and 10 minutes turnaround times between most flights)

3. Focus on passenger business (no large air freight and no U.S. mail)

4. Serving short-haul, mass-transit commuter market (flight segments under two hours and fare structure competitive with bus and auto travel)

6   As of March 15, 1980, Southwest had grown to 1,600 employees, 31 aircraft, 1,852 total system-wide weekly flights, and an average load factor of 68.3 percent (based on 1979 figures and a 118 seat capacity). Exhibit 1 illustrates their growth in passenger boardings over the years in operation, and Exhibit 2 shows their operating statistics in relation to income.

7   Between 1972 and 1979, the number of passengers carried grew at an annual rate of 48.9 percent. The reason for this growth, according to Southwest's management, was that they offered a good product in a receptive market at a fair price that the average person could afford.

8   In late 1978, Southwest Airlines served 11 major Texas cities as an intrastate carrier subject to the economic regulation of the Texas Aeronautics Commission. However, in December of that year, Southwest received their Certificate of Public Convenience and Necessity from the Civil Aeronautics Board, providing them the authority to extend their service beyond Texas. The first route outside Texas was to New Orleans almost immediately, and routes were added to Oklahoma City on April 1, 1980 to Tulsa on April 2, and to Albuquerque on April 3.

The Market

9   Nineteen seventy-nine was a year of considerable change within the airline industry. Deregulation had precipitated many fare reduction programs; however by the end of the year, the fuel crisis had seemingly reversed this policy, and fares had increased once again.

10   Fuel costs in 1978 averaged $.37 per gallon, while 1979 saw an increase to $.80 per gallon by the year's end. Southwest Airlines' management projected that fuel costs would exceed $1.00 per gallon in 1980, representing 40 percent of their budget for operating costs.

11   The deregulation trend, however, afforded Southwest the opportunity to expand service into new markets, and their business philosophy pointed to three cities with apparent growth potential. The Oklahoma City, Tulsa, and Albuquerque markets are described briefly in Exhibit 3. It was felt that expanding air service to these cities from their Dallas headquarters offered a profitable strategy to capitalize on the regulatory changes. Exhibit 4 illustrates the relative location of these new markets.

Exhibit 1

Southwest Airlines passenger boardings

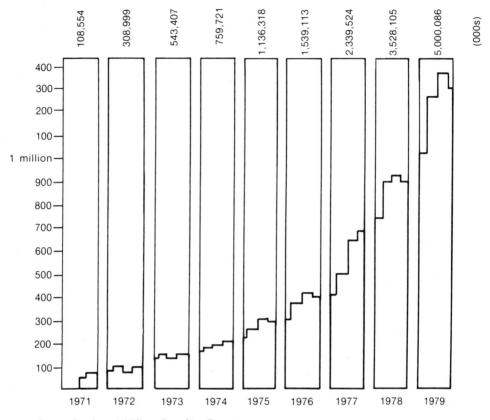

Source: Southwest Airlines Boarding Reports.

Marketing Research

12   The potential for expanding service appeared profitable given the trends evident in executive class boardings (see Exhibit 5), total passenger boardings (see Exhibit 6), the 1979 load factors (see Exhibit 7), and the projected growth (see Exhibit 8). To supplement these data, however, a research project was conducted in the fall of 1979. A random, system-wide survey of 7,900 Southwest Airlines' passengers was conducted on board flights to identify the frequency of flying and the attributes deemed important by these passengers.

13   Each respondent was asked how many round-trip flights he had taken on Southwest during the past year. The results (shown below) indicated

Exhibit 2

Southwest Airlines financial statements

Consolidated balance sheet
for the years ended March 31
($000)

	1980	1979
Assets		
Current:		
Cash and commercial paper	$ 8,936	$ 8,374
Accounts receivable..................	11,678	5,447
Other	1,590	1,058
Total current assets	22,204	14,879
Flight and ground equipment,		
at cost less reserves	169,507	112,763
Other noncurrent assets	877	366
Total assets	$192,588	$128,008
Liabilities and Net Worth		
Liabilities:		
Current:		
Accounts payable and		
accrued liabilities	$ 10,615	$ 6,287
Current maturities of		
long-term debt	4,720	1,750
Total current liabilities	15,335	8,037
Long-term debt less		
current maturities	98,487	63,250
Deferred federal income tax	14,186	10,398
Deferred other........................	942	387
Total liabilities	128,950	82,072
Net worth:		
Common stock and		
paid-in capital	15,828	14,448
Retained earnings	47,810	31,488
Total net worth.................	63,638	45,936
Total liabilities and net worth	$192,588	$128,008
Share data:		
Common stock issued		
and outstanding		
(Note A) (000s)	4,567	4,500
Book value per share	$ 13.94	$ 10,21

Consolidated statement of income
three months ended March 31
($000)

	1980	1979
Operating revenues:		
Passenger	$ 38,878	$ 24,732
Package express	1,116	799
Other...............................	192	146
Total operating expenses	40,186	25,677

	1980	1979
Operating expenses:		
Flight operations excluding fuel	3,470	2,453
Fuel and oil	12,631	5,286
Maintenance.........................	2,383	1,521
Passenger services	1,654	1,173
Terminal operations	4,485	3,126
Promotion and sales.................	1,808	1,479
Insurance, taxes, and		
administrative	2,662	1,895
Depreciation	2,638	1,858
Employee profit sharing		
expense............................	923	688
Total operating expenses	32,654	19,479
Total operating income	7,521	6,198
Nonoperating expense (income):		
Interest and other income	(1,020)	(40)
Interest expense	2,459	1,813
	1,439	1,773
Income before federal income tax	6,093	4,425
Provision for federal income tax	1,784	1,097
Net income...........................	$ 4,309	$ 3,328
Weighted average common		
and common equivalent		
shares outstanding		
(Note A) (000s)	4,544	4,500
Net income per share	$ .95	$ .74

Comparative operating statistics
three months ended March 31

	1980	1979
Number of flights	18,833	15,935
Passengers carried	1,189,745	1,038,657
Passenger miles flown (000)	383,773	317,806
Passenger load factor	63.9%	67.9%
Operating revenues per flight	$2,134	$1,611
Operatings expenses per flight	1,734	1,222
Operating income per flight	$ 400	$ 389

Note A: All share data adjusted to reflect the effect of the 3-for-2 stock split on February 23, 1979.

Basis of Presentation—The consolidated financial statements include the accounts of the Company and its wholly owned subsidiary Midway (Southwest) Airway Co. All significant intercompany accounts or transactions have been eliminated in consolidation. Certain reclassifications of amounts previously reported in the financial statements at March 31, 1979, have been made to conform to the presentation at March 31, 1980.

Exhibit 3

Southwest Airlines new markets

Oklahoma City, the capital of Oklahoma, is the largest municipality in the state with a population of 368,164 (1970 census). Located in Central Oklahoma on the North Canadian River, the city represents the state's financial, commercial, and industrial center built on rich oil and gas lands. Its industry includes meat packing, electronic components, production of transportation equipment, and oil field supplies. A frequent convention center, it has also grown into an aeronautical complex, housing Federal Aviation Administration facilities and Tinker Air Force Base. Additionally, a variety of tourist attractions such as the National Cowboy Hall of Fame and the Western Heritage Center are located in Oklahoma City, approximately 181 air miles from Dallas.

Tulsa, Oklahoma, a city of 330,350 (1970 census), has been dubbed "The Oil Capital of the World" and is the western-most inland water port in the United States. Next to oil, aviation and aerospace industries are the next largest employers. A beautiful city of parks and old homes, Tulsa is also the home of the University of Tulsa and Oral Roberts University. Located at the base of the Ozark Mountains, the city is surrounded by lakes, and is a water-sports haven. Tulsa is approximately 237 air miles from Dallas.

Albuquerque, New Mexico is the largest city in New Mexico with a population of 243,751 (1979 census). Located in North-Central New Mexico on the Upper Rio Grande, it is a fast-growing center of trade, small industry, federal agencies, and a famous health resort. Following World War II, growth accelerated rapidly due primarily to Sandia Corporation's nuclear weapons laboratory and Kirtland Air Force Base, a nuclear effects research laboratory and satellite tracking station. Albuquerque's manufacturing industry includes brick and tile, wood products, Indian jewelry, clothing, and business machines. Additionally, several railroad shops, lumber mills, and food processing plants are located there, as well as the University of New Mexico. Albuquerque is approximately 580 air miles from Dallas.

Exhibit 4

Southwest Airlines air miles between new markets

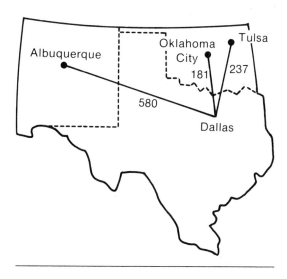

Exhibit 5

Southwest Airlines executive class boardings, 1979

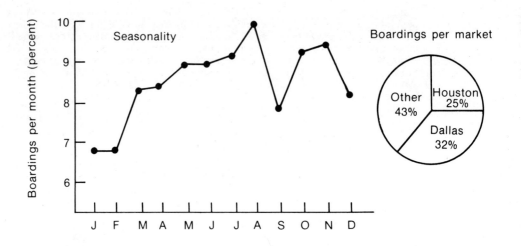

Exhibit 6

Southwest Airlines total passenger boardings, 1979

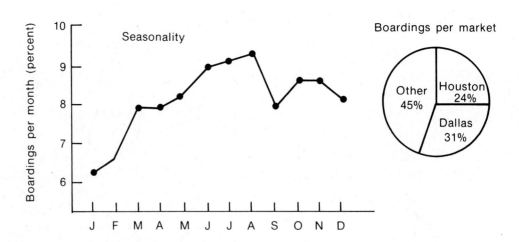

Exhibit 7

Southwest Airlines 1979 load factors

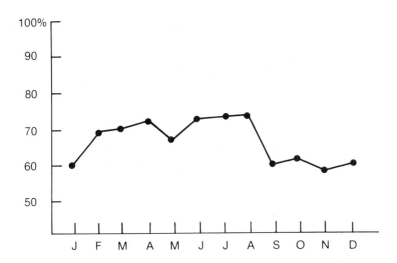

Exhibit 8

Southwest Airlines 1980 forecast

	1979	1980	Increase Number	Percent
Total passenger boardings	5,000,000	7,000,000	2,000,000	40
Total trips	76,000	105,000	29,000	38
Available seat miles	2,500,000,000	3,500,000,000	1,000,000,000	40
Revenue passenger miles	1,500,000,000	2,500,000,000	1,000,000,000	67

that 18.7 percent of the respondents accounted for 55 percent of the total trips.

No. of flights	Percent of respondents	Percent of trips
1-2	22.9%	3%
3-6	29.0	11
7-12	16.7	13
13-20	12.7	18
21-40	10.9	28
41+	7.8	27
	100.0%	100%

14   Respondents were also asked to evaluate various airline attributes in terms of importance, using a four-point rating scale (4 = very important; 1 = not important at all). As shown below, departing on time was rated as the most important attribute by the majority of those surveyed.

Attribute	Rank	Percent of respondents rating important
On-time departure..........................	1	98.61
Frequency of scheduled departures..........	2	97.86
Friendly ground personnel	3	97.12
Convenient departure times	4	96.99
Courteous hostesses	5	95.51
Baggage handling	6	93.01
Lower fares	7	91.05

15   After assessing what passengers generally wanted in air service, respondents were also asked to indicate their particular likes and dislikes concerning Southwest Airlines. Low fares was the highest ranked positive attribute (see below).

Attribute	Rank
Low fares..................................	1
Convenient airports	2
Pleasant hostesses	3
Convenient (in general)	4
On-time departure.........................	5
Frequency of scheduled departures..........	6
Prompt and efficient service	7

16   In another independent survey, *Texas Business* polled their subscribers concerning airline service. The results of this survey coincidentally appeared in their February 1980 issue, just as Southwest Airlines was granted their three new interstate routes. The results (shown below) indicated Southwest was rated as "excellent" or "good" by over 90 percent of those 795 respondents.

	Meals	Ticketing performance	Luggage handling	Hospitality	Overall performance
Southwest	*	1	1	1	1
American	2	2	3	2	3
Delta	3	3	2	3	2
Continental................	1	4	4	4	4
Braniff	4	7	7	6	7
Eastern....................	5	5	5	5	5
Texas Int'l................	6	6	5	7	5

*No meal service.
Source: Texas Business, February 1980.

Marketing Strategy

17   Besides maintaining a consistent growth pattern in previously established routes, Southwest Airlines management's highest priority in 1980 was the introduction of the new routes to Oklahoma City, Tulsa, and Albuquerque on April 1, 2, and 3, respectively. Service from Dallas' Love Field to these new markets was established as follows.

Market	Schedule
Oklahoma City	7 round-trips daily
Tulsa	7 round-trips daily
Albuquerque..........	4–5 round-trips daily

18   Passengers arriving from these cities to Dallas' Love Field could connect with flights to the rest of the Southwest Airlines' system from Love Field. Likewise, passengers from other destinations could travel to these new cities through a connection at Love Field. However, Southwest did not plan to have any direct flights from the new cities to other Southwest Airlines' markets until passenger load factors to Dallas' Love Field were deemed successful.

19   To assist in the planning and development of these new routes. Southwest obtained a traffic history analysis of the 1978 origins and destina-

tions (O&D) from each of the new markets. Dallas/Ft. Worth was the O&D leader from each of the new cities, Houston ranking a strong second (particularly from Tulsa and Oklahoma City). The latter was hypothesized to be the result of petroleum-related industry traffic. Albuquerque, was marked not only by an increasingly growing business community (particularly in electronics) but also as a pleasure travel market. The New Mexico area was becoming a very popular ski market to Texans. Exhibit 9 illustrates the 1978 O&D's from each new market.

Advertising Strategy

20   The introduction of the new routes was supported by a heavy radio and newspaper advertising campaign created by the Bloom Agency, South-

---

Exhibit 9

Southwest Airlines 1978 origins and destinations report

From Oklahoma City

150,000	Dallas/Ft. Worth
115,000	Houston
30,000	New Orleans
26,000	San Antonio
13,000	Midland/Odessa
12,000	Austin
10,000	El Paso
27,000	N/A
383,000	

From Tulsa

160,000	Dallas/Ft. Worth
150,000	Houston
34,000	New Orleans
15,000	New Orleans
15,000	San Antonio
13,000	Midland/Odessa
9,000	Austin
3,000	Rio Grande Valley
29,000	N/A
413,000	

From Albuquerque

108,000	Dallas/Ft. Worth
50,000	El Paso
40,000	Houston
20,000	San Antonio
11,000	New Orleans
11,000	Midland/Odessa
10,000	Lubbock
24,000	N/A
274,000	

west's advertising agency of record. Two weeks before the inaugural flights, the campaign broke with small "teaser" advertisements in the new market newspapers. The advertisements contained headlines such as "Here Comes Love, Southwest Style" and listed a phone number to make reservations.

21   That same week also began 60-second radio spots, running primarily in the morning and late afternoon, designed to reach the businessman during drive time. It was felt by both Southwest's marketing team and the agency that businessmen represented the heaviest travelers and the appropriate target audience for these messages.

22   The week before the initial flights, the newspaper advertisements were stepped up to twice daily, and the radio schedule was doubled. Nearly every radio station in the new markets was running Southwest Airlines' spots. On Monday, March 31, just days before the inaugural flights, full-page advertisements appeared in addition to the teaser newspaper advertisements in each of the local markets.

23   Monday also marked the posting of 30 outdoor posters with messages such as "Tightwads Rejoice" and "Big D, Little $" on the major arterials throughout the new market cities. The full-page advertisements ran once daily through each inaugural flight, and radio stations continued to broadcast "That's Love, Southwest Style." Exhibit 10 illustrates another print advertisement which appeared in *Southwest,* their in-flight publication.

24   On the day of each inaugural flight, Howard Putnam (President of Southwest Airlines) joined Tom Volz and Camille Keith to welcome new passengers personally, and later dignitaries at banquets held after each new route opening. Billboards proclaimed each city's welcome to Southwest, and four-color, truck newspaper advertisements announced that air service had officially begun.

25   The advertising blitz in those first three weeks was designed to reach approximately 90 percent of the households in each new market, and the combination of newspaper, radio, and outdoor advertising was meant to add breadth to the media coverage. Although no television or magazine advertising was conducted during this period, a number of news stories appeared, reflecting Southwest's public relations releases.

Effectiveness Research

26   While Southwest regularly conducts on-board passenger surveys, the occasion of these route extensions prompted them to supplement their research program. On-board surveys were administered randomly by flight attendants to new market customers one week after the expansion of service to garner some general feedback on how passengers in the new markets had heard about Southwest and the new routes. Further, there was some feeling at Southwest that the radio buy had been too wide, and they wanted to see

Exhibit 10

Southwest Airlines print advertisement

THANKS TO YOU, WE'RE STILL IN LOVE.

On February 15, 1980, a compromise bill authorizing limited interstate service from Love Field was signed into law. The bill permits Southwest Airlines to use Love Field both for flights within Texas and to states bordering Texas. It also signals the end of a long and heated controversy over Love Field's use as a satellite airport.

We at Southwest have held fast in the belief that Love Field represents a valuable service to our passengers, both for intrastate and interstate travel. And hundreds of thousands of Texans feel the same way. The strength of those convictions was demonstrated when Love Field was threatened by a bill proposing total elimination of all interstate flights from Love.

Last November when the contents of that proposed bill became public, supporters of Southwest and of Love Field made their feelings known in editorials, letters, mailgrams, and over 160,000 signatures on petitions circulated by Southwest. One particularly heartwarming show of support was the response to our "Now is the time to fight for Love" ad asking for endorsement in the form of a mail-in coupon. We ran that ad only one time and received an overwhelming response of over 16,000 coupons.

These massive demonstrations of support by citizens throughout the state helped convince the U.S. Congress that Southwest Airlines and Love Field do indeed provide a valuable service to Texans.

The generous support of our passengers and friends was particularly meaningful to all of us here at Southwest. Not only because it aided in a compromise bill which permits our continued growth, but also because it shows that the service we provide is important to you. And we're reaffirming our service commitment by opening flights to Oklahoma City, Tulsa and Albuquerque in April.

In the meantime, we hope you'll accept a less tangible display of gratitude in the form of one simple statement: thank you.

Herbert D. Kelleher
Chairman of the Board

Howard D. Putnam
President and Chief Executive Officer

SOUTHWEST AIRLINES

if that was correct.

27   The results of the three surveys conducted by Southwest (see Exhibits 11, 12, and 13) were somewhat confusing to Ms. Keith as she reviewed them, along with a variety of other information, in preparation for her meeting the next morning. For example, how could television have ranked so highly in advertising recall when no television advertising had run? What explanations could be offered for the differential results obtained between the new market cities? What were the managerial implications of the survey results, and what action was next appropriate? Was more research needed? These were the types of questions that were bound to come up in the meeting, and she knew she had less than 24 hours to prepare the answers.

Exhibit 11

Southwest Airlines advertising recall study: Oklahoma City service

1. Where do you recall seeing or hearing the Southwest Airlines advertising of the new route service?

Newspaper	145
Radio	92
TV	743
Billboard	29
Magazine	16
Don't know	24
Other	14

2. In which newspaper(s) did you see this advertising?

Ft. Worth Star Telegram	6
Dallas Morning News	53
Dallas Times Herald	40
Daily Oklahoman	69
Oklahoma Journal	11
Other	12

3. On which radio station(s) do you recall hearing this advertising?

KBYE, Oklahoma	0
KEBC, Oklahoma	21
KFNB, Oklahoma	0
KOCY, Oklahoma	7
KOFM, Oklahoma	7
KOMA, Oklahoma	7
KTOK, Oklahoma	13
KXXY, Oklahoma	1
KZUE, Oklahoma	5
WKY, Oklahoma	5
KAAM, Texas	1
KBOX, Texas	3
KFJZ, Texas	2

Exhibit 11 (continued)

KNTU, Texas	0
KOAX, Texas	3
KRLD, Texas	17
KVIL, Texas	9
WFAA, Texas	5
WRR, Texas	2
Other	4

4. On which television station(s) do you recall seeing this advertising?

KOCO, (Ch. 5) Oklahoma	19
KTVY, (Ch. 4) Oklahoma	15
KWTV, (Ch. 9) Oklahoma	4
KDFW, (Ch. 4) Texas	5
KERA, (Ch. 13) Texas	3
KTVT, (Ch. 11) Texas	2
KXAS, (Ch. 5) Texas	6
WFAA, (Ch. 8) Texas	11

5. Do you recall seeing or hearings NEWS coverage about the new routes? Where?

Newspapers	63
Radio	43
TV	35
Magazine	6

6. Did you hear about the new route service from a travel agency?

Yes	29
No	215

7. What in the advertising attracted you?

Convenience of SWA	132
Low fares	140
High frequency	78
Friendly service	59
Close in airports	124

8. What is your occupation?

Professional/technical	118
Managers/administrators	107
Sales workers	37
Clerical workers	3
Craftsmen/foremen	1
Operatives	0
Service workers	2
Student	5
Retired	3
Unemployed	5
No answer	1

9. Into which of the following age categories do you fall?

18–24	18
25–34	78

Exhibit 11 (concluded)

35–44	90
45–54	57
55–64	26
65 over	8

10. Into which of the following categories does your total yearly household income fall?

$10,000 and under	5
$10,000–$14,999	9
$15,000–$19,999	57
$20,000–$24,999	16
$25,000 over	210
No answer	26

11. How frequently do you fly?

Once a week or more	76
Two or three times a month	129
Seldom	73

Exhibit 12

Southwest Airlines advertising recall study: Tulsa service

1. Where do you recall seeing or hearing the Southwest Airlines advertising of the new route service?

Newspaper	131
Radio	90
TV	51
Billboard	40
Magazine	16
Don't know	26
Other	17

2. In which newspaper(s) did you see this advertising?

Ft. Worth Star Telegram	8
Dallas Morning News	64
Dallas Times Herald	32
Tulsa Tribune	53
Tulsa World	82
Other	21

3. On which radio station(s) do you recall hearing this advertising?

KAKC, Oklahoma	7
KCFO, Oklahoma	1
KELI, Oklahoma	8
KFMJ, Oklahoma	0
KMOD, Oklahoma	17

Exhibit 12 (continued)

KRMG, Oklahoma	33
KTOW, Oklahoma	2
KVOO, Oklahoma	13
KXXO, Oklahoma	2
KAAM, Oklahoma	2
KBOK, Texas	7
KFJZ, Texas	4
KLIF, Texas	2
KNTU, Texas	1
KOAX, Texas	4
KRLD, Texas	10
KVIL, Texas	8
WFAA, Texas	8
WRR, Texas	0
KNUS, Texas	7
Other	2

4. On which television station(s) do you recall seeing this advertising?

KOTV, (Ch. 6) Oklahoma	17
KTEW, (Ch. 2) Oklahoma	18
KTUL, (Ch. 8) Oklahoma	21
KDFW, (Ch. 4) Texas	14
KERA, (Ch. 13) Texas	4
KTVT, (Ch. 11) Texas	5
KXAS, (Ch. 5) Texas	5
WFAA, (Ch. 8) Texas	16

5. Do you recall seeing or hearings NEWS coverage about the new routes? Where?

Newspapers	106
Radio	56
TV	58
Magazine	9

6. Did you hear about the new route service from a travel agency?

Yes	49
No	242

7. What in the advertising attracted you?

Convenience of SWA	127
Low fares	206
High frequency	84
Friendly service	82
Close in airports	141

8. What is your occupation?

Professional/technical	112
Managers/administrators	105
Sales workers	49
Clerical workers	8
Craftsmen/foremen	4
Operatives	2

Exhibit 12 (concluded)

Service workers	3
Student	4
Retired	6
Unemployed	7
No answer	7

9. Into which of the following age categories do you fall?

18–24	6
25–34	61
35–44	52
45–54	46
55–64	13
65 over	3

10. Into which of the following categories does your total yearly household income fall?

$10,000 and under	10
$10,000–$14,999	11
$15,000–$19,999	13
$20,000–$24,999	35
$25,000 over	239
No answer	13

11. How frequently do you fly?

Once a week or more	96
Two or three times a month	143
Seldom	94

Exhibit 13

Southwest Airlines advertising recall study: Albuquerque service

1. Where do you recall seeing or hearing the Southwest Airlines advertising of the new route service?

Newspaper	104
Radio	49
TV	20
Billboard	24
Magazine	13
Don't know	17
Other	18

2. In which newspaper(s) did you see this advertising?

Ft. Worth Star Telegram	8
Dallas Morning News	64

Exhibit 13 (continued)

Dallas Times Herald	32
Albuquerque Journal	36
Albuquerque Tribune	9
Other	5

3. On which radio station(s) do you recall hearing this advertising?

KABQ, New Mexico	
KDQQ, New Mexico	6
KJOY, New Mexico	9
KKIM, New Mexico	1
KOB, New Mexico	11
KPAR, New Mexico	
KQED, New Mexico	1
KRKE, New Mexico	4
KRST, New Mexico	1
KZIA, New Mexico	
KZZX, New Mexico	1
KAAM, Texas	
KBOX, Texas	2
KFJZ, Texas	1
KLIF, Texas	6
KNTU, Texas	
KOAX, Texas	5
KRLD, Texas	14
KVIL, Texas	12
WFAA, Texas	4
WRR, Texas	
KNUS, Texas	4
Other	4

4. On which television station(s) do you recall seeing this advertising?

KGGM, (Ch. 13) New Mexico	7
KMXN, (Ch. 23) New Mexico	
KOAT, (Ch. 7) New Mexico	10
KOB, (Ch. 4) New Mexico	6
KDFW, (Ch. 4) Texas	12
KERA, (Ch. 13) Texas	3
KTVT, (Ch. 11) Texas	1
KXAS, (Ch. 5) Texas	14
WFAA, (Ch. 8) Texas	16

5. Do you recall seeing or hearings NEWS coverage about the new routes? Where?

Newspapers	44
Radio	32
TV	28
Magazine	5

6. Did you hear about the new route service from a travel agency?

Yes	16
No	130

Exhibit 13 (concluded)

7. What in the advertising attracted you?

Convenience of SWA	72
Low fares	116
High frequency	23
Friendly service	50
Close in airports	60

8. What is your occupation?

Professional/technical	75
Managers/administrators	58
Sales workers	18
Clerical workers	3
Craftsmen/foremen	0
Operatives	3
Service workers	1
Student	2
Retired	2
Unemployed	3
No answer	2
Other	1

9. Into which of the following age categories do you fall?

18–24	25
25–34	96
35–44	97
45–54	60
55–64	37
65 over	9

10. Into which of the following categories does your total yearly household income fall?

$10,000 and under	3
$10,000–$14,999	9
$15,000–$19,999	22
$20,000–$24,999	13
$25,000 over	131
No answer	10

11. How frequently do you fly?

Once a week or more	41
Two or three times a month	87
Seldom	53

case **16** A Note on the
Forest Products
Industry

Historical Development

1   The major products of the forest product industry—paper, lumber, veneer, and plywood—date back to antiquity. The Chinese were first credited with making paper from the pounded bark of the mulberry tree. By 4000 B.C., the Egyptians had 8-foot-long metal saws which they used to cut both stone and wood. In approximately 1500 B.C., the Egyptians were manufacturing veneered furniture, which was later found by archeologists in the tombs of the Pharaohs.

2   The first sawmills in the United States were believed to have been established at Jamestown, Virginia around 1625 and at Berwick, Maine around 1631. These initial sawmills were likely water powered frame saws which had been employed in Europe since about 1200 A.D. The initial lumber industry of the early colonies was centered in the white pine forests of the New England states. As the nation grew and expanded, so did its need for more wood. The lumber industry moved to the white pine forests of Michigan, Wisconsin, and Minnesota, and later in the early 1900s to the southern pine forests of the southeastern United States. The great timber stands of the Pacific Northwest were also being opened up, and by the 1920s, they were supplying a large portion of the nation's lumber needs.

3   The early lumber industry in the United States was blessed with a low-

This case was written by Steven A. Sinclair, Associate Professor of Forest Products Marketing, Virginia Polytechnic Institute and State University. The helpful comments of Larry D. Alexander are gratefully acknowledged. Copyright © 1985 by Steven A. Sinclair.

cost plentiful supply of raw material. Markets were relatively strong because the nation needed considerable quantities of lumber and other wood products to support its rapid growth. By 1909, lumber production in the United States reached its all-time peak of 45,000,000,000 board feet.

4   Although paper had been manufactured dating back to the Chinese mulberry bark paper and the Egyptian papyrus, the early manufacture of paper was not from wood. It was not until approximately 1840 that the manufacture of wooden pulp was accomplished. This early manufacture of wood pulp was accomplished by forcing a log against a rotating stone in a water slurry. The rotating stone ground off small fibers of wood which were carried away in the water slurry. This new process for making pulp was called the ground wood process and was introduced into the United States in the early 1860s.

5   The first United States paper mill actually had been built much earlier in 1690 to produce paper from the fibers of old rags and not from wood pulp. These early paper mills produced paper sheet by sheet in a slow time consuming process. The first paper machine was installed in the United States in 1827 allowing the continuous production of a long, wide sheet of paper. This new technology was a significant boost to the paper industry.

6   By the 1880s, chemical methods of pulping wood appeared. In 1880, the sulfite process was available and by 1884, the Kraft or sulfate process was available to produce wood pulp. Both of these methods relied on using chemicals to dissolve the part of the wood that held its fibers together. In 1909, the first Kraft mill using southern pine was built in Roanoke Rapids, North Carolina beginning the growth of the strong southern pulp and paper industry.

7   Between the two world wars, early leaders in the forest products industry began to utilize their raw material resources more completely. Several large predominantly western lumber companies, such as Weyerhaeuser, led the way by moving into the pulp and paper field. Prior to this point, firms in the industry specialized in either the lumber or paper segments of the industry.

8   The addition of pulp and paper capacity to a traditional lumber manufacturing firm allowed it to make optimum use of its resources. This was accomplished by taking the waste material from lumber production and the timber unsuitable for lumber production from company lands and using it as raw material for their pulp and paper mills. Increasing timber prices further encouraged better utilization practices, and other western lumber companies followed the lead of Weyerhaeuser by purchasing or building pulp and paper facilities in the 1940s and 1950s.

9   At the same time, companies that had traditionally been pulp and paper companies, such as St. Regis Paper Company and International Paper Company, began to move into the lumber business. The paper companies moved into the lumber business to enable them to process their high quality timber into more valuable lumber products rather than paper.

10   Producing both lumber and paper products also helped to diversify company earnings because the sales of paper and lumber tended to be somewhat counter cyclical. In addition, paper prices have historically been more stable than lumber and plywood prices as shown in Exhibit 1. By the late 1950s and early 1960s, the forest products industry was taking on the appearance that it still had in the 1980s. That was an industry increasingly dominated by large fully integrated firms in most product and market segments as shown in Exhibits 2 through 5.

Exhibit 1

Relative price indexes of softwood plywood, softwood lumber, and paper compared to indexed housing starts from 1967–1983

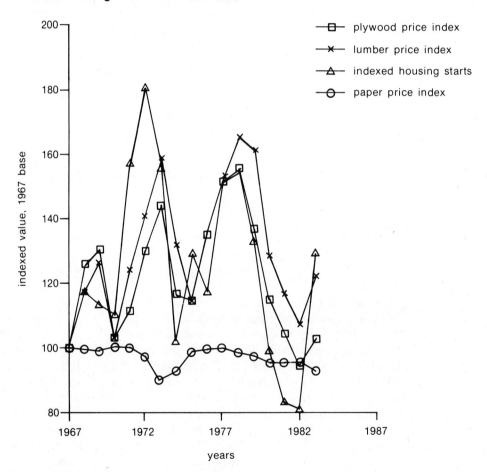

Source: Alice H. Ulrich, *U.S. Timber Production, Trade, Consumption and Price Statistics 1950-83,* (Washington D.C.: U.S. Dept. of Agriculture, 1984), pp. 53-72.

Exhibit 2

1983 sales data for major U.S. forest-products firms

Forbes 1983 sales 500 rank		Total sales ($ mil)	% of sales by business segment		
			Wood products	Paper products	Other
82	Georgia-Pacific	6,469	61	27	12
121	Weyerhaeuser	4,883	53	39	8
144	International Paper	4,357	17	81	2
151	Champion International	4,264	41	59	0
197	Boise Cascade	3,451	35	65	nm
210	Kimberly-Clark	3,274	nm	98	2
245	St. Regis	2,775	15	84	1
248	Crown Zellerbach	2,709	9	90	1
276	Scott Paper	2,465	4	81	5
284	Mead	2,367	nm	95	5
311	James River Corp.	2,104	0	100	nm
365	Union Camp	1,688	9	75	16
380	Hammermill Paper	1,623	9	91	0
400	Great Northern Nekoosa	1,565	6	87	7
401	Westvaco	1,564	nm	89	11
496	Temple-Inland	1,175	25	72	7
*	Louisiana-Pacific	1,265	85	15	0
*	Willamette Industries	1,045	30	70	0

*Unranked.
nm = not a meaningful %.
Sources: "The Nation's Largest Companies Ranked Four Ways," *Forbes*, April 30, 1984, pp. 172–178. Also Corporate annual reports for 1983.

Exhibit 3

1983 U.S. lumber market-share estimates

Company	Production (MMBf)	Estimated market share
Weyerhaeuser	3,123	8.7%
Georgia-Pacific	1,802	5.0%
Louisiana-Pacific	1,680	4.7%
Champion International	1,272	3.6%
Boise Cascade	844	2.4%
Top 5 Total		24.4%
International Paper	760	2.1%
St. Regis	583	1.6%

Total 1983 consumption = 35,695 MMBf.
Source: "Lumber Firms Enjoyed '83 But '84 Outlook Is Dimmer," *Forest Industries*, July 1984, p. 16.

Exhibit 4

1983 U.S. plywood market-share estimates

	Production (mm sq f, 3/8″ basis)	Estimated market share
Georgia-Pacific	4,872	23.9%
Champion International	1,822	8.9%
Boise Cascade	1,381	6.8%
Weyerhaeuser	1,319	6.5%
Willamette	1,282	6.3%
Top 5 Total		52.4%

Total 1983 consumption = 20,348 mm sq f (3/8″ basis).
Sources: Corporate annual reports for 1983. Also Robert G. Anderson, *Regional Production and Distribution Patterns of the Structural Panel Industry* (Tacoma, Wash.: American Plywood Association, 1983), p. 11.

Exhibit 5

1981 U.S. pulp and paper capacity, by category and top five companies

Category	Company	1000 short tons
Newsprint*	Bowater	1,313
	St. Regis	815
	Boise Cascade	610
	Publishers Paper	537
	Kimberly-Clark	526
		3,801
		(57% of total capacity)
Printing and Writing Papers	International Paper	1,525
	Boise Cascade	1,390
	Great Northern Nekoosa	1,238
	Champion International	1,126
	Mead	903
		6,182
		(42% of total capacity)
Tissue	Scott Paper	1,060
	Proctor and Gamble	900
	Kimberly-Clark	532
	Fort Howard Paper	530
	Georgia-Pacific	500
		3,522
		(83% of total capacity)

Exhibit 5 (concluded)

Category	Company	1000 short tons
Unbleached Kraft	St. Regis	861
	Georgia-Pacific	547
	Union Camp	454
	Continental Group	370
	International Paper	260
		2,492
		(64% of total capacity)
Bleached Packaging	International Paper	320
	James River	230
	Hammermill Paper	189
	Crown Zellerbach	140
	Longview Fibre	140
		1,019
		(67% of total capacity)
Paperboard	International Paper	3,205
	Container Corp. (Mobil Oil)	1,941
	Weyerhaeuser	1,900
	Champion International	1,553
	Mead	1,485
		10,084
		(33% of total capacity)
Market Pulp*	Weyerhaeuser	1,213
	Georgia-Pacific	871
	ITT Rayonier	871
	International Paper	500
	Brunswick Pulp & Paper	467
		3,922
		(53% of total capacity)

*Canadian companies have a substantial share of the North American capacity in these categories.
Source: Thomas P. Clephane and J. Carroll, *Timber Survey* (New York: Morgan Stanley and Company, 1982), pp. 52–63.

Major Competitors in the Forest Products Industry

11   The forest products industry typically produced large bulky products that were relatively expensive to transport. As a result, the early stages of development in the U.S. forest products industry centered on local sawmills and paper mills supplying products for local markets. With the advent of rail and steamship transportation, however, strong competition was possible between firms some distance apart. This competition has intensified and continued to this day.

12   Several major competitors in the two major segments of this industry are profiled here. The segments are those firms predominately producing paper

products and those firms predominantly producing lumber and other wood products. In addition, two new entrants to the industry are profiled in this section.

Paper Products Firms

Boise Cascade

13   In 1957, 36-year-old Robert Hansberger, the President of Boise Payette Lumber Company, arranged a merger with another lumber producer of similar size, the Cascade Lumber Company. The merger of these two Idaho lumber companies formed the new Boise Cascade Corporation. Boise Cascade Corporation, under Hansberger's leadership, grew at a rapid rate through a long series of acquisitions during the late 1950s and 1960s.

14   Boise Cascade's initial acquisition strategy was that of integrated utilization. That is, Boise grouped complementary timber conversion operations together in order to achieve the maximum return from each log. In a typical sawmill as much as 50% of the round log became waste materials as square lumber was produced. In the past, many firms simply burnt this waste. However, by utilizing this waste as a raw material to produce other forest products, such as paper or particleboard, Boise Cascade began to integrate its utilization facilities achieving higher returns from its logs.

15   Through additional mergers in the 1960s, Boise Cascade also became a significant producer of paper and packaging products. It also ventured into home building and land development. Hansberger noted at that time that his company was in the shelter business. Boise Cascade further integrated its operations to include retail level concerns within the building products industry, becoming one of the very few major integrated forest products firms to have a significant building products retail group.

16   Hansberger was caught up in diversification fever in the late 1960s and proceeded to turn Boise Cascade into a conglomerate. One of the more unusual acquisitions was the Cuban Electric Company, for which Boise had had claims against the Cuban government since 1960. For a while, it seemed this diversification strategy was working and Boise Cascade became one of the glamour conglomerates. In the 1970s, however, this strategy almost proved disastrous and Hansberger was forced to resign.

17   In 1972, the board of directors chose John B. Fery as the new Chairman and Chief Executive Officer of Boise Cascade. Fery sold off much of the earlier diversified operations acquired by Hansberger. The income generated by selling these non-forest products assets was reinvested back into its core forest products businesses. As a result of Fery's actions, many credit him with rescuing Boise Cascade from near disaster.

18   Fery instituted a sophisticated planning system for Boise Cascade with 5

and 10 year plans along with comprehensive business reviews. These became the basis for strategic decision making at Boise Cascade headquarters and in its operating units. Since the early 1970s, Boise spent nearly $3,000,000,000 to move the corporation into what Fery believed were young markets with high growth potential. Boise moved rapidly into white paper production, the demand for which was being constantly strengthened by the office computer and copy machine. At the same time, Fery lessened Boise's dependence on wood and building materials, which were very vulnerable to the cyclical nature of the housing market.

19   When Fery took over, Boise Cascade was largely a lumber company with wood products accounting for half of its total sales. Even in 1983, the company was the fifth largest lumber producer and the third largest plywood producer in the U.S. As a result of Fery's actions, however, paper operations for Boise Cascade had grown and accounted for approximately two-thirds of 1983 sales. In addition, Fery pursued a niche strategy in the wood products business by emphasizing distribution to the remodeling market rather than materials for new construction. By 1983, Boise Cascade owned 87 retail building material centers, which served primarily the small remodeling contractors and do-it-yourself consumers. These retail building material centers were supported by 15 wholesale distribution units. All of these facilities were located in high growth areas of the West and southwestern United States.

20   Boise Cascade also operated a string of 40 office products distribution centers which served all 50 states. These distribution centers gave it a strong position in the office products market and provided a unique marketing outlet for Boise's fast growing white paper production.

21   In 1983, Boise Cascade had total sales of $3,500,000,000 and 28,708 employees. It owned 3,200,000 acres of timberlands and controlled another 4,500,000 acres through long-term leases and contracts.

International Paper

22   International Paper was incorporated in 1898. For most of the time since then, it has been the largest paper manufacturer in the world. The acquisition of St. Regis Corporation by Champion International in 1984, however, gave Champion International claim to that title.

23   International Paper was quick to apply new technology to achieve a dominant position in the paper industry during the early part of this century. However, by the 1960s, the rate of return on net worth for International Paper and its growth in sales were much lower than competing paper companies (Exhibit 6). Rumors on Wall Street that a group of investors were attempting to buy sufficient shares of International Paper stock to control the company shocked the directors out of complacency.

24   Under the leadership of Edward Hinman and Frederick Kappell (a for-

Exhibit 6

Selected financial data for major U.S. forest-products firms from Value Line's value/screen data base, January 1985

	Return on net worth	Price/ book value	5 year earnings per share growth	Financial strength	Long term debt/ total debt
James River Co.	17.1%	1.60	20.5%	C++	43%
Kimberly-Clark	12.7%	1.40	8.0%	A+	25%
Union Camp	11.0%	1.40	3.5%	A	34%
Great Northern Nekoosa	9.3%	1.00	5.5%	A	34%
Georgia-Pacific	8.7%	1.20	-11.9%	B++	39%
Scott Paper	8.3%	1.10	4.0%	B++	27%
Crown Zellerbach	7.7%	0.90	-16.9%	B+	35%
Westvaco Corporation	7.6%	1.20	3.5%	A	28%
Hammermill Paper	7.5%	1.00	6.0%	B+	38%
Temple-Inland	6.8%	1.30	nm	B	22%
Weyerhaeuser	6.3%	1.30	-11.9%	A	29%
International Paper	5.8%	0.80	1.5%	A	20%
Champion International	4.6%	0.70	-18.9%	B++	35%
Willamette Industries	4.5%	1.30	-18.9%	B	37%
Boise Cascade	4.3%	0.80	-10.9%	B++	30%
Louisiana-Pacific	3.8%	0.90	-26.9%	B++	19%
Mead Corporation	3.4%	1.20	-18.9%	B	40%

nm = not a meaningful %.
Source: Value/Screen Data Base (New York: Value Line Inc., 1985).

mer chairman of AT&T), International Paper began a drive in the late 1960s to expand and diversify. International Paper moved into the consumer tissues and disposable diapers market, purchased a producer and distributor of specialty health care products, and spent over $1,000,000,000 to increase its paper capacity by 25%. All of this served to leave International Paper strongly in debt after having almost no debt as late as 1965. To better manage this situation, Paul Gorman took over the helm of International Paper in early 1971. Gorman was apparently chosen because of his strong financial abilities.

25   Gorman immediately began to close and/or sell the unprofitable acquisitions and to modernize International Paper's financial systems. With these new controls in place, he began to manage more to turn a profit and not just to attempt to be the largest paper company.

26   After Gorman's retirement in 1974, the new chairman, J. Stanford Smith, signaled a new strategy indicating that International Paper was no longer just in the paper or even the forest products business, but rather was in the land resource management business. This thinking led International Paper to acquire new companies that had the expertise needed to develop oil deposits that had been discovered on the company's large land holdings.

In addition, a new emphasis was placed on solid wood products in the mid to late 1970s when the markets for lumber and other wood products were strong.

27   In 1979, when Dr. Edwin A. Gee assumed the chairmanship of International Paper, another strategic change was signaled. Gee moved to consolidate International's Paper's operations around its original central core of basic forest products. The oil and gas subsidiaries were sold along with other assets which were not directly related to its core business. Cash raised through these sales was plowed back into a five-year capital spending program to upgrade aging paper mills. Between 1979 and 1984, International Paper spent approximately $4,000,000,000 in modernizing its facilities.

28   International Paper had a stated goal to become a low-cost producer of white paper, packaging, container board and bleached board. To achieve this goal, International Paper began the process of converting and modernizing some of its paper mills to produce uncoated white papers. At the same time, the firm announced its intention to move out of the newsprint business and converted newsprint mills to produce other paper products or sold them.

29   In 1983, International Paper owned 15 pulp and paper mills, 22 wood products manufacturing facilities, and 57 packaging plants. These operations generated sales of approximately $4,400,000,000 that year. International Paper had the largest timberland base in the forest products industry, totaling approximately 7,000,000 acres, and employed 33,600 people in 1983.

Wood Products Firms

Weyerhaeuser

30   By 1900, Frederick Weyerhaeuser had already been active in the lumber and timber industry for 43 years. He led a group of midwestern lumbermen to Tacoma, Washington, in that year to organize a new lumber company. This new company was incorporated as Weyerhaeuser Timber Company. When many people think of the forest products industry, Weyerhaeuser is the name that first comes to mind. Furthermore, six of the nine men who led this giant had the Weyerhaeuser name.

31   Weyerhaeuser first purchased 900,000 acres of timberland from the Northern Pacific Railroad and later purchased its first sawmill in Everett, Washington in 1902. The company expanded slowly, opening Weyerhaeuser Sales Company in St. Paul, Minnesota, in 1919 and acquiring its first sulfite pulp mill in 1931 in Longview, Washington. Weyerhaeuser was an early leader in the industry in promoting integrated utilization by

purchasing pulp mills to use the residues available from its sawmilling operations. Weyerhaeuser was also an early leader in the development of tree farms and the reforestation of cut-over forest land. In addition, Weyerhaeuser was one of the first major forest products firms to institute a research and development program.

32   Weyerhaeuser remained in the Pacific Northwest until the mid-1950s, at which time it moved into the Southeast and south central United States through a strong acquisition program. Timberlands were first acquired in Mississippi and Alabama in 1956, then in North Carolina and Virginia in 1957. One of the largest southern timberland acquisitions came in 1969 when Weyerhaeuser acquired Dierk's Forests Inc., adding 1,800,000 acres of timberlands in Arkansas and Oklahoma, along with various forest products mills.

33   Weyerhaeuser tended to be a leader in the forest products industry, instituting such slogans in early advertising as "we're the tree-growing company" and "high-yield forestry." Beginning in mid-1961, George Weyerhaeuser, then the executive vice president of Weyerhaeuser Timber Company, announced a basic shift from commodity selling of lumber to end-user marketing of wood products. This signaled Weyerhaeuser's move into the consumer market with specialty products and a decreasing emphasis on the commodity grades of lumber. The company's huge reserves of prime high-quality timber supported this move and allowed them to produce many high-quality specialty wood products such as prefinished paneling, glue-laminated trusses, pre-primed siding, and molded wood products. This same product policy was extended to the pulp and paper division. The emphasis there shifted to a wide variety of printing papers and finished paper products. The marketing-to-end-users theme carried forward into the 1980s when Weyerhaeuser even became the largest U.S. manufacturer of private-labeled disposable diapers.

34   While emphasizing end-user marketing, Weyerhaeuser also became the tenth largest home builder in the United States in 1983 and one of the country's largest mortgage bankers. Weyerhaeuser developed a system of 64 wholesale customer service centers with the stated goal of becoming a lending force in the wholesale marketing of building products in the 1980s. Weyerhaeuser's current advertising theme "first choice" was keyed upon making each customer service center a separate profit center, giving the manager considerable autonomy to provide a mix of products appropriate for the local building markets.

35   Beginning in the late 1950s, Weyerhaeuser began to expand its operations into various foreign countries. By 1983, 22% of the net corporate sales were from overseas subsidiaries.

36   Weyerhaeuser was the only major U.S. forest-products producer that had sufficient timberlands to support 100% of its wood and fiber needs. While this approach had its advantages and disadvantages, it did free the corporation from a heavy dependence on expensive government timber con-

tracts in the Pacific Northwest and from privately owned timber in the Southeast. In all, the company owned approximately 5,900,000 acres of commercial timberland, 54% in the South and 46% in the Pacific Northwest.

37   In 1983, Weyerhaeuser was the leading U.S. lumber producer with an 8.7% market share. Its total corporate sales in 1983 were $4,880,000,000, second behind Georgia-Pacific, with a net income after taxes of $204,843,000. In the same year, the company employed 42,600 people, principally in its forest-products businesses.

Georgia-Pacific

38   In 1927, a Virginian named Owen Cheatham borrowed $12,000 and purchased a wholesale lumber yard in Augusta, Georgia. It wasn't long before Cheatham enticed his college friend, Robert Pamplin, to join him in this new business. Together these two men built the company known as Georgia-Pacific.

39   The early years of Georgia-Pacific were marked by the Great Depression and World War II; however, by 1946 the company owned five lumber mills in Alabama, Arkansas, Mississippi, and South Carolina along with its original lumber yard in Georgia. In addition, sales offices were established in New York City and Portland, Oregon.

40   Beginning in the late 1940s, Georgia-Pacific entered into an era of tremendous growth. The company moved into the plywood business by purchasing and building several West Coast plywood mills. This was considered quite risky at that time because plywood was a very new product with an unsure market potential. Beginning in the 1950s, Georgia-Pacific moved aggressively into the pulp and paper field and began to acquire some of the last remaining large tracts of old growth West Coast timberlands. The corporation borrowed very heavily to acquire these lands and then, through accelerated harvesting schedules, generated enough cash to repay its short-term creditors and bring its long-term debt down to a manageable level.

41   The corporate offices were moved from Augusta, Georgia to Portland, Oregon. However, beginning in the 1960s, Georgia-Pacific made a strong move back to its original base in the southern U.S. Large tracts of land were acquired in the Crossett, Arkansas area and in other deep south states. In 1963, Georgia-Pacific built the first southern pine plywood plant. Later that same year four additional plants were running which gave it about a one-year head start over its major competitors. Georgia-Pacific continued its emphasis on plywood and other specialty panels and was the world's largest plywood manufacturer producing approximately 4,900, 000, 000 square feet of plywood in 1983.

42   Georgia-Pacific tried to emphasize market positions in fast-growth fields throughout its history. Early on, it chose to emphasize plywood production

over that of lumber and also emphasized the rapidly expanding pulp and paper segment. Like Weyerhaeuser, it decided to emphasize the distribution of building products to building material retailers, believing this gave it a strong advantage in the marketplace. By 1983, Georgia-Pacific's 145 wholesale distribution centers made it the world's largest distributor of building products.

43   Perhaps the largest set back to Georgia-Pacific's growth resulted from a 1972 Federal Trade Commission ruling. It held the company had illegally restricted competition within the softwood plywood industry. The settlement resulted in the company selling 20% of its assets centered in Louisiana. As a result, the Louisiana-Pacific Corporation was created and was immediately the sixth largest domestic producer of lumber. In addition, the Georgia-Pacific Corporation was prohibited from purchasing any additional softwood plywood producers in the United States for 10 years.

44   In the early 1980s, Georgia-Pacific began construction of a new corporate headquarters in Atlanta, Georgia. It decided to move its corporate headquarters from Portland to Atlanta to be nearer the major part of Georgia-Pacific's assets. By 1983, the corporation owned 4,600,000,000 acres of timberlands in North America, of which 65% was in the southern U.S., 16% in the Pacific Northwest, and 19% in the eastern U.S. and eastern Canada. In that same year, Georgia-Pacific had total sales of $6,500,000,000, ranking it 82nd in sales on the Forbes 500 list and 1st among forest products corporations.

45   Back in the late 1950s, Georgia-Pacific diversified into the chemical industry to manufacture the resins necessary for its plywood plants. Georgia-Pacific's corporate goals in the 1980s, as articulated by Chief Executive Officer T. Marshall Hahn, were to liquidate all but the most profitable of its chemical operations and to invest the proceeds in modernizing the core forest-products businesses of the corporation.

New Entrants into the Industry

46   The threat of new entrants building greenfield plants in the forest-products industry continued to be limited. The tremendous cost of a new pulp and paper mill ($500,000,000 to $1,000,000,000) and the necessary timberland base to support such a facility presented an almost insurmountable barrier for a new company. In addition, the new firm would be forced to develop its own marketing channels, manufacturing skills, etc.

47   While the threat of new entrants was low, the threat of other established firms taking over undervalued forest-products firms was a significant threat. A number of acquisition attempts, takeovers, and spin-offs of forest-products business units occurred. This activity continued to the mid-1980s, and it seems likely to continue in the future. Clearly, it has the potential to alter the traditional structure of the industry.

Louisiana—Pacific

48 A 1971 complaint to the Federal Trade Commission against Georgia-Pacific ultimately resulted in Louisiana-Pacific Corporation. On January 5, 1973, Georgia-Pacific spun off $327,000,000 of assets to create Louisiana-Pacific. Harry A. Merlo, a former Georgia-Pacific executive, was named president of the new corporation. Merlo wasted no time getting started and in 1973 the company made 17 acquisitions, invested over $21,000,000 in capital improvements, and added 1,800 employees.

49 On January 5, 1973, 26,320,000 shares of Louisiana-Pacific stock began trading on the New York Stock Exchange. Later in that same year the stock was split 2 for 1. Net sales in that first year of operation were approximately $417,000,000. By 1974, company ownership of timberlands climbed to 625,000 acres, and the company had the capacity to supply 2,500,000 seedlings per year to reforest cut-over timberlands.

50 While its 1979 annual sales reached $1,300,000,000, they declined to $1,100,000,000 in 1983 due to a weak building-products market. Louisiana-Pacific remained primarily a lumber and plywood producer. In 1973, 92% of its sales were from building products and 8% were from pulp and paper operations. By 1983, the distribution of sales between these two segments had changed slightly. Building products contributed 85% of net sales, and pulp and paper products contributed 15%. Of the major integrated forest-products firms, Louisiana-Pacific had the largest exposure to the highly cyclical building-products market.

51 Louisiana-Pacific had two principal market areas where it was trying to establish a strong leadership position. The first market area involved the new structural composite panel market. Louisiana-Pacific had a stated goal of 1,000,000,000 square feet of capacity in this market segment by 1985. When the plants under construction in 1985 went into production this goal was met. Louisiana-Pacific produced an oriented waferboard product under the brand name of Waferwood. This particular product had the necessary grade stamps from the American Plywood Association to compete as a substitute product against traditional plywood sheathing and underlayment and also against oriented strandboard products. Its 1,000, 000,000 square feet of capacity made Louisiana-Pacific one of the top two producers in this product category along with Georgia-Pacific.

52 The second area where Louisiana-Pacific had stated goals of market leadership was in the southern pine lumber industry. The company stated, in 1981, that its goal was to have 1,000,000,000 board feet of southern pine lumber capacity by 1985. The company pursued this goal by acquiring southern pine sawmills and by constructing new mills in the southern states.

53 Louisiana-Pacific largely concentrated on the development of its manufacturing base and somewhat ignored the development of its distribution system for building products. However, in 1979 Louisiana-Pacific did ac-

quire a chain of 15 building-material centers in Southern California from Lone Star Industries. By 1983, Louisiana-Pacific operated 12 building products distribution centers in California, one in Texas, and one in Florida. Louisiana-Pacific employed approximately 13,000 employees and operated 111 manufacturing facilities in 1983.

Temple-Inland

54   Temple-Inland made the most dramatic entry as an independent company into the forest-products industry of any firm in the 1980s. It began operations on January 1, 1984 following its spin-off from Time's forest-products operations. Temple-Inland was formed from two subsidiaries of Time, Inc., Temple-Eastex and Inland Container, which each had long operating histories.

55   T.L.L. Temple acquired 7,000 acres of timberland in Texas and established the Southern Pine Lumber Company in 1893. By 1894, the Southern Pine Lumber Company's first sawmill was operating in Diboll, Texas, cutting approximately 50,000 board feet of southern pine per day. During the early years of this company, it was primarily a producer of basic lumber products for the construction and furniture industries. In the late 1950s and early 1960s the company moved into the production of particleboard, gypsum wall board, and other building materials, along with entering the mortgage banking, insurance, and construction businesses.

56   In 1964, the Southern Pine Lumber Company's name was changed to Temple Industries, Inc., and the company's initial 7,000 acres of timberland had grown to more than 450,000 acres.

57   In the early 1950s, Time, Inc. entered into a joint verture with the Houston Oil Company and established the East Texas Pulp and Paper Company. In 1956, Time purchased Houston Oil's ownership in the East Texas Pulp and Paper Company. Later in 1973, Time acquired Temple Industries, which was merged with Eastex Pulp and Paper Company to form Temple-Eastex, Inc.

58   Herman C. Krannert was responsible for the origin of Inland Container Corporation. Krannert started the Inland Box Company in Indianapolis in 1925 and soon acquired a second box plant in Middleton, Ohio. Then, in 1938, the company was re-incorporated as Inland Container Corporation. Up until 1946, Inland was primarily a multi-plant box converter relying solely on outside sources for its paper supply. Through a joint venture with Mead Corporation, that same year, the Georgia Kraft Company was formed and a new liner board mill was constructed in Macon, Georgia. Inland Container Corporation was acquired by Time, Inc. in 1978, to be operated as a subsidiary. In the 1980s, Georgia Kraft, 50% owned by Inland Container, operated three liner board mills with five paper machines, plywood and lumber mills, and owned approximately 1,000,000 acres of timberland in Alabama and Georgia.

59   The formation of Temple-Inland Corporation from the Time subsidiaries of Temple-Eastex and Inland Container produced an integrated forest-products firm. Its 1983 sales of approximately $1,200,000,000 ranked 16th among major U.S. paper and forest-products companies. Temple-Inland had four main areas of operation: paper, containers, building materials, and financial services. The paper activities of Temple-Inland concentrated on two paper grades, container board and bleached paper board. Both of these served as raw materials for its container-producing operations.

60   Temple-Inland had a diversified building-products product line, designed to serve the rapidly growing Texas and southeastern U.S. markets. In addition to manufacturing operations, the company also owned six building-materials retail distribution centers in Texas and Louisiana. Its financial services group produced 16% of earnings in 1983. This group was comprised primarily of mortgage banking and insurance operations.

61   Temple-Inland had a substantial timberland base consisting of 1,100,000 acres of timberland in east Texas and 50% ownership of Georgia Kraft Company, which had approximately 1,000,000 acres of timberland in Georgia and Alabama.

Industry Trends

62   The commitment to strong captive distribution systems was reiterated by several industry leaders in the early 1980s; they publicly stated that expansion of their distribution systems for building products was a top priority. One of the reasons for developing a strong distribution system was to address the increasingly important repair and remodeling market better. This market's potential was better understood when one looked at the ages of existing housing. In 1980, the total U.S. housing inventory consisted of approximately 90,000,000 units. Of these, approximately 45,000,000 were single-family homes that were at least 20 years old, making them prime candidates for expenditures on upkeep and improvement.[1]

63   In 1983, 22% of the U.S. softwood lumber consumption and 29% of the U.S. structural panel consumption was utilized in the repair and remodeling market, as shown in Exhibits 7 and 8. Total retail sales in the repair and remodeling market were predicted to reach over $65,000,000,000 in 1984 and $116,000,000,000 by 1990.[2] The fastest growing segment of the repair and remodeling market was the do-it-yourself market. Sales in this market were predicted to expand at a compound rate of 12.5% annually between 1984 and 1990, reaching total sales of $75,400,000,000 in 1990.[3] Furthermore, the total repair and remodeling market was strong enough to be called recession proof. If this market continues to expand as predicted, the major forest-products producers can be expected to continue their strong push into it by expanding their distribution systems.

64   An earlier trend in the 1960s and early 1970s was a diversification move

Exhibit 7

1983 U.S. softwood lumber consumption by end-use markets

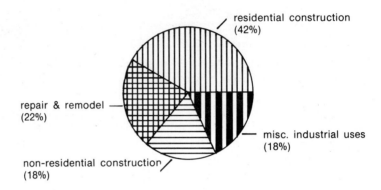

Source: Stuart U. Rich, "Sawmillers Can Profit By Knowing Market Trends," *Forest Industries,* October 1984, p. 21.

Exhibit 8

1983 U.S. structural panel consumption by end-use markets

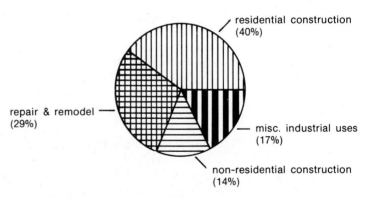

Source: Robert G. Anderson, *Regional Production and Distribution Patterns of the Structural Panel Industry,* (Tacoma, Wash.: American Plywood Association, 1983), p. 11.

by many forest-products firms. Georgia-Pacific, International Paper, and Boise Cascade, among others, moved into unrelated businesses they knew little about. These acquisitions included oil and gas, land development, chemicals, and in the case of Boise Cascade, even such exotic adventures as Latin American utilities. The forest products industry was highly dependent upon housing starts and general economic trends; however, the diversification schemes of most companies failed to produce the expected result of protecting against cyclical swings in their forest-products businesses. Beginning in the mid-1970s and continuing until the mid-1980s, many companies started to sell off assets not related to their core forest-products businesses.

65   A consolidation of firms in the industry occurred. The number of sawmills and planing mills in the United States decreased from 12,189 in 1963 to 7,544 in 1977 and further decreased to 5,881 in 1981.[4] During this period of consolidation, the major forest-products firms increased their market shares. Georgia-Pacific and Weyerhaeuser increased their combined share of the United States lumber market from 6.8% in 1960 to 13.9% in 1981. During the same period, these two companies managed to increase their share of the softwood plywood market from 8.4% in 1960 to 28.8% in 1981.[5]

66   Another trend was the continued over capacity within the lumber industry, which was capable of producing enough lumber to support housing starts of 2,300,000 units per year in the early 1980s.[6] Although 20% of the western sawmills had gone out of business since 1978, newly built mills and renovations by larger companies kept capacity high. A fair number of old and inefficient plywood plants were in the Pacific Northwest. Many of these were independent operations which were expected to shut down over the next several years. This will reduce the production capacity to bring it more in line with current levels of housing construction, as well as increasing the market share of the major U.S. companies.

67   An additional trend in the paper segment was to build larger and larger plants to attain economies of scale. The strategy of most major paper producers was to concentrate their production on certain grades of paper to achieve the necessary economies of scale and market clout. Scott Paper Company, for example, continued to emphasize its strength in tissue paper products, including bathroom tissues, paper towels, facial tissues, and napkins. Boise Cascade, a leader in printing and writing papers, continued to strengthen its position in this market segment by bringing two new ultramodern paper machines on line by mid-1980.

Recent Changes in the Forest-Products Industry

68   The recent federal timber bailout legislation, which was signed into law in late 1984, will likely have a far reaching impact on the forest-products

industry. Many Northwest forest-products firms relied heavily on public timber for their supply. During the late 1970s and very early 1980s, the prices bid for this public timber sky rocketed, reaching a peak in 1980 of $429 per thousand board feet for Douglas fir sawtimber. By 1984, that figure had dropped to $139.59 per thousand board feet for the same timber but, unfortunately many Northwest firms were still locked into these earlier contracts at much higher prices. Many of these firms subsequently appealed to the federal government for relief. Industry analysts speculated that many Northwestern forest-products companies would go bankrupt without federal relief. In fact, some firms owed more money on their timber contracts than their company's net worth.

69   The new legislation provided that the companies can buy out up to 55% of their cutting contracts up to a maximum of 200,000,000 board feet of contracted volume. The other 45% must be harvested under the terms of the original contracts. Timber cutting contracts generally run for a number of years so that some contracts signed in the early 1980s may not need to be cut until 1989.

70   The part of this legislation which impacted the greatest upon the long-term future of the industry was the restrictions on future timber sales. These restrictions required that annual timber sales in the region not exceed 5,200,000,000 board feet and that timber under contract at the end of any fiscal year not exceed 12,300,000,000 board feet. The annual sales volume for the years 1978 through 1984 was approximately 5,000,000,000 board feet. However, the region in early 1985 had 18,300,000,000 board feet of timber under contract, which greatly exceeded the limitation of 12,300,000,000 board feet at the end of any fiscal year. For the future, this legislation means that in times of strong wood demand the timber offered for sale in the Pacific Northwest from public lands cannot be increased above the current harvest levels.

71   The production of structural panel products began in the Pacific Northwest in the 1940s with early plywood mills, and this region remained dominant in plywood production until the early 1980s. In the early 1960s, the technology became available to produce plywood from southern pine, and by the early 1980s, the production of southern pine plywood exceeded that of plywood produced in the Pacific Northwest. Recent trends in timber costs and harvesting restrictions in the Pacific Northwest have further enhanced this trend.

72   Several knowledgeable industry analysts predicted in the early 1980s that the last southern pine plywood mill had been built. They speculated that all new expansion in the structural panel business would come from new, highly engineered composite panels such as waferboard and oriented strand board. These two new products used lower-cost timber and had a more highly automated production process. These two factors significantly lowered production and operating costs for these products versus the traditional plywood panel. Most of the major forest-products companies that

had strengths in wood products staked out a position in this new market.

73   The demand for coated paper stock used for magazine production had been growing at approximately 10% per year. This strong increase in demand was spurred by increased magazine advertising and also rapid increases in the number of special interest magazines dedicated to such subjects as personal computers, physical fitness, self-improvement, and sports in the early 1980s. Demand increased so fast that U.S. coated paper machines operated at 100% of capacity, and yet approximately 425,000,000 tons of coated paper stock were still imported to fill the increasing demand in 1984.

74   Uncoated white paper used for business purposes and computer printers were also experiencing strong production with operating rates of approximately 95%. The expanding personal computer market was predicted to continue to increase demand for uncoated papers in coming years.

75   U.S. newsprint production was also up approximately 8% from 1983 levels, reaching approximately 95% of productive capacity in 1984. Canadian imports, however, were very strong in this market, and some U.S. firms appeared ready to pull out of this market altogether.

Threats to the Forest Products Industry

76   One of the major threats to the forest-products industry, which surfaced several times over the last 20 years, was government timber-cutting policies on federal forest lands. Through the pressure of the environmental movement over the last 15-20 years, a large amount of federal timberlands had been withdrawn from future timber production. This placed increasing pressure on the remaining federal timberlands. In addition, the increasingly stringent environmental regulations on federal timber contracts increased the cost of cutting some timber.

77   The companies hurt most by these policies were those in the West and Northwest that depended heavily upon federal timberlands for their raw material needs. Many of the companies hardest hit were small- to medium-sized operations with little or no timberland holdings of their own.

78   Another threat to the forest-products industry was the large role that the federal government played in the housing market. Every time government policies altered interest rates up or down, housing starts typically moved in the opposite direction. The interest cost of a new home represented such a large part of its total cost that any time interest rates were increased, the number of new houses built typically fell. This was especially important to the forest-products industry because in 1983, for instance, 42% of the softwood lumber and 40% of the softwood plywood consumed in this country was used in new residential construction.

79   Over the years, the federal government supported home ownership. This

was evidenced by the interest deduction for home mortgages permitted on individual tax returns. In addition, the government sponsored various programs to make government-backed mortgage money available. If the U.S. Congress were to change the existing laws, this could pose a strong threat to the housing industry and in turn to the forest-products industry. Such proposals as the flat tax legislation that would eliminate the interest deduction for second homes and perhaps limit the interest deduction on first homes could severely damage the new home construction market.

80   Many segments of the forest-products industry, particularly plywood and most paper segments, were oligopolistic in nature. They were characterized by large firms with fairly large market shares, where price leadership was the norm. A number of times in the past, the Justice Department accused various firms in these oligopolistic segments of the industry of price fixing. These law suits consumed considerable time and effort for forest-products firms and many times resulted in large fines or out-of-court settlements. For instance, in recent plywood price fixing litigation, Georgia-Pacific, Weyerhaeuser, and Willamette reached a settlement of $165,000,000 after an unfavorable jury verdict. They did not admit any guilt, but rather said that the settlement was preferable to the expense and time required for an appeal.

81   Although the U.S. forest-products industry has been largely free of strong import pressure in most of its product lines, the Canadians had a strong market share in softwood lumber and newsprint. The Canadians had been gaining a larger share of the U.S. softwood lumber market. The National Forest Products Association estimated that Canadian firms supplied approximately 19% of the softwood lumber consumed in the United States in 1975. By 1983, the Canadian share of the U.S. softwood lumber market had risen to almost 34%. In the early 1980s, several major forest-products firms combined forces and filed a countervailing duty petition with the U.S. International Trade Commission. After a major investigation was conducted, the Commission chose to take no action, and Canadian softwood lumber remained free to enter the U.S. without duties.

Suppliers to the Forest Products Industry

82   Timber supply was the number one ingredient for the forest-products industry. In the production of softwood lumber, for example, the cost of timber comprised approximately 71% of the total cost of lumber production, and for the production of liner board, a paper product, the cost of timber comprised approximately 32% of the total cost of production in the early 1980s.[7] With such high-cost components, it was easy to understand the power that timber supply could have over a forest-products facility. This helped to explain the great concern that forest-products firms had over

federal timber-cutting policies and the industry's large privately-owned timber base.

83   The production of most lumber and panel products was done with relatively little energy consumption; however, the production of pulp and paper products tended to be very energy intensive. The energy crisis of the early and mid-1970s spurred many pulp and paper firms to develop the ability to generate their own energy. As a result, pulp and paper firms and other segments of the forest-products industry helped make the industry one of the most energy self-sufficient industry groups in the U.S.

Buyers of Forest Products

84   Although several major corporations had strong captive distribution systems at the wholesale level, most of the lumber and plywood still moved through small independently-owned building-materials wholesalers. In the early 1980s, independently owned wholesalers controlled approximately 76% of the sales volume within the lumber, plywood, and millwork markets. With 6,928 wholesalers, mostly small independents, wholesalers exerted relatively little power over the production of forest products by major integrated firms.

85   The retail side of the wood-products segment was controlled almost entirely by firms without significant manufacturing capabilities. There were 24,940 retail building-material dealers in the early 1980s. The vast majority of these building-material dealers were small, independent firms; however, several large retail building-material chains such as Lowe's, Wickes, and Payless Cashways, all had sales over $1,000,000,000. Wood products sales, however, were only one segment of their total sales. Nonetheless, the size and the growing number of large building-material chains will probably increase their power over the producers of building materials.

86   The paper segment of the forest-products industry was still highly influenced by the availability and cost of the timber needed to produce paper. However, unlike the wood-products segment, the paper segment sold to buyers in some of its markets that were large enough to influence strongly the price of the product and terms of the sale. One paper market characterized by large buyers was the newsprint market. Most newsprint was sold on the basis of long-term contracts with large established newspapers. Newsprint moved directly from the producing mills to the newspaper firms. In addition, many large newspapers integrated backwards and built or purchased their own newsprint mills, often on a joint venture basis.

87   The light-weight coated-paper segment of the paper market was also one that dealt with very large buyers. This paper was used in the printing of high quality magazines. Large magazine printers purchased this particular grade of paper in large enough quantities to influence the supplier.

Also, buyers in this paper segment had a tendency to integrate backwards into the production of this grade of paper.

88   For many grades of paper commonly used in everyday life, the major paper producers marketed these products through paper merchants/wholesalers. In 1983, approximately $24,100,000,000 of paper products were sold through the 5,351 paper merchants/wholesalers in the United States. Approximately 80% of these paper merchants were independently owned firms; however, the 20% owned by manufacturers controlled approximately 50% of the sales volume.[8] With so many independent wholesalers and a strong captive wholesaler segment in the paper wholesale market, it was unlikely that any group of buyers could exert undue influence over paper manufacturers.

Substitute Products

89   Certain segments of the forest-products industry were sensitive to substitute products. One good example was hardwood flooring. Prior to the advent of wall-to-wall carpeting and the introduction of better quality vinyl flooring, hardwood strip flooring enjoyed a large market in the United States. After the advent of these substitute flooring products, however, the hardwood flooring market declined precipitously. From 1969 to 1982, shipments of oak flooring decreased from 387,800,000 board feet to 75,000,000 board feet.

90   Fortunately most segments of the forest-products industry were not affected to that extent by substitute products. One industry analyst predicted a decrease in the strong relationship between real GNP and paper demand for certain categories of paper products in the late 1980s. This decrease was predicted due to plastic substitutes for certain packaging products and a slight negative influence of electronic transmission of information on newsprint and white-paper demand.

91   Within the wood-products side of the forest-products industry, the largest market was still for housing. Several substitution trends had the potential to affect the future market for wood building products adversely. Many consumers not able to afford a traditional single-family home were substituting apartments, townhouses, and other multifamily dwellings. A multifamily dwelling consumed approximately half as much lumber and plywood during construction, per housing unit, as the traditional single-family dwelling. Between 1976 and 1980, single-family units represented approximately 71% of total housing starts. By 1981, their market share had dropped to 64%, and Morgan Stanley predicted that in the 1986 to 1990 period, the share of single-family dwellings will drop to approximately 52% of total housing starts.[9]

The Future Outlook

92 Despite various trends, threats, and substitute products, the outlook for the wood industry as a whole remains strong. In the United States about as much wood, by weight, was used each year as steel, cement, plastics, aluminum, and all other materials combined.[10] With this tremendous usage and a timber supply that is still increasing, the wood-industry future looks bright.

93 In the wood-products arena, the major forest-products companies need to learn to address better the growing repair and remodelling market. With such firms as K-Mart entering into the retail building material market, many observers predict a competitive shake out in this market place.

94 Within the paper-products side of the industry, the overall outlook is good. Although electronics and plastic packaging are predicted to impact upon the demand for certain grades of paper, new products on the horizon may boost paper demand even further. One new product is ovenable paper. The increasing use of the microwave in the family kitchen stimulated the need for a tray to hold frozen foods that could be used in a microwave oven. Traditional aluminum packaging for frozen foods like TV dinners was not usable in a microwave. As a result, a new category of paper products was developed. This product allowed frozen foods to be heated in a microwave oven without damage to the microwave circuitry.

95 Additional interesting paper products on the horizon include aseptic containers made from laminents of paperboard, aluminum foil, and plastic. These containers, used for packaging perishable goods, could keep these goods fresh for long periods of time without refrigeration. Kimberly-Clark recently began test marketing a new treated facial tissue that kills most of the viruses that cause colds and flu. The product is expected to help fight the spread of virus between family members.

96 A potential cloud on the horizon for many forest-products companies resulted from relatively low stock prices and high initial investments required for new paper capacity. This led to a rash of takeover attempts of paper firms. The largest recent move involved St. Regis, which, after fending off several takeover attempts, finally accepted a friendly offer to merge with Champion International. Continuing mergers and takeovers of this type have the capacity to influence strongly the future shape of the forest products industry.

Notes

1. Stuart U. Rich, "Sawmillers Can Profit By Knowing Market Trends," *Forest Industries,* October 1984, p. 20.

2. "Home Improvement Market Nailing Up New Growth Records," *Building Products Digest,* May 1984, p. 10.

3. "Making Do," *Forbes,* June 1984, p. 8.

4. Rich, p. 21.

5. Thomas P. Clephane and J. Carroll, *Timber Survey,* (New York: Morgan Stanley & Co., 1982), p. 133.

6. Standard and Poor's Industry Survey, *Building and Forest Products,* December 1984, p. b65.

7. Clephane, p. 6.

8. *Who's Who in Paper Distribution and Fact Book,* (Great Neck, New York: National Paper Trade Association, 1984) p. 14.

9. Clephane, p. 126.

10. James L. Bowyer, "Wood: What Are the Alternatives?" *Northwestern Lumberman,* February 1980, p. 41.

Scott Paper
Company:
Reassessing
the Strategic Plan

Introduction

1   Scott Paper Company, headquartered in Philadelphia, Pennsylvania, was
a multinational forest-products firm that grew, harvested, and sold timber.
More importantly, it also manufactured and sold a variety of paper products such as toilet paper, paper towels, napkins, facial tissues, baby
wipes, food wraps, and nonwoven materials. In fact, Scott was the world's
leading producer of sanitary tissue products for both home and commercial
use.

2   Competition within the paper products industry had grown increasingly
intense since the early 1970s. At first, Scott responded rather lethargically;
consequently, its market share declined for several key products and its
overall profitability suffered. With lower profitability and worsening economic conditions in the late 1970s, Scott Paper became a prime candidate
for a takeover. Even though it had millions of acres of valuable timberland,
a reputable name, and quality products, its stock price was clearly undervalued. In 1979, Brascan Limited, a Canadian investment firm, began a
serious attempt to acquire a majority of Scott Paper Company's stock.

3   In 1981, Scott Paper Company initiated an aggressive strategic plan that

---

This case was written by Fred C. Walters and Larry D. Alexander of Virginia Polytechnic
Institute and State University. Copyright ©1985 by Fred C. Walters and Larry D. Alexander.

called for the firm to concentrate on its strengths and divest itself of unprofitable operations. In part, this plan was taken to avoid a possible takeover by Brascan Limited or some other firm in the future. The plan appeared to be making some progress after three years, but many analysts still wondered if the effort was too little and too late. Thus, in 1984, Scott Paper Company was considering what additional actions it might take to improve its financial performance and to prevent a takeover from outsiders. Phillip E. Lippincott, Scott Paper's newly promoted President, had actively helped to formulate the plan and was to have prime responsibility for its implementation.

History of Scott Paper Company

4   In 1867, T. Seymour Scott and E. Irvin Scott left their family farm in Saratoga, New York and moved to Philadelphia, Pennsylvania. There, they opened a store that sold straw paper to local merchants. The brothers incorporated their business in 1879 under the name Scott Paper Company Limited. They bought pulp from other firms and converted it into coarse and straw paper which they sold. They soon added toilet paper (also known as bathroom tissue), which was a new innovation. A major problem in marketing this product was the established business norm of not advertising such personal products. As a result, Scott Paper Company started to ghost manufacture toilet paper under the name of the merchants who sold their product.

5   Later, in 1910, the Scott brothers decided it was time to produce toilet paper under their own name. They bought their first fully integrated paper mill in nearby Chester, Pennsylvania. This plant was capable of first making the pulp and then producing the paper product itself. Arthur Scott joined his brothers around this time, and he developed ScotTissue, America's first paper towel. The Scott brothers' philosophy was to produce quality products in high volume, sell them at low prices, and advertise extensively.

6   The Chester mill grew from one paper-making machine to six machines in 1923. By then, Scott Paper had become the leading toilet paper manufacturer in the world. Four of the five products Scott Paper Company produced at that time had not even been invented when the company first was established. Scott so successfully marketed its products that the name Scott became a household word and even a generic name for some of its products.

7   Scott Paper Company grew rapidly from 1927 through 1939, even during the heart of the depression. Its plants and machinery were greatly expanded to handle the increased sales during this period. The Chester mill alone increased to nine separate paper machines. A research and engi-

neering department, which had been established, was given the charge to keep the firm at the forefront of the paper industry. To ensure a continuous supply of pulp, Scott joined with Mead Corporation and constructed a chemical pulp mill under the name of the Brunswick Pulp and Paper Company.

8   In the 1940s, Scott further expanded its operations by purchasing two West Coast pulp mills along with several mills owned by the Marinette Paper Company. By the end of World War II, Scott had acquired seven new plants and introduced three new products, including a line of facial tissues.

9   In the 1950s, Scott further expanded its operations and began to diversify its product mix. The company introduced Scotkins, a paper napkin of unusually high quality. Scotkins was so popular that customer demand exceeded the available supply for several years. By 1954, when Scott Paper celebrated its 75th year as an incorporated business, it manufactured five basic product lines, which included toilet paper, paper towels, facial tissues, wax paper, and paper napkins.

10   In the 1960s, Scott further diversified by acquiring the S. D. Warren Company, which produced fine printing, publishing, and specialty papers. While Scott looked to the 1970s and 1980s as an opportunity to participate in new growth markets, these decades, unfortunately, brought adversities to this leading supplier of paper products.

11   Several factors in the 1970s significantly impacted on Scott's progress. Crippling strikes in 1971 hurt Scott's credibility as a reliable paper supplier. High inflation that racked the decade slowed the growth of the paper industry and many other industries that used paper products. Competition within the sanitary paper products market became more intense as the industry growth rate slowed. For example, Procter & Gamble introduced Bounty paper towels and Charmin toilet paper, which cut deeply into Scott's respective market shares. Scott was also hurt by several generic paper manufacturers which launched an all-out attack on the low price segment of the toilet paper market.

12   As a result of these competitive challenges, Scott Paper's pretax margins dropped from 16% in the early 1960s to just 7% in 1981. Scott's return on stockholders' equity was 10.6% over the 1976-1981 period. That ranked a disappointing 22nd in profitability out of the 23 leading firms in the forest-products industry.

Scott's Strategic Plan

13   On February 24th of 1981, Scott Paper Company announced its strategic plan for the 1980s. It was an aggressive five-year strategic plan whose prime objective was to reverse Scott's 20-year downward trend. The plan

was designed to improve the profitability of Scott Paper in those core businesses where it had unique competitive strengths. The plan was the result of a thorough two-year analysis of Scott's worldwide operations, its past strategies, and its competitive position within each market segment where it competed.

14   Scott Paper's new strategy focused on those business segments where it had or could achieve competitive advantages. These included:

1. Value brands and high-quality paper towels and toilet paper for the consumer sanitary-paper market.
2. Paper and nonwoven products for the away-from-home commercial customers.
3. High quality coated commercial printing and publishing papers.
4. Sanitary paper products that were sold internationally.[1]

Within these segments, Scott's strategic plan sought growth in unit volume and market share if, and only if, they could result in improved profitability. To improve its competitive position, the plan called for Scott aggressively to lower its cost position in those manufacturing facilities which produced these core products. One way that costs were to be lowered would be to simplify Scott's product offerings within each product line. If it could concentrate on fewer, more popular brands, it could increase volume for fewer products, which would lower unit costs, and help increase profitability.

Manufacturing/Operations

15   Scott Paper's extensive worldwide operations, as shown in Exhibit 1, were located in 21 countries. Within the United States alone, it operated 18 manufacturing facilities in 12 states as shown in Exhibit 2. Its largest papermaking mills were located in Chester, Pennsylvania; Everett, Washington; Mobile, Alabama; Muskegon, Michigan; and Westbrook and Winslow, Maine. These and other facilities were grouped into four divisions. They were (1) the Packaged Products Division, (2) the S. D. Warren Division, (3) the Natural Resources Division, and (4) the Nonwovens Division.

16   The Packaged Products Division, headquartered in Philadelphia, made both consumer sanitary paper products and commercial paper products. J. Richard Leman, age 49, has headed up this division since early 1982. This division was very important to Scott Paper since it accounted for the majority of Scott's total sales. It had been reducing its manufacturing costs since the strategic plan started by improving pulp use, thus completing various cost-reducing capital projects, and by emphasizing its more profitable brands.

Exhibit 1

Scott Paper Company's worldwide operations

Scott Paper Company
Executive Offices
Scott Plaza
Philadelphia, Pa. 19113
(215) 522-5000

Packaged Products Division
Philadelphia, Pa.

Consumer:
Chester, Pa.; Dover, Del.; Everett, Wash.; Ft. Edward, N.Y.; Marinette and Oconto Falls, Wis.; Mobile, Ala.; Winslow, Me.; Lester, Pa. (Excell Paper Sales Company)

Commercial:
Chester, Pa.; Everett, Wash.; Hattiesburg, Miss.; Marinette, Milwaukee and Oconto Falls, Wis.; Mobile, Ala.; Winslow, Me.

S.D. Warren Division
Boston, Mass.

Mobile, Ala.; Muskegon, Mich.; Skowhegan, Westbrook and Winslow, Me.

Managed for Scott Paper International, Inc.:
Belgium (Scott Graphics International, a division of Scott Continental)

Natural Resources Division
Philadelphia, Pa.

Everett, Wash.; Mt. Vernon, Ala.; Timberlands in Alabama, Maine, Mississippi and Washington; Timberlands in Georgia, Florida and South Carolina (Scott Timber Company); Alabama (Escuhbia Oil Company); Maine (Greenville Forest Products, 50% owned; Skylark, Inc.); Washington (Three Rivers Timber Company)

Supplier Affiliates:
Brunswick, Pearson and Sterling, Ga.; McCormick, S.C. (Brunswick Pulp & Paper Company, 50% owned); Brunswick, Ga. (Brunswick Pulp Land Company, 50% owned); Tacoma, Wash. (Mountain Tree Farm Company, 50% owned)

Managed for Scott Paper International, Inc.:
New Glasgow, Nova Scotia (Scott Maritimes Limited; Canso Chemicals Limited, 33.3% owned); Parrsboro and Upper Musquodoboit, Nova Scotia, and Timberlands in Nova Scotia (Canadian Timberlands Division; Cape Chignecto Lands Limited); Brazil (Amapá Florestal e Celulose S.A.—AMCEL, 49% owned)

Nonwovens Division
Philadelphia, Pa.

Landisville, N.J.; Rogers, Ark.

Managed for Scott Paper International, Inc.:
Germany (Federal Republic of Germany) (Scott Paper GmbH Nonwovens)

Other Consolidated Operations
Bermuda (Riscott Insurance, Ltd.); Nova Scotia (Owikeno Finance Ltd.)

Scott Paper International, Inc.
Philadelphia, Pa.

Consolidated Operations:
New Glasgow, Nova Scotia (Scott Maritimes Limited); Parrsboro and Upper Musquodoboit, Nova Scotia, and Timberlands in Nova Scotia (Canadian Timberlands Division; Cape Chignecto Lands Limited); Nova Scotia (Owikeno Lake Timber Company Limited); Delaware (Discott II, Inc.); Liberia (Scott Finance Liberia, Ltd.); Germany (Federal Republic of Germany) (Scott Paper GmbH Nonwovens)

Supplier Affiliate:
New Glasgow, Nova Scotia (Canso Chemicals Limited, 33.3% owned)

International Affiliates:
Argentina: Celulosa Jujuy, S.A. (33.3% owned)

Australia: The Bowater-Scott Corporation of Australia Limited (50% owned; The Bowater Corporation of Australia Limited owns 50%)

Belgium: Scott Continental and its Scott Graphics International Division

Brazil: Amapá Florestal e Celulose S.A.—AMCEL (49% owned; Indústria e Comércio de Minérios S.A.—ICOMI owns 51%); COPA—Companhia de Papéis (49% owned; Companhia Auxiliar de Emprésas de Mineração—CAEMI owns 51%)

Canada: Scott Paper Limited (50.05% owned)

Colombia: Papeles Scott de Colombia, S.A. (49% owned)

Costa Rica: Scott Paper Company de Costa Rica, S.A. (50% owned)

France: Bouton Brochard Scott, S.A.

Germany (Federal Republic of Germany): Scott Paper GmbH Nonwovens (a consolidated operation)

Hong Kong: Scott Paper (Hong Kong) Limited (50% owned; Hong Shem & Sons Limited owns 50%)

Italy: Scott S.p.A.

Japan: Sanyo Scott Company Limited (50% owned; Sanyo-Kokusaku Pulp Co., Ltd. owns 50%)

Korea (Republic of Korea): Ssangyong Paper Co., Ltd. (34% owned)

Malaysia: Scott Paper (Malaysia) Sdn. Bhd. (50% owned; SPP Limited owns 50%)

Mexico: Compañia Industrialde San Cristóbal, S.A. (48.8% owned)

Philippines: Scott Paper Philippines, Inc.

Singapore: Scott Paper (Singapore) Pte. Ltd. (50% owned; SPP Limited owns 50%)

Spain: Gureola-Scott, S.A. (92% owned)

Taiwan (Republic of China): Taiwan Scott Paper Corporation (66.7% owned)

Thailand: Scott Trading Limited (49.8% owned) and Thai-Scott Paper Company Limited (50% owned)

United Kingdom: Bowater-Scott Corporation Limited (50% owned; The Bowater Corporation Limited owns 50%)

(Unless otherwise indicated, Scott or Scott Paper International, Inc. owns 100% of each listed operation.)

From *Scott Paper Company 1983 Annual Report,* p. 48.

Exhibit 2

Scott Paper's manufacturing facilities in the United States

Packaged Products Division
Chester, Pennsylvania—consumer and commercial
  paper products
Dover, Delaware—consumer paper products
Everett, Washington—consumer and commercial
  paper products and pulp
Ft. Edward, New York—consumer paper products
Hattiesburg, Mississippi—commercial paper
  products
Marinette, Wisconsin—consumer and commercial
  paper products
Milwaukee, Wisconsin—commercial paper products
Mobile, Alabama—consumer and commercial
  paper products and pulp
Oconto Falls, Wisconsin—consumer and
  commercial paper products
Winslow, Maine—consumer and commercial paper
  products

S.D. Warren Division
Mobile, Alabama—paper and pulp
Muskegon, Michigan—paper and pulp
Skowhegan, Maine—paper and pulp
Westbrook, Maine—paper and pulp
Winslow, Maine—paper

Natural Resources Division
Mt. Vernon, Alabama—lumber
Parrsboro, Nova Scotia—lumber
New Glasgow, Nova Scotia—pulp

Nonwovens Division
Landisville, New Jersey—nonwoven products
Rogers, Arkansas—nonwoven products

From *Scott Paper Company Form 10-K for 1983,* p. 9.

17   The S. D. Warren Division, headquartered in Boston, manufactured commercial printing, publishing, and specialty papers. Robert E. McAvoy, its 55-year-old President, has only held this position since December of 1983. This division operated five pulp and/or paper mills located in Maine, Michigan, and Alabama. A new paper machine was added in 1983 at its Showhegan, Maine facility at a cost of over $200,000,000. This new machine helped increase the production of lighter weight coated printing paper. In addition, a paper machine at the Muskegon mill was rebuilt during that same year to increase output and lower its unit costs.

18   This division provided professional advice and technical assistance to more than 800 private landowners through its S. D. Warren tree farm program. Much of the timber harvested from these private woodlots was

purchased by Scott Paper Company for use in its mills.

19   The Natural Resources Division, headquartered in Philadelphia, had responsibility for managing the company's 3,080,000 acres of timberlands and mineral resources. Stephen J. Conway was its vice president for Natural Resources—Timberlands. Scott owned some 2,800,000 acres of timber and had long-term cutting rights (or leased or had purchase rights) for the remaining 280,000 acres. Scott's timberlands, which were located in the United States and Canada, supplied nearly half of the wood fiber it required for pulp and papermaking. Each year, approximately half of the harvested logs was sold worldwide as logs or converted into lumber to be sold to the commercial market. The other half of the harvested logs was used as raw materials for Scott's pulp manufacturing operations to produce various paper products.

20   In recent years, Scott's timberlands provided an important fuel source for operating its plants and mills. About 55% of Scott's total energy consumption was supplied from a mix of wood biomass and liquid residues resulting in the conservation of nearly 6,000,000 barrels of crude oil per year. Scott Paper had also placed a heavy emphasis on environmental stewardship wherever it operated. Every mill was in full compliance with both federal and state environmental regulations. The effort to comply with various governmental standards had not come cheaply, since Scott's expenditures totaled over $250,000,000 since the mid-1970s.

21   The primary objective for Scott's manufacturing operations was to become one of the most cost efficient operations within the paper industry. When Phillip Lippincott was promoted to president and chief operating officer in 1980, Scott had a number of older mills and processing plants. Some of the projects completed already in its five-year capital-spending program included:

1. A new $200,000,000 paper machine at Skowhegan, Maine.
2. A $85,000,000 biomass and coal cogeneration facility at Westbrook, Maine.
3. A $69,000,000 woodyard modernization project at Mobile, Alabama.
4. A $28,000,000 modernization of a papermaking machine at Muskegon, Michigan.
5. A $25,000,000 fiber recycling facility at Winslow, Maine.
6. A $20,000,000 commercial products converting plant at Hattiesburg, Mississippi.
7. A $100,000,000 energy facility at its Chester, Pennsylvania paper mill.

In addition, Scott Paper Company also planned to continue its $300,000,000 project to modernize and upgrade extensively the energy generation facilities at its Mobile, Alabama plant, which was scheduled to be completed in 1985. Despite these capital improvements, Scott Paper still had other old mills that handicapped its production efficiency.

Marketing/Sales

22 Scott Paper's products were marketed differently depending on the type of product and market involved.

23 The Packaged Products Division had sales of $1,570,778,000, which accounted for 63.7% of Scott Paper's total sales in 1983. The various consumer and commercial products offered by this division are shown in Exhibit 3.

24 The Packaged Products Division's consumer products were targeted at different segments of the market; however, its value segment (sometimes called economy or family pack) was given the most emphasis. Irrespective of the segment, these consumer products were sold primarily through grocery stores, drug stores, general retailers, and discount stores. Scott's four value line products included ScotTissue toilet paper, ScotTowels paper towels, Scotties facial tissues, and Scott Family napkins. These products

---

Exhibit 3

Scott's Packaged Products Division's various products

Packaged Products Division. Trademarked and other products manufactured by the Company's Packaged Products Division, other than pulp, include the following:

Consumer Products

Bathroom Tissues	*Disposable Towels*	*Napkins*
Cottonelle, Family Scott, ScotTissue, Soft 'n' Pretty Soft-Weve, Waldorf	Job Squad, ScotTowels, Viva	Scott Family, Viva
Facial Tissues	*Wax Paper*	*Baby Wipes*
Scotties	Cut-Rite	Baby Fresh, Wash a-bye Baby

Commercial Products

Washroom Products	*Food Service Products*	*Fixtures*
Bathroom Tissues— Escort, ScotTissue, Soft-Weve, Soft Blend, Waldorf Towels— Scott, Premiere Facial Tissues— Scotties Repete	Mealmates, Scottex, Scottlin and Windsor napkins; Cut-Rite wax bags; American placemats, tray covers, table covers, doilies, portion products, fluted containers, specialty cups	Towel, facial tissue, napkin and windshield towel dispensers; bathroom tissue and wiper holders

Wiping Products

Paper—*Assembly Wipes, Micro-Wipes, Sani-Prep, Soft-Cote, Sturdi-Wipes II, Utility Wipes,* Windshield Towels
Scrim Reinforced—
   Dura-Weve

Air Lay—*Heltlon II, Ultralon,* Shop, Service, Autoshop and Roll Wiper Control Towels
Carded Rayon—*Heftlon*
Bonded Cellulose—*Dry-Up, WypAll, WypAll* Blue, Professional Towel

From *Scott Paper Company Form 10-K for 1983,* pp. 2–3.

were all targeted at the medium-priced market segments. In the higher quality segments, Scott brands included Cottonelle and Soft 'n' Pretty toilet paper, Job Squad and Viva paper towels, and Baby Fresh baby wipes. Under Scott's five-year strategic plan, some of the better known brands such as Cottonelle and Soft 'n' Pretty were being milked for whatever cash they could generate; otherwise they might be dropped entirely.

25   This division's commercial products, by definition, were used in the away-from-home markets, which were growing faster than the home-use market. They included industrial, institutional, commercial, food service, hotel/motel, and government establishments. Whereas the consumer products were generally sold directly to the retail firms themselves, Scott's commercial products were usually sold through distributors, which primarily competed on the basis of price, product quality, and service.

26   The Packaged Products Division products were noted for high quality, their value for the price, and the Scott name. While the Packaged Products Division had 16 mills, a number of them were older, less efficient production facilities. Scott's natural resources supported this division by providing an unlimited base of raw materials.

27   The S. D. Warren Division, which manufactured commercial printing, publishing, converting, and specialty papers, posted sales of $686,957,000 in 1983. That represented a 20% increase over 1982. Its principal products were high-quality coated papers used for print advertising, annual reports, and magazines. It also produced uncoated publishing papers of various grades and qualities for a wide range of printed books. The division had made excellent progress in 1983 towards implementing its two-fold strategy. One aspect of it was to expand its market share for lighter weight grades of printing and publishing paper. The other aspect of the strategy was to retain its long standing quality and market position in heavier weight papers.

28   This division's products were mainly distributed through independent wholesalers throughout the United States. Most of the converting and specialty papers were sold to converters for further processing into a final end-user product. The principal methods of competition in the markets where these products went included price, product quality, and customer service. Many of this division's products had a strong market position and were supported by an effective sales force.

29   The Natural Resources Division's sales of $86,004,000 for 1983 did not reflect its importance to the other two major divisions. This division had two major objectives. One was to supply wood, pulp, and biomass fuel wood to other Scott operations at the lowest possible cost. The other objective was to become a reliable, long-term supplier of pulp within the pulp-wood market. Half of the logs this division harvested each year were processed into square lumber and the remainder were used by Scott in its pulp manufacturing operations. Scott sold the pulp it made in both the domestic and international markets.

Finance/Accounting

30   Scott Paper Company's statement of consolidated earnings for 1981-1983 is shown in Exhibit 4. For 1983, its net sales of $2,465,088,000 were an all-time record but so were its costs of goods for that same year. Its 1983 net income after taxes of $123,679,000 was a substantial improvement over the $74,457,000 for 1982, but down somewhat from the previous three years. Scott's consolidated balance sheets for 1982 and 1983 are shown in Exhibit 5. A summary of Scott's business segments for 1981-83 appears in Exhibit 6. Its income from operations of $140,125,000 for 1983 breaks down as follows: $127,063,000 for the Packaged Products Division, $54,189,000 for

Exhibit 4

Consolidated earnings for 1981–1983 (in thousands, except on a per share basis)

	1983	1982	1981
Sales	**$2,465,088**	$2,293,436	$2,309,444
Costs and expenses			
Product costs	**1,753,698**	1,592,053	1,580,409
Marketing and distribution	**416,430**	440,977	484,519
Research and development	**29,293**	29,957	31,344
Administration and general	**93,532**	86,401	73,792
Interest expense	**32,010**	21,744	32,642
	2,324,963	2,171,132	2,202,706
Income from operations	**140,125**	122,304	106,738
Other income and (expense)	**18,561**	86,102	58,292
Income before taxes	**158,686**	208,406	165,030
Taxes on income			
Current	**41,223**	19,555	23,297
Deferred	**20,397**	74,610	44,368
	61,620	94,165	67,665
Income before share of earnings of international affiliates	**97,066**	114,241	97,365
Share of earnings (loss) of international affiliates	**26,613**	(39,784)	35,975
Net Income	**123,679**	74,457	133,340
Dividends on preferred shares	**6,262**	5,740	255
Earnings for common shares	**$ 117,417**	$ 68,717	$ 133,085
Earnings per common share	**$2.58**	$1.61	$3.22
Dividends per common share	**$1.00**	$1.00	$1.00
Average common shares outstanding	**45,534**	42,652	41,375

From *Scott Paper Company 1983 Annual Report*, p. 30.

Exhibit 5

Consolidated balance sheets for December 25, 1982 and December 31, 1983 (in thousands)

		1983		*1982*
Assets:				
Current assets				
Cash		$ 7,654		$ 4,769
Marketable securities		2,352		3,325
Time deposits		136,185		15,646
Receivables		253,093		224,021
Inventories		173,500		211,666
Prepaid items		24,287		14,282
		597,071		473,709
Plant assets, at cost	$2,665,485		$2,548,249	
Accumulated depreciation	(1,116,873)	1,548,612	(1,042,423)	1,505,826
Timber resources, at cost less				
timber harvested		95,440		95,061
Investments in and advances to				
international affiliates		280,686		232,218
Investments in supplier affiliates		44,696		40,207
Construction funds held by trustees		114,521		1,577
Other assets		42,130		33,765
Total		**$2,723,156**		**$2,382,363**
Liabilities and Shareholders' Equity:				
Current liabilities				
Payable to suppliers and others		$ 371,438		$ 344,546
Current maturities of long-term debt		13,895		10,645
Accrued taxes on income		43,910		18,842
		429,243		374,033
Long-term debt		566,343		445,176
Deferred credits, principally deferred				
income taxes		246,411		227,477
		1,241,997		1,046,686
Redeemable preferred shares		17,608		45,000
Non-redeemable preferred shares		7,128		7,128
Common shareholders' equity				
Common shares	$ 514,590		$ 396,254	
Reinvested earnings	1,010,682		944,787	
Cumulative translation adjustment	(58,835)		(47,212)	
Treasury shares	(10,014)	1,456,423	(10,280)	1,283,549
Total		**$2,723,156**		**$2,382,363**

From *Scott Paper Company 1983 Annual Report,* p. 31.

the S. D. Warren Division, $25,315,000 for the Forest Products and Materials Division, $9,636,000 from other operations, and $76,078,000 deducted for corporate interest expense. Finally, a ten-year financial summary, from 1974 through 1983, is shown in Exhibit 7.

Exhibit 6

A summary of Scott's business segments for 1981–83 (in thousands)

	1983	1982	1981
Sales			
Packaged Products			
Sanitary paper products	$1,505,741	$1,473,265	$1,481,631
Market pulp	65,037	71,960	69,450
	1,570,778	1,545,225	1,551,081
S.D. Warren			
Printing, publishing, converting, and			
specialty papers	666,575	558,916	564,117
Market pulp	20,382	12,899	11,025
	686,957	571,815	575,142
Forest Products and Minerals	86,004	64,118	69,309
Other Operations	121,349	112,278	113,912
	$2,465,088	$2,293,436	$2,309,444
Operating Profits			
Packaged Products			
Sanitary paper products	$ 143,280	$ 121,480	$ 69,844
Market pulp	(16,217)	(1,925)	14,781
	127,063	119,555	84,625
S.D. Warren			
Printing, publishing, converting and			
specialty papers	57,343	39,203	56,819
Market pulp	(3,154)	(3)	2,999
	54,189	39,200	59,818
Forest Products and Minerals	25,315	14,526	21,077
Other Operations	9,636	7,902	9,069
Corporate	(76,078)	(58,879)	(67,851)
Income from operations	140,125	122,304	106,738
Other income and (expense)	18,561	86,102	58,292
Income before taxes	$ 158,686	$ 208,406	$ 165,030
Depreciation and Cost of Timber Harvested			
Packaged Products	$ 69,974	$ 67,482	$ 61,363
S.D. Warren	44,729	30,252	28,288
Forest Products and Minerals	25,087	26,390	23,277
Other Operations	2,578	2,741	2,243
Corporate	2,204	1,519	1,823
	$ 144,572	$ 128,384	$ 116,994

Exhibit 6 (concluded)

	1983	*1982*	*1981*
Capital Expenditures			
Packaged Products	$ **137,055**	$ 145,416	$ 142,494
S.D. Warren	**41,369**	204,621	136,083
Forest Products and Minerals	**29,108**	32,477	30,817
Other Operations	**2,129**	5,688	8,300
Corporate	**11,289**	527	3,405
	$ **220,950**	$ 388,729	$ 321,099
Identifiable Assets			
Packaged Products	$**1,145,374**	$1,158,142	$1,143,131
S.D. Warren	**755,036**	678,022	572,556
Forest Products and Minerals	**198,596**	161,682	160,955
Other Operations	**—**	67,707	64,973
Corporate	**624,150**	316,810	357,068
	$**2,723,156**	2,382,363	$2,298,683
Identifiable assets include investments in supplier affiliates of:			
Packaged Products	$ **39,249**	$ 33,804	$ 39,830
S.D. Warren	**5,100**	6,059	6,324
Forest Products and Minerals	**347**	344	339
	$ **44,696**	$ 40,207	$ 46,493

From *Scott Paper Company 1983 Annual Report,* p. 43.

31   Scott's financial objective was to increase its stockholders' return on investment, which hovered around 5% in 1981, up to around 12% to 15% by the end of 1986. Several actions were taken in the early 1980s to realize these objectives.

32   One action was to commit $1,600,000,000 towards a five-year capital spending program as a part of Scott Paper's 1981 strategic plan. The capital spending was needed to upgrade aging plants, buy new machinery, and to expand capacity. This capital spending program was already helping Scott Paper to lower its costs and to increase its productivity. Phillip Lippincott noted:

> The capital investment program and the financial strengthening and rationalization measures weren't matters of choice so much as matters of necessity if we were going to maintain, much less improve, our standing in the industry.[2]

Exhibit 7

A ten-year financial summary from 1974 through 1983 (in millions)

	1983	*1982*	*1981*	*1980*	*1979*	*1978*	*1977*	*1976*	*1975*	*1974*
Sales	**$2,465.1**	$2,293.4	$2,309.4	$2,083.2	$1,908.1	$1,724.9	$1,520.2	$1,373.8	$1,191.9	$1,109.5
Costs and expenses										
Product costs	**1,753.7**	1,592.0	1,580.4	1,399.9	1,268.7	1,174.3	1,067.9	941.1	827.3	796.9
Marketing and distribution	**416.5**	441.0	484.5	478.2	399.1	344.7	274.9	233.0	195.4	155.3
Research and development	**29.3**	30.0	31.4	31.2	30.0	26.8	25.9	24.4	24.2	23.0
Administration and general	**93.5**	86.4	73.8	65.8	60.4	55.6	46.2	44.8	37.9	34.9
Interest expense	**32.0**	21.7	32.6	32.4	33.4	34.7	32.6	30.2	28.7	18.1
	2,325.0	2,171.1	2,202.7	2,007.5	1,791.6	1,636.1	1,447.5	1,273.5	1,113.5	1,028.2
Income from operations	**140.1**	122.3	106.7	75.7	116.5	88.8	72.7	100.3	78.4	81.3
Other income and (expense)	**18.6**	86.1	58.3	61.0	21.2	(2.1)	(10.8)	4.7	1.7	—
Income before taxes	**158.7**	208.4	165.0	136.7	137.7	86.7	61.9	105.0	80.1	81.3
Taxes on income	**61.6**	94.2	67.6	47.9	45.1	26.4	19.5	40.7	33.4	31.1
Income before share of earnings of international affiliates	**97.1**	114.2	97.4	88.8	92.6	60.3	42.4	64.3	46.7	50.2
Share of earnings (loss) of international affiliates	**26.6**	(39.7)	35.9	44.2	43.9	32.7	19.2	8.5	17.7	18.9
Income before cumulative effect of accounting change	**123.7**	74.5	133.3	133.0	136.5	93.0	61.6	72.8	64.4	69.1
Cumulative effect of accounting change	—	—	—	—	—	—	37.1	—	(.6)	—
Net income	**123.7**	74.5	133.3	133.0	136.5	93.0	98.7	72.8	63.8	69.1
Dividends on preferred shares	**6.3**	5.8	.3	.3	.3	.3	.3	.3	.3	.3
Earnings for common shares	$ **117.4**	$ 68.7	$ 133.0	$ 132.7	$ 136.2	$ 92.7	$ 98.4	$ 72.5	$ 63.5	$ 68.8
Dollars per common share	**$2.58**	$1.61	$3.22	$3.41	$3.50	$2.40	$2.55	$2.00	$1.84	$1.99
Earnings	**$2.58**	$1.61	$3.22	$3.41	$3.50	$2.40	$2.55	$2.00	$1.84	$1.99
Dividends	**1.00**	1.00	1.00	1.00	.90	.80	.76	.72	.68	.62
Market price—high	**$32\frac{1}{4}$**	21	$28\frac{1}{2}$	$23\frac{1}{2}$	$20\frac{7}{8}$	19	$20\frac{3}{4}$	$24\frac{1}{8}$	19	$18\frac{1}{8}$
low	**$18\frac{5}{8}$**	$13\frac{5}{8}$	15	$13\frac{1}{4}$	$13\frac{5}{8}$	$12\frac{1}{2}$	13	$14\frac{1}{4}$	$12\frac{1}{4}$	$9\frac{5}{8}$

	1983	1982	1981	1980	1979	1978	1977	1976	1975	1974
Percent of income from operations to sales	5.7%	5.3%	4.6%	3.6%	6.1%	5.1%	4.8%	7.3%	6.6%	7.3%
Debt as a percentage of total capitalization	25.1%	22.6%	26.4%	28.6%	28.1%	27.9%	37.8%	29.1%	32.4%	29.4%
Return on common shareholders' equity	8.6%	5.3%	11.0%	12.4%	14.1%	10.6%	11.8%	10.2%	10.0%	11.7%
Pro forma amounts										
Net income	$123.7	$74.5	$133.3	$133.0	$136.5	$93.0	$61.6	$95.8	$70.5	$72.3
Earnings per common share	2.58	1.61	3.22	3.41	3.50	2.40	1.59	2.64	2.04	2.09
Total assets at year end	$2,723.2	$2,382.4	$2,298.7	$2,012.6	$1,827.9	$1,620.3	$1,588.1	$1,464.8	$1,283.5	$1,107.5
Long-term debt at year end	566.3	445.2	500.7	474.8	422.3	371.1	430.2	374.1	352.2	270.5
Redeemable preferred shares	17.6	45.0	—	—	—	—	—	—	—	—
Capital expenditures for plant and timber	221.0	388.7	321.1	252.4	182.2	134.0	149.4	198.6	210.2	147.0
Depreciation and cost of timber harvested	144.6	128.4	117.0	109.4	104.3	97.7	88.4	67.7	60.1	54.2
Investments in affiliates	53.0	(54.7)	33.4	30.8	46.1	30.0	19.9	12.7	20.1	23.1
(Thousands)										
Common shares										
Average shares outstanding	45,534	42,652	41,375	38,896	38,885	38,722	38,619	36,225	34,574	34,573
Number of shareholders	59.1	65.0	70.1	74.7	77.7	78.3	75.4	75.9	79.4	82.5
Number of employees	17.0	18.6	20.3	20.5	20.8	20.4	21.3	20.6	20.1	20.4

From *Scott Paper Company 1983 Annual Report*, p. 46.

Capital expenditures, including equity investments in affiliates, were $350,000,000 for 1981, $402,000,000 for 1982, and $270,000,000 for 1983. An additional $750,000,000 was allocated for 1984 and 1985 combined.

33   Another action taken towards increasing its stockholders' return on investment focused on how Scott Paper financed its needed capital. Scott used external sources to finance about 50% of its capital spending plan. While not noted for being financially creative, Scott Paper was rather ingenious in how it financed this plan. It sold approximately $50,000,000 worth of tax benefits under the safe harbor provision of the Economic Recovery Tax Act of 1981. It also financed well over $100,000,000 in equipment purchases by using relatively cheap foreign financing, which took advantage of an international tax loophole. Scott also raised $7,000,000 by leasing its equipment to two banks in England as a form of two-country tax shelter. Scott also raised another $91,000,000 by transferring ownership of a new biomass processing boiler to General Electric Corporation under a 25 year contract whereby Scott would buy back the power it uses.

34   Scott Paper also generated cash internally through the divestiture of several of its affiliates and landholdings. In November of 1983, Scott agreed in principle to sell its Brown Jordan Furniture and Lighting Division to Integrated Resources, Inc. for $83,000,000. Scott was also in the process of selling 220,000 acres of its Northwest timberlands for a sum expected to run in the hundreds of millions of dollars. In addition, these divestitures helped to increase Scott's return on stockholders' investment by spinning off weak performing units, generating needed cash, and emphasizing products in markets where Scott Paper had a competitive advantage.

Research and Development

35   Scott Paper Company's research and development efforts were conducted primarily at facilities located in Philadelphia, Pennsylvania and Westbrook, Maine. Scott spent approximately $30,000,000 per year for various R&D programs. Some of these ongoing programs included research efforts on pulp and papermaking, process control, paper converting, and the development of new and improved paper products.

36   Ongoing research was also directed at helping Scott achieve its environmental and energy conservation goals. Scott had made significant strides in reducing its use of crude oil through its biomass fuel wood and liquid residue program. For example, Scott was experimenting with a prelogging harvest operation at its Mobile, Alabama papermill. This operation recovered hardwood and small pine stems for fuel, which reduced its use of fuel oil. The project improved Scott's operations at that facility in several ways. Site preparation costs were substantially lower, and logging costs had been reduced by up to $4.00 per cord. As a result of this program,

approximately 55% of the mill's fuel needs were supplied from a mix of biomass fuel wood and liquid residuals.

37   Scott also emphasized research efforts to improve its forest productivity. Scott's Monroeville, Mississippi, orchard bred genetically superior super trees which were used to replant its harvested timberlands. Scott's foresters believed that the improved seedlings it will plant by the year 2005 will yield at least 40% more volume than ordinary pine trees. Trees which it experimented with in the 1950s were yielding 10% greater volume per acre by the 1980s than ordinary trees. Other projects to increase forest productivity included research to develop trees that can grow in poor soils, shorten the tree growth cycle, and breed disease- and insect-resistant pine trees.

Human Resources/Personnel

38   Since Lippincott took charge in 1981, Scott Paper had been streamlining its work force. Scott had reduced the number of salaried and hourly domestic employees by 15%. In fact, its 17,000 total U.S. employees were down some 1,600 from just the previous year. In 1983, it had 10,800 employees engaged directly in manufacturing operations and 6,200 in administrative, technical, clerical, and sales positions. Scott had also reduced the number of levels in the organization and had increased the average span of management. These actions were taken to reduce overhead costs and to streamline its various business operations to remain competitive.

39   Scott was placing a greater emphasis on managerial excellence. It tried to create a climate that encouraged its employees to realize their full potential. Scott had adopted new management procedures that gave its employees a greater role in managing Scott's operations. Along with this increased responsibility, Scott had also modified its incentive programs so they would be based more on bottom-line financial measures. The firm believed that tying in personal financial rewards to the overall corporate plan would help improve its return on equity to an acceptable level.

40   Approximately 9,900 of Scott's hourly-paid work force were represented by labor unions. Since 1981, Scott had taken three costly strikes in an effort to reform work rules to reduce labor costs. A nine-month strike from late 1982 to mid-1983 at Scott's Maritime pulp mill alone was estimated to have cost Scott almost $.10 a share after taxes.[3] However, Scott management believed that it had to take strikes, if necessary, to demonstrate its determination to become a low-cost producer of paper products.

The External Environment: The Art of Papermaking

41   The modern day steps used to manufacture pulp and paper products operated in a very sophisticated manner. Pulp wood via truck, rail, or water

arrived at the mill where it was unloaded and transferred to the barking drum area. The barking drum was a large revolving drum that removed the bark from the tree. The bark was salvaged as fuel for the mill's energy requirements—fuel that cut down on the use of crude oil.

42   The stripped logs were then taken by conveyor to the chipper, which reduced the logs to tiny chips. The chips were then sorted and packed into large tanks known as digesters. Here, the chips were cooked by steam in an alkaline solution to dissolve the lignin, a glue like substance, which binds the cellulose wood fibers together.

43   The pulp was then washed in vacuum washers to remove the alkaline chemicals. The pulp could be sold at this point in the pulp wood market or converted into paper products at the papermill.

44   Within the papermill, the pulp was put through disc refiners to flatten the fibers so they would knit together on the paper making machines. The papermaking machines, some as long as a football field, had an endlessly moving screen, known as a fourdrinier wire, on which the pulp slurry was spread. It had a consistency of about 99.5% water and 0.5% wood fiber. As the mixture was deposited on the fourdrinier wire, the excess water poured down through the screen. The paper was then transferred to continuously moving felt blankets to remove still more water.

45   In the final process, the paper passed through colanders, which were heavy revolving steel rollers, that gave the sheet a finished, glazed surface. The paper was then wound onto jumbo rolls about 21 feet long and 8 feet in diameter. The jumbo rolls were cut into smaller rolls which were made to the buyer's specified size.

The Paper Products Industry

46   Paper manufacturing was the ninth largest industry in the United States. Paper mills directly employed over 263,000 workers while another 413,000 people were involved in converting and distributing paper products.

47   The paper industry was characterized by a high degree of vertical integration. Large companies owned or controlled their own timber resource base, saw mills, pulp and paper mills, and converting facilities. Large companies owned or controlled their own timber resource base, saw mills, pulp and paper mills, and converting facilities. In addition, the industry was highly leveraged with average debt to capital ratios between 30% and 40% as shown in Exhibit 8. The exhibit also shows the return on assets ratios for leading firms which varies from 0% up to 10% for 1983. Finally, the industry was very capital intensive. A new papermill cost up to $250,000,000 and took four years to build.

48   Historically, paper and paperboard production were closely tied to the health of the U. S. economy. Furthermore, sales for many paper and paperboard items were based on a derived demand for some other product

Exhibit 8

Debt to capital and return on assets ratios for leading forest-products firms

Debt/Capital Ratio (%)

Company	1979	1980	1981	1982	1983
Paper and Forest Products					
Boise Cascade	31.0	36.8	35.0	34.8	28.0
Champion International	31.7	28.7	31.5	34.1	33.1
Chesapeake Corp. of Virginia	22.6	20.4	26.7	26.6	19.4
Consolidated Papers	8.7	7.3	5.5	4.4	3.4
Crown Zellerbach	31.5	25.9	30.2	34.6	33.5
Domtar Inc.	21.8	22.4	24.4	29.5	28.0
Fort Howard Paper	16.4	15.1	10.2	6.9	16.4
Georgia-Pacific	32.2	32.8	35.7	37.1	33.9
Glatfelter (P.H.)	6.9	4.9	3.3	1.8	0.5
Great Northern Nekoosa	27.4	23.9	22.3	27.5	30.5
Hammermill Paper	35.2	31.7	35.4	38.3	33.1
International Paper	25.4	21.4	17.6	20.7	18.9
Kimberly-Clark	13.4	20.4	15.8	17.4	22.2
Longview Fibre	NA	NA	38.5	41.9	42.2
Louisiana-Pacific	17.5	14.8	12.8	17.2	16.2
MacMillan Bloedel	24.4	32.0	33.8	39.3	34.0
Mead Corp.	32.9	33.9	41.6	48.9	37.8
Pentair Inc.	19.5	32.0	37.4	17.7	20.6
Potlatch Corp.	36.1	36.0	32.6	32.3	28.8
St. Regis Corp.	27.1	32.3	32.5	35.4	29.6
Scott Paper	27.4	27.8	26.0	22.2	27.7
Sonoco Products	8.8	13.6	11.2	12.2	13.4
Southwest Forest Inds.	49.6	47.8	47.4	50.0	54.5
Stone Container	36.4	32.5	39.9	41.9	63.4
Union Camp Corp.	18.6	21.9	20.0	25.3	29.6
Wausau Paper Mills	34.8	50.6	45.6	43.3	41.5
Westvaco Corp.	29.0	27.2	24.8	23.5	25.1
Weyerhaeuser Co.	32.3	31.2	31.4	28.7	26.5
Willamette Inds.	22.1	32.9	39.4	43.8	38.6

NA—Not available. NM—Not meaningful.
Definition: Long-term debt as a % of invested capital.

that varied with the economy. For example, corrugated box production depended upon the derived demand that various consumer and industrial products had for shipping containers. Similarly, newsprint production depended upon the level of newspaper advertising, which in turn fluctuated with the economy. Because the paper industry was so closely tied to the economy, it experienced an upswing in demand during the second half of 1983 as the economy rebounded. Industry analysts expected the paper industry to continue to prosper well into 1985 and perhaps beyond. This positive outlook was based upon an expectation of record paper production, further price increases for paper products, and a high operating utilization rate.

Exhibit 8 (continued)

Return on Assets (%)

Company	1979	1980	1981	1982	1983
Paper and Forest Products					
Boise Cascade	8.2	5.5	4.4	0.3	2.2
Champion International	8.2	5.7	3.5	1.1	2.3
Chesapeake Corp. of Virginia	9.6	10.8	10.3	2.8	2.9
Consolidated Papers	16.8	14.4	13.4	9.1	10.4
Crown Zellerbach	6.5	4.3	3.0	NM	3.6
Domtar Inc.	10.7	8.1	4.7	0.7	3.0
Fort Howard Paper	15.3	14.7	15.3	15.1	10.9
Georgia-Pacific	8.9	5.6	3.3	1.0	2.1
Glatfelter (P.H.)	14.1	11.7	8.5	10.0	9.3
Great Northern Nekoosa	8.8	8.6	7.5	5.6	5.1
Hammermill Paper	5.7	5.8	6.0	3.2	3.2
International Paper	7.7	6.2	9.8	2.9	4.6
Kimberly-Clark	16.0	8.3	8.8	7.7	6.8
Longview Fibre	16.8	0.6	3.7	0.9	4.0
Louisiana-Pacific	10.1	5.4	2.3	NM	2.2
MacMillan Bloedel	9.6	5.9	NM	NM	0.1
Mead Corp.	8.8	7.3	5.3	NM	1.3
Pentair Inc.	14.7	12.0	6.2	7.4	6.2
Potlatch Corp.	8.1	4.9	5.2	1.9	3.5
St. Regis Corp.	7.2	6.9	6.4	1.6	1.9
Scott Paper	7.9	6.9	5.9	3.2	4.6
Sonoco Products	11.1	11.4	12.0	8.3	10.0
Southwest Forest Inds.	4.9	4.4	2.0	NM	NM
Stone Container	7.0	8.8	8.1	4.0	NM
Union Camp Corp.	11.3	10.7	9.8	6.5	6.0
Wausau Paper Mills	10.3	8.3	2.5	NM	3.6
Westvaco Corp.	7.8	8.0	8.3	4.8	4.3
Weyerhaeuser Co.	10.8	6.3	4.2	2.4	3.4
Willamette Inds.	11.2	8.2	3.4	0.6	2.4

NA—Not available. NM—Not meaningful.
Definition: Net income divided by average total assets.

From Standard and Poor's Industry Survey, *Building and Forest Products,* September 27, 1984, pp. B85–B86.

49   Because the paper industry incurred huge fixed costs for plant and equipment, operating utilization rates had a critical impact on profitability. The paper industry's overall operating utilization rate was around 97% of capacity in early 1984 and was expected to be even higher by the end of the year. An industry rule of thumb is that below 93% of capacity, gross operating margins for paper firms plummet as in the recession years 1982 and 1975, when rates were 88% and 81%, respectively, because competitors started discounting prices just to keep their machines running.

50   In the 1980s, industry leaders had become conservative about increasing capacity. They feared that huge federal budget deficits would have an adverse impact on the economy that would particularly hurt their industry. Consequently, most new production capacity and capital spending plans

were for smaller projects located in the South. The advantages for locating new production facilities in that region were its longer growing season, proximity to sun belt markets, and its lower labor costs.

51   The prices and production levels for all grades of paper were up sharply in 1984. Kraft and coated paper production facilities were operating at full capacity. Linerboard production was at full capacity and commanded a price of $320 per ton. Tissue paper products were at 95% capacity, and prices were slightly higher than in 1983. Finally, market pulp, which was used by paper companies to make paper products, was selling for $540 per ton, approximately $100 higher than in 1983.

Industry Threats and Problems

52   Many of the large vertically integrated paper companies also sold forest products, such as lumber and poles. These products were even more affected by fluctuating interest rates and the general health of the economy. Rising interest rates since the beginning of the 1970s had decreased yearly housing starts, which caused profits to decrease significantly. The early 1980s marked the most severe recession in the forest-products industry since the 1930s. The timber side of the forest-products industry was still facing tough times in 1984, and some firms tried to raise cash by selling off some of their timberlands. The result was a glut of timber on the marketplace, which brought about a substantial decline in the market price of timberland throughout the United States.

53   The relative strength of the U. S. dollar abroad in 1984, along with the devaluation of some foreign currencies, reeked havoc with the profitability of some multinational paper companies. A continuing strong U. S. dollar would exacerbate the high U. S. trade deficit, thereby generating even greater political pressure for protectionist trade measures. This in turn could threaten future prospects for increased paper product exports. The devaluation of foreign currencies affected operating earnings of foreign affiliates, creating considerable exchange losses. For instance, Scott Paper Company noted a substantial drop in its Mexican affiliate's earnings due to the devaluation of the peso by approximately 83% in 1982.

54   The stocks of most forest products firms were selling at low multiples of their earnings. This made many of them vulnerable to possible acquisition. In fact, St. Regis was acquired in 1983 by Champion International, and Fort Howard Paper Company had merged with Maryland Cup Corporation. Other firms like Southwest Forest Industries and Scott Paper Company had faced serious takeover attempts. Acquisitions were popular in this industry because buying additional production capacity was usually cheaper than building it from scratch.

55   Another threat to the paper firms was their heavy reliance on outside energy sources. Since 1970, the price for crude oil had risen substantially

during the 1970s and its availability became less certain. Consequently, many paper firms had made a concerted effort to become more energy self-sufficient. Many firms had started to utilize more fully wood scraps and mill residues to run their mill operations. Some firms had spent hundreds of millions of dollars to convert plant boilers to coal or wood use in an effort to reduce dependency on limited fossil fuel reserves.

56 Still another threat was the increasing use of plastic as a substitute product for paper bags, sacks, and wraps. Many grocery stores and retailers were switching to plastic because it was stronger and cheaper than paper. Furthermore, plastics were increasingly being used to make disposable cups, bags, and plates.

57 Three innovations posed a threat to the paper industry. First, the increasing use of computers enabled firms to store tremendous amounts of information on computer files rather than on countless paper reports and documents. Fortunately, at least computers were creating the need for more and more computer paper. Second, the increasing use of microfilm and microfiche, made from plastic, reduced the need for storing bulky paper documents and library materials. Third, the advent of electronic mail, electronic banking, and teleconferencing may well reduce the demand for envelopes, white paper, bank checks, and even newspapers.

Buyers of Paper Products

58 The paper products industry offered a highly diverse assortment of products including consumer packaged products, specialty papers, pulp- and wood-based chemical derivatives, and timber products. As a result, a variety of distribution methods was used to reach customers in these diverse markets.

59 Generally, consumer packaged products were sold to supermarkets, grocery stores, and other mass merchandisers either through a direct sales force or wholesale distributors. Commercial packaged products were marketed to industrial and commercial users such as food services, chemical companies, furniture manufacturers, textile operations, and government institutions. These products were generally sold through a direct sales force because most products were specially made to the customer's needs.

60 Paper products which included specialty and printing papers were usually sold to converters and wholesale distributors. Once again, a direct sales force was used to market these products because orders were specially tailored to the individual customer's needs.

61 Wood products and pulp were usually sold in the commercial lumber market via a network of wholesalers and distributors. Buyers of these products included contractors, builders, and home-improvement supply centers.

62 Wood-based chemicals, which were by-products of pulp mill operations,

were used mainly in coating, adhesives, printing inks, soaps, detergents, and plastics. Many of these types of products were bought by chemical companies and primary manufacturing operations. In turn, they marketed their products either through a direct sales force or wholesale distributors.

Competitor Profiles

63   The severe recession in the early 1980s brought about dramatic changes in the strategies used by many paper companies. Before this recession, many paper firms believed that capacity expansion and diversification were the keys to success. Since then, many firms re-evaluated and changed their strategies. Many paper companies were trying to become more cost competitive and starting to emphasize those products in which they had a competitive advantage. Many firms began to divest themselves of poor performing, nonessential business units. Conversely, the proceeds from these divestitures were being plowed back into their high-performance businesses. Capital spending programs were undertaken to lower operating costs and reduce energy dependence rather than increasing capacity. The paper firms hoped that these various actions would help improve bottom-line profitability. Scott Paper's key competitors in the paper and pulp industry are overviewed in the following profiles.

International Paper Company

64   International Paper (I.P.), headquartered in New York City, was the world's largest papermaker. It manufactured and sold products primarily in three business segments: (1) pulp and paper, (2) packaging and packaging materials, and (3) wood products and resources. I.P.'s 1983 sales totaled $4,357,100,000, up some $342,000,000 from the previous year.

65   Pulp and paper, and packaging were its two dominant business segments. I.P. had invested over $4,000,000,000 since 1979 alone to modernize its plants. Paper and packaging products were sold through its own sales force directly to users or converters for manufacture. International Paper maintained manufacturing plants and sales offices throughout the United States as well as in various locations throughout the world. The firm owned approximately 7,000,000 acres of timberlands in the United States. Of this total, 67% was located in the South, 26% in the Northeast, and 7% in the West. These timberlands collectively supplied most of the raw materials for its mills.

66   Because of prospects for a continued slump in timber demand, I.P. was in the process of changing its product mix. In coming years, it planned to take the following actions: (1) increase its dependence on the white paper business, (2) eventually phase out its newsprint business, and (3) substantially cut back on timber harvesting.

67   In stressing its pulp and paper product segments, International Paper's new strategy was to improve the quality of its products. I.P. planned to do this by: (1) coordinating marketing and manufacturing review of product specifications, (2) emphasizing continually effective customer technical service and product development activities, (3) upgrading process control equipment, and (4) providing additional technical resources and training for its production and management employees.[4]

Westvaco Corporation

68   Westvaco Corporation was one of the major producers of paper and paperboard in the United States. Westvaco was also headquartered in New York City and employed approximately 15,000 people, of which 7,000 were unionized. It operated facilities in both the United States and Brazil.

69   Westvaco divided its businesses into three major segments: (1) bleached pulp, papers, and paper products, (2) unbleached papers and paper products, and (3) specialty chemicals. In 1983, Westvaco generated sales of $1,500,000,000, which was a 3% increase over 1982's sales. Ninety percent of its 1983 sales were in the pulp and paper products businesses. The principal markets for Westvaco's products were in the United States, and these markets were reached through the firm's own sales force.

70   Westvaco owned 1,373,650 acres of timberland in the United States and Brazil, which supplied 37% of its wood fiber needs. Another 1,022,000 acres of additional wood fiber were made available through its cooperative forest management program with private landowners.

71   Like Scott Paper, Westvaco had unveiled a five-year growth program that was designed to emphasize its strongest products and businesses. The overall objective of this program was to produce significant growth in its earning power and competitive position. Particular emphasis would be placed on increasing productivity, cost reduction, environmental protection, and maintaining its high business ethics and business conduct standards. During these five years, which ran from 1984 through 1988, Westvaco anticipated making capital expenditures of $1,600,000,000 to increase its papermaking capacity by 21%. Westvaco planned to expand and emphasize its bleached board and coated paper business. Finally, Westvaco planned a major increase in its R&D efforts for its products and services.

Union Camp Corporation

72   Union Camp, headquartered in Wayne, New Jersey, produced and sold paper, paperboard, packaging products, building materials, and chemicals. Almost all of Union Camp's sales were made east of the Rocky Mountains. Its 1983 sales totaled $1,688,254,000 with its paper and paperboard business segments contributing the most to its overall net income after taxes of $132,736,000.

73   Union Camp employed approximately 17,000 people of which 53% were represented by unions. It had exceptional relations with its unions and had not experienced a strike at any major facility since 1974. Union Camp used four mills to produce paper and paperboard. It satisfied approximately two-thirds of its mills' energy requirements by burning wood waste and spent liquor, which was a by-product of the pulping process. Union Camp owned or controlled 1,700,000 acres of timberland scattered throughout the Southeast, which provided 35% of its wood fiber requirements. Its remaining wood fiber needs were purchased from private landowners, other paper companies, and the federal government.

74   Union Camp's paper and paperboard operations produced paper bags for grocery outlets, merchandise bags for retailers, and multiwall bags for holding cement, feed, fertilizer, pet food, and mineral products. It also produced corrugated containers used to store and ship canned, bottled, and packaged products. Paper and paperboard were sold both by its own sales force and through wholesale distributors. Using Union Camp's own sales force, packaging materials were sold directly to industrial and agricultural users.

Hammermill Paper Company

75   Hammermill Paper Company, headquartered in Erie, Pennsylvania, was the largest producer of fine writing papers in the United States. Hammermill had five business groups, which were as follows: (1) fine and printing papers, (2) industrial packaging, (3) converted paper products, (4) wholesale distribution, and (5) forest products. Hammermill's 1983 sales were $1,622,695,000 with net profits after taxes of $32,548,000. It employed 13,000 people and owned 35 manufacturing or processing plants, which were all located within the United States. The company also owned or controlled 425,000 acres of timberland.

76   Hammermill's strategies were aimed at increasing market position and profit growth. They included:

1. Building leading positions in targeted market segments.
2. Achieving cost competitiveness in all of its operations.
3. Balancing five distinct but related businesses.
4. Expanding productive capacity by increments.
5. Maintaining a strong flexible financial position, which assures the availability of long-term capital.[5]

77   The prospects for Hammermill for 1985 and beyond were a bit cloudy. Several competitors were planning to start up new white paper machines during 1984 and 1985. This and the continued influx of imported white papers could cause a softening in the market.

Chesapeake Corporation of Virginia

78   Chesapeake Corporation of Virginia, headquartered in West Point, Virginia, was a major manufacturer of pulp and paper products. They included unbleached kraft paperboard and paper, and bleached hardwood market pulp. Its 1983 total sales were $273,800,000; net income after taxes was $12,500,000.

79   Chesapeake operated one paper mill located in West Point that employed 2,700 people. It owned 376,000 acres of timberland that supplied approximately 20% of its yearly wood requirements.

80   In 1983, Chesapeake launched the largest expansion program in its history. It allocated $73,000,000 to construct a new linerboard machine at its West Point mill, which was expected to be fully on line by 1985.

Scott Paper's Outlook for the Future

81   Scott Paper did better in 1983 than it did in 1982; however, its net profits after taxes from 1979 through 1981 had been even higher. Still Scott Paper was optimistic about the future. The general upturn in several key foreign economies along with a strong U. S. economy in 1984 provided hope for increased sales in the future. On the cost side, greater efficiency and higher productivity were beginning to show results from Scott's strategic plan and its five-year capital spending program. In addition, Scott found out that it could raise prices on some of its core products and so widen operating margins.

82   The product/market opportunities that Scott might pursue were numerous. The U. S. paper market was booming, and analysts expected the paper industry's operating capacity rates to remain high through 1985. Foreign competitors could not match the U. S. wood fiber base. Furthermore, Scott's steady capital spending in the 1980s in its domestic facilities had made many of Scott's mills some of the most efficient in the world.

83   With the demand for paper and forest products rapidly increasing in developing countries, Scott Paper might decide to pursue further this largely untapped market. As it stood in 1984, Scott Paper already had a number of international affiliates. While foreign markets might be very lucrative, they were subject to even greater economic swings than the U. S. economy. In effect, when the U. S. economy made a downturn, it had an even greater effect on economies in many foreign countries.

84   Scott's tree farm program for private landowners provided another opportunity to increase its wood fiber supply. Scott provided professional advice and technical assistance to private landowners in Maine and New Hampshire. This program could possibly be expanded to include private landowners within the southeastern and western regions of the United States as well. The opportunity to increase future yields and provide pro-

fessional assistance might go a long way toward ensuring Scott's fiber needs for the future.

85   By increasing the use of its prelogging operations, Scott also had the opportunity to reduce further its dependence on fossil fuels. By expanding the use of this effective program to include other mill locations, Scott might be able to save a substantial amount of crude oil.

86   Unfortunately, Scott was involved with several legal matters. On September 17,1981, Scott Paper Company, along with virtually all other pulp producers in the United States, Canada, Portugal, and Scandinavia that sold pulp in the Common Market, was charged with price fixing. If infringement was established, the firms could be fined and required to stop such practices. The case was still pending as of late 1984.

87   Domestically, Scott Paper Company faced another legal threat. It received a request from the Federal Trade Commission for information to determine whether Scott and numerous other U. S. pulp manufacturers had engaged in unfair methods of competition in violation of section 5 of the Federal Trade Commission Act. The investigation into the above allegation was likewise unresolved by 1984's end.

88   Finally, Scott was very concerned with another legal issue, namely the possibility of being acquired by Brascan Limited in the future. The situation was at a standstill in 1984, with Brascan holding 23.5% of Scott Paper's stock, and prohibited from increasing its stock holding above 25%. Unfortunately, the agreement between the two parties was set to expire on January 1, 1986, and Brascan's executives had expressed serious interests in gaining a majority control of Scott Paper's stock, whose board of directors already included four Brascan executives. Clearly, the future possibility of a takeover posed a serious threat that Scott's top management wanted to prevent at any costs.

Notes

1. Scott Paper Company, *Scott Paper Company Annual Report 1981,* pp. 6, 9.
2. "Down to the Core: Scott Paper Cuts Back to its Basic Business, Records a Rebound in Earnings," *Barron's,* April 16, 1984, p. 9.
3. Ibid., p. 10.
4. International Paper, *International Paper Company 1983 Annual Report,* p. 11.
5. Hammermill Paper Company, *Hammermill Paper Company Annual Report, 1983,* pp. 2-3.

case **18** **The Georgia-Pacific Comply Dilemma**

The Problem

1   In 1979, management at Georgia-Pacific Corporation, a manufacturer of forest products, was considering the introduction of a new item into its product line. Called comply, it was a wood product substitute for plywood that utilized more of the tree than did traditional plywood products. Comply was, therefore, considered a more efficient use of resources.

2   The efficient use of timber resources was a factor of growing importance for Georgia-Pacific. Studies had shown that demand for timber was increasing more rapidly than was the available supply. Although comply seemed to help alleviate the scarcity problem, it had only recently been developed. A complete study of comply, along with assessments of Georgia-Pacific's strengths and weaknesses, the wood products industry, and Georgia-Pacific's competitors, was necessary before a decision regarding full-scale production could be made.

The Company

3   Georgia-Pacific Corporation was founded in Atlanta, Georgia, in 1927 by Owen R. Cheatham with an investment of $12,000. In its early years, Georgia-Pacific grew steadily, becoming an industry giant through explosive expansion between 1955 and 1965. The company increased its size by seven times during that period.

4   The Federal Trade Commission considered the tremendous growth to

This case was prepared by Professor John A. Pearce II of the University of South Carolina.

have resulted from Georgia-Pacific's, illegally restraining competition within the softwood-plywood industry. Thus in 1972, Georgia-Pacific was forced to agree to the sale of 20 percent of its assets. These assets were used to form a new independent corporation, Louisiana-Pacific. At birth, Louisiana-Pacific was the sixth-largest domestic producer of lumber. The agreement also prohibited Georgia-Pacific from acquiring an interest in any softwood-plywood producer in the United States for 10 years and limited its purchases of timberland.

5   Despite this setback, Georgia-Pacific's management continued to pursue a policy of growth and diversification related to the core business of wood products, and it quickly grew as a truly diversified natural-resources firm. Its holdings included gypsum, coal, natural gas, oil, and 6 million acres of timberlands—assets totaling more than $4.4 billion. The company diversified into three major areas: (1) building products, (2) pulp and paper, and (3) chemicals. Diversification did not slow the growth of the company's core business, wood products, which grew to include: plywood, particleboard, lumber, paper bags and sacks, corrugated packaging, facial and bathroom tissue, paper plates, check safety paper, and package labels.

6   By 1979, Georgia-Pacific had sales of more than $3.7 billion and had grown into the nation's 56th-largest industrial corporation with over 200 plants in the United States, Canada, Indonesia, Brazil, and the Philippines. It also had 151 building-materials distribution centers across the United States, as well as numerous sales offices throughout the world. Through the strengths of its distribution system and material resources base, Georgia-Pacific had become the largest producer of forest products in the world. It ranked first in plywood production, third in lumber production, third in gypsum production, and eighth in paper production. It was also trying to become a dominant force in the chemical business.

7   Management saw the opportunity to enter the chemical business as a natural outgrowth of its manufacture of plywood, pulp, and paper products. Many chemicals were produced as by-products, and many more were used in the manufacturing processes. In 1959, Georgia-Pacific built its first resin plant to supply its building-products manufacturing operations, and by 1975, the firm's chemical division supplied most of the major chemicals necessary for its building-products and paper-manufacturing operations. Production in excess of company needs (approximately two thirds of total production) was sold to outside customers. Chemicals manufactured included phenol, methanol, acetone, chlorine, caustic soda, polyvinyl chloride, household bleaches and detergents, swimming pool chemicals, alcohol, sulfuric acid, turpentine, and charcoal. Top management regarded its diversified product offering as one of the company's big strengths. Company sales by industry for the years 1975–79 are shown in Exhibit 1.

8   In its efforts to become a leader in the wood industry, Georgia-Pacific made several major decisions that seemed very risky at the time. In 1946, the company began manufacturing plywood in Washington. Plywood was

---

Exhibit 1

Sales by industry segment for the period 1975–1979 (in millions)

Sales	1975		1976		1977		1978		1979	
Building products:										
Plywood	$ 713	30%	$ 960	32%	$1,222	33%	$1,343	30%	$1,338	26%
Lumber	429	18	660	22	884	24	1,178	27	1,283	25
Gypsum	95	4	117	4	160	4	203	5	229	4
Other	191	8	244	7	275	8	393	9	478	9
Total	$1,428	60%	$1,981	65%	$2,541	69%	$3,117	71%	$3,328	64%
Pulp, paper, and										
paperboard products	691	29	763	25	780	21	875	20	1,269	25
Chemicals	183	8	243	8	301	8	344	8	542	10
Other operations	57	3	51	2	53	2	67	1	68	1
Total sales	$2,359	100%	$3,038	100%	$3,675	100%	$4,403	100%	$5,207	100%

Source: Georgia-Pacific, 1981 Annual Report to Shareholders on Operating and Financial Results, p. 22; and Georgia-Pacific, 1977 Annual Report to Shareholders on Operating and Results, p. 29.

a new product at that time, and industry competitors felt it lacked profit potential. Georgia-Pacific began manufacturing plywood from hardwoods in 1949 and, in 1963, was the first company to produce plywood from southern pine trees successfully. By the end of 1979, Georgia-Pacific was the largest manufacturer of plywood and plywood products in the world.

9   Another strategic decision that helped to strengthen Georgia-Pacific was its move into actual ownership of timber. The company purchased its first lumber company in Oregon in 1951 and, by 1979, controlled about 6 million acres of timberlands throughout the world. Within the company, this timber became known as "green gold." These vast timber holdings supplied the company's resource needs, eased the dependence on government and private landowners, and served as collateral for the firm's financial activities. The decision to purchase timberlands exemplified management's drive for self-sufficiency in the resources needed to operate. Although the company's forest-resource base was among the largest in the industry, an active timber- and forest-acquisition program ensured its continued expansion. Top management considered timberland a sound investment because it made the company more self-sufficient and financially stronger since the timberholdings tended to appreciate in value.

10   Along with expansion of timber holdings came recognition of the need for the prudent management and increased utilization of these valuable resources. The company continually looked for new products and better planting and harvesting techniques that would permit more efficient usage of its trees. The company's search for new and innovative products enabled it to be the first in the world to use redwood waste particles in the manufacture of paper. Productivity was also increased through company research

in the development of faster-growing, more disease-resistant strains of trees, which increased wood yielded per acre. By using wood residuals—such as bark and fine sawdust, which were otherwise economically unusable—to fire boilers in several of the company's plants, the company achieved nearly 50 percent energy self-sufficiency.

11   The corporation's marketing arm for most of its building products was its distribution division. Since competition was based primarily on service, particularly product availability, Georgia-Pacific believed its 151 distribution centers, strategically located to serve U.S. markets, gave it a favorable competitive position. These centers furnished plywood, lumber, gypsum, and other materials to building-material dealers, industrial accounts, and major contractors, which helped make Georgia-Pacific a very efficient, high-volume commodity marketer. At the same time, these centers also enabled the company to keep a finger on the pulse of the marketplace. New products could be test-marketed easily by selection of individual distribution centers for new-product introduction. Exhibit 2 shows sales by distribution centers.

12   From its beginning, Georgia-Pacific enjoyed a good working relationship with the financial community. When Owen Cheatham, the company's founder, needed money to begin his operation, he went to his lenders with a detailed plan and payout schedule. Over time, the firm continued to follow this same practice, which has contributed to its ability to tap financial markets for needed capital.

13   Growth and initiative on the part of management was encouraged by a highly decentralized structure that gave executives and plant managers individual responsibility and freedom to manage their operations in their own ways. Such a management structure also allowed for smooth transitions during management personnel turnover.

14   Georgia-Pacific showed remarkable growth in the 1970s. Their five-year goal to double earnings, begun in 1973, was achieved more than one year early, in 1976. In 1977, Robert Floweree, the chairman of the board, announced another five-year growth plan for the corporation. Sales goals for 1981 were set at $5.25 billion with earnings targeted to reach $430 million, or double the 1976 earnings level. The five-year plan included a $2 billion expenditure goal for plant and equipment. Exhibit 3 shows the breakdown of these expenditures for the years 1977 to 1979.

15   In looking ahead, Georgia-Pacific intended to continue to increase its timber base near its U.S. manufacturing operations, thereby ensuring supply and reducing transportation costs. Since three fourths of its products are sold in the Eastern states, the corporation decided to move its corporate headquarters from Portland, Oregon, to Atlanta, Georgia.

16   Operating profits, as defined by Georgia-Pacific, represented income from operations before corporate, general, and administrative expenses, interest income and expense, and income taxes. Exhibit 4 shows the operating profits by division for the years 1975–79.

Exhibit 2

Dollar sales of Georgia-Pacific's distribution centers

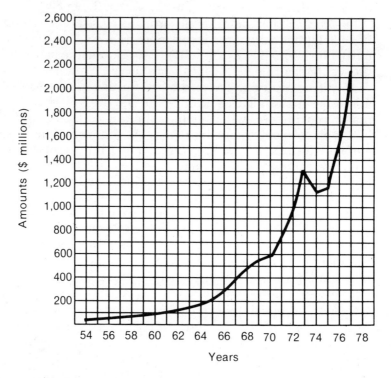

Source: John R. Ross, *Maverick: The Story of Georgia-Pacific Corporation,* 1980, p. 312.

17   Georgia-Pacific had consistently maintained a philosophy of growth and expansion. The consolidated income statements (Exhibit 5) and balance sheets (Exhibit 6) show the company's performance.

The Industry

18   Georgia-Pacific was directly affected by a variety of economic conditions. Changes in the level of housing starts, commercial building activities, cost of money, inflation, energy shortages, and unemployment all had their impact on the sales and net income of the company.

19   Housing construction had historically been strongly influenced by changes in the nation's population, wealth, and wood prices, all of which affected demand for wood-based products such as housing, furniture, and

Exhibit 3

Capital expenditures for 1977–1979 ($ millions)

	1977		1978		1979	
Property, plant, and equipment:						
Building products:						
New plants, distribution centers, and equipment	$70		$95		$115	
Replacement and modernization	60	$130	70	$165	90	$205
Pulp and paper:						
New plants and equipment	75		45		95	
Replacement and modernization	70	135	50	95	90	185
Chemicals:						
New plants and equipment	90		90		120	
Replacement and modernization	10	100	15	105	10	130
Total property, plant, and equipment		$365		365		$520
Natural resources:						
Timber and timberlands	75		95		260	
Natural gas and oil properties	10	85	20	115	35	295
Total capital expenditures		$450		$480		$815

Source: Georgia-Pacific, 1982 Annual Report to Shareholders on Operating and Financial Results, p. 21.

Exhibit 4

Operating profits for the period 1975–1979 ($ millions)

Operating profits	1975		1976		1977		1978		1979	
Building products	$ 97	34%	$190	47%	$347	69%	$434	73%	$329	52%
Pulp, paper, paperboard	123	42	113	28	50	10	61	10	154	24
Chemicals	60	21	91	22	96	19	87	15	137	22
Other operations	10	3	13	3	11	3	15	2	13	2
Total operating profits	$290	100%	$407	100%	$504	100%	$595	100%	$633	100%

Source: Georgia-Pacific, 1981 Annual Report to Shareholders on Operating and Financial Results, p. 22; and Georgia-Pacific, 1977 Annual Report to Shareholders on Operating and Financial Results, p. 29.

paper. Exhibit 7 shows the U.S. population from 1920 to 1970, with projections to the year 2000.

20   According to the Department of Commerce, the demand for housing was expected to increase 15 percent annually by the year 2000. New residential construction and home remodeling accounted for about two thirds of all softwood plywood produced. Exhibit 8 shows softwood plywood production

---

Exhibit 5

Georgia-Pacific Corporation statements of consolidated net income for the years ended December 31, 1975–1979 (in thousands of dollars except per share data)

	1975	1976	1977	1978	1979
Net sales	$2,358,600	$3,038,000	$3,675,000	$4,403,000	$5,207,000
Costs and expenses:					
Cost of sales..............	1,798,900	2,331,900	2,920,000	3,410,000	4,100,000
Selling, general, and administrative	144,600	161,000	194,000	231,000	279,000
Depreciation and depletion................	133,800	151,000	175,000	194,000	228,000
Interest expense	49,800	38,000	33,000	38,000	66,000
Provision for income taxes....................	83,500	141,000	191,000	228,000	208,000
Gross income	2,210,600	2,823,000	3,513,000	4,101,000	4,881,000
Net income	$ 148,000	$ 215,000	$ 262,000	$ 302,000	$ 326,000
Income per share of common stock:					
Primary...................	$ 1.60	$ 2.12	$ 2.54	$ 2.93	$ 3.11
Fully diluted	$ 1.53	$ 2.05	$ 2.47	$ 2.84	$ 3.02

Sources: Georgia-Pacific, 1981 Annual Report, p. 23; and Georgia-Pacific, 1977 Annual Report to Shareholders on Operating Income and Financial Results, p. 31.

from 1970 to 1979. Softwood plywood, used most often in construction, was made from pine and fir trees; hardwood plywood, made from maple and gum trees, was mainly used for furniture making. About 20 percent of softwood plywood was used for nonresidential construction, the remainder directed to industrial and miscellaneous markets. Exhibit 9 shows the cycles and trends of residential and nonresidential construction in the United States from 1969 to 1977.

21   Plywood had experienced strongly increased usage in residential construction during the 1970s, when the amount of plywood used for the average single-family home had approximately doubled.

22   Past studies have shown that price increases in timber products had relatively little effect on demand in the short run. However, in the long run, as price continued to rise, demand for timber products declined, and the use of competitive materials increased.

23   In 1973, America experienced a lumber shortage, and as a result, the U.S. Forest Service conducted a study of the future supply and demand of timber products in the United States. This study reported that the demand for lumber, plywood, woodpulp, and other forest products was increasing more rapidly than the available timber supply, much of the rise in demand resulting from the population growth. The problem of increased demand

Exhibit 6

Georgia-Pacific Corporation consolidated balance sheets for the years ended December 31, 1975–1979 (in thousands of dollars)

	1975	1976	1977	1978	1979
Assets					
Current assets:					
Cash......................	$ 31,800	$ 25,000	$ 11,000	$ 21,000	$ 22,000
Marketable securities	16,600	—	—	—	—
Receivables	250,000	295,000	256,000	418,000	502,000
Inventories*..............	376,700	423,000	449,000	496,000	585,000
Prepaid expenses	6,600	10,000	9,000	9,000	14,000
Total current assets....	$681,700	$753,000	$825,000	$944,000	$1,123,000
Natural resources, at cost less depletion:					
Timber and timberlands	319,900	331,000	385,000	453,000	683,000
Coal, minerals, natural gas, and oil	26,800	30,000	36,000	52,000	81,000
Total natural resources............	$346,700	$361,000	$421,000	$505,000	$764,000
Property, plant, and equipment:					
Land, buildings, machinery, and equipment at cost........	2,049,900	2,285,000	2,657,000	2,988,000	3,476,000
Less: Reserves for depreciation.............	721,900	836,000	995,000	1,123,000	1,283,000
Total property, plant, and equipment.......	$1,328,000	$1,449,000	$1,662,000	$1,865,000	$2,193,000
Noncurrent receivables and other assets	47,500	21,000	21,000	30,000	38,000
Total assets	$2,403,900	$2,584,000	$2,929,000	$3,344,000	$4,118,000

was compounded because the number of trees grown each year was decreasing. Commercial forests were shrinking at a rate of about 500,000 acres per year, while the demands for forest products and lands for recreation were expanding. Commercial forest land was that which had the capability of growing commercial quantities of timber suitable for harvest. Of the 500 million acres of commercial forest land in the United States, private citizens owned 59 percent, the government owned 27 percent, and the forest-products industry owned 14 percent. Because of the declining timber supply, the United States would have to increase its reliance on wood imports. The U.S. Forest Service projected that by the year 2000, the softwood timber supply would fall short of demand by at least 2 billion board feet.

24   The 1973 Forest Service study also projected that the demand for ply-

Exhibit 6 (concluded)

	1975	1976	1977	1978	1979
Liabilities					
Current liabilities:					
Current portion of long-term debt	$ 98,600	$ 36,900	$ 46,000	$ 60,000	$ 70,000
Accounts payable and accrued liabilities	130,100	206,700	254,000	321,000	400,000
Income taxes	25,600	67,200	65,000	28,000	32,000
	$254,000	$310,800	$365,000	$409,000	$502,000
Commercial paper and other short-term notes supported by confirmed seasonal bank lines of credit	—	222,600	13,000	52,000	159,000
Total current liabilities.............	$254,300	$533,400	$378,000	$461,000	$661,000
Long-term debt, excluding current portion....................	606,900	317,700	607,000	702,000	984,000
Convertible subordinated debentures:					
5¾% due 1994..............	75,000	—	—	—	—
5¼% due 1966	125,000	125,000	125,000	125,000	125,000
6⅕% due 2000	100,000	—	—	—	—
Deferred income taxes	215,000	250,000	280,000	325,000	380,000
Employee stock purchase plan	—	5,800	10,000	5,000	9,000
Redeemable preferred stock......................	—	—	—	—	165,000
Capital stock and surplus:					
Common stock	48,300	79,000	82,000	82,000	82,000
Paid-in surplus.............	701,300	905,700	1,021,000	1,023,000	1,023,000
Earned surplus	279,900	368,800	428,000	625,000	827,000
Less: common stock held in treasury, at cost	(1,800)	(1,400)	(2,000)	(4,000)	(138,000)
Total capital stocks and surplus	$1,027,700	$1,352,100	$1,529,000	$1,726,000	$1,794,000
Total liabilities	$2,403,900	$2,584,000	$2,929,000	$3,344,000	$4,118,000

*Inventories recorded at the lower of cost or market.

Sources: Georgia-Pacific, 1976 Annual Report; Georgia-Pacific, 1977 Annual Report to Shareholders on Operating and Financial Results, pp. 32–33; Georgia-Pacific, 1978 Annual Report, pp. 30–31; Georgia-Pacific, 1980 Annual Report, pp. 34–35.

Exhibit 7

U.S. population 1920–1970, with projections to the year 2000

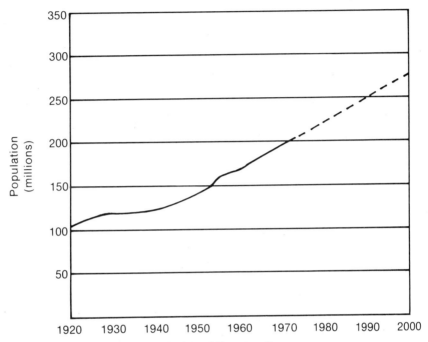

Source: *Eastern Air Lines, Inc., 1982 Annual Report*, p. 31.

Exhibit 8

U.S. softwood plywood production

Year	Softwood plywood production (million square feet)
1979	19,744
1978	19,492
1977	19,721
1976	17,841
1975	15,706
1974	15,306
1973	17,929
1972	17,843
1971	16,353
1970	14,149

Source: Department of Commerce, National Forest Products Association, Standard & Poor's Industry Surveys, 1981, p. B127.

Exhibit 9

Residential and nonresidential construction, seasonally adjusted (indexed, 1967 = 100)

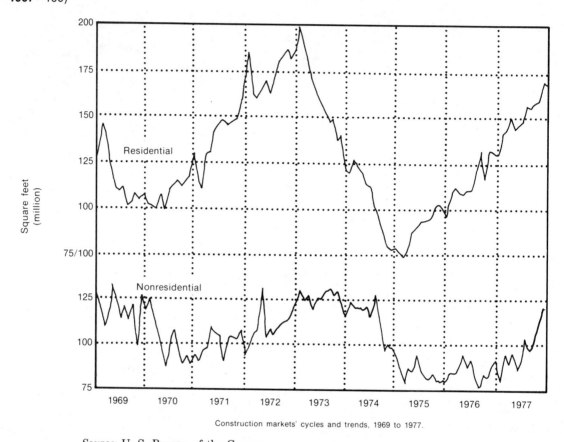

Construction markets' cycles and trends, 1969 to 1977.

Source: U. S. Bureau of the Census

wood would increase more rapidly than the demand for lumber for the remainder of the century. While lumber use in housing was expected to increase 50 percent by the year 2000, plywood usage was expected to double. The use of plywood in nonresidential construction was also expected to double from 1970 levels of 17.8 billion square feet to 36.8 billion square feet by the year 2000.

25   One of the problems Georgia-Pacific and the forest-products industry faced was the government's restriction of timber cutting in national forests. National forest lands contained 52 percent of the country's softwood timber, the type of timber from which most plywood was made. Despite this large inventory, the national forests supplied less than 30 percent of the

nation's softwood timber requirements. The majority of softwood timber was being supplied by the forest-products industry lands, which contained only 17 percent of the nation's softwood timber. Although the United States had 70 million more acres of hardwood forest than softwood forest, much of this resource was relatively untapped.

26   Another problem that plagued the forest industry was the government's demand that it refrain from the practice of "clear-cutting"—harvesting all the trees from a given area at the same time. Clear-cutting offended environmentalists and violated provisions of the Organic Act of 1897.

27   However, in September 1976, Congress passed legislation to alleviate part of the timber-supply problem and improve the long-term outlook for timber production in this country. The National Forest Management Act amended the 1897 Organic Act and permitted a greater share of the nation's timber requirements to be harvested from the national forests. It also allowed clear-cutting and other modern forestry practices.

28   After passage of this act, environmentalists demanded that more national forest lands be included in the Wilderness System (established by Congress through the Wilderness Act of 1964). When land was protected, insect disease and fires were controlled. No roads could be built and no motor vehicles were allowed. In 1977, as a result of pressure from environmentalists, President Carter called for a study of 62 million acres of national forest land that had the potential to be set aside as wilderness. During the study period, which was expected to last for two years, no timber cutting would be permitted on that land. The forest industry was concerned that results of the study could strike an even harder blow to the nation's future timber supply.

29   Because fewer timberlands would be available for harvest, the cost of timber would increase, meaning that profits of fewer companies would keep pace with sales growth. Thus Georgia-Pacific's management anticipated that timber ownership would become the critical determinant of a company's ability to grow with controlled manufacturing costs.

The Competitors

30   Since the early 1970s, Georgia-Pacific had taken many risks to get ahead. During that time, the company borrowed heavily from banks and insurance companies when the other companies were not doing so, using the money to finance the acquisitions that had always been a key element in its corporate growth strategy. By the mid 1970s, Georgia-Pacific's strategic risk-taking was paying off as the company began to capture market share from its major competitors.

31   Competition was intense in the plywood and wood-product specialties markets, but although many competitors existed, Georgia-Pacific faced its main competition from three giants: Boise Cascade, Champion Inter-

Exhibit 10

Selective data on Georgia-Pacific's key competitors (in thousands of dollars)

	1975	1976	1977	1978	1979
Total sales:					
Boise Cascade	$1,458,050	$1,931,530	$2,315,780	$2,573,110	$2,916,160
Champion Int'l.	2,530,000	3,079,000	3,127,000	3,475,145	3,750,960
Weyerhauser	2,421,271	2,868,379	3,282,768	3,799,400	4,422,000
Softwood plywood sales:					
Boise Cascade	*	*	*	*	*
Champion Int'l.	315,000	450,000	496,000	647,159	636,958
Weyerhauser	238,000	362,000	453,539	555,000	599,000
Net income:					
Boise Cascade	63,890	100,830	115,610	132,800	174,920
Champion Int'l.	61,020	135,940	138,620	168,688	247,120
Weyerhauser	164,740	305,970	303,890	370,700	511,600
Total assets:					
Boise Cascade	1,569,324	1,731,242	1,799,048	1,981,947	2,309,057
Champion Int'l.	2,180,000	2,564,000	2,465,000	2,856,104	3,040,485
Weyerhauser	2,421,271	2,868,379	3,282,768	4,466,922	4,961,673
Stockholders' equity:					
Boise Cascade	866,241	945,371	959,088	1,058,397	1,178,400
Champion Int'l.	980,000	1,162,000	1,257,000	1,358,964	1,535,028
Weyerhauser	1,788,839	1,981,886	2,179,485	2,313,792	2,731,168

*Plywood sales dollars not provided.
Sources: Boise Cascade, 1977 Annual Report, p. 22; Boise Cascade, 1981 Annual Report, p. 32; Champion International, 1977 Annual Report, pp. 18, 42, 68–69; Champion International, 1981 Annual Report, p. 1; Weyerhauser, 1977 Annual Report, pp. 24, 55; Weyerhauser, 1981 Annual Report, pp. 27, 32, 33, 52, 53.

national, and Weyerhauser. Exhibit 10 contains selective data on these companies.

32   Each of these competitors had strategies and goals for their organizations, and it was necessary for Georgia-Pacific to analyze their strategies, goals, and product lines to ascertain where its competitors were headed.

33   Boise Cascade and Georgia Pacific were involved in different product lines within the paper and wood industries. Boise Cascade placed its emphasis on paper manufacturing. Capital expenditures in this area stressed efficiency and flexibility to enable Boise Cascade to capitalize on the growing demand for its papers. The company also planned to grow as a converter and distributor of paper and wood products, and these operations were well positioned in favorable markets. Boise was a leading producer of composite cans, a product being marketed as a substitute for other types of packaging. It was a leader in distribution of office products, but with a market share of less than 3 percent, there was room for growth. The building-materials distribution and manufactured-housing operations were expected to grow along with the housing industry. Of all of Boise Cascade's divisions, only the wood products manufacturing was not expected to ex-

perience any significant growth since sufficient capacity existed within the industry to handle demand for the foreseeable future. Instead, this company sought to increase efficiency in its wood products manufacturing.

34   Champion International changed its strategic objectives in the 1970s. Management wanted to withdraw from any nonforest products businesses, and in 1977, this objective was achieved along with expansion into the paper-packaging business. Divisions included timberlands, building materials, paper, and paper packaging. The company planned to spend $1.9 billion for capital projects from 1978 to 1982, using this money for business preservation, expansion, maintenance of competitive cost-effective management, and profit improvement.

35   Weyerhauser, another Georgia-Pacific competitor, was the only large forest-products company to have net self-sufficiency in its raw-material supply. This gave it both a materials-cost advantage and more manufacturing flexibility than any of its competitors. Its timber stands appreciated each year at a higher rate than inflation. Weyerhauser, like Georgia-Pacific, used forestry programs to manage its lands for increased productivity. Weyerhauser believed that the future industry environment would require different product mixes and processes, which would mean a change in raw materials. The firm believed that the industry's future leaders would be those who were in the forefront of the effort to increase timber growth and raw-material utilization, replace obsolete manufacturing processes, and reduce energy and chemical uses. Weyerhauser exported a large percentage of their goods. Their forests were located principally in the Pacific Northwest, which provided easy access to ports. In the short term, the company planned to reduce manufacturing costs and increase productivity through capital investment and efficient cost-effective management with emphasis on the Pacific Northwest operations.

The Strategic Decision—Comply

36   To meet the need for increased demand of wood products, the American Plywood Association and the U.S. Forest Service and Department of Housing and Urban Development initiated a research program to develop products that would utilize timber in a more efficient manner. About one third of the timber cut in U.S. forests was wasted in logging and milling operations. One result of the research was the development of comply, a name which stood for composite plywood. Comply was made by sandwiching a panel of oriented fiberwood flakes between sheets of pine veneer; heat, pressure, and a special glue were used to bond the panel to the sheets of pine veneer.

37   Comply was stronger than plywood for most uses and met the American Plywood Association's quality standards. Designed as a substitute for plywood, Comply looked and performed like plywood and would have the

same market applications. However, comply could make use of more wood from each tree than conventional plywood. About 45 percent of a tree's wood volume could be used in making plywood, with the rest ending up as residue. Comply, on the other hand, could use all of the tree, except sawdust and bark. A comply plant would require half as many trees as raw materials for a plywood plant to produce an equivalent number of panels.

38   Other differences existed between comply and plywood production: much-smaller trees could be used in manufacturing comply, and sound portions of dead and damaged trees and wood residues, such as limbs and tree tops, could be used for the core. This was not feasible in plywood manufacturing. Whereas most plywood was made from softwood timber, a variety of tree species, including both hardwood and softwood, could be used for the core of comply. One negative quality of comply was that a panel was heavier than a plywood panel and, therefore, more difficult to handle on a construction site.

39   In 1977, as a result of the government's co-operative research on comply, Potlatch Corporation took the initiative and opened (in Idaho) the country's first factory for manufacturing comply. The executives at Georgia-Pacific were considering producing and marketing the new product, as were at least four other companies, but none of the companies had made a firm commitment. Georgia-Pacific, upon talking with Potlatch, found they would welcome Georgia-Pacific, or any other large company, into the market, recognizing it would speed the acceptance and use of comply by the building industry.

40   Potlatch claimed it had patented rights on comply production technology and would sell this technology to Georgia-Pacific at a cost of $250,000 for the first comply plant built and $100,000 for each additional plant built by Georgia-Pacific during the next 10 years. However, the legal staff of Georgia-Pacific determined the patents were not valid and such payments would not be required. Since the patents were invalid, Georgia-Pacific's management felt that if it decided to manufacture comply, a one-time payment of only $50,000 would be sufficient to secure a working relationship with Potlatch. This would allow Georgia-Pacific to consult Potlatch for working out bugs in the manufacturing system.

41   Before Georgia-Pacific would seriously consider comply as an alternative product, the cost of the resources necessary for its production had to be investigated, and in 1977, the company hired an outside consulting firm to conduct a feasibility study on comply and its related costs. Norman Springate and Associates looked at the requirements for building a plant for comply-manufacturing purposes. Exhibit 11 provides the result of this study on relevant start-up costs.

42   The consultant also conducted financial analyses to determine the type of revenue that would be generated with the comply plant. Exhibit 12 gives a brief summary of the estimated revenues.

43   Georgia-Pacific itself did a cost analysis of producing one piece of plywood

Exhibit 11

Costs of a comply plant

Site	$ 470,000
Building	1,596,000
Machinery and equipment	14,597,000
Contingencies and escalations	1,477,000
Construction capital required	$18,140,000

Source: Norman Springate and Associates, 1977.

Exhibit 12

Estimated financial data if comply is produced (year 1)

Net sales to be generated	$14,572,000
Net profit before taxes	4,042,000
Net profit after taxes	2,021,000
Net cash flow	3,768,000
Investment credit	1,475,000

Source: Norman Springate and Associates, 1977.

versus one piece of comply of the same dimension (four by eight feet) in one of their existing factories. The results, as shown in Exhibit 13, demonstrated that production of comply would be less expensive than plywood. The company felt comply had the potential to command a premium price because its solid core resisted hole punctures and the sealed edges reduced expansion from water absorption. Also, comply, by its design, was stronger than an equivalent panel of plywood.

44   Georgia-Pacific was faced with the need to examine the diverse data it had available and decide whether to proceed with the production of comply.

Exhibit 13

Comparison of cost of plywood versus comply

	Comply panel	Plywood panel
Wood	$1.28	$1.74
Resin and wax	.70	.62
Labor	.84	.62
Overhead	1.19	1.24
Total	$4.01	$4.22

Source: Norman Springate and Associates, 1977.

case 19 Weyerhaeuser in the 1980s Revised

1   In 1980, the Weyerhaeuser Company, a forest-products company with sales of $4,535,800,000, qualified as the largest lumber manufacturer in the United States and one of the top 100 in *Fortune* magazine's list of the 500 leading industrial corporations. Further, Weyerhaeuser was the only major U.S. forest-products company that produced, on the balance, more raw materials from its own timberlands than it used. As of June 1980, the company listed owned timberlands of 1,716,000 acres in Washington state; 1,154,000 acres in Oregon; and a total of 3,089,000 acres in Mississippi, Alabama, Arkansas, Oklahoma, and North Carolina. The company also had harvesting rights on 9,102,000 acres in Canada and 1,495,000 acres in Indonesia and Malaysia. The combination of such forest resources plus a heavy research commitment to better ways of growing and processing forest products and an orientation towards the future had helped propel Weyerhaeuser to a position of strength and industry leadership in both forest practices and international operations by 1980.

2   Although engaged primarily in the ownership and management of timberlands, the processing of timber, and the marketing of those resources, the company was not limited solely to such activities. Weyerhaeuser had interests in real estate development and construction, financial services, chemicals, and ornamental nursery supplies, in addition to the manufac-

This case was written by Stephen E. Barndt, Professor of Strategic Management, Pacific Lutheran University. The author gratefully acknowledges the substantial assistance of Michael Staudinger who helped in collecting the data upon which the case was based and who contributed to the preparation of the first two sections. The author also thanks Larry D. Alexander for some additional material included in this revised case. Copyright © 1985 by Stephen E. Barndt.

turing, distribution, and sale of lumber, plywood, pulp, paper, newsprint, paperboard, corrugated shipping containers, milk cartons, hardboard, particleboard, disposable diapers, laminated, and other structural wood products, and assorted other wood and wood-fiber products.

History

3   The company was started in 1900 when Frederick Weyerhaeuser and a group of Midwest investors purchased 900,000 acres from Northern Pacific Railroad, incorporated in the state of Washington, and opened an office in Tacoma, Washington.

4   The Weyerhaeuser Company purchased its first sawmill, located in Everett, Washington, in 1902. More sawmills were added through the teens and twenties by acquisition, new site construction, and expansion. At the same time, timberland holders were also growing, more than doubling to 2,013,404 acres by 1916.

5   During the early years, Frederick Weyerhaeuser set the tone for the company's view toward forest management practices. In 1905, he told a national forestry conference that "only by tremendous effort can the lumberman himself, the legislator, and the voter be made to realize its [forestry or timberlands'] importance and its possibilities."[1] Then in 1913, he testified before a congressional committee and sought action concerning fire prevention and regulation of logging activities in the hopes that such legislation would help prevent soil erosion and preserve seed sources. During this period, he also pointed out that the existing property tax laws encouraged cut and run, the practice of buying timberland, clear-cutting, and then leaving the area. In 1929, partly as a result of Weyerhaeuser-sponsored lobbying, Oregon became the first state to declare that reforestation, not deforestation, was a prime objective of property tax laws.

6   Company expansion through the thirties, forties, and most of the fifties was relatively slow. Weyerhaeuser expanded into the pulp industry in 1931, acquiring its first pulp mill in Longview, Washington. Then the company moved into the plywood industry in 1947, containerboard in 1949, composition board in 1954, packaging in 1957, and paper in 1961. Through the mid-fifties, all plants remained in the Pacific Northwest.

7   A particularly significant move on behalf of Weyerhaeuser came in 1934. J. P. Weyerhaeuser, Jr., then president, implemented the first full-scale reforestation policy of the company and began using the slogan "timber is a crop." Seven years later, Operation Rehab began in Montesano, Washington. This land rehabilitation plan covered 130,000 acres of burned land, which under the guidance of Weyerhaeuser's intensive forest management policies, became the nation's first large-scale tree farm.

8   A second significant advance by Weyerhaeuser came in 1952 when J. P. Weyerhaeuser, Jr., began implementation of a new advertising policy. According to *Nation's Business* magazine, Weyerhaeuser was quoted as saying that "unless an institution merits goodwill and understanding, it cannot maintain a position as part of our American industrial structure."[2] This marked the beginning of a nationwide advertising attempt aimed not at selling products, but instead at selling ideas and information. One resulting advertising effort, Weyerhaeuser's "Wildlife Series," which ran 15 years, was one of the longest continuous advertising campaigns ever to run in the United States.

9   A third major change of direction began in the mid-1950s when the company geographically expanded outside the Northwest. Significant timberland acquisitions took place in the southern pine regions of the Southeast and south central United States, giving Weyerhaeuser sources of materials closer to eastern markets.

10   A fourth important advance by Weyerhaeuser came in 1958 when the company entered the foreign market, with the formation of Weyerhaeuser International. By 1980, the company reported that overseas markets regularly consumed about one-third of its total production.

11   The four cornerstones of (1) forest research and management, (2) advertising the company, (3) geographic expansion, and (4) international marketing had been associated with rapid company growth from the late 1950s into the 1970s. This growth, both internationally and domestically, was reflected in its 1980 employment of 45,700 people, in more than 30 United States and 12 foreign major operating locations, and well in excess of 100 locations with smaller scale activities.

Company Objectives

12   A company general policy statement formalized in 1971 stated its objective and the means of realizing it:

> The basic objective of Weyerhaeuser Company is to operate a vigorous, growing, diversified, and profitable business in the balanced best interest of its customers, shareholders, employees, suppliers, and the economy at large by generating earnings, and profits at levels which will assure payment to shareholders of dividends sufficient to warrant their continued investment in the company and at the time sufficient for retention of funds in the business to assume growth and improvement.

13   To this end, the company shall:

> a. Energetically seek and develop opportunities for accelerating profitable growth both at home and abroad, with particular emphasis in fields where the company may occupy an advantageous position because of raw materials, facilities, or management skills.
>
> b. Seek constantly to devote company land to those uses which will produce

optimum long-term economic returns, and . . . maintain ownership of strategically located forestlands. . .

c. Constantly seek optimum profitability by adopting timber harvesting schedules in accordance with broad sustained yield principles . . . and by providing plants with the most favorable supplies of raw material, both as to volume and log mix. . .

d. Produce and market customer oriented products of appropriate quality and price under a policy which recognizes the integrated nature of the company's operations and places at appropriate operating levels (i) responsibility for the establishment of goals relating to volume, productivity, and profitability, supported by programs to meet these goals, and (ii) accountability for results achieved.

e. Be the most efficient operator, producer, distributor, and merchandiser in the industry by continually introducing modern cost-reducing processes, methods, and equipment, and by making the most effective use of facilities, capital, personnel, and management skill.

f. Pursue intensively, research and related programs that will establish and assure continuing leadership in . . . products and services . . . efficient processes and methods . . . and improve the growth, quality, and utilization of forest resources.

g. Build and maintain an organization able to meet present and future needs by attracting competent personnel with growth potential. . .

h. Build and maintain a favorable employee attitude that will encourage maximum contribution. . .

i. Build and maintain in customers, employees, shareholders, and the public, a reputation for honesty, fairness, and good corporate citizenship. . .

j. . . .exercise the highest level of responsibility stewardship of natural and environmental resources, practicing wise use of all resources throughout its activities, responding positively to opportunities for environmental, ecological, and social problem-solving, and encouraging others toward the same commitments.[3]

14   Subsequently, growth, productivity and efficiency, and energy independence had been singled out as major topics for more definitive objectives.

15   The objectives of growth were to build a new and significantly larger earnings base, to upgrade the mix of products and markets, and to become a more balanced and international company. In the effort to research these objectives, Weyerhaeuser had engaged in numerous activities to acquire forestlands and production operations, as well as to build new production facilities. In addition, emphasis had been placed on expanding the company's export market to include pulp, newsprint, containerboard, dimension lumber, and plywood, as well as logs. Further, the company had entered product lines that, although forest-product related, were much further removed than in the past, e.g., disposable diapers; lines that were only indirectly related through the land base, e.g., home building and salmon and shrimp growing; and lines that were not related, e.g., mortgage lending and restoration of buildings.

16   The objectives of increased productivity and efficiency and, hence, greater profit margins had resulted in efforts to gain economies of scale; to develop new technologies, to modernize capacity, to obtain higher harvest utilization, and to realize greater product yields; to strengthen market coverage sales and distribution efforts; to keep abreast of developments that could impact the industry and the company, anticipate them, and influence them in the way most favorable to the company; and to increase energy self-sufficiency.

17   Energy self-sufficiency had been singled out as a special area for company efforts. Weyerhaeuser aimed to be completely free from the direct use of petroleum fuels for plant production by the end of the 1980s and, in addition, wanted to maximize cogeneration of electrical power. The company expected to accomplish these objectives through a heavy commitment to research and development, increased use of wood wastes, and partial conversion to coal.

Operations

18   Many domestic U.S. Weyerhaeuser operations were concentrated in the states of Alabama, Arkansas, Mississippi, North Carolina, Oklahoma, Oregon, and Washington. Washington accounted for the greatest employment by far as shown in Exhibit 1. That exhibit also shows that the most important foreign operations were found in Canada, Indonesia, Malaysia, and, to a much lesser extent, France. The relatively more minor production and service operations were scattered over a significantly larger number of states and countries as shown in Exhibit 2. The geographical spread of operating locations and facilities was a function of access to raw materials, costs of transporting them versus the converted intermediate or final products, need for customer responsiveness, and, in the case of acquired companies, their original locations. Production facilities for lumber, paper, plywood, and other bulky end products plus intermediate products tended to be located in close proximity to the company's large timber holdings. On the other hand, production facilities for some specialized end products such as milk cartons and shipping containers tended to be located closer to their markets. Warehouses (wood products customer service centers), nurseries, and residential or commercial building construction operations likewise located close to markets for reasons of transportation economy and customer service.

19   Growth through acquisition and internal expansion since 1975 had placed greater relative emphasis on increasing output of wood fiber end products, manufactured construction materials, and new initiatives in less closely related product lines. Shifts in the company's emphasis on various products were reflected in the relative changes in production volume among the various types of wood products shown in Exhibit 3. While the production of

Exhibit 1

Principal timberlands and manufacturing facilities

Area	Number of locations	Timber holdings	Employ-ment	Products
Washington	8	1,716,000 acres	15,000	Softwood lumber, plywood, cedar shakes, paperboard, pulp, paper, newsprint
Oregon	5	1,154,000 acres	7,400	Softwood lumber, plywood, laminated products, hardboard siding, particleboard, linerboard
Oklahoma and Arkansas	9	1,841,000 acres	5,400	Gypsum board, fiberboard, hardboard siding, insulating board, treated lumber and timbers, softwood lumber, softwood veneer, plywood, bag paper, linerboard, corrugating medium, pulp
North Carolina	5	586,000 acres	4,200	Softwood plywood, softwood lumber, fiberboard, pulp, bleached paperboard, corrugating medium, linerboard, paper
Mississippi and Alabama	6	662,000 acres	2,000	Softwood lumber, softwood plywood
North Central	11		2,400	Hardwood lumber, hardwood plywood, particleboard, laminated products, paper, hardwood veneer, hardwood doors
Canada	9	9,102,000 acres	2,200	Softwood lumber, hardwood lumber, pulp, hardwood veneer
Other foreign: Malaysia, Indonesia, France	3	1,495,000 acres (harvesting rights)	3,500	Hardwood lumber, paperboard, shipping containers

Source: *Weyerhaeuser Handy Facts*, June 1980.

the two largest revenue earners, logs and lumber, had remained almost the same between 1976 and 1980, the production of plywood, particleboard, paperboard, paper, and containers had increased. Further, recent expansion in the real estate construction, nursery supply aquaculture, and soft disposables product lines provided additional evidence of change in product-line emphasis.

20   Weyerhaeuser's major kinds of product or service producing operations were sufficiently varied that they could be thought of as different kinds of businesses. Thus, even though there were sometimes materials, process, or locational interdependencies, the products and operations of the company could be categorized as falling in either the construction materials (solid wood products), fiber products, international, real estate, or special business segment operations.

Exhibit 2

Other Weyerhaeuser operations

Product/Service	Geopolitical areas	Number of locations
Panel products	VA, CA	3
Milk cartons	WA, CA	2
Chemicals	WA, NC, AR, OK	6
Fireplace logs	WA, OR, NC	4
Research and development	WA, MS, FL, CA, AR, OR, NC, OK	12
Secondary fiber	NC, WA, OR, MD, OK, CA	8
Shipping containers	CA, Spain, GA, MN, NJ, IL, Canary Islands, OR, IA, Greece, MI, France, NC, Belgium, HI, VA, TX, AL, KY, OH, NE, NY, ME, WA, WI	41
Environmental resources	WA, MS, AR, NC, OR, WI, Canada	7
Shelter group (real estate)	WA, FL, TX, CA, NJ, NC, MD, AZ, CO, NV, OR, SC	25
Aquaculture	OR, FL	2
Nursery supply	CT, FL, TX, CA, Washington, D.C.	7
Soft disposables	IL, PA, CA, GA	4
Energy and environmental equipment	CA	1
Wood products	CA, GA, NC, MD, OR, AL, NY, IA, OH, TX, MI, CO, MN, IN, PA, ND, IL, NJ, WI, CT, WA, KY, MO, TN, FL, LA, KS, AR, OK, AZ, RI, UT, SC, SD, MA, Canada, Australia	75

Source: *Weyerhaeuser Handy Facts,* June 1980.

21   The construction materials business was Weyerhaeuser's largest and involved the harvesting of timber; production of logs, lumber, plywood, panels, hardboard, particleboard, veneers, and other solid wood products; and their distribution directly to the buyers or through the company's 75 wood products customer service centers. Recent expansion and improvement had been through acquisition and modernization, as well as new plant construction. Because large tracts of timber were not readily available, the company had been effectively restricted to acquisitions of smaller tracts, more intensive use of its existing timber resource, and to the acquisition of small firms that contributed to product line and regional market expansion. The recent availability and stiff bidding for Bodcaw Company and its extensive forestlands in Louisiana highlights the scarcity of desirable large tracts. Weyerhaeuser actively bid for Bodcaw, but withdrew when International Paper's offer exceeded the value Weyerhaeuser had placed on the assets. The failure to acquire Bodcaw left the 1969 acquisi-

Exhibit 3

Production of wood products

Product	Basis	1980	1979	1978	1977	1976
Solid wood						
Logs	1000 cunits*	8,248	8,713	9,253	9,162	9,015
Lumber	million board ft.	2,747	2,914	3,068	2,898	2,701
Softwood plywood						
& veneer	million sq. ft. ($\frac{3}{8}''$)	1,192	1,454	1,406	1,207	1,070
Hardwood plywood						
& veneer	million sq. ft.	687	887	995	963	857
Particle board	million sq. ft. ($\frac{3}{8}''$)	385	41	44	386	325
Oriented strandboard		0	0	2		
Hardboard	million sq. ft. ($\frac{1}{8}''$)	110	416	420	374	304
Fiber products						
Market pulp	1000 air dry metric tons	1,073	912	917	858	923
Newsprint	1000 tons	176	63	—	—	—
Paper	1000 tons	509	521	527	471	358
Paperboard &						
containerboard	1000 tons	1,890	1,973	1,999	1,797	1,758
Shipping containers	1000 tons	1,177	1,241	1,178	1,046	1,010
Cartons	1000 tons	88	144	144	150	145

*Cunit $= 100 \text{ ft}^3$.
Source: 1980 10K Report.

tion of Dierks Forestry, Inc., and its 1,800,000 acres of forestland, as the company's last large acquisition. The current use of small company acquisitions in attempting to increase product and market competitiveness is evident in Exhibit 4. Major modernization improvements involved introducing more efficient and productive small-log production processes, introducing new processes and control technology to increase yield of the product mix, and converting from petroleum fuel as the primary energy source.

22   The fiber-products business was involved with the production of pulp, bleached paper boards, paper, newsprint, milk cartons, shipping containers and containerboard, and recycling fiber products. This fast-growing business had seen major expansion. A multiphase plant construction project at Columbus, Mississippi, planned to provide a lightweight coated paper and wood pulp mill in 1982, to be followed later by another lightweight coated paper mill, a kraft pulp mill, and an uncoated free sheet paper machine. Other major expansion projects included an increase in the linerboard capacity at the Valliant, Oklahoma, mill and a second newsprint machine at the company's Longview, Washington, facility.

23   Weyerhaeuser's international business included both the international marketing of forest products produced in the U.S. and the foreign production of forest products for marketing within the producing nation or inter-

Exhibit 4

Planned and completed acquisitions, 1979–1980

Company	Location	Benefit
Dixieline Lumber Co.	Southern California (San Diego)	Market expansion
Delta Industries	Mississippi-Alabama	Plywood production
Northwood Mills	British Columbia	Lumber production
Travers Lumber	Alabama (Mobile)	Export marketing of southern lumber
Eclipse Timber Co.	Washington (Port Angeles)	Market expansion
Menasha Corp. (West Coast operations only)	West Coast (North Bend, Ore.; Anaheim, Cal.; Portland and Eugene, Ore.)	Corrugating medium, waste paper collection, and containerboard operations
Everitt Lumber Co. and Union Manufacturing & Supply Co.	Colorado (Fort Collins)	Distribution
Northwest Hardwoods, Inc.	Washington (Chehalis and Arlington)	Alder lumber mills

nationally. The exporting of U.S. produced products, primarily pulp, liner-board, lumber, and plywood to Europe, and pulp, logs, wood chips, and newsprint to the Far East (principally Japan) accounted for approximately 20% of Weyerhaeuser's gross sales, as shown in Exhibit 5. In 1980, approximately 60 to 65% of such exports were solid wood (e.g., logs) and 35 to 40% were pulp products. However, this mix was expected to change as more finished or semi-finished products were exported, particularly in fiber form. For instance, in mid-1979, the North Pacific Paper Corporation, a new joint venture of Weyerhaeuser and a Japanese paper company, started producing newsprint at Longview, Washington, for sale in the United States and Japan on a 50-50 basis. At the same time, Weyerhaeuser had not shown any evidence that it wished to relinquish its position as the largest United States log exporter. Weyerhaeuser's planned marshalling yard and port at Dupont, Washington, will allow cutting exporting costs by $10 per ton from the $20 to $70 per ton otherwise required. This facility, when completed, was expected to allow Weyerhaeuser to compete more effectively.

Exhibit 5

Volume of international business

Year	Total sales of products exported from U.S.	Total net sales from operations outside the U.S.	Total net sales from all operations, domestic & international
1979	$978,000,000	$482,000,000	$4,423,000,000
1978	729,000,000	370,000,000	3,799,000,000
1977	658,000,000	325,000,000	3,283,000,000

Source: 1979 10K Report.

24   The other aspects of international operations included the harvesting of timber, processing of timber into lumber, and the production of intermediate and finished products, principally shipping containers, in other nations. Canadian lumber and pulp were used domestically in Canada and, in addition, were marketed in the eastern U.S., Europe, and Japan. Southeast Asian timber and lumber were principally marketed in Japan, and a joint-venture company in which Weyerhaeuser was a partner was planning to construct up to five processing plants in Indonesia in addition to the one in operation. Each plant was expected to be able to produce 4,200,000 cubic feet per year. Besides the timber processing plants in Southeast Asia, Weyerhaeuser had a paperboard plant in France, situated to supply the company's European container plants, which also supplied European markets.

25   The real estate business, centered around the Weyerhaeuser Real Estate Company and its subsidiaries, made Weyerhaeuser the seventh largest home builder and the seventh largest mortgage lender in the U.S. The Weyerhaeuser Real Estate Company employed approximately 2,000 of the company's 45,700 employees and built, sold, and financed single and multi-family dwelling units. Recent initiatives included plans to build an 800 housing unit and resort development in Oregon, consideration of entering the savings and loan field, and the formation of Cornerstone Development Corporation, a joint venture in which Weyerhaeuser held the majority interest. Cornerstone was formed both as a profit making venture and to serve a social purpose through rehabilitating and redeveloping run-down urban areas. The first project, planned for completion in the mid-1980s, was the renovation of a five-block area of the Seattle waterfront into housing, retail, and parking facilities.

26   Special products businesses included aquaculture and the production of energy and environmental equipment, paper disposable diapers, nursery supplies, and chemicals. Two of these diversification efforts, (i.e., production of energy and environmental equipment by Combustion Power Company and production of chemicals,) provided Weyerhaeuser control over products for its internal use as well as profit. Chemical production capitalized on some by-products, (e.g., turpentine and tall oil), but was involved primarily with production of chlorine and caustics used in pulping, and with the production of urea fertilizers used in forestry. Weyerhaeuser's entry into the disposable diaper field had left them the largest private label supplier (to Sears Roebuck and other chains) with approximately 8 to 9% of the total domestic market. Recent company interest in aquaculture operations in Florida, Oregon, and Brazil offered long-range potential to capitalize on the company's waterfront properties, providing a social benefit and profit as population pressures on the food supply made commercial shrimp growing and salmon ocean ranching feasible. In the latter line, Weyerhaeuser estimated that if even only one percent of the salmon released to the sea eventually reached harvestable size and returned to be harvested, the company would break even.

27   An important aspect of Weyerhaeuser's operations was the management

of its resource base: 2,800,000 acres of forestland concentrated in the Douglas fir region of western Washington and Oregon and the Ponderosa pine region of eastern Oregon; 3,100,000 acres in the southern pine region of North Carolina, Mississippi, Alabama, Arkansas, and Oklahoma; and 10,500,000 acres of harvest rights in interior British Columbia, Eastern Ontario, Malaysia, and Indonesia. Weyerhaeuser was alone among major companies since it had enough trees on an ongoing basis to supply its own needs. This resource allowed Weyerhaeuser to sell logs for export. Not only did the company export logs, but it also produced more logs than it needed for its own manufacturing and converting and thus sold to its competitors. However, Weyerhaeuser at the same time, bought timber from others because of qualities needed for specific products or because it was more economical to do so from a logistics cost standpoint, even at locations where the company had an excess supply.

28   Weyerhaeuser was the largest private landowner on Mount St. Helens in southern Washington. It grew Douglas fir and hemlock on nearly 500,000 acres. Unfortunately, this dormant volcano started showing signs of life in early 1980, which escalated into a cataclysmic eruption on May 18, 1980. This instantly uprooted and knocked down almost all of its trees on 68,000 acres of Weyerhaeuser's forestland, of which 15,000 acres contained mature trees. Weyerhaeuser also lost 39 railcars, 30 trucks, 22 crew buses, and three logging camps from the mud slides that occurred as a result of the eruption. Fortunately, the eruption occurred on a Sunday when no Weyerhaeuser crews were on duty; thus, no employee lost his life. In the subsequent months, Weyerhaeuser used 650 employees to clean up the logging camps and salvage the damaged timber. By September of 1980, Weyerhaeuser had salvaged about 60% of the 10,000,000 cubic feet of trees carried away by floods and mud after the eruption.

29   The company's basic policy was to manage lands to provide the highest yield on its investment consistent with a continuous supply of wood in the future. An early leader in tree farming, Weyerhaeuser did about 16% of U.S. forest regeneration by 1980. Weyerhaeuser had, over time, improved its techniques so that its high yield forestry program could double production in a given replanted area over what nature unassisted could do. Forests selected for the high yield forestry program were planted with genetically improved trees within one year of harvest, fertilized, and thinned as necessary. As a result of this program, Weyerhaeuser forecasted a dramatic increase in the southern wood supply in the 1990 to 2010 period. However, improved forestry practices were not without cost—Weyerhaeuser estimated that it would spend approximately $140,000,000 per year on forestry through the 1980s.

30   Weyerhaeuser's size had scale implications not only for forestry management but also for logistics and movement into new areas. A high volume of export shipments combined with capital made the logistics cost-saving Dupont export-facility possible. Similarly, volume and capital made

operation of its own transportation system possible. For example, Weyerhaeuser had been able to develop a network of 32,000 miles of internal roads on its lands, owned and operated six short line common carrier railroads with 3,600 owned and leased rail cars, and chartered 18 ocean-going ships. Eight of the ships, two 660 foot Japanese built and Norwegian owned and operated ships used to carry newsprint, pulp, and other products from the West Coast to Japan, and six similar ships, which operated between the West Coast and Europe, were specially configured for efficient loading and were scheduled to serve Weyerhaeuser. Similarly, its railroads were dedicated to Weyerhaeuser, both schedules and rail cars being tailored to the company's needs.

31   Weyerhaeuser continued to expand and build new plants in 1980. This expansion included a new pulp and paper complex in Mississippi, a new linerboard manufacturing plant in Oklahoma, an enlarged disposable diaper plant in Georgia, and plans to build a corrugated container plant in Oregon. Weyerhaeuser also bought lumber warehouses and manufacturing facilities from Everitt Lumber Company and Union Manufacturing & Supply Company. In addition, Weyerhaeuser attempted to purchase some of Menasha's assets, but the Federal Trade Commission moved to block the purchase on antitrust grounds. While Weyerhaeuser was expanding in many areas, it also closed down some saw mill plants that were located near old-growth lumber.

Research and Development

32   Research and development at Weyerhaeuser has been conducted by a work force of some 145 doctoral degree holders in 40 disciplines plus 338 other degree holders in 60 disciplines plus 376 technicians working approximately 500 projects. These efforts were supported by an annual budget of approximately $50,000,000.

33   In the late 1970s, the company consolidated major research activities in a new 450,000-square-foot technology center located at corporate head-quarters at Tacoma, Washington. Here, researchers worked on exploratory research projects that may produce usable results in three to ten years and on applied research that had been advanced from the exploratory stage because of its high potential and lower risk. Such applied research was expected to have actual payoff in one to three years.

34   Two major thrusts dominated research—forest production and production plant technology. In the former direction, much effort had been aimed at genetically improving trees and developing techniques used in cultivating replanted forests. For example, research had developed a technique for planting new seedling trees that requires only 160 days of growth in a greenhouse before replanting and results in fast growth after replanting. This was contrasted with the next best technology that required two years

of growth in a nursery before replanting and then produced a medium rate of growth. Production plant technology research and development was aimed at improving efficiency. A major area had been improving machinery to improve yield from logs in sawmills. Largely with the development of computer scanning equipment that permitted saws and edgers to be positioned to maximize recovery, Weyerhaeuser's research and development effort had, in eight years, provided the means to double the volume of usable wood obtained from logs. Weyerhaeuser's scale of operations allowed the company to capitalize on this advancement not at just a single plant, but at 20 or more sawmills. Another major area of research and development interest had been the development of technology specifically aimed at maximizing the recovery from small logs. As a result, a number of small log sawmills had been constructed, the latest of which replaced an older inefficient mill at Raymond, Washington, in 1980.

Marketing

35   Strong competition from other forest-products companies and producers of wood-products substitutes was reflected in a marketing approach oriented toward flexibility and service. Flexibility was evident in several ways. First, marketing decision making was decentralized to the various business and product groups. Each used its choice of a channel or channels of distribution tailored to the nature of the product and user. Construction materials were sold through wholesalers and directly to retailers and industrial users. Pulp, newsprint, and paperboard were sold directly to industrial users, processors, and converters, while paper was sold through wholesalers or jobbers. Containers and packaging products were usually sold directly to industrial or agricultural users. Second, marketing was operating in an adaptive mode, focusing on matching the products that could be economically produced at each of its operating regions with the markets that could be economically served by each. In particular, this adapting had taken the direction of shifting to the most profitable geographical markets as transportation economics effectively closed out long-standing markets, such as the Midwest and East Coast for western timber products. Third, the company's marketing efforts were aimed at anticipating and adapting to change in user tastes and locations. This involved changing the product mix as consumer preferences and technology shifted demand from lumber and plywood to hardboards and particleboards, for example. A major change that Weyerhaeuser saw was a growing Asian market, particularly Japan, Korea, and Taiwan in the 1980s, and later China. This change had shaped the company's emphasis on international operations, organization, export facilities, and sales.

36   Customer service as a marketing strategy showed itself in the company's plant location practices and its commitment to special facilities. For exam-

ple, container and milk carton plants were located near their markets. This closeness coupled with technical advice and service provided customers with a higher level of service than otherwise. Similarly, the operation of more than 70 distribution centers in high-growth or high-volume areas, each carrying a full line of produced and purchased products, provided retailers and industrial users better service. Use of its own ships, under charter, was yet another means of providing increased speed and reliability of service, this time for foreign customers.

Financial Performance

37   Weyerhaeuser experienced a general growth trend in assets, net sales, net earnings, and earnings per share during the decade of the 1970s. Assets were nearly tripled, while long-term debt was doubled as shown in Exhibit 6. As indicated in Exhibit 7, earnings, although erratic, increased severalfold. After tax return on equity was characterized by a slight increased trend and considerable variability with rates of 12.2%, 9.7%, 14.1%, 25.0%, 18.5%, 10.6%, 15.4%, 13.8%, 16.0%, and 18.7% in 1970 through 1979.

38   Part of the realized rate of return was related to the long-term holding of trees purchased in the past at very low prices (relative to 1980). Any positive difference between the value for tax purposes (based on 1980 bids for future harvests of similar stands of government-owned timber) and the value of the timber at the time it was acquired, plus growing and harvesting expenses, was treated as a long-term capital gain subject to the lower rate capital gains tax.

39   Although growing, the rate of growth in total revenues had been decreasing in recent years, without even considering the undervaluation of assets associated with inflation and the generally increased price levels. Had materials and resources been priced at current values rather than historical costs, net earnings and return on equity would have been less. For example, had assets been valued at current cost, net owners' equity would have been $4,775,164,000, rather than the $2,735,867,000 reflected in the 1979 balance sheet. Net earnings of $512,200,000 for 1979 represented a 10.7% return on equity when adjusted for specific prices while the rate of return unadjusted for price changes was 18.7%.

40   The greatest rate of growth (in sales and contributions to earnings) was attributable to other, non-building materials and fiber products sales. Based on data from Exhibit 8, between 1977 and 1979 alone, this class of products increased its contributions 130% while increasing identifiable assets only 43%.

41   The company's commitments to growth and modernization of its asset base were reflected in its capital expenditure outlays that had exceeded after-tax earnings in nine out of ten years in the 1970s. Operations had been the primary source of funds for capital expenditure and other corpor-

Exhibit 6

Consolidated balance sheet end of calendar year ($ millions)

	1980	1979	1978	1977	1976	1975	1974	1973	1972	1971
Assets										
Current assets										
Cash	68.8	176.1	141.1							
Short-term investments	40.7	186.8	105.6							
Receivables	491.7	429.5	392.5							
Inventories	480.9	465.4	407.1							
Prepaid expenses	19.1	33.9	29.8							
Total current assets	1,101.2	1,291.7	1,076.1	1,009.5	981.4	782.8	657.6	476.9	404.3	412.7
Investments and other assets										
Weyerhaeuser Real Estate Co.	222.3	201.7	182.4							
Other	140.2	49.5	41.6							
	362.5	251.1	224.0	212.6	206.8	220.2	210.9	195.6	197.2	195.1
Property and equipment, at cost, less depreciation	2,520.3	2,485.2	2,199.1	2,044.4	1,848.4	1,579.7	1,238.8	1,111.8	1,101.3	765.6
Construction in progress	441.1	170.8	252.3	238.9	167.2	204.7	291.0	102.9	33.0	291.1
Leased property, under capital leases, principally ships, less amortization	135.7	150.6	166.1	181.1	—	—	—	—	—	—
Timber and timberlands (& other)	677.9	608.3	545.9	532.6	477.9	458.9	452.8	422.5	405.2	417.2
Total Assets	5,238.7	4,957.9	4,463.6	4,219.1	3,681.7	3,246.3	2,851.0	2,309.6	2,141.0	2,081.8
Liabilities and shareholders' interest										
Current liabilities	618.0	645.9	589.5	488.4	469.4	395.2	378.0	349.2	210.2	338.5
Long-term debt	1,269.5	1,185.0	1,187.1	1,211.9	1,093.4	929.4	915.6	526.4	780.5	531.6
Deferred income taxes	152.0	57.5	55.0							
Deferred pension and other liabilities	186.6	155.7	127.5							
Capital lease obligations	147.3	157.6	167.6							
Minority interest in subsidiaries	28.7	20.4	19.0							
Shareholders' interest										
Preferred shares	4.0	4.0	4.0							
Preference shares	.3	.3								
Common shares	241.2	241.2	241.1							
Other capital	246.6	251.1	249.9							
Retained earnings	2,448.1	2,347.5	1,980.5							
	2,940.1	2,844.0	2,475.5							
Treasury shares	103.3	108.1	157.7							
Total shareholders' interest	2,836.8	2,735.9	2,317.9	2,177.1	1,981.9	1,784.5	1,491.2	1,390.5	1,127.0	1,189.0
	5,238.7	4,957.9	4,463.6							

Source: 1980 Annual and 10K Reports.

Exhibit 7

Consolidated earnings (millions except per share figures)

	1980	1979	1978	1977	1976	1975	1974	1973	1972	1971
Net sales	4,535.8	4,422.6	3,799.4	3,282.8	2,868.4	2,421.3	2,529.0	2,301.7	1,675.9	1,299.5
Weyerhaeuser Real Estate Company earnings	51.2	57.1	51.8	47.1	16.9	5.1				
Other income, net	33.3	37.0	19.9	14.6	12.5	(10.5)				
	4,620.3	4,516.7	3,871.1	3,344.6	2,897.8	2,416.0				
Operating costs	3,594.5	3,325.7	2,872.1	2,543.9	2,181.5	1,842.5				
Selling, general and administrative expenses	336.4	302.5	255.1	228.6	207.5	182.9				
Research and development expenses	52.2	45.0	51.0	46.3	30.3	22.9				
Interest expense	121.5	113.3	113.0	103.4	78.8	82.5				
Less interest capitalized	13.8	8.7	9.2	8.0	13.1	15.2				
Earnings before income taxes and extraordinary charge	529.5	738.9	592.6	430.4	412.8	299.4				
Income taxes	208.0	226.7	180.0	128.9	106.8	110.6				
Earnings before extraordinary charge	321.5	512.2	412.6	301.5	306.0	188.8				
Extraordinary charge	43.5	—	41.5	—	—	—				
Net earnings	278.0	512.2	371.1	301.5	306.0	188.8	277.0	348.4	158.9	114.8
Average common shares outstanding	125.6	124.8	126.1	127.4	127.2	126.9	127.5	126.6	125.7	125.5
Net earnings per common share	2.12	4.02	2.85	2.28	2.32	1.48	2.17	2.72	1.17	.82
Dividends paid	1.30	1.07½	.85	.80	.80	.80	.80	.47	.41½	.40

Source: 1980 Annual Report and 10K Report.

Exhibit 8

Major product class performance ($ millions)

	1980	*1979*	*1978*	*1977*	*1976*
Net sales					
Building materials	2,482	2,710	2,346	1,950	1,627
Pulp, newsprint, paper and paperboard products	1,149	888	753	715	680
Container and packaging products	730	685	590	539	514
Other	175	140	110	79	47
	4,536	4,423	3,799	3,283	2,866
Approximate contribution to earnings[a]					
Building materials	548	726	671	515	418
Pulp, newsprint, paper and paperboard products	158	181	87	69	152
Container and packaging products	21	26	13	18	18
Other	26	23	20	10	7
	753	956	791	612	592
Identifiable assets					
Building materials	2,479	2,293	2,094	1,919	
Pulp, newsprint, paper and paperboard products	1,672	1,435	1,351	1,321	
Container and packaging products	250	295	254	240	
Other	209	173	141	121	
	4,610	4,196	3,840	3,601	

[a] Excludes: general, administrative, certain research and other expenses; interest expense; income taxes; earnings of unconsolidated real estate and finance subsidiaries; and other unallocatable income such as dividends, interest, and royalties.
Source: 1980 Annual Report.

ate requirements, new debt and new equity providing only 21% of the needed funds during 1975-1979.

42   The Mount St. Helens eruption during 1980 had a significant adverse financial impact on the company. Weyerhaeuser wrote off all of the costs associated from this disaster during the third quarter of 1980. The costs included losses of standing timber, harvested logs, buildings, equipment, and transportation systems. This $43,500,000 extraordinary charge reduced 1980's net income after taxes of $321,500,000 to $278,000,000. This single event reduced net earnings per share of common stock by $.29 to $2.12, down from $4.02 in 1979.

Corporate Citizenship

43   Once termed "the best of the SOB's,"[4] Weyerhaeuser evidenced corporate citizenship in a number of ways beyond providing jobs, products, and profits. Responsible and complete use of forest resources, forest regeneration, resource development, energy conservation, protection of the environment, active involvement in the public policy-making process, and

corporate giving were all means by which the company may be considered by some to have contributed to the well-being of society.

44   Forest use practices pointed toward full use of its forestland resources—from efficient conversion of timber into wood products, use of by-products, reduction of waste and scrap, to the regeneration of logged-off lands for greater yields in the future. A major thrust of the company's research and development effort had been in these directions. The scientific tree farming that began in the 1930s and that evolved into the high yield forestry program had been expanded to include commitments to nonsilviculture activities such as design of more efficient processes and new product developments, both forest products based and others, such as aquaculture.

45   Energy conservation had been another subject of company policy and expenditure. Substantial research, development, and engineering modification efforts had been directed toward the use of waste products as sources of energy. As a result of these efforts, Weyerhaeuser was rated most energy efficient of 18 paper and forest products companies surveyed by Kidder, Peabody and Company, in 1978.[5] Concern with energy conservation had also been manifested in a company-sponsored car-pooling program. Under its van-pooling program, Weyerhaeuser bought and provided vans for groups of employees wishing to share rides. Members paid only a periodic fee calculated to pay the costs of the van, over time. The van-pool driver-sponsor, in return for organizing, collecting, and driving, had limited use of the van for personal travel in off-work hours.

46   With an early start in pollution abatement and expenditures on environmental costs that amounted to between 10% and 15% of its capital expenditures budget, Weyerhaeuser had been a leader in regulatory compliance among the large companies in its industry. Such pollution control efforts had sometimes been combined with those aimed at other objectives such as the recovery and reuse of chemicals used in pulp making.

47   The company's approach to solving problems concerning conflicts between profitable company operations and protection of the ecology and the environment had been both proactive and accommodating. The company policy concerning use of resources was to "perform in concern and harmony with nature and the public interest by: exercising the highest level of responsible stewardship of natural and environmental resources, practicing wise use of all resources throughout its activities, responding positively to opportunities for environmental, ecological and social problem, and encouraging others toward the same commitments."[6] Carrying out this policy had involved attempting to anticipate environmentalists' concerns, using their input in planning, and then actively championing the resultant plan. The proposed Dupont export facility was a case in point. Arguments against the facility had been based on two issues. The first and most emotional issue was whether or not the port facilities and activity would have an adverse effect on the fish and wildlife of the nearby Nisqually River delta and wildlife refuge. Second, opponents argued that

exporting logs from the facility meant exporting jobs and forest resources that were needed in the United States. Weyerhaeuser's response was to study the economic and environmental consequences of operations, solicit inputs from concerned governmental bodies, private groups, and the public, and to attempt to present facts and arguments on both sides of the issue to the public and government officials. Basically, the company stressed that the facility should not be expected to have any significant impact on the surrounding environment and that adequate precautions would be taken to prevent any unforeseen impacts that were humanly controllable. With respect to the arguments against exporting logs, Weyerhaeuser had taken every opportunity to explain that the facility was designed for manufactured product exports and that any logs shipped from Dupont would be in lieu of exporting them from other ports, that logs exported were from surplus trees, that jobs were actually created because people were employed in the export business in addition to those needed for meeting domestic demand, that employment was stabilized because foreign demand and sales did not follow U.S. seasonal patterns, and that the nation was better off because of the net benefit to the U.S. trade balance. Despite the company's efforts, it had not yet won approval of the port.

48   The proactive approach to public policy making was visible in George Weyerhaeuser, chief executive officer of the company, who had been outspoken both as a supporter of U.S. national interests, such as log exporting, and a critic of federal government economic policy. However, the company does not rely solely on personal opinion leadership. Organizationally, Weyerhaeuser operated a liaison office in Washington, D.C., employed the services of lobbyists, belonged to and supported national and state general business interest groups and industry interest groups, and sponsored a political action committee. The political action committee typically channeled its campaign contributions to candidates who were believed to consider information from multiple sources, and who were from states where the company had sizable operations.

49   The Weyerhaeuser Company Foundation was the primary vehicle through which the company supported selected social goals. The foundation had two missions: to improve the quality of life in employees' living environments and to provide leadership, information, and understanding of significant issues impacting both industry and society, specifically as they related to forestland use. Toward these purposes, grants totaling over $32,000,000 had been made since 1948 to social, health, educational, cultural, and civic organizations, primarily in communities where the company had a high level of employment. In 1979 alone, the Foundation distributed over $4,000,000 to organizations. In 1980, the Foundation was administering two ongoing programs, the quality-of-life program and general education grants, and a third, the forestland-use grants program was in the planning stage. The quality-of-life program was aimed at improving basic services and amenities in communities where Weyerhaeuser operated.

Based on priorities and guidelines approved by local-employee review committees, grants were selectively made in these communities to support social services, health, recreation, culture, the arts, civic causes, employment training, and supplemental educational projects. General education grants covered three traditional programs, scholarships, fellowships, and matching gifts to private colleges and universities.

50   Although Weyerhaeuser had been long recognized as a leader in the responsible use of resources, it had at the same time been the subject of criticism. Among the criticisms in addition to those associated with the export of logs and the building of a port at Dupont, Weyerhaeuser had been accused of:

   a. Genetically tampering with salmon and thus possibly weakening them in their natural environment.

   b. Growing uniform forests of a single species of trees, thus creating a monotonous landscape and tampering with the balance of plant life.

   c. Establishing tree farms only where they can be seen, leaving other forestland in nature's hands after the timber was cut.

   d. Continuing to pollute. For example, notwithstanding expenditures on pollution control, the company was cited for failure to meet standards at its Longview, Washington, plant in a suit by the Environmental Protection Agency.

   e. Unethical or illegal behavior. In the late 1970s, the company was the subject of several criminal and civil actions for alleged price-fixing practices and was fined $632,000 by a federal judge after pleading no contest to one charge. Despite failure to obtain indictments, an acquittal in federal court, and the settlement of most civil suits out of court, the company's name was associated with the price-fixing scandal.

51   In the effort to preclude further evidences of unethical behavior by employees, George Weyerhaeuser had expressed his and the company's concern, to employees, about the company's image and had been adamant concerning adherence to the letter and intent of the law. As an aid to employees faced with doubtful decision situations, the company developed a business conduct committee that could be contacted for advice, guidance, and clarification, before the fact; disseminated written policies concerning employee behavior; and developed criteria by which employees could certify their compliance with the policies.

Organization and Management

52   Growth, primarily since the 1950s, into new products, new geographical areas, and international operations, often through acquisition, had

spawned structural changes. The added complexities associated with centralized management and coordination of multiple materials sources, production plants, and markets for several different kinds of products caused Weyerhaeuser to decentralize operations decision making to regions and to assign each of its various products to a business grouping of similar product lines. This reorganization, initially effected in 1972 with the formation of five business groups and eleven geographical regions evolved into a structure that involved four major kinds of organizational units, each with its distinct role. These four organizational groupings or units were senior management, businesses, operating regions, and corporate staff.

53   Senior management included the president and chief executive officer and seven senior vice presidents who assisted the president in overseeing the corporation and providing general direction. Each member of this top management group was charged with coordinating the efforts and needs, evaluating the performance, and assisting in establishing appropriate policy and plans for those assigned businesses or staff functions. Exhibit 9 shows the assignment of major staff functions, businesses, and operating regions among the president and senior vice presidents.

54   As of 1980, 12 major businesses or resource groups reported to senior management. The vice presidents of pulp, paper, newsprint, and paperboard packaging reported to the senior vice president for pulp, paper, and paperboard. The vice presidents of land and timber; raw materials; lumber; panels, hardwood, and consumer products; plywood; and wood-products sales and distribution reported to the senior vice president for timberlands, wood products, and international relations. The vice presidents for shelter and special businesses (aquaculture, chemicals, nursery supply, soft disposables, and Combustion Power Company) reported to the president and the senior vice president for finance and planning, respectively.

55   The businesses were the primary units for strategic planning and marketing. Each was a profit center responsible for business planning, including the formulation of objectives, strategies, and policies. Each was held accountable for developing marketing strategy; developing supporting financial plans; selling, distributing, secondary manufacturing of products, and planning new manufacturing facilities, processes, and product developments. In addition to the responsibility for log, timber, and chip marketing and planning, the raw materials business provided functional guidance to operating regions for maximizing raw-materials values. The land and timber resources group was responsible for management and analysis of the timber asset, including directing the high yield forestry program; nursery and seed-orchard management; timber and seedling sales; land classification; recreation development; mineral and agricultural development; road-use agreements; and land acquisition, sales, or transfers.

56   Although the major business strategy was formulated and effected from the business groups at corporate headquarters, decision making with re-

Exhibit 9

Weyerhaeuser organizational relationships.

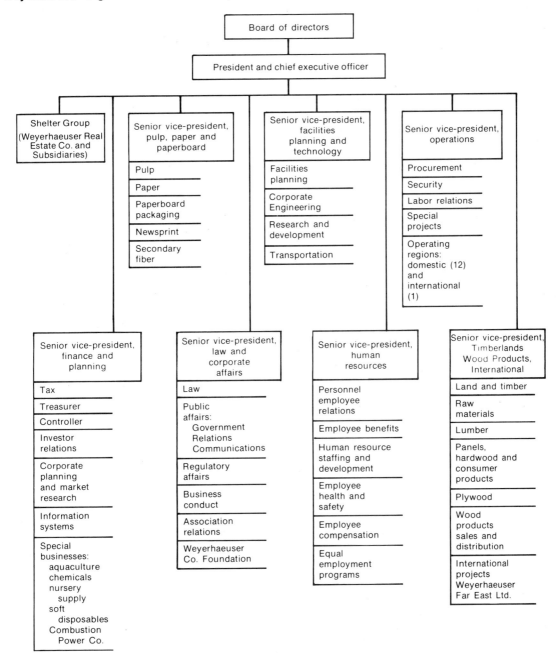

Source: Weyerhaeuser Company Profile, 1979, Management Bulletin No. 861, and *Weyerhaeuser Handy Facts,* June 1980.

spect to operations was decentralized, resting with the 12 domestic and two international regions. As the primary unit for operations, the regions were responsible for maximizing production efficiency of timber and primary manufacturing operations and achieving optimum value from the raw materials available. Within regions, this profit responsibility and decision making was further delegated to local plant managers. The vice presidents for the regions of eastern Oregon, Willamette (Oregon), southwest Oregon; northern Washington; Twin Harbors (Washington); southwest Washington; central Arkansas; Mississippi/Alabama; North Carolina; north central Oklahoma; southwest Arkansas, and the president of Weyerhaeuser Canada Ltd. reported to the senior vice president of operations. The only other operating region, Weyerhaeuser Far East Ltd., reported to the senior vice president of timberlands, wood products, and international.

57   Corporate staff units, under vice presidents or directors, were clustered for reporting purposes by functional groupings. Generally, the staff served to perform three functions:

a. Assisted in the planning process through fact gathering, analysis, and counseling service.

b. Supported the chief executive officer, operating units, and the corporation as a whole by providing advice and expert services in specialized areas.

c. Assisted management in setting objectives, policies, and budgets; developing procedures; and evaluating performance.

58   Management of foreign-based businesses and resources followed two forms. In the case of Canadian and European operations, management was usually accomplished through subsidiaries (e.g., Weyerhaeuser Canada Ltd. and Cartoonpack S.A.) which functioned at units in the operating region of business structure. The other case applied to the management of Far Eastern enterprises, in which joint ventures represented a significant portion of Weyerhaeuser's activity. In this case, the president of Weyerhaeuser Far East Ltd., in the role of Weyerhaeuser's shareholder representative, represented Weyerhaeuser's interests in its joint ventures. In addition, Weyerhaeuser Far East Ltd. performed as the operating and administrative reporting unit for all Weyerhaeuser subsidiaries and offices in that part of the world.

59   Acquired and newly-formed subsidiaries played an increasingly noticeable role in Weyerhaueser's production, manufacturing, and marketing efforts. Even before the latest round of acquisitions, the company had integrated a substantial number of subsidiaries into its existing businesses, regional operations, and international organization. As listed in Exhibit 10, the majority of these subsidiaries were wholly owned.

60   With some 45,700 employees working in more than 100 locations in and outside the United States under 12 business/resource groups, 14 geograph-

Exhibit 10

Weyerhaeuser's subsidiaries

Name	State or country	Percent owned
Camad Veneer, Inc.	Oregon	50
Chehalis Western Railroad Company	Washington	100
Columbia & Cowlitz Railway	Washington	100
Combustion Power Company, Inc.	Delaware	100
Curtis, Milburn and Eastern Railroad Company	Washington	100
De Queen and Eastern Railroad Company	Arkansas	100
Dixieland Lumber Company	Delaware	100
Dixieland Builders Fund Control, Inc.	California	100
Fisher Lumber Company	California	100
Golden Triangle Railroad	Mississippi	100
Malibu Lumber and Hardware Company	California	100
Mississippi & Skuna Valley Railroad Company	Mississippi	100
Mountain Tree Farm Company	Washington	50
North Pacific Paper Corporation	Delaware	90
Northwest Hardwoods, Inc.	Delaware	100
Oregon Aqua-Foods, Inc.	Oregon	100
Oregon, California & Eastern Railway Company	Nevada	100
Shemin Nurseries, Inc.	Delaware	80
Texas, Oklahoma & Eastern Railroad Company	Oklahoma	100
Union Manufacturing and Supply Company, Inc.	Delaware	100
Westwood Shipping Lines, Inc.	Washington	100
Weyerhaeuser Export, Inc.	Delaware	100
Weyerhaeuser Construction Company	Washington	100
Weyerhaeuser International, Inc.	Washington	100
The Capricorn Corporation	Philippines	100
Cartonpack, S.A.	Greece	100
Cargal Hallas L.L.C.	Greece	100
de Bes' Insurance Ltd.	Bermuda	100
Kennedy Bay Timber Sendirina Berhan	Malaysia	100
Pacific Hardwoods, Sdn. Bhd.	Malaysia	49
Silam Forest Products, Sdn. Bhd.	Malaysia	49
Timber Trading (International), S.A.	Panama	65
Weyerhaeuser (Aust.) Pty. Ltd.	Australia	100
Weyerhaeuser Canada Ltd.	Canada	100
Weyerhaeuser Deutschland Gmbh	Germany	100
Weyerhaeuser Europe, S.A.	France	99.5
Cartonneries du Forez	France	100
Dropsy Carton	France	100
Societe Novelle des Paperteries de La Descartes S.A.R.L.	France	100
Weyerhaeuser (Far East) Limited	Hong Kong	100
P.T. International Timber Corporation	Indonesia	65
Weyerhaeuser Italia, S.r.l.	Italy	100
Weyerhaeuser, S.A.	Panama	100
Weyerhaeuser Overseas Finance Company	Delaware	100
Weyerhaeuser Townsite Company	Arkansas	100
Weyerhaeuser Real Estate Company	Washington	100
The Babcock Company	Florida	100
Centennial Homes, Inc.	Texas	100

Exhibit 10 (continued)

Name	State or country	Percent owned
Cornerstone Development Company	Washington	80
Duma, Inc.	New Jersey	100
Par-West Financial	California	100
Marmount Realty Company	California	100
Pardee Construction Company	California	100
Pardee Construction Company of Nevada	Nevada	100
Westwood Associates	California	100
Weyerhaeuser Mortgage Company	California	100
Weyerhaeuser Insurance Agency	California	100
Weyerhaeuser Venture Company	Nevada	100
The Quadrant Corporation	Washington	100
Quadrant Development Limited	Canada	100
Quill Corporation	New Jersey	100
Scarborough Corporation	Delaware	100
Scarborough Corporation	New Jersey	100
Scarborough Constructors, Inc.	Florida	100
Trendmaker Homes, Inc.	Florida	100
Westmark Development Company	Washington	100
Westminister Company	North Carolina	100
Weyerhaeuser Real Estate Company of Nevada	Nevada	100
Winchester Homes, Inc.	Delaware	100

Source: 1980 10K Report.

ical regions, or other staff and operational units, capable managers and executives were needed to effect decisions and coordination. Accomplishing this task involved the efforts of a large number of executives and senior managers. This team included, in addition to the various plant and operations managers, 45 executives of vice president or similar status, and a top management group of the president or similar status, and a top management group of the president and seven senior vice presidents. The top eight executives, identified in Exhibit 11, represented a total of 166 years of experience in the company. All of the top executives except two, Ben Borne and William Ruckelshaus, were appointed to their present positions from within the company.

Beyond 1980

61   Weyerhaeuser Company faced both economic and environmental challenges in 1980. Double digit U.S. inflation brought about the highest interest rates ever domestically. In turn, this had a devastating effect on the housing market and commercial construction. In addition, a totally unexpected

Exhibit 11

Senior management

Name and position	Age	Years with Weyerhaeuser	Background (Weyerhaeuser unless otherwise noted)
George H. Weyerhaeuser, President & Chief Executive Officer	54	31	Yale (B.S., Ind. Adm.); manager, V.P.; exec. V.P., wood products; exec. V.P. operations; President and CEO since 1966.
Charles W. Bingham, Senior Vice President, timberlands, wood products & international	47	20	Harvard (LL.B.); law dept. wood chip supply manager; corp. raw materials manager; area manager; V.P. wood products.
Ben W. Borne, Senior Vice President, human resources	56	2	Spring Hill College (B.A.), Loyola Univ. (J.D.); FBI; industrial relations V.P. Litton Industries division; V.P. & director human resources, Motorola.
Alexander M. Fisken, Senior Vice President, facilities planning and technology	57	35	Yale (B.S. Engineering); engineering, development, new business; manager in several products divisions; engineering director; V.P. facilities planning and engineering.
Harry E. Morgan, Jr., Senior Vice President, operations	58	34	Stanford (A.B.); wood & plant operations; asst. logging superintendent; admin. asst.; branch manager; manufacturing manager; V.P. timberlands division, Corp. V.P.
William D. Ruckelshaus, Senior Vice President, law and corporate affairs	48	4	Princeton (B.A.), Harvard (LL.B.); attorney in private practice; deputy attorney general & chief counsel, State of Indiana; minority attorney, Indiana Senate; member Indiana House of Representatives; asst. attorney general, U.S. Dept. of Justice; Federal Administrator, EPA; acting director, FBI; Deputy Attorney General, U.S.; senior partner in private practice.
Robert L. Schuyler, Senior Vice President, finance and planning	44	14	Nebraska (B.S. in B.A.), Harvard (M.B.A.); manager, financial analysis; manager, investment evaluation; V.P. finance & planning.
John Shethar, Senior Vice President, fiber business	53	26	Yale (B.S. in Econ.); sales representative; manager, pulp sales; pulp division manager; pulp & paper division V.P.; V.P. pulp, paper, & consumer packaging.

volcanic eruption had destroyed valuable timberland and required an extraordinary charge. This too adversely impacted on earnings per share of common stock. Still, as 1980 came to a close, George Weyerhaeuser was cautiously optimistic about the future. He noted, "We believe that 81 will be a more 'normal' year, with interest rates declining to levels that, while high by historical standards, will permit a gradual recovery in home construction."[7]

Notes

1. "The Tree Farm and How It Grew," *Nation's Business*, January 1971, pp. 94-95.
2. Ibid., p. 95.
3. Weyerhaeuser Company, *Policy-General: Company Objective.* August 16, 1971.
4. John G. Mitchell, "The Best of the SOB's," *Audubon,* September 1974, pp. 48-59.
5. Pamela G. Hollie, "Slow Growth for a Giant," *New York Times,* April 20, 1979, p. 9.
6. Company draft statement concerning intentions and use of the Dupont site, June 8, 1979.
7. Weyerhaeuser Company, *Weyerhaeuser Company 1980 Annual Report,* p. 2.

case **20** **Note on the Grocery Industry**

History

1   Prior to the 1920s, the grocery business was probably the least advanced of all retail industries. Separate stores existed for baked goods, meat, fish, and dry foods. It was not until the mid-1920s that the concept of a supermarket emerged so that customers could make all their purchases at one store. The pioneers of the industry included John Hartford of The Great Atlantic & Pacific Tea Company, Inc., Michael Cullen of King Kullen, Barney Kroger of The Great Western Tea Company, and Clarence Saunders of Piggly Wiggly.

2   The year 1932 saw the first time in the industry's history that profits were down. Throughout the Depression years of the 1930s, numerous supermarkets started and went bankrupt. Even then, however, the larger-volume stores were beginning to dominate the scene.

3   By 1939, the corner mom-and-pop grocery store was having difficulty maintaining competitive prices with the high-volume supermarkets. As a result, Congress passed a series of laws with the intent of keeping these larger stores from running the small, family-owned stores out of business.

4   In the 1940s, The Great Atlantic and Pacific Tea Company, Inc. (A&P) forged ahead as the nation's Number 1 food retailer. All chains, however, suffered stock shortages during the war years and had trouble attracting customers from any appreciable distance due to gas rationing. When the war ended grocery sales skyrocketed. Sales for 1947 increased 20 percent

This case was written by William Reese and Larry D. Alexander of Virginia Polytechnic and State University with the assistance of J. Kay Keels of the University of South Carolina. Copyright © 1985 by William Reese and Larry D. Alexander.

from the previous year. Inflation and low levels of unemployment also helped stimulate the demand for groceries.

5   With the 1950s came the introduction of frozen foods and nonfood items and the merging of many of the leading chains as industry consolidation occurred.

6   The early 1960s brought the emergence of the convenience store and the discount store. By 1965, standard supermarkets retaliated by issuing millions of stamps in an effort to boost sales. S&H Green Stamps and Top Value Stamps became a fixture in every family's repertoire of goods to help them stay within their budget. Food prices climbed dramatically in the late 1960s—enough that discounting became the major theme by the decade's end.

7   Rising costs and falling profit margins led to more good price increases in the 1970s. Meat prices climbed so fast that many shoppers began to remove it from their weekly grocery lists. A new concept in store design also emerged. The larger size superstore helped keep prices on food items in line through higher volume and the sale of more high profit, nonfood items.

8   The late 1970s and early 1980s saw an increase in stores' packaging foods in containers featuring their own labels to cut costs. Other retailers attempted more drastic cost-cutting measures by opening no-frills warehouse stores where shoppers marked their own prices and bagged their own groceries but were compensated with lower prices.

9   In the mid 1980s, there seemed to be a pull on grocery stores from each end of the spectrum. On one end, the warehouse stores were trying to see how low they could cut costs by offering the customer only bare necessities. On the other end, the larger chains were offering more and more nonfood items in an effort to build volume with the attraction of one-stop shopping. Each store type seemed to satisfy important niches in the grocery industry.

National Supermarket Chains

10   National chains are perhaps the best-known representatives of the grocery industry. Exhibit 1 shows the top U.S. grocery chains, four of which are profiled in the following paragraphs.

Kroger

11   In January 1983, Kroger became the industry leader in U.S. sales with its acquisition of the Dillon Company. Kroger reached this lofty position primarily through the aggressive store-building campaign it began in 1972 and through its substantial manufacturing capabilities.

Exhibit 1

Leading U.S. grocery chains, 1982

Chain	Sales ($ billion)	Total number of stores
Safeway Stores, Inc.	17.0	2,400
		(1,888 U.S.)
The Kroger Co.............................	11.5	1,258
Lucky Stores, Inc..........................	7.5	1,576
Food store sales	5.0	541
American Stores Co.	7.5	1,100
Food stores		680
Winn-Dixie Stores, Inc..	7.0	1,220
The Great A&P Tea Co., Inc.................	4.7	1,055
The Grand Union Co.	4.0	725
Albertson's, Inc..	3.5	412
Jewel Cos., Inc.............................	5.4	
Food stores	3.4	347
Supermarkets General Corp..................	3.0	
Food stores	2.7	117
Dillon Cos., Inc..	3.0	485
Publix Supermarkets, Inc.	2.6	265
Vons Grocery Co.	2.4	167
Stop & Shop Cos., Inc.	2.2	
Food stores	1.3	125
Giant Food, Inc.	1.9	130
Ralphs Grocery Company	1.3	104
Waldbaum, Inc.	1.5	140

Sources: Newspaper Advertising Bureau: and Kenneth W. Clarfield and Jean Kozlowski, "Supermarkets and Grocery Chains," *Standard & Poor's Industry Surveys* (May 26, 1983), p. R 177.

12   The Kroger Company was founded in 1883 by Barney Kroger, starting as a single store in Cincinnati called The Great Western Tea Company. Barney Kroger headed the business himself until 1928. By then, the chain had spread to several other states and was one of the nation's 10 largest grocery chains.

13   When Kroger entered a second expansion phase in the 1970s, it did so with a clearer idea of what it wanted to accomplish. Because CEO James Herring felt that customers would respond to larger stores with a wider selection of nonfood items, Kroger became the first chain to open superstores. These superstores emphasized one-stop shopping by continually adding new services like delicatessens, wine shops, and floral centers.

14   Kroger stores were heavily concentrated in the midwestern and southeastern portions of the country. Unfortunately, since those areas were hit hard by the 1981-1983 recession, many Kroger stores did not experience the sales growth they had hoped for in the early 1980s.

15   All Kroger stores were unionized. This meant that the company was

forced to pay a premium for its labor. Often, Kroger was the only unionized chain in many of its markets and was forced to make up for higher labor costs with higher store volume. So far, Kroger had been able to do so.

16   In addition to Kroger and Dillon food stores, Kroger owned and operated Super X drug stores, usually located next to Kroger stores. Kroger also operated Barney's warehouse store and Bi-Lo box stores, which were located only in the Cleveland, Ohio, area.

17   Traditionally, Kroger did not offer many of the promotional gimmicks that other chains did, but relied heavily on print advertising and the advertising of its private-label brands. In 1981, Kroger initiated cost-cutter brands, a generic labeling of national and Kroger-manufactured products that offered lower prices than most national brands.

Safeway

18   Although Kroger held the number 1 spot in U.S. sales, Safeway stores sold the most groceries worldwide. With about one fourth of its sales outside the United States, Safeway was the only major U.S. chain to have moved significantly into foreign markets.

19   In the United States, Safeway stores were located in the far western states and in the area surrounding Washington, D.C. These locations proved especially beneficial during the 1981-83 recession, as they included some parts of the country hit least by the resulting unemployment. When high unemployment hit an area, people bought fewer of the high-margin items on which supermarkets had come to depend.

20   Safeway's 2,454 stores were located as follows: 1,919 in the United States, 294 in Canada, 98 in the United Kingdom, 28 in West Germany, and 115 in Australia. In addition to its supermarkets, Safeway operated a series of warehouse food stores called Food Barns and Liquor Barn discount liquor stores located in California and Arizona. The 67 Liquor Barns together with the 700 Safeway stores that carried liquor made Safeway the world's largest retailer of alcoholic beverages.

21   During the mid-1970s, Safeway's management seemed to be led by the conservative influence of its legal department. According to current C.E.O. Peter Magowan, "Safeway adopted the strictest possible interpretation of government antitrust and other regulations. Lawyers nixed plans to create health-food departments in stores because of possible legal hassles over insect infestation. They curtailed advertising of loss leaders because of possible legal exposure if stores ran out of items."[1] Wall Street also recognized the problem. In 1981, Safeway's stock was still selling at the same price for which it sold in 1964.

---

[1]"Safeway Stores: Back to Price Wars for a Company that Played It Too Safe," *Business Week,* April 5, 1982, pp. 108-9.

22   In 1980, Safeway attempted to turn things around by hiring 37-year-old Peter Magowan as chairman and chief executive officer. Magowan's father had guided the company during its growth years of 1955-69, and the company hoped that the son would be equally effective.

23   The younger Magowan immediately curtailed the heavy legal influence by putting retailers in control of the company. The company closed stores that were located too close to other Safeway stores and began opening 100 new superstores per year. These new stores were called superstores because their size was typically in the 40,000- to 60,000-square foot range. Safeway also reorganized its organizational structure, which, according to Magowan, had been "decentralized to a fault."

24   It appeared that Safeway was following Kroger's strategy of 10 years earlier. However, Safeway did take a different route with private-labeled products by concentrating on national brands rather than its own labels. In the early 1980s, Safeway started to regain some of the momentum it lost during the 1970s, and it appeared unlikely that another food chain would take over its number 1 position in the near future.

Winn-Dixie

25   Winn-Dixie's 1,222 grocery stores, including 11 Buddies stores, were located only in the southeastern region of the United States. A third of them were located in Florida alone. The firm began in 1914 with a single store owned by William M. Davis. Davis was one of the first grocery merchants to employ the idea of cash-and-carry grocery stores. His four sons, two of whom were still with the company in the mid-1980s, helped him open 34 Table Supply Stores located in South Florida.

26   In 1944, the company negotiated several mergers that helped it become the fourth largest food retailer in the country. The Table Supply chain's first merger resulted in the Winn & Lovett food stores. The Davis family located their new headquarters in Jacksonville.

27   After World War II ended, Winn & Lovett merged with or acquired Steiden stores in Kentucky, Margaret Ann stores in Florida, Wylie Company stores in Alabama, Penney stores in Mississippi, King stores in Georgia, and the Eden and Ballentine stores in South Carolina. In 1955, when it combined with Dixie Home stores in North and South Carolina, it changed its name to Winn-Dixie. Winn-Dixie went on to acquire the Ketner and Milner stores in North and South Carolina and the Hill stores in Louisiana and Alabama.

28   Through these acquisitions, Winn-Dixie gained many experienced grocery people, some of whom have become its top executives. In contrast, many of its competitors tended to promote managers and executives from only their base companies.

29   Winn-Dixie was slow to move toward the superstore concept. As a result,

many markets were already saturated with regular grocery stores and superstores, and Winn-Dixie had trouble obtaining financing for its own new store construction. So the company changed its strategy in favor of remodeling its existing stores.

30   Winn-Dixie climbed to the number 4 position in sales nationally despite the facts that it was located in a relatively small portion of the country and that it had been built from many small, diverse chains. The synergies resulting from its integration efforts contributed to Winn-Dixie's success.

The Great Atlantic & Pacific Tea Company, Inc. (A&P)

31   The Great Atlantic & Pacific Tea Company, Inc., was established in 1869 by George Hartford. A&P was the oldest chain in the industry, and for many years the firm dwarfed its competition. In the last decade, however, the company suffered substantial losses and was forced to close stores and move out of entire cities. In 1981, the company declared a $231 million loss for the year. Since then, the company has made a desperate attempt to rescue itself from the brink of bankruptcy. But competition from larger chains has made A&P's recovery attempt difficult.

32   Though A&P continued to grow, it always seemed to be responding to strategy moves of competitors rather than initiating change itself. For example, A&P began building supermarkets in 1937 but only in response to King Kullen stores that had already proved to be so successful. The later addition of nonfood items, trading stamps, and the discount approach were all ideas that A&P picked up after someone else in the industry first introduced them.

33   In 1969, A&P's sales of $5.7 billion made it the world's largest food retailing firm. Stores seemed to be located everywhere, and weekly sales topped $100 million. So great was its size and power that A&P influenced all aspects of the food industry from farmers to food processors to wholesalers to competitors.

34   In the early 1970s though, Safeway and Kroger began challenging A&P's number 1 ranking, and in 1972 Safeway passed A&P in total sales. Industry observers blamed A&P's decline on small, poorly located stores, insufficient service, and haphazard sales promotion. Even in the 1980s, A&P stores still had a dull, old-fashioned image that was reinforced by the fact that many of A&P's employees were old.

35   In the spring of 1972, A&P decided to take aggressive action to try to regain its place as the industry leader. It initiated a "Where Economy Originates" (WEO) campaign, a drastic price-slashing move designed to increase market share. The program seemed to be working at first, but the company couldn't maintain profitability with its low prices and consequently had to raise them again.

36   The price wars that the WEO campaign brought about left A&P badly bruised. While all of its attention was focused on prices, unfortunately,

A&P paid little attention to its deteriorating stores. Throughout the late 1970s, sales and profits continued to decline.

37   In 1979, A&P began opening low-overhead Plus stores that carried only a limited assortment of items sold at discount. Unfortunately, these Plus stores were not successful. By 1981, A&P had dropped to fifth place in grocery sales and was forced to discharge a third of its work force.

38   When things seemed darkest for A&P, a bit of good fortune occurred. A $250 million surplus was found in the company's pension fund. As of late 1982, A&P had not yet received the money, but chances looked good that the courts would turn it over to the firm in the next year or so.

39   In 1981, A&P pulled out of Philadelphia. But in 1982, it reopened 18 stores in the city with new labor union contracts. In exchange for getting their jobs back, union members gave back 25 percent of their wages and benefits, a $10 million savings for the company. However, employees gained the right to share in decisions with A&P managers. They would divide 1 percent of the stores' annual sales, but only if labor costs were 10 percent of sales or less. A&P's former Philadelphia labor-cost average had been 15 percent. A&P made this arrangement in hopes that employees would be motivated to treat customers well so that they would remain loyal to A&P. For 1982, A&P posted $32 million in earnings. This was its first year in the black since 1977.

Regional Grocery Chains

Mick-or-Mack

40   Mick-or-Mack food stores were founded in 1927 by Norman MacVay, who ran the business until he died in 1975. In October of 1981, Peter McGoldrick and Conrad Stephanites jointly purchased the company, and in 1983 Stephanites became the chief executive officer.

41   There were only 13 Mick-or-Mack stores, most located in the Roanoke Valley of Virginia. Until August of 1983, two additional stores operated in the small Virginia towns of Blacksburg and Christiansburg. Since Mick-or-Mack was not publicly owned, it did not have to disclose figures on sales and earnings. However, a company spokesman reported that Mick-or-Mack stores averaged $4 million in sales annually. Stores averaged 21,000 square feet in size.

42   When Stephanites and McGoldrick bought the chain, it was not doing well and was not keeping up with new trends in the industry. According to CEO Conrad Stephanites, "Things that were taken for granted by a regional chain, we weren't even doing. We weren't open Sundays, we were still giving stamps, we were not aggressive in price, and our stores were

blah. We were working from a base that was 10 years behind the times."[2]

43   Mick-or-Mack bought its groceries from a wholesaler because there was no advantage to operating its own warehouse to serve just 13 stores. The wholesaler that Mick-or-Mack used was Fleming Company, the number 2 rated wholesaler in the United States.

44   Mick-or-Mack attempted to take advantage of its regional status by emphasizing to its customers that their food dollars were being recycled back into the local economy. The company further attempted to build up its local image by taking part in fund raising for charity events.

45   Mick-or-Mack did not carry as many private-label brands as did Kroger and Winn Dixie, its two biggest local competitors. Instead, it carried a wider assortment of national brands in an attempt to differentiate itself from its rivals.

46   In contrast to their national chain competitors, all Mick-or-Mack stores were nonunionized. In order to preserve this advantage, Mick-or-Mack management offered employees benefits that union contracts would be hard-pressed to match. One example was the Mick-or-Mack fun check. When taking a two-week paid vacation, an employee was paid for three weeks.

Fisher Foods

47   Fisher Foods was another example of a regional chain. It operated the Fazio's regional supermarket chain. As of 1983, there were 40 Fazio's in the Cleveland, Ohio, area and 17 located elsewhere in Ohio.

48   When it first started in 1908, the chain was known as Fisher Brothers Co. It changed its name to Fisher Foods in 1961. During the 1960s, Fisher was a growth-oriented company that did little wrong. It was known for its high-quality meats and other fine food and could afford to operate on a high margin. In 1968, Fisher acquired Dominick's Finer Foods. Dominick's had 71 supermarkets in the Chicago area, and these accounted for much of Fisher's income during the middle and late 1970s. In September 1981, Fisher Foods sold the Dominick's stores for $100 million, a figure which greatly exceeded its book value.

49   Fisher Foods' most publicized developments in the late 1970s came in the courtroom, rather than in the grocery aisles. Fazio's, along with the two other Cleveland-area supermarket chains, was found guilty of fixing prices over two periods during 1976-78. The three chains were ordered to pay collectively a $2 million fine and to distribute $20 million in free groceries to area residents from 1982 to 1987. In 1982, Fisher Foods faced another lawsuit from May Co. for the sum of $180 million. May brought this suit

---

[2]Personal interview with Conrad Stephanites, president of Mick-or-Mack Stores, August 16, 1983, at company headquarters in Roanoke, Virginia.

because Fisher Foods discontinued a trading stamp program for which Fisher had contracted with May.

50   The Fazio's food stores experienced regular growth throughout most of the 1970s, reaching a peak in 1978. However, the company lost $5.3 million in 1979 on a no-frills warehouse venture. Since then, other problems have continued to mount.

51   Fazio's has always tried to project an image of a high-quality, premium-price supermarket. During the inflationary years of the 60s and early 70s, that strategy proved to be quite successful in the suburban areas of northeastern Ohio. Shoppers who wanted to get the best meats and the freshest produce shopped at Fazio's. The image did not appeal to everyone, but it attracted enough customers to allow the company to continue its expansion.

52   With the 1981-1983 recession and the resulting high levels of unemployment (14 percent in Cleveland), shoppers in Fazio's stores became willing to trade some quality for price. With Fazio's resulting drop in sales, losses from its warehouse store, and its legal problems, Fisher Foods experienced a loss for 1982. As a result, the company tried to streamline operations in 1983 by selling nonvital assets to obtain cash needed to move into more favorable markets.

Convenience Stores

53   Convenience stores, typically smaller than grocery stores, carried fewer items, had higher prices, and tried to attract customers by quickly providing supplemental grocery items and extended shopping hours.

54   While large supermarkets targeted their marketing efforts toward women in the 18 to 49 age range, convenience-store customers were typically men from 18 to 35. Since working men had less free time, they used convenience stores as a way to pick up a few needed items quickly. However, as more women entered the work force, they also relied more on the nearby convenience store to supplement their shopping needs.

55   Convenience stores fared exceptionally well in low-income areas though area residents could least afford to pay the higher prices charged by convenience stores. Two reasons for this phenomenon were offered. First, many lower-income people did not own cars and the local convenience store was the closest grocery store to their homes. Second, most supermarket chains were reluctant to build stores in low-income, high-crime urban areas.

56   Grocery items in convenience stores were marked up as high as 30 percent over conventional grocery store prices. Health and beauty aids typically were marked up even higher. The exceptions were milk, bread, beer, and wine. Milk was often sold below cost in an effort to attract customers. Bread, beer, and wine were often priced fairly close to super-

market prices.

57   All the large convenience store chains and most of the small ones were members of the National Association of Convenience Stores. Promotional ideas, new products, and different strategies were openly discussed among representatives of competing chains at various workshops and conventions. In many ways, the association was more like a cooperative effort than firms competing ruthlessly against one another.

58   In the mid-1980s, two major threats faced the convenience stores. The biggest threat was the oil companies who were beginning to sell convenience items at their gas stations. Many stations had 15 to 20 gas pumps, which generated a large daily volume of customer traffic. Furthermore, gas stations got their customers in and out in just a few minutes, just as convenience stores did. When gas stations started selling milk, tobacco products, and bread, most of these customers were drawn away from the convenience stores.

59   The other major threat was large supermarkets that began staying open 24 hours a day. One of the big advantages enjoyed by convenience stores had been their extended hours. However, with the option of shopping late at night at either a convenience store or a supermarket, a customer often chose the lower-priced supermarket. At odd hours, either alternative could provide the same quick service.

60   Surveys showed that convenience stores attracted most customers from a one-mile radius of the store. This meant it was essential that they be located near homes, apartments, or businesses. However, as more and more convenience store chains opened, it became apparent that the successful ones might be firms that would identify neglected products and untapped dimensions of customer service.

Southland Corp. (7-Eleven)

61   The modern day American institution named 7-Eleven was originally named for its long hours of operation, 7 A.M. to 11 P.M. 7-Eleven's sales of $6.76 billion in 1982 made it the nation's 10th largest retailer and its leading convenience store.

62   Over 7,000 7-Eleven stores were located in 42 states, the District of Columbia, and five provinces of Canada and served almost 7 million customers every day. Forty percent of these stores were operated by franchisees and the remainder by managers hired by Southland.

63   7-Eleven stores benefited from putting gasoline pumps in front of its stores. Forty percent of the stores had self-service pumps as of 1983, and gas sales accounted for 26 percent of total store sales.

64   One of Southland's basic strategies with 7-Eleven was to make each store a clone of the rest. One company executive boasted that he could walk into most stores blindfolded and find any item requested.

65   Southland had always been an innovator with its 7-Eleven stores. It was the first grocery chain that had stores open 24 hours. More recently, Southland began opening stores in the inner city, an innovation some industry observers felt might also start a trend.

66   Southland's expansion plans involved opening about 400 new stores around the country each year. However, about 250 stores were closed each year. Though store sites were carefully selected and a net gain of 150 stores occurred each year, it was costly to close so many stores.

67   Southland described its 7-Eleven stores this way:

> Generally, the stores are open every day of the year and are located in neighborhood areas, on main thoroughfares, in shopping centers, or on other sites where they are easily accessible and have ample parking facilities for quick in-and-out shopping. The company emphasizes personal, courteous service and clean, modern stores. The stores attract early and late shoppers, weekend and holiday shoppers, and customers who may need only a few items at any one time and desire rapid service. Typical stores contain approximately 2,400 square feet, carry more than 3,000 items, and have distinctive and easily recognizable facades.[3]

To maintain a modern store appearance, older stores were remodeled by Southland. Most of the items carried were nationally or locally advertised brands. In addition, 7-Eleven stores carried a sizable portion of private-label products.

Silverwood Industries (Hop-In)

68   Silverwood Industries, which operated Hop-In Convenience Stores located in North Carolina, Tennessee, and Virginia, was founded in the mid-1960s by John Hudgins. Hop-In started as a single store in southwestern Virginia with Hudgins as the owner-operator. The number of Hop-In stores grew so rapidly in the 1970s and early 1980s that the company's logo of a rabbit seemed most appropriate.

69   This large regional convenience-store chain was acquired by Silverwood Industries, a publicly owned Canadian firm, in early 1982. Silverwood also owned 700 stores that made up the Max Convenience Stores chain. After this acquisition, Hop-In began to experience some growing pains. Twenty-six of the company's 160 stores were closed due to ongoing losses.

70   Many Hop-Ins had four gas pumps located in front of the store. While little money was made on gas sales, it did help bring customers into the store. Hop-In marketing analyst Lara Nance commented, "Most gas customers only buy gas at the time of the sale; however, they will often return later to buy milk and bread. If they get in the habit of stopping at Hop-In to

---

[3]Southland Corporation, Form 10-K (Washington, D.C.: Securities & Exchange Commission, 1983), pp. 1-2.

buy gas, they'll stop here on their way home to get some higher-margin food items."[4]

71   A typical Hop-In was 2,200 square feet and had sales of $312,000 per year. Those sales were achieved with very little advertising since it was not given a high priority at Hop-In. In fact, advertising was always the first thing to be cut when money was tight. With significantly fewer advertising dollars than 7-Eleven, Hop-In attempted to draw its customers to its stores by offering coffee mugs and bunny bonus cards. Shoppers could collect stamps to get free coffee when they purchased gas. Both of these promotional gimmicks emphasized Hop-In's coffee, which the company felt was one of its biggest assets. They also tried to get business people to stop at Hop-In for coffee on their way to work each day.

72   Since Hop-In did not issue franchises, all stores were run by a store manager and were coordinated out of the headquarters office. Although each Hop-In contained basically the same items on the same shelves, individual managers had requested that their stores be allowed to carry some different items. If the central office approved this request, store managers could modify their offerings to serve their unique customer groups better. This especially might benefit stores located in areas that served different ethnic groups with distinct food wants and needs.

Warehouse Stores

73   In industry surveys taken from 1978 through June 1983, the main reason customers selected or changed grocery stores was price. Good service, friendly employees, and clean stores were nice, but what the shoppers really wanted were low prices. In response, warehouse stores, a totally new type of grocery store, emerged to provide those lower prices.

74   Warehouse stores were quite different from traditional grocery stores. The food was usually stacked in boxes: there were no service clerks, and often customers had to price items themselves. The floors were often concrete instead of tile, and the building had a drab appearance. Some warehouse stores did not supply bags (or else you paid a few cents for each one you used), and there was no one to help carry the groceries out to the car. However, in exchange for these inconveniences, customers saved 10 to 30 percent over traditional supermarket prices on nearly every item in the store.

75   Different warehouse stores met with various levels of success. Some were owned by a major national chain, with the warehouse stores operating under a different name. For example, Kroger ran both the Barney's warehouse store and the Bi-Lo stores, Grand Union operated Basics warehouse

---

[4]Personal interview with Lara Nance, marketing analyst for Hop-In Stores, August 16, 1983, in company headquarters in Roanoke, Virginia.

stores, and Safeway ran the Food Barn stores. These operations had all proven to be successful. On the other hand, A&P's Plus warehouse stores and Fisher Food's Warehouse stores both had to be closed at a financial loss.

76   Despite the setbacks experienced by some warehouse stores, the concept appeared to be firmly established in the industry. By 1983, there were 1,800 warehouse (or depot) stores that had captured 7.4 percent of all grocery sales in the United States. Customers remained loyal due to the warehouse's promise to keep prices down as much as possible. Ninety-two percent of the warehouse customers in one survey expressed satisfaction with their stores and rated them favorably on providing high-quality products, low prices, and product variety. Furthermore, when people were asked why they did not shop at a warehouse store, the number 1 reason given was that there was no such store in their local area.

77   Warehouse-store operators cited a number of reasons for the format's popularity and success. First, such stores were less expensive to build than conventional grocery stores. Second, many stores generated more money per week than did regular grocery stores in the same location. Third, some customers perceived that warehouse stores had the freshest food because their high volume meant quick turnover.

78   Two independent warehouse stores that had been a part of that growing trend were the Warehouse of Groceries in Jeffersonville, Indiana, and Pick 'N Save in Lake Geneva, Wisconsin. The owners of both stores credited their success to keeping prices down while still offering customers essentially what they looked for in a conventional supermarket.

79   One industry observer suggested two factors that kept customers from returning to warehouse stores. One was a dirty, dingy store. The other was a limited selection of products.

80   Pick 'N Save was one warehouse that avoided these two pitfalls. Its stores had a low ceiling, used bright lights, and had a tile floor. Its produce and meat departments were almost on a par with that of the average national chain's. However, cut boxes were stacked 10 feet high or on 86-inch-high warehouse racks to keep stocking costs down. Pick 'N Save's typical 10,000 store items made them comparable to many grocery stores, except their prices were lower.

Basics

81   Basics, a division of Grand Union, operated 19 stores in Florida, Maryland, Virginia, and New Jersey. Basics was a typical warehouse store except that its shelves stocked mostly national label brands, instead of the label of its parent company. Basics described its stores as follows:

82   When customers enter a Basics, they immediately notice that, except for the main produce aisle, the rest of the store follows a different shopping pattern.

Once inside the store, the customers are greeted by endless displays of garden-fresh produce. The produce line consists of some 165 items, as compared to a supermarket selection of about 300. At the tip of the produce aisle is the Basics deli, stocking all of the popular cold cuts. A special slicing machine cuts row after row of cold cuts, and they are bulk displayed. From the deli, the customers walk down a long aisle, spanning the width of the store, filled with fresh meat on one side and a wall of soda on the other. The abbreviated meat section contains all of the traditional favorites, like roasts, chicken, and steaks, but there is no service butcher. Many products are also sold in larger, family packs for added savings.[5]

In addition, Basics stores contained a dairy section, frozen foods, and some general merchandise.

Wholesalers

SuperValu

83   SuperValu, the nation's largest food wholesaler, engaged primarily in selling food and nonfood products on a wholesale basis to independently owned retail food supermarkets throughout most of the United States. About 85 percent of the SuperValu's sales and earnings were from wholesale groceries. Total sales for 1983 were $5.2 billion with net earnings of $68 million.

84   SuperValu operated 16 grocery warehouses and also owned and operated some 111 retail grocery stores. Although SuperValu was called a wholesaler, it saw itself in the retail grocery support business. It provided retail services to 2,345 retail grocery stores. Its services included advertising and sales promotion, consumer research, professional retail training programs, professional retail counseling, management assistance and development, contract negotiation assistance, retail accounting services, retail labor scheduling, merchandising services, insurance services, and tax counseling. In sum, SuperValu helped people operate better supermarkets. It also helped companies find new sites, design and equip new stores, display merchandise, train employees, and write advertisements.

85   SuperValu's success came partly from its ability to help independent retailers improve their bottom-line performance without burdening them with the overhead of a large corporation. Large chains were not as likely to use its services because they did most of these things themselves. Generally, the retailers SuperValu served had no national marketing plan, no single image, and no vertical integration. Still, these independents performed well, earning $1\frac{1}{4}$ percent to 3 percent net profit after taxes and

[5]Grand Union Company, "Grand Stand," March 1983, p. 4.

after paying SuperValu. The average for the grocery industry as a whole was under 1 percent. SuperValu seemed to be in the business of helping independent grocery retailers prosper by beating the chains with its array of expert services.

Co-ops

86   Co-ops usually formed because a group of individuals wanted something that traditional grocery stores in their area did not offer, such as natural foods or low prices. These people opened their own store, operated it themselves, bought their own food, and sold it at their own established prices. Unfortunately, many co-ops lacked grocery expertise and managerial ability, were under-capitalized, and had perpetual cash flow problems.

87   People who shopped at co-ops usually did so because they liked the atmosphere. Generally, co-ops were all self-serve, and customers made purchases in bulk quantities. Some co-op employees would provide free advice on the foods customers were purchasing. Co-ops usually seemed to be more concerned with what people bought than the dollar amount of their order. A customer shopping at a co-op often found no air-conditioning, drab walls, and hand-printed promotional signs.

88   Supermarkets were not necessarily avoided by most co-op customers; most of them did some shopping there anyway. However, as supermarkets expanded to include nutrition and health-food centers, some of the co-ops' customers were drawn away. One Kroger store manager in a city of over a 100,000 people felt that there were over 900 people in that city alone who ate nothing but health foods. He felt that his store would do well if it put in a nutrition center to serve these and other health-conscious customers. The future of co-ops appeared promising. As people became more educated about food, many would be attracted to a co-op for at least part of their nutritional needs.

89   There were two national associations for co-ops—the Consumer Cooperative Alliance located in Ann Arbor, Michigan, and the Consumer League in the United States of America with headquarters in Washington, D.C. Unfortunately, neither association had active members who were willing to work cooperatively.

90   Co-ops seemed to meet the needs of a select group of people. While they did not pose a serious threat to the larger supermarkets, they definitely had carved out a niche in many communities. Approximately 15,000 food co-ops operated in the United States in 1983. Although they served a small percentage of the total public, their combined annual sales still amounted to billions of dollars.

The Roanoke Natural Food Cooperative

91   The Roanoke Natural Food Cooperative was started in 1973 by nine area individuals who felt that the traditional grocery stores in the area did not meet their needs. They formed a co-op which has grown into the largest one operating between Washington, D.C., and Atlanta. However, with gross sales of $400,000 per year and a store with only 3,000 square feet of space, the Roanoke co-op was only a bit larger than a convenience store. It was owned by its 950 shareholders and run by two full-time managers and volunteer workers. The full-time staff received a 32 percent discount on all co-op items in addition to their regular salary.

92   Volunteers who worked 30 or more hours per month at the co-op received a 31 percent discount on all purchases. Those who worked less than 30 hours per month received an 18 percent discount, and those members who chose not to work in the store still were granted a discount of 7 percent. Nonmembers could also shop at the co-op but had to pay full price. Interestingly, 40 percent of the co-op's sales went to nonmembers.

93   The Roanoke co-op had a very simple strategy for setting prices—every item was marked up 47 percent over cost. This was to establish the non-members' price. The co-op did most of its business in natural foods, but also sold books, crafts, and greeting cards. Many of these other items were marked up much more than 47 percent. The foods sold often were not found in a typical grocery store, and customers had to weigh or measure items for themselves. Exotic teas and coffees, spices, nuts, jams, and a limited assortment of fresh produce lined the shelves. Natural junk food and ice cream were popular items.

94   Approximately 170 customers per day shopped at the Roanoke Natural Food Cooperative ranging in age from 17 to 75. Although some customers were people leading alternative lifestyles, others were doctors, lawyers, and business people, all of whom were very concerned about what they ate.

95   The Roanoke co-op purchased its foods from a wide variety of suppliers. Most were large food suppliers on the East Coast. It took time for a co-op to locate good sources of supplies for nontraditional foods, because many of these suppliers did not advertise. All suppliers were carefully screened to ensure that only natural foods were sold in the co-op.

96   The Roanoke co-op advertising was limited compared to that of the supermarket chains, but occasionally ads with coupons were run in the local newspaper. When they had a fair amount of cash on hand, they sometimes promoted a sale on a local AM radio station. Most advertising, though, was done through word of mouth and specialized newsletters sent out by other organizations that were also interested in natural foods.

97   Some of the key characteristics that distinguished these representative firms in the grocery industry are summarized in Exhibit 2. Exhibit 3 shows how the number of chains, independents, and convenience stores has changed during the last 10 years. Exhibit 4 compares store types according to operating characteristics.

Exhibit 2

Key operating characteristics of profiled companies

Name	Corporate headquarters	Primary region	Number of stores	1982 sales (in thousands of dollars)	1982 profits (in thousands of dollars)	Average size of stores (square feet)	Known for
Kroger	Cincinnati, Ohio	Midwest	1,200	$11,901,892	$143,758	36,000	Superstores
Safeway	Oakland, California	Far West	2,454	17,632,821	159,660	28,000	Stores in other countries
A&P	Montvale, New Jersey	North	1,016	4,607,817	31,211	25,000	Struggling for survival
Winn-Dixie	Jacksonville, Florida	Southeast	1,222	6,764,472	103,513	27,000	Mergers
Mick-or-Mack	Roanoke, Virginia	Roanoke, Virginia	13	60,000	n.a.	21,000	A single-city chain
Fisher Foods	Cleveland, Ohio	Northeast Ohio	45	524,328	(176)	30,000	High price, high quality
7-Eleven	Dallas, Texas	United States	7,165	6,756,973	108,051	2,400	Identical stores
Hop-In	Roanoke, Virginia	Virginia, North Carolina, Tennessee	134	80,000	n.a.	2,200	Good coffee
SuperValu	Minneapolis, Minnesota	United States	16 warehouses	5,197,081	68,031	n.a.	Wholesalers
Roanoke Co-op	Roanoke, Virginia	Roanoke, Virginia	1	400	n.a.	3,000	Natural foods

n.a. = not available.

Exhibit 3

Sales and number of food stores, 1973–1982 ($ millions)

Year	Chains		Independents		Convenience stores	
	Sales	*Units*	*Sales*	*Units*	*Sales*	*Units*
1982	125,582	18,330	111,318	104,970	15,100	38,700
1981	119,905	19,070	106,875	108,130	14,120	37,800
1980	108,115	18,700	105,285	112,600	12,400	35,800
1979	93,375	18,725	96,025	116,050	10,000	34,125
1978	84,280	19,350	88,670	117,650	8,710	32,500
1977	76,250	20,930	79,160	124,890	7,380	30,000
1976	71,340	21,550	74,340	134,750	8,300	27,400
1975	66,750	23,080	70,300	143,730	5,480	25,000
1974	61,240	24,190	842,755	151,240	5,320	22,700
1973	52,975	25,025	55,805	154,235	4,350	20,300

Sources: Progressive Grocer; Kenneth W. Clarfield and Jean Kozlowski, "Supermarkets and Grocery Chains," *Standard & Poor's Industry Survey* (1983), p. R 174.

Trends in the Grocery Industry

Store Size and Type

98   The trend in stores has been toward two extremes—low cost and wide selection. The low-cost warehouse stores were beginning to offer some services in addition to lower prices. The superstores and combination stores (grocery and drug stores together or adjacent) continued to increase in size. They also offered more and more nonfood items. Exhibit 5 shows what customers felt was important in choosing a store.

99   *Progressive Grocer* magazine noted trends in store size and type in its 1983 "Annual Report on the Grocery Industry" as follows:

100   The variety of store formats also keeps expanding. Warehouse style outlets, a concept reminiscent of the earliest supermarkets, have flourished recently and carved out substantial market shares in a number of areas. Subtypes ranging from basic bare bones to fashionably frugal are being developed. Hybrids, combining a warehouse core with specialty and boutique perimeters, have been successful.

101   Combination stores are growing in importance as the choice of customers who want one-stop shopping. Convenience stores, providing their own distinct service, now number 38,700 and are going strong. With sales in excess of $15 billion (not counting gasoline), their market share has reached 6 percent. But the star performers are superstores. These 30,000 square-feet and up heavyweights annually take a larger share of total sales and are judged by industry leaders to have the best prospects for future success. At present,

Exhibit 4

Characteristics of various store types

Estimated	Limited assortment store	Warehouse store	Conventional supermarket	Superstore	Combination store	Convenience store
Weekly volume	$65,000	$110,000	$100,000	$230,000 ($150,000 min.)	$270,000 ($150,000 min.)	Gas $15,000 No gas, $6,700
Selling area (sq. ft.)	9,000	18,000	17,000	Min. 30,000	Min. 30,000	2,500
Checkouts	3	7+	7	9+	9+	1+
Employees equivalent	8	26	30	60	60	4
Full-time	3	14	20	40	40	2
Part-time	10	24	20	40	40	4
Gross margin (percent)	12	16	21	23	25	30
Number of items	Under 1,500	1,500-7,500+	8,000-12,000	15,000+	20,000+	3,100
Share of supermarket dollar sales (percent)	1.5	3.1	68.1	23.5	3.8	n.a.
Percent of total supermarkets	2.7	3.3	80.3	12.0	1.7	n.a.

n.a. = not applicable.
Sources: *Progressive Grocer*; Kenneth W. Clarfield and Jean Kozlowski, "Supermarkets and Grocery Chains," *Standard & Poor's Industry Survey* (1983), p. R 176.

Exhibit 5

What's important in choosing a store?

1. Lowest possible prices

| 78.9 percent |

2. Pleasant shopping experience/
   helpful personnel/good service

| 75.3 percent |

3. One-stop shopping

| 72.1 percent |

4. Prices marked on individual
   packages

| 70.0 percent |

5. Store located nearby

| 68.3 percent |

6. Selection or variety of store
   brands and lower-priced products

| 63.6 percent |

7. Finish shopping as quickly as possible

| 54.4 percent |

8. Open late hours

| 43.5 percent |

9. Double coupons or other special
   incentives

| 41.7 percent |

10. Special departments, such as deli
    or bakery

| 38.7 percent |

Note: Each factor was rated as not at all important, slightly important, of medium importance, very important, or extremely important. Answers were converted to scores on a 0-to-100 scale.
Source: Robert Dietrich et al., "What's Important in Choosing a Store," *Progressive Grocer,* October 1981, p. 52.

3,200 superstores account for an estimated 16.5 percent share of the market and 23 percent of supermarket sales.

102   Despite the proliferation of formats, the standard, conventional model still represents 79 percent of all supermarkets and checks out 47.2 percent of total volume (65.7 percent of sales by supermarkets). Its dominance is likely to decline, however. As the American public divides into more and more segments, each with specific buying motives, and as retailers increasingly adopt positioning strategies to attract those segments, undifferentiated stores will find it harder to compete.[6]

103   Exhibit 6 shows the number of each type of store in the United States over the last seven years. As can be seen by viewing the chart, the superstore was by far the most popular type, but the biggest advances over the past few years were made by warehouse stores.

---

[6]Walter H. Heller, "50th Annual Report on the Grocery Industry," *Progressive Grocer,* April 1983, p. 56.

Exhibit 6

Formats: Superstores still lead the pack

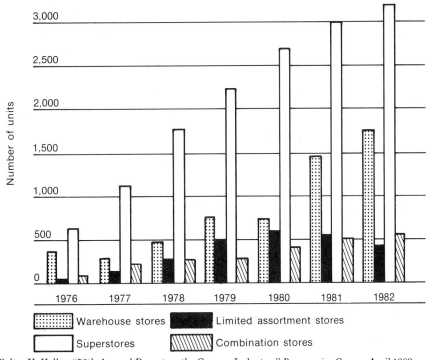

Source: Walter H. Heller, "50th Annual Report on the Grocery Industry," *Progressive Grocer,* April 1983, p. 82.

104   Though warehouse stores were growing in sales and number of stores, superstores, which had only been in vogue since 1975, already outnumbered all other types. By 1981, 75 percent of all new grocery stores constructed in the United States were superstores.

105   A very definite trend for all segments of the industry was longer store hours to satisfy the growing need for more shopping time during evenings and early morning hours. The changing character of the work force justified the extended hours and thus made store operation more cost efficient.

Marketing

106   Over the years, the grocery industry has consistently used newspaper advertising more than any other media, as is shown in Exhibit 7. However, large national chains found that television advertising reached more potential customers than did other media. Newspaper advertising was also

Exhibit 7

Newspapers slip a notch—percent share of advertising budget (independents)

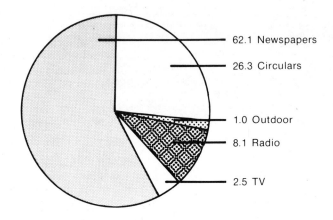

62.1 Newspapers

26.3 Circulars

1.0 Outdoor

8.1 Radio

2.5 TV

Newspapers are far and away the favorite advertising medium of independent operators, garnering 6 of 10 ad dollars from the 68 percent of operators who use them. Compared to the previous year, however, newspapers slipped 4 percent in share of budget and 2 percent in number of operators. The difference went mainly to circulars, which grew 4 percent in share of dollars while increasing 8 percent in number of operators using. Results vary by region, the West is the biggest user of newspapers and TV but the smallest user of circulars.

Source: Walter H. Heller, "50th Annual Report on the Grocery Industry," p. 80.

beginning to decline in popularity due to large drops in the circulations of major newspapers in recent years.

107   Most of the space that food retailers bought in newspapers was devoted to coupons. Couponing emerged in earnest in the mid-1970s and continued in the 1980s as the most widely used food-promotional advertising technique. In 1965, manufacturers distributed 10 billion coupons. In 1982, the figure had increased tenfold to 100 billion. The cost savings for customers who used them was significant. For example, the redeemed value of coupons in 1974 amounted to $220 million, which more than doubled to $550 million by 1979. Although coupons remained popular, other types of games and gimmicks seemed to be on their way out.

108   In the mid-1980s, stores also began emphasizing the size of the sale-per-customer-visit in contrast to earlier years when stores had focused their marketing efforts mostly on getting new customers into the store. With store loyalty on the decline, the concern was with maximizing the number of dollars customers spent once they were in the store.

Product Line

109 More and more shoppers bought house-label brands in the 1980s to save money, even though in the late 1970s, ultra-low-priced generic brands were not well received. Many grocers moved away from them since customers did not trust products that no one claimed. However, they were willing to purchase items with the store's name on it even if it was not a national brand.

110 With customers trading down to many private-label brands, stores increasingly relied on the sale of nonfood items to boost their overall profit margin to an acceptable level. In fact, Kroger and Safeway committed up to 50 percent of the sales space in new stores to nonfood items. Major types of nonfood purchases included housewares, pet supplies, greeting cards, and toys.

111 A major trend in the meat department is seen in declining beef consumption, while chicken sales have continued to grow. Some industry observers speculated that by 1985, chicken would be the primary meat item carried by grocery stores.

112 Other trends included more purchases of fresh produce, health foods, and ethnic items, particularly Hispanic foods.

Market Growth

113 The rapid growth rate that the grocery industry experienced during the late 1970s began to slow down significantly in the early 1980s. High unemployment, less inflation, and a slowdown in the population growth rate all were contributors.

114 While total supermarket sales for grocery items increased steadily during the 1970s, the early 1980s had zero real increases when adjusted for inflation. For 1981, real sales decreased 1.2 percent as compared to 1980. Because of the high interest rates accompanying the 1981-1983 recession, only 270 new stores were built in all of 1982.

Innovation

115 The biggest innovation in the grocery industry in the early 1980s was the large-scale introduction of computer scanners. Approximately 23 percent of all supermarkets, some 6,500 stores, already were using optical scanners by 1980. These computer-assisted devices allowed clerks to check out items more quickly, helped store managers analyze inventory, assisted in shelf-space allocation decisions, and analyzed the effectiveness of various promotional campaigns.

116 The potential uses of the scanner in the near future are promising. As

one Kroger official put it:

> With hand-held micro computers in the aisle, minicomputers in the office, scanning at the front end, electronic ordering and invoicing in the warehouse, sophisticated analysis of item movement, computerized assistance on promotional decisions, and the availability of sensitive programs to fine tune shelf space allocation, the stage is set for extraordinary advances in operating and merchandising precision.[7]

Customer Profile

117   It was announced in July of 1983 that for the first time since 1978, low price had been dethroned as the main reason a customer changed or selected a food store. According to the Food Marketing Institute, the new number 1 reason customers selected a store was because it had a quick checkout. The number 2 reason was its national brand variety. Third was a tie between courteous employees and low prices.

118   Exhibit 8 shows a profile of grocery customers. Regular shoppers were classified according to sex, age, size of household, household income, and education. According to *Progressive Grocer,* the following generalizations could be made:

119   Conventional supermarkets have the oldest, poorest, least-educated customers, a fact which augurs poorly for their long-term prospects. The income patterns of superstore and economy format customers are quite similar, although the latter can claim an edge with better-educated households. In shopping behavior, those who regularly patronize economy format stores are the most compulsive or at least the best organized, reading ads, making lists, and clipping coupons. Shoppers of combination stores are the least likely to shop at drug and discount stores, presumably because their major needs are fulfilled via one stop shopping.

120   The most clear-cut difference among the shopper segments is evidenced by the evaluation of the importance of price marking on individual packages, a practice revered by the older, more-conservative shoppers of conventional stores, but of little importance to shoppers of economy format stores (warehouse stores) who've learned to love the scanner and the precisely annotated register tape it produces.

121   Patrons of economy format stores aren't too satisfied about the store's ambience, its selection of national brands, or some of its departments, but these are the trade-offs they're willing to make for their very high satisfaction with the one thing they're really interested in, everyday (low) pricing.[8]

---

[7]Ibid., p. 60.

[8]Robert Dietrich et al., "Competitive Dynamics in the Marketplace," *Progressive Grocer,* October-December 1981, pp. 51-53.

Exhibit 8

Who shopped where

	Type of store				
Regular shoppers	*Conven-tional*	*Super-store*	*Combi-nation*	*Ware-house*	*Other*
Sex:					
Male	25% +	33% +	22% +	13% +	7% = 100%
Female	25	29	20	17	9
Age:					
Under 25	21	36	16	23	4
25 to 34	13	39	23	20	5
35 to 44	21	35	23	14	7
45 to 64	26	23	10	17	15
65 and over	45	21	18	9	7
Size of household:					
One	33	28	22	10	7
Two	26	29	21	13	11
Three............................	21	33	17	21	8
Four or more	23	29	19	20	9
Household income:					
Under $10,000	56	18	15	8	3
$10,000–$15,000	34	28	12	16	10
$15,000–$25,000	20	33	17	19	11
Over $25,000	10	35	27	18	10
Education:					
Less than high					
school graduate	57	18	5	12	8
High school graduate.............	25	33	16	16	10
Attended college..................	18	34	28	13	7
College graduate	10	27	29	22	12

Source: Robert Dietrich et al., "Customer Profiles—Who Shops Which Format," *Progressive Grocer,* October 1981, pp. 48–49.

122   Exhibit 9 shows the results of a study of persons who shop in two or more different type grocery stores. Men frequented grocery stores that were open late. Coupons generally didn't mean much to them nor did special prices. Warehouse-type stores were preferred more by people with incomes over $15,000 than those in worse economic situations. The more affluent shoppers appreciated a store with special service departments regardless of the prices charged. Few basic differences existed between working women and housewives as to store choice. However, working women did prefer a store that was open late hours. They also liked a complete store so they could avoid going to a second grocery store. On the other hand, housewives were more likely to be influenced by coupons. Younger shoppers liked stores that were open late hours, including convenience stores, and they were more receptive to new grocery innovations, such as generics or in-store drug services.

Exhibit 9

Percent who shop at two or more different-type stores

	Percent naming as regular store	Percent naming as store also shopped in	Total shopping format
Conventional supermarket	25.3	17.1	42.4%
Superstore.............................	29.3	22.8	52.1
Combination store	20.0	19.1	39.1
Warehouse store.........................	16.1	22.7	38.8
Other	4.2	12.3	16.5

Source: Robert Dietrick, et al., "How Formats Fight It Out for Share of Sales," *Progressive Grocer,* November 1981, p. 46, 50, & 52.

Threats to the Grocery Industry

123   Exhibit 10 summarizes how independents and chain grocery store managers rated various problems facing the grocery industry. Some of these threats are discussed below.

Legal/Political

124   Many grocery industry insiders agreed that the two biggest legal/political threats to stores were unit pricing and bottle bills. Many municipalities had passed ordinances that required all grocery stores to mark the sales price on every item in the store. Pressure for the passage of these laws came mostly from senior-citizen groups. Most stores practiced unit pricing, but with the increased use of scanning, there was a tremendous potential reduction in labor cost if hand-stamping every item could be avoided. Price changes could be facilitated by one simple change in the computer. Unfortunately, unit-pricing laws (which required putting the price on every store item) hindered stores from capitalizing on potential productivity increases offered by scanners.

125   Bottle-bill legislation, which was typically enacted at the state level, was designed to reduce highway litter. Proponents of these bills claimed that by placing a mandatory deposit on all beverage containers, people would be less likely to discard them improperly. Where such bills were in effect, merchants that sold cans and bottles served as a recycling center. The grocery industry opposed such bills because it felt that the inconvenience of recycling and paying deposits for disposable containers was an undue hardship.

Exhibit 10

Independent and chain grocery store managers ratings for key problems

Energy costs lead the problem parade

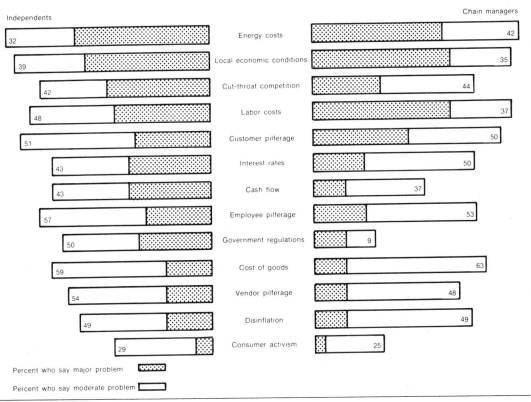

	Independents		Chain managers
Energy costs	32		42
Local economic conditions	39		35
Cut-throat competition	42		44
Labor costs	48		37
Customer pilferage	51		50
Interest rates	43		50
Cash flow	43		37
Employee pilferage	57		53
Government regulations	50		9
Cost of goods	59		63
Vendor pilferage	54		48
Disinflation	49		49
Consumer activism	29		25

Percent who say major problem

Percent who say moderate problem

Source: Kenneth W. Clarfield and Jean Kozlowski, "Supermarkets and Grocery Chains," *Standard and Poor's Industry Surveys* (May 26, 1983), p. R 175.

Costs

126   There was a constant threat that costs would escalate faster than sales. The costs of operating a grocery store continued to rise and many people in the industry were concerned that there was no apparent way to contain these increases.

127   Energy and labor costs were the biggest problems. In 1982, energy costs rose 11 percent, and labor costs rose 6 percent. Exhibit 11 summarizes 1982

Exhibit 11

Going wage rates for independent chains—1982 (dollars per hour)

	Part-time clerk		Full-time clerk		Journeyman meat cutter	
	I	*C*	*I*	*C*	*I*	*C*
Sales volume:						
$2–$4 million	$3.99	$4.53	$4.79	$5.64	$ 7.91	$ 8.52
$4–$8 million	4.31	4.82	5.19	5.97	8.64	9.12
$8–$12 million	4.87	5.93	5.56	6.69	9.45	10.31
$12 million + ...	5.69	5.92	6.48	6.41	10.80	10.83
Region (unweighted):						
North Atlantic	4.21	4.78	4.95	6.04	8.10	9.21
Great Lakes	4.08	5.56	4.96	6.05	8.99	10.69
Plains	4.05	4.66	5.13	6.35	8.71	11.00
South Atlantic	3.77	4.07	4.38	5.16	6.39	7.32
South Central	3.58	4.26	4.31	5.37	7.21	9.05
West	5.84	8.32	6.63	8.38	10.30	11.73
Format:						
Warehouse	4.59	4.93	5.39	5.97	9.00	9.90
Superstore/combo	4.98	5.86	5.60	6.48	9.63	10.89
Average supermarket	$4.21	$5.03	$5.03	$6.08	$ 8.35	$ 9.37

A very regular pattern can be observed in hourly wage rates. Chains average higher wages than independents due to higher organization of the labor force. For both groups the higher the store volume, the higher the wage rate. The West, as always, is far ahead as the region with highest labor costs for chain and independent alike. Lowest wage rates prevail in the South Atlantic for chains and in the South Central for independents. It should be noted that union wages are higher than the all-store averages. For instance, a full-time unionized independent clerk costs $1.58 an hour more than the average for both union and nonunion stores. A union independent journeyman meat cutter costs $2.55 per hour more than the average for independent union and nonunion stores combined.

I = independents. C = chain.

Source: Walter H. Heller, "50th Annual Report on the Grocery Industry," p. 102.

wage rates for key store jobs in various regions and for various store types.

128   Labor costs were highest for the largely unionized chains. In 1982, 54 percent of the clerks and 55 percent of the meat cutters in chains were unionized compared to only 17 percent and 22 percent, respectively, for independent stores. Smaller stores, regional chains, and stores located in the South all tended to be less unionized.

129   Federal legislation was proposed in 1983 that would make labor costs even more critical. This union-backed bill sought to mandate automatic yearly pay increases for workers to protect their real income from decreases due to inflation. In an industry that traditionally paid a fair share of its workers more than the minimum wage, such legislation would burden store owners with locked-in cost increases for labor.

130   Exhibit 12 shows grocery store costs as a percentage of sales over a five-year period. With costs increasing so rapidly, the key difference between

Exhibit 12

Percent various grocery store costs represented (food chains—gross margin, expenses, earnings)

Item	53 Chains 1977-78	46 Chains 1978-79	55 Chains 1979-80	61 Chains 1980-81	50 Chains 1981-82
	Percentage of sales				
Gross margin	21.74	21.50	21.71	22.03	22.32
Expense					
Payroll	12.34	12.23	12.39	12.70	12.66
Supplies	1.03	0.99	1.08	1.07	1.07
Utilities	1.08	1.04	1.04	1.15	1.24
Communications	0.08	0.08	0.07	0.07	0.07
Travel	0.09	0.08	0.09	0.09	0.09
Services purchased	1.29	1.13	1.20	1.14	1.20
Promotional activities	0.40	0.31	0.35	0.32	0.41
Professional services	0.06	0.06	0.07	0.08	0.05
Donations	0.01	0.01	0.01	0.01	0.01
Insurance	0.90	0.88	0.85	0.90	1.02
Taxes and licenses (except on income)	1.00	0.90	0.98	0.94	1.04
Property rentals	1.25	1.13	1.18	1.12	1.20
Equipment rentals	0.18	0.14	0.14	0.17	0.14
Depreciation & amortization	0.69	0.81	0.79	0.88	0.87
Repairs	0.61	0.83	0.59	0.65	0.64
Unclassified	0.97	1.19	1.09	0.90	1.14
Total expense before interest	21.40	20.57	20.84	21.16	21.60
Total interest	0.57	0.61	0.15	0.25	0.19
Total expense (including interest)	21.97	21.18	20.99	21.41	21.79
Net operating profit	0.22d	0.32	0.73	0.62	0.53
Other income or deductions					
Credit for imputed interest	0.41	0.42	0.41	—	—
Cash discounts earned	0.59	0.61	0.52	0.52	0.56
Other revenue, net[1]	0.06	0.34	0.14	0.31	0.34
Total net other income	1.07	1.37	0.66	0.84	0.91
Total net earnings before income taxes	0.84	1.70	1.89	1.46	1.44
Total income taxes	0.33	0.77	0.59	0.57R	0.56
Total net earnings after income taxes	0.51	0.93	0.80	0.89R	0.88
Earnings as % net worth Aftertax earnings	7.48	13.27	11.66	12.55R	11.53
Number of stockturns	12.43	13.54	12.77	13.42	13.59
Sales (in thousands of dollars)					
Average, per store	4,535	5,852	5,864	6,937	8,216
Average, per identical store	4,470	5,906	5,893	6,947	8,199

d = Deficit. R = Revised.
[1]Includes profit or loss on real estate.
Source: Kenneth W. Clarfield and Jean Kozlowski, "Supermarkets and Grocery Chains," *Standard and Poor's Industry Surveys,* May 26, 1983, p. R 182.

successful and unsuccessful stores in the last half of the 1980s would be their ability to control costs.

The Economy

131 During 1983, recession, along with fiscal and monetary policies, produced a sharp drop in the inflation growth rate. Despite this, interest rates remained high , and real interest rates (difference between actual interest rates and the inflation rate) reached historic highs. Many grocery chains and independents found themselves burdened with high costs, but were unable to raise their prices. Profitability was substantially threatened.

132 The economic situation just described is known as disinflation. It was a new situation for grocers. Store owners had been accustomed to high growth in sales and profits, largely due to inflation. Under the current situation, however, they did not have an extra 10 to 12 percent built into their figures.

133 Industry experts were divided in their opinion of how disinflation would affect the grocery industry. Surveys did show, however, that store managers felt the overall economic climate was their biggest worry, followed by energy costs.

Competition

134 Over the years, history has shown that supermarkets, as a group, had a tendency toward self-destruction. Price wars often resulted in store closings for the losers and huge losses for the winners. Industry price wars followed a predictable pattern. A recession slowed down inflation, which caused margins to be reduced; supermarkets attempted to attract their competitors' customers and steal market share; destructive price wars resulted as stores sought to protect their customer base and often, all grocery stores involved lost in the process.

135 The economic climate of the early 1980s seemed to be just right for price wars, but no major wars broke out during 1982 or 1983 since the major chains were showing uncharacteristic restraint. While no one in the industry wanted to take part in a price war, few avoided one if challenged. Kroger CEO Lyle Everingham explained why: "We intend to defend the customer base we worked so hard to get, and this has an effect on the behavior of the more reckless competitors in the marketplace."[9]

136 What made price wars an even more likely and deadly occurrence was the increasing lack of store loyalty among grocery shoppers. One recent study showed that 23 percent of over 800 shoppers interviewed had switched

---

[9]Jonathan Greenberg, "Supermarkets," *Forbes,* January 3, 1983, p.204.

their regular supermarket in the past 12 months. It appeared that the grocery industry's biggest threat was internal. In addition to price wars, a variety of promotional techniques was employed to attract customers. Exhibit 13 summarizes their frequency of use.

The Industry Outlook

137   Despite rising costs, a slowing population growth, and intense competition, industry insiders tended to be optimistic. Most felt that the supermarkets' future prospects looked very bright. The most important determinants would be the ability to adapt to a rapidly changing environment, to find ways to curtail cost increases, and to find creative ways to better satisfy various customer groups.

138   Some industry observers believed that major corporate chains would emphasize super and combination stores and concentrate their activities on markets with enough population density to support them. The smaller-sized regular grocery store would be operated typically by independents and located in outlying sections of big cities or in smaller-sized cities.

139   Conrad Stephanites, Mick-or-Mack's CEO, summed up the industry's

Exhibit 13

Promotion techniques: Small supers, big effort (percent using)

		Total U.S.	$2-$4 million	$4-$8 million	$8-$12 million	$12+ million
Merchandise	Independent	50	50	53	41	38
(Dinnerware, etc.)	Chain	59	55	60	61	56
Bonus (2x) coupons ...	Independent	30	30	30	25	26
	Chain	32	30	32	31	35
Register tapes	Independent	19	17	24	16	19
	Chain	27	26	27	30	31
Games	Independent	24	28	19	12	7
	Chain	26	33	27	16	18
Saver plans..........	Independent	13	15	11	11	7
	Chain	16	23	14	12	12
Trading stamps.......	Independent	12	14	9	7	5
	Chain	15	21	15	11	9
Sweepstakes	Independent	8	9	7	10	5
	Chain	10	13	9	11	10
None of these........	Independent	25	24	25	36	43
	Chain	22	24	21	22	23

Note: About three of four independent managers/owners and chain managers make use of these seven promotional lures, but large variations exist, depending upon store volume. The lowest volume supermarkets, for example, use games, saver plans, and trading stamps at rates two to four times greater than some of the other stores. Note that the larger volume independent supers depend upon these seven techniques the least.
Source: Walter H. Heller, "50th Annual Report on the Grocery Industry," *Progressive Grocer*, April 1983, p. 102.

future prospects by saying, "It is going to have problems, and there are going to be setbacks, but that has been inherent in this business since day 1. It is a business that continually changes, but in some ways, some things never change. People still want clean stores, friendly service, fair prices, and personalized care."

case **21** **7-Eleven Stores: Convenience 24 Hours a Day**

1   There was little doubt in 1984 that Southland's 7-Eleven stores division continued to be very successful. Approximately 85% of Southland's profits were generated by 7-Eleven. Revenues had increased along with earnings per share for the last 22 years. Cash dividends had been declared each of the past 27 years, and the annual dividend rate had been raised 12 times in the past 13 years.

2   Despite this success, 7-Eleven stores were facing heated competition as more firms entered various overlapping segments of the grocery industry. Would 7-Eleven remain the undisputed industry leader and hold on to its 20% share of the convenience store segment? How would 7-Eleven's stores fare against the mini-marts that gas stations were adding to their franchises? Would supermarkets, superstores, and warehouse stores take away sales by appealing to 7-Eleven's customers in different ways? In sum, how would 7-Eleven address a number of significant threats facing it in the 1980s and beyond?

This case was written by Jeremy B. Fox and Larry D. Alexander of the Virginia Polytechnic Institute & State University. Copyright © 1985 by Jeremy B. Fox and Larry D. Alexander.

Company History

3   Joe C. Thompson, Jr., was the predominant figure in Southland corporation's history. He grew up in Dallas and started working for a salary at the age of eight. J. O. Jones, a neighbor who owned the Consumer's Ice Company, initially hired the young Thompson to clean the stalls of the horses that delivered ice throughout the city. After Thompson graduated from the University of Texas at Austin, he went to work full-time at Consumer's Ice in management. In the summer of 1924, Thompson started offering ice cold watermelon to the public at Consumer's ice dock. By 1927, Thompson was in a key position at Consumer's. When the company was acquired in a merger with several other small ice companies, he was given a full directorship in the new Southland Ice Company.

4   During the summer of that same year, the convenience store concept came into realization. J. J. Green, owner of a small ice dock in Dallas began stocking a few grocery items at the urging of a number of customers. As fall came and the demand for ice decreased, he noticed that the demand for his grocery items continued to be strong. He suggested to J. C. Thompson that groceries, which Thompson would buy, be continued through the winter, and the profits be split later in the spring. By the spring of 1928, Southland was $1,000 richer and the idea of the convenience store became a viable reality.

5   The Southland Ice Company also continued to grow by acquiring other small, but successful, ice companies throughout Texas. Grocery shelves were installed at many of their ice docks to further develop the convenience store business. Southland soon acquired Tot'em retail stores, which were clearly identified by an Alaskan totem pole standing by the street.

6   Shortly after being named president of Southland, in 1931, the 30-year-old Thompson had to deal with the company's financial problems. The collapse of an affiliate threw Southland into bankruptcy and Thompson was named receiver. Since Southland was in a fair financial situation itself, the receivership freed it from many hindering interest payments caused by its affiliate's bankruptcy.

7   During the depression years, Thompson and his management team were still able to expand the number of Tot'em Ice and Grocery Stores. In anticipation of further expansion, Southland formed Oak Farms Dairy in 1936 to supply dairy products to the Tot'em stores. Oak Farms also sold to restaurants, hospitals, and grocery chains. Oak Farms initially operated at a loss; however, it became a profitable unit in the Southland group by 1938.

8   By 1939, there were 60 Tot'em stores in the Dallas-Ft. Worth area alone. World War II brought about the building of Hood Army Base in Temple, Texas. Southland bid and won the contract to supply ice to the base. This proved to be a very significant move, one that stabilized the firm's sales.

9   At the conclusion of World War II, Thompson decided to put all of Southland's grocery stores and Tot'em Stores under the 7-Eleven logo. This

name was taken from the extended hours that the stores were open at the time, from 7 a.m. to 11 p.m. The Southland Ice Corporation's name was shortened to Southland Corporation at the same time.

10   Southland expanded beyond Texas in 1954 by opening a store in Miami, Florida. That same year, the firm's operating profits exceeded $1,000,000 for the first time. Up until 1956, 7-Eleven stores were all located in warmer climates, and had an open store front. That year, however, Southland opened its first northern 7-Eleven store. It was located in the Washington, D. C. area and was a fully enclosed building, a necessity in colder climates. This first northern store was such a hit, that 20 new stores were opened in the D. C. area within the next 18 months. This milestone hinted at the potential available to the firm. At the 1958 opening of the 300th 7-Eleven store, Thompson said, "This new shift toward convenience store shopping is not only evident in Texas, Florida, and Washington, D. C.; it will be evident throughout the United States in the years to come."[1]

11   These early milestones for 7-Eleven were preliminary to its later expansion, which paralleled the American population shift to suburbia and exburbia. This caused people to make longer commutes to work by car. With fewer leisure hours, the idea of a convenience store fit perfectly into the American life style, and by 1961, 7-Eleven stores numbered almost 600. During this period, Southland's dairy and ice divisions had also registered strong gains. When Joe C. Thompson died in mid-1961, control of the company was passed to his oldest son, John Thompson.

12   All 7-Elevens were owned by Southland up until 1964. Southland was introduced to franchising, however, with its acquisition of California Speedee Marts, which were all franchised. Southland quickly came to realize that there were advantages associated with franchising. Speedee also brought to Southland new methods of owner training and support for franchisees.

13   Two additional key changes were initiated at 7-Eleven during the 1960s. First, a 7-Eleven store near the University of Texas at Austin freqently started staying open 24 hours a day. This idea spread to many other 7-Eleven stores since the experiment improved the store's sales and profitability. By 1984, approximately 95% of all stores were open 24 hours a day. Second, was the establishment of an electronic, centrally controlled, distribution center in Florida. This started in 1969, but several other centers were added quickly in other regions. These centers helped meet the day-to-day needs of the individual stores in less time and at a lower cost to Southland. Later, Southland started distributing food products to other companies, which by the 1980s, included such firms as Bonanza Steak Houses, Arthur Treacher's, Dunkin' Donuts, Rustler Steak House, and even competing convenience store chains.

14   The number of 7-Eleven stores continued to grow in the 1970s and early 1980s. During 1972, Southland's sales exceeded $1,000,000,000 for the first time. There were 4,114 stores, and its stock had just been listed on the New York Stock Exchange. Between the years 1972 and 1984, approximately

3,000 new stores were opened by Southland in the United States and Canada. In addition, almost 3,000 stores were added in foreign countries.

Southland's Functional Operations

Marketing/Sales

15   Convenience had always been emphasized in Southland's stores. All early 7-Elevens in the southern states featured curb service. It was literally true that a customer could make a purchase without leaving his car. A person came into the old ice dock to buy ice, and the ice was brought out to the vehicle and strapped to the running board. When groceries were added, 7-Eleven decided to provide the same level of convenience. In the 1980s, Southland was still stressing convenience by serving customers who wanted to pick up a few items quickly rather than take more time to go to the supermarket.

16   7-Eleven's products and product lines continued to evolve through the years. Products or services that no longer sold well, such as television tube testing machines, shotgun shells, and cold watermelon were discontinued. Conversely, Southland exploited many new ideas that were profitable. For example, when hot coffee was introduced and proved successful, it wasn't long before other hot items were added. The stores had microwave ovens added by the late 1950s. From its emphasis on hot food to go, Southland had become one of the top dozen or so fast-food outlets in the 1980s. Its position was strengthened with such staggering figures as the 50,000,000 burritos that it sold annually.

17   More recently, Southland became concerned with its stores' image. The image it wanted its stores to project was that of a family store that stood ready to help by providing everyday items for everyday type people. For example, Southland had removed all cigarette rolling paper from its thousands of stores in 1979 to protect its image. Jere Thompson, Southland's President and second son of J. C. Thompson, ordered this action because he felt that in selling the papers the company gave "credibility to the use of drugs, an area in which I don't want my company associated."[2]

18   In July of 1984, 7-Eleven's image was put to a test. Citizens in a small Pennsylvania town picketed their 7-Eleven store for the removal of Playboy type magazines. Southland considered this a significant threat since it was the nation's largest seller of Playboy magazine. After consultation with headquarters, store management complied with the demand and removed all "girlie" type magazines. Southland's top management went along with this decision and viewed it as a test market to determine the effect on the store's image, sales, and profits.

19   Southland initiated various image-building programs that portrayed the firm standing behind America. First, Southland started an annual Jerry Lewis muscular dystrophy fund-raising drive in all of its stores. Second, the firm became one of the top corporate sponsors of the 1984 Olympics. Two new velodromes were constructed for the track bicycling events in Los Angeles at a cost to Southland of over $4 million. In the months before the Olympic Games, its television ads told how various U. S. Olympic hopefuls were getting a chance to become the best because of 7-Eleven's major Olympic sponsorship. Most ads closed by stating that the dream begins with freedom, which clearly sounded very pro-America.

20   In its stores, 7-Eleven still followed J. C. Thompson's philosophy of giving the customer what he wanted when he wanted it. Exhibit 1 shows the major product categories for 7-Eleven stores and their percent of total sales from 1979 through 1983. Each of the new stores was laid out in a similar fashion as other newer 7-Eleven stores, as shown in Exhibit 2. Therefore, a hurried customer knew that if cold soft drinks were stocked in one particular location in his local 7-Eleven, they would also be in that same location in other 7-Eleven stores he might enter. Southland did this so its customers would not waste time trying to locate these items. Southland also stocked only one or two leading brand names for many of its items to help customers quickly decide which brand to purchase. This also helped Southland since its stores averaged only 2,000 square feet compared

Exhibit 1

Major product categories for 7-Eleven Stores and their percent of total sales for 1979–1983

	1983	*1982*	*1981*	*1980*	*1979*
Gasoline	25.5%	25.3%	25.3%	23.0%	17.2%
Tobacco products	13.8	13.1	12.1	12.3	12.9
Beer/Wine	11.8	11.9	11.7	11.7	12.4
Groceries	10.5	10.8	11.5	12.4	12.6
Soft drinks	10.4	9.8	10.0	10.1	10.3
Non-foods	7.5	8.7	8.1	8.0	8.7
Dairy products	5.7	5.9	6.3	6.7	8.4
Other food items	4.6	5.0	5.2	5.6	6.2
Candy	3.9	3.9	4.0	4.0	4.3
Baked goods	3.5	3.0	3.2	3.4	3.8
Health/Beauty aids	2.8	2.6	2.6	2.8	3.2
Total	100.0%	100.0%	100.0%	100.0%	100.0%

Percent convenience store sales (by principal product category)

The Company does not record sales by product lines, but estimates the percentage of convenience store sales by principal product category based upon total store purchases.

From *Southland Corporation 1984 Annual Report*, p. 12.

Exhibit 2

A typical 7-Eleven store floor plan

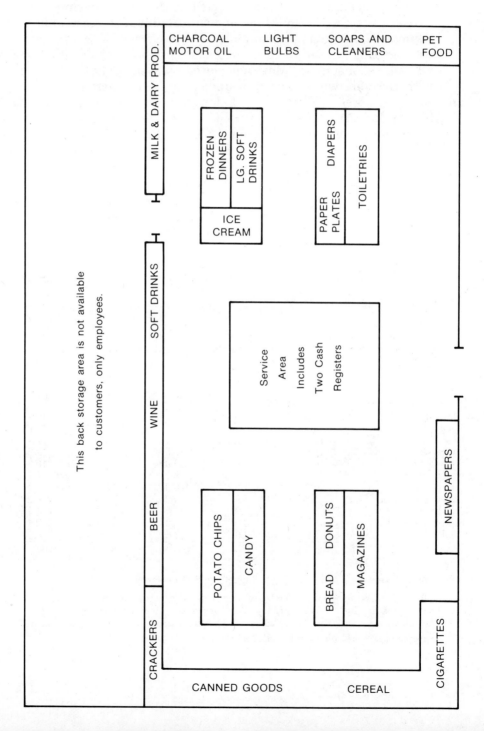

to over 20,000 square feet for most grocery stores. Other products such as beer could be found in a more extensive selection, but the number of brands was still limited.

21   Southland also took action to reduce the number of items carried within a specific brand. For example, while Campbell's made over 20 types of soups, 7-Eleven stocked only the 11 top selling types on its shelves. 7-Eleven stores had previously carried almost all of Campbell's different types of soup. Surprisingly, 7-Eleven found that when it reduced its Campbell's soup offering to the 11 top sellers, its Campbell soup sales went up 19.2%

22   While approximately 950 daily customers got in and out of the average 7-Eleven store, each in only a couple of minutes, they paid a price for that convenience. In general, 7-Eleven had 10% to 30% higher prices for most of its products. However, it equaled supermarket prices for a few staples such as milk. As a leader, 7-Eleven charged lower prices in the 1980s for gasoline than did many of the national gas station chains.

23   Store location was another important marketing element for Southland. Proximity to established neighborhoods, traffic flows on the main arteries, and property costs were major considerations. After the oil embargo of 1974 caused many corner gas stations to close, new 7-Eleven stores were almost always located on corner lots. This change was made because Southland discovered that its corner lot stores typically had 50% more sales than did similar mid-block stores.

24   In September of 1978, 7-Eleven opened a store on Manhattan's east side, which initiated its move into city center stores. Whereas 7-Eleven's earlier stores in the suburbs attracted customers who lived nearby, the city center stores appealed primarily to walk-in traffic from customers who worked nearby. Since then, 7-Eleven city center stores were opened in New York, Philadelphia, Boston, Seattle, and San Francisco.

25   Advertising for Southland and 7-Eleven was handled by the Stanford Agency. Bob Stanford, a Texas radio personality turned advertiser, founded this in-house advertising company. Southland corporation was the first convenience store that used the media for advertising. In 1965, the Stanford Agency helped 7-Eleven successfully introduce the frozen Slurpee drink. Later, it coined the slogan "Thank heaven for 7-Eleven." Stanford Agency's advertising work for other clients, such as its famous "Pepsi Challenge" campaign, helped generate additional profits for Southland. By the 1980s, 7-Eleven still did considerably more advertising in all media than all other convenience stores combined.

26   Advertising was directed primarily at the typical male customer. He was under 35, married with two children, lived less than one mile from the store, and earned in the lower middle income range. The average customer spent only a couple of dollars per trip and came into the store about 1.25 times per week. While this was considered typical among its 7 million daily customers, 7-Eleven had started to include some advertising directed at the growing number of working women.

27   In 1981, Bruce W. Krysiak was named marketing vice president of retail. He immediately started looking for an outside advertising agency that could handle the full-scale network television advertising that was being planned, particularly for the 1984 Olympic Games. Krysiak explained that one reason for this change was that large, national agencies had more bargaining power with the television media; thus, 7-Eleven could get more time for the same money. The Stanford Agency, however, still handled radio, print, and any regional advertising used by the stores.

Operations

28   In 1969, Southland started a small pilot distribution program in Florida that supplied 22 stores. This pilot program was later expanded to establish a massive distribution system that supplied 4,900 7-Eleven stores from just four warehouses by 1983. These warehouses were located in Orlando, Florida; Champaign, Illinois; Fredericksburg, Virginia; and Tyler, Texas. They totaled almost two million square feet of storage space and served 66% of the 7-Eleven stores located in 33 states. A new distribution center was scheduled to open in 1984 in Southern California. Southland's Distribution Center (SDC) operation also supplied products for in-flight meal caterers, several restaurant chains, and even some other convenience store chains.

29   The operation of Southland's sophisticated, computerized distribution centers is shown in Exhibit 3. Individual stores prepared and submitted their orders directly to their respective SDC. Handheld terminals, which read orders from an order book using bar codes, were installed in many 7-Eleven stores in 1982 to make store ordering even easier. This information was then transmitted via telephone to a computer at the SDC which received the store's order. At the SDC, the order filling system was largely automated. Computers helped to decide what to load on which truck and then even determined the route it should travel. Routinely, merchandise arrived within 72 hours at each 7-Eleven store. This quick turnaround permitted stores to place less than case lot orders; thus, they used most of their store space for selling rather than storage.

30   7-Eleven processed its own fast foods at six food centers. These centers produced about 30 different types of sandwiches, pizzas, burritos, and snack cakes for distribution to 7-Eleven stores and its other customers. These centers operated on high volume. For example, they produced 1.3 million gallons of syrup for Slurpee drinks alone in 1982.

31   Operations within each 7-Eleven store tended to follow uniform procedures while still permitting individual store freedom. For example, when new products were introduced by Southland, individual stores could accept or reject them. In reality, most stores accepted these new items because they trusted Southland's marketing expertise, which closely monitored the sales of individual items. The majority of stores used Southland distribution

Exhibit 3

Southland's computerized, sophisticated distribution system

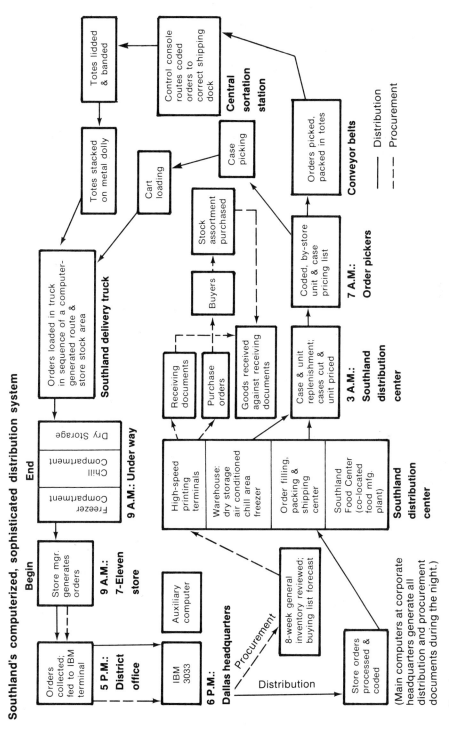

From Anonymous, *Restaurants and Institutions*, October 15, 1981, p. 14.

centers as the source for most of their goods, which made the ordering operation fairly uniform across most stores.

32   Over the years, Southland strove to standardize many items within its 7-Eleven stores. All product wrappers, containers, employee uniforms, and company trucks promoted 7-Eleven with this uniformity. This helped 7-Eleven stores become a familiar and recognized part of American life. In turn, this made stopping at a 7-Eleven an ordinary event for millions of customers.

33   By 1984, approximately 40% of the stores were franchise operations. Store profits were split as follows: 52% for Southland and 48% for the owner. Under this agreement, Southland reserved the right to open new stores at any distance from an existing 7-Eleven store. The average cost of a 7-Eleven franchise was $17,500, which was inexpensive when compared to other chains. Advertising was paid for exclusively by Southland. In addition, while headquarters offered support to an ailing store, it would shut one down rapidly if there was little hope of making the store profitable. As John Thompson bluntly put it, "We won't carry unprofitable stores."[3] For example, while Southland opened 498 new stores in 1983, it also closed 364 stores during that same year.

34   Southland basically turned a ready-to-run store over to each newly trained franchisee. The franchisee paid business licenses, permits, and put up cash equal to the value of the stock in the store. Operating expenses were born by the franchisee. The franchisee was not required to purchase merchandise from Southland or to sell the company's merchandise at its suggested prices. If the store franchise was terminated, Southland repurchased the owner's part of the store stock and equipment.

35   Headquarters monitored a wide variety of potential store problem areas and brought them to the attention of a store manager when warranted. In addition, Southland headquarters was so interested in learning more about store level problems that it established the Managers' Advisory Council. This committee of store managers came to Dallas periodically to exchange views with top management on various operating problems.

36   The expansion of new 7-Eleven stores into several European countries, Japan, and other Pacific areas had not been done by either direct ownership or franchising. Rather, this expansion was accomplished by licensing agreements. These licensed stores had little direct contact with Southland. The agreement basically allowed the licensee to use the 7-Eleven logo in exchange for a fee. The profits from these stores were not included in Southland's earnings statement. Royalties from licensees, however, were reported as other income. There were also eight area licensees in the United States that were treated in a similar financial manner.

Finance/Accounting

37   The consolidated balance sheets for the years ending December 31, 1982 and 1983 are shown in Exhibit 4. The consolidated statement of earnings

Exhibit 4

The Southland Corporation and subsidiaries consolidated balance sheets for the years ending December 31, 1982 and 1983 (in thousands of dollars)

	1983	*1982*
Assets		
Current assets:		
Cash and short-term investments	$ 22,120	$ 34,685
Accounts and notes receivable	476,393	158,217
Inventories	954,916	309,739
Deposits and prepaid expenses	55,257	36,908
Investment in properties	76,200	76,800
Total current assets	1,584,886	616,349
Investments in affiliates	84,280	31,359
Property, plant and equipment	1,437,492	990,925
Capital leases	152,432	168,412
Other assets	50,365	35,209
	$3,309,455	$1,842,254
Liabilities and shareholders' equity		
Current liabilities:		
Commercial paper and notes payable to banks	$ 26,438	$ 11,696
Accounts payable and accrued expenses	908,802	420,294
Income taxes	8,913	43,490
Long-term debt due within one year	42,813	12,052
Capital lease obligations due within one year	15,065	15,805
Total current liabilities	1,002,031	503,337
Deferred credits and other liabilities	106,819	52,589
Long-term debt	940,878	386,304
Capital lease obligations	184,765	196,676
Commitments for operating leases		
Shareholders' equity:		
Preferred stock without par value, authorized 5,000,000 shares in 1983, none issued or outstanding	—	0
Common stock, $.01 par value, authorized 150,000,000 and 40,000,000 shares, issued and outstanding 46,852,348 and 36,106,841 shares	469	361
Additional capital	624,483	347,786
Retained earnings	450,010	355,201
	1,074,962	703,348
	$3,309,455	$1,842,254

From *Southland Corporation 1984 Annual Report,* p. 34.

are shown in Exhibit 5 for 1981–1983. Finally, a financial summary of Southland's business segments is shown in Exhibit 6 for 1981–1983. During 1983, Southland had total revenues of $8,772,067,000 and a net income after taxes of $131,768,000. 7-Eleven stores division represented 76% of Southland's revenues in 1983. As a result, Wall Street tended to assess the

Exhibit 5

The Southland Corporation and subsidiaries consolidated statements of earnings for the years ending December 31, 1981–1983 (dollars in thousands, except per-share data)

	1983	1982	1981
Revenues:			
Net sales	$8,772,067	$6,756,933	$5,693,636
Other income	32,943	25,450	40,524
	8,805,010	6,782,383	5,734,160
Cost of sales and expenses:			
Cost of goods sold	7,177,147	5,350,453	4,454,774
Selling, general and administrative expenses	1,349,574	1,174,886	1,050,073
Interest expense	52,636	27,390	24,539
Imputed interest expense on capital lease obligations	20,638	21,345	23,048
Contributions to Employees' Savings and Profit Sharing Plan	19,426	19,568	16,965
	8,619,421	6,593,642	5,569,399
Earnings before income taxes	185,589	188,741	164,761
Income taxes	53,821	80,690	71,901
Net earnings	$ 131,768	$ 108,051	$ 92,860
Net earnings per share:			
Primary	$3.26	$3.02	$2.61
Fully diluted	$3.21	$2.94	$2.54

From *Southland Corporation 1984 Annual Report*, p. 35.

future of Southland almost entirely upon the outlook for the convenience store industry.

38   Between the years of 1977 and 1980, 50% of capital expenditures and needed working capital were financed from internally generated funds. Southland reinvested 11% of its earnings during this same period, of which about 85% went into the 7-Eleven stores division. Since the vast majority of purchases at 7-Eleven stores were for small dollar amounts, approximately 85% of total sales were cash or check transactions, which were quickly converted to cash.

39   Conservative fiscal policies at Southland were the result of the Great Depression. John Thompson commented, "Early exposure to the Depression era had a lot to do with our understanding of the need to control expenses. We have passed this understanding down to the first-level supervisors."[4]

40   Investors were concerned over the future of Southland during 1980. Southland's common stock price was down dramatically as was its first quarter earnings. At that time, a study prepared for the National Association of Convenience Stores on the industry outlook for the 80s was not

Exhibit 6

Financial summary of Southland's business segments (000s omitted)

	1983	1982	1981
Revenues:			
Stores	$6,693,417	$5,721,099	$5,144,087
Gasoline refining and supply	2,871,339	1,259,493	103,754
Dairies	601,564	584,422	568,560
Special operations	204,017	165,154	140,904
Corporate	11,478	9,031	7,725
	10,381,815	7,739,199	5,965,030
Intersegment revenues:			
Gasoline refining and supply	(1,305,811)	(713,238)	(18,472)
Dairies	(254,968)	(229,833)	(198,329)
Special operations	(16,026)	(13,745)	(14,069)
Consolidated revenues	$8,805,010	$6,782,383	$5,734,160
Operating profits:			
Stores	$ 236,757	$224,916	$ 219,887
Gasoline refining and supply	22,731	23,009	2,994
Dairies	16,998	12,457	13,333
Special operations	1,403	(3,137)	(9,503)
Consolidated operating profits	277,889	257,245	226,711
Equity in earnings of pipeline companies	7,446	—	—
Interest expense	(73,274)	(48,735)	(47,587)
Corporate expense—net	(26,472)	(19,769)	(14,363)
Consolidated earnings before income taxes	$ 185,589	$ 188,741	$ 164,761
Identifiable assets (including capital leases) at December 31:			
Stores	$1,412,029	$1,253,280	$1,216,037
Gasoline refining and supply	1,390,419	139,676	89,472
Dairies	118,778	114,799	120,313
Special operations	111,903	97,122	96,463
Corporate	276,326	237,377	132,313
Total identifiable assets	$3,309,455	$1,842,254	$1,654,598
Capital expenditures (excluding capital leases):			
Stores	$ 190,682	$ 184,677	$ 150,301
Gasoline refining and supply	317,350	15,681	14,700
Dairies	13,686	15,966	14,213
Special operations	15,256	11,164	11,462
Corporate	94,409	109,800	33,215
Total capital expenditures	$ 631,383	$ 337,288	$ 223,891
Depreciation and amortization expense:			
Stores	$ 114,822	$ 99,200	$ 85,009
Gasoline refining and supply	7,282	3,571	203
Dairies	8,966	8,648	7,930
Special operations	6,487	5,327	4,538
Corporate	7,548	4,955	3,151
Total depreciation and amortization expense	$ 145,105	$ 121,701	$ 100,831

From *Southland Corporation 1984 Annual Report,* p. 48.

encouraging. It noted that real sales, adjusted for inflation and not including sales of gasoline, showed no gain whatsoever. However, nationwide sales of gasoline had decreased since the first oil embargo in 1974. The report further stated that Southland's sales gains had come exclusively from gasoline, while traditional sales leaders such as groceries, dairy products, and candy, had shown a decline in sales.

41   Investors were also concerned about Southland's new Chief Auto Parts group, which had some 300 stores. Some investors and company observers did not see any commonality or synergies between the Auto Parts operations and its more profitable 7-Eleven stores. Interestingly, while Southland's 7-Eleven stores competed on the basis of convenience and didn't worry about price, its Chief Auto Parts stores focused primarily on price competition.

42   Although Southland wanted to maintain its annual earnings growth at a 15% level, its earnings grew by about 20% in 1983 alone. Not surprising, Southland announced in January of 1984 a 9.5% dividend rate increase, which was the ninth consecutive year its dividends increased.

Human Resources/Personnel

43   Southland executives frequently referred to themselves as a family. Even its in-house publication that was distributed to its stores was called "Family." The July 1984 issue of that magazine, for example, was devoted to articles describing how Southland was working with recent emigrants to the United States. Southland also helped these people develop the needed skills to work in a 7-Eleven. This program was aimed at Haitians, but it had focused on Vietnamese and Cubans in the past. Clearly, Southland was a strong believer in the American dream, that everyone could have a chance to earn a good living and advance in their job by doing good work.

44   The 7-Eleven stores group employed about 43,738 regular employees and 1,069 temporary or call-in employees in 1983. These represented more than 80% of the employees that worked for Southland. Store personnel were not covered by collective bargaining contracts. In addition, the vast majority of store managers were Southland employees, rather than franchisee owners, a situation that gave headquarters more direct control over store operations. To help stimulate sales, the majority of sales and supervisory staff personnel in 7-Eleven stores were under some form of incentive pay plan.

45   Southland looked after its existing store managers, whether or not they were franchisees. Some 2,600 of the 7,300 7-Eleven stores were operated by franchisees. Southland originally offered a training program to franchisees that introduced them to the actual nuts and bolts of running a store. Recent programs, however, were aimed at also helping store owners become successful small business operators. The program started with a

mandatory 10-to-12 day training program that dealt with real store problems. After these initial topics, other sessions focused on managerial skills needed to increase a store's profits, time management, auditing store performance, and stress management. Southland felt that these and other topics helped bring about better profits for the franchise holder and Southland itself. This training program was initiated by headquarters at the request of a number of independent owners. Unfortunately, even with this preparation, the average store franchisee lasted only five years. Some industry observers felt this was partially due to the long hours that franchise holders and store managers put in, which averaged 80 hours per week.

46   Southland's training program had been taken from one developed by Speedee Mart. When that California chain was acquired in the 1960s, Southland adopted Speedee's training methods by developing its own simulated 7-Eleven store. Real store problems were discussed along with ideas about being in business for oneself. This realism was felt to be invaluable for trainees when they finally started their own stores.

Innovation

47   Southland had always been an innovator. From that day in 1927 when the first additional items were stocked on its ice dock shelves, Southland always looked for new convenience products and services. For example, 7-Eleven tried making money orders available in its stores. This idea was so successful that 7-Eleven was the largest seller of money orders after the post office in 1983. While 7-Eleven welcomed innovation, products and services that did not work out were dropped quickly.

48   Southland introduced a number of innovations in its 7-Eleven stores over the years. One such innovation was its extended store hours, from 7 a.m. to 11 p.m. Clearly, being open whenever customers wanted to make a purchase helped in 7-Eleven's efforts to provide convenience to its customers. Later on, most 7-Eleven stores extended their hours so they were open 24 hours a day. Another innovation was a willingness to expand from just a Texas operation to a national chain of convenience stores.

49   A major innovation at 7-Eleven stores was installing gasoline pumps outside many of their stores. This was a unique move at the time for a chain of small grocery stores. Yet, by September of 1983, Southland became the nation's largest, independent gasoline retailer when it purchased Citgo Petroleum from Occidental Petroleum. This was done to secure a reliable source of gasoline.

50   The gasoline pumps innovation accounted for 25% of 7-Eleven's sales from 1981 through 1983. Although gasoline sales accounted for only 8% of Southland's profits, 34% of the gasoline customers also made other purchases when they went inside the store to pay for their gas. Thus, the real

innovation with gasoline perhaps was pricing it lower than many national gas stations so that it drew customers into 7-Eleven stores to purchase higher-priced convenience items.

51   By 1984, automatic teller machines (ATMs) had been installed at 1,680 7-Eleven stores. These ATMs provided 7-Eleven with a monthly rental fee from the bank and an additional transaction-based fee. J. P. Thompson, Southland's Chairman, felt that the machines followed the public shift towards more convenience products and services, including self-service ones.

52   Southland's entry into the food distribution through its warehouses was innovative for a convenience store chain. It helped reduce its dependency on independent suppliers. It also turned a cost center into a profit center and made profits on sales to other retail firms. Sales to these outside concerns increased 50% in 1983 alone, pushing sales of the distribution centers to over $1 billion for the first time.

Management

53   Southland's management team throughout the decades had been family run. With the death of Joe Thompson, Sr., in 1961, some industry analysts felt that the company might undergo significant changes. However, this did not occur. With John Thompson, as chairman of the board and chief executive officer, and Jere Thompson, as president, the original Thompson philosophy was well maintained. In fact, many actions taken since Joe Thompson's death appeared to be very consistent with what he might have done himself.

54   Management at Southland practiced promotion from within. Thus, loyal, competent employees were almost always moved up into management positions rather than bringing in outsiders unfamiliar with 7-Eleven. In fact, 24 of the top 29 people in corporate management in 1984 had been with the company for at least ten years.

55   When there was a need for some hard-to-find expertise, however, Southland did not hesitate to hire someone from the outside. For example, when Southland decided to create its distribution centers, to gain the needed expertise, it hired Joseph S. Hardin, head of the U. S. Army's P. X. system. A major task he initially focused on was the establishment of the electronic data processing component of the distribution system. He even hired other outsiders that he felt were needed to handle the day-to-day workings of the data processing system.

Security

56   Security was a particular problem at the average 7-Eleven. With the typical store open 24 hours a day, a lone clerk with a cash register full of money

was a very attractive target for potential robbers. One clerk, working the night shift, reported first selling rope to two customers who then used it to tie him up in the cooler and rob the store at gun point. In one year during the 1970s, Southland had over 17,000 robberies at its 7-Eleven stores.

57   Southland sought help from a consultant that specialized in robberies. He made a number of changes in day and night operations in its stores. Signs in store windows were removed so the cash register could be seen from the street. Taxis were encouraged to use 7-Eleven parking lots and thereby discourage crime in its stores. Training films were shown to 7-Eleven employees dealing with the topic of robberies and security. Most importantly, Southland installed a timed access safe in each store called Tidel. These safes accepted deposits and dispensed money in only small quantities after a programmed amount of time had elapsed.

58   These measures were very successful in cutting robberies. Between 1976 and 1980, the number of robberies was cut about in half, and the average amount stolen dropped from $200 to $66. Tidel was so successful that Southland set it up as a separate division for use by its 7-Eleven stores and outside businesses. Southland also created a robbery prevention kit, which contained training materials, that was sold to the public and other convenience stores for $10.

The Task Environment

59   The convenience store industry was actually considered to be a segment of the grocery industry. A convenience store could be defined as an extended hours retail store that got customers in and out of it quickly, but charged higher prices on most items than did supermarkets. Convenience stores provided groceries, take-out food and beverages, gasoline, dairy products, nonfood merchandise, specialty items, and incidental services.

60   Convenience stores were facing a growing array of different competitors. They were forced to compete with a variety of national, regional, and independent grocery stores in most cities where they operated. Furthermore, their expanded offerings into nonfood items meant the stores competed directly with various discount retail stores, such as K mart and drug stores. Similarly, their hot foods also meant the stores competed directly with a whole host of fast-food restaurants. Finally, they were now competing with their mirror image, gas stations that had added food stores. Clearly, competition had become more intense; furthermore, it was coming from a number of different, overlapping industries.

61   The convenience store segment of the grocery industry faced a periodic common problem or threat. It was the U. S. economy. When the economy was performing poorly, more and more people started going to grocery stores for all of their food needs. While they still liked convenience, they were forced to protect their financial resources by searching out the lowest

possible prices for food items. While past economic downturns had not significantly hurt the convenience industry, they had slowed the market growth rate during those periods. However, when the construction of new housing was in a downturn, there had been a corresponding downturn in convenience store sales. This was due to construction workers out spending money and fewer suburbs being built for convenience stores to expand into. If future economic downturns come more frequently or last longer, then the convenience store industry could be damaged.

62   The stronger the local market, the less likely a downturn in the economy would have an adverse impact. Irrespective of the health of the economy, most convenience stores continued to stress the idea of convenience to their customers. This meant that the store needed to be in a readily accessible location; the store needed an appropriate range of products (usually this meant little depth) and long business hours. Most successful convenience stores stayed open 24 hours in the 1980s and had attempted to get corner lots on busy two-way streets. Many stores had added gasoline pumps since it spurred sales of other items as well as provided up to $1,000 per month in profits from gas sales alone.

63   Two of 7-Eleven's competitors in the convenience stores segment are worth examining. While these chains were not nearly the same size as 7-Eleven, they did represent a loss of customers. However, as recently as 1978, Southland had sales greater than twice the total sales of the next eight chains.

64   Munford Inc. was the only other convenience store chain listed on the New York Stock Exchange. The company operated and franchised Majik Markets stores which seemed to be staggering until 1981. Then, Munford took corrective action by closing marginal stores and relocating Majik Markets stores to high volume gasoline locations. Because of these actions, there was a healthy increase in earnings. Its earnings per share went from $.16 in 1980 to $2.07 just two years later.

65   Munford was planning a steady expansion of stores, which amounted to some 900 new stores in 1983. There had been no word, however, whether expansion to areas outside Florida and Georgia would be attempted.

66   Circle K convenience stores, like Southland and Munford, espoused the idea of linking convenience stores with gasoline sales. Furthermore, this Phoenix-based firm, which operated in twelve western states, was going about this linking in much the same way as was Southland. Thus, gas pumps were installed at existing convenience stores.

Threats to 7-Eleven

67   One of the biggest threats to 7-Eleven's well-being was the many gas stations that were converting their service bays into convenience stores. The building and necessary space was already there to make the convenience store. Thus, it was easier and cheaper to add convenience foods to

a gas station than to do the opposite. For one thing, it cost approximately $80,000 to add gas pumps and storage tanks to an existing convenience store, as 7-Eleven did. In addition, most gas station self-service customers were used to going into the station anyway to pay for their gas. Once inside, they could easily get a few needed items before continuing on their way. By 1982, six oil companies had about 2,000 convenience stores attached to their stations, while 2,800 7-Eleven stores had gas pumps.

68   Southland's Citgo refinery represented another threat. If gas sales at 7-Eleven stores were to decline significantly in the future, Southland would be hurt by its backward vertical integration move into oil refining. Furthermore, if gas sales declined, it would have an adverse impact on impulse items that were marked up much more than was gasoline. Thus, Southland had come to count on gasoline sales to keep up store performance.

69   Still another threat was supermarkets remaining open 24 hours per day. The fact that, over the years, 7-Elevens had been one of the few businesses open around the clock was a big reason why people went to them. However, in the 1980s a customer, late at night, could choose to go to a 24-hour supermarket, with a larger brand selection, and get almost any item cheaper without facing any delay at the checkout counter at that hour. This was obviously cutting into the oddball-hour customer base of 7-Eleven and represented a factor that could continue to hurt 7-Eleven increasingly.

70   Another threat facing Southland was its publicized tax bribery trial that was litigated in New York in 1984. Apparently a company employee, hoping to save Southland a $1,000,000 back tax bill, tried to bribe a New York state tax official. The legal issues concerned questions of (1) whether there was actually a conspiracy to bribe and (2) whether Southland's corporate management was aware of the attempted bribe.

71   The resulting conviction on June 11th of 1984 made the corporation a felon. In most states that 7-Eleven operated in, felons were not allowed to hold licenses to sell beer or wine, which not only represented 12% of its sales, but also helped to stimulate the sales of related items. However, Southland felt that the conviction might not have a major impact on the company. Still, it remained to be seen if individual states would place Southland's liquor licenses in jeopardy.

Possible New Product/Market Opportunities

72   Over the years, Southland Company had tried, or at least considered, a number of different opportunities. Through acquisition or new start-up ventures, the stores group had tried hardware stores in the late 1950s, candy manufacturing (Lofts and Barriccini brands), and grocery stores (Gristede's still operated 124 stores in the New York City area), department stores (Thomas and Hart), and gasoline stations (Super Seven stations on

the west coast). In the 7-Eleven stores themselves, the company had already tried everything from television tube testing machines to garden seeds, from Slurpees to film processing, and from automatic teller machines to cancer insurance. Some worked well, while others failed miserably.

73   One major opportunity for 7-Eleven stores would be to begin keying in on the woman of the house, who traditionally shopped at the supermarket. While its strength with men should not be ignored, women might be attracted to convenience stores by a different mix of products. Southland could advertise the fact that 7-Eleven had what women were looking for when doing last minute shopping. For example, a *Progressive Grocer's* survey identified that the five most important ways women chose a super-market were (1) cleanliness, (2) prices clearly marked, (3) low prices, (4) accurate and pleasant checkout clerks, and (5) freshness date marked on products.[5] 7-Eleven could match most of these requirements except price. Furthermore, if the price was kept low on key grocery products and adver-tised as such, perhaps even this factor could be partially overcome. This was not to suggest that 7-Eleven would become the Saturday grocery mecca for women; however, satisfying these five important considerations could help siphon off some customers from supermarkets during the week.

74   7-Eleven might add new services to its stores. Local 7-Eleven stores could serve as convenient bill paying centers for common utility and city bills. These unstamped envelopes could be left inside a 7-Eleven store for a small fee. Perhaps it could be done for free just to generate sales on other items. The store could then gather them, sort them, and deliver them daily to the respective utilities.

75   By the same token, 7-Elevens could be a drop for packages being delivered by one of the overnight freight services. Since the freight company would make one stop to pick up several packages, they might charge less, allow-ing room for 7-Eleven to make a small profit. Perhaps delivery at the other end could also be to the neighborhood 7-Eleven store. This might be even more convenient, particularly when the receiving party was not at home during delivery hours.

76   With the emphasis that 7-Eleven puts on fast food, the company might bring out a microwave-ready package of French fries. Southland could work out an agreement with one of the processed potato companies to develop a product that would equal the quality of French fries available at the local fast-food chains. This could be made available in single servings at a competitive price. If it were successful, then other fast-food menu items could be added later on.

77   Along the same line, 7-Eleven could sell a frozen solid milkshake, avail-able in popular flavors. The product could be thawed in the microwave to a cold, but drinkable consistency. Preparation of the drink would be at a food processing center, shipped by one of Southland's delivery trucks, and

placed in the freezer compartment at the store. Little work by the clerk would be necessary, compared to the work required by the very popular slurpee drink.

78   Southland's stores division also operated the Gristede's grocery chain of 50 stores in the New York City area. The company could expand this chain to other East Coast metropolitan areas. These stores, which offered premium quality groceries, might be seen as a good compliment to existing 7-Eleven stores. Expanding into more full-scale grocery stores might help Southland compete directly against the supermarket chains.

79   In 1977 John Thompson noted, "We're thinking about adding pharmacy items."[6] But the idea never got off the ground. However, if an all-hours pharmacy could somehow be established in 7-Eleven stores, it might help win the mother of the house over to its convenience stores. The biggest obstacle would be how to process prescription items that would require a doctor's signature, since a licensed pharmacist would have to fill the prescription. Still, the idea might be workable.

80   Still another opportunity would be to appeal to nontypical customers. Since 7-Eleven stores appealed to younger and middle-aged men, this clearly suggested that there remained a large untouched customer base that was being ignored or at best poorly served. For example, older citizens were not shopping very frequently at these stores. Women were another nontypical customer for 7-Eleven stores. Perhaps women could be grouped by age to identify patterns and preferences in product offerings. Young school children were another nontypical customer group that might be exploited. Finally, perhaps Southland could more effectively cater to the concentrations of various minority groups living in major metropolitan areas of the United States.

81   Over the years, 7-Eleven had succeeded in building a solid business on people spending only a few dollars on an average visit. The nature of the store and pricing structure made it difficult to raise that figure significantly. However, with an increase in store traffic, larger overall sales figures could be generated and increased pressure could be placed on the competition by taking away their potential customers. Both these ends were desirable as 7-Eleven considered which opportunities to pursue in the mid-1980s and beyond.

Concluding Note

82   While 7-Eleven had been very successful in previous decades, the 1980s and beyond would probably not be as hospitable. The numerous competitive threats facing it from different store formats might make a significant dent in its sales and profits. 7-Eleven's success, in part, will rest upon its

ability to keep identifying and exploiting new products and services people want in a convenience store. In addition, its future success will also rest upon its ability to develop appropriate responses to a variety of competitive threats, from mini-marts to superstores to warehouses.

Notes

1. Allen Liles, *Oh Thank Heaven!* (Dallas: The Southland Corporation, 1977), p. 117.
2. *The Wall Street Journal,* Sept. 13, 1979, p. 1.
3. "Convenience stores: A $7.4 billion mushroom," *Business Week,* March 21, 1977, p. 64.
4. *Restaurants and Institutions,* October 15, 1981, p. 33.
5. "42 ways to choose a super," *Progressive Grocer,* May, 1984, p. 58.
6. "Convenience stores: A $7.4 billion mushroom," *Business Week,* March 21, 1977, p. 64.

case 22 A&P's James Wood Tries to Turn Grandma Around

1   The Great Atlantic and Pacific Tea Company, Inc. (A&P) was still thought of by many as an American institution. Although A&P had faced many problems over the last couple of decades, the firm was showing signs of rejuvenation in the 1980s. With 1983 sales of $5,222,013,000 and profits of $47,551,000, A&P had completed eight consecutive quarters of profitability. While many competitors had long since written A&P off as a major force to contend with, the gray old lady of the grocery industry was starting to regain her strength.

2   James Wood had taken a number of steps to turn around A&P's performance since becoming its chief executive officer in 1980. So far, many of them had proven to be successful. Further actions obviously needed to be taken to prevent A&P from sliding back to its dismal performance of past years. A number of key questions needed to be addressed. Which store formats should A&P concentrate on? How should it try to reduce further its high operating costs? Should the unions be asked to make further concessions or will this provoke a strike? How should A&P counteract the superstores and warehouses? These and countless other questions need to be considered before A&P can determine which further steps will best help it continue its initially successful turnaround strategy.

   This case was written by Gregory P. Watson and Larry D. Alexander of Virginia Polytechnic Institute and State University. Copyright © 1985 by Gregory P. Watson and Larry D. Alexander.

History

3   In 1859, George F. Gilman, with the help of his sole employee, George Hartford, started importing tea as a sideline product for his leather shop in New York City. With the advent of the clipper ship, which traveled twice as fast as the traditional sailing ships, they were able to slash tea prices by 50% on shiploads imported from China. At that price, tea soon became the mainline product of Gilman's leather shop.

4   By 1864, the main store had been relocated and several other stores added in the Wall Street and Lower Broadway areas of New York City. In addition, the name had been changed to The Great American Tea Company. The stores were decorated with crystal chandeliers, red, white, and blue gas lights out front, gilt-edged Chinese panels on the walls, and a cockatoo to welcome the customers. However, even with all this decor, the main lure was still the low prices on the various blends of tea.

5   In 1869, the firm was incorporated under its present name in order to separate it from the mail-order tea business that had been started. The Great Atlantic and Pacific Tea Company, Inc. was the name chosen in celebration of the joining of the Atlantic and Pacific Oceans by railroad.

6   The company later expanded into other states. It reached as far west as St. Paul, Minnesota and as far south as Norfolk, Virginia. Much of the success was due to the innovative marketing strategy of offering gifts to each customer visiting the stores and to the brass bands that played in front of the main store every Saturday.

7   In 1878, George Gilman retired from his duties, leaving Hartford with exclusive management responsibility of the million-dollar-a-year business. Soon, two of Hartford's five children, George and John, started working for the company. Mr. George, as he was called by A&P employees, was known for his conservatism and financial genius. Mr. John was known for his ability to merchandise and to communicate with people. Together, the two sons and their father made a very good team.

8   By 1900, A&P had sales of $5,600,000 and operated nearly 200 stores. It also had a growing wagon route system that sold door to door and introduced rural customers to A&P. When credit was introduced, its merchandise lines expanded rapidly. Still, low prices remained the primary attention getter.

9   When sales had grown to $23,600,000 and stores to 480 in 1912, Mr. John persuaded his father and his brother George to try a cash-and-carry economy type store. With the rising cost of living and the public unrest about grocery prices, Mr. John felt this approach might allow them to reduce prices further and rely more on volume. The first store was received by the public with such success that A&P soon began opening other similar stores by the hundreds each year. By 1916, sales had risen to $76,000,000 and A&P had 2,000 stores located in 29 states. Later, in 1925, A&P's sales totaled $440,000,000 and its stores numbered a staggering 14,000.

leaving the ownership of the company to his grandchildren; however, Mr. George and Mr. John retained all administrative power. however, Mr. George becoming the chairman of the board and Mr. John the company's president.

11   The two brothers made major changes at A&P in their new leadership roles. They decentralized the company into five geographical divisions and established several buying offices throughout the country. This action was taken when they realized A&P had become too large to run entirely from corporate headquarters. In addition, the firm moved into manufacturing to give its customers better value. Stores were enlarged and new product lines added. For example, the stores started carrying produce, fresh meat, and expanded their dairy offerings. Over time, however, A&P stores changed from economy to combination stores with still some emphasis on low prices.

12   With the widespread use of the automobile, consumers increasingly drove past their nearby independent grocery stores to shop at lower-priced chain stores. This quickly started hurting sales of many of A&P's smaller competitors. These independents countered by lobbying the U. S. Congress. As a result of this and other pressures, the Robinson-Patman Act was passed in 1936. In part, this act further restricted firms from acquiring, or merging with, other firms within the same industry. As a result of this act's passage, A&P started to manufacture more of its own products. It also started purchasing more from smaller manufacturers to avoid violating the act.

13   Even that action by A&P did not keep it out of legal entanglements. The Antitrust Division of the U. S. Department of Justice filed suit against A&P in 1942, charging it with criminal violation of antitrust laws. After 12 years of litigation, however, A&P was fined only $175,000. Still, the ordeal had cost the firm millions for its defense. To be on the safe side, A&P started manufacturing even more of its products to avoid further lawsuits. A&P even avoided taking any quantity discounts when buying national brand products. In sum, it was fearful of doing anything that might give the appearance of combination in restraint of trade which various laws prohibited.

14   Mr. John died in 1951 and then Mr. George followed him in 1957. Soon thereafter, A&P's family-owned business became a public corporation. Ralph Burger, a long time A&P executive and friend of the Hartfords', took over as both the chairman of the board and president of the Hartford Foundation. That foundation held all of Mr. John's and Mr. George's A&P stock.

15   In the early 1960s, A&P's profits and sales began to level off, but it continued paying large dividends and put little back into store development. By the end of the decade, profits had turned to losses. Since then, the company's financial performance has been inconsistent, with profitable years few and far between.

16   In 1973, Safeway stores took over as the number one sales leader in the supermarket industry, moving A&P to the number two spot. In 1975, A&P started a major consolidation program, and by 1984 was operating only about one quarter of the stores that existed when Mr. George died. In 1979, Karl Haub, a German grocer, bought out A&P stock held by the Hartford Foundation and one other heir of George Hartford, Sr. As a result, Haub owned 50.7% of the chain's stock.

Management

17   Up until 1974, all top management officials had worked their way up through the ranks from local stores. That year, however, A&P's board felt pressure from its large stockholders to look outside the company for fresh leadership. This pressure stemmed from the reality that four different internally promoted men had been A&P C.E.O.'s since 1965 alone. Furthermore, A&P's troubles had steadily worsened during those years. Much of the pressure the board felt came from the John Hartford Foundation. This foundation owned 33% of A&P's stock and its board included many past A&P executives, who had been very complacent. More recently, however, the restructured board included a majority of men who had no connection with A&P.

18   In late 1974, Booz, Allen, and Hamilton, a leading management consultant group, recommended A&P make Jonathan Scott an offer to become chief executive officer. Previously, Scott had been a very successful C.E.O. at Albertson's, where he was known as an innovator and team builder. As A&P's C.E.O., he quickly identified many problems that the grocery chain had and set out to address them. Because he was a firm believer in decentralized management, he allowed store managers to make their own decisions about how to market their own merchandise and what private label goods to carry. Unfortunately, this freedom was something that A&P managers were unaccustomed to, and it proved to be harmful.

19   Scott lured away many senior executives from other grocery chains, including Albertson's. By 1977, Scott had appointed 28 out of 46 top managers from outside of A&P. Thus, promotion from within as a management policy was being de-emphasized. In addition, many of A&P's past top managers were demoted down to regional level management.

20   Scott's obvious goal was to turn A&P around. Unfortunately, several of his major changes were being ignored by A&P managers, who were to implement them. Some industry observers felt that Scott's biggest problem was that he was too nice a guy. They felt he was not tough enough to get his programs really implemented at A&P. In April of 1980, Scott resigned to start his own investment firm in Texas.

21   The search process for Scott's replacement weeded down the candidates to James Wood, the C.E.O. at Grand Union grocery chain. Several industry observers portrayed Wood as a veteran turnaround artist, because of his

recent success at Grand Union, another leading national chain. Karl Haub, A&P's major stockholder, was a major force behind getting Wood to become A&P's C.E.O. Wood's lucrative five-year contract included $300,000 to transfer, $400,000-a-year salary, a potential annual bonus of up to $300,000, and an option to buy 10% of Haub's personal stock in A&P at $4 per share.

22   Wood immediately started to change A&P's organization structure. Within two months, he combined the buying and merchandising functions at the corporate level. This made the same person who purchased the merchandise also responsible for setting policies on how the merchandise would be sold in the stores. He also formed nine different geographic groups that would order, market, and merchandise for a number of divisions. The functional managers in these geographic groups reported directly to the vice president of their own geographic group. At the same time, they also indirectly answered to their respective functional managers at the corporate level. Prior to this change, each of the 19 operating divisions did its own merchandising and buying while also handling day-to-day operations. Exhibit 1 shows a simplified organizational chart of A&P after Wood made his initial management changes.

23   Since Wood retained almost all of the top managers from Scott's era, this reorganization met with a great deal of resistance. Later, when Wood assumed a more forceful stand, several of his top managers resigned, enabling him to implement his reorganization more easily. By 1984, Wood had replaced many of these top level managers with executives from outside of the organization.

24   Wood also increased the number of operating divisions that made up the nine geographical regions from 19 to 27. Before the change, the individual divisions had anywhere from 27 to 130 stores. Under the new plan, the biggest division had just over twice as many stores as the smallest division, 71 to 31 stores. Wood undertook this reorganization because he felt that top management was too far removed from individual stores with so many levels in between. Wood hoped that this change would (1) give him closer access to store managers, (2) help him get more specific weekly information about store performance, and (3) help eliminate unnecessary jobs. The reorganization did eliminate a number of jobs. Administrative offices in both Patterson and Indianapolis were closed, and the overhead expenses were reduced from 2.2% to 1.7% of sales.

25   Wood formed a management executive committee that met on a monthly basis to improve communications throughout A&P. The committee studied reports on operations, evaluated current programs, and helped shape overall corporate direction. It was comprised of executives from all different functional areas at corporate headquarters. Each committee member also chaired a subcommittee for his respective area of management. These subcommittees informed all A&P store managers of new programs and policies and gave subordinates the opportunity to provide feedback through

Exhibit 1

Simplified organizational chart of A&P after Wood made his initial management changes

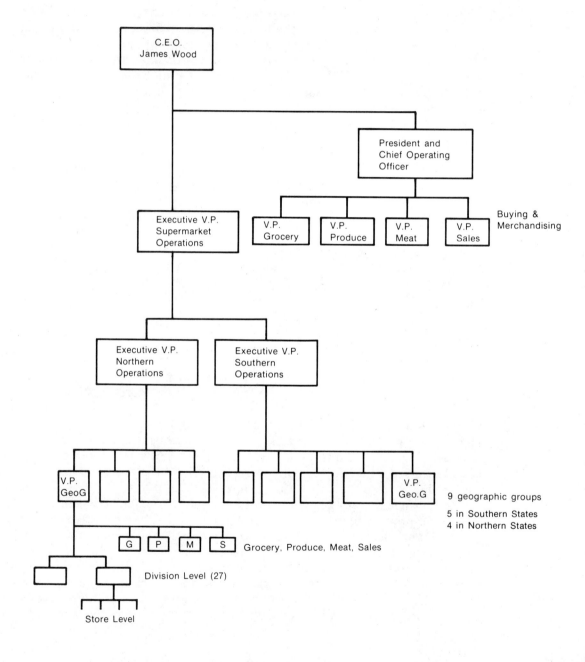

their superiors. A&P hoped this program would enhance not only communication and management control, but also help create an atmosphere of cooperation within the organization.

26   At the store level, Wood required each manager to formulate an annual plan and growth objectives. Each manager was then expected to achieve these goals and was later evaluated against them. Wood insisted that managers aggressively try to improve each store's market share by being sensitive to the needs of the local market. Thus, while Wood established a more centralized management structure at A&P, he also insisted that A&P decentralize day-to-day store operations, with store managers being the basic building block.

Operations Within Functional Areas

Marketing/sales

27   Marketing never seemed to be a major concern for A&P until James Wood became C.E.O. A&P's stores were small and dingy. The shelves were normally understocked, except for the numerous private label items. There was only a limited variety of national brands to choose from. Service was typically slow and the prices were consistently higher than its competitors'. In sum, there were few signs of trying to meet customer needs.

28   When Scott became A&P's C.E.O. in 1975, he made a number of changes in its marketing approach. Scott eliminated the W.E.O. (Where Economy Originates) program of the early 1970s. He switched A&P's $6,000,000 a year advertising program over to a price and pride medley. Scott also put an added emphasis on national brand grocery products, but still retained A&P's extensive private label offerings. In addition, general merchandise was added to some A&P stores. Scott also experimented with keeping stores open 24 hours a day, using trading stamps, and opening large combination, food-drug Family-Marts.

29   When Karl Haub bought the majority of A&P's stock in 1979, he sought to implement his German Plus store idea at A&P. The Plus stores, which had a limited assortment, had been very successful at his Tengelmann Group, the second largest grocery chain in Germany. Haub felt that it would be as successful in America. Even though Scott was not convinced that it would work, Haub pressured him into implementing it.

30   Plus stores gave customers a limited grocery offering, but at prices 30% lower than other grocery stores. The stores only carried about 850 items in stores that ranged in size from 5,000 to 12,000 square feet. A typical Plus store carried 500 grocery, 80 frozen food, 40 dairy, 25 bakery, 20 meat (which excluded fresh meat), 20 deli, 15 produce, 50 general merchandise, 95 health and beauty aid products, and a few other items. About 60% of the products were private label items. It was hoped that these stores would

increase sales at A&P and also increase the utilization of its manufacturing facilities.

31   Plus stores had no frills, which helped lower their overhead. Customers had to bag their own groceries and even pay three cents a bag, unless they brought their own. In addition, employees were all part-time and nonunion, earning about $3.50 an hour compared to a $7.50 average wage for unionized part-timers. Although weekly sales per store increased from $35,262 in 1974 to $60,621 the next year, A&P still sustained an overall loss in 1975.

32   When James Wood became C.E.O. in 1980, A&P had 1,543 stores, including 35 Plus stores. For the first year and a half, he stuck with the basic marketing strategy that Scott had developed. The main difference was that Wood did not close any more stores; rather, he focused his attention on other major internal problems, such as high labor cost and an inadequate management information system.

33   Once he improved A&P's internal management control system, top management was able to evaluate an individual store's profitability. Subsequently, Wood did eliminate some individual unprofitable stores. He also closed entire divisions when unions did not give him the wage and work rule concessions he sought. Some Super Fresh Food Markets were closed. By 1984, there were only about 60 of these A&P type stores located throughout Philadelphia, Northern Delaware, and Southern New Jersey.

34   Wood was initially not certain what to think of the Plus limited assortment store concept. He commented, "I made it clear that...[Haub] might have to accept the black balling of Plus before I agreed to take the job."[1] However, Wood did continue to open Plus stores at Haub's insistence, but only on a limited basis. Then, in late 1981, Wood changed his mind and started closing Plus stores after a long battle with Haub over their slumping performance. All of the Plus stores were finally eliminated in August of 1983, when the last 25 units were sold.

35   After A&P completed the closing of 500 poor performing stores in early 1982, 1,016 total stores remained that were located throughout the United States and Canada. Exhibit 2 breaks down these stores according to geographical region.

36   A&P's thousand plus stores fell into one of four store types. They were traditional A&P supermarkets, Family Marts, Super Fresh Food Markets, and Super Plus Warehouse Stores (different from Plus limited assortment stores). A&P's strategy was to locate each of these type stores where customer needs matched their offerings.

37   All four store formats merchandised food in a similar fashion. Each strongly emphasized national brand grocery products, with the new A&P private labels and its P&Q generics complementing them. The perishable departments, produce and meat, were emphasized because A&P felt they were major strengths. Advertising campaigns stressed its perishables departments, which offered some 140 to 150 varieties of produce and meat, which were carried in economy family packs and gourmet cut packages.

Exhibit 2

Store breakdown by geographic region

New England States:	Connecticut	36	
	Maine	5	
	Massachusetts	25	
	New Hampshire	6	
	Rhode Island	3	
	Vermont	4	
	Total		79
Middle Atlantic States:	Delaware	10	
	District of Columbia	1	
	Maryland	65	
	New Jersey	120	
	New York	102	
	Pennsylvania	63	
	Total		361
Central States:	Illinois	10	
	Indiana	20	
	Michigan	60	
	Ohio	11	
	Total		101
Southern States:	Alabama	22	
	Florida	34	
	Georgia	36	
	Kentucky	7	
	Louisiana	48	
	Mississippi	26	
	North Carolina	77	
	South Carolina	29	
	Tennessee	4	
	Virginia	58	
	West Virginia	15	
	Total		356
	Total United States		897
Canadian Provinces:	Ontario	104	
	Quebec	15	
	Total Canada		119
	Total Stores		1,016*

*Note that this 1,016 store figure included 31 Plus Limited Assortment Stores that do not exist as of 1984. From The Great Atlantic & Pacific Tea Company's *10-K Annual Report*, February 26, 1983, p. 4.

38   A&P's most frequent store type was still the traditional supermarket. By May of 1984, A&P operated 990 of these supermarkets. They carried a full line of national brand groceries, complemented by A&P brand private label and P&Q generic products. At A&P supermarkets, the goal was to

offer the customer value, quality, and good prices. Some of the larger stores offered a wide line of general merchandise items and some specialty departments to increase gross profit margin. The supermarkets recently started adding bakeries and delicatessens in these stores in an attempt to reach working wives and young people.

39   Family Mart stores emphasized one-stop shopping through a variety of merchandise and heavily emphasized service departments. Traditional grocery departments were supplemented with such specialty departments as gourmet cheese shops, sit-down restaurants, delicatessens, seafood departments, floral shops, liquor shops, and other food departments throughout the store. These stores also offered prescription drugs and general merchandise that typically had a high profit margin. Family Mart stores numbered 65 in 1984 and were located primarily in the sun belt states. So far, these type of stores had proven to be profitable.

40   The Super Plus Warehouse stores' game plan centered on low price and no frills. Merchandise was displayed in shipping cases rather than stocked on shelves. Super Plus carried a complete line of products including national brand grocery items, private labels, and perishables. There were only six of these stores in 1984, however, all were located in the Chicago area. A&P planned to expand them into other areas where it felt they would be successful.

41   Although A&P's stores were not as large as many of its competitors', the firm was striving to overcome this deficiency. Some $300 million had been allocated for 1983 through 1985 to remodel its existing stores and build new ones, primarily in the suburbs. A&P was trying to change its image by shifting to a large superstore format with lower prices, better service, and a wider range of goods. A&P believed that this approach added up to better value for its customers.

42   In the early 1980s under Wood's leadership, A&P adopted a new insignia for its private label products. That insignia replaced as many as 19 different private labels at A&P. The strategy behind the new general label was to show that A&P stood behind its products and would vouch for their quality. A&P also recently converted its traditional black and white labeled generic brand products to P&Q generics. The idea here was to upgrade the product's image while offering generic prices. This change had proven to be successful.

43   Advertising at A&P was directed at attracting new customers. It tried to project an image of outstanding value to appeal to potential customers. Ads focused heavily on its meat and produce departments, areas where A&P felt it had a competitive advantage. Price and quality were also emphasized through A&P's well known commercial theme, "We watch our P's and Q's." Some other advertisements emphasized A&P employees' willingness to help and to serve customers.

44   A&P utilized a variety of advertising media; however, television and radio were emphasized in the early 1980s. In 1983, A&P spent $4,696,000 on television advertising, a 15% increase over its 1982 level. Still, this ranked

only ninth among the top ten supermarket chains for television dollars spent. A&P had developed a co-op advertising program that shared the cost with national brand manufacturers. A&P tried to coordinate its store displays and newspaper advertisements with television advertising. The movement of the products advertised was kept on record, and when a promotion proved successful, that specific advertisement and media were used again.

Manufacturing

45   When Scott became C.E.O. in 1975, he took actions to eliminate over half of A&P's stores. Exhibit 3 shows various store statistics for each year from 1969 through 1983. Scott closed stores on an individual basis, rather than by city or region. He particularly emphasized trying to close stores in the stagnant urban Midwest and northeast regions and expand stores in the suburbs and the South. Compass Foods, a wholly owned subsidiary, was also formed during Scott's era in an attempt to increase the utilization of A&P's manufacturing facilities. Compass distributed food to A&P stores in the U.S. and in several foreign countries where it operated.

46   On April 1, 1982, A&P closed its mammoth 1.5 million square foot food processing plant in Horsehead, New York. It was the biggest such plant in the United States. The huge plant had been opened in 1963 with the intention of serving 4,000 stores with low priced, private label products.

Exhibit 3

Store statistics from 1969 through 1983 (sales and profits in thousands)

Year	Sales	Profit	No. of stores	No. of employees	Average per week sales per store
1969	5,436,325	45,247	4,713	131,500	22,182
1970	5,753,692	53,302	4,575	130,100	24,185
1971	5,664,025	50,129	4,427	125,000	24,604
1972	5,508,508	14,619	4,264	113,600	24,844
1973	6,368,876	(51,277)	3,940	123,600	31,086
1974	6,747,689	12,227	3,680	113,800	35,262
1975	6,537,847	(32)	2,074	93,000	60,621
1976	7,235,859	18,742	1,978	90,000	70,349
1977	7,288,577	569	1,905	81,000	73,577
1978	7,469,659	(52,186)	1,771	72,000	81,111
1979	6,684,179	(3,807)	1,542	63,000	83,361
1980	6,989,529	(43,049)	1,543	60,000	87,112
1981	6,226,755	(101,633)	1,055	45,000	113,503
1982	4,607,817	31,211	1,016	40,000	87,216
1983	5,222,013*	47,551	—	—	—

*Unaudited.
    Data taken from *The Great Atlantic & Pacific Tea Company, Inc., Annual Reports* for 1973, 1976, 1981, and 1982. 1983 data was taken from a March 20, 1984 A&P news release.

When Scott took over, A&P was the number one food processor in the U.S. It manufactured 1,500 private label grocery, dairy, bakery, and fish products that accounted for about 15% of the chain's total sales. Scott, however, felt that A&P was overemphasizing its private labels and started to put national brands back onto the grocery shelves. Not surprisingly, Scott's vast store-closing program left A&P with considerable unused manufacturing capacity. Some industry observers estimated that the huge facility operated at only 25% to 50% of full capacity.

47   Upon his arrival, James Wood commented that it was A&P's "manufacturing orientation that has created an overemphasis on private label as opposed to branded products in A&P stores."[2] One independent market research study conducted in 1982 concluded, "Consumers still perceived A&P as a private label house and that they found the practice of having competitive private labels to be deceptive."[3] Although Scott had started emphasizing national brands, customers apparently felt that he had not de-emphasized A&P's private labels enough.

48   A&P often made decisions based on what was best for its manufacturing facilities rather than its customers. This was done to utilize as much of its manufacturing facilities as possible. As one past A&P manufacturing executive noted:

> I think at one time A&P got into a situation where we decided we were a manufacturing company instead of a company serving the consumer. We were giving the consumer what we wanted to make a profit on rather than what she wanted to buy.[4]

He referred to this approach as the tail wagging the dog. Clearly, manufacturing had been the tail at A&P for quite some time.

49   Rumors started flying when James Wood arrived that A&P might get out of manufacturing. However, Wood took no immediate action due to A&P's weak financial position and Haub's urging that its manufacturing facilities should remain open. When Wood won a power struggle with Haub later the next year, production was drastically cut at Horsehead. Product lines were cut back from 800 to 200, and some 400 of the 1,500 employees at the plant were permanently laid off. Finally in 1982, the plant was closed.

50   By 1984, A&P had withdrawn almost entirely from manufacturing, except for four coffee roasting plants and two bakeries. Wood noted, "This will free A&P buyers to get the best possible purchases, while steering the mix of goods offered in our stores more in line with the customer's demands."[5] So, by the mid-1980s, the dog was starting to wag the tail, as A&P tried to meet its customers needs.

Finance

51   In 1973, A&P lost its number one sales position to Safeway. While its sales rose in 1974, they did not rise as fast as those of some other chains. Later,

the massive store-closing program under Scott's chairmanship caused sales to fall again. When Kroger's sales moved ahead of A&P in 1978, the old gray lady was bumped to third position in the industry. Later, sales took another dip in 1981 as the result of Wood's closing one third of the chain's stores. This caused A&P to fall to fifth position in sales behind Safeway, Kroger, Lucky, and American Stores. By 1984, A&P had dropped further to seventh position in the grocery industry. Its 1983 sales were over two billion dollars less than they had been as recently as 1978.

52   During the ten-year period from 1972 to 1982, A&P's market share fell from 10% to 2.5%. Similarly, it only made a profit five out of the last eleven years, but its 1982 and 1983 profits were the highest since 1971. 1983 profits were the highest since 1971. Finally, things were looking much better from a financial viewpoint. Top management hoped first to prune its chain down to a profitable core and then to pursue a growth strategy in the future. As James Wood noted, "It's no secret that in the past we allowed a lot of divisions to just go to hell. Well the days are over when A&P will stand around and let the competition eat us up."[6]

53   Traditionally, A&P had been a very conservatively financed organization. Until the early 1970s, A&P had never incurred any long-term debt, but had relied totally on issuing stock to raise needed capital. However, when sales and profits started eroding in the early 1970s, A&P was forced finally to leverage itself with debt.

54   A&P traditionally had paid very high dividends and put very little back into the company. This dividend policy was done to satisfy pressure on A&P for dividends by the Hartford Foundation. Over time, this caused A&P to be stuck with smaller, outdated stores since it lacked the resources to modernize them. As a result, many stores started incurring losses.

55   Scott cut back A&P's traditional 60% to 70% pay-out ratio to about 30%. He started reinvesting more money back into new store openings and old store modernization. Unfortunately, Scott's capital spending program for redeveloping stores was allocated in a haphazard manner, due to inadequate financial controls. Later, after a 1981 $200 million write-off, James Wood remarked that "80% of the stores [that] remained after my write-off make money compared to the 50% [remaining] after Scott's [earlier] $200 million dollar write-off."[7] As it turned out, A&P only made a profit two out of the five years when Scott was C.E.O. and was able to pay only two very small dividends.

56   Scott increased A&P's long term debt from $39,000,000 to $134,000,000 in 1977. This put pressure on Wood later to turn the company around quickly because in 1983 A&P's long-term debt would begin to mature at an accelerated rate. That year the accelerated rate increased to $11,800,000 per year as opposed to the $1,700,000 per year figure the previous year.

57   In January of 1979, Karl Haub bought up 42% of A&P's 24,900,000 shares in two separate stages for over $77,000,000. He paid $7.38 a share for 7,300,000 shares and had an option to buy 3,100,000 additional shares for

$7.50 each. While some people criticized Haub for this purchase, he did understand the American grocery business in which he had started his career in America with the Jewel grocery chain and later with Alpha Beta. Haub continued to purchase A&P stock and by 1984 held 50.7% of its total outstanding stock.

58   Wood established several key goals when he came to A&P. They were (1) to increase return on sales to at least the industry average, (2) to establish consistent profits, (3) to increase earnings per share, and (4) to increase A&P's market share. One of the first things Wood did was to install an adequate management information and control system so that he would have sufficient data upon which to launch what he hoped would be a successful turnaround strategy.

59   Once this was accomplished, he still needed capital to finance efforts to modernize A&P's existing stores. He considered issuing stock but knew few people would be willing to take that risk. Then, in May of 1981, a multimillion dollar gift was discovered. A consulting firm that A&P had hired found a $250,000,000 surplus in A&P's employee pension plan. This surplus was the result of higher interest rates and fewer total employees than expected when the pension plan was created. Wood wanted to use the surplus to build new stores and modernize existing stores, but he was met with resistance from Haub. After a hard summer of rampant price wars and a loss to the company, Wood finally convinced Haub to let him dip into the surplus. However, when Wood finally publicly announced that A&P would use the pension surplus, a former A&P vice president, William Walsh, took A&P to court. He contested that management had changed the language in the original pension plan. A&P won this court case and took $200,000,000 of the surplus for the company. While the ruling was appealed in late 1981, A&P was still able to add a $130,000,000 extraordinary credit to its assets because the annuities it had bought to cover the pension liability would earn future benefits for an additional $200,000,000 write-off.

60   A&P made several acquisition attempts in the early 1980s. Two of them fell through; however, two were successful. A&P acquired 11 Stop and Shop stores in metro New York in 1981 and 63 Kohl's Food Stores in Wisconsin in 1983. When asked why A&P was acquiring stores, Wood indicated that A&P wanted to latch on to some earnings in order to recoup at least some of its $170 million in loss carry forwards and investment tax credits that began to run out in 1982. Fortunately for A&P, the federal government changed laws that extended tax loss carry forwards.

61   A&P leased a substantial portion of its stores and other facilities. It did this because it believed that its capital could be invested more productively in inventories and store equipment. In 1977, A&P also started leasing some of its equipment and delivery trucks for financial and tax purposes.

62   By the mid-1980s, A&P was in a much better financial position because of Wood's shrewd financing, changing laws that extended tax loss carry forwards, and a top-of-the-line computerized information and cost control

system. In March of 1984, A&P received a final decision from the Third Circuit Court of Appeals concerning the anticipated pension fund surplus. The ruling provided the company with a tax-free $275,000,000, instead of the original $200,000,000. This increased amount was the result of good investments producing the long awaited surplus. Early 1984 brought more good news. The company announced then that it made a profit of approximately $47,551,000 in 1983, thus completing eight consecutive profitable quarters.

63   A&P's stock performance in 1984 reflected an improved outlook for the company. Early spring found its stock price at around $15 per share, which was a sizable increase over its $3.50 price for much of 1981. Value Line rated A&P's stock as an above-average market performer, but below average for safety. Moody's increased A&P's rating from a speculative grade rating to a lower medium grade. Reports from other investment companies, plus information coming from within A&P, suggested that the firm does have a bright future. Value Line forecasted that A&P's three-to-five-year prospects looked promising and felt that its accelerated capital spending program would allow the firm to sustain a 25% compounded annual earnings gain through 1986-88.[8]

64   Several exhibits provide more specific information about A&P's financial performance. Exhibit 4 compares the 1982 earnings with the 1983 preliminary earnings (fiscal year ending February 25, 1984). Then, Exhibit 5 shows the statement of consolidated operations and the statement of consolidated stockholders' equity for 1980 through 1982. Since A&P closes its financial year on February 26th of the next year, this meant that the 1982 income statement, for example, ended on February 26, 1983. Finally, Exhibit 6 shows the consolidated balance sheets for the years ending February 26, 1983 and February 27, 1982.

Human Resources

65   When James Wood arrived at A&P, he viewed the 63,000 employees more as a liability than an asset for the company. With labor costs at two or three percent of sales higher than the industry average, it was next to impossible for A&P to make a profit in such a highly competitive, low margin industry. Wood stressed right from the start that excessive labor costs were one of A&P's fundamental problems.

66   A&P was the first grocery chain to be unionized. Since then, its unions had pressured management to sign some very tough, long-term contracts. These contracts contained job security and seniority provisions that came back to haunt A&P in the form of increased labor costs. In the 1970s when Scott closed over half of A&P's stores, on a store-by-store basis, senior employees bumped less senior employees out of their jobs. This caused the average rate of pay to skyrocket from its already high level and made it

Exhibit 4

1982 earnings compared with 1983 preliminary earnings (in thousands)

	February 25, 1984	*February 26, 1983*
Sales	$5,222,013	$4,607,817
Income before income taxes and extraordinary items	63,951	45,061
Provision from income tax	(32,550)	(23,700)
Income before extraordinary items	31,401	21,361
Credit from tax loss carryforward utilization	16,150	9,850
Net income	47,551	31,211
Income per share before extraordinary items	.84	.57
Credit from tax loss carryforward utilization per share	1.27	.83

From Great Atlantic and Pacific Tea Company, Inc. *A&P News Release,* March 20, 1984.

that much harder for A&P to make a profit. The average age of A&P's employees also rose and productivity declined drastically. At one time during this period, the average age of employees in the Long Island and Pittsburgh divisions was 56 years old. As a result, the old gray lady was paying more than its competitors for the same jobs; unfortunately, many of these older employees were not able to produce as much.

67   When Wood was asked about the labor problems in June of 1980, he seemed very optimistic. As he put it, "I don't see it as any problem we cannot solve. We are in the course of some negotiations this year. We are hoping for release from some contract restrictions."[9] Wood's first 18 months in office did not bring about any promising results. He did not close many stores because he felt that his firm needed to catch its breath from all of the past management changes. Instead, he relied on tough labor negotiations to drive down labor costs. He started by negotiating at the national level with the employees union, the United Food and Commercial Workers. This broke an industry pattern of negotiating locally. However, this plan failed because the regional differences made it too difficult to cut labor costs. Also, Wood's demands for a two-year wage freeze and suspension of all staffing and scheduling restrictions were just too much for any union to accept.

68   Wood finally got Haub's permission to close some stores. Wood did even more than that. He threatened to close down entire divisions during the prolonged 1981-83 recession unless major concessions were granted. By closing down an entire division, Wood would escape the seniority and

Exhibit 5

Statement of consolidated operations (dollars in thousands, except per share figures)

	Fiscal 1982 (52 weeks)	Fiscal 1981 (52 weeks)	Fiscal 1980 (53 weeks)
Sales	$4,607,817	$6,226,755	$6,989,529
Cost of merchandise sold	3,575,901	4,903,227	5,512,202
Gross margin	1,031,916	1,323,528	1,477,327
Store operating, general and administrative expense	914,404	1,251,584	1,421,457
Depreciation and amortization	49,870	67,411	67,902
Income (loss) from operations	67,642	4,533	(12,032)
Interest (expense) income			
Interest expense	(30,132)	(35,596)	(36,465)
Interest income	7,551	6,430	12,448
Interest expense—net	(22,581)	(29,166)	(24,017)
Income (loss) before income taxes, revitalization program and extraordinary credit	45,061	(24,633)	(36,049)
Anticipated cost of revitalization program	—	(200,000)	—
Income (loss) before income taxes and extraordinary credit	45,061	(224,633)	(36,049)
Provision for income taxes	(23,700)	(7,000)	(7,000)
Income (loss) before extraordinary credit	21,361	(231,633)	(43,049)
Extraordinary credit—tax loss carryforward utilization	9,850	—	—
Extraordinary credit—pension	—	130,000	—
Net income (loss)	$ 31,211	$ (101,633)	$ (43,049)
Per common share:			
Income (loss) before extraordinary credit	$ .57	$ (6.19)	$ (1.35)
Extraordinary credit—tax loss carryforward utilization	.26	—	—
Extraordinary credit—pension	—	3.47	—
Net income (loss)	$ .83	$ (2.72)	$ (1.35)

security provisions of the union contracts that permitted employees to bump lower labor cost employees.

69   After several union locals refused to grant concessions, Wood closed down several divisions such as Philadelphia and Altoona, to prove he did mean business. Employees and union officials took notice and their attitudes changed drastically. One union local president surprisingly remarked:

> "I think Wood has finally got a handle on some of the company's problems. If we can get some assurances that A&P is willing to invest in our area, we are ready to make concessions, and I don't give a damn what anyone else does."[10]

Subsequent negotiations with local unions helped Wood to reduce A&P's

---

Exhibit 5 (concluded)

Statement of consolidated stockholders' equity (dollars in thousands)

	Fiscal 1982 (52 weeks)	*Fiscal 1981* (52 weeks)	*Fiscal 1980* (53 weeks)
Common stock:			
Balance forward	$ 37,393	$ 37,393	$ 24,893
Exercise of options	12	—	—
Increase due to rights offering	—	—	12,500
	$ 37,405	$ 37,393	$ 37,393
Capital surplus:			
Balance forward	$ 421,052	$ 421,052	$377,301
Exercise of options	57	—	1
Increase due to rights offering	—	—	43,750
	$ 421,109	$ 421,052	$421,052
Cumulative translation adjustment:			
Balance beginning of year	$ (4,218)	$ —	$ —
Exchange adjustment	157	—	—
	$ (4,061)	$ —	$ —
Retained earnings (deficit):			
Balance forward	$(156,292)	$ (54,659)	$ (11,610)
Net income (loss)	31,211	(101,633)	(43,049)
	$(125,081)	$(156,292)	$ (54,659)

From *The Great Atlantic & Pacific Tea Company, Inc., Annual Report 1982,* p. 14.

---

labor cost. For example, in one collective bargaining agreement covering western Maryland and some West Virginia stores, workers agreed to waive a 60-cent-an-hour wage increase about to come due and even took a 70-cent-an-hour reduction in hourly rate. These same employees also waived a cost of living adjustment, forfeited one paid personal holiday, and gave up one week paid vacation.

70   Wood also brought into practice a rather innovative concept of worker management cooperation in an attempt to lower wages. As mentioned, he closed the entire Philadelphia division in 1981 when the local union did not agree to contract concessions. After the closing, Wendel Young, the U.F.C.W. local president persuaded Wood into reopening it. Later in the spring of 1982, this same division was reopened as a wholly owned subsidiary under the name of Super Fresh Food Markets. Under the new agreement, the workers conceded 25% of their previous wages and benefits. But the workers did gain the right to share with management in making such decisions as to what products would be shelved. The workers would also be allowed to divide 1% of their store's sales under the stipulation that labor costs were 10% of sales or less. This agreement, it was hoped, would give

Exhibit 6

Consolidated balance sheets (in thousands)

	February 26, 1983	February 27, 1982
Assets		
Current assets:		
Cash and short-term investments	$98,449	$ 55,638
Accounts receivable	58,094	49,066
Inventories	414,650	478,103
Properties held for development and sale	17,809	17,989
Prepaid expenses	3,799	7,331
Total current assets	592,801	608,127
Property:		
Land	10,443	11,211
Buildings	45,026	49,643
Equipment	244,850	274,144
Store fixtures and leasehold improvements	144,956	152,032
Total—at cost	445,275	487,030
Less accumulated depreciation and amortization	(199,940)	(202,842)
	245,335	284,188
Real property leased under capital leases	104,083	107,489
Property—net	349,418	391,677
Other assets (includes $130 million prepaid pension)	145,176	141,875
	$1,087,395	$1,141,679
Liabilities and stockholders' equity		
Current liabilities:		
Current portion of long-term debt	$ 11,859	$ 1,817
Current portion of obligations under capital leases	10,679	11,162
Accounts payable	232,410	268,487
Accrued salaries, wages and benefits	61,381	66,077
Accrued taxes	30,872	26,293
Current portion of closing reserves and other accruals	60,531	58,529
Total current liabilities	407,732	432,365
Long-term debt	116,557	128,416
Obligations under capital leases	143,160	153,975
Deferred income taxes	8,811	4,417
Closing reserves and other liabilities	81,763	120,353
Stockholders' equity:		
Preferred stock—no par value; authorized— 3,000,000 shares; issued—none		
Common stock—$1 par value; authorized—80,000,000 shares; outstanding 37,404,784 shares	37,405	37,393
Capital surplus	421,109	421,052
Cumulative translation adjustment	(4,061)	—
Retained earnings (deficit)	(125,081)	(156,292)
Total stockholders' equity	329,372	302,153
	$1,087,395	$1,141,679

From *The Great Atlantic & Pacific Tea Company, Inc., Annual Report 1982*, p. 15.

employees an incentive to improve sales and productivity. This was definitely a step in the right direction, considering labor cost averaged 15% of sales in this division.

71   At the end of fiscal year 1982, A&P only had 40,000 employees, some 23,000 fewer than when Wood took office in 1980 and 53,000 fewer than when Scott took office in 1975. Of these 40,000 employees, approximately 85% were covered by union contracts. In addition, 60% of the total employees were part-timers who had fewer fringe benefits. The key difference after the division reopened was that the average cost of labor had been lowered to only about 11.5% of sales. This was only about 1 percentage point above the average for unionized competition.

Training and Development

72   In 1980, Wood felt that A&P was weak in its training and development of its personnel. He felt that since the company was in a customer-oriented business, a great deal depended on the quality of employees and their service to put A&P back on its feet. Therefore, he made developing A&P's human resources one of his top priorities throughout the entire organization. A&P came out with a major communications program, called Turning Point 82, as one way of gaining the commitment of its employees. This program stressed friendly customer service and competency on the job. Training for this program took place both on the job and in the classroom. In training sessions, A&P tried to create an atmosphere that it hoped would be implemented in its stores. The desired store changes included fair treatment of employees, responsiveness to their problems and suggestions, and discipline used to demonstrate A&P's commitment to high standards of customer service.

73   Division managers and store managers were, in part, trained and then appraised on how well they developed successors for their own jobs. Store management was also required to stimulate a climate in which employees were encouraged to achieve their maximum potential and felt that they would be able to move up. Wood's objective here was to enhance morale, give the best possible customer service, and also to develop employees to manage A&P in the future.

Innovation

74   Over the past several decades, A&P had not been an innovator. It had been more concerned with paying high dividends and making large profits from its private label products than with upgrading its stores and equipment. As a competitor's executive noted, "A&P always seemed one step behind. I remember when other stores were computerized, A&P clerks were still using pens and pencils. They continued to do things in the old style."[11]

75   When Scott came to A&P, it was hoped that his innovative leadership would help increase its sales and profits. Although Scott had been noted for being an innovator at Albertson's, many of his new ideas just did not seem to work at A&P.

76   A&P had also been innovative in its use of four store formats to appeal to a broad range of customer needs. A&P felt that since it operated in so many different type markets, it was impossible to use just one single store format to reach many, diverse customer segments. With consumers' taste and needs continuously changing, perhaps other supermarket chains may follow A&P's lead in diversified store formats.

77   A&P was also one of the industry leaders in developing a generic food program. Many competitors followed A&P's lead with their own generic products, such as Kroger's Cost-Cutter program. By the mid-1980s, A&P modified its traditional black and white label to a more appealing P&Q label.

78   The Compass Food distribution subsidiary had also been an innovation of A&P. This subsidiary was originally developed to increase the utilization of A&P's manufacturing capacity. It proved to be successful and carved out $100 million a year in sales. In recent years, however, the subsidiary's sales were much lower due to the elimination of almost all of A&P's manufacturing facilities, although it still distributed A&P's famous Eight O'Clock coffee.

The Task Environment

The Supermarket Industry

79   The supermarket industry was a highly competitive one. It was composed of a number of national chains, regional chains, and independents. The store formats found in this industry included conventional grocery stores, larger supermarkets, superstores, warehouse stores, convenience stores, and combination grocery-drug stores. Clearly, the industry had become very competitive, particularly since there were so many different store formats. This intense rivalry brought about an ongoing reliance on price competition to attract new customers and retain existing ones. Grocery retailers also utilized service, store design, store location, and overall product offering to be successful.

80   The industry typically had a low markup on its food products and depended on high volume to make a profit. Unfortunately, the typical grocery firm's net profits after taxes usually averaged around 1% of sales. The industry historically had been labor intensive with labor costs averaging about 60% of a firm's average gross margin. Furthermore, labor costs had been increasing at a rapid pace in recent years.

81   The ability of a grocery firm to meet the needs of its customers and

anticipate societal changes was vital for success. This was particularly important since numerous grocery stores competed for a fixed dollar amount in many cities. A&P's history clearly demonstrated what can happen when a grocery chain became out of sync with a changing environment.

Threats to the Industry

82   The cost of operating a supermarket had been rising at a rapid pace since the early 1970s. Although the average gross margin had increased because of the addition of many high margin departments, record-high operating expenses had lowered net profits. The major contributors of increasing operating expense were labor cost, rent for property and equipment, energy cost, and the cost of technological improvements. Supermarket officials had taken various steps to cut down on some of these costs, but they were still rising. Therefore, rising operating costs were probably going to continue as a major problem in this industry for quite some time.

83   The 1983 spring floods and summer drought caused many supermarket prices to go up in 1984. Prices in produce and meat departments, which were very hard hit, went up substantially. This forced many consumers to substitute lower margin canned goods for fresh produce and meat. This hurt the industry's gross margins and sales. Spring of 1984 was much like a year earlier, and with a dry summer being forecast, the grocery industry might be prepared for lower gross margins.

84   This industry faced a number of other major threats. Somewhat surprisingly, one threat was that food price inflation was lower than it had been quite a while, a situation the industry was unaccustomed to. In a 1983 survey, a slight majority of supermarket executives expressed regret over disinflation and felt that it had adversely affected the industry's health. Another economic threat that had to be faced was the questionable long-run stability of the U.S. economy itself. With a projected $180,000,000,000 national deficit for 1984 alone, an increasing defense budget, and rising interest rates, consumer spending at the grocery store might not increase much in coming years.

85   A number of governmental threats also faced the grocery industry. One of the most publicized of these was the recent push for a national minimum drinking age of 21 years old. This might significantly lower the sales of beer, wine, and liquor in supermarkets. Although grocery stores in both New Jersey and Maryland reported little change in traffic or purchasing patterns since their states adopted a 21-year-old minimum law, reduced grocery sales might occur in other states as a result of the same action.

86   President Reagan's program to eliminate food stamp program abuses through tighter state controls was also a threat. His changing food stamp policies were already requiring banks to charge fees for redeeming food stamps. More basic, however, far fewer food stamps were being issued

under the Reagan Administration, which reduced grocery purchases from low-income customers.

87   Several other legal threats existed. A bill in Congress that would end mandatory retirement might cause employee productivity for the average grocery firm to decrease. A farm bill that allowed additional dairy and grain price supports would cause increased supermarket prices. Finally, a proposed Federal bottle bill would force consumers to pay deposits on beer and soft drink bottles and cans. If passed, this would cause increased prices and inconveniences to supermarkets that would be forced to recycle them.

88   Probably the biggest threat to the industry in 1984 was bitter price wars initiated by the competitors themselves. Although the Value Line Investment Survey predicted a reduction in such competitive activity, the supermarket executives were predicting more of these wars.[12] Even though market share gains from such price wars often proved to be only temporary, increased competition and the advent of warehouse stores caused price wars. Unfortunately, with a projected doubling in the number of new stores that grocery firms expected to open in 1984 over just the year before, the industry might encounter even more price wars in the future.

Industry Trends

89   By 1984, the economy was in better shape than it had been in for quite some time. It was hard to predict how long it would last, but with less inflation and lowered unemployment, consumers were becoming less apprehensive about spending money in grocery stores. Thus, an improved economy would probably help both sales and maybe even profits in this volume-oriented business.

90   There were also trends in the store formats being used in recent years. For the past several years, superstores, warehouse stores, and combination stores had been taking market share away from the conventional stores. Furthermore, the industry would soon see the introduction of the super triad, a new format which combined three stores in one. These stores will be centered around an indoor mall with fountains, trees, and skylight ceilings. The three stores would be separate, but all under one roof. One triad might contain a warehouse store, a combination type store, and a superstore with fresh perishables. Only time will tell just how popular this new type of store will be.

91   Another trend was the increased number of mergers and acquisitions in the last few years. In part, this was due to the relaxed attitude of the Antitrust Division of the Department of Justice under the Reagan Administration. The recession caused many chains with high cost structures to shut the doors of their unprofitable stores. Often, independent grocery firms would then reopen the stores at a lower-cost structure and operate profitably. Most industry observers expected additional mergers and ac-

quisitions in the future, particularly given the excessive number of stores that existed in many cities.

92   Many regional chains and independents competing in the same markets had nonunionized work forces. This gave them a lower cost structure and added flexibility in running their stores. With this growing trend, unionized chains, such as A&P and Kroger, were at a competitive disadvantage. Furthermore, grocery store customers were not particularly loyal to any one particular store. In general, grocery customers were very price sensitive and shopped where the best prices were offered.

93   There was also a trend in the industry for stores to include high margin service and specialty departments. These departments were being added to facilitate the growing needs of consumers who preferred one-stop shopping for as many different items as possible. Such sections included cheese shops, fish shops, health food departments, meat sections, pasta shops, floral shops, automotive maintenance shops, and a variety of other nonfood departments.

94   Several other key trends were impacting on this industry. Growing trends included (1) the growing use of new electronic technology in supermarkets, such as electronic scanners, (2) an intensified use of price specials and coupons, and (3) new warehouse stores continuing to outpace all other new store types. One industry trend saw the use of generics and private labels losing market share.

Competition

95   In a nut shell, the grocery industry was highly competitive and was comprised of numerous national chains, regional chains, and independents. By 1982, Safeway had $17,700,000,000 in sales followed by Kroger with $11,900,000,000. Other large nationals included Winn Dixie, Lucky Stores, Acme, Alpha Beta, Publix, Pathmark, A&P, and Jewel. Together, regional chains and independents numbered in the thousands. Another organization that was rarely thought of as a competitor was the U.S. military commissary business. This business was spread throughout 38 states and achieved $3,500,000,000 in sales each year.

96   The various national and regional chains did not compete against one another in any one local market. This was because they covered different, yet somewhat overlapping geographical areas. For example, a national chain might compete against only one other national chain, a couple of regionals, and some independents in any one specific city.

97   With the advent of warehouse type stores, competition was becoming increasingly keen. Cutthroat pricing, coupons, and many special promotions had made their way into competitive tactics used by grocery retailers. With the growing number of nonunionized competitors and no-frills type stores, price will probably become a more important marketing element in each competitor's marketing strategy in the coming years.

Substitute Products for Supermarkets

98   Just a few years ago, restaurants and convenience stores were the primary substitutes for grocery stores. But with the recent trend in the supermarket industry of adding service and specialty departments, additional retailers existed as substitute products. In the mid-1980s, a shopper can find substitute products at a bakery, florist, fresh seafood shop, health foods store, discount clothing store, and discount appliance store, among others.

99   Clearly, supermarkets no longer competed for market share only against other supermarkets, convenience stores, restaurants, and produce stands. Since they were increasing their nonfood items, many grocery stores were directly competing against drug stores, discount houses, variety stores, toy stores, etc. Clearly, the boundaries where the grocery industry started and stopped were becoming blurred and overlapped with some other industries.

Supermarket Customers

100   Because of rampant price wars that spread throughout the grocery industry in 1983, consumers were able to buy more grocery items for less money. Consumers only spent 15.6% of their disposable income for food, of which 11.4% was at the supermarket. These figures were down from 1982 figures, 15.7% and 11.6% respectively, and were both record lows. Because consumers eased up on their budget-minded shopping, the decrease in grocery spending was clearly due to the price wars.

101   Consumers rated a clean store as the number one factor in selecting a supermarket in several recent surveys. Earlier, at the start of the 1980s, consumers had rated a good selection of private label and generic products much lower than they had in the past. This may reflect the many specials on name brands offered by stores because of price wars. Low income consumers, however, rated a good selection of private label products and generics as important to them in selecting a store. They also rated low prices and frequent sales important. High income shoppers rated a good selection of national brands, a good produce department, and a supermarket that had a deli/bakery as important to them in store selection.[13]

102   More men were shopping for groceries than ever before. In a recent survey, 47% of the consumers surveyed reported that men shopped at the supermarket as either the primary shopper in the household or as a participant. This was quite a change from past years when women did most of the shopping.

103   Consumers were also more health conscious than ever before. This had been reflected in the opening of health and nutrition centers, labeling of nutrients on products, and the low sodium food additions that were starting to appear. In recent years, the sales growth in produce departments were also reflecting this trend towards healthful foods. Overall, consumers were

becoming more demanding than they had been in the 1970s. Supermarkets in the grocery industry would not have added all of the service and specialty departments had not the consumer already responded favorably to them.

Current and Future Issues and Problems

New Product/Market Opportunities for A&P

104   In order to increase its sales, market share, and profitability, A&P needed to continue to exploit appropriate product and market opportunities. Still, A&P needed to avoid expanding its product lines where it lacked expertise and avoid markets that were already adequately served.

105   One approach A&P might pursue would be to become a more aggressive marketer of its products in existing markets. A&P could increase the number of stores it had in these markets through acquisitions along with new store openings. The advertising budget could be increased and research could be undertaken to determine the advertising medium with the greatest potential. Existing stores could be redesigned and refocused to satisfy emerging customer needs. The use of flexible fixtures for easy redepartmentalization might be an alternative to remodeling. Prices could be lowered by offering such incentives as coupons and possibly even giving customers credit cards so that they could be billed later.

106   A&P could also add additional brands of merchandise to its shelves for more variety and selection. It could look for new service and specialty departments to add to its stores. Such departments might include financial centers, dry cleaning services, fashion apparel, full meal restaurants, beauty salons, bulk foods sections, and a host of other gourmet foods. While the list of new departments is endless, A&P should keep its customers' needs in mind when making its decisions.

107   A&P might also consider the Super Triad store since it already operated a warehouse store, combination store, and a superstore. By combining these three together in a mall, A&P would go beyond one stop shopping, as was emphasized by its two largest competitors, Kroger and Safeway.

108   A&P could also consider easing back into food manufacturing, which would involve vertical integration. It should remember, however, its past problems with excessive manufacturing at the expense of serving its customers.

109   Moving to new markets is also a possibility, but it should be done with some caution. A&P should not hopscotch hundreds of miles away from its nearest stores because of the increased transportation costs and lost economies in advertising. But with its varied store formats, A&P should be able to meet many customer needs in other markets.

110   A&P might also consider following Safeway's strategy and expand overseas. This might be very profitable, but A&P must determine if it has the
support capabilities for such a move. Many overseas markets in developing
countries might not be ready for a superstore or a warehouse store, but
regular supermarkets might do very well and face limited competition.
A&P could even consider changing its store formats to meet customer
needs in foreign countries. For example, it could start a chain of open air
markets if they work well in some underdeveloped country. It could also
consider reopening its Plus limited assortment stores in Europe where
Haub had success with them.

111   A&P might start emphasizing one or two of its store formats as opposed
to operating all four of them. For example, A&P could start building more
warehouse stores or even converting some of its other stores to warehouse
stores. Since A&P's employees were part of the total product it offered,
A&P might use the Super Fresh Food Markets' labor-management cooperation idea in its other type of stores. This would not only give A&P a
lower-cost structure, but with the incentive offered, it could also give A&P a
more attractive overall package.

A&P's Future

112   Clearly, A&P needs to decide how to address many of the threats and
strategic issues facing it in the mid-1980s. A&P's management needs to ask
itself a number of critical questions. Is it keeping up to date in store format
and are each of them being effectively managed? Can it remain competitive with the advent of the many nonunionized grocery chains? Does the
public still perceive A&P as a private label house? If so, how can that
image be corrected? How will the economy act in the future, and what can
A&P do to prepare for various ups and downs in it? Should A&P expand
into other markets, remain set, or close stores that are not making it? What
new food or nonfood departments should be added to its stores? Clearly,
the answers to these and other questions are very important ones for A&P
to address.

113   James Wood had been able to get the old gray lady back on her feet in the
early 1980s. But, what additional measures should A&P take to insure
continued growth and to prevent its profits from eroding just after grand-
ma started regaining her strength?

Notes

1. Christopher Lorenz, "A Foreign Tonic for an Ailing U.S. Grocer," *Financial Times,*
September 12, 1980, p. 15.

2. *Great Atlantic and Pacific Tea Company, Inc., Annual Report 1981* (Montvale, New
Jersey: Great Atlantic and Pacific Tea Company, Inc.), p. 2.

3. "A&P New Private Label Program a Practical Approach," *Processed Prepared Foods,* p. 16.

4. "The Travels of Ann Page," *Forbes,* June 15, 1977, p. 85.

5. *Great Atlantic and Pacific Tea Company, Inc., Annual Report 1981,,* p. 3.

6. Larry Schaeffer, "Fit and Feisty," *Progressive Grocer,* October 1983, p. 69.

7. Gwen Kinkead, "The Executive-Suite Struggle Behind A&P's Profits," *Fortune,* November 1, 1982, p. 90.

8. "Grocery Story Industry," *The Value Line Investment Survey,* March 2, 1984, p. 1508.

9. Barbara Ettmorre, "New Chief Reshapes Ailing A&P Chain," *The New York Times,* June 27, 1980, p. 104.

10. "Local Unions May Give A&P its Best Bargains," *Business Week,* May 3, 1982, p. 32.

11. Fran R. Schumer, "Embattled A&P, New Management Fights to Revive the Old Chain," *Barrons,* January 25, 1982, p. 4.

12. "Grocery Store Industry," p. 1508. Walter H. Heller et al. "51st Annual Report of the Grocery Industry," *Progressive Grocer,* April 1984, pp. 47, 57.

13. "51st Annual Reports of the Grocery Industry," p. 58.

Introduction

1   In 1982, after three years of below-average financial performance, Safeway Stores, Inc., sold its 70-store Nebraska-Iowa division. Company officials said they could not keep prices competitive because of the region's limited population growth and the influx of nonunionized stores. They gave similar reasons for moves out of the company's Memphis and southwest Missouri markets. Some industry experts interpreted these drastic cutbacks differently. They wondered if recent poor financial performances and dwindling market shares suggested that Safeway, the world's largest food retailer, was about to fall as the once-mighty A&P had fallen in years past.

2   The picture appeared somewhat brighter in 1983 as this Oakland, California, headquartered firm posted its first earnings increase in four years. Some of the credit for this improvement was due to a 3 percent real increase in sales and higher profit margins. However, a significant portion of the credit could also be attributed to revenues gained from the 1982 divestments, as well as lower first-in, first-out accounting changes. Had Safeway indeed reversed its four-year slide? Would this grocery giant continue to make other improvements necessary to retain its industry leadership? As one skeptical competitor noted, "Safeway is not driving a PT boat, but a battleship, and you just can't move that fast."[1]

This case was prepared by Barbara Spencer of Clemson University. Copyright © 1984 by Barbara Spencer.

[1]"Safeway Stores: Back to Price Wars for a Company that Played It Too Safe," *Business Week,* April 5, 1982, p. 109.

History

3   Safeway had its beginnings in American Falls, Idaho, where a Baptist minister by the name of Skaggs built a tiny grocery store. His aim was to help poor local wheat farmers who were dependent on storekeepers offering credit at exorbitant interest rates. Skaggs's idea was to sell groceries for cash at a savings. He operated the store until 1915 when one of his six sons, Marion Barton "M. B." Skaggs purchased the company for $1,088.

4   M. B., who is generally recognized as Safeway's founder, decided that by accepting a small profit margin, he could build his one small store into a larger business. He reduced costs by buying directly from food manufacturers and eliminating as much wasted operating expense as possible. In less than 11 years, he expanded the organization to 428 retail units operating in 10 states. His motto, "Distribution without Waste," continued with the company through the 1970s.

5   In 1926, M. B. merged his stores with the Sam Seelig stores of Southern California and incorporated under the name of Safeway. He then embarked on a five-year period of rapid expansion, mainly through acquisitions. By 1931, the company was serving virtually the same geographical markets in the United States and Canada as it did later on in the 1970s and 1980s. Amazingly, Safeway operated the most stores in its entire history during 1931, when it had 3,527 outlets.

6   Skaggs, a practical businessman, also rapidly moved into warehousing. By 1925, he had established a wholesaling operation in the Pacific Northwest. By 1929, this operation had expanded to include branch warehouses in 20 cities throughout the western United States and Hawaii. Although Skaggs relinquished the presidency to Lingan A. Warren in 1931, Safeway continued to grow. By the mid-1930s, Safeway had 21 bakeries, 6 coffee roasting plants, 3 meat-distributing plants, a milk condensery, a candy and syrup factory, a mayonnaise plant, and a produce-purchasing company.

7   While the total number of stores declined from its 1931 record high, the average number of square feet per store increased dramatically from around 1,000 square feet in 1926 to 3,000 square feet in the 1930s. It later increased to between 5,000 and 6,000 square feet in the early 1940s and up to 10,000 square feet by the end of that decade. This increase in store size corresponded to the shift from consumer walking to driving. As a side note, every new Safeway store came with a parking lot by 1938.

8   Under Warren, Safeway prospered throughout the 1930s and 1940s, but net income dropped from $14.7 million in 1950 to $7.3 million in 1952. Net income as a percent of sales fell from 1.2 percent in 1950 to .4 percent during this same period, even though sales increased by $429 million to $1.6 billion in 1952.

9   When Robert Magowan took over in 1955, he quickly turned the company around. Net income rose to $25.4 million in 1956, and net income as a

percent of sales returned to its former level of 1.2 percent and continued to rise to 1.8 percent in 1966. Magowan remained a key force behind Safeway's strategic moves as chairman of the board from 1966 until his retirement in 1971. His staunchly conservative management style became a company trademark.

10   Magowan's successor, Quentin Reynolds, served as president from 1966 to 1971 and then as board chairman from 1971 to 1974. Like Magowan, Reynolds was an extremely successful corporate leader and had worked his way up through the ranks from his first position as a food clerk. During Reynolds's tenure as CEO, Safeway earned more money than any other food chain. During this period, first inflation and then price controls, instituted under President Nixon in the early 1970s, reduced supermarket profits to an average of less than a half a cent on a dollar of sales. Yet, Safeway earned at least three times as much as the industry average by making every penny count.

11   Safeway did several things during that period that really helped profitability. For example, instead of spending money on a glamorous corporate headquarters, the company's 250 corporate-level employees worked in an old converted warehouse. In addition, all bills were paid within 30 days to take advantage of discounts. Yet there was no skimping where customers were concerned. Rather, all stores were large and modern, offered unit pricing, and provided nutritional labeling.

12   During these same years, the company also experimented with nonfood discount stores. In some instances, these Super-S stores were located right next to its own supermarkets. Under the management of food executives, who were admittedly out of their league, these stores failed dismally, causing Safeway to retreat rapidly back to the low-margin food business. Later on, when Safeway expanded its supermarkets to 25,000 square feet, only 1,000 square feet were devoted to higher-margin, nonfood items.

13   It was during Reynolds's tenure that a number of social issues exploded in the external environment. For example, minority civil rights concerns and consumerism reached peaks of activity in 1968. Riots erupted in Washington, D.C., and housewives boycotted supermarkets all across the country. Reynolds took several actions to respond to these problems. He joined the National Business Council for Consumer Affairs, improved the company's affirmative-action program, and established a program to develop minority businesses. He even initiated the innovative process of labeling ground beef according to its fat content, as opposed to the cut of beef from which it came, to avoid misleading customers.

14   While Reynolds was focusing on the external environment, President William Mitchell was in charge of internal operations. Mitchell, who joined Safeway in 1936 as a clerk in the accounting department, was extremely conservative and cautious. Some of his deliberateness was probably due to the variety of lawsuits against Safeway in the early 1970s.

15   Several of Safeway's lawsuits focused on store prices. In 1973, the Feder-

al Trade Commission accused Safeway of advertising food at sales prices but actually selling it at regular prices. Safeway, Kroger, and several other chains were convicted of this charge in 1977. In 1974, the company was charged with employment discrimination against women and minorities in a $10 million class-action suit. During that same year, Safeway also was the number 1 target of Cesar Chavez's United Farm Workers Union, which demanded the firm sell only produce with their union label. Also, in 1974, a U.S. Senate committee headed by Senator William Proxmire found identical prices on 2,969 out of 3,959 items checked in the Kansas City stores of Safeway and A&P. Proxmire pointed out that Safeway made more profits than the rest of the industry, but never offered lower prices than competitors. Moreover, his survey showed that Safeway had higher prices in 13 areas across the United States where it dominated the market. In 1975, several price-fixing charges were brought against Safeway, with the best known probably being the case in which 500 cattle feeders charged that Safeway, A&P, Kroger, American Stores, Jewel, Winn-Dixie, Food Fair, Grand Union, and Supermarket General conspired to pay low cattle prices to farmers but still charged high prices to consumers. This suit was later dismissed.

16   As a result, it was little wonder that President Mitchell increasingly surrounded himself with financial and legal executives. Under their influence, Safeway adopted the strictest possible interpretation of government antitrust and other regulations. Lawyers vetoed plans to create health food departments in stores because of potential legal hassles over insect infestations. They even curtailed advertising of loss leaders because of possible legal exposure if stores ran out of items.

17   In 1973, Safeway passed A&P and became the world's largest food chain in terms of sales, net income, market value of shares, and stockholders' equity. Because of this feat, Mitchell was honored as the most outstanding chief executive officer in the grocery industry in 1975. It was at that point, paradoxically, that Safeway began losing market share in key cities. Exhibit 1 shows how Safeway's market share and rank among competitors fared between 1976 and 1981 in 14 key cities.

18   With Mitchell planning to retire in 1980, the company named Dale Lynch, formerly head of Safeway's successful 253-store northwestern region, as president in late 1977. Earnings bounced back to $146 million in 1978, up 43 percent on a 12 percent increase in sales. However, in the first quarter of 1979, net income dropped 8 percent below the first quarter earnings of 1978, and the 57-year-old Lynch suffered a heart attack, which caused Mitchell to change his mind about promoting Lynch to chairman and C.E.O. Mitchell still insisted on retiring but submitted 10 names to the board of directors for consideration as a successor.

19   In a surprise move, the board selected Peter Magowan, the 37-year-old son of Robert Magowan, the former C.E.O., as the new chairman and chief executive officer. Despite concerns about nepotism and his youth, Ma-

Exhibit 1

Safeway's market-share changes in key cities

Key cities	1976	1981	Rank among competitors in 1981
Baltimore	6%	8%	3
Dallas	31	28	1
Denver	42	39	2
Des Moines	15	13	3
Houston	12	16	2
Kansas City	25	·20	2
Los Angeles	9	8	4
Phoenix	10	11	3
Portland	25	18	3
Salt Lake City	19	17	2
San Diego	20	19	1
San Francisco/Oakland	26	27	1
Seattle	30	35	1
Washington, D.C.	32	30	2

Source: Jeff Blyskal, "A&P West," *Forbes*, April 12, 1982, p. 62.

gowan seemed to give the giant company a new life. Before coming to Safeway, the younger Magowan had earned a B.S. degree at Stanford and a master's degree at Oxford and had studied international relations at Johns Hopkins University. He started at Safeway as a real estate negotiator, managed a 15-store district in Houston, and held posts of increasing responsibility in both Safeway's U.S. and international divisions. Most recently, he had been vice president of Canadian and overseas subsidiaries.

20   Magowan's top priorities when he took office in January of 1980 were to regain market share, expand superstores and nonfood merchandising, and make Safeway the lowest-cost operator in the industry again. His task was a formidable one since earnings had slid since 1978, and Safeway's 10.6 percent return on equity was one third lower than the retail food industry average. Furthermore, its market share had fallen in 9 of 14 major cities.

21   Magowan immediately started making major changes. He soon added over 200 superstores with bakeries, delicatessens, natural food departments, cosmetic centers, and pharmacies. Superstores derived their name from their enormous size, usually above 30,000 square feet, and many of these enormous one-stop shopping centers stocked more than 12,000 different items. In addition, Magowan moved Safeway into Liquor Barns, discount Food Barns, and gourmet food outlets. By 1981, it appeared that Safeway had stopped the erosion of sales and market share, but some industry observers questioned the company's ability to maintain these improvements.

Safeway's Operations in the 1980s

Marketing/Sales

22   Marketing at Safeway was headed up by John Prinster, senior vice president of marketing. Prinster, 52 years old, was appointed to this position in 1981.

23   Safeway stores offered customers a full line of food and nonfood products in large grocery store and superstore formats. Food items at a typical Safeway store included fresh fruits and vegetables, meats, poultry and fish, frozen foods, dairy products, baked goods, delicatessen and gourmet foods, dry goods, and other items. Nonfood items, which varied depending on the store size, often included soaps, health and cosmetic products, magazines and paperback books, paper products, hardware, electrical appliances, cameras and photography equipment, toys, garden supplies, auto accessories, and cigarettes.

24   Health and beauty aids were doing so well that they accounted for 40 percent of the nonfood sales. Furthermore, these products tended to be high-profit items. By 1982, Safeway also had pharmacies in 300 stores. Health and beauty aids sales were much higher in stores that also had a pharmacy.

25   New ways were constantly being used to appeal to customers and to make shopping enjoyable. Many stores soon housed video games, floral shops, wine and cheese shops, bakeries, and even live lobsters. Over 250 automatic teller machines were installed in stores in 1983, and the company began experimenting with computer sales, aluminum recycling, salad bars, and bulk items such as sugar, flour, and nuts.

26   The use of innovative store layout was also utilized to attract shoppers. For example, instead of the usual box shape, Safeway's 61,000 square foot Arlington, Texas, superstore was constructed with broad sections meeting to form a wide-based V as shown in Exhibit 2. Within this V, an island contained many of the store's specialty items. Shelves were built lower than usual so that customers could always see the service island. Open around the clock, this new store held about 20,000 items, almost double the number for conventional stores.[2] Magowan chose Arlington for his first super, superstore because with the area's excellent competition, it provided a good test.

27   Safeway had long tailored its individual stores to local markets and continued this policy in the 1980s. Stores in affluent areas featured gourmet shops while those in ethnic neighborhoods offered freshly baked tortillas or tofu. Moreover, to meet the needs of today's health-conscious

---

[2]Manuel Schiffres and Joseph Benham, "As Supermarkets Get Even More Super," *U.S. News & World Report,* June 13, 1983, p. 66.

Exhibit 2

Floor layout for Safeway's 61,000-square-foot superstore—Arlington, Texas

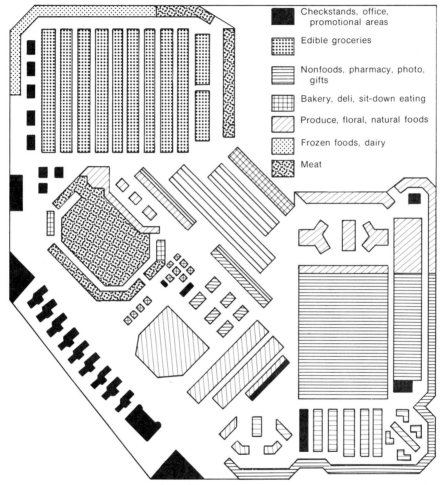

Checkstands, office, promotional areas

Edible groceries

Nonfoods, pharmacy, photo, gifts

Bakery, deli, sit-down eating

Produce, floral, natural foods

Frozen foods, dairy

Meat

Source: Safeway Stores, Inc., Annual Report, 1982, p. 32.

consumers, the company sold leaner beef cuts as well as more poultry and seafood. Produce sections tripled their offerings with over 180 different items. Low-sugar fruits and low-sodium vegetables appeared on shelves, and natural foods became one of the firm's biggest-selling items.

28   In 1982, the company began reducing its emphasis on private-label groceries. Private-label grocery products often were manufactured by the same firms that packaged various national brands, but then they put a

different label on the package. Some private-label products were packaged by the grocery chains themselves, if they had vertically integrated backwards into such operations. While such house-label products were described as the downfall of A&P, other grocery chains had been helped by them. For example, Kroger grocery stores achieved a great deal of its profits from lower-priced private-label brands sitting right next to higher-priced national brands.

29   Safeway aggressively promoted its wares and took the lead in using magazine advertising while decreasing its emphasis on newspapers. They also used radio during weekday rush hours and television during evening prime time. For example, one television ad series showed customers interacting with Safeway employees and products as the background lyrics said, "Proud to be part of your life." This theme was further reflected in the company's sponsorship of the U.S. Olympic training site near Colorado Springs. In that capacity, it supplied the center with food products and financial backing through the end of 1984.

30   In the early 1980s, Safeway clearly was willing to do battle against the competition in important cities to protect its volume and customer base. This was clearly a changed policy from years past when Safeway's motto seemed to be to let the other chain initiate action. Not so any more. For example, Safeway lost up to as much as $50 million during the summer of 1981 in Washington, D.C., alone. In a brutal price war initiator Giant Food was equally hurt, but two other competitors were forced to vacate the nation's capitol. In another recent price-war battle in Denver, Safeway's actions caused Dillon Company, the city leader, to suffer its first profit decline in almost 20 years. No longer was Safeway going to let others damage its market position without a fight.

31   Safeway's development of foreign markets has led the industry. Safeway first entered foreign markets in 1962, and by 1982, it had 535 international stores: 294 in Canada, 98 in the United Kingdom, 115 in Australia, and 28 in West Germany. During that same year, these four regions provided about 50 percent of Safeway's profits, although they only accounted for 20 percent of its sales. These financial returns were achieved despite severe economic conditions in Canada and intense price competition in Australia.

32   The company's British operations registered a 4 percent increase in profits during 1982. Safeway's British unit then attempted to purchase a 98-store chain from Fitch Lovell PLC for $54 million in April of 1983. Fitch Lovell initially accepted the offer, but two weeks later, it reneged when Linfield Holdings Company offered them $59.3 million, thus initiating a bidding war. Finally in June of 1983, Safeway gave up when the bid had climbed to $70.3 million. Undaunted, Magowan expressed plans to continue Safeway's expansion in the United Kingdom. He was also looking at Japan, Taiwan, Hong Kong, Singapore, and Malaysia. As he put it:

We should do a lot better abroad once those currencies stabilize against the U.S. dollar and those foreign economies begin picking up, because there's even greater growth potential in those markets than in the United States.[3]

33   Magowan formed an international-development division to develop foreign markets more systematically. John Kimball headed up this division and managed the directors of operations in Australia, Germany, and the United Kingdom. In addition, he helped set up a joint venture to run 13 stores in Mexico and 4 more in Saudi Arabia through a management contract. Other significant international activities thus far have included the signing of technical-assistance agreements to manage supermarkets in Kuwait and Oman and the signing of an import-export agreement with Allied Imports, a Japanese marketing group that would provide a market for the overseas distribution of Safeway's private-label items. In addition, the company acquired a 49 percent interest in a Mexican food retailer, partly to learn more about selling to the growing U.S. Hispanic market.

Manufacturing/Operations

34   Safeway had 2,454 stores at the start of 1983, 1,806 of which were conventional grocery stores averaging 24,000 square feet. However, Safeway also had approximately 500 superstores averaging 40,000 square feet in size. Finally, the firm had 81 Food Barn warehouse-type stores and 67 Liquor Barn discount liquor stores. Food Barns were primarily in Los Angeles, Kansas City, and Washington, D.C., whereas the Liquor Barns were all located in California and Arizona.

35   In addition, Safeway operated 55 fast-food outlets selling chicken and seafood, operated 8 food variety combination stores, was involved in a joint venture for 3 egg production facilities, owned 3 wholesale outlets in Mexico, owned 2 clothing stores, owned 55 percent of Holly Enterprises, and owned 49 percent of Casa Ley.

36   Out of its total of 2,454 stores, 1,919 were located in the United States— 1,690 in 22 of the 24 states west of the Mississippi River and the remaining 229 in the Mid-Atlantic region. Safeway's heaviest concentration was along the West Coast and the western providences of Canada. Its biggest competitor, Kroger, on the other hand, was strongest in the mid-western states and the southeastern portions of the United States.

37   Safeway clearly excelled at replacing older stores in saturated areas with newer, more modern outlets. As one frustrated competitor commented, Safeway hasn't even required its customers to change their habits. On some occasions, it has simply built the new store on part of the old parking lot and torn down the old building over a weekend. On Monday, there was

---

[3]Mitchel Gordon, "Safeway Stores Again Poised for Back-to-Back Profit Records," *Barron's,* March 7, 1983, p. 47.

a brand new store, but it was at the same old familiar place.

38   Safeway was late in spotting the trend toward superstores but then quickly became committed to the concept. It had no superstores as of the end of 1978. However, starting in 1979, the company added over 100 super-stores per year, each averaging 40,000 square feet. These one-stop shopping superstores doubled Safeway's volume in more profitable nonfood items in five years to well over 20 percent of total sales. Furthermore, most super-stores were able to show a profit within one year.

39   The company had equipped 915 stores with computer-assisted power management systems by the end of 1982 to monitor and control all energy uses within the store. Safeway also developed a fuel-reduction program for its extensive truck fleet. In fact, Safeway's various energy conservation programs had been so successful that the firm received an award from the Federal Energy Administration.

40   The company streamlined its manufacturing and processing facilities. In 1981 and 1982, for example, Safeway reduced the number of meat prefabricating plants from 11 to 3, discontinued several produce prepack-aging operations, combined production of two biscuit plants into one facil-ity, and reduced its nonstore work force by over 3,000 positions. Still, the extent of its manufacturing capabilities remained significant.

41   As of 1983, Safeway operated 105 manufacturing plants. They included 21 milk plants, 18 bakeries, 17 ice cream plants, 9 produce prepackaging plants, 5 soft drink bottling plants, 5 egg candling plants, 4 fruit and vegetable processing plants, 3 meat processing plants, 3 fresh beef fabrica-ting plants, 3 coffee and tea plants, 3 dressing and salad oil plants, 2 jam and jelly plants, 2 household chemicals plants, 1 edible oil refinery, 1 spice plant, 1 dry pet food plant, and 7 other various plants. In all, approximate-ly 12 percent of Safeway's employees were engaged in these various pro-cessing and distribution functions.

42   Each Safeway retail division, and the stores that comprised it, was supported by these modern distribution centers, which were actually a collection of specialized warehouses. Thus, groceries, meats, dairy products, frozen foods, and produce were all kept in separate warehouses depending on their maintenance needs. Safeway, which pioneered the distribution concept, had established a network of 29 distribution-warehouse centers by 1983.

43   A key function of the various distribution-warehouse centers was to receive thousands of items and then assemble them into truckloads that were sent out to the stores. The supporting fleet of vehicles needed to dis-tribute supplies to its countless stores included 2,500 tractor-trailers plus 2,600 additional trailers, comprising the largest private trucking fleet in the country. Because of its tremendous size, management believed it stood to gain more than the competition from the Transportation Act of 1980, which permitted backhauling, longer trailers, and heavier payloads. To exploit this potential advantage, Safeway started examining trucking routes and store delivery schedules. It then announced plans to reduce fuel

expenses and make maximum use of trailer space by combining deliveries and mixing loads as well as by vigorously pursuing backhaul opportunities. In this way, the expense of the return trip was covered, many times at a profit.

Finance/Accounting

44 Harry Sunderland, age 47, was the chief financial officer and treasurer for Safeway. He had been an officer with Safeway since 1972.

45 Several exhibits provided here review the company's financial performance. Exhibit 3 shows Safeway's balance sheet for calendar years 1980 through 1982. Exhibit 4 shows the consolidated statement of income and retained earnings for the same three years. For the year ending December 31, 1982, sales were $17.6 billion, and net income was $159,660,000. Exhibit 5 sheds some light on where the sales and profits came from by overviewing the financial performance of the stores by major geographical areas. Finally, Exhibit 6 provides a five-year summary of earnings, financial statistics, and other statistics.

46 Since overall statistics are sometimes hard to comprehend, one can consider what individual stores were expected to do. A conventional Safeway store did about $5 million in annual sales and was run by 65 people. Superstores, on the other hand, did between $10 and $15 million in sales and employed 120 to 150 people. Within each store, the goal was to be competitive with its pricing. That translated into being competitive with other stores offering comparable value on products of similar quality.

47 Arch competitor Kroger used 15 percent market share as a make-or-break point for each of its stores. If a store couldn't stay above that level, it was closed down. In contrast, under Magowan, Safeway had downplayed the importance of market share in favor of store volume. Magowan once stated that he would rather close down three stores with $100,000 weekly sales and open up one large store with a $250,000 weekly volume. He used this example to stress he was more interested in sales and profits in individual stores than in market share. Consequently, when Magowan closed stores, he did it more on the basis of low-store volume.

48 The company has also taken care to cut its losses in cities or regions when necessary. One past example was its 1962 decision to abandon the large New York market. Due to excessive pilferage, unions, and a small market share, it was unable to turn a profit and sold all 163 stores. The most recent divestiture decision was the closing of its 70-store Nebraska-Iowa division in 1982, which was mentioned earlier. However, 65 of those stores were sold at a $6 million profit, generating sizable funds to invest in other areas with a greater potential return. The five remaining stores were transferred to another division.

49 When Magowan first took office in 1980, the company's stock price had not increased since 1964. Even in 1982, Standard & Poor's actually advised

Exhibit 3

Safeway Stores, Incorporated, and subsidiaries consolidated balance sheet as of January 1, 1983, January 2, 1982, and January 3, 1981 (in thousands of dollars)

	1982	*1981*	*1980*
Assets			
Currents assets:			
Cash	$ 63,808	$ 44,075	$ 115,758
Receivables	73,105	72,180	56,633
Merchandise inventories:			
FIFO cost	1,627,440	1,496,775	1,269,560
Less: LIFO reductions	289,450	276,339	256,093
	1,337,990	1,220,436	1,013,467
Prepaid expenses and other current assets	142,646	128,984	83,809
Total current assets	1,617,545	1,465,675	1,269,667
Other assets:			
Licenses, notes receivable, and investments	49,616	40,814	31,775
Deferred income tax charges	7,220	—	—
Excess costs of investment in subsidiaries over net assets at date of acquisition, less amortization	14,301	16,234	2,859
Total other assets	71,137	57,048	34,634
Property:			
Land	174,623	159,113	138,201
Buildings	279,736	232,139	176,631
Leasehold improvements	403,413	375,407	363,143
Fixtures and equipment	1,610,584	1,497,632	1,336,333
Transport equipment	165,761	155,189	161,763
Property under capital leases	1,140,436	1,187,204	1,217,075
	3,774,553	3,606,684	3,393,146
Less: Accumulated depreciation and amortization	1,572,602	1,477,092	1,363,906
Total property	2,201,951	2,129,592	2,029,240
Total assets	$3,890,633	$3,652,315	$3,333,541
Liabilities and stockholders' equity			
Current liabilities:			
Notes payable	$ 88,028	$ 141,208	$ 116,679
Current obligations under capital leases	45,564	46,384	44,855
Current maturities of notes and debentures	13,845	10,406	5,880
Accounts payable	948,632	868,143	726,429
Accrued salaries and wages	149,492	136,628	129,457
Other accrued expenses	142,603	128,075	102,074
Income taxes payable	11,257	21,912	30,108
Total current liabilities	1,399,421	1,352,756	1,155,482
Long-term debt:			
Obligations under capital leases	767,309	809,393	844,011
Notes and debentures	488,877	328,223	207,218
Total long-term debt	1,256,186	1,137,616	1,051,229
Deferred income taxes	—	5,102	1,529
Accrued claims and other liabilities	97,931	81,743	69,614

Exhibit 3 (concluded)

	1982	1981	1980
Commitments and contingencies			
Stockholders' equity:			
Common stock—$1.66⅔ par value			
Authorized 75,000,000 shares			
Outstanding 26,149,743, 26,115,917,			
and 26,115,917 shares	43,583	43,527	43,527
Additional paid-in capital	64,573	63,436	63,436
Cumulative translation adjustments	(96,042)	(66,414)	(45,441)
Retained earnings	1,124,981	1,034,549	994,165
Total stockholders' equity	1,137,095	1,075,098	1,055,687
Total liabilities and stockholders' equity	$3,890,633	$3,652,315	$3,333,541

Source: Safeway Stores, Inc., Annual Report, 1982, pp. 22-23.

Exhibit 4

Safeway Stores, Incorporated, and subsidiaries consolidated statement of income and retained earnings for the 52 weeks ended January 1, 1983, the 52 weeks ended January 2, 1982, and the 53 weeks ended January 3, 1981 (in thousands of dollars)

	1982	1981	1980
Sales	$17,632,821	$16,580,318	$15,102,673
Cost of sales	13,628,052	12,945,923	11,816,733
Gross profit	4,004,769	3,634,395	3,285,940
Operating and administrative expenses	3,653,561	3,363,478	2,999,130
Operating profit	351,208	270,917	286,810
Interest expense	129,484	120,393	99,614
Other (income), net	(26,536)	(15,822)	(16,486)
Income before provision for income taxes	248,260	166,346	203,682
Provision for income taxes	88,600	58,062	74,544
Net income (per share: $6.11, $4.15 and $4.94)	159,660	108,284	129,138
Retained earnings at beginning of period	1,034,549	994,165	932,911
Cash dividends on common stock			
(per share: $2.65, $2,60, and $2.60)	(69,228)	(67,900)	(67,900)
Additions resulting from stock acquisitions	—	—	16
Retained earnings at end of period	$ 1,124,981	$ 1,034,549	$ 994,165

Source: Safeway Stores, Inc., Annual Report, 1982, p. 21.

Exhibit 5

Financial information by geographic area (in thousands of dollars)

	1982	1981	1980
U.S. sales...	$13,252,699	$12,491,852	$11,518,993
Gross profit...	3,128,111	2,815,057	2,576,021
Operating and administrative expenses...................	2,921,505	2,688,571	2,424,175
Operating profit....................................	206,606	126,486	151,846
Income before provision for income taxes................	110,199	21,050	70,283
Provision for income taxes	34,090	(6,007)	18,735
Net income...	76,109	27,057	51,548
Net working capital including merchandise			
inventories at FIFO cost.............................	384,744	277,160	229,099
Less: LIFO reductions	289,450	276,339	256,093
Net working capital (deficit)	95,294	821	(26,994)
Total assets	2,838,616	2,675,569	2,461,407
Net assets..	559,389	532,185	566,909
Culumative translation adjustments	—	—	—
Canada sales	2,569,717	2,404,972	2,190,917
Gross profit...	549,112	504,543	449,339
Operating and administrative expenses...................	452,170	410,701	357,894
Operating profit	96,942	93,842	91,445
Income before provision for income taxes................	93,387	103,256	95,263
Provision for income taxes	41,902	47,011	42,761
Net income...	51,485	56,245	52,502
Net working capital including merchandise			
inventories at FIFO cost.............................	—	—	—
Less: LIFO reductions	—	—	—
Net working capital (deficit)	135,108	150,681	161,428
Total assets	619,486	578,281	518,702
Net assets..	365,767	430,063	372,197
Cumulative translation adjustments	(54,219)	(40,362)	(41,806)
Overseas sales......................................	1,810,405	1,683,494	1,392,763
Gross profit...	327,546	314,795	260,580
Operating and administrative expenses...................	279,886	264,206	217,061
Operating profit	47,660	50,589	43,519
Income before provision for income taxes................	44,674	42,040	38,136
Provision for income taxes	12,608	17,058	13,048
Net income...	32,066	24,982	25,088
Net working capital including merchandise			
inventories at FIFO cost.............................	—	—	—
Less: LIFO reductions	—	—	—
Net working capital (deficit)	(12,278)	(38,583)	(20,249)
Total assets	432,531	398,465	353,432
Net assets..	211,939	112,850	116,581
Cumulative translation adjustments	(41,823)	(26,052)	(3,635)

Source: Safeway Stores, Inc., Annual Report, 1982, pp. 30–31.

investors to avoid Safeway stock. Safeway's management responded and took several steps to increase its stock's attractiveness. The quarterly dividend was increased to 70 cents per share of common stock starting with the fourth quarter of 1982. In early 1983, the board of directors declared a two-for-one stock split. A dividend reinvestment and stock pur-

Exhibit 6

Five-year summary of earnings, financial statistics, and other statistics

	1982	*1981*	*1980*	*1979*	*1978*
Earnings:					
Sales	$ 17.6B	$ 16.6B	$ 15.1B	$ 13.7B	$ 12.6B
Percent of annual increase	6.3—	9.8%	10.1—	9.3%	11.6%
Cost of sales	$ 13.6B	$ 12.9B	$ 11.8B	$ 10.8B	$ 9.8B
Gross profit	4.0B	3.6B	3.3B	2.9B	2.7B
Percent of sales	22.7%	21.9%	21.8%	21.3%	21.7%
Operating and administrative expenses........................	$ 3.7B	$ 3.4B	$ 3.0B	$ 2.6B	$ 2.4B
Percent of sales	20.7%	20.3%	19.9%	19.1%	18.9%
Operating profit	$351.2M	$270.9M	$286.8M	$306.6M	$352.9M
Interest expense	129.5M	120.4M	99.6M	91.3M	74.1M
Other income—net................	(26.5M)	(15.8M)	(16.5M)	(13.9M)	(10.8M)
Income taxes	88.6M	58.1M	74.5M	81.5M	130.6M
Net income........................	159.7M	108.3M	129.1M	147.7M	159.0M
Cash dividend per share of common stock	2.65	2.60	2.60	2.60	2.30
Average shares of common stock outstanding	26.1B	26.1B	26.1B	26.1B	26.1B
Financial statistics:					
Working capital	218.1M	112.9M	114.2M	127.1M	211.6M
Addition to property..............	511.9M	518.3M	493.0M	435.9M	303.1M
Depreciation and amortization....................	242.4M	226.0M	204.5M	180.9M	162.9M
Total assets	3.9B	3.7B	3.3B	3.1B	2.8B
Long-term debt	1.3B	1.1B	1.1B	955.7M	880.7M
Equity of common stockholders	1.1B	1.1B	1.1B	994.4M	903.2M
Per share of common stock........	43.48	41.17	40.42	38.08	34.61
Cash dividends on common stock	69.2M	67.9M	67.9M	67.9M	60.0M
Other statistics:					
Employees at end of year	156.5K	157.4K	150.0K	148.9K	144.2K
Stores opened during year........	153.0	159.0	160.0	104	111.0
Stores closed during year.........	176.0	98.0	169.0	115	103.0
Total stores at end of year	2,454	2,477	2,416	2,425	2,436
Total store area at year-end (in square feet)	66.8M	65.5M	62.1M	59.5M	57.5M
Average annual sales per store.......................	$ 7.2M	$ 6.7M	$ 61.M	$ 5.6M	$ 5.1M

K = thousands; M = millions; B = billions.
Source: Safeway Stores, Inc., Annual Report, 1982, p. 18.

chase plan was approved allowing stockholders to buy more shares—at 5 percent below market price. In addition, Safeway filed a $200 million stock issuance with the SEC. The proceeds were to be used to reduce short-term debt and for general corporate purposes. As 1982 came to an end, Safeway's common stock had made progress on the New York Stock Exchange. It started the year at $26.50 and closed at an impressive $45.75. During that same year, the Dow Jones averages rose by only 19.6 percent.

Research and Development

50   True to its name, Safeway had traditionally followed the safe route of letting others take the risks and then trying to play catchup. However, under Magowan, the company attempted to become more innovative. Magowan tried out many new ideas, moved Safeway into new businesses, such as Liquor Barns and fast-food chains, and was even considering the company's potential to provide a complete customer financial network similar to that provided by Sears. By 1983, this new philosophy had resulted in only one major failure—in-store home repair centers, which were a complete flop.

51   Unlike Kroger, Safeway did not use a formal customer research department. In fact, the company did not spend anything on research and development activities from 1980 through 1982. Nor did it conduct customer research related to the development of new products or services or the improvement of existing products, services, or techniques. However, by 1983 the picture had changed. According to one Safeway executive, "In the past, we ran our business by giving the consumers what we thought they wanted. Now we've got to find out what they want and then develop the products."[4] Under this new philosophy, the chain began using its scanner checkout system to test the results of price and display changes and to help figure out shelf-space allocations. The marketing staff also started to monitor customer attitudes by providing check-cashing privileges and discounts to those who filled out questionnaires on a regular basis.

Human Resources/Personnel

52   This functional area was headed by John Repass, senior vice president of human resources. Aged 51, Repass had been in this present position since only 1979 but had been a company officer since 1973.

53   With over 156,000 full- and part-time employees, labor was among Safeway's biggest costs, particularly so since the company had always been one of the most heavily unionized of all the retail food chains, with over 1,300 separate three-year contracts. It had paid higher-than-average wages for a long time; however, extended strikes still plagued the firm, sometimes resulting in temporarily shutting down stores in large regions. For example, a meat cutters' strike in 1973 forced the temporary closing of over 100 stores. In 1978, the Teamsters Union went out on strike for four months, which caused major disruptions of the company's northern California stores.

---

[4] "Safeway Jilts the Family of Four to Woo the Jogging Generation," *Business Week,* November 21, 1983, p. 99.

54   When the bulk of these union contracts were renegotiated in 1983, Safeway's management felt it had made considerable progress in achieving parity with competitors for labor costs. Working with union leadership, Safeway negotiated lower wage rates and got less restricted work rules included in many contracts.

55   Safeway also beefed up its employee communication program to provide workers with greater understanding of the organization's promotion system and how their roles meshed with the rest of the operation. To this end, several policies were installed. Notices of job openings were distributed to all Safeway stores and put up on bulletin boards. Career counseling sessions were held to explain how to prepare for future job openings. Employees were advised about the growth plans of the company and the number of each type of jobs it would be needing in the future. Employees were encouraged to use the educational reimbursement plan to a greater extent. Local colleges were utilized to teach specialized skills and supervisory courses. Finally, divisional newsletters were used to publicize employees who had been promoted and to explain how they got their jobs.

56   With more than 2,000 stores, the need to promote employees into new positions of responsibility was a never ending proposition for Safeway. In the late 1970s and early 1980s, Safeway felt it needed to train about 350 new store managers, 350 new meat department managers, 700 new assistant store managers, and 800 new produce managers. Furthermore, this had to be done each year during that period to satisfy the demand caused by retirements, promotions, transfers, resignations, and the opening of new stores.

57   Working on better ways to assess candidates for promotion, management developed a retail career development center program that put assistant store managers through simulated exercises resembling actual situations faced by store managers. This provided employees with a good understanding of their own strengths and weaknesses, while the company got an objective evaluation of promotion candidates.

58   Paradoxically, at the uppermost levels of the organizational structure, Magowan no longer promoted almost exclusively from within. On many occasions, he hired outsiders skilled in running pharmacies, delicatessens, health food departments, liquor stores, and other nongrocery operations. This was clearly a departure from Safeway's past tradition of almost always promoting from within.

Management

59   Safeway had been decentralized to a fault under Mitchell. While leaving most merchandising decisions with local stores, Magowan tightened controls in certain areas. For example, he centralized the organization's purchasing and advertising departments as well as its processing of fresh meat. Moreover, he brought regional managers back to headquarters and

fundamentally reorganized headquarters. He created an office of the chairman, which he ran along with four senior vice presidents whom he promoted to share this new office.

60   In addition to these moves, Magowan took the company away from the lawyers, who ruled during Mitchell's reign, and turned it over to executives with strong retail experience. He also brought in more young managers from the outside with fresh ideas to help turn the conservative Safeway around. Youth was clearly being emphasized. Safeway's 1982 annual report even profiled 17 key middle managers on the rise who ranged in age from 31 to 45.

61   Safeway was organized on both a functional and a geographic basis. It was functionally organized at the corporate level with vice presidents (or equivalents) heading up retail, supply, and a variety of corporate services, which included (1) personnel and public relations, (2) general counsel, (3) grocery merchandising, (4) advertising and market research, (5) treasurer, (6) controller, (7) management information and services group, and (8) real estate construction and engineering. All of these people reported directly to Dale Lynch, who was the president and chief operating officer. In turn, the 61-year-old Lynch reported to the 40-year-old Peter Magowan, chairman of the board and chief executive officer, who was clearly the firm's chief strategist.

62   Within the retail functional area, however, Safeway was organized according to regional locations. Among those people who reported to John Bell, the vice president regional manager—retail, were three U.S. regional managers. Vice President Bell also functioned as one regional manager and had 847 stores grouped under his 7 divisions. The Los Angeles division had 185 stores; Phoenix, 88; Richmond, 77; Sacramento, 92; San Diego, 52; San Francisco, 203; and the Washington, D.C. division, 150. A second U.S. regional manager, Fred MacRae, had responsibility for 497 stores grouped in six divisions. The Butte division had 28 stores; Denver, 146; Portland, 94; Salt Lake City, 59; Seattle, 129; and the Spokane division, 41. William Maloney, the third and final U.S. regional manager, had 575 stores under him. The Dallas division had 153 stores; El Paso, 54; Houston, 99; Kansas City, 79; Little Rock, 65; Oklahoma City, 68; and the Tulsa division, 57. Stores in Canada and overseas were similarly grouped and first reported to a division manager who in turn reported to a regional manager in that country or a major geographic region.

63   In 1982, Safeway's first strategic management program was established to help the company adapt to the changing environment. As spelled out in its 1982 annual report, the corporate mission included the following five elements:

1. To be a growing company.
2. To be a profitable company.

3. To be a worldwide company.

4. To be a retailer of groceries.

5. To be a retailer of related consumer goods and services.[5]

The External Environment

The Grocery Industry

64   The grocery industry has been described as dynamic, complex, and very competitive. Billion dollar chains were operating on a bottom line of less than 1 percent profit. Thus, there was little room for error for the managers who made them run. In the 1980s, competitive pricing made already slim margins even smaller.

65   With all this competition, it was not uncommon for supermarkets to engage in price wars in specific markets. Unfortunately for the stores, usually the only winner in these wars was the customer. These price wars took many forms. Sometimes the stores just lowered their prices. Other times, they offered double, triple, or even quadruple savings on coupons. At still other times, gimmicks such as stamps, games, or giveaways were initiated. No matter what the method, the reason was always the same. One store or chain in an area decided it needed to improve its market share, so it offered an incentive to customers to shop there for a change. Since the larger volume could lead to greater revenues than the cost of the promotion, it seemed like a good idea. It made further sense since statistics showed that many of the shoppers stayed with the new store as regular customers, even after the promotion was over.

66   The extra volume had to come from somewhere, and it was usually from the other grocery stores in the area. Naturally, they had to lower their prices or offer some sort of promotion to protect their share, and another price war was on. One industry observer explained that chain promotions were very important to generate new customers and protect the ones a store already had.

67   One major trend in the 1980s was the sizable increase in the number of superstores, which represented a major shift in how a growing number of Americans did their grocery shopping. Their higher store profitability was often attributed to very high volume, many more high margin food and nonfood items, and fixed and variable costs being spread over a larger volume.

68   Safeway's Chairman Peter Magowan accurately assessed the situation when he commented, "It's not going to be good enough to be just the best in

---

[5]Safeway Stores, Inc., *Safeway Stores, Incorporated, Annual Report, 1982* (Oakland, California Safeway Stores, Inc., 1982), p. 1.

running a conventional grocery store."[6] Not surprisingly, the majority of stores closed in the 1980s were conventional grocery stores, while, conversely, about 70 percent of the new stores opened were superstores. Furthermore, many existing stores were being rapidly converted to larger, superstore-type formats.

69   Interestingly, the industry trend toward superstores appeared to be incongruent with the traditional three premises of supermarket operation:

1. Convenience and fast service.

2. Mass merchandising of volume items.

3. High productivity and efficiency.

70   Anyone who had ever entered a supermarket knew that walking through one of them took time. Walking through a 30,000 or more square foot superstore obviously would take even more time. With the recent increases in energy and labor costs, it was questionable just how much money these stores actually saved. In fact, one study showed that as store size exceeded 27,000 square feet, productivity tended to decrease.

71   Despite these potential problems, customer acceptance of superstores was high. Consumers seemed to enjoy the easy access to a variety of competitively priced goods and services under one roof. It was even predicted that price wars would lessen in number and intensity as higher profits arrived all around.

Changing Demographics

72   One demographic change that Safeway and other grocery chains had to deal with was the reality that more women than ever before were in the labor force. Over half of all women aged 16 and over held jobs outside the home, and it was anticipated that another 7 million women would do so before the 1980s were over. While this meant that many women had more money for shopping, they also had less spare time to do it in. In addition, more males began to share the grocery shopping duties. Recent studies have confirmed that in households where both spouses hold jobs, the male is twice as likely to share in the shopping. A second reason for this increase in male shoppers was the growing number of single male households in the United States, including both young, single men and those who have been divorced.

73   Supermarkets needed to be aware of this demographic change because males approached grocery shopping from a rather different perspective than did females. In general, men considered the task to be a bother. Therefore, convenience was emphasized instead of bargains. Clearly, they

---

[6]"Safeway Stores," p. 108.

were willing to pay more to save time. In addition, men were more loyal to particular brands; thus, they preferred shopping at stores that offered a wide variety of major brands.

74   A second key demographic change was the shifting population among regions of the United States. The migration to the Sun Belt was increasing in the early 1980s, causing unprecedented population growth in Texas, Florida, California, and other southern states. Furthermore, the ethnic make-up of the population itself was changing. According to the 1980 census, about 12 percent of the U.S. population was black and 8 percent Hispanic. However, it was expected that the number of Hispanics would surpass blacks by 1990. In fact, they were predicted to account for 50 percent of California's population by the year 2000.

75   A third key demographic change was that the population was getting older. The 25 to 44 age group was growing three and a half times faster than the total population, and the number of people over 65 was expected to reach 31 million by 1990. Also, a new baby boom was expected to peak between 1985 and 1989 with 4 million expected births per year.

76   This older population was more educated and more affluent than ever before. As such, they demanded superior quality and a wide selection of items to choose from. Many of them were also very interested in health and nutrition and had changed their eating patterns. For this subgroup, their consumption of beef, whole milk, coffee, and eggs had dropped while their purchases of chicken, low-fat milk, and cheese had soared. In addition, ethnic foods, wines, and easy-to-prepare foods were gaining increasing popularity among this older group.

Industry Threats and Problems

77   The industry's sales had increased in recent years, but at a decreasing rate. First, the economic downturn from 1981 to 1983 hurt even the strongest of retail chains. Second, grocery shoppers started purchasing cheaper-priced private-label brands and generics to a greater extent. Third, more grocery shoppers reduced their purchase of higher-margin, nonfood items when they went to the grocery store.

78   An increasingly major expense item for grocery stores was wages. In the late 1970s and early 1980s, wage increases outpaced increasing grocery sales. It was even worse for those chains that linked cost-of-living increases with rises in the consumer price index. When inflation finally began to slow down, unionized grocery stores were stuck with annual wage increases negotiated when inflation was increasing rapidly. This caused operating margins to erode further. Some grocery chains responded by closing their least profitable stores, particularly in the depressed Midwest. These closings and the threat of additional closings elsewhere helped some grocery chains obtain wage and benefit concessions from their respective unions.

79   Although union concessions had helped to alleviate the problem for some chains in the short run, the situation was expected to change. Since many unions had agreed to pay cuts to assist their companies during hard times, it was doubtful they would sit by idly when profits began to go up again. Moreover, some experts felt that labor unions would attempt to recoup the losses they suffered during those weak economy years of 1981-1983.

80   As for managerial pay, some experts feared that the U.S. Labor Department's Wage and Hour Division would adopt new white-collar salary test levels to determine who was exempt from overtime pay. If this legislative threat were to materialize, assistant store managers and supervisors who currently worked long hours, but were not paid for it, would acquire non-exempt jobs requiring overtime pay. This could mean that their salaries would increase by up to 50 percent.

81   Energy costs were a bigger problem than ever. Especially because of their refrigeration systems, supermarkets were large users of energy. During 1982 alone, energy costs for chains climbed by over 15 percent. Many stores installed glass doors on their refrigeration units to reduce these costs.

82   Finally, consumers were also becoming more vocal when confronted with defective merchandise or dissatisfied with it for any seeming reason. A defect was legally defined as anything wrong with a product that might cause harm. It could refer to something omitted from a product or something that should not be a part of it. This could include not only the product itself but also packaging, misleading or inadequate warnings, instructions, or other literature. For the grocery industry, there was an extra catch. Even though food products could be spoiled or impure through no fault of the manufacturer or seller, the law allowed courts to hold stores liable even though no fault or lapse of conduct on their part had taken place. Thus, supermarkets not only had to monitor carefully the products they sold but also had to prevent misuse or abuse of their products if at all possible.

83   Although it was still many years away, some industry executives saw a possible revolutionary change coming. Some added that they did not view it so much as a threat but rather as a technological change that they would have to adjust to. It seemed quite possible that some day customers might be able to order their groceries from a monitor in their home. Some cable networks already had established a television channel devoted to listing the prices of commodities at various local grocery stores, and viewers were able to compare prices without leaving their living rooms. It may not be too long before they would select grocery items with a keyboard attached to their television sets. The grocery store would then deliver the order later the same day.

The Future for Safeway

84   With its aggressive entrepreneurial chief executive officer, Safeway had come a long way from its former conservative posture. In 1983, it had

adopted a more innovative stance than ever before and was willing to try out new ideas, even before its competition did.

85   The company had chosen to continue expansion, both inside and outside of the country, despite its already gigantic size. It had also expanded the size of its new stores to well over 30,000 square feet in what seemed to be a response to a rather well-established industry trend.

86   An industry report in 1982 concluded that perhaps the companies best positioned to emerge from the recession of the early 1980s would be the ones that carried a light debt load, sported a strong cash flow, and found the means to finance expansions internally.[7] Whether Safeway meets these goals may ultimately depend on its ability to react quickly given its size. The environment of the grocery industry was currently so dynamic that predictions as to what lay down the road were very tenuous. If interest rates did not rise again, if profit margins continued to grow through the continued expansion of superstores, if costly price wars could be avoided, if union negotiations continued to fare well, and if overseas currencies stabilized in the countries where the company did business, then Safeway would probably do well. But what if some of these assumptions did not hold true? What would lie ahead for Safeway then? Large battleships, like grocery giants such as Safeway, have lots of momentum once they get going, but how long does it take them to put on the brakes and change their basic direction?

---

[7]"Supermarkets and Grocery Chains—Disinflation Squeezing Retail Profits," *Standard & Poor's Industry Surveys* (New York Standard & Poor's, 1982), p. R182.

case **24** **Note on the Oil Industry**

History, Structure, and Government Regulations

Background

1   The existence of crude oil has been acknowledged for hundreds of years. It was not until the middle of the 19th century, however, that crude oil became popular. Its popularity coincided with the search for an improved source of lighting and the development of a suitable refinery process. The crude oil used as feedstock was refined into a lighting oil known as kerosene. The oil was found in natural seeps in the earth's surface and initially sold for about $20 a barrel.

2   In 1859, Edwin L. Drake struck oil in Titusville, Pennsylvania by drilling a well 69 feet. This was the first time that oil had been obtained by drilling through rock. This event has been classified as the birth of the oil industry. The market and a price had been established and, finally, substantial quantities were available.

3   The price, however, did not remain at $20 a barrel. As a result of Drake's discovery, many men rushed to Pennsylvania to search for crude oil. This surge in exploration soon spread to other states and to other countries. As the available supply increased, the price plummetted. By 1861, the price of a barrel of crude oil averaged fifty cents.

This note was written by Mary Pat Cormack, Coordinator of the MaGuire Oil and Gas Institute of Southern Methodist University and M. Edgar Barrett, Director of the same institute.

4   **Original Refined Products.** The primary product of the unsophisticated refineries of the 1860's was kerosene. Lubricants, which became more in demand as the United States moved into a new technological age, were also produced. Another product resulting from the refining process was natural gasoline. However, it had no use at the time and was considered to be a waste by-product.

5   The Civil War hastened the development of a new technological age. This, consequently, increased the need for petroleum. Some new industrial processes were developed. In addition, existing factories worked at capacity producing materials needed for the war. These factories required both kerosene and lubricants.

6   The need for petroleum, however, did not decrease when the war ended. Many cities needed to be rebuilt and a railroad system, which brought with it a movement to settle the Western United States, had been established. Petroleum and petroleum-based products became more and more a part of the American life-style.

7   At the turn of the century, the development of the internal combustion engine and the birth of the auto industry resulted in a variety of new applications for products derived from crude oil. This caused still another increase in the demand for crude oil. Gasoline, a product which had been considered a waste by-product, found a market.

The Structure of the Industry

8   As the foreign oil industry evolved, it divided itself between the major companies and the independent companies. Majors were defined as integrated companies: those involved in exploration, production, transportation, refining, and marketing. Independents, for the most part, were involved in only one phase of the industry. The domestic oil industry, however, evolved into three distinct groups: the top eight, the lesser majors, and the non-integrated independents.

9   The top eight domestic oil companies in 1982, in terms of total assets, were: Exxon, Mobil, Texaco, Standard (Indiana), Standard Oil of California, Gulf, Atlantic Richfield, and Shell. Their split from other majors was recognized because these companies so clearly separated themselves from the other integrated oil companies. In 1982, the top eight companies owned 44.5% of all domestic oil reserves and produced 39.1% of all crude oil in the United States.[1] Total assets for members of this group ranged from $21.4 billion to $62.3 billion at year-end 1982.[2]

10   Although differences of opinion existed concerning the classification of certain oil companies, a group of 14 companies were classified by many as

[1]*Market Shares and Individual Company Data for U.S. Energy Markets: 1950–1982,* American Petroleum Institute, 1983.

[2]"Annual Reports," reprinted from *National Petroleum News Factbook Issue,* 1983.

the lesser majors in 1982, bringing the total number of majors to 22. Total assets for this group ranged from $1.2 billion to $17.4 billion.[3]

11   **The Evolution of the Industry's Structure.** The production of crude oil in the United States has always been widely dispersed among numberous producers. The faith and determination of many individuals, not just a few companies, played a vital role in shaping the oil industry. For example, independents discovered 14 of the 15 large oil pools in Texas and Oklahoma between 1912 and 1926. Many of the discoveries were in areas that the majors would not touch.

12   In addition to sheer will on the part of the independents, a dominance by the major producers did not develop domestically due to the laws that governed *mineral rights* in the United States.[4] The mineral rights in most foreign countries belonged to the government. Major companies often negotiated contracts that granted concessions that allowed them a near, or absolute, monopoly in the exploration and production of oil in a specific foreign country. Consequently, a small number of producers controlled the mineral rights underlying a vast amount of land.

13   Ownership of land in the United States, however, included what was below it (the mineral rights). Therefore, the right to drill often involved negotiations with a large number of landowners. As a result of these circumstances, the ownership of the mineral rights in the United States belonged to many individuals or companies, not a small number of large companies. Given a choice between focusing their efforts upon large tracts, often consisting of an entire country, and small tracts, often as small as a few hundred acres, the majors chose the former.

14   Although the production phase of the industry was not dominated by a few companies, that was not the case in other phases of the industry. In their early stages, both refining and transportation operations were controlled by one company—the Standard Oil Trust. In 1870, the Trust controlled 10% of the nation's refining capacity. Nine years later, its control had increased to 90%. This increase was achieved, in large part, through control of transportation, both pipelines and railroads.

15   It was feared that the production of crude oil would also become concentrated. Many people hypothesized that the Trust would determine which producers could get their crude transported and refined. Therefore, the Supreme Court dissolved the Standard Oil Trust in 1911. The result of this action was the creation of 34 independent operating companies, each positioned in one or two phases of the industry.

16   Many, if not most, of these newly created companies found themselves to be partially or totally lacking in one or more key facets of the overall oil and gas business. Standard Oil (Indiana), for example, found itself with

---

[3]Ibid.

[4]Those tems underlined are in the glossary, shown as Appendix A.

neither crude oil nor pipelines. However, not long afterwards, the newly divided companies resumed their growth and began striving to attain balance as integrated companies.

17   The period, 1920 to 1935, was one of the most active periods in the history of the industry with respect to integration. Management realized that by operating their companies across two or more levels of the industry, they would gain considerable protection against wide fluctuation in their profit positions. Another factor, however, played an even greater role in the substantial forward integration movement that took place during this period. This was the existence of an abundant supply of crude oil.

18   The property laws in the United States with respect to oil and gas were based on the "rule of capture." Thus, the producers of a well on a tract of land acquired title to all the oil and gas produced from their well despite the fact that some of the oil and gas could have been drained from under adjoining properties. Newly discovered oil was usually produced at maximum rates regardless of the price of the oil or the requirements of the market. Obviously, it was to the advantage of the producers to sell their oil at any price in excess of their direct lifting costs, rather than to lose it entirely to a neighboring producer.

19   Many *prorationing laws* were enacted between 1930 and 1935. These laws put an end to this situation of maximum production rates. However, until this time, an acute condition of oversupply existed. Many crude oil producers integrated their companies into refining activities as a means of disposing of their crude oil. Due to the large number of companies that followed this pattern, the competition in this phase of the industry increased greatly. This situation stimulated forward integration into marketing activities by refiners who needed outlets for their processed crude.

20   Another wave of extensive integration occurred between 1935 and the 1950s. This wave resulted from both forward integration by producers and backward integration by refiners. The latter, however, was the more prevalent situation during this period. Backward integration by refiners was due primarily to the characteristics of the refining business. This facet of the oil industry was very capital intensive and, for the most part, was not a profitable business unless refineries were run at 75% capacity or better. For this reason, joined with the fact that the supply of crude oil was at times scarce, many refiners acquired producing companies or potential acreage to insure the supply of crude oil for their refineries.

Government Involvement: Tax Regulations

21   In 1974, the federal level, corporate tax bill for the 19 largest oil companies in the United States averaged 7.6% of their income before taxes.[5] Consider-

---

[5]John M. Blair, *The Control of Oil,* (Vintage Books, 1978), p. 187.

ing that the corporate tax rate was 48%, the tax code applicable to the oil industry obviously contained special provisions. These provisions not only set the industry apart from other industries, they also contriuted significantly to the evolution of its structure. They did this, primarily, by providing multiple incentives to explore for oil, both at home and abroad.

22   Three provisions of the tax code had, by far, the most impact: the percentage depletion allowance; the cost of intangible drilling costs; and, the foreign tax credit.

23   *Percentage Depletion.* This tax allowance was established in order to allow various taxpayers to reflect the exhaustion of a natural resource by way of a deduction from their taxable income. It was analogous to the depreciation allowance, which usually reflected the reduction of the unexpired cost of a tangible asset. However, the percentage depletion allowance gave taxpayers the right to deduct from operating revenue an amount which was based upon the selling price of the natural resource. On the other hand, the depreciation allowance was usually based upon the cost of the asset. In addition, under rules that governed depreciation, an allowance could not be taken after the cost of the property had been fully depreciated. Tax deductible depletion allowances, however, were historically taken as long as the well was producing. "Studies have indicated that percentage depletion allowances have provided deductions that over the life of a productive property recovered from 10 to 20 times the cost."[6]

24   From 1925 to the late 1960s, the percentage depletion allowance was calculated by taking $27 \frac{1}{2}\%$ of gross income from the sale of crude oil from each unit of property. This amount was limited to 50% of net income from the sale of crude oil from each unit of property. When the law was revised in the late 1960s, the percentage allowed was reduced to 22%, and the deduction was limited to the revenue generated from 2,000 barrels of oil per day.

25   Again, substantial reductions were placed on the allowance as a result of the Tax Reduction Act of 1975. Similar acts in the following years had much the same effect. As of 1978, the only oil companies allowed to use the percentage depletion allowance were independent oil producers. Independent producers, for purposes of determining taxable status, were defined as those who received no more than 5% of their gross revenues from retailing or refining.

26   Other restrictions that were placed upon the allowance included the reduction of the barrel per day limit and of the percentage used to calculate the allowance. By 1980, the limit of barrels per day (b/d) used to calculate the allowance was to be reduced from 2,000 b/d to 1,000 b/d. Also, the percentage of gross income allowed was to be reduced gradually from 22%

---

[6]Ibid., p. 189.

in 1980 to 15% after 1983. In addition, the percentage depletion allowance was disallowed in connection with foreign production.

27   **Intangible Drilling Costs.** Approximately 75% to 90% of total drilling costs, such as wages, fuel, drilling mud, and machine tool rentals, have historically been classified as intangible drilling costs. Many of these costs, if incurred in another industry would have been classified as capitalized costs and would have been capitalized and then depreciated over the useful life of the property. In the oil industry, however, all costs classified as intangible drilling costs were allowed to be listed as expenses for tax purposes in the year in which they were incurred.

28   As with the percentage depletion allowance, recent changes in the tax code have affected the provisions that allowed for the expensing of intangible drilling costs. Previously, costs that were incurred abroad could be used to offset domestic income for tax purposes. This rule was disallowed in 1975. As of 1980, only the intangible drilling costs incurred in domestic operations could be used to offset domestic income. Similarly, only the intangible drilling costs incurred abroad could be used to offset foreign income.

29   **Foreign Tax Credit.** In the United States, a producing company that leased mineral rights from a landowner usually paid the landowner for these rights. On the other hand, payment to acquire the right to foreign production was usually paid to the state in the form of taxes. The foreign tax credit allowed companies operating internationally to use the taxes paid to one country as direct offsets against taxes owed to another. As credits, 100% of the payment was used to offset taxes payable in the United States, whereas, had domestic companies paid the foreign governments in the form of royalties, the payment would have been worth approximately 48 cents (assuming a 48% tax rate).

30   As with percentage depletion and the expensing of intangible drilling costs, the effect of the foreign tax credit was lessened in recent years. By 1980, the maximum amount of foreign tax credits allowed could not exceed 48% of foreign income emanating from oil and gas operations.

The Main Processes Inherent in the Industry

Exploration and Production

31   During the 1970s, the United States became increasingly more dependent on foreign oil. In 1970, only 9% of the total domestic demand for crude oil was supplied by foreign crude oil imports. Domestic crude oil production accounted for 64% of the total consumption. By 1979, 34% of the total

domestic demand was supplied by imports, and domestic crude oil production accounted for only 45% of the total consumption. This trend, however, changed and by 1981 only 26% of demand was supplied by imports and domestic crude oil accounted for 51% of total consumption.

32   Simultaneous with the development of this trend, the oil companies began focusing more attention on the domestic exploration and production aspects of the industry. According to one industry analyst, "the greatest stock market reward has been and will continue to be accorded those companies who demonstrate superior exploratory expertise."[7] The same analyst outlined three factors that investors should focus their attention on when evaluating a company. He believed that the firm should have: (1) long-lived reserves in the United States and Canada; (2) large inventories of undeveloped acreage; and (3) healthy cash flows to ensure evaluation of the acreage.

33   Drilling in the United States reached a record level in 1956 which was not surpassed until 1980. However, these levels of drilling activity were not sustained during the two decades between these peaks. The upswing did not begin until the early 1970s.

34   The substantial increase in the price of crude oil during the 1970s was the cause of the increased interest in domestic drilling. Free-market crude prices in some parts of the United States topped $40/bbl. at times in 1980. The average price of crude oil in May of that year was $21, compared to $3.89 per barrel in 1973.

35   The United States accounted for 80% of all wells completed in the entire free world during 1980. In the same year, in the state of Texas alone, more wells were drilled than in the total of the rest of the free world. In addition to established drilling areas in Texas, Oklahoma, and Louisiana, the most widely discussed prospective areas included: the *Outer Continental Shelf,* the Western Overthrust Belt, the Tuscaloosa Trend and the Williston Basin. (See Exhibit 1.)

36   **Offshore Activities.** The *Department of Interior* announced plans in 1979 to conduct five offshore lease sales a year extending into 1985. The Outer Continental Shelf was believed to hold great potential for oil and gas discoveries. For this reason, these lease offerings were expected to command very substantial *bonuses.* Past sales had substantiated this belief. The July 1979 offshore lease sale for properties lying off the Louisiana Coast commanded total bonuses of $1.24 billion. The 90 offshore Texas tracts that were put up for sale in November of 1979 brought $1.91 billion in bonus payments. The next month, more than $1 billion was spent in the federal and state lease sale in the Beaufort Sea, an area offshore northern Alaska. Exxon, Union Oil and Atlantic Richfield were the largest spenders, accounting for more than half of the total outlay.

---

[7]William H. Furth, "Oil Industry Fundamentals," Bear Sterns, 1980.

Exhibit 1

Domestic exploration and production areas

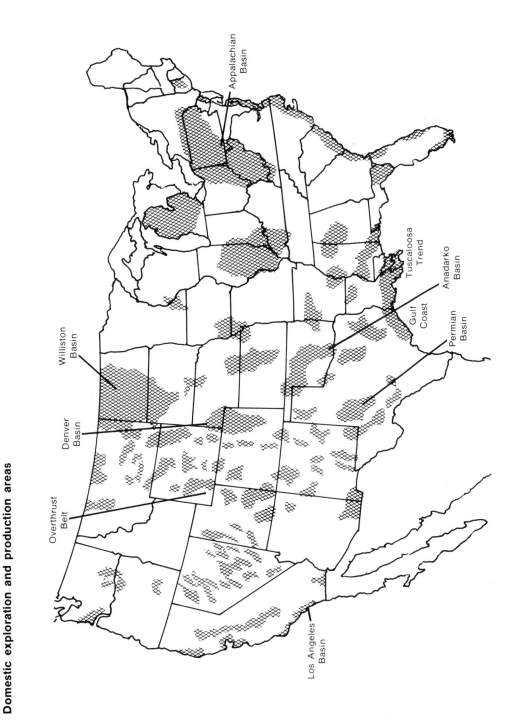

37   **The Western Overthrust Belt.** This prospective oil producing area extended from the Canadian Rockies through the United States and into Mexico. Drilling activities, however, were heavily concentrated in a 20- by 70-mile fairway in southwest Wyoming and northeast Utah. This area did not receive active exploration until the mid to late 1970s. American Quasar's and Amoco Production Company's discoveries sparked a rush to the area.

38   **The Tuscaloosa Trend.** This trend extended some 200 miles. It ran from northeast of New Orleans, Louisiana, through Baton Rouge to the Louisiana-Texas border. Virtually all the major oil companies were active in the area.

39   **The Williston Basin.** This basin was located in North Dakota and Montana. It was expected to remain an active area of exploration and production. Unlike other major producing areas, the smaller independents were highly visible in this area. They sought smaller, but highly profitable, finds.

The Future

40   Drilling fell sharply during 1982 in both the United States and Canada. For the short term the future was predicted to be a time of declining exploration and development. This was primarily due to the surplus of oil and gas that existed at year-end 1982 and because of the uncertainty about how much lower crude oil prices would fall. (In March 1983, members of OPEC reduced the price of marker crude from \$34/bbl. to \$29/bbl.)

Transportation

41   Crude oil is transported from producing areas to refineries by a vast system of pipelines, ocean tankers, barges, tank cars, and tank trucks. Similar modes of transportation move the refined products from the refining centers to the marketing areas. Generally, the crude oil and petroleum products that are transported through this distribution system are not owned by the company that carries them.

42   **Pipelines.** As of the beginning of 1980, over 100 companies delivered more than 6.7 billion barrels of crude oil and over 4.4 billion barrels of product through their pipelines. These companies owned 168,976 miles of pipeline. Investment in liquid pipelines was almost \$19 billion at the end of 1979. The combined operating revenue of the pipeline companies was about \$5.8 billion, while net income was over \$1.6 billion.

43   In late 1979, the National Petroleum Council noted some significant

trends in the petroleum pipeline system in the United States.[8] They were: (1) due to the decrease in domestic petroleum supplies from the lower 48 states, more crude oil was being imported through water terminals and transported to inland refineries by pipeline; (2) in an effort to move petroleum more efficiently, crude oil, liquified petroleum gas (LPG), and refined products were being frequently *batched* through the same lines; and, (3) with the advent of higher priced crude oil, refined products, and LPG, more precise methods of measurement were being implemented.

44   **Railroad.** As of July 1979, there were 202,811 tank cars, representing a 3.6 billion gallon capacity, in the U.S. rail car fleet. Of that total, 107,522 cars of 2.2 billion gallon capacity were considered to be suitable for carrying crude oil and petroleum products. This represented a 28% increase in capacity since 1967. However, the number of cars decreased by 24%, reflecting the industry trends of replacing older, smaller equipment with cars of greater capacity.

45   **Other Modes of Transportation.** As of December 1978, U.S. tankships had a capacity of 97 million barrels. The 3,971 barges suitable for hauling petroleum had a capacity of 71.4 million barrels. Tank trucks had a total capacity of 364 million gallons. There were approximately 50,000 tank trucks, each with a capacity of over 3,500 gallons.

Refining

46   Domestic refining capacity on January 1, 1983 was almost 16.2 million b/d. This represented a 8.5% decrease over the capacity of the previous year. The top 20 refiners in the U.S. represented almost 12.5 million b/d or 77% of the total capacity. These 20 companies operated 95 refineries, with an average capacity of 131,000 b/d. The largest domestic refinery was owned by Exxon. It was located in Baytown, Texas and its capacity on May 1, 1982 was 640,000 b/d. The remaining 3.7 million b/d were refined by 113 companies in 130 refineries. Average capacity for this group was 28,000 b/d.

47   **Reductions and Shifts in Product Demand.** Due to forecasts that called for the demand for petroleum products to remain unchanged or even decline slightly during the 1980s, the refinery capacity that existed in the United States in 1983 was believed to be basically adequate for the next several years. However, the basic configuration of many refineries was

[8]*U.S. Petroleum Inventories, and Storage and Transportation Capacities*, Volume I, National Petroleum Council, November 1979, p. 27.

scheduled to be, or had recently been, revised due to changes in the demand for specific products. The decline in the demand for heating oil and residual fuel oil was offset by increased demand for commercial jet fuel, liquified gases, petrochemical feedstocks, and lubricants. In addition, the industry concentrated much of its efforts on improving percentage yields of unleaded gasoline as lead phasedown regulations became stricter.

48   **Availability of Crude.** Many of the expected alterations to refineries were also made due to a shift in availability of types of crude oil. *Light sweetcrudes,* those with low sulfur content and low "gravity," were in the greatest demand and the least supply. North American crude was generally classified as light, sweet crude. However, the majority of foreign crudes were *heavy, sour-crudes.*

49   In 1978, approximately 46% of the crude oil processed in domestic refineries was of medium to high sulfer content. This percentage was projected to increase to 49% in 1980 and 51% in 1982.[9] Therefore, refiners were focusing much of the upgrading efforts on producing basically the same amount of *light products* (gasoline and middle-distillate fuel) from inferior crudes.

50   To accomplish this goal, refiners will be required to install desulferization equipment such as *hydro-treating* facilities. However, this equipment could be restricted to the large refineries due to cost. The restructuring of a refinery was expected to come close to the building of a new refinery in terms of cost. For example, Chevron spent over $750 million during 1980 for two high-sulfur processing projects.

Marketing

51   Retail outlets operated directly by the major refiners numbered approximately 5% of the industry total in 1980. This was about the same percent that prevailed ten years earlier. The distribution of gasoline was done primarily through *jobbers* and *franchised dealers.* The major oil companies, however, influenced distribution patterns by acquiring properties (potential service station locations) and, subsequently, leasing the properties to independent operators under franchise-type arrangements.

52   The number of *service stations* in the United States was reduced by more than 35% from its peak of 226,000 in 1972 to 144,690 in 1982. However, average annual sales revenues per station increased from $149,000 in 1972 to $736,000 for 1982.[10] The service stations eliminated were, for the most part, outlets where the monthly volume was less than 50,000 gallons. New stations were usually quite large, many with sales significantly greater than 100,000 gallons monthly.

---

[9]*Refinery Flexibility,* National Petroleum Council, 1980, p. 10.
[10]*National Petroleum News Factbook,* 1983, p. 100.

53   In addition to the increase of high volume stations at the expense of smaller units, the industry also experienced a notable trend in the 1970s concerning self-service stations. The amount of gallons of gasoline sold through self-service stations increased continually during the 1970s. By 1982, self-service stations held about a 72% share of the motorist gasoline market in the United States. This was up from 26% in 1975 and 47% in 1978.

54   Amoco was the number one gasoline marketer in the United States in 1982 for the second year in a row. Shell ranked second and Exxon ranked third in both 1981 and 1982.

International Oil

55   Most of the world's known reserves, outside the Communist countries and North America, were found in few locales: the Middle East, Libya, Algeria, Nigeria, Venezuela, and Indonesia.[11] As previously mentioned, ownership of foreign mineral rights generally resided in the state or the ruler. Therefore, companies seeking exploration rights did not have to deal with numerous private owners of the surface land. Early concession agreements between foreign governments and a few large companies granted monopoly rights for the exploration of oil in huge areas, extending over long periods of time.

Historical Background

56   **Early Concessions.** By 1920, nearly all the major American oil companies were actively seeking foreign reserves. These actions were strongly encouraged by the U.S. government. Fear of an oil shortage had been on the minds of many politicians since the First World War. As a result, the State Department declared the doctrine of the "Open Door," which demanded that the Allies should not discriminate against each other in oil supplies.

57   Despite the efforts on the part of the oil companies and the U.S. government, access to foreign concessions, especially in the Middle East, was not easily obtained. It was not until 1928 that any American companies were granted concessions in the Middle East. In that year, Exxon and Mobil became part owners of the Iraq Petroleum Company. In 1933, Gulf entered the area through Kuwait, and, in the same year, Socal and Texaco were granted concessions in both Bahrain and Saudi Arabia.

---

[11]Data in the International Oil section of this note was taken from two primary sources: John M. Blair, *The Control of Oil,* and Anthony Sampson, *The Seven Sisters,* Bantam Books, 1975.

58   **Expansion of Aramco.** During the second half of the 1940s, the management of Socal and Texaco were becoming aware of the vast quantity of oil reserves that existed in Saudi Arabia. The potential of the fields was far greater than they had anticipated and certainly far larger than could be accommodated by the companies' marketing systems. Thus, it was decided to permit companies with marketing outlets and positions to acquire an interest in their company, Aramco.

59   During November of 1948, a formal agreement was signed that gave Exxon a 30% interest in Aramco and Mobil a 10% interest. (Each company had originally been offered 20%; but Mobil's management did not believe that the company could absorb the amount of oil the commitment would require.) As a result of the new arrangement, Aramco's output was to be sold worldwide.

60   **Venezuela's Influence.** A chain of events, which was to have a dramatic effect on the oil industry in the following years, had its origin in Venezuela in 1948. The country had been a vital source of oil for Exxon, Shell, and Gulf. During that year, the government demanded a fifty-fifty share in all oil profits. (At the time, the companies were paying 12% in the Middle East.) Naturally, the companies resisted the government's attempts. However, they finally gave in when they realized the advantage of having a foreign government as a partner. It gave them greater security against the attacks of local nationalists.

61   Presumably as a result of the deal made in Venezuela, the King of Saudi Arabia began to increase his demands. Aramco obliged by building hospitals, schools, roads, and railroads. They were fearful of losing their concessions. At the same time, however, they were not willing to give up 50% of profits.

62   Aramco's officials met with members of the State Department in November 1950 to discuss the King's demands. They found a sympathetic ear due to the fact that the U.S. government was worried about the Communist influence in the Middle East. It was a result of this meeting that the "Golden Gimmick" was developed.

63   **The Golden Gimmick.** Payments to Saudi Arabia were raised from 12% to 50%. However, the incremental amount was considered a tax. Due to the Federal Tax Credit, such payments could be used to offset taxes payable in the United States. It had been estimated that this plan cost the U.S. Treasury $50 million in its first year of existence. However, the federal bureaucrats did not see themselves as the losers in this deal. It was a means for them to provide foreign aid to Saudi Arabia without having to submit the proposal to Congress. The Golden Gimmick had two long-term effects. First, other companies were soon allowed to make the same deal that was made in Saudi Arabia. Thus, there was a great incentive to invest abroad rather than in the United States. As a consequence, in 1973, the five

American "sisters" were making two thirds of their profits abroad and paying no taxes on those earnings.[12] In addition, internal accounting systems were altered as companies attempted to show maximum amounts of profits on upstream (exploration and production) operations. Both the change in strategies and the change in accounting procedures were at the expense of downstream (refining and marketing) activities.

64   **The Iranian Concession and Anti-Trust Action.** The oil concession for the entire country of Iran had been held by British Petroleum (BP) for forty years. However, in 1952, under a new leader, Dr. Mohammed Mossadegh, the British holdings in Iran were nationalized. BP appealed to the other "sisters" to boycott Iranian oil and to help them increase production in other areas. The six companies cooperated, as each was aware of what could happen to their own concessions.

65   Over two years after the Iranian oil fields had been nationalized, Mossadegh was forced out of office and the deposed Shah returned to Iran. This was accomplished with the aid of the C.I.A. A new consortium was established to develop the oil fields in Iran. The group consisted of the seven sisters and France's CFP (Compagnie Francaise de Petrole).[13] In 1955, however, each of the five American companies gave up an eighth of their holdings, allowing a consortium of nine American "independents" to share the resulting 5%.

66   **The Independents.** It was the Iranian concession that allowed the independents to get their foot in the door in the Middle East. Once they found an opening, they aggressively sought more concessions. Libya, determined not to be dominated by the majors, provided the next major opportunity. The country granted 51 concessions to 17 companies in 1956. Within a few years, the independents were responsible for one-half of all the oil production from Libya. By 1957, a glut of oil was developing. Simultaneously, the independents were undercutting the majors, forcing down the price of oil. Domestic producers argued that they could not compete with cheap imports. As a result, import controls were mandated in 1959, limiting oil imports to 12% of domestic production.

67   **OPEC.** In September 1960, the Organization of Petroleum Exporting Countries (OPEC) was formed by Iran, Iraq, Kuwait, Saudi Arabia, and Venezuela. The founding of OPEC, however, did not lead to any immediate reversal of relations between the oil companies and the producing countries. Throughout the 1960s, the companies continued to deal separately with each, often playing them against each other. From the beginning, though, OPEC

---

[12]*Senate Multinational Subcommittee Hearings*, Volume 4, pp. 12 and 95.

[13]The original agreement gave the companies the following percents of interest: BP—40%; Royal Dutch Shell—14%; CFP—6%; and, each American company—8%.

achieved one important goal. It prevented further reductions in the posted price. This was accomplished despite the fact that competition was continually becoming more intense.

64   The process by which OPEC developed its strength took 13 years, reaching a peak during what became known as the energy crisis of 1973-74. Three separate actions were taken by OPEC during this time.[14] They were: an oil embargo, a production cut, and a substantial price increase.

69   After the outbreak of the Yom Kippur War on October 6, 1973, many Arab members of OPEC participated in an oil embargo against the United States and the Netherlands. The Arab oil exporters were expressing their support of Egypt and Syria in this war against Israel. Due to their friendship with the Israelis, the United States and the Netherlands were to be cut off completely.

70   These same countries, for the most part, simultaneously announced that they would cut production by a minimum of 5% per month until the Israeli withdrawal was completed from the whole of the Arab territory occupied in June 1967.

71   Finally, OPEC announced an increase in the price of *marker crude* (Saudi Arabian light) from $3.00 to $5.11 per barrel. On January 1, 1974, the price was raised to $11.65. OPEC had put an end to price-setting negotiations between the oil companies and the producing countries.

72   The embargo ended on March 18, 1974, less than six months after it began. During the first quarter of 1974, oil was generally available throughout the world. However, it was available at new price levels.

73   A situation in which the United States would be faced with a severe shortage of crude never developed. This was due primarily to two factors. First, the Arab countries' output had been sharply increased during 1973. Thus, the curtailments simply offset the earlier accelerations. Second, and more important, the major oil companies controlled the world's network of tankers and refineries. These companies were the ones that allocated the available crude throughout the world. As a result, the shortage was fairly evenly distributed. However, some European countries and Japan, in which imported oil constituted a greater percentage of the total energy consumption than in the United States, felt the effects of an even reduction in oil imports more than did the United States.

74   Up to the time of the energy crisis, oil companies operated as concessionaires. They shared the oil with the host governments (often on a 50–50 basis). The oil that the oil companies received as their 50 percent share was known as *equity oil*. The additional oil that the oil companies bought from the governments was known as *participation oil*. Payment for this category of oil was not regarded as a tax, but as a business expense.

75   After the end of the embargo, OPEC governments began to increase their

---

[14]Members of OPEC in 1973 were Abu Dhabi, Algeria, Ecuador, Gabon, Indonesia, Iran, Iraq, Kuwait, Libya, Nigeria, Qatar, Saudi Arabia, and Venezuela.

control over petroleum operations and the income that they received from a barrel of oil. They accomplished this by increasing their proportion of participation oil to the point where many controlled full ownership. Thus, the international oil companies became a combination of contractor and sales agent for OPEC countries. In 1960, private companies managed 100% of the international crude oil flow and owned 80% of it. By 1970, these percentages had been reduced to 70% and 40%. By 1980, private companies managed only 50% and owned only 17% of the international crude oil flow.[15]

76   As a result, oil companies' profits on the production of crude sharply declined. However, the product was then far more expensive than it had been before. Smaller profit margins yielded larger absolute amounts. In addition, the profitability of the companies' *downstream* operations was substantially increased.

Appendix

Glossary of terms

Aramco. The Arabian American Oil Company, the original owners of which were Exxon, Standard (California), Texaco and Mobil.

Batch. A measured amount of oil or refined product in a pipeline or a tank.

Bonus. Consideration paid by an oil and gas firm to a property owner in order to obtain an oil and gas lease on a specific piece of property for a specified period of time.

Condensate. Hydrocarbons that are in the gaseous state under reservoir conditions and that become liquid either in passing up the hole or at the surface due to the reduced pressure.

Department of Interior. An organization of the United States government that has jurisdiction over the outer continental shelf of the United States.

Development well. A well drilled within a reservoir that contains proved oil and gas reserves to a depth already known to be productive.

Downstream operation. A term referring to industry operations beyond the producing phase of the business, i.e., refining and marketing.

Equity oil. Crude oil that is received by oil companies under their role of either concessionaire or joint venture partner with the host government. Additional payment is usually made to the host government in the form of taxes.

Exploratory well. A well drilled to find oil or gas in an unproved area, to find a new reservoir in a productive field, or to extend an existing well to new depths.

Franchised dealer. A person who leases and operates marketing facilities from an oil company under franchise-type arrangements.

Heavy crude. Thick, sticky crude oil of heavy specific gravity.

Hydrotreating. A refining process used to convert residual to lighter product. It is also used to remove sulfur and other contaminants.

Jobber. A wholesaler who buys and resells petroleum products.

Light crude. Thinner, freely flowing crude oil of light specific gravity.

Light products. The more volatile components or fractions of petroleum, such as butane, gasoline, and middle-distillates.

Marker crude. Arabian light crude oil. It provides the benchmark price for oil of other qualities or oil produced at other locations.

Mineral rights. The rights of ownership, conveyed by deed, for gas, oil, and other minerals beneath the surface of the earth. In the United States, the mineral rights are the property of the surface owner unless disposed of separately.

---

[15]*International Petroleum Encyclopedia* (PennWell Publishing Co., 1982), p. 11.

Outer Continental Shelf (OCS). All submerged lands (1) that lie seaward and outside the area of lands beneath the navigable waters as defined in the Submerged Lands Act (67 Stat. 29) and (2) of which the subsoil and seabed appertain to the U.S. and are subject to its jurisdiction and control.

Participation oil. Crude oil, the ownership of which accrues directly to the account of the host government as a result of their joint venture interest in a particular producing field.

Primary recovery. The initial production of hydrocarbons from a well or field. The natural energy contained in the reservoir is employed to remove the product.

Prorationing laws. Laws that restrict oil and gas production, usually on the basis of market demand.

Proved reserves. Those quantities of crude oil and natural gas that appear with reasonable certainty to be recoverable in the future from known oil and gas reserves.

Secondary recovery. The extraction of oil from a field beyond what can be recovered by normal methods of flowing or pumping. The use of water flooding, gas injection, and other methods to recover additional amounts of oil are all examples of secondary recovery methods.

Service station. A real outlet that earns 50% or more of its income from sales and services related to petroleum products.

Sour crude. Crude oil that contains 2.5% or more of sulfur.

Sweet crude. Crude oil that contains 0.5% or less of sulfur.

Wildcat well. A well drilled in an unproved area. It is an exploratory well in the truest sense of the word.

Crude oil supplies by states (percent of total)

	1981	1980	1975	1970	1965
New York	.03	.03	.03	.03	.06
Pennsylvania	.14	.11	.11	.12	.17
West Virginia	.10	.07	.08	.09	.12
East	.27	.21	.22	.24	.35
Illinois	0.88	0.73	0.85	1.24	2.24
Indiana	0.18	0.15	0.15	0.21	0.40
Kansas	2.23	1.91	1.93	2.41	3.68
Kentucky	0.23	0.19	0.25	0.33	0.68
Michigan	1.00	1.04	0.80	0.33	0.52
North Dakota	1.50	1.27	0.67	0.63	0.93
Ohio	0.46	0.40	0.31	0.28	0.45
Oklahoma	5.02	4.83	5.34	6.36	7.14
Midwest	11.50	10.52	10.30	11.79	16.04
Alabama	0.63	0.21	0.44	0.70	0.66
Louisiana	14.52	14.84	21.29	25.78	20.88
Mississippi	1.05	1.16	1.52	1.85	1.97
New Mexico	2.25	2.40	3.11	3.64	4.18
Texas	29.31	30.99	39.97	35.53	35.13
South & Southwest	47.76	49.60	66.33	67.50	62.82
Alaska	19.61	18.80	2.28	2.38	0.39
California	12.72	11.33	10.54	10.58	11.11
Colorado	0.97	0.94	1.25	0.70	1.18
Montana	0.98	0.94	1.07	1.08	1.15
Wyoming	3.75	4.11	4.45	4.56	4.86
West	38.03	36.12	19.59	19.30	18.69
All Other States	2.44	3.55	3.56	1.17	2.10

Source: Twentieth Century Petroleum Statistics, DeGolyer and MacNaughton, 1983, p. 22.

U.S.crude oil reserves and production
(millions of barrels)

Year	Estimated Proved Reserves January 1	New Reserves Proved During Year	Production During Year	Estimated Proved Reserves December 31
(API Estimates)				
1945	19,785	1,894	1,737	19,942
1950	24,649	2,563	1,944	25,268
1955	29,561	2,870	2,419	30,012
1960	31.719	2,365	2,471	31,613
1965	30,990	3,048	2,686	31,352
1970	29,632	12,689[1]	3,319	39,002
1975	34,250	1,318	2,886	32,682
1976	32,682	1,085	2,825	30,942
1977	30,942	1,404	2,860	29,486
1978	29,486	1,347	3,030	27,803
1979	27,803	2,206	2,958	27,051
(DOE Estimates)				
1979	31,355	1,410	2,955	29,810
1980	29,810	2,970	2,975	29,805
1981	29,805	2,570	2,949	29,426
1982	29,426	1,587	2,951	27,858
1983	27,858	—	—	—

Source: *Twentieth Century Petroleum Statistics*, DeGolyer and MacNaughton, 1983, p. 18.
[1]Includes 9.6 billion barrels for Alaska's Prudhoe Bay Field.

Proven U.S. crude oil, condensate, and
natural gas liquids reserves (percent of total U.S. reserves)

Company	1982	1981	1980	1975
Atlantic Richfield	7.3	7.0	7.0	5.8
DuPont (Conoco)	1.0	1.1	1.1	1.3
Exxon	8.1	7.7	7.8	10.3
Getty	3.5	3.6	3.8	4.2
Gulf	2.3	2.4	2.5	3.3
Marathon	1.7	1.8	2.1	2.0
Mobil	2.6	2.5	2.4	2.6
Phillips	1.4	1.3	1.6	1.8
Shell	6.3	6.1	6.2	4.8
Standard Oil (California)	3.4	3.4	3.5	4.5
Standard Oil (Indiana)	4.7	4.6	4.6	5.8
Standard Oil (Ohio)	8.1	9.4	10.0	11.7
Sun	2.0	2.0	2.1	2.3
Texaco	3.0	3.1	3.4	7.3
Union	1.5	1.5	1.4	1.6

Source: *Market Shares and Individual Company Data for U.S. Energy Markets: 1950*-1982, American Petroleum Institute, 1983.

Top 15 U.S. crude oil production companies (percent of total U.S. production)

Company	1982	1980	1975	1970
Atlantic Richfield	6.0	5.5	3.7	3.6
Conoco (DuPont)		—	1.9	1.7
Exxon	7.3	7.7	8.5	8.4
Getty	2.7	2.7	2.9	2.8
Gulf	3.2	3.6	4.3	5.5
Marathon (U.S. Steel)	1.6	1.7	1.7	1.5
Mobil	3.0	3.1	3.4	3.4
Occidental	1.5	1.5	2.0	1.8
Phillips	2.5	2.7	2.4	2.4
Shell	5.1	5.0	5.5	5.3
Standard Oil (California)	3.3	3.3	3.8	4.2
Standard Oil (Indiana)	4.0	4.6	5.3	4.1
Standard Oil (Ohio)	6.8	7.0	—	—
Sun	2.1	2.0	2.3	2.3
Texaco	3.5	4.1	6.7	7.2
Union	1.7	1.7	2.6	2.8
Top 15 Companies	54.2	56.2	57.0	56.9

Source: *Market Shares and Individual Company Data for U.S. Energy Markets: 1980-1982*, American Petroleum Institute, 1983.

Percentage of world crude oil production by area

	North America	South America	Eastern Europe	Western Europe	Africa	Middle East	Far East
1982	23.59	6.37	23.26	5.48	8.38	24.15	8.67
1980	20.08	6.10	20.84	4.13	10.39	31.01	8.13
1975	19.83	6.70	19.07	1.23	9.37	36.80	7.00
1970	24.86	10.40	15.86	1.01	13.25	30.85	3.77
1965	29.47	14.15	17.00	1.54	7.34	27.70	2.80
1960	37.24	16.47	15.15	1.60	1.37	25.14	3.03
1955	48.06	16.18	10.46	1.45	0.25	21.20	2.40
1950	54.56	16.94	7.84	0.88	0.44	17.15	2.19
1938	63.38	13.22	12.75	0.49	0.08	6.72	3.36

Source: *Twentieth Century Petroleum Statistics*, DeGolyer and MacNaughton, 1983, p. 3.

Worldwide estimated proved oil reserves (million barrels)

	1-1-84	1-1-82		1-1-84	1-1-82
ASIA-PACIFIC			AFRICA		
Australia	1,586	1,709	Algeria	9,220	8,080
Brunei	1,390	1,630	Angola - Cabinda	1,700	1,450
India	3,485	2,672	Cameron	520	480
Indonesia	9,100	9,800	Congo Republic	400	1,300
Malaysia	3,000	2,800	Egypt	3,450	2,930
New Zealand	170	171	Gabon	490	480
Pakistan	83	240	Libya	21,270	22,600
All Other	155	129	Nigeria	16,550	16,500
Total	18,969	19,151	Tunisia	1,820	1,690
			Zaire	110	145
			All Other	1,377	517
				56,907	56,172

	1-1-84	1-1-82
WEST EUROPE		
Austria	122	134
Denmark	324	470
Germany, West	304	342
Greece	51	73
Italy - Sicily	800	625
Norway	7,660	7,620
Spain	160	123
United Kingdom	13,150	14,800
All Other	448	447
Total	23,029	24,634
MIDDLE EAST		
Abu Dhabi	30,400	30,600
Bahrain	185	209
Divided (Neutral) Zone	5,695	6,500
Dubai	1,440	1,270
Iran	51,000	57,000
Iraq	43,000	29,700
Kuwait	63,900	64,480
Oman	2,790	2,570
Qatar	3,330	3,434
Saudi Arabia	166,000	164,600
Syria	1,490	1,890
Turkey	370	280
All Other	501	307
Total	370,101	362,840

	1-1-84	1-1-82
WESTERN HEMISPHERE		
Argentina	2,429	2,650
Bolivia	160	104
Brazil	1,800	1,325
Chile	748	790
Colombia	560	516
Ecuador	1,675	850
Mexico	48,000	56,990
Peru	775	801
Trinidad and Tobago	630	600
Venezuela	24,850	20,300
United States	27,300	29,785*
Canada	6,730	7,300
All Other	50	56
Total	115,707	122,067
COMMUNIST AREAS		
U.S.S.R.	63,000	63,000
China	19,100	19,895
All Other	2,500	2,950
Total	85,600	85,845
TOTAL WORLD	669,303	670,709

Source: "Worldwide Oil and Gas at a Glance," *Oil and Gas Journal,* December 26, 1983, and December 28, 1981.

U.S. motor gasoline sales

	1982		1981		1980		1975	
	Rank	Share	Rank	Share	Rank	Share	Rank	Share
Amoco	1	7.3	1	7.3	3	7.4	3	7.2
Atlantic Richfield	8	4.7	8	3.8	8	3.9	8	4.0
Chevron	7	4.8	7	5.2	6	5.8	7	4.6
Exxon	3	6.6	3	6.8	1	7.5	2	7.3
Gulf	4	5.8	5	5.7	7	5.4	5	6.3
Mobil	5	5.6	6	5.4	4	6.0	6	6.0
Phillips	10	2.7	10	2.9	10	2.8	9	3.9
Shell	2	6.8	2	6.9	2	7.5	4	7.0
Sun	11	2.6	11	2.6	11	2.7	10	3.5
Texaco	6	5.6	4	5.8	5	6.0	1	7.9
Union	9	3.2	9	3.3	9	3.5	11	3.2

Source: Market Shares and Individual Company Data for U.S. Energy Markets: 1950-1982, American Petroleum Institute, 1983.

Worldwide refining capacity—January 1, 1984 (thousand barrels per day)

Country	Capacity
Algeria	137
Argentina	678
Australia	722
Bahamas	500
Bahrain	250
Belgium	694
Brazil	1,301
Canada	806
Chile	141
Colombia	211
Denmark	174
Egypt	369
Finland	299
France	2,670
Germany	2,386
Greece	369
India	779
Indonesia	387
Iran	530
Iraq	168
Israel	190
Italy	3,050
Japan	5,020
Korea	776
Kuwait	623
Libya	125
Malaysia	205
Mexico	1,269
Netherlands	1,552
Netherlands Antilles	740
Nigeria	247
Norway	243
Okinawa	153
Panama	100
Peru	169
Philippines	286
Portugal	282
Puerto Rico	121
Saudi Arabia	860
Singapore	1,101
South Africa	338
Spain	1,493
Sweden	453
Switzerland	137
Syria	229
Trinidad	375
Turkey	472
United Kingdom	2,092
United States	15,930
Venezuela	1,224
Virgin Islands	600
Yemen, S.	130
All Other Free World Countries	2,851
Total Free World	58,007

Source: Oil and Gas Journal, December 26, 1983.

Percentage of total U.S. consumption by sources of energy

Year	Crude oil	Natural gas	Hydro	Nuclear	Coal	Total consumption (trillion Btu's)
1920	13.3	4.4	3.9	—	78.4	19,782
1930	25.4	9.9	3.5	—	61.2	22,288
1940	31.4	12.4	3.8	—	52.4	23,589
1950	37.2	20.3	4.7	—	37.8	34,153
1960	41.6	31.6	3.6	—	23.2	44,816
1970	40.3	36.5	4.0	0.3	18.9	67,143
1975	43.0	31.6	4.6	2.6	18.2	70,635
1980	42.0	29.9	4.1	3.5	20.5	76,186
1981	40.1	30.3	4.0	3.9	21.7	74,289
1982	39.7	29.0	4.9	4.3	22.1	70,812

Source: *Twentieth Century Petroleum Statistics*, DeGolyer and MacNaughton, 1983, p. 107.

Net income (millions of dollars)

	1982	1981	1980	1979	1978
Amerada Hess	$169	$213	$540	$507	$139
American Petrofina	54	74	104	83	32
Ashland	181	90	432	370	245
Atlantic Richfield	1,676	1,671	1,651	1,166	804
Cities Service	—	(49)	478	348	118
Diamond Shamrock	250	308	281	173	101
Exxon	4,186	5,568	5,650	4,295	2,763
Getty	692	857	872	604	330
Gulf	900	1,231	1,407	1,322	785
Kerr-McGee	210	211	182	160	118
Marathon	—	344	379	323	225
Mobil	1,380	2,433	2,813	2,007	1,131
Murphy	158	163	151	104	47
Phillips	646	879	1,070	891	718
Shell	1,605	1,701	1,542	1,126	814
Standard of California	1,377	2,380	2,401	1,785	1,106
Standard (Indiana)	1,826	1,922	1,915	1,507	1,076
Standard (Ohio)	1,879	1,947	1,811	1,186	450
Sun	537	1,076	723	700	415
Tenneco	819	813	940	678	455
Texaco	1,281	2,310	2,643	1,759	852
Union	804	791	647	501	382

Source: "Annual Reports," reprinted from *National Petroleum News Factbook Issue*, 1979-1983.

Operating Revenue (millions of dollars)

	1982	1981	1980	1979	1978
Amerada Hess	$8,394	$9,434	$7,955	$6,813	$4,739
American Petrofina	2,242	2,504	2,098	1,587	1,168
Ashland	9,110	9,506	8,365	6,837	5,426
Atlantic Richfield	26,991	28,208	24,156	16,677	12,739
Cities Service	—	8,564	7,786	6,276	4,661
Diamond Shamrock	1,791	1,868	1,691	969	669
Exxon	103,559	115,148	103,143	79,106	64,886
Getty	11,971	13,252	10,150	4,831	3,515
Gulf	30,630	30,461	28,463	26,140	20,094
Kerr-McGee	3,777	3,826	3,478	2,683	2,104
Marathon	9,098	9,301	8,180	6,681	4,509
Mobil	60,969	64,488	59,510	44,721	35,383
Murphy	2,602	2,447	1,967	1,596	1,218
Phillips	15,698	16,288	13,377	9,503	7,422
Shell	20,214	21,629	19,830	14,431	11,123
Standard of California	35,218	46,609	42,919	30,938	14,598
Standard (Indiana)	28,073	31,729	26,133	18,610	14,961
Standard (Ohio)	13,529	13,810	11,023	7,916	5,198
Sun	16,258	15,967	12,945	10,666	7,494
Tenneco	14,979	15,462	3,624	2,705	2,015
Texaco	48,019	57,628	52,485	39,095	29,124
Union	10,390	10,746	9,984	7,568	5,955

Source: "Annual Reports," reprinted from *National Petroleum News Factbook Issue,* 1979–1983.

Total assets (millions of dollars)

	1982	1981	1980	1979	1978
Amerada Hess	$6,147	$6,322	$5,895	$4,899	$3,504
American Petrofina	1,166	1,146	1,188	1,080	982
Ashland	4,210	4,097	3,358	3,113	3,038
Atlantic Richfield	21,633	19,733	16,605	13,833	11,989
Cities Service	—	6,048	5,538	4,772	4,005
Diamond Shamrock	3,194	3,016	2,376	2,004	2,057
Exxon	62,289	62,931	56,577	49,490	41,531
Getty	9,924	9,536	8,267	6,014	4,684
Gulf	20,436	20,429	18,638	17,265	14,936
Kerr-McGee	3,763	3,415	2,807	2,399	2,022
Marathon	9,624	5,994	5,043	4,321	3,758
Mobil	36,439	34,776	32,705	27,506	22,880
Murphy	2,990	2,777	2,308	1,887	1,515
Phillips	12,097	11,264	9,844	8,519	6,834
Shell	21,376	20,118	17,615	16,127	10,453
Standard of California	23,490	23,680	22,162	18,103	16,761
Standard (Indiana)	24,289	22,916	20,167	17,150	14,109
Standard (Ohio)	16,016	15,743	12,080	9,209	8,326
Sun	12,019	11,822	10,955	7,461	6,052
Tenneco	17,378	16,808	3,836	2,917	2,343
Texaco	27,114	27,489	26,430	22,992	20,463
Union	8,511	7,593	6,772	6,013	5,429

Source: "Annual Reports," reprinted from *National Petroleum News Factbook Issue,* 1979–1983.

case **25** # Mobil Corporation: Acquisitions with an Unusual Purpose

Company Overview

1   Mobil Corporation was the third largest industrial company in the United States (behind Exxon and General Motors), with revenue from operations in 1983 of nearly $55 billion. Mobil consisted of one of the world's largest petroleum operations, a growing chemical business, a paperboard packaging business, and a nationwide retailing operation. Mobil companies conducted business in more than 100 countries and employed more than 178,000 people.

2   The company had total assets in 1983 of $35 billion. Net income was $1.5 billion. Total return to investors in 1983 was 22.39%. Over the previous ten years, Mobil averaged a 15.17% total return to investors—highest among the major oil companies.[1] With a 5.69% share of the domestic market, Mobil ranked as the fifth largest gasoline retailer in 1983.

Historical Background

3   Mobil's corporate roots could be traced in one direction back to the formation of Vacuum Oil in 1866, and in another, to John D. Rockefeller's Standard

This case was written by Robert R. Gardner, Associate Director of the MaGuire Oil and Gas Institute, under the direction of M. Edgar Barrett, Director. It was based, in part, on earlier versions written by Bill Clark and Mary Pat Cormack.

[1]"The 500 largest U.S. Industrial Corporations," *Fortune*, April 30, 1984, pp. 276-77. (As measured by *Fortune*, "total return to investors" includes both price appreciation and dividend yield to an investor in the company's stock.)

founded by Hiram Bond Everest and Mathew Ewing, who had invented in 1865 a new process of distilling crude oil under a vacuum. At that time, a gallon of kerosene sold for twice as much as a barrel of crude oil, and Ewing believed that his vacuum process could produce more kerosene from a barrel of crude than was possible with other known refining methods. Everest, on the other hand, recognized the possibilities of using the oily residue from the distilling process as a petroleum lubricant for machinery and leather. Everest decided to finance the new venture, and Vacuum Oil was founded in 1866.

4   After some initial consumer resistance, the quality and utility of Everest's lubricants were proven in the marketplace, and Vacuum Oil began growing rapidly. The favorable reputation of Vacuum Oil finally attracted the attention of Rockefeller's Standard Oil Company, and in 1879, Rockefeller bought a controlling interest in the smaller company. Under Standard's aegis, Vacuum Oil evolved into a company whose primary functions were refining, domestic and foreign marketing, domestic manufacturing, and distribution of specialty products. By 1912, Vacuum had become an international lubricating oil company, two thirds of whose business volume was outside the United States.

5   Standard Oil Company of New York (Socony), was the other of Mobil's immediate ancestors. When the huge Standard Oil Trust was broken up in the historical antitrust action of 1911, Socony was one of 33 fragments of the original company. In 1912, Socony had both an extensive export business and a wide marketing outlet system. However, the company had no crude oil resources, nor was it involved in the lubricating products business. In fact, after leaving the Standard Oil Trust, neither Socony nor Vacuum Oil had any significant strength in exploration or production. Consequently, both companies began trying to integrate operations in the United States and abroad in order to shore up their respective weaknesses. In 1918, Socony acquired 70% of the stock of a Texas oil producing company called Magnolia Petroleum Company, which had crude oil production, reserves, refineries, and pipeline in the Southwest. Later, in 1925, Socony, which had assets of $90 million, acquired all of the properties of Magnolia Petroleum Company. Other acquisitions included the General Petroleum Corporation of California (1926), which had production properties, refineries, and marketing facilities on the West Coast, and the White Eagle Oil & Refining Company of Kansas City (1930), which had refineries in Wyoming and Kansas. These acquisitions provided considerable new oil reserves and strengthened the company's marketing network throughout the United States.

6   Socony and Vacuum Oil merged in 1931, forming Socony-Vacuum, with international capabilities to produce, refine, and market petroleum products. Thus, Socony-Vacuum (later to become Mobil) emerged as the youngest and the smallest of the American "sisters." In 1933, Socony-Vacuum pooled its properties and business operations in the Far East with properties

owned by Standard Oil Company of New Jersey. Each company owned 50% of the stock of the newly formed company called Standard-Vacuum Oil Company, which handled Far Eastern operations.

7   In 1936, Socony-Vacuum and Texaco, Inc. each acquired a 50% interest in South American Gulf Oil Co., and a 49.94% interest in Columbian Petroleum Company. Mobil sold its interest in these companies in 1972. In 1955, the company changed its name to Socony Mobil Oil Corporation. (The company later dropped "Socony" from its name and was known as Mobil Oil Corporation until 1976, after which time it was known simply as Mobil Corporation.) By this time, Mobil was already heavily dependent on the Middle East, which supplied 50% of the company's total crude oil. In 1961, Mobil acquired the oil and gas properties and other assets of Republic Natural Gas Company. In the following year the company transferred its business and assets in the Far East, representing its 50% ownership of Standard Vacuum Oil Co., to a new company called Mobil Petroleum Company, Inc. The new firm's affiliates and branches were later brought under the single management of Mobil International Oil Company (1965).

8   Other acquisitions in the '60s and'70s included Kordite Corporation (1962); Goliad Corporation, a gas processor in Louisiana and Texas (1962); Forum Insurance Company (1963); the worldwide paint and chemical coatings interests of Martin Marietta Corporation.(1962); Virginia-Carolina Chemical Corporation (1962); Northern Natural Gas Producing Company (1962); Industrias Atlas S.A., a manufacturer of industrial and consumer paints in Mexico (1965); Goodling Electric Company, Inc. (1968); Aral Italiana, an Italian subsidiary of Aral AG, West Germany (1971); Pastucol Companies, three Italian firms which manufactured and marketed polyethylene film products (1971); Marcor Corporation, which operated through two subsidiaries, Montgomery Ward & Company, Inc., and Container Corporation of America (1974); W. F. Hall Printing Company (1979); the oil and gas operations of General Crude Oil Company (1979); and TransOcean Oil Inc. (1980).

9   In terms of the petroleum business proper, Mobil spent the three decades following its formation in 1931 consolidating its diverse holdings and subsidiaries. Throughout its corporate evolution, Mobil contined to be well known as a manufacturer of high grade industrial lubricants. In 1969, Albert Nickerson, chief executive officer at Mobil, noted:

> In most of the world after World War II, the company had really been just a lubricant marketer. Then we started to expand into one European market after another; we constructed refineries; we improved our crude oil sufficiency.[2]

10   Even so, Mobil continued to be short of crude oil reserves relative to the other majors, and its reputation in lubricants had followed the company Oil Trust, which later absorbed the smaller company. Vacuum Oil was

---

[2]"How to Rob Peter...," *Forbes*, June 15, 1969, pp. 30-31.

into more recent times. An article from the August 1978 issue of *Industrial Marketing* highlighted Mobil's current emphasis on industrial lubricants:

> Mobil Oil Corp. announced a new print ad campaign...that will emphasize the company's service and technological expertise in the industrial lubrication market...the new ads are part...of an evolutionary communications effort which for the past ten years has been positioning Mobil as the leader in supplying total lubrication programs to industry.[3]

11   Thus, Mobil Corporation, now the second largest oil company in the United States, still retained part of its heritage, which could be traced to Vacuum Oil, a small producer of petroleum lubricants that had been capitalized in 1866 for $10,000.

Corporate Structure

12   Many of the smaller subsidiaries which had been acquired by Socony and Vacuum had not been fully integrated into Mobil's corporate structure. These companies often retained their original staffs, operating procedures, and corporate identities. In 1959, Albert L. Nickerson, chief executive officer of Mobil, initiated an extensive company-wide program of reorganization that included the full integration of some of the more independent of Mobil's subsidiaries. Concerted efforts were made to cut fixed costs in the form of redundant staff services, to improve efficiency in exploration and production through better co-ordination among subsidiaries, and to redefine corporate strategy.

13   From 1969 until the present, Mobil has been led by two men: Rawleigh Warner, Jr., chairman, and William P. Tavoulareas, president and (later) chief operating officer. Both men rose through the ranks of the company on the financial side. This was somewhat unique, as the engineering ladder was, for most oil companies, the more traditional route. Warner had received a liberal arts degree from Princeton. Tavoulareas started with Mobil in 1947 in the accounting department, and later received a law degree.[4] Tavoulareas was named the first manager of the newly-formed planning department in 1959, part of Nickerson's program of reorganization. One oil analyst who worked in planning and finance at Mobil for ten years said, "Mobil is a lawyer-businessman company rather than an oilman-geologist company. Planning is the real essence of this company."[5]

14   As head of planning, Tavoulareas set out to shake up a company said to be extremely slothful and badly in need of reorientation. Though incurring the ire of some of Mobil's more traditional executives, Tavoulareas and his

---

[3]"New Mobil Pro Ad Campaign Stresses Expertise in Industrial Lubricants," *Industrial Marketing*, August 1978, p. 22.

[4]"What Makes Mobil Run," *Business Week*, June 13, 1977, pp. 80–85.

[5]Ibid.

planning department set in motion a procedure of carefully scrutinizing all projects and killing those that failed to measure up financially.[6]

15 Both Warner and Tavoulareas continued the earlier trend toward leaner staffing and greater consolidation. In 1973, Mobil's U.S. marketing force, which had previously been operating through seven divisions, was consolidated into four regional offices, whose greater efficiency was expected to save the company about $10 million a year.[7]

16 Prior to 1974, Mobil was organized into four operating divisions. The North American Division was Mobil's operating petroleum division for the United States and Canada. The International Division coordinated the petroleum operations of Mobil affiliates outside the United States and Canada. Mobil Chemical Company was an operating division formed in 1960 that co-ordinated the chemical operations of Mobil affiliates in the United States and several other countries. This division was involved in the manufacture of agricultural and industrial chemicals, plastics, paints, chemical coatings, and petrochemicals. The fourth division, Transportation, was comprised of domestic trucking, pipelines, and deep sea carriers.

17 In 1974, the North American Division was reorganized to exclude Canada; the resulting divisions were U.S. Operations and Foreign Operations. Two years later, on July 1, 1976, a holding company was formed called Mobil Corporation, encompassing the Mobil Oil Corporation (which included domestic and foreign energy operations), the Mobil Chemical Company, Montgomery Ward, and Container Corporation. So there were still four operating segments, but they were now distinguished as follows: Energy Operations, including the subdivisions of United States Energy Operations and Foreign Energy Operations; Chemical Operations; Retail Merchandising; and Paperboard Packaging.

18 Further belt-tightening moves were put into effect in the early 1980s, paralleling efforts made by other industry members. As part of an overall attempt to trim fixed costs, Mobil closed various plants, refineries, and gasoline terminals. The company also scrapped surplus tankers, cut back on travel, and shrank an administrative unit in Europe.

19 Another reorganization took place in late 1982. This most recent restructuring was said to be setting the stage for the retirement of Warner and Tavoulareas. Warner was scheduled to retire in 1986 and Tavoulareas in 1983. (However, during 1983, the board extended Tavoulareas's tenure until November of 1984.)

20 Two major operating units were established under Mobil Corporation, which remained responsible for overall policy and strategy decisions. All oil- and gas-related activities became the responsibility of Mobil Oil. Allen E. Murray was named president of this unit. All other activities, such as

---

[6]"Mobil's Maverick: Tavoulareas Puts Firm on a Separate Course From Most of Big Oil," *The Wall Street Journal,* February 14, 1980, p. 18.

[7]"Mobil Reshuffle Aims at Cost-Cutting," *National Petroleum News,* September 1973, p. 145.

chemicals, paperboard packaging, retailing, and alternative energy interests, became the responsibility of Mobil Diversified Business. The creation of this new division lumped the company's most severely troubled businesses into a single group. Richard F. Tucker was named president of this unit. Warner and Tavoulareas were, in turn, named chairman and vice chairman of Mobil's Executive Committee.

21   Murray and Tucker were often compared to Tavoulareas and Warner and were considered to be heirs apparent. "Murray is a numbers man, and he came in from the bottom, like Tavoulareas. Tucker is extremely effective in public and came to Mobil at a later stage—and at a fairly high level—as Warner did."[8] Shortly after the reorganization, Warner was quoted as saying, "We will rate these individuals on their capacity to meet established plans."[9]

Exploration and Production

22   Mobil's commitment to a strong exploration program can be traced back to the Suez crisis in 1956, when Mobil's Middle East oil supplies were seriously disrupted and the company paid dearly to acquire crude. A tangible sign of an increased emphasis on exploration was Mobil's increased acreage position, which doubled to nearly 100 million acres throughout the 1960s.

23   Despite this apparent strategy, the period of the '60s and early '70s was a frustrating one for the explorationists at Mobil. The company still concentrated a great deal on downstream (refining and marketing) activities. A number of instances could be cited in which Mobil sold or passed up the opportunity to buy into certain prospects, Alaska being the most costly. Mobil's staff was one of the first to perform seismic work on Alaska's North Slope and vigorously encouraged Mobil's participation. However, the company did not bid aggressively on what later became the Prudhoe Bay field. "The financial people in this company did a disservice to the exploration people," Warner was quoted as saying. "The poor people in exploration were adversely impacted by people (in the company) who knew nothing about oil and gas."[10]

24   Oil prices substantially increased during the 1970s and Mobil, like the other majors, stepped up its exploration activities. By the late 1970s, Mobil's strategy was finally paying off. The company held an interest in nine giant oil and gas fields which were discovered during 1979 and the first half of 1980, each of which could net Mobil the equivalent of at least 100 million barrels of new reserves. "We've hit on some kind of formula in exploration," said Tavoulareas. "We hope we are in a cycle where each

---

[8]"Mobil's Costly Saudi Strategy," *Business Week*, October 17, 1983, p. 76.

[9]Ibid.

[10]"Mobil's Successful Exploration," *Business Week*, October 13, 1980, p. 112.

year we can find a big field, and if we do, I'm not worried about our future."[11]

25 **Saudi Arabia.** During the late 1940s, Texaco and Standard Oil Company of California (Socal), who were then co-owners of Arabian American Oil Company (Aramco) offered 40% of Aramco to Jersey Standard and Mobil. Being a bit nervous about its ability to absorb its share of crude oil, Mobil opted for 10% rather than the 20% it could have bought.
Commented Warner in 1971:

26 That (decision) cost us a tremendous amount of money.... The oil companies that year in and year out make the most money make it because they are balanced. They move their own crude, they refine their own crude, and they sell their own crude.[12]

27 By the mid '50s, the Middle East was supplying approximately 50% of Mobil's crude oil. The company's dependence on Mideast oil was particularly evident during the Arab-Israeli war in 1956. Mobil's earnings suffered much more than those of its competitors with the closing of the Suez Canal during that conflict.

28 William Tavoulareas first went to the Middle East on mobil business in late 1950. He possessed a no-nonsense manner and a determination to build a strong relationship with the Saudis. As his stature in Mobil grew, Tavoulareas's conviction that the company's best prospects lay in enhancing its access to Saudi oil became ingrained in Mobil's strategy. For years this strategy handsomely benefitted the traditionally crude-poor oil company. During the mid 70s, he skillfully negotiated a five-year contract to acquire another 5% of Aramco.

29 Originally, the Aramco partners (Exxon, Mobil, Texaco and Socal) owned the production, and the Saudi government was paid a royalty. During the mid 1970s, however, the Saudis began negotiations to buy out the Aramco partners. This process was completed in 1980. The partners were granted priority access to significant volumes of Saudi Arabian oil. The price of this oil put the partners at both an advantage and at a disadvantage compared to their competitors during the four years that followed the buyout.

30 Saudi Arabia, with its small population and vast reserves, had traditionally possessed sufficient foresight to cut back production in times of surplus. Special access to Saudi crude, therefore, was likely to pay off only in an expanding market.

31 Access to Saudi oil was especially beneficial from 1979 to 1981, when the Saudis were flooding the market with relatively cheap oil to retain world

---

[11]Ibid.

[12]"The Lively Tortoise," *Forbes,* August 1, 1971, pp. 18–19.

prices. The so-called "Aramco advantage" added some $200 million to Mobil's 1980 earnings.[13]

32   In 1981, the Aramco advantage became a burden. When world oil prices started declining, Saudi oil became among the world's most expensive, because the country adhered rigidly to OPEC's price structure. As other members of Aramco slashed their purchases, Mobil increased its take, buying as much as 35% of Aramco's contracted volumes. Tavoulareas explained, "We made a commitment to believing continued reliance on Saudi crude would be a benefit to our company. Every time we set out to lift more than our share, other guys (in Aramco) cut back more...so we lifted a bit more than we wanted to."[14] Mobil's European refining and marketing arm, once a principal profit center because it used competitively priced Saudi crude, lost $280 million in 1982, a drop of more than $1 billion from 1980.

33   To further cement its ties to the Saudis, Mobil, in 1980, agreed to build two vast export facilities for the Saudis: an oil refinery and a petrochemical complex in Yanbu, a new industrial city on the Red Sea. In return, Mobil won the right to buy an extra 1.4 billion barrels of extra crude over 19 years. Tavoulareas defended the deal by pointing to the favorable financing and low-cost materials that the Saudis had promised. However, he stated, "These projects must be judged as part of the Saudi 'insurance policy' rather than by their own economics."[15]

34   Mobil's bold moves in Saudi Arabia were not without criticism from skeptical industry members. Warned one highly placed industry source:

> Mobil's serious risk is that the market won't grow. They made their big, expensive moves in Saudi Arabia in an expansive environment. The expenses they made there have drawn resources that could have been used elsewhere.[16]

35   Nonetheless, Mobil's Saudi commitment has never waivered. By year-end 1983, $600 million had been spent at Yanbu. In addition, many hours of manpower had been employed to train Saudis to run the complexes. In February 1984, Mobil directors held their board meeting in Saudi Arabia—a first for any U.S. corporation.

36   In early 1984, Mobil was receiving less than 30% of its total crude supply from Saudi Arabia. Though Mobil was lifting the full amount of oil to which it was contractually obligated, the Saudi portion of Mobil's total crude supply was down from some 50% in 1982.

37   **Offshore Activities.** During the early 1970s, Mobil decided to confine

---

[13]"What Makes Mobil Run."

[14]"Mobil's Costly Saudi Strategy."

[15]Ibid.

[16]Ibid.

most of its domestic exploration to a search for big fields in offshore waters. The Gulf of Mexico was the area in which Mobil spent the most and received the greatest rewards. Between 1970 and 1983, the company spent over $2.5 billion to acquire federal lease bonuses, second in the industry. For the most part, Mobil has been successful in maintaining U.S. reserves through a combination of exploration efforts in the Gulf of Mexico and a series of acquisitions of producing companies.

38   Mobil acquired 20,000 acres in the Mobile Bay, offshore Alabama, in a state lease sale in 1969 for a low price. The company completed a discovery well in 1979 that flowed 12.2 million cubic feet per day of natural gas. The company then acquired drilling permits for four additional wells, and, in 1981, bought two more leases near the discovery. Mobil estimated reserves on the acreage to be between 200 and 600 billion cubic feet. However, industry analysts believed that the potential of the area was much higher— nearly one trillion cubic feet.[17]

39   Mobil's long record of success in the Gulf of Mexico continued with a significant discovery in the Green Canyon area of the central Gulf. In a 1983 central Gulf lease sale, Mobil added considerably to its holdings in the area, spending more than $400 million for interests in 38 leases. Some of these tracts were located in the vicinity of the Green Canyon discovery.

40   The company's exploration efforts in other domestic offshore areas have not been as prosperous. Following the launching of a sophisticated $14 million geophysical vessel in 1978, Mobil bid aggressively in a 1979 federal drilling lease sale for tracts located off Massachusetts. Mobil spent $222 million, more than one quarter of the money the government took in.[18] People in the industry questioned whether Mobil had simply overbid or had seen more valuable structures in the area because it had better data. Unfortunately for Mobil, the former turned out to be closer to the truth. The company spudded its first well in the area in 1981. As of 1984, no hydrocarbons had been discovered.

41   Other offshore U.S. areas have also proved to be disappointing. Expenditures in the Baltimore Canyon, where Mobil began drilling in 1978, have been largely written off.

42   Mobil's partnership with Sohio in a promising offshore Alaska exploration effort ended in further disappointment. Mobil had paid $288 million for 14 federal tracts in the Mukluk area. Failure to discover commercial quantities of oil and gas in the well drilled there caused Mobil to write off its share of the costs to drill the well, as well as part of its investment in tracts in the Mukluk area. This amounted to a $98 million after-tax write-off against 1983 income.

43   Mobil's efforts to find hydrocarbons in offshore areas in other parts of the world have proved more fruitful, however. In 1971, Mobil discovered

[17]"Research Brief, Mobil Corporation," Goldman Sachs, April 1, 1981.

[18] "Mobil's Successful Exploration."

Arun, a 13-trillion-cubic-feet gas field in Indonesia, which ranked as the second largest gas field of the decade. To exploit the field, a liquefied natural gas plant was built by Pertamina, the Indonesian state oil company. Arun has been Mobil's most profitable single property, annually contributing more than $300 million to net income.

44   Mobil was the holder of the largest private interest in the Statfjord Field. This field had been discovered by Mobil and was located off the coast of Norway in the North Sea. The company's interest in this project was almost 13%, the largest of any of the twelve company partners except Statoil, the Norwegian State Oil Company. Production from the Statfjord Field, which had reserves of more than 3 billion barrels of oil and 2.5 trillion cubic feet of natural gas, began in November 1979 and reached a total of 391,000 barrels daily in 1983.

45   The largest single North Sea addition, however, was the Beryl oil and gas field in the British sector. Mobil held a 50% interest in Beryl, and production was expected to begin during the summer of 1984.

46   Mobil was also active in the offshore areas of Nigeria, where the company produced some 65,000 barrels per day in 1983.

47   The company paid $37,00 for the rights to 13 million acres off Newfoundland in 1965. It performed seismic activity in the area, which was enough to satisfy the minimal work requirements of the 12-year leases. (Other companies had previously drilled nearly 50 unsuccessful wildcats in the vicinity.) Presumably in an attempt to hold onto their leases, yet unwilling to commit the money needed to drill, Mobil offered farm-outs that eventually reduced its share to 28.1%. Then, in 1980, the massive Hibernia field was discovered in the area by a Chevron-operated rig. It was estimated that the field would eventually yield 3–4 billion barrels of oil.

48   Another promising find was the Venture gas field near Sable Island off the coast of Nova Scotia. Mobil held a 42% share in an estimated 4 trillion cubic feet of natural gas at that location.

49   Mobil officials announced in early 1984 that the company's 1984 capital budget would total $3.4 billion, about the same as that for the previous year, and would be funded entirely from cash flow. Some 70% of the budget was to be devoted to exploration and development, while some 70% of that was earmarked for North American activities. Mobil's attention in the near future was to be focused on four plays—the central Gulf of Mexico, state and federal waters off Alabama, the Canadian Atlantic, and Offshore Alaska.[19]

50   **Domestic Onshore Activities.** With the exception of the large field that Mobil discovered in Mobile Bay, the company's record at finding domestic reserves had been considered to be only average. While it was

---

[19]"Mobil's Spending to Concentrate on Regions in North America," *Oil & Gas Journal,* February 20, 1984, p. 33.

"hunting for elephants" offshore, Mobil missed much of the early action in such promising plays as the Rocky Mountain Overthrust, the Williston Basin of the Dakotas, and the Anadarko Basin of Oklahoma.

51 The company paid dearly during the early 1980s in an attempt to catch up to competitors such as Amoco, Shell and Chevron. Since 1978, Mobil had devoted 67% of its $5 billion exploration budget to the United States. Without acquisitions, however, Mobil would not have managed to replace the reserves it produced. Since 1979, Mobil had made more attempts to purchase other oil companies than any other major.

52 By and large, Mobil's U.S. hydrocarbon reserves were primarily in the form of natural gas. Price regulation on some of that gas, along with a growing natural gas surplus, had made much of Mobil's domestic reserves uneconomic. In 1983, the company's domestic gas production fell 20% (to 1,506 million gross cubic feet per day) as a result of flagging demand. Production in the Hugoton field in Kansas proved to be particularly susceptible.

Refining

53 With the merger of Socony and Vacuum Oil in 1931, the company emerged as one of the strongest refiners in the industry. In terms of refining capacity, Socony-Vacuum was the second largest refiner in the United States. By 1960, however, mobil had dropped back to third place, and its U.S. refining capacity relative to the other major oil companies continued to decline in the following years. By 1978, Mobil was in seventh place behind Exxon, Standard of California, Standard of Indiana, Shell, Texaco, and Gulf. In 1960, Mobil's U.S. refining capacity was 716,700 barrels per day, or 7.4% of the U.S. total. By 1983, however, the company's domestic refining capacity had been restored to 750,000 barrels per day.

54 As of December 31, 1983, Mobil owned or had operating interests in 29 refineries in 17 countries. Mobil's total crude oil refinery capacity was 2,186,000 barrels per day, 34% of which was located in the United States. The company's domestic refineries ran at 82% of capacity during 1983, while foreign refineries ran at 68% capacity.

55 Mobil's petroleum product operations were fairly evenly divided among the United States, Europe, and the Far East. Foreign downstream earnings had suffered during 1982, owing to the relatively high cost of Saudi Arabian crude. Foreign margins recovered somewhat in 1983, following a $5/barrel price reduction by the Saudis.

56 At home, Mobil was still seriously short of crude. Just 45% of the oil used in its domestic refineries came from Mobil's own wells in the United States.[20] Gasoline markets in 1983 were particularly competitive in the

---

[20]"Mobil's Costly Saudi Strategy."

Table 1

Refining Statistics (thousands barrels daily)

	1983	*1982*	*1981*	*1980*	*1979*
Domestic Runs	618	644	639	734	797
Domestic Capacity	750	860	860	910	901
Domestic Runs/Capacity	82%	75%	74%	81%	88%
Foreign Runs	976	1067	1134	1225	1266
Foreign Capacity	1436	1534	1647	1709	1770
Foreign Runs/Capacity	68%	70%	69%	72%	72%

Source: Mobil Corporation Financial and Operating Statistics, 1983.

United States. Without inventory profits, Mobil would have lost money on its domestic refining and marketing operations in that year.[21]

57   Speaking before a group of New York security analysts in early 1984, Tavoulareas said that downstream strategic plans called for Mobil to be "the lowest cost operator wherever we do business or get out."[22] Evidence of this strategy in action was Mobil's announcement in May of 1983 that it would close its refinery in Augusta, Kansas, within a year. Accordingly, Mobil would gradually withdraw from marketing gasoline and distillates in Kansas, Nebraska, South Dakota, and parts of Iowa, Missouri, and North Dakota.

Marketing

58   Between 1950 and 1970, the major oil companies had been competing fiercely to penetrate as many regional markets as possible. Market share, rather than profitability, had been the primary marketing objective. Mobil, on the other hand, had followed a different strategy. Albert L. Nickerson, who was then chairman of Mobil, made the decision to limit domestic marketing expenditures in the effort to develop European markets. In 1969, Nickerson commented on this period of the company's growth:

> From 1948 to 1964 we really starved our marketing people in this country. We just said, "Look, there are many jobs this company has to do.... Give us a chance to strengthen some other elements of the company, and the day will come when we can come back to you.... " We had a program that almost required us to lose position.[23]

59   Mobil's domestic market share dropped from 9.9% in 1948 to 6.7% in 1967.

---

[21]"Company Analysis: Mobil Corporation," Donaldson, Lufkin & Jenrette, March 20, 1984.

[22]"Mobil's Spending to Concentrate on Regions in North America."

[23]"How to Rob Peter...."

By 1965, when foreign sales were approaching domestic sales, Mobil finally began to increase its domestic marketing expenditures. By 1969, Mobil's European market share was about 5%. Since earnings had improved every year since 1958, Nickerson's strategy was viewed as an overall success.

60   Since the early '70s, however, there had been a steady decline in the number of marketing outlets for all companies. Even as late as 1977, Texaco was marketing to every state in the union. At the same time, Mobil was in 48 states, Exxon in 44, Shell in 40, and Socal and Gulf in 39.

61   By the late '70s, Mobil had decided to get out of the Rocky Mountain States because the firm had no refineries in that area. The decision called for pulling out of five states by 1981, and included closing 276 retail outlets that were supplied directly or indirectly by Mobil. As previously mentioned, Mobil later announced its intention to withdraw from several Midwestern states. From 1969 to 1983, Mobil decreased the number of its retail outlets nationwide from 25,513 to 15,403.

62   Both at home and abroad, Mobil's strategy was to close down marginal service stations and to consolidate areas of marketing strength. Part of Mobil's domestic marketing retrenchment included the introduction of secondary brands, beginning with the "Sello" brand in the Southwest in 1972, and later with "Big-Bi" stations in the Midwest, and "Reelo" in North Carolina. Most of these secondary outlets were marginal Mobil stations that were converted to self-serve operations designed to compete with lower-priced private brands. The introduction of these secondary brands caused some confusion among competitors and jobbers, since Mobil was not supplying these outlets with its own product, nor was it closing all of its branded outlets in the areas where secondary brands had been introduced. Amid considerable speculation, Mobil consistently maintained that it did not intend to withdraw the Mobil brand from those areas where secondary outlets had been introduced. The company claimed that it was looking at each of its branded outlets on an individual basis to see if they met various investment criteria.

63   As of December 31, 1983, Mobil's petroleum products were marketed in more than 100 countries. Worldwide the company had approximately 33,000 retail dealer outlets, 47% of which were located in the United States. Thirty-four percent of Mobil's petroleum product sales were in the United States. Mobil ranked as the fifth-largest gasoline retailer.

64   During October of 1983, Mobil announced plans to install point-of-sale terminals in 2,400 of its outlets around the country.[24] Station attendants would swipe debit or credit cards through a reader on the terminal, allowing the company to benefit from automated credit checks, inventory controls and electronic funds transfer. Mobil's announcement followed a 2-1/2 year

---

[24]"Mobil One-Ups Others with Debit Card System," *National Petroleum News,* December 1983, p. 29.

study and $10 million in testing debit card systems. The move was expected to put Mobil in the lead among the majors in a race toward a national electronic fund transfer system.

65   In February of 1984, Mobil made known its intention to turn as many as possible of its full-service stations into self-service gas islands in combination with convenience stores.[25] The company called them "snack shops." Although many of the majors, including Arco, Texaco, Amoco and Tenneco, had already introduced combination gas stations and convenience stores, none were on the scale reportedly envisioned at Mobil.

Transportation

66   At year-end 1983, Mobil owned 38 ocean-going tankers and had another 20 vessels under charter. The company also made use of voyage charters. Mobil had traditionally been extremely adept at handling its tanker commitments, thus benefitting from consistently low transportation costs.

67   Mobil's U.S. pipeline system, including partly-owned facilities, consisted in December 1983, of 18,855 miles of crude oil, natural gas liquids, natural gas, and carbon dioxide trunk and gathering lines, and 9,158 miles of product lines. The company's pipeline system outside of the United States, including partly-owned facilities, consisted of 7,969 miles of trunk and gathering lines, and 1,893 miles of product lines.

68   Mobil held a 4% interest in the Trans Alaska Pipeline System (TAPS), a 48-inch pipeline system that moved crude oil some 800 miles from the Prudhoe Bay field on Alaska's North Slope to the port of Valdez on the southern coast of Alaska.

Other Energy Sources

69   Anticipating the future importance of alternative energy sources, Mobil, in the mid '70s, began investing more in research and development for new sources of energy. The objectives of Mobil's energy research efforts were to improve technology for finding and extracting current energy resources and to find viable alternatives to petroleum-based energy.

70   Mobil held proved and probable coal reserves of 4.3 billion tons located in Wyoming, Montana, North Dakota, Colorado, and Illinois. The company first commenced shipments from a mine near Gillette, Wyoming, in late 1982. Production from the mine was soon expected to reach 2.5 million tons annually.

71   Initially, coal was thought to be a very attractive alternative if it could be economically liquified or gasified for transportation through the oil indus-

---

[25]"Mobil Wants to be Your Milkman," *Forbes*, February 13, 1984, p. 44.

try's huge pipeline system. The major oil companies had, accordingly, increased their ownership of coal reserves since 1970. By the early 1980s, however, serious doubts remained about whether coal liquification and gasification would ever become economical.

72   Mobil was a majority shareholder in a venture that began exploration for coal in Indonesia in 1983. In Australia, the company was involved in coal exploration, as well, and held reserves of 60 million tons through a joint venture.

73   The company had had a significant position in oil shale lands for many years and was active in shale research. No commercial oil shale operations had yet begun, however.

74   In New Zealand, a Mobil synthetic fuel plant, which would manufacture gasoline from locally produced natural gas, was expected to come on stream in late 1985.

75   Mobil had, as well, devoted considerable effort to researching solar technology. Mobil Solar Energy Corporations, a wholly-owned subsidiary, planned to build a solar-powered desalination plant in Abu Dhabi. Mobil Tyco Solar Energy Corporation, another subsidiary, was meanwhile involved in the production of solar panels for use in the residential consumer market.

76   Mobil held proved and probable uranium reserves of 33.5 million pounds, and sold 207,000 pounds of uranium domestically during 1983.

Non-Energy Diversification

77   Mobil's diversification into areas outside of petroleum included operations involving chemicals, real estate, paperboard packaging, and retail merchandising. Like some of the other major oil companies, Mobil found it difficult to achieve profit margins in these businesses that approached those of its core business. In 1983, for instance, Mobil netted just $49 million in net income out of $10 billion in revenues from chemicals, paperboard packaging, and retail merchandising.

78   **Chemicals.** The Mobil Chemical Company was formed to bring the company's worldwide chemical business into one integrated operating division. This division was equipped with its own research and development, manufacturing, and marketing facilities. The primary domestic facilities produced basic petrochemicals such as ethylene, propylene, and butadiene, and aromatics such as benzene and toluene.

79   Mobil's strategy in chemicals was said to be one of concentrating on selected areas of business with good growth opportunities, primarily in those fields where the company already had a strong competitive position and could profit from its structural integration and traditional expertise. In addition, Mobil Chemical used much of its output of basic petro-chemicals in other manufacturing operations. This large degree of internal utili-

Table 2

Non-petroleum earnings, 1979-83 (millions)

	1979	*1980*	*1981*	*1982*	*1983*
Chemicals	$113	$119	$ 93	$ 24	$ 8
Paperboard packaging	40	71	57	24	1
Retail merchandising	54	(162)	(160)	(93)	40
Total	$207	$ 28	$(10)	$(45)	$ 49

Source: "Company Analysis: Mobil Corporation," Donaldson, Lufkin & Jenrette, March 20, 1984.

zation made the company somewhat less sensitive to the fluctuations of the petrochemical market.

80   The company owned or had interest in 63 facilities located in ten countries. Mobil's principal chemical products included: plastics used in the home and in packaging by industry; basic petrochemicals sold to producers of plastics, synthetic fibers, and other chemical products; phosphate rock and di-ammonium phosphate products sold to fertilizer producers; coatings used in packaging, furniture, shipping, and maintenance applications; and specialty industrial chemicals. Brand names identifying Mobil's chemical products included "Hefty," "Kordite," and "Baggies."

81   Mobil Chemical was, in fact, the largest manufacturer of plastic packaging in the United States, producing such products as garbage bags, food bags, bread wrapping, and industrial packaging. Another highly successful product of the plastics division was polystyrene foam, which was used in the manufacture of egg cartons, fast-food containers, and disposable tableware. There had also been considerable growth in sales of a product called Mobilrap, which was a heavy-duty polyethylene stretch film used to wrap pallet loads for industrial distribution

82   Mobil also produced "oriented polypropylene" (OPP) under the brand name BICOR, which was a packaging film replacement for cellophane. This product was receiving rapid acceptance because of its lower cost and higher quality as a cellophane substitute. Mobil was the world's largest producer of this fabricated plastic, and had OPP manufacturing plants in the United States, Canada, and Europe.

83   Mobil had attained leadership in the field of high performance chemical coatings, and was the third largest U.S. producer of phosphate rock, as well.

84   The company's chemical earnings were barely break-even in 1983, partly because of $23 million of pre-operating expenses related to the Saudi petrochemical facility.

85   **Real Estate.** Mobil made its first significant real estate investment in 1966 when it moved its Hong Kong terminal, thereby vacating a choice 40-

acre site. Mobil decided to build a huge middle-class apartment complex rather than sell the land for an estimated $15 million. This complex was completed in 1979, and housed more than 70,000 people.

86   In 1970, a management team was formed to explore further opportunities in real estate. The company's first U.S. purchase was a residential community comprised of 3,300 bayfront acres near San Francisco.

87   Early in 1977, Mobil began bidding for southern California's Irvine Company, which was the owner of America's largest real estate development. Beginning with an offer of $24 per share (or $202 million), Mobil finally bid more than $336 million for the property before losing out to a private group that included Henry Ford II, John Irvin Smith, Max M. Fisher (a Detroit industrialist), and others. In July of 1978, Mobil purchased the undeveloped half of Reston, Virginia from Gulf Oil for over $30 million. Gulf previously had sizable interests in real estate, but later divested itself completely of these projects. Gulf maintained that they were not closely enough related to the company's basic business, and that they had not made a meaningful contribution to corporate profits.

88   The majority of Mobil's real estate was owned by Mobil Land Development Company, a non-consolidated subsidiary located in San Francisco. Mobil's holdings were generally large tracts of land strategically located in high growth areas, and were well suited to large-scale communities of at least 1,000 homes.

89   Despite these investments, real estate remained a relatively minor part of Mobil's overall operations.

90   **Marcor.** In 1968, Mobil made a decision to diversify outside of the energy business in a significant way. A diversification study team was formed to analyze various industries and select individual companies as possible candidates for acquisition. Mobil's objective was not to become a large conglomerate, but to acquire one major diversification subsidiary. Mobil's Rawleigh Warner, Jr., commented on Mobil's motivation:

> We had become aware that governments would interfere with our business. We thought they would be oil-producing countries, not consuming nations. But after the oil embargo we realized that the consuming nations would also play a greater role. That impelled us forward with the diversification program.[26]

91   Senior management established certain criteria for any potential acquisitions. These criteria required that any company being considered have a strong management team, considerable experience in its own field, good earnings growth and rate of return possibilities, different business cycles and business risks from the oil industry, and a strong competitive position within its own markets.

92   After reviewing over a hundred companies in a five-year period, Mobil began looking very closely at Marcor, Inc., a holding company formed in

---

[26]"Big Oil's Move into Retailing," *Chain Store Executive,* September 1976, pp. 29–32.

1968 that consisted of two main subsidiaries, Montgomery Ward and Container Corporation. Montgomery Ward was a retailer in the United States, and Container Corporation was the largest U.S. producer of paperboard packaging.

93   In 1973, Mobil bought 4.5% of Marcor's stock for an average cost of $23 per share. When the Arab oil embargo hit, the stock market fell sharply and oil prices skyrocketed. By 1974, Mobil had a lot of extra cash on hand, and Marcor's stock looked like more of a bargain than ever. In August of 1974, Mobil made a tender offer for shares that would give it a majority interest in the smaller company. The price at that time was still below $25 per share. Marcor's price per share rose sharply that same year. Later in 1974, three Marcor executives were elected to Mobil's Board of Directors, and four officers of Mobil, including Warner and Tavoulareas, were elected Directors of Marcor.

94   In July of 1976, Mobil bought the rest of Marcor. The 1976 Annual Report contained the following message to the stockholders:

> By merging with Ward and Container, Mobil effectively realized its major diversification objective. Both firms are extremely well managed and have the growth potential to contribute materially to Mobil's U.S. based earnings. They helped Mobil to increase significantly the percentage of total earnings produced in the U.S. Moreover, they operate in business areas with different cycles and risks from oil's and are not subject to the vagaries of oil industry regulation.[27]

95   During the period of acquisition, Mobil drew considerable criticism from members of Congress and the Federal Energy Administration. John C. Sawhill, chief of the FEA, who had previously defended higher oil profits as necessary for capital investment in domestic exploration and production, said the Mobil offer to acquire controlling interest in Marcor was "like having a wet dishrag thrown in your face." Walter F. Mondale (D-Minn.) said in July 1974 that the proposed acquisition:

> is the best sign yet that the oil industry is engaged in a desperate search for ways in which to get rid of embarrassingly high profits. (It) lends substantial weight to the wisdom of repealing the oil depletion allowance immediately.[28]

Sen. Thomas J. McIntyre (D-N.H.) called the acquisition plan "irresponsibility at its worst."[29]

96   Warner's reply to the criticism that the Marcor acquisition siphoned off cash that should have been used in exploration and production was that Mobil was already exploiting as many E&P opportunities as it could find.

97   While Mobil never revealed the total price for Marcor, it was estimated that it must have paid about $1.8 billion, spending around $800 million for

---

[27]Mobil Annual Report, 1976.

[28]"Congressional Barbs Hit Mobil-Marcor Deal," *Oil and Gas Journal,* July 1, 1974, p. 32.

[29]Ibid.

Table 3

Montgomery Ward earnings, 1979-83 (millions)

1979	1980	1981	1982	1983
$54	$(162)	$(160)	$(93)	$40

Source: Mobil Corp. Annual Reports, 1981–83.

the first 54% in 1973 and 1974. Mobil put $200 million of cash directly into Marcor's treasury in exchange for new preferred stock, but maintained that it had no plans to pump additional capital into the retailing chain. Ward was definitely expected to pull its own weight, and Mobil emphasized that its new subsidiary would be granted operational autonomy in the conduct of its business.

98   Although the Marcor acquisition was seen by some analysts as one of the boldest diversification efforts by a major oil company into a non-energy field, some oilmen viewed the acquisition as overly conservative. One oil executive said:

> They were far ahead with the idea, but maybe they were too timid. Why not diversify into drugs, instruments, office equipment, electronics, or computers—all of which have higher rates of return?[30]

99   By 1980, Mobil's management was admitting that the scenario surrounding Marcor had not panned out as they had predicted. "We probably wouldn't buy Marcor this year, right now," conceded Tavoulareas.[31]

100   In order to maintain Montgomery Ward's bond rating in 1980, Mobil was forced to pump $200 million into the company. Mobil took great care to label the transaction an interest-free loan. At year-end 1980, Montgomery Ward showed a loss of $162 million. Early in 1981, Mobil granted the retailer an additional $155 million in interest-free loans. Earnings, however, continued to deteriorate.

101   A 1983 turnaround at Montgomery Ward was attributed to rising retail sales, lower interest rates, more sophisticated merchandising techniques, and cost savings related primarily to a reduction in the number of employees. Credit was also widely given to the guidance of Stephen Pistner, who became chief executive of Ward in 1981.

102   Results at Marcor's Container Corporation of America, meanwhile, were less than encouraging. Though the paperboard packaging firm showed a $1 million profit in 1983, it would actually have shown a loss, had gains on sales of properties been excluded. Moreover, the company had proved to be a drain on capital to Mobil for several years.

---

[30]"The New Diversifications Oil Game," *Business Week,* April 24, 1978, pp. 76–88.

[31]"Mobil's Successful Exploration," *Business Week,* October 13, 1980, p. 112.

Table 4

Container Corporation Funds Flow (millions)

	1979	*1980*	*1981*	*1982*	*1983*
Funds from operations	$128	$141	$147	$117	$100E
Capital expenditures	116	141	206	229	132
Surplus/(deficiency)	$ 12	$ 0	$(59)	$(112)	$(32)

Source: "Company Analysis: Mobil Corporation," Donaldson, Lufkin & Jenrette, March 20, 1984.

103   Mobil's 1983 annual report stressed that a management reorganization, major cost-cutting programs, and the introduction of more efficient labor practices were expected to lay the groundwork for better margins at Container Corporation in the years ahead.

Public Relations

104   Beginning in the early 1970s, Mobil developed a public relations strategy that was outspoken, controversial, and decidedly atypical compared with that of other members of the conservative and usually silent oil industry.[32] This strategy did not appear to have resulted from any single decision by senior management. Rather, "Mobil's 'high profile' operation developed gradually," according to *Fortune* magazine, "in response to an increasingly perceived need for the company to become more visible and articulate."[33]

105   By the late 1970s, Mobil was also well known for its efforts to sponsor and promote cultural events on both public and commercial television networks. Its first grant was made in 1970 to launch the very successful "Masterpiece Theatre."

106   Another facet of Mobil's public relations strategy was revealed in the company's willingness to address "issue-oriented" or "advocacy" questions in the media. While much of its advocacy advertising was aimed at problems within the oil industry, Mobil also editorialized on other controversial issues that the company thought were of national interest. Mobil was quick to attack any treatment of the oil industry (by the media or the government) that it perceived as unfair. At the same time, many of its views were somewhat surprising when first aired. For example, the endorsement of an effective mass transit policy for the nation's largest metropolitan areas initially surprised many observers. At one time or another, Mobil's readi-

[32]See the case "What Ever Happened to Fair Play? Public Relations at Mobil," by Clark and Barrett, for a thorough description of Mobil's PR efforts.

[33]Ross, Irwin, "Public Relations Isn't Kid-Glove Stuff at Mobil," *Fortune,* September 19, 1976, pp. 106–202.

ness to defend its interests had led it into extended public conflicts with such powerful media forces as the CBS and ABC television networks, the *Washington Post,* and the *Wall Street Journal.* Mobil had also not hesitated to break ranks with the other members of the oil industry on particularly sensitive issues, such as the question of oil price controls.

Mobil on the Prowl

107 Throughout the late '70s and early '80s, Mobil redirected its exploration and production efforts toward properties in North America. At the same time, Mobil made repeated attempts to bolster its paltry domestic reserves through acquisition—attempts that met with mixed success.

108 **General Crude Oil Company.** Mobil entered the high-stakes bidding war for General Crude Oil Company (a subsidiary of International Paper) in the spring of 1979. Gulf had originally reached a tentative agreement to buy General Crude's oil and gas operations, but was later outbid by a joint offer from Tenneco and Southland Royalty Company. Mobil offered in March of 1979 to buy the operations for $765 million, thus topping the previous offer. General Crude's reserves, located primarily in the United States, were said to approach 160 million barrels. Mobil eventually raised its offer, and a sale for $792 million was completed in July of 1979.

109 **Belridge Oil Company.** In May of 1979, Belridge Oil Company let it be known that it was actively seeking a merger with a large oil comapny. Mobil, the largest single shareholder with 18%, was thought to have an inside track. Belridge attracted a good deal of interest. This was due in part to Belridge's substantial proven reserves, mostly heavy crude located in California. Some speculated, however, that the interest in Belridge was better explained by the company's vast and largely unexplored reserves of light, high quality oil located in deep geologic formations. A group of big oil companies (which included Mobil) lost out on the bid for the closely-held target to Shell Oil, which ultimately purchased Belridge for $3.6 billion. Mobil, in turn, sold its interest in Belridge in January of 1980.

110 **Texas Pacific Oil Company.** Some months later, Sun Oil bid $2.3 billion for the U.S. oil and gas properties of Texas Pacific Oil, a subsidiary of Joseph E. Seagram & Sons, Inc. Texas Pacific was one of the nation's five largest non-integrated petroleum producers, with proven U.S. reserves of 120 million barrels of oil and 300 billion cubic feet of natural gas. Sun's bid was a record for proven reserves, and amounted to $12 per barrel. Despite a last minute, secret effort by Mobil to bid for the properties, Sun and Seagram signed a definitive agreement. Mobil was said to have offered to match Sun's price, but with different terms.

111   **TransOcean Oil.** TransOcean Oil was the exploration unit of Vickers Energy Group, which in turn was a subsidiary of Esmark, Inc. In the summer of 1980, Mobil successfully bid $715 million for TransOcean, which owned considerable property in the Overthrust Belt in the Rockies. The deal was structured so that Esmark would be free of capital gains tax. To accomplish this, Mobil bought Esmark common stock, then swapped those shares with Esmark for TransOcean shares—a tax-free transaction. This arrangement was said to have saved Esmark some $100 million in capital gains taxes.

112   **Conoco.** In July of 1981, Mobil made a $7.7 billion tender offer for slightly more than 50% of the stock of Conoco, Inc. Mobil thus became Conoco's third major suitor, along with Dupont Company and Seagram. Mobil's offer was immediately rebuffed. Conoco filed an antitrust suit against Mobil, while continuing to press for a DuPont merger.

113   Mobil continued to press its attack, however, quickly raising its offer to $8.2 billion, and later $8.82 billion. Conoco was an attractive target to crude-short Mobil. Conoco offered stable and abundant acreage, half of which was located in the United States and the remainder in Europe and Canada. Moreover, a Mobil-Conoco merger would more than double Mobil's interest in the North Sea's Statfjord field.

114   In response to continued reference to possible antitrust violations, Mobil offered to dispose of certain U.S. marketing operations in order to speed the purchase.

115   Ultimately, Mobil lost out to DuPont when a federal appeals court refused to issue a temporary restraining order to delay a DuPont deal. Mobil had been spurned again, despite a final offer, which was $1.28 billion more than DuPont's.

116   **Marathon.** In the fall of the same year, still smarting from the failed Conoco takover attempt, Mobil made a $5.1 billion ($85 a share) bid for Marathon Oil. Like Conoco, Marathon held reserves in politically secure areas. Marathon, the nation's 17th largest oil company, actually offered greater reserves in the United States and Canada than did Conoco. A merger with Marathon at Mobil's bid price would have yielded oil and gas reserves at an equivalent of less than $3 a barrel. Moreover, such a merger would boost Mobil's U.S. oil reserves by some 80%.

117   Though Mobil had structured its offer so as to entice Marathon stockholders to tender their shares quickly, Mobil's bid was immediately stalled by a court restraining order. That gave Marathon time to search for a white knight (or, friendly suitor). Marathon managed to secure a $100 a share offer from U.S. Steel (subsequently raised to $106 a share).

118   In a last-ditch effort to salvage the merger attempt, Mobil announced plans to purchase as much as 25% of the outstanding stock of U.S. Steel, its rival bidder. Industry observers questioned the sincerity of Mobil's threat.

Though many labeled the announcement "scare tactics," others speculated that a future attempt to buy all of U.S. Steel was not out of the question. Were that to happen, Mobil would pick up massive mineral reserves and could conceivably write down the target company's steel mills, using the loss to shield oil profits.

119   In order to counter antitrust concerns in the Marathon takeover bid, Mobil offered to bid jointly for Marathon with Amerada Hess. Mobil would then sell Amerada Hess all of Marathon's existing marketing, refining, and transportation properties. A lower court rejected this plan, however.

120   Though Mobil eventually raised its offer for Marathon to slightly above the U.S. Steel bid, it finally lost out to the steel company when the U.S. Supreme Court rejected a Mobil appeal. Mobil officials would not rule out a run at U.S. Steel in the future, however.

121   **Anschutz.** In 1982, Mobil acquired a working interest in certain domestic oil and gas reserves and exploration acreage from Anschutz Corporation. Industry sources estimated the purchase price exceeded $500 million. The acquisition was said to net Mobil some 100 million barrels of oil from a giant field located in Utah, and straddling the southwestern corner of Wyoming. Mobil was also said to have received 250,000 acres of undeveloped exploration leases elsewhere. A report from one investment broker called the Anschutz field "potentially one of the most significant finds in North America since the Prudhoe Bay discovery" on the North Slope of Alaska.[34] It was expected that the Anschutz field would be expensive to develop, however.

122   It had earlier been reported that Anschutz had been seeking a buyer for part of its interest in the field because it was in need of more money to develop the property.

123   While adding significantly to Mobil's reserves, the acquisition reflected a desire on Mobil's part to bolster its domestic reserves through private, friendly transactions. Mobil thus avoided many of the antitrust complications that hindered earlier takeover attempts.

124   **Superior.** Having twice failed to acquire an integrated oil firm, in March of 1984 Mobil turned its attentions to Superior Oil Company, the nation's largest independent. Industry experts viewed Mobil's interest in Superior as a calculated effort to avoid the antitrust accusations of Mobil's previous attempts. Superior owned neither gasoline stations nor refineries. It did possess, however, vast reserves in the United States and Canada.

125   A Mobil-Superior merger would increase Mobil's U.S. and Canadian oil reserves by 15% and 48% respectively. Growth in natural gas reserves would be even more dramatic, with U.S. reserves increasing by 29% and

---

[34]"Mobil Buys Part of Utah Oil Field From Anschutz," *The Wall Street Journal,* August 12, 1982, p. 2.

Canadian reserves by 92%. In fact, Superior's 1983 reserve increases would more than offset Mobil's 1983 reserve declines.

126   In sharp contrast to its maverick reputation, Mobil's strategy in attempting a takeover of Superior was uncharacteristically couched in secrecy and aimed at achieving a friendly deal. Mobil officials first met with members of the founding Keck family, who owned 22% of Superior. Mobil's management knew that the Keck family members, who had recently been fighting among themselves, were willing to sell. Mobil offered them $45 a share and received their agreement to make the purchase for the Kecks' 22% share.

127   While negotiating with the Kecks, Mobil was simultaneously attempting to strike a deal with Superior's top executives.

128   On March 11, Mobil made public its agreement with the Kecks and announced its intention to purchase the remaining shares at the same $45 price. The total bid of $5.7 billion would make this deal the fifth-largest oil merger in history. Mobil would gain reserves of about one billion barrels of oil and oil equivalent at a price of less than $6 a barrel.

Exhibit 1

Mobil Corporation income statement (millions)

	1983	1982	1981	1980	1979
Revenues					
Sales and services					
Petroleum operations....................	$43,433	$49,182	$53,298	$49,189	$35,403
Chemical...............................	2,230	2,034	2,235	1,812	1,562
Paperboard packaging	1,685	1,869	1,998	1,880	1,600
Retail merchandising	6,003	5,584	5,742	5,497	5,251
Services and other	1,256	1,277	1,215	1,132	905
Total sales and services...........	54,607	59,946	64,488	59,510	44,721
Excise and state gasoline taxes...........	3,389	3,168	3,129	3,313	2,764
Interest	513	460	335	414	339
Dividends and other income	92	142	19	22	80
Equity in earnings of certain					
affiliated companies....................	397	392	616	467	388
Total Revenues	58,998	64,108	68,587	63,726	48,292
Costs and Expenses					
Crude oil, products, merchandise, and					
operating supplies and expenses	38,404	43,997	46,178	41,301	30,477
Exploration expenses	618	847	803	524	359
Selling and general expenses	4,967	5,312	5,181	4,957	4,265
Depreciation, depletion, and					
amortization	1,892	1,736	1,586	1,399	1,086
Interest and debt discount expense........	814	663	608	479	459
Taxes other than income taxes					
Excise and state gasoline taxes	3,389	3,168	3,129	3,313	2,764
Windfall profit tax.....................	447	630	936	267	—
Import duties	3,395	3,500	3,825	4,155	3,756
Property, production, payroll,					
and other taxes	858	949	941	655	564
Total taxes other than					
income taxes	8,089	8,247	8,832	8,390	7,084
Income taxes............................	2,711	2,093	2,966	3,863	2,555
Total Costs and Expenses..........	57,495	62,895	66,154	60,913	46,285
Income Before Extraordinary Item	1,503	1,213	2,433	2,813	2,007
Extraordinary Item—Gain on sale					
of interest in Belridge Oil Company					
(less income taxes of $189)...............	—	—	—	459	—
Net Income.............................	$ 1,503	$ 1,213	$ 2,433	$ 3,272	$ 2,007
Memo:					
Income less foreign inventory profits					
(before extraordinary item)...............	$ 1,503	$ 1,213	$ 2,332	$ 2,169	$ 1,707

Source: Mobil Corporation Financial and Operating Statistics, 1983.

Exhibit 2

Mobil Corporation balance sheet (millions)

	December 31				
	1983	*1982*[a]	*1981*	*1980*	*1979*
Assets					
Current assets					
Cash..................................	$ 507	$ 542	$ 782	$ 698	$ 621
Marketable securities, at cost	1,046	1,133	1,262	1,220	1,257
Accounts and notes receivable	4,832	5,135	5,440	5,718	5,060
Inventories					
Crude oil and petroleum products	3,070	3,678	4,320	4,518	3,114
Chemical products	317	338	333	315	237
Paperboard packaging	128	137	172	181	158
Retail merchandising	937	893	937	975	1,080
Other, including materials and					
supplies..............................	626	737	718	474	362
Total inventories	5,078	5,783	6,480	6,463	4,951
Prepaid expenses.......................	427	367	256	203	174
Total current assets	11,890	12,960	14,220	14,302	12,063
Investments and long-term					
receivables............................	2,854	2,563	2,423	2,213	2,030
Properties, plants, and equipment,					
at cost................................	31,673	30,029	27,612	24,581	20,676
Less accumulated depreciation,					
depletion, and amortization	11,795	10,714	9,902	8,741	7,573
Net properties, plants,					
and equipment	19,878	19,315	17,710	15,840	13,103
Deferred charges and other assets	450	378	423	350	310
Total Assets......................	$35,072	$35,216	$34,776	$32,705	$27,506
Liabilities and Shareholders' Equity					
Current liabilities					
Notes and loans payable...............	$ 1,185	$ 2,187	$ 1,692	$ 949	$ 1,064
Accounts payable and accrued					
liabilities............................	6,847	7,332	7,604	7,880	7,113
Income, excise, state gasoline,					
and other taxes payable	2,246	2,393	2,486	3,218	2,377
Deferred income taxes	163	316	704	546	467
Long-term debt and capital lease					
obligations maturing within					
one year	372	198	219	126	170
Total current liabilities	10,813	12,426	12,705	12,719	11,191

Exhibit 2 (concluded)

	December 31				
	1983	*1982*[a]	*1981*	*1980*	*1979*
Long-term debt...........................	5,162	4,404	3,284	3,256	2,962
Capital lease obligations	328	313	320	315	342
Reserves for employee benefits	336	385	410	412	398
Deferred credits and other non-current obligations	1,074	845	653	605	294
Accrued restoration and removal costs	315	265	208	148	114
Deferred income taxes	3,000	2,665	2,442	2,087	1,605
Minority interest in subsidiary companies	92	106	97	94	87
Shareholders' equity	13,952	13,807	14,657	13,069	10,513
Total Liabilities and Shareholders' Equity	$35,072	$35,216	$34,776	$32,705	$27,506

[a] Restated.
Source: Mobil Corporation Financial and Operating Statistics, 1983.

Exhibit 3

Mobil Corporation changes in financial position (millions)

	1983	*1982*[a]	*1981*	*1980*	*1979*
Sources of Funds					
Operations					
Income before extraordinary item	$ 1,503	$1,213	$2,433	$2,813	$2,007
Depreciation, depletion, and amortization	1,892	1,736	1,586	1,399	1,086
Deferred income tax charges	487	166	425	482	585
Dividends in excess of (less than) equity in income of unconsolidated companies	(158)	44	(41)	129	(50)
Funds available from operations	3,724	3,159	4,403	4,823	3,628
Extraordinary item	—	—	—	459	—
Book value of properties, plants, and equipment sold	(30)	195	123	410	84
Funds available before financing	3,834	3,563	4,642	5,791	3,790
Application of Funds					
Cash dividends to shareholders	813	836	851	733	541
Capital expenditures	3,073	3,821	3,571	3,525	2,641
Major acquisitions[b]	—	500	—	715	792
Increase (decrease) in:					
Accounts and notes receivable	(303)	(302)	(278)	658	870
Inventories.............................	(705)	(545)	17	1,512	823
Prepaid expenses.......................	60	111	53	29	32

Exhibit 3 (concluded)

	1983	1982[a]	1981	1980	1979
Investments and long-term receivables	133	77	169	312	136
(Increase) decrease in:					
Accounts payable and accrued liabilities..............................	485	266	276	(767)	(1,437)
Income, excise, state gasoline, and other taxes payable	147	93	732	(841)	(637)
Foreign exchange translation effects on working capital, debt, and other items, net	206	203	—	—	—
Application of funds before financing	3,909	5,060	5,391	5,876	3,761
Increase (decrease) in funds before financing	(75)	(1,497)	(749)	(85)	29
Total Financing*					
Increases in long-term debt	1,208	1,424	375	525	202
Decreases in long-term debt..............	(450)	(304)	(347)	(231)	(287)
Increase (decrease) in capital lease obligations............................	15	(7)	5	(27)	(20)
Increase (decrease) in notes and loans payable..........................	(1,002)	495	743	(115)	461
Increase (decrease) in long-term debt and capital lease obligations maturing within one year...............	174	(21)	93	(44)	1
Purchase of common stock for treasury.................................	(11)	(471)	—	—	%
Issuance or sale of common stock.........	19	12	6	17	10
Total financing increase (decrease).........................	(47)	1,128	875	125	367
Increase (Decrease) in Cash and Marketable Securities	$ (122)	$ (369)	$ 126	$ 40	$ 396
*Excludes the increase (decrease) in financing of two major unconsolidated subsidiaries:					
Mobil Oil Credit Corporation.............	$ (16)	$ (101)	$ —	$ 193	$ 187
Montgomery Ward Credit Corporation	36	(315)	(281)	(99)	498
Total	$ 20	$ (416)	$ (281)	$ 94	$ 685

[a]Restated.

[b]Includes acquisition of a working interest in certain holdings of The Anschutz Corp., 1982, and acquisition of operations of TransOcean Oil, Inc., 1980, and General Crude Oil Co., 1979.

Source: Mobil Corporation Financial and Operating Statistics, 1983.

Exhibit 4

Mobil Corporation distribution of earnings and assets—segments (millions)

1983	*1983*	*1982*[a]	*1981*	*1980*	*1979*
Total Revenues					
Petroleum—United States	$14,291	$14,759	$15,701	$14,560	$10,820
—Foreign	35,745	42,073	44,827	43,226	31,814
Chemical................................	2,424	2,246	2,437	2,027	1,718
Paperboard packaging	1,779	1,953	2,068	1,946	1,647
Retail merchandising	6,646	6,143	6,122	5,916	5,652
Other	22	46	24	33	13
Adjustments and eliminations	(1,909)	(3,112)	(2,592)	(3,982)	(3,372)
Total	$58,998	$64,108	$68,587	$63,726	$48,292
Segment Earnings					
Petroleum—United States	$ 774	$ 877	$ 1,174	$ 953	$ 689
—Foreign	979	677	1,512	2,012	1,345
Chemical................................	8	24	93	119	113
Paperboard packaging	1	24	57	71	40
Retail merchandising	40	(93)	(160)	(162)	54
Other	(133)	(136)	(99)	(42)	(83)
Corporate expenses	(166)	(160)	(144)	(138)	(151)
Income before extraordinary item	$ 1,503	$ 1,213	$ 2,433	$ 2,813	$ 2,007
Capital Expenditures					
Petroleum—United States	$ 1,458	$ 1,617	$ 1,485	$ 1,215	$ 1,160
—Foreign	1,074	1,389	1,236	1,424	825
Chemical................................	210	328	274	248	146
Paperboard packaging	129	273	255	180	182
Retail merchandising	121	69	144	322	250
Alternative energy	16	68	107	48	27
Corporate and other	65	77	70	88	52
Total	$ 3,073	$ 3,821	$ 3,571	$ 3,525	$ 2,642
Depreciation, Depletion, and Amortization					
Petroleum—United States	$ 1,045	$ 1,033	$ 856	$ 751	$ 540
—Foreign	495	394	445	396	334
Chemical................................	95	82	76	67	58
Paperboard packaging	107	93	88	79	71
Retail merchandising	106	105	101	88	74
Corporate and other	44	29	20	18	9
Total	$ 1,892	$ 1,736	$ 1,586	$ 1,399	$ 1,086
Total Segment Assets at Year-End					
Petroleum—United States	$10,878	$10,560	$ 9,686	$ 9,107	$ 7,651
—Foreign	15,457	16,519	17,137	16,692	13,681
Chemical................................	2,266	2,044	1,797	1,547	1,160
Paperboard packaging	1,866	1,942	1,820	1,649	1,519
Retail merchandising	4,183	4,076	4,154	3,942	3,746
Other	410	391	337	275	271
Corporate assets	483	483	443	221	115
Adjustments and eliminations	(471)	(799)	(598)	(728)	(637)
Total	$35,072	$35,216	$34,776	$32,705	$27,506

[a]Restated.
Source: Mobil Corporation Financial and Operating Statistics, 1983.

Exhibit 5

Mobil Corporation distribution of earnings and assets—geographic (millions)

	1983	*1982*[a]	*1981*	*1980*	*1979*
Total Revenues					
United States	$23,934	$23,844	$24,936	$23,318	$18,908
Foreign					
Canada	1,203	1,072	835	850	723
Other	35,399	41,898	44,901	43,189	31,806
Total foreign........................	36,602	42,970	45,736	44,039	32,529
Adjustments and eliminations	(1,538)	(2,706)	(2,085)	(3,631)	(3,145)
Total Revenues	$58,998	$64,108	$68,587	$63,726	$48,292
Geographic Earnings					
United States	$ 659	$ 660	$ 1,041	$ 826	$ 739
Foreign					
Canada	104	80	33	97	100
Other	906	633	1,503	2,028	1,319
Total foreign........................	1,010	713	1,536	2,125	1,419
Corporate expenses, net of income taxes..................................	(166)	(160)	(144)	(138)	(151)
Income before extraordinary item	$ 1,503	$ 1,213	$ 2,433	$ 2,813	$ 2,007
Geographic Assets at Year-End					
United States	$18,706	$18,123	$16,898	$15,644	$13,696
Foreign					
Canada	1,329	1,314	1,138	969	788
Other	15,200	16,265	17,049	16,765	13,716
Total foreign........................	16,529	17,579	18,187	17,734	14,504
Corporate assets	483	483	443	221	115
Adjustments and eliminations	(646)	(969)	(752)	(894)	(809)
Total Assets	$35,072	$35,216	$34,776	$32,705	$27,506

[a] Restated.

Source: Mobil Corporation Financial and Operating Statistics, 1983.

Exhibit 6

Mobil Corporation capital, exploration, and other outlays (millions)

	1983	1982ᵃ	1981	1980	1979
Segment Distribution					
United States					
Petroleum—	$ 1,742	$ 2,061	$ 1,804	$ 1,429	$ 1,301
—Acquisitionsᵇ	—	500	—	712	700
Chemical	195	311	258	200	130
Paperboard packaging	101	224	208	131	144
Retail merchandising	121	69	144	322	250
Alternative energy	12	82	123	61	40
Corporate and other	145	162	165	139	72
Total	$ 2,316	$ 3,409	$ 2,702	$ 2,994	$ 2,637
Foreign					
Petroleum—	$ 1,400	$ 1,774	$ 1,697	$ 1,715	$ 1,026
—Acquisitionsᵇ	—	—	—	3	92
Chemical	15	17	16	48	16
Paperboard packaging	28	49	47	49	38
Alternative energy	12	4	7	6	3
Total	$ 1,455	$ 1,844	$ 1,767	$ 1,821	$ 1,175
Worldwide					
Petroleum—	3,142	$ 3,835	$ 3,501	$ 3,144	$ 2,327
—Acquisitionsᵇ	—	500	—	715	792
Chemical	210	328	274	248	146
Paperboard packaging	129	273	255	180	182
Retail merchandising	121	69	144	322	43
Corporate and other	145	162	165	139	72
Total	$ 3,771	$ 5,253	$ 4,469	$ 4,815	$ 3,812
Geographic Distribution					
United States	$ 2,316	$ 3,409	$ 2,702	$ 2,994	$ 2,637
Canada	153	138	148	222	206
Other foreign	1,302	1,706	1,619	1,599	969
Worldwide	$ 3,771	$ 5,253	$ 4,469	$ 4,815	$ 3,812
Research Expense	$ 209	$ 196	$ 179	$ 143	$ 115

ᵃRestated.
ᵇIncludes acquisition of a working interest in certain holdings of The Anschutz Corp., 1982, and acquisition of the operations of TransOcean Oil, Inc., 1980, and General Crude Oil Co., 1979.
Source: Mobil Corporation Financial and Operating Statistics, 1983.

Exhibit 7

Mobil Corporation top 11 domestic retail gasoline marketers

	1983		1982		1981		1980		1979		1978		1977	
	Rank	% Share	Rank	% Share	Rank	% Share	Rank	% Share	Rank	% Share	Rank	% Share	Rank	% Share
Amoco	1	7.23	1	7.32	1	7.28	3	7.40	2	7.48	2	7.70	2	7.30
Shell	2	6.97	2	6.77	2	6.89	2	7.44	3	7.30	1	7.71	1	7.53
Exxon	3	6.90	3	6.75	3	6.81	1	7.54	1	7.65	3	7.28	3	7.14
Texaco	4	5.80	6	5.62	4	5.77	5	5.95	5	6.01	4	6.75	4	7.11
Mobil	5	5.69	5	5.68	6	5.38	4	6.01	6	5.78	6	5.55	6	5.59
Gulf	6	5.30	4	5.78	5	5.69	7	5.39	4	6.36	5	5.83	5	5.91
Chevron	7	5.06	8	4.84	7	5.21	6	5.77	7	5.30	7	4.76	7	4.75
Arco	8	4.82	7	4.64	8	3.80	8	3.87	8	3.89	8	3.79	8	3.85
Union	9	3.52	9	3.31	9	3.31	9	3.50	9	3.49	9	3.28	11	3.08
Phillips	10	2.61	10	2.77	10	2.88	10	2.83	11	2.85	11	3.02	10	3.15
Sun	11	2.54	11	2.64	11	2.55	11	2.74	10	3.01	10	3.20	9	3.39

Source: 1984 National Petroleum News Factbook, p. 117.

Exhibit 8

Mobil Corporation share price data

	High	*Low*
1974	14 1/4	7 3/4
1975	12 1/4	8 5/8
1976	16 3/8	11 7/8
1977	17 7/8	14 5/8
1978	18 1/8	14 5/8
1979	30 1/4	17
1980	44 7/8	24 7/8
1981	41 1/8	24 1/8
1982	28 5/8	19 1/2
1983	34 5/8	24 1/4

Adjusted for stock splits.
Source: Standard NYSE Stock Reports, Standard & Poor's Corp., December 6, 1984.

1   It was early March 1981 and Thomas Baiman had just completed a four-hour review of his file on Houston Oil and Minerals Corporation (HOM). He sat back in his chair on the 46th floor of Universal Petroleum's Houston office building and tried to sort out his thoughts prior to returning to the as-of-yet uncompleted task.

2   Mr. Baiman, vice president of Exploration and Production at Universal, had been interested in HOM for quite some time. Along with many other industry executives, he had regarded HOM as a "star" performer. However, during 1979 and 1980, its increasing size caught up with this once innovative and highly successful independent oil and gas producer. Finally, in December 1980, a merger with Tenneco was announced.

3   Although Mr. Baiman knew that HOM was not regarded as highly as it had once been, he still was impressed by its rapid rise to the top. It was his hope that a thorough review of HOM would allow him to determine some of the factors which led to its success and some reasons for its ultimate merger with Tenneco. The results of this analysis, he had hoped, would be applicable to Universal, thereby improving its exploration and production division.

This case was prepared by Katherine B. Penn and M. Edgar Barrett, Director of the Maguire Oil and Gas Institute.

General Background

4   HOM was classified as an independent oil company. Like most independents, HOM was not involved in every phase of the industry. For instance, it had no refineries, no chemical operations, and no retail gasoline outlets. Although HOM was involved in some transportation and trading activities, it was primarily known as an oil and gas exploration company. In fact, during 1977, the company sank more exploratory footage in the United States than all but five other oil companies.[1]

5   Despite this concentration on one area, HOM's financial results were large enough that the company ranked not far behind many of the integrated majors. Among the leading oil companies in 1979, HOM ranked 42nd in terms of revenues. It ranked 38th in terms of net income and 34th in respect to total assets.[2]

Company Background

6   Houston Royalty Company was incorporated in 1966 in the state of Nevada. It was the successor of two Texas companies, Houston Royalty Company and Royalties Management Corporation, both of which had been organized in 1928. At the time of the 1966 merger, the company had assets of $2.8 million and annual revenues of $674,000. Two years later the name of the company was changed to Houston Oil and Minerals Corporation in order to reflect the decreasing importance of royalty interests for the overall firm.

7   By the end of 1980, HOM's assets totaled $1,708 million and annual revenues amounted to $383 million. The firm also reported $319 million in capital expenditures and an annual net income of $79.6 million. Clearly, the preceding 15 years had seen a great deal of growth.

The Late 1960s

8   Joseph C. Walter, Jr., HOM's president, and F. Fox Benton, Jr., its chief financial officer, made two policy decisions in 1968. The first was that HOM would try to retain a 100-percent working interest in whatever prospects the company undertook for exploration purposes. This was—and still is—an unusual practice in the oil and gas business, particularly among independents. Most oil companies routinely formed partnerships for the purpose of leasing and exploratory drilling over a diverse group of exploration sites. Company managements seemed to feel that the risks associated

[1]"Why an Oil-Patch Legend Joined Tenneco," *Fortune*, January 12, 1981, p. 49.
[2]*The Oil Daily*, May 8, 1980.

with drilling dry holes were lessened by taking a less than total interest in multiple projects.

9   The second major policy decision concerned the type of leases that HOM would purchase. The decision was made that the company would buy both producing and non-producing properties.[3] However, it was decided that HOM would endeavor to buy only those producing properties that offered potential for the discovery of previously unknown reserves. It was felt that buying producing properties of this type would serve two purposes: they would provide potential exploration sites; and, they would lessen the risk of the overall company by providing an assured level of production. The company's top management also set a corporate goal of 100% compounded annual growth in revenues, profits, production, and reserves over the next eight years.

10   HOM's management was also active in capital spending and investment during 1968. The company bought Blessing Dryer and Warehouse, Inc., a rice-drying and -storage company. Although it was held only during the last half of the year, Blessing generated 25% of HOM's total revenues for the year. HOM also participated as operator and part owner in the formation of Southwest Minerals Exploration Corporation. It soon owned over 120,000 acres of leases, most of which were bought for sulfur exploration.

11   HOM began to strengthen its domestic oil and gas exploration program in 1969. The firm quadrupled the total size of its leaseholds of oil and gas properties to 122,758 net acres. It also bought Sunflower Royalties Company, which served to increase the firm's royalty revenues by 10 percent. To manage the enlarged exploration program, HOM hired John Walters to be manager of exploration and production. Mr. Walters, a geologist by training, came to HOM from Kerr-McGee, another independent oil company. Mr. Walters had been involved with exploration in the Frio and Miocene regions of the Gulf Coast for most of his career.[4]

12   In April 1969, HOM made its first public offering of common stock. The company sold 140,000 shares at 8 3/4 per share, and netted over $1.2 million from the sale. The proceeds of the offering were used to acquire Good Hope Refineries, Inc. Good Hope, which was to be HOM's only refinery venture, had a throughput capacity of 8,500 barrels per day (b/d). This was 14 times HOM's crude oil production at the time.

13   The refinery's main product was JP-4 jet fuel, which it sold to the Department of Defense under six-month contracts. The refinery was profitable during the first five months of its operation by HOM. After that time, however, a decline in jet fuel prices resulted in a drop in revenues and a marginally profitable operation. HOM then invested another $650,000 in the construction of additional facilities designed to provide greater flexibility of product mix and to increase profit margins at the refinery. The

---

[3]Producing properties are those on which oil and/or gas is currently being produced.

[4]The terms Frio and Miocene refer to geological formations. Both are found extensively in the Gulf Coast region.

company sold Good Hope the next year for less than half of the original purchase price.

The Early 1970's

14 In 1970, HOM reported a loss on continuing operations, the only reported loss in the history of the company. The decline in profits was due to two factors: increasing interest charges, and a large number of unsuccessful exploration attempts.[5] The company drilled four wildcat wells,[6] and participated in drilling an additional three wells, all seven of which turned up dry. At that time, the company was paying for all dry hole costs in the year they were drilled.

15 HOM reversed some of its recent expansion activities during 1970. Southwestern Mineral Exploration Corporation (SMEC) relinquished all of its sulfur and uranium leases, and HOM subsequently reduced its financial interest in the company to a nominal amount. With the disposition of SMEC and Good Hope Refineries, all remaining operations except Blessing Dryer and Warehouse were directly related to oil and gas exploration.

16 The 1970 annual report stated that:

> . . . in 1971, the Company will concentrate its activity along the Gulf Coast. The Company is currently negotiating for leases on several prospects along the Texas Gulf Coast in a deep gas trend.[7]

17 In February of 1971, the company purchased properties for $4 million that produced at an average daily rate of approximately 1,500 barrels of oil and 4 million cubic feet of gas. All of the acquired properties were in Louisiana and Mississippi. In December, HOM bought the 10,500-acre Bolivar property in Galveston Bay. The company paid the sellers, Occidental Petroleum, and Alied Chemical, $2.7 million for the lease. At the time of the purchase, the Bolivar acreage had 4 shut-in oil wells at about 9,000 feet in the Miocene formation. The property had no production and no proven reserves.

18 The focus on buying leases and exploring for oil and gas continued through 1972. The company spent $2.6 million during the year for new leases, all of which were in Southern Texas and Louisiana. An additional $4.6 million was spent on exploration and development drilling.[8]

---

[5]The financial impact of the disposition of Good Hope Refineries, Inc., and Southwestern Minerals Exploration Corporation was shown as additional losses above and beyond those from continuing operations.

[6]A "wildcat" well is an exploratory well drilled in an area that is not in the vicinity of oil and gas production. A well may be called a wildcat even though it is in the vicinity of oil and gas production if the well is drilled substantially deeper to a different geological formation. The terms "wildcat well" and "exploration well" are used interchangeably.

[7]*HOM 1970 Annual Report*, p. 3.

[8]A development well is a well drilled near a successful exploration well for the pupose of production from the field already discovered.

The Bolivar Discovery

19   HOM drilled five wildcat wells in 1972. Four of them proved to be unsuccessful. The fifth one, however, located in the Bolivar Point area of Galveston Bay, struck a natural gas field in the Frio sands section at a depth of 12,500 feet. After the second well was drilled in January 1973, the reserves were estimated to contain 50 billion cubic feet of natural gas. Its discovery more than doubled HOM's known gas reserves. The price of the company's stock, which had never before risen above $10 per share, rose to a third quarter high of 18 $\frac{1}{8}$. In the fourth quarter of 1972, as more test wells were drilled, HOM's share price rose to 34 $\frac{3}{8}$. HOM's common shares were listed on the American Stock Exchange in October, and in December the company announced a four-for-three stock split.

20   The Bolivar discovery served to reinforce management's decision to emphasize oil and gas exploration and development. The company spent $28.5 million of new leases and on exploration activities during 1973. Most of that amount was spent in the Galveston Bay area. Only one of the company's wildcat wells drilled in the Galveston Bay area that year was successful. That well hit a gas field in the North Point Bolivar area that the company had leased just after the original Bolivar discovery.

21   In November 1973, HOM entered into a contract with Lone Star Gas, the intrastate pipeline subsidiary of Enserch Corporation. The contract called for the sale of not less than 80% of the natural gas production from the Bolivar field through the year 1993. The contract allowed, at the option of the seller, for price renegotiation every two years. Between 1973 and 1978, HOM had twice renegotiated a higher price for the gas.

22   Seagull Pipeline Corporation was also formed at the end of 1973 as a wholly owned subsidiary of HOM. The principal asset of the subsidiary consisted of an eleven-mile-long "gathering" pipeline, which delivered gas from the North Point Bolivar field to an onshore pipeline owned by Lone Star Gas. HOM began natural gas deliveries from the Bolivar field in November 1973. Revenues earned from the sale of natural gas from Bolivar during November and December were 20% of total corporate revenues for the year.

23   Several factors appear to have made possible HOM's singular success in the Bolivar area. The history of exploration in that area up to the time of HOM's Bolivar discovery discouraged competition by the major oil companies. Texaco had drilled in the 1950s in an area adjacent to the Bolivar discovery and got a dry hole. Gulf had also drilled just south of this area in the 1960s. After a discovery, three offsetting dry holes were drilled, but the overall project proved discouraging. These experiences caused the area to be viewed as an unattractive prospect. When HOM's discovery occurred, the image of this area may well have dampened the enthusiasm of the major oil companies to follow up on their discovery.

24   Thus, HOM was able to acquire other tracts in the area even after their discovery. The North Point Bolivar gas field was discovered on a tract that

HOM was able to lease while their earlier discovery was still, to some extent, inside information. Although the log from the earlier discovery became available at about the time that the bid was awarded, HOM's bid was high enough to ensure their success. According to an industry observer, "At that point, no other company would even have considered bidding that high for tracts in that area. They left a lot of money on the table unnecessarily."

25   HOM was also protected from competition during this period by its relative youth and inexperience in exploration. It appears to have been considered young, aggressive, and much more willing to take risks than were the majors. The price of gas at the time of HOM's discovery was so low that the potential rewards of exploring such an historically unattractive area were not considered sufficient to attract other companies.

Turbulence in Petro-Land

26   HOM's North Point Bolivar discovery came at a time just before the average selling price for oil and natural gas began to rise rapidly. In October 1973, the Organization of Petroleum Exporting Countries (OPEC) announced that the posted price for crude oil for export would be doubled to over $5 per barrel. The United States was importing 37% of its crude oil from OPEC-member countries at the time. Also in October 1973, King Faisal of Saudi Arabia announced an embargo against petroleum exports to the United States. King Faisal was reacting to the pro-Israel posture of the United States during the 1973 Middle East War. The embargo was supported by all of the other Arab members of OPEC.

27   The net effect of the Arab oil embargo was a worldwide shortage, rather than curtailed supplies only in the United States. This was largely due to the fact that the major oil companies were able to shift supplies to the United States from other, non-embargoed, importing countries. It was in this climate of international shortage that the Shah of Iran announced an increase of crude oil prices to $11 a barrel in January 1974. The other OPEC members quickly followed suit.

28   The United States government constructed a price regulation structure as a partial reaction to the oil embargo and the pursuant quadrupling of crude oil prices. The explicit purpose of the new structure was to encourage expanded domestic exploration and production. The price of "old" oil, defined as oil flowing from wells drilled in 1972 or before, was initially controlled at $5.25 per barrel. The price of "new" oil, defined as oil emanating from fields developed after 1972, could be sold at world market prices. The world market price of natural gas also showed a dramatic rise over the 1973–74 period. Natural gas brought prices in the uncontrolled market that were comparable to oil prices per Btu.[9]

---

[9]A British thermal unit (btu) is the amount of heat required to raise the temperature of one pound of water by one degree Fahrenheit.

29   The average selling price for natural gas sold in the United States did not rise nearly so dramatically as world market prices for oil. The reasons for the relatively slower increase were two. First, natural gas was sold domestically through long-term contracts. Until recently, the selling price of the gas was fixed for the life of the contract, usually 20 years. Therefore, rising world market prices had no effect on natural gas already contracted for sale. The second reason for the relatively slower increase was that most natural gas was sold in the interstate market, which was price-controlled by the U.S. Federal Power Commission. The highest price that a producer could receive in an interstate sale, even after the world market price rise, was $1.42 per thousand cubic feet (MCF), which was 40% below the uncontrolled price in the intrastate market.

30   Most of HOM's major oil discoveries occurred after 1972. Thus, the oil revenues received moved in line with the world market price. HOM's average revenue per barrel of crude oil, for example, increased from $4.53 in 1973 to $8.29 in 1974.

31   The firm's Bolivar discovery was also made after the emergence of a price disparity between the interstate and the intrastate markets. As noted earlier, HOM's major contract for the sale of natural gas from the Bolivar Field contained a price renegotiation clause. The firm's average revenue per MCF of natural gas rose from $ .36 in 1973 to $ .77 in 1974.

The Middle 1970s

32   HOM's revenues in 1974 were almost quadruple 1973 levels. This increase was due to the doubling of prices for natural gas in the intrastate market and to increased natural gas production. The company's net profit for the year was 470% of 1973 profits, despite a blow out and fire at a producing well in the North Point Bolivar field.

33   HOM drilled sixteen wells during 1974. Half of these resulted in oil or gas discoveries. In addition to these exploration expenditures, the company spent $2.3 million on the purchase of oil and gas leases from the State of Texas. These leases were located in Galveston Bay and other Texas bays. The company also bought leases in Louisiana and Mississippi and additional leases in Texas.

34   HOM also expanded its interests in 1974 with both the addition of a Gas Processing and Products Division and the initiation of a small foreign exploration effort. The Gas Processing and Products Division was formed in order to provide flexibility in the marketing of gas liquids from the company's oil and gas production. No capital expenditures were planned for the division, however, until legislation was enacted that would indicate whether more favorable price and tax treatment would be given to natural gas or to products derived from it.

35   Seagull Pipeline Company added 11 miles to its gathering pipeline facility during 1974. The addition doubled the length of the pipeline and reflected

the increasing number of successfully completed development wells in the Bolivar field.

36   HOM's 1974 Annual Report attributed much of the company's success and growth to "decisions and strategies adopted in 1968."[10] The report went on to state that "they are the company's policies today."[11] The annual report gave this explanation of the company's exploration strategy:

> Houston Oil and Minerals has developed a basic exploration philosophy which is unique for a company its size. The company generates virtually all its exploratory prospects internally and retains all of the working interest in its prospects. This policy and the larger interest maximizes the potential gain.[12]

1975

37   More than half of the company's capital budget in 1975 was spent drilling 30 wildcat wells along the Gulf Coast. The drilling discovered several small fields and one large field, Texas City Dike, in Galveston Bay. The Texas City Dike field was important for two reasons. First, it added reserves, and second, it confirmed the existence of a trend of productive Frio sands under Galveston Bay. At this point, 60,000 acres, or 10 percent of HOM's leased acreage, was in and around the Galveston Bay area. The company drilled 47 development wells in 1975. Twenty-six of these resulted in successful oil producing wells, while 12 resulted in successful gas producing wells.

38   The year also saw the widening of HOM's geographical areas of interest. The company acquired a 100%-working interest in three foreign leases located, respectively, in Australia, the United Arab Emirates, and offshore Sharjah. None of these leases contained producing properties. The company also expanded its exploration activities into the Rocky Mountain and Upper Midwest regions of the United States.

39   In 1975, HOM began to pay cash dividends at an annual payout rate of 19% of earnings. With large increases in revenue and a relatively low dividend rate, HOM was able to reinvest substantial amounts of after-tax income in the form of increased exploration and development activities. Despite this, only 20% of the 1975 capital expenditures were funded from operating income. The balance was funded by bank debt, production payments, prepayments for natural gas deliveries and the proceeds received from offerings of securities.

40   An additional source of funds for the company has been deferred taxes. In 1975 the company's deferred taxes amounted to $8.4 million. HOM was paying no federal income taxes whatsoever as of 1976.

---

[10]Source: *HOM 1974 Annual Report,* inside cover.
[11]Ibid.
[12]Ibid, p. 4.

1976

41   The company's series of gas discoveries in Galveston Bay continued into 1976. In January, HOM announced a gas discovery in the Half Moon Shoal field, just east of the Texas City Dike field discovered in 1975. The discovery of an oil and gas field contiguous to the north side of the Texas City Dike field was announced in March.

42   The largest discovery of the year, however, was in the Shipwreck Channel field. This discovery was made outside Galveston Bay, 10 miles south of the North Point Bolivar field. The company quickly drilled 15 development wells in the Shipwreck field. All of them proved successful. The additional 1976 discoveries resulted in a 42% increase in gas reserves and a 32% increase in oil reserves.

43   The company's revenues and earnings for 1976 more than doubled those of a year earlier. HOM used most of the resulting increase in cash flow for exploration. The increased capital spending was necessary, in part, to keep up with the rising prices of leases. In a 1976 State of Texas sale, HOM paid an average $117 per acre for mineral lease in Galveston and Aransas Bays. In a sale two years earlier, HOM had paid an average $55 per acre for leases in the same general area.

44   In other leasing activity, HOM bid in a Federal lease sale for four blocks in the Baltimore Canyon, offshore New Jersey on the outer continental shelf. HOM bid alone and was the only independent to bid successfully in the sale. One of the tracts, for which HOM paid $5.7 million was contiguous to a tract for which Shell paid $45 million. In a second Federal lease sale, HOM bid successfully for Vermilion Block 50 located 15 miles off the Louisiana coast.[13]

45   The company also created a new minerals division in 1976. This division was based in Denver, Colorado, and was charged with prospecting for precious metals, base metals, and uranium in Alaska, New Mexico, Colorado, Utah, Montana, and Washington State. Finally, while conducting exploratory drilling for oil and gas, the company's wholly-owned subsidiary— Houston Oil and Minerals, Australia, Inc.—encountered seams of coal and methane gas. The company then initiated a long-range feasibility study designed to assess the prospects for commercial production from the deposits.

1977

46   HOM revenues and earnings in 1977 were both double 1976 levels. The source of the increase was primarily the increase in production from the

---

[13]These were the first two Federal lease sales in which the company had participated. Because they were Federal leases, any forthcoming production from the leasehold property would have to be sold in the interstate market. Thus, the price for any natural gas produced from these properties would probably have to be sold at prices lower than could be commanded for the same gas sold in intrastate markets.

Shipwreck field and secondarily from higher gas prices. Capital expenditures increased to $229 million, almost half of that amount going for oil and gas exploration. Most of the exploration during the year was spent in the Gulf Coast area, and all of the company's seven discoveries were located there.

47   Despite the addition of substantial oil and natural gas reserves in 1977, net reported, proved reserves of oil and natural gas decreased by 5 and 9 percent, respectively. Some of the decrease was caused by production during the year. The major portion, however, resulted from a downward revision of the company's estimated reserves by independent engineers. Shortly after the late 1977 announcement of the downward revision of estimated reserves, the company's common share price fell to its lowest price in almost two years.

48   Most other oil companies estimated their own reserves internally. In HOM's case, however, the company had to obtain an independent estimate of reserves as part of an agreement with the financial institutions that lent HOM funds against those reserves. Over the past several years, HOM had borrowed as much as their lending institutions would allow, and all of the company's reserves were used as collateral.

49   Most of the leaseholds that the company acquired during 1977 were in large contiguous blocks in state and federal waters offshore Texas and Louisiana. Despite the continuing emphasis on oil and gas exploration in the Gulf Coast area, the company did spend 7 percent of its exploration budget abroad and another 4 percent on mineral exploration that was primarily in the Rocky Mountain area of the United States.

50   The 1977 annual report contained an announcement that:

> In 1978, the Company's strategy is to continue to concentrate exploration activities in the highly productive Gulf Coast area and to develop and expertise in other areas which are believed to have profitable opportunities.[14]

Financial Considerations

51   The major financial issue within HOM had been how to raise the funds necessary to finance an ever-growing program of capital expenditures. Such expenditures, which reached a level of $229 million in 1977, averaged four times earnings during the 1974 to 1977 period. The funds involved had been used primarily for four purposes: the purchase of oil, gas and mineral lease rights; exploratory drilling for oil and gas; geophysical research; and development drilling for oil and gas.

52   HOM had relied upon a mixture of internally generated funds, bank debt, convertible subordinated debentures, prepayments, deferred taxes, and stock offerings to supply the capital for its exploration program. Of

---

[14]*HOM 1977 Annual Report*, p. 4.

these, the least significant source of funds had been direct recourse to the public equity markets. HOM's last public offering of common stock occurred in 1969, when the company sold 140,000 shares.

53   Despite the absence of public stock offerings, the number of HOM common shares outstanding increased from 382,750 in 1968 to 29,000,000 in 1977. This increase in common shares outstanding could be attributed to three major sources: the existence of stock dividends and stock splits; the conversion of convertible debt intruments; and the exercise of stock options and stock warrants. Solely as a result of stock dividends and stock splits, 10 HOM shares in existence at December 31,1968 would have constituted 200 shares on December 31, 1977.

54   The company issued $37 million in convertible subordinated debentures between December 1968 and the end of 1977.[15] Of the total amount issued during this period, only $361,000 worth remained unconverted at the end of 1977. The conversions that occurred during the nine-year period, in terms of December 1977 shares, represented 11 million of the 29 million shares outstanding as of December 1977.

55   The company also issued stock to its employees under a "thrift plan," which had been in operation since 1973. Under the terms of the plan, an employee was allowed to contribute up to 6 percent of the employee's salary to the fund. The company then contributed matching funds, and the total amount was used to purchase shares of the company's stock. HOM also gave stock options to employees on the basis of outstanding performance. Approximately 9 million shares, which represent approximately 30% of the company, were issued during the December 1968 to December 1977 period through stock options, stock warrants, and the thrift plan. At the end of 1977, 1 million shares were reserved for unexercised options and warrants.

56   In addition to convertible debt, a great deal of money was raised through the issuance of straight long-term debt. The amount of long-term debt owed by the company grew from $14 million in late 1968 to $279 million in late 1977.

Accounting Methods

57   HOM had used the "full cost" method for reporting the financial impact of exploration and development costs since 1971. Under this method of accounting, the company capitalized all costs of exploration and development. The sum of both dry hole costs and the costs of drilling successful

---

[15]Convertible debentures are debt instruments issued by a company at a specified interest rate and, often, with specific sinking fund provisions. The debenture holder has the option to convert the debenture to common stock, receiving one share for a specified amount of debt principal. This amount of prinicipal is generally set somewhat higher than the market price for the stock at the time that the debentures are issued.

wells was capitalized, placed on the balance sheet as an asset, and amortized over the life of the producing fields.

58   Most major oil companies used the "successful efforts" method of accounting. Under this method, all costs incurred in drilling exploratory wells that resulted in dry holes were treated as an expense in the period incurred. Only those costs that were incurred in drilling that resulted in the discovery or further development of oil and gas fields were capitalized.

59   In 1978, the Financial Accounting Standards Board (FASB) issued Statement No. 19, which, if it had been enacted, would have required all companies to use the successful efforts method.

60   According to commentary contained in HOM's 1977 Annual Report, the restatement of prior years' earnings using the successful efforts method would have had the effect of reducing the company's reported retained earnings by $64 million. Such a reduction would have left the 1977 consolidated earnings at 36% of the level actually reported.

Production Activities

61   HOM had oil and gas exploration activities from the outer continental shelf in the Atlantic Ocean, to the Gulf Coast area of the Southern United States, and on to the Rocky Mountain area. It also had such activities in the United Arab Emirates, the Phillipines, Australia, and Tunisia. As of 1977, the international facets of this program were still in the exploration stages. All of HOM's prospects were generated internally by the company's staff of geologists and geophysicists.

62   In addition to the company's petroleum activities, HOM also had an exploration program for minerals other than oil and gas. HOM held leases for mineral exploration in Alaska, the Rocky Mountain States, and Australia. As of 1977, the company had no mineral production other than oil and gas. It had no production of any kind outside the United States.

63   Like most oil companies, HOM used its exploration expertise to find and develop oil and gas properties. It was through the production of the developed properties that the company received the major portion of its revenues. The company had total revenues of $256 million in 1977. Of that amount, 86% could be attributed to the sale of oil and gas. Seventy-one percent of the total came from natural gas sales alone. Pipeline revenues and product trading activities provided the remaining 14% of total revenues.

64   HOM did not own any of the drilling rigs used in its exploration program. Instead, the company contracted with independent drilling operators for drilling services. HOM was the operator of all properties in which the company had a majority interest. The company's policy had been to retain a working interest of 100% wherever possible in its leases. Therefore, HOM was the operator of almost all of the properties in which the company had an interest. Where HOM was the operator, the exploratory drilling was

supervised by the company's engineering staff. If large quantities of oil and gas were found through exploratory drilling, HOM's staff also supervised development and production from the field.

65   HOM's success in oil and gas exploration had been attributed by some observers to the quality of its geological staff. According to an article in *Business Week,* HOM managed to attract a top-flight staff because of the autonomy that HOM allowed its employees.[16] Autonomy for the company's geological staff meant decision-making power on what and where to drill. "Once the basic budgets are drawn up, we give the geologists almost complete autonomy in how they want to spend the money," said HOM President J. C. Walter in the article.[17]

66   HOM also provided incentives to the company's employees to find oil; the reward for a discovery in stock options was sometimes several thousand shares for a large find. From 1972 to 1977, options on 600,000 shares were granted to HOM employees. The system of autonomy with incentives allowed HOM to retain its streamlined management by allowing more decisions to be made in the field. According to Walter, it also allowed HOM to avoid overhead costs that were part of the difference between HOM's average finding costs of $2.50 per barrel of oil and the industry average of $5.00 per barrel.

The Late 1970s and After

1978

67   HOM reported net earnings of $55.6 million on revenues of $325.7 million in 1978. This represented an increase of 7% and 21%, respectively, over figures for the previous year. The primary source of increased revenues was due to the first full year of production from the Shipwreck, Ship Channel, and Giddings fields. In addition, the company began production in the Vermilion Block 50 located offshore Louisiana, and in the West Lopez field west of Corpus Christi.

68   HOM continued to be active in acquiring offshore lease properties. The company paid an average of $114 per acre for 100% working interest for 31 tracts in a State of Texas sale. Later in the same year, HOM paid as much as $906 per acre for interest in five tracts located on the outer continental shelf in the Gulf of Mexico. The company bid with Kerr-McGee, an independent oil company, for four of the five tracts. This action reversed an established strategy of obtaining 100% interest in properties.

69   Outside of the Gulf Coast area, HOM bought a 50% interest in a 630,000 acre petroleum concession in the Emirate of Dubai, United Arab Emirates.

[16]"Houston Oil's Freehand Approach to Growth," *Business Week,* June 13, 1977, p. 97.
[17]Ibid.

SEDCO, Inc., a Dallas firm primarily known as an independent drilling contractor, owned the other half interest in the joint venture, and was to be the operator of the properties. Houston Oil International, Inc., a wholly-owned subsidiary of HOM, was formed in July 1978, with responsibility for the Dubai concession, as well as activities in the Phillipines. A service contract for oil exploration was awarded to HOM by the Republic of the Phillipines in March 1978. The 865,000 acres covered by the contract were in Central Luzon, north of Manila.

70   The company also sold half of its interests in the Baltimore Canyon to Phillips Petroleum Company for $4.1 million. In addition to the $4.1 million that Phillips paid in cash, Phillips was to bear 100% of the cost of the first two exploratory wells. Both wells turned out dry and were capped. Neither firm had plans for further exploration.

71   During 1978, revenues from Seagull pipelines nearly doubled to $42 million, while net earnings were up 33% to $13.6 million. By year-end Seagull operated 85 miles of gathering pipelines and had 40 additional miles under construction. Seagull aggressively sought business from firms other than HOM. Sixteen of the 18 transmission contracts signed were with outside customers.[18]

72   Late in the year, HOM's oil and gas operations were decentralized to form five individual operating divisions defined by geographical boundaries. Each division operated with its own staff of exploratory and support personnel. Performance was evaluated on "sustained additions to proved reserves at a profitable cost."[19] This move was not favorably viewed by many industry observers. "Several veteran geologists from its most active region, the Texas coast, were shifted to the Louisiana and offshore regions, leaving a good many comparatively inexperienced geologists to cover Texas, where the company spent the largest portion of its exploration dollars."[20]

1979

73   Net earnings increased 18% to $65.6 million while total revenues were up 14% to $352 million. Capital expenditures, which continued to emphasize the Gulf Coast area, totalled $383 million. Year-end net equivalent reserves were up 7% over 1978 figures to 223 million net equivalent barrels. HOM's inventory of undeveloped domestic acreage rose over 24% to 964,000 acres during the year.

74   In November 1979, Houston Oil Colombiana, S.A. (HOCOL), a wholly-owned subsidiary, acquired Petroleos Colombo-Brasileros, S.A. for $55 million. Estimated proved reserves of HOCOL were 80 million barrels of oil

---

[18]*HOM 1978 Annual Report,* p. 6.

[19]Ibid.

[20]"Why an Oil-Patch Legend Joined Tenneco," *Fortune,* January 12, 1981, p. 50.

and 6.6 billion cubic feet of gas. Oil produced in the country was sold exclusively to a government-owned oil company. The sales contract provided incentive to increase production through development drilling, prices increasing on total production as production increased. At year-end, HOCOL received $3.79 per barrel on production of 15,000 b/d. Contract prices were to rise to $5.17 per barrel when production reached 21,800 b/d.

75   HOM also reduced its equity interest in the Oaky Creek coal project in Australia from 90% to 42.5%. However, the company remained operator of the property. HOM realized $43.3 million from the sale, but it reinvested $19.9 million back into the development. The total estimated investment to complete the development of the operation was $300 million.

76   Joe Walter became less active in the company following a heart attack in November 1978. He returned to the office in mid February of 1979 for shortened work days. Fox Benton filled in during Walter's absence. In May, Benton was named president and chief executive officer. Walter retained his role as board chairman.

1980

77   The year held great promise for HOM. The company discovered another major gas field (the Cavolla field) in the coastal waters southwest of Galveston Bay. When fully developed, the field was estimated to be capable of sustaining production of one trillion cubic feet of natural gas.[21] In addition, domestic activities included exploratory and development drilling in nine states. By year-end, HOM's domestic undeveloped oil and gas acreage position totaled some 1,939,116 gross acres, 1,422,738 net acres. Also, the company brought into production its precious metals operations in Nevada.

78   However, by 1980, HOM's rapid growth began to catch up with the company. At year-end, HOM was responsible for almost $450 million in debt, about 70% of which floated with the prime rate. "Both Walter and Benton, who have the wildcatters' spirit, disliked the constraints that came with HOM's rapid growth."[22]

79   The company felt the constraints as the bankers, who once lent freely on HOM's reserves, held back. As a result, capital expenditures were down 17% from 1979. The company was able to drill only in what was considered to be the best places, while many prospects stacked up. In addition, HOM sold its Australian coal properties because it could not put up the $300 million which was necessary to develop the property.

---

[21]Ibid.

[22]"A Texas Wildcatter Cashes in His Chips," *Business Week,* December 22, 1980, p. 21.

Financial Reporting Revisited

80 HOM was not required to use the Successful Efforts method of accounting as had been earlier anticipated. However, as of 1980, information concerning a firm's oil and gas reserves and its producing activities prepared on the basis of Reserve Recognition Accounting (RRA) was required by the SEC to appear as supplemental disclosures. Under this new method, a company's income would be measured by the increase in recoverable reserves, less the expenses incurred during the period.

81   The results of HOM's oil and gas producing activities on the basis of RRA, which appeared in the notes to its 1980 annual report, were $364 million for 1979 and $122 million for 1980 (results of oil and gas producing activities in the United States during 1980 were $90 million, foreign results being reported at $212 million). The corresponding amounts under the full cost method, which were reflected in the primary financial statements, were $237 million for 1979 and $259 million for 1980.

The Merger

82 In December 1980, HOM accepted a friendly merger offer from Tenneco, Inc. The deal was estimated to have been worth nearly $2 billion. Tenneco saw the acquisition as an opportunity to achieve its goal of replacing each year's production with new oil and gas finds. For HOM, the deal meant money—the capital necessary to develop its properties and the realization of the company's value by its shareholders.

Exhibit 1

Houston Oil and Minerals Corporation letter to stockholders—1980

To Our Stockholders

1980 was a year of developments which will significantly affect the Company's future operating structure. The spin-off of Seagull Pipeline Corporation, the proposed property trust, and the subsequent merger with Tenneco should provide substantial benefits to our stockholders. These events should not, however, overshadow the record financial and operating results achieved during 1980. Revenues from continuing operations were $383 million, up 27 percent from 1979. Earnings from continuing operations were $71 million, an 18 percent increase and funds from continuing operations rose 19 percent to $238 million. Total production of oil and gas was 23 million net equivalent barrels, an 11 percent increase over 1979.

Oil and Gas

During 1980, the Company enjoyed another successful exploration year worldwide, by adding a total of 40 million net equivalent barrels of oil and gas to proved reserves. Seventeen million net equivalent barrels were added in the U.S., and an additional 23 million net equivalent barrels were discovered in Colombia. Domestic production decreased slightly to 18 million net equivalent barrels in 1980, reflecting continued weakness in the Texas intrastate

Exhibit 1 (continued)

gas market and a decline in deliverabilities from some of the Company's more mature fields. Foreign oil production, however, increased substantially. Houston Oil Colombiana produced 5 million barrels of oil during 1980, raising its daily net production rate by 50 percent during the year. Revisions to previous estimates were primarily responsible for lower estimated total reserve quantities at year-end 1980. However, price increases maintained the net present value of these reserves at $1.7 billion, as calculated under SEC guidelines.

The Company has budgeted $306 million for oil and gas capital spending in 1981. Of this amount, $172 million has been allocated to exploration activities and $134 million for development of previous discoveries. Our exploration joint venture with Tenneco will ensure the funding required to maintain the Company's aggressive domestic drilling program. 76 domestic exploratory wells are planned in 1981, a 69 percent increase over the 45 domestic wildcats drilled in 1980.

Pipeline

In early March 1981, we completed the spin-off of Seagull Pipeline Corporation. Seagull continued to post record operating results in 1980, earning $8 million on revenues of $61 million. Its opportunities for future growth as an independent company should be excellent.

Minerals

In 1980, the Company consolidated its worldwide minerals activities into a new Denver-based subsidiary, Houston International Minerals Corporation (HIMCO). During 1980 HIMCO made significant progress on the Comstock and Manhattan projects which improved gold and silver production rates. Exploration activity was highlighted by the confirmation of a gold and silver deposit at the Borealis prospect near Hawthorne, Nevada. Feasibility studies have been completed and development of the property is underway. Initial metals production is scheduled to commence late this year.

In Australia, HIMCO completed the divestiture of its remaining interest in the Oaky Creek metallurgical coal project. Early in the year a twelve percent equity interest was sold to two European firms. Prompted by a governmental ruling which required additional Australian equity in the project, the Company sold its remaining 38 percent interest late in the year to a major Australian mining firm. HIMCO realized a substantial gain on its total investment in Oaky Creek, but it is unfortunate that the project's long-term potential to the Company was precluded from being realized.

The Merger

Our Company grew to a size which made it difficult to sustain its past growth rates. Oil and gas discoveries which could provide dramatic growth for Houston Oil became by definition very large. With ever-increasing exploration and development costs, additional financial resources to achieve our potential were needed. Many alternatives were considered, and we decided that a merger with another company would be most advantageous to our stockholders and employees. After carefully considering corporations which could provide the needed resources, Tenneco emerged as the best positioned to help exploit our excellent exploration prospect inventory and to carry forward our other business lines. On December 9, 1980, we signed a definitive agreement with Tenneco Inc. which provides for the merger of Houston Oil into Tenneco after the spin-off of Seagull and the creation and distribution of a new property trust to our stockholders. The new Houston Oil Trust will own a 75% net profits interest in all the Company's domestic productive oil and gas properties, a 5% overriding royalty in nearly all domestic exploratory acreage, and various net profits interests in certain of the Company's foreign oil and gas properties.

As a result of these transactions, the Company's stockholders will have a continuing interest in oil and gas properties and prospects developed by the Company, with the opportunity to receive income from the production of existing proved reserves. The Trust will also benefit from any future reserve additions on the Company's productive properties and future exploratory efforts on the Company's existing domestic and certain foreign unevaluated

Exhibit 1 (concluded)

prospects. The Trust distribution permits the Company's stockholders to participate in any future increases in oil and gas prices, and to realize any tax benefits associated with the ownership of non-operating interests in oil and gas properties. At the same time, our stockholders will be provided with new equity ownership of an exciting diversified corporation.

Words are inadequate to convey our appreciation for our employees' efforts throughout this and past years. Without them, the Company's dramatic success would not have been possible. We are confident that our new relationship with Tenneco will provide an equally rewarding and challenging atmosphere for them, and that their efforts will provide significant contributions to our new parent organization.

Finally, we take this opportunity to thank you, our stockholders, for your long-standing interest and support. Together, we have made significant accomplishments, and we are confident that stockholder benefits will continue under the new operating structure.

Sincerely,

J. C. Walter, Jr.
Chairman of the Board

F. Fox Benton, Jr.
President and Chief Executive Officer

March 1981

Exhibit 2

Houston Oil and Minerals Corporation selected excerpts from consolidated balance sheet and notes (year ended December 31) (in thousands)

	1980	*1979*
Assets		
Current assets:		
Cash	$ 10,511	$ 35,081
Receivables:		
Trade accounts—net of allowance for doubtful accounts of $674,000 (1980) and $572,000 (1979)	80,967	64,147
Other (Note 5)	41,478	36,446
Inventories	30,943	23,040
Prepaid expenses	2,883	3,024
Total current assets	166,782	161,738
Property, plant and equipment—at cost (Notes 1, 2 and 7):		
Oil and gas properties and equipment—full cost	1,070,676	867,411
Pipeline facilities and equipment (Note 4)	51,687	40,894
Minerals properties and equipment (Note 5)	71,780	84,221
Other	12,764	9,916
Total cost	1,206,907	1,002,442

Exhibit 2 (continued)

	1980	1979
Accumulated depletion, depreciation and amortization	350,890	223,455
	856,017	778,987
Notes and long-term receivables (Note 5)	50,752	
Deferred charges and other	4,141	4,914
Total assets	$1,077,692	$ 945,639
Liabilities and stockholders' equity		
Current liabilities:		
Accounts payable	$72,618	$ 75,277
Accrued expenses and other current liabilities	28,640	22,369
Income taxes payable (Note 11)	4,006	
Notes payable (Notes 6 and 10)	18,000	22,891
Current maturities on long-term debt	27,193	13,535
Total current liabilities	150,457	134,072
Long-term debt (Note 10)	431,772	411,088
Deferred income taxes (Note 11)	182,689	141,391
Deferred compensation	129	3,670
Stockholders' equity:		
Capital stock:		
Preferred stock, $1 par value: authorized 10,000,000 shares; issued and outstanding 2,295,438 shares (1980) and 2,999,900 shares (1979) (Note 13)	2,295	3,000
Common stock, $.10 par value: authorized 50,000,000 shares; issued and outstanding 30,142,341 shares (1980) and 29,179,479 shares (1979) (Note 12)	3,014	2,918
Additional paid-in capital	122,408	115,616
Retained earnings	184,928	133,884
Total stockholders' equity	312,645	255,418
Total liabilities and stockholders' equity	$1,077,692	$ 945,639

Note 3. Proposed Merger of the Company and Tenneco Inc.

On December 9, 1980, the Company entered into a definitive acquisition agreement providing for the merger of the Company and a wholly-owned subsidiary of Tenneco Inc. The agreement has been approved by the Boards of Directors of both companies and is subject to approval by stockholders of the Company. The agreement contemplates that the Company will create a trust, consisting of an approximately 75% overriding royalty interest (equivalent to a net profits interest) in its presently productive domestic oil and gas properties, a 5% overriding royalty interest in substantially all of its domestic exploratory oil and gas properties and varying net profits interests in certain foreign oil and gas properties. Units in the trust would be distributed to the Company's common stockholders prior to the merger. In addition, the agreement provides that the Company may proceed with the previously announced distribution of Seagull to the Company's stockholders. Under the agreement, and after giving effect to these distributions, each share of Company common stock will be converted in a tax free exchange into 0.31 of a share of Tenneco common stock. Assuming completion of the entire transaction, a total of about 10.1 million Tenneco common shares would be issued in the merger.

Note 4. Distribution of Seagull Pipeline Corporation to Stockholders

On January 30, 1981, the Board of Directors of the Company declared the distribution of all of the outstanding common stock of Seagull Pipeline Corporation ("Seagull") to the Company's stockholders. All of the outstanding Seagull common stock will be distributed on or about March 9, 1981, to the Company's stockholders on the basis of one share of Seagull common stock for each six shares of the Company's common stock outstanding and owned of record at the close of business on February 13, 1981. No consideration was payable by company stockholders to the Company or to Seagull in connection with the distribution. As a result of the distribution, Seagull has become independent of the Company and has its own directors, officers and employees.

Exhibit 2 (continued)

Seagull was incorporated in Texas in 1973 as a wholly-owned subsidiary of the Company. Seagull was formed to gather and transport gas for delivery to intrastate pipeline companies. In January 1981, the Company conveyed to Seagull its interest in certain gas processing facilities under construction and granted Seagull the right to process certain gas produced from the Company's Cavallo and Block 525-L fields located offshore Matagorda County, Texas.

Seagull Pipeline Corporation condensed balance sheets (in thousands)

	December 31	
	1980	*1979*
Current assets	**$19,544**	$22,848
Property, plant and equipment—net	**34,283**	29,080
Other assets	**117**	68
Total assets	**$53,944**	$51,996
Current liabilities	**$ 8,983**	$13,042
Non-current liabilities	**21,129**	23,258
Stockholders' equity	**23,832**	15,696
Total liabilities and stockholders' equity	**$53,944**	$51,996

Condensed statements of earnings (in thousands)

	Year ended December 31		
	1980	*1979*	*1978*
Revenues	**$60,770**	$51,187	$42,667
Expenses	**46,893**	43,741	35,103
Earnings before taxes	**13,877**	7,446	7,564
Income taxes	**5,741**	2,193	3,138
Net earnings	**$ 8,136**	$ 5,253	$4,426

Note 5. Disposition of Remaining Interest in Oaky Creek Coal Project

Prior to November 1979, Houston Oil & Minerals Australia, Inc. ("HOMA"), a wholly-owned subsidiary of the Company, held a 100% interest in a coal project ("Oaky Creek") not yet in production, in Queensland, Australia. In November 1979, HOMA sold a 40% interest to Mount Isa Mines Limited ("Mount Isa") and a 10% interest to Hoogovens Delfstoffen BV. The two sales were for cash and resulted in a net gain of $5,797,000. In July 1980, HOMA finalized agreements with Finsider International SPA ("Finsider") and Empresa Nacional Siderurgica SA ("Ensidesa"), whereby these companies acquired a 7% and 5% interest, respectively, out of HOMA's remaining 50% interest in the Oaky Creek project. HOMA also finalized an agreement with Mount Isa under which Mount Isa acquired HOMA's remaining 38% interest in the Oaky Creek project as of December 31, 1980. These transactions received approval by the Australian Foreign Investment Review Board and other governmental authorities along with approval of the other parties in the project. The 1980 sales to Finsider, Ensidesa and Mount Isa of HOMA's remaining 50% interest resulted in a gain of $33,960,000 net of income tax expense of $8,630,000, which was recognized in the fourth quarter. A portion of the $81,538,000 in receivables from the sale, which are due over the next six years, in the amount of $37,238,000 has been determined to be a marketable security and is classified as a current asset based on its expected realization within one year. The remaining $44,300,000 is shown as long-term. HOMA will continue to conduct oil, natural gas, and other mainerals exploration and development activities elsewhere in Australia.

Exhibit 2 (continued)

Note 6. Acquisition of COLBRAS

On November 29, 1979, Houston Oil Colombiana, S.A. ("HOCOL"), a wholly-owned subsidiary of the Company, completed the acquisition of Petroleos Colombo-Brasileros, S.A. ("COLBRAS") for approximately $55,000,000. HOCOL is engaged in oil and gas exploration and production in Colombia. Its production is sold under a sales contract to Ecopetrol, the government-owned oil company. A $50,000,000 credit facility with a group of banks was arranged to finance the acquisition and a development drilling program. A total of $49,057,000 in debt was outstanding under this facility at December 31, 1980. This debt consisted of two long-term notes, one for $5,057,000 at an interest rate of 18.625% per annum as of December 31, 1980, and another for $44,000,000 at an interest rate of 18.1875% per annum as of December 31, 1980. An additional $10,000,000 of various indebtedness at an interest rate of 13.75% per annum was incurred in connection with the acquisition of COLBRAS. The amount of this indebtedness may be reduced in certain events subject to an escrow agreement. The amount of this indebtedness outstanding as of December 31, 1980 was $5,000,000 plus accrued interest. The acquisition was accounted for as a purchase and the results of its operations since December 1, 1979 have been included in the consolidated results of the Company. Reported net earnings would not have been significantly different if this acquisition had been reflected as of the beginning of 1979.

Note 7. Sale of Houston Oil Royalty Trust

On April 15, 1980, the Company's Registration Statement with the Securities and Exchange Commission relating to the underwritten public offering and sale by the Company of $60 million of units of beneficial interest in the Houston Oil Royalty Trust became effective. On April 22, 1980, the Company assigned to the Houston Oil Royalty Trust overriding royalty interests in certain of its productive oil and gas properties as of March 1, 1980, and in all of its unevaluated oil and gas prospects offshore of Texas and Louisiana in the Gulf of Mexico as of February 22, 1980. The reserves attributable to the Houston Oil Royalty Trust, as estimated by Keplinger and Associates, Inc., independent petroleum engineers, as of March 1, 1980 were 478,000 barrels of oil and 19,399 MMcf of natural gas. The financial statements of the Company reflect the sale as of March 1, 1980. No gain was recorded for financial reporting purposes as it is the Company's policy to charge or credit accumulated DD&A unless the sale of oil and gas properties is significant. The proved reserves attributable to the Houston Oil Royalty Trust, as estimated by Keplinger and Associates, Inc., as of January 1, 1981 were 359,000 barrels of oil and 18,833 MMcf of natural gas.

Note 10. Long-term and short-term debt

	December 31	
	1980	1979
Unsecured notes payable to insurance companies:		
Series 1 10¾%, due April 1, 1990	$ 38,000	
Series 2 10¼%, due April 1, 1991	35,000	
Series 3 9%, due April 1, 1989	42,000	
Unsecured notes payable to banks, due February 1, 1986; interest rate fluctuates with prime rate (the rate was 22% at December 31, 1980)	250,000	
First mortgage notes payable to banks and insurance companies:		
Series A 10½%, due April 1, 1990		$ 40,000
Series B, due April 1, 1981; interest rate fluctuates with prime rate		15,710
Series C 10%, due April 1, 1991		35,000
Series D, due April 1, 1983; interest rate fluctuates with prime rate		135,000
Series E 8¾%, due April 1, 1989		42,000

Exhibit 2 (continued)

	1980	*1979*
Pipeline mortgage notes payable to banks, due March 1, 1985; interest rate fluctuates with prime rate (the rate was 21% at December 31, 1980)	**21,000**	23,000
Unsecured note payable to bank, due August 31, 1981		50,000
Unsecured note payable to bank, due September 30, 1981		50,000
Secured notes payable to banks, due November 11, 1985; interest rate fluctuates with London Interbank Offering Rate (the rate was approximately 18% at December 31, 1980)	**49,057**	20,000
Other long-term debt with various interest rates and maturities	**23,908**	13,913
	458,965	424,623
Less payments due within one year	**27,193**	13,535
Total long-term debt	**$431,772**	$411,088

Refinancing of Notes to Banks and Insurance Companies

On February 19, 1980, the Company repaid in full the principal amount then outstanding on the Series B notes. On August 28, 1980, the Company exchanged with a group of insurance companies the Series 1, 2 and 3 unsecured notes for the Series A, C and E first mortgage notes, respectively. Also on August 28, 1980, the Company sold to a group of banks pursuant to a revolving credit agreement variable rate unsecured notes due February 1, 1986 and used the $217,000,000 of proceeds to retire the principal amount of the Series D notes then outstanding and the principal amount of the two unsecured notes to banks due August 31, 1981 and September 30, 1981. The indenture of mortgage under which the Series A, B, C, D and E notes were issued was cancelled effective August 28, 1980. Terms of the note exchange agreements for the Series 1, 2 and 3 notes require mandatory sinking fund payments for each series of notes as follows:

Series 1—$2,000,000 semi-annually which began October 1, 1980
Series 2—$1,750,000 semi-annually, beginning October 1, 1981
Series 3—$5,250,000 semi-annually, beginning October 1, 1985

Under certain conditions, the Series 1, 2 and 3 notes and the unsecured notes payable to banks due February 1, 1986, require contingent sinking fund payments in amounts based on net revenues from the Company's domestic oil and gas properties. The agreements covering these notes include restrictive provisions regarding mergers or consolidations, incurring additional debt, making certain investments, sales of properties and payment of cash dividends on or repurchase of capital stock. The two agreements also require the Company to maintain current assets, as defined, equal to or greater than current liabilities, as defined. In the case of the note exchange agreements, there is an additional requirement to maintain current assets, as defined, plus unused long-term debt commitments equal to at least 125% of current liabilities, as defined.

The revolving credit agreement provides that without the bank lenders' consent, the Company may not declare or pay any dividend on common stock or make any payments for the purchase, redemption or retirement of capital stock if such total declarations or payments during the previous two years exceeds the sum of 15% of "funds from operations" of the Company during such previous two years. Funds from operations is equal to the sum of net earnings after federal income taxes plus "non-cash" charges, including, but not limited to, deferred federal income taxes, excess capitalized costs and depletion, depreciation and amortization. Under the most restrictive provisions of the debt agreements, $7,700,000 of retained earnings are available for payment of cash dividends on common stock and repurchase of capital stock as of December 31, 1980.

Although there is no formal agreement to do so, the Company has agreed to maintain compensating balances equal to 5% of the total commitment plus 5% of the amount outstanding under the revolving credit agreement. The total commitment from the banks under this agreement is currently $275 million.

Secured Notes Payable to Banks

In 1979, a whooly-owned foreign subsidiary of the Company (HOCOL) acquired virtually all of the outstanding capital stock of a company with oil and gas operations in Colombia. The Company has pledged the stock and assets of HOCOL to a group of banks under a loan agreement. The total commitment from the banks is $50,000,000.

Exhibit 2 (continued)

Long-Term Maturities

The aggregate amounts of long-term debt maturities for the five years following December 31, 1980 with respect to long-term debt outstanding at December 31, 1980 (excluding the debt of the Company's discontinued pipeline operations) are estimated as follows:

1981	$27,193,000
1982	$20,066,000
1983	$40,016,000
1984	$85,494,000
1985	$60,209,000

Short-Term Lines of Credit

During 1980, the Company arranged unsecured lines of credit with banks under which it could borrow amounts not to exceed $30,000,000. No commitment fees are required for these facilities, but the Company is required to maintain compensating balances of 5% of the commitment. Debt outstanding under these lines of credit at December 31, 1980 was $18,000,000, at varying interest rates which fluctuate with the banks' prime interest rates or cost of funds, as chosen by the Company. These lines of credit can be withdrawn at the banks' option.

Note 11. Income Taxes

Provisions for income taxes applicable to continuing operations consisted of the following:

	Year ended December 31		
	1980	**1979**	**1978**
	(in thousands)		
United States federal:			
Current	**$ 2,089**	$	$ 611
Deferred	**32,006**	38,270	40,941
Foreign:			
Current	**672**		
Deferred	**4,684**	221	
Total federal and foreign	**39,451**	38,491	41,552
State income tax	**419**		
Total	**$39,870**	$38,491	$41,552

Note 12. Common Stock and Stock Options

The number of shares used in the computation of earnings per common share for the three years in the period ended December 31, 1980 was:

	1980	**1979**	**1978**
Common and common equivalent shares	**29,515,880**	29,219,898	29,124,550
Fully diluted shares	**32,047,416**	31,742,751	30,531,378

At December 31, 1980, common shares were reserved for:

Conversion of $1.69 cumulative convertible preferred stock	1,912,265
Exercise of options granted under qualified stock option plans	145,970
Exercise of options granted under non-qualified stock option plans	382,765
Exercise of options not granted pursuant to stock option plans	13,800
Issue of stock for tax reduction act stock ownership plan	178,989
Issue of stock for restricted stock plan	1,900
	2,635,689

Exhibit 2 (concluded)

Under the employee stock option plans, unexercised options have been granted to purchase Common Stock at prices ranging from $10.00 to $41.75 per share. The options are exercisable 20 percent annually and expire five years after date of grant. Changes in stock options are summarized as follows:

	1980 Reserved	1980 Granted	1979 Reserved	1979 Granted	1978 Reserved	1978 Granted
Shares at beginning of year	753,425	691,826	843,275	687,126	979,775	827,426
Granted		26,260		137,950		62,650
Forfeited		(45,330)		(43,400)		(66,450)
Exercised	(224,690)	(224,690)	(89,850)	(89,850)	(136,500)	(136,500)
Shares at end of year	528,735	448,066	753,425	691,826	843,275	687,126

At December 31, 1978, options were exercisable under the qualified and non-qualified stock option plans as to 147,740 shares ($3,323,000 aggregate proceeds). At December 31, 1979, options were exercisable under the qualified and non-qualified stock option plans as to 236,383 shares ($5,889,000 aggregate proceeds). At December 31, 1980, options were exercisable under the qualified and non-qualified stock option plans as to 176,401 shares ($5,204,000 aggregate proceeds). In the proposed merger agreement with Tenneco, the Company's approved and granted options will be accelerated in order that all options will be exercisable prior to the merger. In September 1980, the Company authorized for issuance 72,475 shares of restricted common stock. At December 31, 1980, 70,575 shares were issued and outstanding.

Source: HOM Annual Report, 1980, pp. 30–43.

Source: *HOM 1980 Annual Report*, p. 50.

Exhibit 3

Houston Oil and Minerals Corporation 10-year summary of earnings

Summary of operations ($000)	1980	1979	1978	1977	1976	1975	1974	1973	1972	1971
Revenues:										
Oil sales	$111,784	$63,464	$49,661	$38,354	$25,614	$21,597	$15,655	$6,580	$3,739	$2,638
Gas sales	214,141	214,389	212,009	182,655	90,239	30,407	20,106	2,809	925	544
Product trading—net and other	57,062	22,771	3,128	2,080	985	481	174	35	20	41
	382,987	300,624	264,798	223,089	116,838	52,485	35,935	9,424	4,684	3,223
Costs and expenses:										
Cost of operations	55,816	39,574	43,851	36,576	22,620	10,941	11,549	2,332	1,202	824
General and administrative	38,871	27,326	18,846	11,699	5,019	2,444	1,135	625	273	178
Interest—net	47,014	32,678	24,199	19,259	10,777	7,869	4,084	1,486	704	545
Depletion, depreciation and amortization	107,386	93,248	78,005	64,691	24,990	12,638	8,666	2,123	1,297	1,037
Excess capitalized cost	13,155	2,779	4,656	6,301	8,963	2,873				
Minerals properties abandonments	9,461	6,130	2,521	742						
	271,703	201,735	172,078	139,268	72,369	36,765	25,434	6,566	3,476	2,584
Earnings from continuing operations before Provision for income taxes	111,284	98,889	92,720	83,821	44,469	15,720	10,501	2,858	1,208	639
Provision for income taxes:										
Current	3,180	38,491	611	423	17,012	3,863	2,704	1,071	461	238
Deferred	36,690		40,941	36,397						
Earnings from continuing operations	71,414	60,398	51,168	47,001	27,457	11,856	7,797	1,787	747	401
Earnings (loss) from discontinued operations and extraordinary items (net of federal income taxes)	8,136	5,253	4,426	4,637	672	394	267	70	67	77
Net earnings (loss)	79,550	65,651	55,594	51,638	28,129	12,251	8,064	1,857	814	478
Preferred stock dividend requirements	5,020	5,070	2,477	12	12	12	12	12	12	12
Net earnings applicable to common stock	$74,530	$60,581	$53,117	$51,626	$28,117	$12,239	$8,052	$1,845	$802	$466
Stockholders' statistics (adjusted for all stock splits)										
Primary earnings per share	$2.53	$2.07	$1.82	$1.78	$1.04	$.51	$.34	$.09	$.06	$.04
Fully diluted earnings per share:	$2.48	$2.07	$1.82	$1.77	$.98	$.48	$.34	$.08	$.05	$.03
Cash dividends paid per common share	$.80	$.80	$.80	$.67	$.33	$.13	$.11			
Stock splits		2-for-1		3-for-2	5-for-4 2-for-1		2-for-1	2-for-1	4-for-3	
Average number of common shares:										
Primary	29,515,880	29,219,898	29,124,550	28,992,140	26,924,478	23,919,153	23,407,395	21,381,039	15,146,970	12,355,035
Fully diluted	32,047,416	31,742,751	30,531,378	29,265,907	29,075,063	26,982,648	23,740,830	23,628,924	21,351,735	15,654,945

Exhibit 4

Houston Oil and Minerals Corporation 10-year summary of operating statistics

Operating statistics	1980	1979	1978	1977	1976	1975	1974	1973	1972	1971
Domestic proved reserves at year-end:										
Oil, condensate and natural gas liquids (000's Bbls)	20,940	23,631	22,645	29,292	30,777	23,299	16,437	15,549	8,600	6,573
Gas (MMcf)	449,655	698,489	647,247	577,562	634,243	445,439	360,250	340,228	92,699	40,638
Foreign proved reserves at year-end:										
Oil (000's Bbls)	95,476	81,989								
Gas (MMcf)	6,027	6,634								
Domestic oil production:										
Net oil, condensate and natural gas liquids production (000's Bbls)	3,370	4,155	4,111	3,410	2,442	2,071	1,888	1,454	1,095	742
Daily average (Bbls)	9,208	11,383	11,264	9,343	6,672	5,675	5,170	3,985	3,000	2,033
Average sales price per barrel	$25.99	$14.97	$12.08	$11.25	$10.49	$10.43	$8.29	$4.53	$3.41	$3.56
Foreign oil production (commencing November 29, 1979):										
Net oil production (000's Bbls)	5,109	385								
Daily average (Bbls)	13,959	11,666								
Average sales price per barrel	$4.71	$3.32								
Domestic gas production:										
Net gas production (MMcf)	86,004	95,606	96,561	86,210	46,748	32,629	26,245	7,700	3,861	2,484
Daily average (Mcf)	234,984	261,933	264,550	236,193	127,727	89,395	71,905	21,095	10,580	6,805
Average sales price per Mcf	$2.49	$2.24	$2.20	$2.12	$1.93	$.93	$.77	$.36	$.24	$.22
Wells at year-end:										
Gross	550	484	544	440	375	369	285	250	161	149
Net	480	435	493	384	322	314	251	224	140	133
Other statistics ($000)										
Working capital	$ 16,325	$ 27,666	$ 19,239	$36,726	$ 23,404	$ 23,056	$ (4,463)	$ 671	$ 636	$ (946)
Total assets	$1,077,692	$945,639	$632,222	$517,924	$333,073	$171,719	$90,059	$51,346	$20,139	$13,324
Long-term debt	$ 431,772	$411,088	$236,166	$279,178	$187,240	$119,610	$50,715	$33,103	$11,656	$ 5,163
Stockholders' equity	$ 312,645	$255,418	$216,554	$122,266	$ 71,782	$ 30,581	$17,470	$10,904	$ 5,907	$ 3,236
Capital expenditures	$ 318,934	$382,776	$215,039	$229,001	$160,499	$ 70,661	$41,015	$29,882	$ 7,207	$ 8,056
Funds from operations	$ 256,639	$211,194	$187,559	$162,643	$ 79,889	$ 31,945	$19,621	$ 5,057	$ 2,668	$ 1,862

Source: HOM 1980 Annual Report, p. 52.

Exhibit 5

Houston Oil and Minerals Corporation cash flow statement, 1971-1980 (in thousands of dollars)

	1980	1979	1978	1977	1976	1975	1974	1973	1972	1971
Source of Funds										
Operations:										
Net earnings (loss)	$ 71,414	$ 65,651	$ 55,594	$ 65,891	$ 38,385	$ 17,099	$10,736	$ 3,627	$ 1,337	$ 788
Deferred taxes	36,219	39,659	42,078	49,444	26,674	8,445	5,279	—	—	—
Depletion, depreciation, amortization	130,002	99,754	82,710	47,308	14,830	6,401	3,606	1,430	1,331	1,074
Sale of interests and discontinued operations	123,428	34,628	7,177	—	—	—	—	—	—	—
Funds provided from operations	$361,063	$239,692	$187,559	$162,643	$ 79,889	$ 31,945	$19,621	$ 5,057	$ 2,668	$ 1,862
Extraordinary item	—	—	—	—	—	—	—	—	380	—
Issuance of Securities:										
Long-term debt										
Banks	393,242	204,229	89,472	90,969	133,228	54,513	19,387	17,600	6,000	5,494
Insurance companies	—	—	—	42,000	35,000	40,000	—	—	—	—
Convertible debentures and preferred stock	—	—	71,345	—	—	30,000	—	—	5,000	—
Other	119,423	27,524	278	2,335	—	1,655	3,606	—	—	—
Common Stock										
Issued in connection with debenture and preferred stock conversion	—	—	356	4,302	20,733	3,722	732	2,987	1,794	551
Issued in connection with exercise of options, warrants & TRASOP plan	6,188	1,574	3,094	3,573	1,230	295	228	164	76	—
Other	4,511	7,301	5,872	1,947	2,915	1,710	128	10,290	—	3,000
Decrease in current assets										
Cash	24,570	—	3,609	—	—	—	—	—	—	—
Accounts receivable	—	—	—	—	—	—	—	—	—	507
Inventories, prepaid expenses	—	—	5,885	—	—	—	—	—	47	—
Increase in current liabilities										
Accounts payable	—	29,363	774	10,328	25,202	—	11,168	3,080	—	934
Accrued expenses, other	10,276	35,483	3,310	4,223	353	1,560	—	229	69	—
Current maturities, long-term debt	13,658	—	7,859	3,177	9,760	—	667	378	14	33
Other	—	—	—	—	—	—	—	—	—	500
	$932,931	$545,166	$379,413	$325,497	$308,310	$195,400	$55,537	$37,785	$16,048	$12,881

Exhibit 5 (concluded)

	1980	1979	1978	1977	1976	1975	1974	1973	1972	1971
Application of Funds										
Additions to Property, Plant and Equipment:										
Oil and gas properties	$257,811	$238,066	$175,076	$198,372	$149,237	$66,821	$42,612	$28,467	$7,114	$8,050
Pipeline facilities, mineral properties, other	61,123	144,710	39,963	30,629	11,262	5,069	2,131	1,415	93	7
Long-term Reductions:										
Debentures and preferred stock conversions	—	—	361	4,450	21,431	3,820	772	3,191	1,941	—
Bank and insurance company debt	474,168	64,779	123,673	35,675	69,371	45,000	—	—	—	—
Current maturities and prepayments	13,658	(8,544)	7,859	3,177	9,760	(157)	667	2,963	2,566	3,495
Other	4,363	596	869	64	36	8,611	3,942	—	—	—
Production Payment Application	—	—	—	—	—	—	—	—	2,375	625
Cash Dividends:										
Common stock	23,486	23,291	23,146	19,018	8,880	3,145	2,445	—	—	—
Preferred stock	5,020	5,070	2,477	12	12	12	12	12	12	12
Notes, long-term receivables, deferred charges and other	56,138	3,925	2,039	3,050	2,658	5,229	5	15	235	(426)
Increase in Current Assets										
Cash	21,852	2,525	3,950	2,019	12,419	17,875	1,189	1,467	635	245
Accounts receivable	7,762	53,514	—	18,807	15,929	3,949	1,374	2,050	—	—
Inventory, prepaid expenses	—	8,690	—	10,224	7,315	150	276	205	495	5
Decrease in Current Liabilities										
Accounts payable	2,659	—	—	—	—	5,719	—	—	82	—
Accrued expenses, other	—	—	—	—	—	—	112	—	—	—
Current maturities, long-term debt	—	8,544	—	—	—	157	—	—	500	868
Decrease in notes payable	4,891	—	—	—	—	—	—	—	—	—
	$932,931	$545,166	$379,413	$325,497	$308,310	$165,400	$55,537	$39,785	$16,048	$12,881

Source: HOM Annual Reports. Some accounts have been reclassified for purposes of comparability.

Exhibit 6

Houston Oil and Minerals Corporation price range of common stock 1973-1980*

Year	Quarter	High	Low
1973	1	$2\frac{5}{8}$	$1\frac{3}{8}$
	2	$2\frac{1}{2}$	$1\frac{3}{4}$
	3	$4\frac{7}{8}$	$1\frac{3}{4}$
	4	$9\frac{1}{8}$	$4\frac{1}{8}$
1974	1	8	$4\frac{3}{8}$
	2	$6\frac{3}{8}$	$4\frac{3}{4}$
	3	$5\frac{1}{4}$	$3\frac{1}{8}$
	4	$8\frac{5}{8}$	$3\frac{5}{8}$
1975	1	8	$5\frac{3}{8}$
	2	$7\frac{3}{8}$	$5\frac{3}{8}$
	3	$7\frac{1}{2}$	$5\frac{5}{8}$
	4	$8\frac{3}{4}$	$5\frac{5}{8}$
1976	1	16	$7\frac{3}{8}$
	2	22	$14\frac{5}{8}$
	3	$23\frac{3}{8}$	$17\frac{5}{8}$
	4	$31\frac{3}{4}$	$21\frac{5}{8}$
1977	1	$40\frac{5}{8}$	$28\frac{3}{8}$
	2	40	$26\frac{1}{8}$
	3	$42\frac{3}{8}$	$33\frac{1}{4}$
	4	37	26
1978	1	$31\frac{5}{8}$	19
	2	$26\frac{3}{8}$	$19\frac{7}{8}$
	3	$27\frac{1}{4}$	$21\frac{1}{8}$
	4	$23\frac{1}{2}$	$13\frac{1}{2}$
1979	1	$20\frac{5}{8}$	$15\frac{1}{2}$
	2	$21\frac{5}{8}$	$16\frac{3}{8}$
	3	$23\frac{5}{8}$	$18\frac{1}{4}$
	4	$24\frac{7}{8}$	$16\frac{1}{4}$
1980	1	$31\frac{7}{8}$	$17\frac{1}{8}$
	2	30	$18\frac{3}{4}$
	3	$39\frac{1}{4}$	$28\frac{1}{8}$
	4	$57\frac{7}{8}$	$36\frac{1}{2}$

*Prices adjusted to reflect stock splits.
Source: HOM Annual Reports.

case **27** Mesa Petroleum Company: The Price of Leadership

1 "It's a waste of corporate assets" said Mr. Lewis, a lawyer and Mesa Petroleum stockholder. His suit against Mesa Petroleum had been filed in March 1980 after Mesa's founder and CEO, T. Boone Pickens, was granted significant new stock options, accompanied by low interest loans. In 1979, Boon Pickens' remuneration had totalled over $2 million. Approximately $1.5 million of this amount had resulted from the exercising of stock options granted earlier. In November 1979, a new option package was approved granting Pickens options to purchase 1.5 million shares of Mesa stock over the next 10 years.

2 Based on stock prices at the end of 1980, the net worth of Pickens's new stock options was over $120 million.[1] At that time, the suit filed by Mr. Lewis had not yet gone to trial.

Origins of the Company and the Early Years, 1956-1973

3 Even though he started his career elsewhere, Boone Pickens played a central role in the formation of Mesa Petroleum. He started his career

This case was prepared by Carol Voelker Bergmann and M. Edgar Barrett, Director of the Maguire Oil and Gas Institute.

[1]Due to a two-for-one stock split on April 25, 1980, Boone Pickens held options for 3 million shares of stock at $23 share. At year-end 1980, the closing price for Mesa stock was $63 1/8/share. Thus, the net worth of Pickens' stock options was over $120 million. [(63.125 − 23)(3,000,000) equals $120,375,000)]

working as a geologist for Phillips Petroleum following his 1951 graduation from Oklahoma State University. In 1956 he formed Petroleum Exploration Inc. (PEI) to do exploration and drilling in the Panhandle-Hugoton area. PEI was started with $2,500 cash from investors and a $100,000 credit line. In 1959, Pickens and his associates formed Altair Oil and Gas Company to explore and drill for oil and gas in Alberta, Canada. Mesa Petroleum, itself, was formed in 1964 in order to consolidate and streamline the PEI and Altair operations.

4   During the early years, Mesa established both an impressive growth record and a reputation as an aggressive, well-managed company. After only three years, Mesa generated an annual net income of $1 million. In 1968, Mesa merged with Hugoton, a Kansas gas producer twice its size. The merger significantly increased Mesa's production levels. It also provided a steady cash flow.

5   During this period Mesa also diversified outside oil and gas exploration and development. Standard Gilsonite, a chemical company, was acquired in 1965. In 1969, Mesa entered the cattle feeding industry. Both operations provided cash to expand Mesa's growth and were later sold.

6   Mesa's growth continued during the late 1960s and early 1970s. In late 1969, Mesa was listed on the New York Stock Exchange. That year net income reached $8.5 million, 20 times that of the first year. In 1970, Mesa acquired a partial interest in several offshore tracts in the Gulf of Mexico. Mesa's first major discoveries were here. Over the years, activity in the Gulf increased substantially until the Gulf of Mexico became one of Mesa's most significant and profitable operations. Additional acquisitions in West Texas, New Mexico, and the Rocky Mountains resulted from the 1973 takeover of Pubco Petroleum.

7   The mergers, acquisitions, and development of the early 1970s required capital in excess of Mesa's operating cash flow. Boone Pickens' ability to negotiate innovative financing quickly earned him a reputation among investment analysts. Following the Hugoton merger, he negotiated a contract for the prepayment of gas production with Kansas Power and Light, the primary purchaser of Hugoton gas. Interest-free loans were also negotiated during this period, gas transmission companies being eager to secure future supplies. Still other financial deals used property as collateral.

Years of Dramatic Growth and Change, 1975-1980

Overview

8   The period between 1975 and 1980 was one of dramatic growth for Mesa. Annual production, revenues, and net income repeatedly reached record levels (see Exhibits 1, 2, & 3 for financial statements and Exhibit 4 for

operational statistics). In general, Mesa's net proved reserves were replaced in spite of production levels that steadily increased (see Exhibit 5). Mesa's common stock posted substantial gains (see Exhibit 6).

9   Two factors were often cited by industry observers to explain Mesa's success during the 1975–1980 period. The first was an aggressive and extremely successful exploration program. Capital expenditures for exploration and development increased steadily and drilling success rates repeatedly reached record levels (see Exhibit 7 for exploration and development statistics). The second factor, a series of financial transactions orchestrated by Boone Pickens, was regarded as even more important. Many of these transactions were considered innovative and attracted the attention of the business media. Gas price renegotiations and acquisition attempts also kept Mesa's name in the news.

Exploration and Development

10   During the 1975–1980 period, Mesa continued its exploration and development efforts within the continental United States. During the mid 1970s Mesa was aggressive in exploration and development efforts in southwest Kansas, particularly in the Adams Ranch and Ashland areas where Mesa had 100% interests. Production increased significantly, and by 1977 the Central Division was Mesa's leading oil-producing division. While development continued in the Ashland area of Kansas, by the end of the decade, continental exploration and development efforts had shifted to other areas. These areas included the Permian Basin in west Texas and the San Juan Basin in northwest New Mexico and southwest Colorado.

11   Throughout most of the 1975–1980 growth period, Mesa's exploration and development efforts were centered around the Gulf of Mexico. Typically, over one half of Mesa's capital expenditures budget was earmarked for Gulf of Mexico operations. For example, in 1977 over $90 million of a $150 million capital budget was spent in the Gulf of Mexico. As a result, acquisitions and development in the Gulf proceeded at a fast pace. Mesa had begun operations in the Gulf of Mexico in 1970 with POGO.[2] By the end of 1974, Mesa had a 5% working interest in 5 platforms. In its 1974 Annual Report, Mesa projected that by 1980 it would have an average 15% working interest in 18 producing platforms. Mesa's actual Gulf of Mexico operations, however, far exceeded these projections. By the end of 1980, Mesa had a 25.4% average interest in 44 platforms. Thirty-five of these were producing and 9 were in various stages of development. An additional 6 platforms were planned for the next year.

12   By the late 1970s Mesa's exploration and development efforts in the Gulf of Mexico began to pay off with significant increases in production and revenue. Annual natural gas production from Gulf of Mexico operations

---

[2]Pennzoil Offshore Gas Operators, Inc., a majority-owned subsidiary of Pennzoil.

Exhibit 1

Mesa Petroleum Company (B) consolidated income statements (in thousands) (year ending 12/31)

	1980	1979	1978	1977	1976	1975	1974
REVENUES							
Natural gas	$200,351	$179,415	$112,238	$92,386	$62,950	$33,956	$25,564
Oil and condensate	73,341	49,308	38,098	34,733	24,942	23,424	16,515
Natural gas liquids	14,041	13,371	11,934	10,861	9,755	6,056	9,048
Total oil & gas revenues	$287,733	$242,094	$162,270	$137,980	$97,647	$63,426	$51,127
Refined products	40,564	24,745	—	—	—	—	—
Interest income	40,608	14,519	781	355	183	238	(a)
Other income	3,458	1,493	3,466	1,722	1,238	301	581
Total	$372,363	$282,851	$166,517	$140,057	$99,068	$63,965	$51,708
COSTS AND EXPENSES							
Operating	39,556	32,975	21,717	16,208	11,217	7,626	4,855
Federal excise tax on oil & condensate	10,657	—	—	—	—	—	—
Refined products	38,962	21,278	—	—	—	—	—
General & administrative	14,416	11,125	9,059	7,486	6,684	5,937	4,851
Interest	68,978	55,796	25,353	13,629	6,860	9,402	9,274
Interest capitalized	(36,323)	(6,195)	(7,053)	(4,789)	(3,476)	(5,693)	(6,228)
Taxes, other than income	4,354	3,366	2,913	2,376	2,736	1,531	1,330
Depreciation, depletion & amortization	80,348	75,652	46,492	33,748	24,213	16,617	12,756
Total	$220,948	$193,997	$98,481	$68,658	$48,234	$35,420	$26,838
INCOME BEFORE OTHER INCOME (EXPENSE) AND INCOME TAXES	$151,415	$88,854	$68,036	$71,399	$50,834	$28,545	$24,870
Foreign exchange gain (loss)	(6,921)	319	(b)	—	—	—	(19,886)
Loss from discontinued operations	—	—	—	—	—	—	—
Gain on sale of marketable securities	15,931	684	—	—	—	—	—
Gain on sale of properties	—	345,328	—	—	—	—	—
Provision for income taxes	(65,189)	(149,563)	(26,270)	(30,100)	(20,100)	(9,375)	—
NET INCOME	$95,236	$285,622	$41,766	$41,299	$30,734	$19,170	$4,984
INCOME PER SHARE (c)							
Primary	$2.78	$8.85	$1.31	$1.33	$1.00	$.62	$.19
Fully diluted	$2.75	$8.85	$1.31	$1.28	$.96	$.62	$.19

Notes:
(a) Interest income reported as other income in 1974.
(b) Prior to 1979 foreign exchange gain (loss) reflected in other income.
(c) Adjusted to reflect 1980 stock split.
Source: Mesa Petroleum Company Annual Reports.

Exhibit 2

Mesa Petroleum Company (B) consolidated balance sheets (in thousands) (year ending 12/31)

	1980	1979	1978	1977	1976	1975	1974
ASSETS							
Cash	$ 8,855	$ 7,441	$ 38,810	$ 36,102	$ 13,774	$ 9,606	$ 4,544
Accounts and notes receivable	103,807	158,163	48,410	42,263	33,727	15,144	13,124
Inventories	22,115	18,216	12,894	6,862	6,144	10,999	6,360
Prepaid expenses	694	747	1,193	618	450	310	287
Total current assets	135,471	184,567	101,307	85,845	54,095	36,059	24,315
Net property	870,083	687,180	822,033	675,757	523,753	455,260	371,299
Marketable securities	86,195	60,346	48,394	35,774	34,473	2,892	1,631
Long-term notes receivable	41,316	46,524	—	—	—	—	—
Term royalty receivable	282,322	284,641	—	—	—	—	—
Deferred charges & other assets	11,463	5,201	3,228	2,834	2,306	2,685	1,825
Total non-current assets	1,291,379	1,083,892	873,655	714,365	560,532	460,837	374,755
Net assets of discontinued operation							5,984
Total assets	$1,426,850	$1,268,459	$974,962	$800,210	$614,627	$496,896	$405,054
LIABILITIES							
Current maturities on long-term debt	48,859	47,388	55,457	20,776	13,656	5,553	6,020
Short-term notes payable	1,300	20,600	—	—	1,175	2,423	545
Accounts payable	107,805	85,634	52,168	49,024	28,503	21,431	21,120
Income taxes payable (a)	5,099	49,401	—	—	—	—	—
Accrued liabilities	16,144	14,063	12,091	8,017	3,771	3,552	4,086
Total current liabilities	179,207	217,086	119,716	77,817	47,105	32,959	31,771
Long-term debt (net of current maturities)	395,357	451,395	384,724	300,677	210,915	145,177	144,151
Production payments	143,030	127,768	11,053	25,436	25,563	31,533	37,621
8½% Subordinated debentures	76,595	—	—	—	—	—	—
Deferred income taxes	122,886	72,029	85,084	59,057	30,561	10,751	1,376
Total non-current liabilities	737,868	651,192	480,861	385,170	267,039	187,461	183,148
Total liabilities	$ 917,075	$ 868,278	$600,577	$462,987	$314,144	$220,420	$214,918

Exhibit 2 (concluded)

	1980	1979	1978	1977	1976	1975	1974
STOCKHOLDERS' EQUITY							
Common stock $1 par value	33,601	16,304	15,901	15,869	12,824	12,547	12,516
Preferred stock, $1 par value	—	—	—	—	3,000	3,069	72
Warrants to purchase common stock	—	—	682	682	682	682	682
Unrealized loss on marketable investment security	—	—	—	—	(1,363)	—	—
Capital surplus	193,530	192,945	180,257	179,492	178,261	177,667	109,610
Retained earnings	282,644	190,932	177,545	141,180	107,079	82,511	67,256
Total stockholders' equity	$ 509,775	$ 400,181	$374,385	$337,223	$300,483	$276,476	$190,136
TOTAL LIABILITIES & STOCKHOLDERS' EQUITY	$1,426,850	$1,268,459	$974,962	$800,210	$614,627	$496,896	$405,054

Note:
(a) Primarily foreign income taxes in connection with the sale of Canadian and British assets.
Source: Mesa Petroleum Company Annual Reports.

Exhibit 3

Mesa Petroleum Company (B) consolidated statement of changes in financial position (in thousands) (year ending 12/31)

	1980	1979	1978	1977	1976	1975	1974
SOURCE OF FUNDS:							
Net income	$ 95,236	$285,622	$ 41,766	$ 41,299	$ 30,735	$ 19,170	$ 24,870
Depreciation, depletion & amortization	80,348	75,652	46,492	33,748	24,213	16,617	12,756
Deferred income tax	59,975	103,994	26,270	30,100	20,100	9,375	—
Gain on sale of marketable securities	(15,931)	(684)	—	—	—	—	—
Gain on sale of properties (a)	—	(299,759)	—	—	—	—	—
Funds provided from operations	219,628	164,825	114,528	105,147	75,048	45,162	37,626
Long-term borrowings, including production payments & debentures	310,493	266,923	147,347	178,144	79,440	29,889	84,852
Cash withdrawn from MTS partnership	159,892	—	—	—	—	—	—
Proceeds from sale of marketable securities	26,035	—	—	—	—	—	—
Proceeds from sale of properties	4,500	1,342	—	—	15,985	—	—
Decrease in term royalty receivable	2,319	466,930	—	—	—	—	—
Proceeds from exercise of stock options							
Other	—	—	—	2,522	1,168	340	319
	$737,233	$912,634	$266,528	$285,813	$171,641	$146,137	$125,605

Exhibit 3 (concluded)

	1980	1979	1978	1977	1976	1975	1974
USES OF FUNDS:							
Capital Expenditures—							
Oil & gas properties, wells & equipment	$425,235	$313,134	$186,635	$179,014	$104,634	$ 99,627	$117,456
Other properties	2,087	6,036	7,634	6,738	4,057	951	1,803
Acquisition of producing properties	—	160,399	—				
Retirement of long-term debt, including production payments & debentures	274,674	81,006	80,214	81,389	11,660	35,326	20,712
Investments	35,953	12,610	12,620	—	31,582	—	—
Cash dividends	3,524	6,267	5,400	7,198	6,167	3,915	785
Increase in term royalty receivable	—	284,641	—	—	—	—	—
Increase in long-term notes receivable	—	46,524	—	—	—	—	—
Gas price increase to be refunded	—	—	—	—	—	2,808	—
Distribution to Royalty Trust—							
Oil & gas properties, wells & equipment	—	(477,464)	—	—	—	—	—
Accumulated depreciation, depletion, & amortization	—	105,864	—	—	—	—	—
Deferred income tax liability	—	170,766	—	—	—	—	—
Reinvested earnings	—	200,834	—	—	—	—	—
Net funds provided by discontinued operations	—	—	—	—	—	(5,125)	(20,738)
Other	6,977	16,128	462	1,913	1,550	1,354	1,939
Increase (decrease) in working capital	(11,217)	(14,111)	(26,437)	9,561	11,992	7,281	3,647
	$737,233	$912,634	$266,528	$285,813	$171,641	$146,137	$125,605

Note:
(a) Net of related income taxes of $45,569,000.
Source: Mesa Petroleum Company Annual Reports.

Exhibit 4

Mesa Petroleum Company (B) production and price statistics (year ending 12/31)

	1980	*1979*	*1978*	*1977*	*1976*	*1975*	*1974*
AVERAGE DAILY NET PRODUCTION (a)							
Natural gas (avg MMcf/day)							
Continental U.S. (b)	134	209(c)	183	189	204	185	211
Gulf Coast	156	98	39	24	18	20.	21
Canada	—	53(d)	78	65	49	48	29
Total	290	360	300	278	271	253	261
Natural gas liquids (Bbls/day)							
Continental U.S. (b)	1697	2720(c)	2803	3038	3360	3270	(e)
Gulf Coast	325	460	376	136	141	102	(e)
Canada	—	591(d)	798	821	872	298	(e)
Total	2022	3771	3977	3995	4373	3670	(e)
Oil and Condensate (Bbls/day)							
Continental U.S. (b)	4932	5217(c)	4059	4373	2842	3325	6664
Gulf Coast	3364	3343	3719	3268	2554	1806	1352
Canada	1	1080(d)	1196	1270	1414	1392	1150
Total	8297	9640	8974	8911	6810	6523	9166
WEIGHTED AVERAGE PRICE							
Natural gas (per Mcf)	$ 1.89	$ 1.37	$ 1.07	$ .93	$ .63	$ .37	$ .27
Natural gas liquids (per bbl)	$18.97	$10.97	$ 8.46	$ 7.54	$6.08	$4.53	$7.18
Oil and Condensate (per bbl)	$24.15	$14.36	$11.84	$10.77	$9.98	$9.86	$7.92

Notes:
(a) "Net" reflects the company's interest in production after deducting royalties.
(b) In 1979 & 1980 combines the production of Hugoton, Mid-Continent, Permian Basin, and Rocky Mountain Divisions. Prior to 1979 combines production of Central, Hugoton, and Permian Basin Divisions.
(c) Includes production from properties purchased from Ashland after 4/30/79. Excludes production from properties transferred to the Royalty Trust after 11/1/79.
(d) Excludes production after 10/4/79.
(e) In 1974 production data for natural gas liquids, oil and condensate is combined.
Source: Mesa Petroleum Company Annual Reports.

increased 151% in 1979 and another 60% in 1980. Mesa continued to commit the majority of its capital expenditures to acreage acquisition and development in the Gulf of Mexico.

13   Mesa's Canadian operations had been an integral part of the business since its inception. This trend continued through the late 1970s. During the mid 1970s, Mesa's exploration and development efforts in Canada were concentrated on shallow gas drilling in Alberta. In 1974, acreage was still available in relatively unexplored areas, yet close to pipeline networks. Exploration was further encouraged by the expectation that the Canadian government would allow gas prices to increase to world commodity levels. During 1975, Mesa drilled more wells than any other company in Canada.

Exhibit 5

Mesa Petroleum Company (B) changes in estimated net proven reserves (a) (b)

	United States		Canada		United Kingdom	Total	
	Oil	Gas	Oil	Gas	Oil	Oil	Gas
July 1, 1974	na	na	na	na	—	37,623	1,696,000
July 1, 1975	na	na	na	na	—	39,305	1,746,000
July 1, 1976	na	na	na	na	—	34,864	1,646,000
July 1, 1977	30,648	1,291,000	4,449	332,000	37,100	72,197	1,623,000
July 1, 1978	30,967	1,303,000	5,468	346,000	37,100	73,535	1,649,000
December 31, 1978	29,047	1,265,083	5,866	354,554	37,124	72,037	1,619,637
Production	(4,285)	(112,107)	(610)	(19,457)	—	(4,895)	(131,564)
Revision of previous estimates	1,361	(36,881)	(315)	(8,522)	—	(1,046)	(45,403)
Extensions, discoveries & other additions	3,917	126,989	1,107	12,979	—	5,024	139,968
Purchase of Tema reserves-in-place	1,348	357,647	—	—	—	1,348	357,647
Sale of reserves-in-place	—	—	(6,048)	(339,554)	(37,124)	(43,172)	(339,554)
Distribution to Royalty Trust	(7,988)	(791,331)	—	—	—	(7,988)	(791,331)
December 31, 1979	23,400	809,400	—	—	—	23,400	809,400
Production	(3,777)	(106,013)	—	—	—	(3,777)	(106,013)
Revisions of previous estimates	1,597	28,965	—	—	—	1,597	28,965
Improved recovery	967	287	—	—	—	967	287
Extension, discoveries & other additions	2,908	124,133	20	1,916	—	2,928	126,049
December 31, 1980	25,095	856,772	20	1,916	—	25,115	858,688

Notes:
(a) "Net" reflects Mesa's interest in reserves after deducting royalties.
(b) Oil is measured in thousands of barrels; gas is measured in millions of cubic feet.
Source: Mesa Petroleum Company Annual Reports.

Exhibit 6

Mesa Petroleum Company (B) securities: market prices, dividends, and shares outstanding

		Common stock			
Year	*Quarter*	*High(a)*	*Low(a)*	*Dividend(a)*	*No. of shares outstanding at 12/31*
1974	First	21 7/8	12 1/5	$ —	
	Second	12 7/8	6 3/8	.0125	
	Third	8 1/2	5 3/8	—	
	Fourth	12 3/8	6 1/4	.0125	12,516,088
1975	First	13 3/8	10	$ —	
	Second	13 3/8	9 1/8	.0125	
	Third	14 1/2	10 5/8	—	
	Fourth	12 7/8	8 7/8	.0125	12,546,914
1976	First	14 1/2	9 1/2	$ —	
	Second	14 1/4	10 5/8	.025	
	Third	16 7/8	13 3/8	—	
	Fourth	18 3/4	14 3/4	.025	12,823,524
1977	First	20	15 1/2	$ —	
	Second	19 4/4	15 1/2	.025	
	Third	23 1/2	19	.05	
	Fourth	23 1/8	18 1/4	.05	15,868,654
1978	First	19 3/4	16 1/4	$.05	
	Second	19 7/8	16 1/8	.05	
	Third	18 3/4	15 1/4	.06	
	Fourth	18 5/8	13	.06	15,900,676
1979	First	21 7/8	16 1/4	$.06	
	Second	32 1/2	20 1/4	.06	
	Third	37 5/8	30 1/2	.06	
	Fourth	37 5/8	22 3/8(b)	.015	16,303,453
1980	First	38 5/8	19 5/8	$.015	
	Second	40 5/8	22 5/8	.03	
	Third	59 1/4	37 5/8	.03	
	Fourth	69 1/4	48 1/4	.03	33,601,000

Notes:

(a) Adjusted to reflect two-for-one stock split on April 25, 1980. A two-for-one stock split approved 2/27/81 is not reflected.

(b) Market price following Royalty Trust distribution.

Sources: Mesa Petroleum Company Annual Reports; *Daily Stock Price Record—New York Stock Exchange* (Standard and Poor's Corporation, 1980).

During the same year, Mesa experienced the highest drilling success ratio of the major explorers in Canada. As a result of this activity, Canadian gas production increased 45% in 1975.

14 Production from Mesa's Canadian wells, however, did not increase as rapidly as one might expect. At times, the lack of pipeline facilities delayed production. In addition, sales were curtailed due to a temporary gas surplus during 1976 and 1977. In spite of lagging production, Mesa's Canadian operations were generating 26% of the company's total gas production and 15% of its total liquid production by 1978. In that year 28% of Mesa's net

Exhibit 7

Mesa Petroleum Company (B) exploration and development data

	1980		1979		1978		1977		1976		1975		1974	
CAPITAL EXPENDITURES ($000)														
Acreage acquisition	$163		$106		$16		$50		$22		$12		na	
Exploratory drilling	98		149		115		42		27		na		na	
Development drilling	84		(a)		(a)		35		33		na		na	
Production facilities	40		34		41		36		18		na		na	
Total	$397		$321		$197		$188		$108		$101		$119	
DRILLING ACTIVITY	gross/net		gross/net		gross/net		gross/net		gross/net		gross/net		gross/net	
Exploratory Wells														
Productive	27	16.6	63	31.8	54	23.7	65	29.9	38	16.9	60	40.3	40	16.5
Dry	26	16.5	34	24.1	29	15.3	57	23.5	48	22.7	64	40.6	74	47.4
Total	53	33.1	97	55.9	83	39.	122	53.4	86	39.6	124	80.9	114	63.9
Development Wells														
Productive	147	75.8	154	72.1	233	122.2	169	79.4	107	58.5	116	80.8	95	47.2
Dry	17	8.6	40	19.4	59	27.5	39	15.3	45	31.5	44	30.9	28	15.8
Total	164	84.4	194	91.5	292	-49.7	208	94.7	152	90.0	160	111.7	123	63.0
Total	217	117.5	291	147.4	375	188.7	330	148.1	238	129.6	284	192.6	237	126.9
Overall Success Rate	79%		71%		77%		74%		58%		63%		50%	
PLATFORMS - GULF OF MEXICO (b)														
Installed & Producing-No.	35		28		14		11		8		7		5	
Mesa's average interest	24.0%		26.7%		28.3%		19.7%		na		na		na	
No. of tracts involved	39		33		14		9		6		na		2	
Installed & in process of development-No.	9		12		23		15		10		7		na	
Mesa's average interest	30.8%		22.1%		17.9%		22.4%		na		na		na	
No. of tracts involved	12		12		27		20		12		na		na	
Planned but not installed-No.	12		9		4		11		11		9		na	
Mesa's average interest	43.3%		47.6%		30.2%		22.2%		na		na		na	
No. of tracts involved	14		9		4		10		14		na		na	
Total No. of platforms	56		49		41		37		29		23		na	
Mesa's average interest	29.2%		29.4%		22.6%		21.4%		na		na		na	
No. of tracts involved	65		54		45		39		32		na		14	

Exhibit 7 (concluded)

	1980 gross/net		1979 gross/net		1978 gross/net		1977 gross/net		1976 gross/net		1975 gross/net		1974 gross/net	
UNDEVELOPED ACREAGE (000's) (as of 12/31)														
Onshore U.S.	2458	1177	2104	1530	1079	863	1239	941	1258	954	1301	991	1484	1183
Offshore U.S.	257	107	268	105	386	130	424	151	382	136	341	108	278	82
Canada	(c)		(c)		3326	1337	3681	1397	3961	1665	4650	2687	5666	3230
North Sea (UK)	—		—		122	34	249	70	249	66	461	119	524	135
Other International (d)	1240	547	648	192	360	45	613	141	613	141	613	141	613	141
Total	3955	1831	3020	1827	5273	2409	6206	2700	6463	2962	7366	4046	8565	4771

Notes:
(a) In 1979 and 1978 expenditures for exploratory and development drilling were not itemized.
(b) Data prior to 1977 is incomplete.
(c) Does not include 12.5% gross overriding royalty interest in Canada.
(d) Includes interests in the West German Sector of the North Sea and Australia.
Source: Mesa Petroleum Company Annual Reports.

income was generated by Canadian operations. By 1978, Mesa felt that higher prices and increased royalty credits from the government justified the expansion of shallow gas drilling from Alberta into the neighboring province of Saskatchewan.

15   In 1976, a spectacular discovery in the North Seas thrust Mesa into the international arena. The discovery was made about 15 miles off the coast of Scotland in 150 feet of water. The area had previously been explored by several major oil companies and abandoned as non-productive. Mesa's reputation was further enhanced by the fact that the discovery was over 100 miles from the nearest producing North Sea well. The discovery was named the Beatrice field in honor of Boone Pickens's wife. Mesa held a 25% interest in the Beatrice field and was operator for a consortium of five companies. The field's total recoverable reserves were estimated at 170 million barrels of oil. During 1977 and 1978, Mesa began development drilling in the Beatrice field.

Renegotiations with KPL

16   In January, 1975, Mesa announced plans to construct a nitrogen rejection plant, at an estimated cost of $17 million, to process gas from the Hugoton field in Kansas. The plant would utilize a cryogenic (i.e., super cold) process to extract liquids such as propane and ethane from the natural gas. Mesa was already extracting 3,100 barrels of natural gas liquids per day. It was projected that the new plant would increase production of natural gas liquids from the Hugoton field by 9,000 barrels/day.

17   The Kansas Power and Light Co (KPL), who was purchasing Hugoton field gas from Mesa, objected to the proposed plant. Construction of the plant would cut the volume of natural gas available for KPL by approximately 22%. Mesa's contract with KPL permitted the removal of natural gas liquids, and specified a minimum Btu content for the remaining vapor. Because of KPL's opposition to the plant, Mesa requested that the District Court of Grant County, Kansas, make a declaratory judgment interpreting the KPL contract, and Mesa's right to extract natural gas liquids.

18   The proposed construction of the plant forced KPL to renegotiate its contract with Mesa. Later in 1975, Mesa and KPL reached a tentative agreement in which natural gas prices were increased by $.28/mcf to $.59/mcf. Mesa agreed to cancel the planned plant construction and give KPL preferential rights to purchase gas in the future. The agreement fell through, however, when the Kansas Corporation Commission denied KPL's request for rate increases to cover the higher gas prices.

19   In February, 1976, the court upheld Mesa's right to construct the nitrogen rejection plant. The next month a supplemental gas purchase agreement was finalized with KPL in which Mesa agreed not to build the extraction plant. According to the agreement, Mesa would sell KPL 78% of the Hugoton gas under the terms of the original contract. The remaining

Hugoton gas production, or the 22% of total gas volume that would have been lost with construction of the plant, would be sold to KPL at an initial price of $1.52/mcf. The agreement subjected 22% of the gas to annual price escalations of $.02/mcf and a price redetermination every two years. The agreement also gave KPL preferential rights to purchase at competitive rates all of the gas from the Hugoton field when the original contract expired in 1989. The Kansas Corporation Commission approved KPL's request for rate increases to cover the increased gas costs, and the new pricing went into effect on May 1, 1976. As a result of the agreement, the average cost of gas Mesa sold to KPL increased 108%, from $.25/mcf to $.52/mcf.[3]

Stock Purchases and Attempted Acquisitions

20 **Aztec Oil.** Early in January, 1976, Mesa made a tender offer of $22/share for any and all of the 5.6 million outstanding shares of Aztec Oil. Just prior to the tender offer, Aztec Oil had been selling at $15.625/share. The Aztec Oil Board of Directors was opposed to the terms of the offer, calling them "inadequate" and not in the best interests of Aztec's stockholders. Both firms initiated lawsuits. Mesa alleged that Aztec was "improperly trying to impede" the takeover bid by refusing either to supply Mesa with a list of their stockholders or mail details of the tender offer to their stockholders at Mesa's expense. Aztec's suit alleged antitrust violations and Mesa's failure to disclose to Aztec's stockholders "material and important information" that was considered necessary to evaluate the tender offer.

21 Aztec appeared to be a popular takeover candidate. Reportedly, at least six companies had scrutinized Aztec during the preceding year and a half, including Mesa. Mesa's management had approached the Aztec management about a merger some two months earlier.[4] During the first part of 1975, Aztec's profits had dropped 40%, primarily as a result of reduced depletion allowances. However, Aztec was virtually debt free and their reserves were substantial—10 million barrels of oil and 1 billion cubic feet of natural gas.

22 A week after Mesa's tender offer, Southland Royalty offered $27 per share for all of Aztec's outstanding stock. The next day Houston natural Gas offered $30/share for up to 2.7 million shares of Aztec stock. Aztec and Houston Natural Gas had discussed merging six months earlier. According to one report, Aztec reinitiated talks with Houston Natural Gas after Mesa's tender offer. Reportedly, Houston Natural Gas agreed to consider a

---

[3]According to an article from the May 14, 1979 issue of *Forbes,* Mesa supplied approximately 70 billion cubic feet of gas to KPL in 1976. The 1976 Mesa Annual Report stated that the Hugoton Field produced roughly 49 billion cubic feet of gas during the year.

[4]"In Hot Pursuit of Aztec Oil," *Business Week,* January 26, 1976, p. 32.

future nontaxable stock conversion in addition to their cash offer.[5]

23   Meanwhile, a Federal judge ruled in favor of Mesa on the issue of access to Aztec stockholders. The court also refused Aztec's request for a temporary restraining order designed to halt Mesa's stock acquisition, pending the trial for Aztec's suit. Following the Houston Natural Gas offer, however, Mesa withdrew its tender offer. At the time, Boone Pickens said, "Mesa considered its cash tender offer to have been at a fair and reasonable price and the company did not intend to enter a bidding contest for Aztec stock."[6] Subsequently, approximately 90% of Aztec's stock was tendered in response to an increased offer of $32/share by Southland Royalty.

24   Mesa owned 632,000 shares of Aztec at year-end 1980. The cost of these shares had been $3.1 million. Their market value was $14.1 million, or roughly $23/share.

25   **General American Oil (GAO).** In late 1976 there was widespread speculation that Mesa was planning a tender offer for GAO stock. Mesa had puchased 495,717 shares, or 7.4% of GAO's outstanding stock for $64/share. In a press release following the stock purchase, a Mesa representative said "that it did not intend to make a tender offer, or to propose a merger or similar transaction. However, it said it couldn't be considered a passive investor as it may change its current intention."[7]

26   Mesa owned 1,787,434 shares of GAO at year-end 1980. The cost of these shares had been $31.7 million. Their market value was $76.7 million, or roughly $43/share.

27   **Imperial-American Energy.** In October 1977, it was announced that Imperial-American Energy had agreed, in principle, to be acquired by Mesa for $51.8 million. With approximately 2.5 million shares outstanding, the offer totalled $20.73/share. A month earlier tender offers of $17/share had been made by Consolidated Oil and Gas, Inc., and Petro-Lewis for 1.3 and 2.5 million shares, respectfully.

28   A week and a half after the announcement of the proposed acquisition, Imperial-American Energy rejected Mesa's offer. Petro-Lewis had raised its tender offer to $20/share. Imperial-American's Board recommended that stockholders accept the Petro-Lewis offer, even though it was approximately $2 million less than Mesa's offer. Reportedly, the Petro-Lewis offer was favored because of its terms and because of uncertainty created by conditions in the Mesa offer.[8] An agreement to liquidate Imperial-American was announced in January 1978. By this time, 71% of Imperial-American's

---

[5]Ibid., p. 32.

[6]"Houston Natural Sets $30 in Cash for Aztec Shares, Mesa Petroleum Withdraws Offer of $22, "*The Wall Street Journal,* January 13, 1976, p. 2.

[7]"Mesa Discloses Price, Seller of 7.4% Stake in General American," *The Wall Street Journal,* November 5, 1976, p. 27.

[8]"Imperial-American Rejects Bid by Mesa," *The Wall Street Journal,* October 17, 1977, p. 17.

stock had been purchased by Petro-Lewis. Petro-Lewis agreed to purchase all of Imperial-American's assets at a price determined by independent appraisers. The agreement required that sale proceeds, net of all costs, be sufficient to make a liquidating distribution of $21 a share.[9]

29   **Equity Oil.** In June 1979, Mesa and individuals affiliated with the company acquired 166,300 shares of Equity Oil. This represented approximately 5.7% of the company's outstanding stock. Once again, Mesa's motives were not clear. Mesa said it "might continue to buy Equity Oil shares in over-the-counter or private transactions or that it might discuss a possible merger with Equity Oil. However, it added that it hasn't any present plans that would lead to merger with, or reorganization of, Equity Oil.[10] Following the Equity Oil stock purchase, the Utah Securities Commission charged that Mesa had violated state security laws requiring that stockholders be notified of an acquisition of more than 5% of outstanding stock prior to such an acquisition.

30   **Beard Oil.** In August, 1979, a possible acquisition of Beard Oil was announced by both Mesa and Beard Oil. Beard Oil was an independent oil and gas exploration and production company with net income of $1.2 million and annual revenues of $8.8 million. A second announcement the following day stated that the two companies were ending discussions.

Major Financial Transations, 1979-1980

Tenneco Partnership

31   In April 1979, Mesa entered into a 50–50 partnership with Tenneco and formed Tema Oil Company. The partnership was formed to acquire mid-continent oil and gas property from Ashland Exploration. Ashland Oil had decided to divest itself of Ashland Exploration, its oil and gas exploration and production subsidiary.[11] Tema paid $321 million for the Ashland property. The purchase was financed with equity contributions of $35.8 million by each partner and a $250 million non-recourse production payment. Terms of the production payment called for repayment from 95% of net lease income, with an interest rate escalating from 105% of prime in 1979 to 125% of prime in 1991. The Ashland acquisition by Tema added 358

---

[9]"Petro-Lewis Agrees to Buy Assets of Imperial-American," *The Wall Street Journal,* January 10, 1978, p. 18.

[10]"Equity Oil Co. Says Mesa Petroleum Co. Has Bought 6% Stake," *The Wall Street Journal,* June 25, 1979, p. 26.

[11]See the *Ashland Oil, Inc.,* case for a detailed discussion of the Ashland Oil divestment decision. Available from Case Publishing.

billion cubic feet of natural gas and 1.3 million barrels of oil and natural gas liquids to Mesa's net proved reserves. Mesa also gained a 50% interest in 398,000 net undeveloped acres.

Sale of Canadian Properties

32   In March 1979, Mesa announced plans to sell all of its oil and gas properties in Canada. According to a Mesa press release, the move reflected Mesa's intention to consolidate its exploration and development activities.[12] Proceeds from the sale were to be used to reduce corporate debt.

33   In October 1979, Mesa sold all of its producing and non-producing oil and gas properties in Canada to Dome Petroleum, Limited. The sale yielded (in Canadian dollars) $656.4 million. Of this, $61.9 million was in cash, $148.2 million was in interest-bearing notes due January 1980, and $446.5 million was structured as a term royalty on the producing properties with an interest rate of 6% per annum. The term royalty provided for monthly production payments beginning in 1980. These payments would increase Mesa's annual cash flow by approximately $35 million.[13] Mesa also retained a 12.5% gross overriding royalty on 1.2 million net undeveloped acres. Dome agreed to spend $70 million over the next 5 years to explore and develop this property. Not including the overriding royalty, the sale resulted in a pretax gain of $314,133,000.

34   Six months after the sale was finalized, the new liberal government in Canada began discussing the need for new Canadian energy policies. The government sought to reduce foreign ownership of Canada's oil industry from the then current amount of 75% to less than 50% by 1990. In a May 1980 speech, Canada's Energy Secretary said, "We are determined to have Canada's resources increasingly developed by Canada and for Canada." He added that the government intended to use a carrot, rather than a stick, approach to reduce foreign ownership.[14]

35   Details of the National Energy Program to "Canadianize" oil assets were announced in October 1980. In general, the program called for changes in land and tax policies to provide incentives for Canadian ownership. The program also provided state-owned Petro-Canada with additional financing and special privileges, including the retroactive right to acquire 25% of any new discoveries on frontier lands. New production taxes were proposed as well as a special consumption tax earmarked for investment capital. Canadian ownership was encouraged with low-cost loans and special subsidies. In some cases, 75% Canadian ownership qualified a company for

---

[12]"Mesa Seeking Buyer For All Its Canadian Oil, Gas Properties," *The Wall Street Journal,* March 14, 1979, p. 14.

[13]*Mesa Petroleum Company Annual Report,* 1979, p. 21.

[14]"Canada Will Favor Domestic Oil Firms In the Search for Petroleum on Frontiers," *The Wall Street Journal,* May 16, 1980, p. 16.

lucrative subsidies of up to $.92 for each $1 spent on exploration.[15]

36   The "Canadianization" energy policies put American oil companies at a distinct disadvantage. Many attempted to sell their Canadian assets, which resulted in depressed prices. Even though Mesa had sold its Canadian assets before the "Canadianization" policies were introduced, they adversely affected the company. At year-end 1979, the estimated present values of the term royalty, at an imputed interest rate of 12%, was $284.6 million. Due to the new royalty tax on production, and price changes resulting from the new policies, it was estimated that the term royalty would ultimately yield only 10.5%.[16]

37   Some commentators considered Canada's new energy policies politically motivated, rather than part of an apparent socialistic trend.[17] Gasoline prices in Canada had escalated dramatically since the 1973 OPEC embargo. Canadians, however, had not experienced the gas shortages seen in the United States that for many Americans had justified the increased gas prices. Oil companies became the scapegoat and Canadian public furor was aimed at the large U.S. oil companies and their Canadian subsidiaries. Trudeau's "Canadianization" energy policy was considered an attack on foreign oil companies and, hence, gained widespread popularity.

38   In addition to capitalizing on popular public opinion, the energy policy was seen as an attempt to increase the power of the Federal government and ease regional conflicts. Changes in the provincial power balance had resulted, in part, from the increased resource wealth of the Western provinces. By shifting financial resources and power from the provinces to the Federal government, the new energy policy furthered Trudeau's nationalistic objectives.

Sale of North Sea Properties

39   In June 1979, Mesa sold all of its interests in the United Kingdom section of the North Sea. The sale of North Sea interests was seen as part of Mesa's overall strategy to reduce foreign activities and concentrate on domestic oil and gas exploration and production. The sale price of $65.3 million paid by British National Oil Company (BNOC) resulted in a before-tax gain of $31,195,000. Mesa received $26.4 million in cash and the balance in notes at 8% interest due over the next three years.

40   Mesa's proven reserves in the North Sea were substantial. As of December 31, 1978, net proven reserves in the North Sea were estimated at 37,124 thousand barrels. Mesa, however, had never realized production from its North Sea Holdings. The company's initial development plan for the

---

[15]"Canada's Oil Policy Starts Biting," *Business Week,* February 16, 1981, p. 25.

[16]*Mesa Petroleum Company Annual Report,* 1980, p. 46.

[17]"One Nation Divisible," *Forbes,* July 20, 1981, p. 67.

Beatrice field was rejected by the British government. The plan was later approved after it was revised to include an underwater pipeline to transport oil to shore. In early 1979, Mesa had estimated that it would cost about $600 million to develop the Beatrice Field.

41   Great Britain had been slow to formulate an oil policy. According to one observer, the policy of all three governments in power since oil was discovered in the North Sea was "remarkedly clear and consistent: to pretend that oil didn't matter."[18] By mid 1980, however, an oil policy was being defined. At that time it was announced that the government intended to slow down the development of North Sea oil fields to delay production. It was hoped that production could be balanced with consumption, extending Great Britain's period of self-sufficiency. Without a slowdown, production would exceed consumption throughout the 1980s and Great Britain would be selling oil on the open market. It appeared that a slowdown trend had begun prior to the policy announcement. By the end of 1979, drilling activity was half that of 1977.[19] To a large extent, Great Britain's slowdown policy was implemented through its licensing procedures. The licensing process for exploration and development of the North Sea oil fields was complex and subjective.[20] Late in 1980, the British government also announced plans to increase taxes on North Sea oil by 20%. Oil industry officials lamented the increase noting that at least 85% of North Sea oil profits could already go to the government under existing royalty arrangements and petroleum revenue tax regulations.[21]

The Royalty Trust

42   Plans to form a Royalty Trust were announced in June 1979. Boone Pickens was credited with pioneering this innovative concept that would later be copied by other gas and oil companies. To form the Royalty Trust, Mesa spun off part of its working interests in three mature, producing properties. Through the Royalty Trust, future income from these properties was transferred directly to the stockholders. In this way, the economic benefits of owning the property were separated from Mesa's other operations and could be realized by the stockholder without incurring corporate income taxes. Stockholders of record on November 5, 1979, received one unit in the Trust for each share of common stock. A stockholder's original Mesa investment was thus converted into two investments: shares of Mesa com-

---

[18]"Getting the Best out of the North Sea," *Financial Times,* October 3, 1980, p. 21.

[19]"Oil Consultant Hits at North Sea 'Chaos'," *Financial Times,* February 5, 1980, p. 8.

[20]Please refer to the *AMOCO (UK) (A)* and *AMOCO (UK) (B)* cases (Case Publishing) for a detailed description of the licensing procedure.

[21]"British Trim Bank Rate, Plan 'Windfall' Oil Tax," *New York Times,* November 25, 1980, p. D1.

mon stock and units of the Royalty Trust. Trust units were expected to trade on the NYSE, separate from Mesa shares.

43   The Royalty Trust received 90% net overriding royalty from Mesa's working interest in the earmarked properties. The royalty consisted of 90% of the net proceeds from production (i.e., the excess of gross production revenues over operating costs). Net proceeds were computed monthly.

44   The Trust properties had served as collateral for some of Mesa's debt. proceeds from the sale of the Canadian and North Sea properties were used to pay off this debt, thus permitting the formation of the Trust. The three properties transferred to the Trust were the Yellow Creek field in southwest Wyoming, the San Juan Basin in northwest New Mexico, and the Hugoton field in Kansas, excluding the new areas recently acquired from Ashland Exploration. The properties selected for the Trust had sufficient reserves to generate significant income over an extended period of time. They were also fully developed; that is, no additional development drilling would be required to establish the size of the reserves. Additional infill development drilling was anticipated, however, Approximately half of Mesa's proved reserves were transferred to the Royalty Trust.

45   **Tax Aspects.**[22] Significant tax advantages were antcipated as a result of the Royalty Trust. Most importantly, as a Trust rather than a corporation, income went directly to the stockholder without being taxed at the corporate level. The initial distribution and the availability of depletion allowances provided additional tax advantages. The anticipated savings were substantial.

46   When the Royalty Trust was formed, its tax status was unclear. It was not known if the IRS would consider the Royalty Trust a corporation, or a Trust, as Mesa hoped. To further complicate matters, there was no clear precedent to indicate the appropriate type of trust. The tax consequences for the investor were different for each type of trust. The IRS did not officially sanction the Royalty Trust until the fall of 1982.

47   For tax purposes, the initial distribution of Trust units to Mesa stockholders was considered a return of capital. The stockholder's basis in each share of Mesa stock was reduced by the market value of the unit at distribution. If the value of the unit exceeded the basis, the excess was taxed as a gain from the sale of the share. This favorable tax treatment was possible because Mesa had had no taxable income in 1979. If Mesa had had income for tax purposes, then the intial distribution of Trust units would have been taxable as a dividend.

48   Because of irregularities in the tax code, the tax consequences of the Royalty Trust were different for individual and corporate investors. The individual investor's basis for a Trust unit was the unit's market value on

---

[22]Much of this section is paraphrased from the September 21, 1979 prospectus for the Mesa Royalty Trust.

the date of distribution. His holding period began on the date of distribution. The corporate stockholder, however, assumed Mesa's long-term holding period and per-unit basis, which was approximately $.02.[23]

49   Through the Royalty Trust, stockholders also reaped the tax advantage of depletion allowances. Generally, depletion was allowable in an amount equal to the greater of cost depletion or percentage depletion. The Tax Reduction Act of 1975, however, eliminated percentage depletion with respect to transferees of proven properties. One exception to this rul concerned natural gas production sold at fixed contract prices. It qualified for percentage depletion.

50   Therefore, much of the income from the Royalty Trust qualified only for cost depletion. Each investor could compute cost depletion using his per unit basis. As noted earlier, the basis for a Trust unit was its market value at distribution. Prior to the formation of the Royalty Trust, cost depletion was calculated on Mesa's basis, which was considerably lower. Thus, the value of the trust's assets was increased, providing significantly higher depletion allowances.

51   As mentioned, due to a special tax code provision for gas sold at fixed prices, a portion of the Trust's income qualified for percentage depletion. Because of long-term contracts with KPL, 78% of the Trust's gas production by volume qualified for percentage depletion at a rate of 22% of gross revenue.

52   **Reactions by the Financial Community.** Investment analysts heralded the Royalty Trust as an ingenious plan, benefiting both the stockholders and Mesa. With reserves in a Trust—rather than as corporate assets—it was thought that the securities market would be more likely to recognize their true value. For this reason, the Royalty Trust was considered a good defense against takeover attempts. With many of Mesa's developed, cash-generating reserves transferred to the Trust, it was felt that the company would be a less attractive takeover candidate. Regarding the Royalty Trust, Boone Pickens was quoted as saying, "The whole idea was to get the true value of our assets across to shareholders and not to sit around and wait for someone to take us over."[24]

53   With the formation of the Royalty Trust, Mesa was split into two separate entities, distinguishable by their assets. The properties transferred to the Trust were fully developed with well-established, proven reserves. These assets were a known quantity, and a more definitive valuation was possible. In contrast, Mesa's remaining properties were not as fully developed.

---

[23]This provided an apparent arbitrage opportunity for the corporate investor. Following the announcement of plans to form the Royalty Trust, Mesa stock could be purchased at an inflated price, reflecting the combined value of the stock and Trust units. Following the distribution of the Trust, the stock could be sold for a short-term loss and the Trust units sold for a long-term capital gain.

[24]"The New Spin in Spin-Offs," *Dun's Review,* March, 1980, p. 123.

These assets represented a good deal of future potential for Mesa and their valuation was more subjective. By dividing Mesa's original assets in this way, one analyst predicted that "the sum of the parts will be worth a lot more than the whole; Mesa is forcing the market to recognize the value of its assets."[25]

Debenture Offering

54   In May 1980, Mesa raised $76.6 million through an unusual debenture offering. The bond was convertible, not into Mesa stock, but into the stock of General American Oil (GAO), which Mesa held in its portfolio. Only four of five companies had offered such a convertible bond during the preceding 10 years. The GAO stock was placed in escrow with Mesa continuing to receive the dividends from the escrowed stock until bondholders chose to exercise their conversion rights. The 20-year subordinated debenture had a coupon rate of 8.5%. The bond covenants called for annual sinking fund payments of $6.1 million to begin in 1991 with the balance to be retired in 2000.

55   Mesa held approximately 7.4% of GAO's outstanding stock. The 1,787,434 shares of GAO had been acquired by Mesa at a cost of $31.7 million. Mesa's GAO holdings were worth $76.7 million at the time of the bond offering, representing an unrealized capital gain of $45 million.

Limited Partnership with Texaco
and Sequoia Petroleum (MTS)

56   In October 1980, Mesa entered into a joint venture to explore for gas and oil with Texaco and Sequoia Petroleum, a subsidiary of the Bechtel Corporation. Mesa's interest in the partnership was 65%, Texaco's 25%, and Sequoia's 10%. Revenues and ongoing exploration costs were to be shared proportionally by the partners according to their interest. As operating partner, Mesa had working control of the partnership. For its share in the partnership, Mesa pledged 1.9 million net acres. This acreage, located in 15 different states, represented nearly all of Mesa's undeveloped gas and oil leases in the United States, aside from those on the outer Continental shelf.

57   When the partnership was intially announced in August 1980, Sequoia was not included. Mesa was to contribute 1.9 million acres and have 75% interest in the partnership. Texaco, on the other hand, was to contribute only cash. Tentative plans were for Texaco to put up approximately $150 million cash and purchase $150 million in preferred stock to be issued by Mesa. Texaco was to be granted certain rights to Mesa's future crude oil production. With respect to the planned partnership, one oil analyst said,

---

[25]"A Gain for Mesa is a Loss for the IRS," *Business Week,* October 8, 1979, p. 111.

"It looks like a good deal for both of them. What it comes down to is Texaco saying 'I got the bucks and you got the acreage, let's get together.'[26] Compared to many other oil companies, a smaller proportion of Texaco's reserves were in the United States. Texaco had been hurt, as many of the foreign oil-producing nations where Texaco operated had gradually assumed greater control of their production.[27]

58   Two weeks after the initial Mesa-Texaco partnership was reported, Sequoia's participation was announced. While Mesa's contribution remained 1.9 million acres, the expanded partnership provided additional funds for exploration. A total of nearly $250 million cash was contributed by Texaco and Sequoia, approximately $178 million by Texaco, and $71 million by Sequoia. Mesa's partners also agreed to spend $210 million for 7% cumulative preferred stock to be issued, at Mesa's option, prior to June 1, 1982. The preferred stock was to be redeemed in installments through 1986. In addition, Texaco and Sequoia were to fund proportionally the first $30.6 million of intangible drilling costs incurred by MTS. Mesa's share of the cash contributed by the other two MTS partners amounted to $160 million. The partnership agreement permitted Mesa to borrow these funds at an interest rate of 10%. Shortly after the partnership was formed, Mesa withdrew these funds to pay down bank loans and its broker margin account.

CEO Compensation

59   Boone Pickens's employment contract, as amended in 1978, was for an initial term through the end of 1989, after which time it was to be renewed annually. (See Exhibit 8 for the provisions of Boone Pickens's employment contract and Exhibit 9 for a history of his remuneration.)

Role of the Stockholders

60   The stockholder appeared to be the critical component of T. Boone Pickens's business philosophy. The fundamental principle he had used to guide Mesa's growth was the maximization of stockholder wealth. It was something he spoke of often: "Our primary function is working for the stockholders. It is management's responsibility to increase the value of the shareholder's investment. They bought the stock to make money, and it is up to us to see that they do."[28]

61   Pickens advocated stock ownership by both employees and manage-

---

[26]"Texaco in Oil Accord with Mesa," *New York Times,* August 14, 1980, p. D1.

[27]Ibid., p. D1.

[28]"Mesa Petroleum Co.: How Boone Pickens Directed the Development of One of the Hottest Companies on the New York Stock Exchange," *Petroleum Independent,* October, 1981, p. 34.

Exhibit 8

Mesa Petroleum Company (B) provisions of Boone Pickens' employment contract

Boone Pickens' employment contract with Mesa Petroleum, as amended in 1978 provided for the following:

1. An initial term expiring December 31, 1989, and continuing from year to year thereafter;
2. An annual base salary of not less than $300,000 (Pickens' 1978 base compensation rate);
3. Continuation of full salary for up to 60 months following death or total disability (reduced by other deferred compensation and disability payments under programs funded by the company);
4. Maintenance by the Company of a $2,000,000 life insurance policy on his life, owned by the company as beneficiary ($49,691 annual premium);
5. Supplemental retirement, disability and/or death benefits to the extent annual limitations required by the Employees Retirement Income Security Act of 1974 ("ERISA") result in a reduction of such benefits to which he would otherwise be entitled;
6. Annual payments to him to the extent his participation in the profit sharing plan or other benefit plans is reduced by ERISA limitations;
7. Payment to him at his election, a termination fee in amount equal to twice his then current salary in the event a change in control of Mesa (by tender offer or otherwise) occurs which is not approved by the Board of Directors; and
8. Acceleration of outstanding stock options, so as to become exercisable in full, in the event of such a change of control not approved by the Board of Directors.

Source: Mesa Petroleum Company Proxy Statement, April 26, 1978.

Exhibit 9

Mesa Petroleum Company (B) remuneration to T. Boone Pickens

Year ending 12/30	*Cash & cash equivalent forms of remuneration*		Aggregating contingent forms of remuneration (amounts expensed by company) (a)	Total
	Salaries, fees, director fees, commissions & bonuses (a)	Securities or property, insurance benefits or reimbursement; personal benefits (a)		
1964-1967	n.a.			
1968	$ 31,333			
1969	44,167			
1970	52,083			
1971	60,833			
1972	71,750			
1973	81,575			
1974	n.a.			
1975	176,556			
1976	243,000			
1977	306,008 (b)			
1978	369,765	$ 28,600	$152,472	$ 550,837
1979	330,006	1,608,635	139,478	2,078,119
1980	415,972	169,145	45,165	630,282

Notes:
(a) Data prior to 1978 is aggregate direct remuneration. In 1978, the SEC broadened its definition of remuneration and required that non-monetary compensation be reported.
(b) Excludes non-monetary compensation, estimated to be less than $10,000.
Source: Mesa Petroleum Company Annual Proxy Statements.

ment. He believed that part of Mesa's success was because 95% of Mesa's employees were Mesa stockholders. Employees could invest in Mesa stock through the company's Profit Sharing Plan, as well as the Employee Stock Purchase Plan. Through the Employee Stock Purchase Plan, Mesa would match the employee's investment, which could be as much as 6% of their base salary.

62   Pickens felt that stock ownership by management was particularly important. He believed that the significant stockholdings of executives provided an incentive to maintain the "proper perspective." He had said, "If more corporate managements held substantial equity interests in their companies, as opposed to serving only as salaried professional managers, the shareholders' interest would more often come first."[29] This philosophy had been reflected in the stock options offered to key Mesa executives.

History of Executive Stock Options[30]

63   Throughout the years, Mesa had granted numerous stock options to its executives and key employees. (Exhibit 10 documents the stock options granted to, and exercised by, Boone Pickens.) Mesa adopted its first stock option program in 1965. A second qualified stock option program was initiated in 1969 and a non-qualified option plan was approved the following year.[31] Two stock option plans, one qualified and one non-qualified, were adopted in 1975 and another option program was introduced in 1978. The provisions of these various stock option plans were essentially the same. Each authorized shares to be used for stock options. Three members of the Board of Directors served on the Stock Option Committee, which was authorized to grant stock options. The exercise price of options was 100% of the fair market value on the date the option was granted. Typically, 25% of the shares granted could be exercised each year, beginning one year after the option was granted.

64   In 1972, Mesa initiated a loan program to assist employees exercising stock options. In some cases, loans were made directly by Mesa; in others, Mesa guaranteed bank loans. The stock being purchased was used to secure Mesa loans to employees. The interest rate on these loans floated at $\frac{1}{2}$ over prime to a maximum of 10%. (See Exhibit 11 for a summary of loans to Boone Pickens.)

65   In 1979, unexercised stock options were amended in order to neutralize the impact of the Royalty Trust distribution. Outstanding stock options

---

[29]Ibid., p. 34.

[30]The source for much of this section and the one that follows is the Proxy Statement issued in anticipation of a special meeting of the stockholders of Mesa Petroleum held on October 26, 1979.

[31]Qualified stock option programs are those that qualify for capital gains tax treatment. With a non-qualified stock option the difference between the market price and the exercise price is taxed as earned income. Non-qualified stock options are tax-deductible for the corporation while qualified stock options are not.

Exhibit 10

Mesa Petroleum Company (B) CEO stock options (a)

	1969(b)-1972	*1973-1977*	*1978*	*1979*	*1980*
SPECIFIC TIME PERIOD	1/1/69– 2/13/73	1/1/73– 2/1/78	1/1/78– 2/1/79	1/1/79– 1/1/80	1/1/80– 12/31/80
OPTIONS GRANTED DURING PERIOD					
Number of shares	52,000	140,000	100,000	1,500,000	—
Average exercise price	$46.33	$25.34	$32.91	$46.00	—
OPTIONS EXERCISED DURING PERIOD					
Number of shares	—	92,650	25,000	297,862	(c)
Net value realized (aggregate market value on dates exercised less aggregate exercise price)	—	$967,382	$484,375	$8,802,727	$7,235,549
OPTIONS UNEXERCISED AT END OF PERIOD					
Number of shares (d)	55,200	113,750	188,750	1,500,000	3,000,000
Average exercise price per share	$43.65	$26.33	$31.27	$46.00	$23.00

Notes:

(a) Data, while drawn directly from the noted sources, may appear inaccurate and/or inconsistent. Inconsistencies reflect adjustment for stock splits, which occurred in 1973, 1980, and 1981; and antidilution adjustments for stock dividends. Other inconsistencies result from amendments to Mesa's option programs. For example, as a result of tax code changes, some qualified stock options were reissued as non-qualified options in 1975. Also options were exercised differently following the introduction of "rights of relinquishment" in 1978.

(b) No stock options were granted to T. Boone Pickens prior to 1969.

(c) Not available.

(d) Data is cumulative and independent of the number of shares granted or exercised during the time period.

Source: Mesa Petroleum Co., Notices of Annual Meetings of Stockholders. Specifically: for the first column, those dated April 17, 1970; March 26, 1971; March 24, 1982; and March 31, 1973; for the second column, March 16, 1978; for the third column, March 16, 1979; for the fourth column, March 17,1980; and for the fifth column, March 16, 1981.

were accelerated so they could be exercised, in full, prior to the distribution of the Royalty Trust. If options were not exercised, the number of shares and the exercise price was adjusted to compensate for the Royalty Trust distribution. The adjustment formulas permitted the option holder to realize any gain in the combined value of the stock and units over the original value of the stock.[32]

[32]As outlined in the Proxy Statement for the special meeting of Mesa Petroleum stockholders held October 26, 1979, the option exercise, price was reduced according to the following formula:

$$\text{new option price} = \text{old option price} \times \frac{\begin{array}{l}\text{common stock market price immediately before distribution}\end{array} - \begin{array}{l}\text{unit price immediately after distribution}\end{array}}{\begin{array}{l}\text{common stock market price immediately before distribution}\end{array}}$$

The number of option shares was increased according to the following formula:

$$\text{new number of shares} = \text{old number of shares} \times \frac{\text{old option price per share}}{\text{new option price per share}}$$

Exhibit 11

Mesa Petroleum Company (B) T. Boone Pickens: stock ownership and indebtedness to Mesa

Year	Maximum aggregate indebtedness and loan guarantee	As of	Number of shares of stock owned (a)		
			Common	$2.20 cumulative convertible senior preferred	$2.20 cumulative convertible preferred
1968		1/25/69	184,920		4,500
1969		3/16/70	176,000	1000	4,100
1970		3/5/71	171,672	1000	3,500
1971	—	3/13/72	116,488	500	
1972	—	3/12/73	148,668	500	
1973	—	4/8/74	318,460	—	
1974	—		n.a.		
1975	—	4/1/76	265,670		
1976	649,328	2/15/77	262,268		
1977	1,419,883	2/1/78	381,128		
1978	1,968,236	2/1/79	870,362		
1979	8,485,727	2/1/80	871,263		
1980	8,547,598	2/1/81	982,486		

Notes:

(a) Not available prior to 1968, or for spring 1975.

Adjusted to reflect 2-for-1 stock split on April 25, 1980.

Excludes shares owned by Mrs. Pickens and by children, either in irrevocable trusts or with Boone Pickens as custodian. For example, as of 2/1/80, 600 and 1,901 shares were thus excluded respectively. Also excludes calls covering 10,000 shares during several years in the early 1970s.

As trustee of Mesa's Profit Sharing & Employee Stock Purchase Plans, Boone Pickens had voting and investment power for shares owned by the former, and investment power for shares owned by the latter. As of 2/1/81 the Profit Sharing Plan owned 23,000 shares and the Employee Stock Purchase Plan owned 134,189 shares.

Source: Mesa Petroleum Company, Notices of Annual Stockholder Meetings.

1979 Stock Option

66   Boone Pickens was granted a special stock option in the fall of 1979, immediately following the distribution of the Royalty Trust. When the option was proposed, the Mesa Board of Directors cited Boone Pickens's leadership qualities and "an unusually perceptive and creative combination of oil and gas, financial administrative, and general business management skills." The Board stated that the Company relied on Pickens's "long-term efforts for continued enhancement of the interests of Mesa and its stockholders." They believed that this required "the granting to him of a special incentive in order to induce him to remain active on a full-time basis with the company for an extended period and to reward him in the event the Company continues to be successful under his leadership, thereby also benefiting all stockholders."[33]

---

[33]*Mesa Petroleum Company Proxy Statement,* September 21, 1979, p. 45.

67   The 1979 Stock Option granted Boone Pickens the right to purchase 1.5 million shares of Mesa stock, with provisions for anti-dilution adjustments. The exercise price was $46 per share. Forty percent of the shares could be exercised after five years of continuous employment, with an additional 12% exercisable at the end of each of the next five years of employment. Early exercise of the options was permitted in three explicit sets of circumstances: (1) termination of employment by Pickens due to a breach of his employment contract by Mesa, (2) a tender offer or similar action resulting in a change of control not approved by the Mesa Board of Directors, or (3) Pickens's death or disability.

68   When the stock option was proposed, the shares of Mesa stock that Boone Pickens either owned or had options to purchase accounted for approximately 2% of Mesa's outstanding stock. With the addition of the 1979 stock option, Pickens's current and potential stock ownership accounted for approximately 10% of Mesa's then outstanding stock, including about 500,000 unissued shares available for stock options of other employees. (See Exhibit 11 for a historical record of stock ownership by Boone Pickens.)

The Lawsuits

69   Boone Pickens's compensation package resulted in two lawsuits being filed against Mesa and its directors. The first, mentioned earlier, was filed in March 1980, by Mr. Harry Lewis, in the U.S. District Court for the Northern District of Texas. A similar suit was filed in August 1980, by Rose Moses in the Court of Chancery of the State of Delaware for New Castle County.

70   The plaintiffs found fault with the 1979 stock option granted to Boone Pickens, the amendments to outstanding stock options precipitated by the Royalty Trust distribution, and the loans to employees exercising stock options at interest rates below Mesa's interest costs. According to the suits these practices were a waste of corporate assets. The suits also alleged violations of federal security laws, and/or breach of fiduciary obligations.

71   Boone Pickens's 1979 stock option had been justified, in part, as an incentive for him to remain active in Mesa's management for an "extended period." In his suit, Mr. Lewis charged that Mesa had failed to "disclose prominently" the fact that Boone Pickens's employment contract obligated him to remain with Mesa through 1989. The suits sought the recovery of damages against the plaintiffs, the restoration to Mesa of excess compensation and benefits received by Boone Pickens, the cancellation of the amendments to outstanding stock options made when the Royalty Trust was established, and the payment of interest, at a rate of $1/_2$% above prime on loans to employees exercising stock option.

A Guide to Industry Analysis

Foreword

In 1980, Professor Michael E. Porter of Harvard University published a book titled *Competitive Strategy*. It propelled the concept of industry analysis into the foreground of strategic thought and business planning. The cornerstone of the book is the following article from the *Harvard Business Review* in which Porter emphasized five forces that shape industry competition. His well-defined analytical framework helps strategic managers to understand industry dynamics and to correctly anticipate the impact of remote factors on a firm's operating environment.

The Authors

Overview

The nature and degree of competition in an industry hinge on five forces: the threat of new entrants, the bargaining power of customers, the bargaining power of suppliers, the threat of substitute products or services (where applicable), and the jockeying among current contestants. To establish a strategic agenda for dealing with these contending currents and to grow despite them, a company must understand how they work in its industry and how they affect the company in its particular situation. This chapter will detail how these forces operate; it will suggest ways of adjusting to them and, where possible, ways of taking advantage of them.

How Competitive Forces Shape Strategy

The essence of strategy formulation is coping with competition. Yet it is easy to view competition too narrowly and too pessimistically. While one sometimes hears executives complaining to the contrary, intense competition in an industry is neither coincidence nor bad luck.

Moreover, in the fight for market share, competition is not manifested only in the other players. Rather, competition in an industry is rooted in its underlying economics, and competitive forces exist that go well beyond the established combatants in a particular industry. Customers, suppliers, potential entrants, and substitute products are all competitors that may be more or less prominent or active depending on the industry.

The state of competition in an industry depends on five basic forces, which are diagramed in Exhibit 1. The collective strength of these forces determines the ultimate profit potential of an industry. It ranges from intense in industries like tires, metal cans, and steel, where no company earns spectacular returns on investment, to mild in industries like oil-field

Exhibit 1

Forces driving industry competition

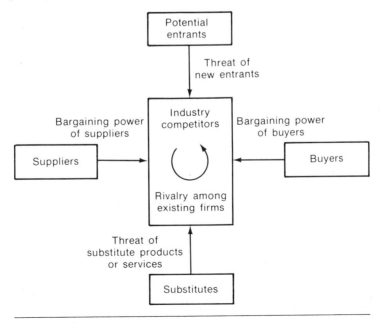

services and equipment, soft drinks, and toiletries, where there is room for quite high returns.

In the economists' "perfectly competitive" industry, jockeying for position is unbridled and entry to the industry very easy. This kind of industry structure, of course, offers the worst prospect for long-run profitability. The weaker the forces collectively, however, the greater the opportunity for superior performance.

Whatever their collective strength, the corporate strategist's goal is to find a position in the industry where his or her company can best defend itself against these forces or can influence them in its favor. The collective strength of the forces may be painfully apparent to all the antagonists; but to cope with them, the strategist must delve below the surface and analyze the sources of competition. For example, what makes the industry vulnerable to entry? What determines the bargaining power of suppliers?

Knowledge of these underlying sources of competitive pressure provides the groundwork for a strategic agenda of action. It highlights the critical strengths and weaknesses of the company, animates the positioning of the company in its industry, clarifies the areas where strategic changes may yield the greatest payoff, and highlights the places where industry trends promise to hold the greatest significance as either opportunities or threats.

Understanding these sources also proves to be of help in considering areas for diversification.

Contending Forces

The strongest competitive force or forces determine the profitability of an industry and so are of greatest importance in strategy formulation. For example, even a company with a strong position in an industry unthreatened by potential entrants will earn low returns if it faces a superior or a lower-cost substitute product— as the leading manufacturers of vacuum tubes and coffee percolators have learned to their sorrow. In such a situation, coping with the substitute product becomes the number one strategic priority.

Different forces take on prominence, of course, in shaping competition in each industry. In the ocean-going tanker industry the key force is probably the buyers (the major oil companies), while in tires it is powerful OEM buyers coupled with tough competitors. In the steel industry the key forces are foreign competitors and substitute materials.

Every industry has an underlying structure, or a set of fundamental economic and technical characteristics, that gives rise to these competitive forces. The strategist, wanting to position his company to cope best with its industry environment or to influence that environment in the company's favor, must learn what makes the environment tick.

This view of competition pertains equally to industries dealing in services and to those selling products. To avoid monotony in this article, I refer to both products and services as "products." The same general principles apply to all types of business.

A few characteristics are critical to the strength of each competitive force. They will be discussed in this section.

Threat of Entry

New entrants to an industry bring new capacity, the desire to gain market share, and often substantial resources. Companies diversifying through acquisition into the industry from other markets often leverage their resources to cause a shape-up, as Phillip Morris did with Miller beer.

The seriousness of the threat of entry depends on the barriers present and on the reaction from existing competitors that the entrant can expect. If barriers to entry are high and a newcomer can expect sharp retaliation from the entrenched competitors, obviously he will not pose a serious threat of entering.

There are six major sources of barriers to entry:

1. Economies of Scale. These economies deter entry by forcing the aspirant either to come in on a large scale or to accept a cost disadvantage. Scale economies in production, research, marketing, and service are probably the key barriers to entry in the mainframe computer industry, as Xerox and GE sadly discovered. Economies of scale can also act as hurdles in distribution, utilization of the sales force, financing, and nearly any other part of a business.

2. Product Differentiation. Brand identification creates a barrier by forcing entrants to spend heavily to overcome customer loyalty. Advertising, customer service, being first in the industry, and product differences are among the factors fostering brand identification. It is perhaps the most important entry barrier in soft drinks, over-the-counter drugs, cosmetics, investment banking, and public accounting. To create high fences around their business, brewers couple brand identification with economies of scale in production, distribution, and marketing.

3. Capital Requirements. The need to invest large financial resources in order to compete creates a barrier to entry, particularly if the capital is required for unrecoverable expenditures in up-front advertising or R&D. Capital is necessary not only for fixed facilities but also for customer credit, inventories, and absorbing start-up losses. While major corporations have the financial resources to invade almost any industry, the huge capital requirements in certain fields, such as computer manufacturing and mineral extraction, limit the pool of likely entrants.

4. Cost Disadvantages Independent of Size. Entrenched companies may have cost advantages not available to potential rivals, no matter what their size and attainable economies of scale. These advantages can stem from the effects of the learning curve (and of its first cousin, the experience curve), proprietary technology, access to the best raw materials sources, assets purchased at preinflation prices, government subsidies, or favorable locations. Sometimes cost advantages are legally enforceable, as they are through patents. (For an analysis of the much-discussed experience curve as a barrier to entry, see Exhibit 2.)

5. Access to Distribution Channels. The new boy on the block must, of course, secure distribution of his product or service. A new food product, for example, must displace others from the supermarket shelf via price breaks, promotions, intense selling efforts, or some other means. The more limited the wholesale or retail channels are and the more that existing competitors have these tied up, obviously the tougher that entry into the industry will be. Sometimes this barrier is so high that, to surmount it, a new contestant must create its own distribution channels, as Timex did in the watch industry in the 1950s.

6. Government Policy. The government can limit or even foreclose entry to industries with such controls as license requirements and limits on access to raw materials. Regulated industries like trucking, liquor retailing, and freight forwarding are noticeable examples; more subtle government restrictions operate in fields like ski-area development and coal mining. The government also can play a major indirect role by affecting entry barriers through controls such as air and water pollution standards and safety regulations.

The potential rival's expectations about the reaction of existing competitors also will influence its decision on whether to enter. The company is likely to have second thoughts if incumbents have previously lashed out at new entrants or if:

The incumbents possess substantial resources to fight back, including excess cash and unused borrowing power, productive capacity, or clout with distribution channels and customers.

The incumbents seem likely to cut prices because of a desire to keep market shares or because of industry-wide excess capacity.

Industry growth is slow, affecting its ability to absorb the new arrival and probably causing the financial performance of all the parties involved to decline.

Changing Conditions. From a strategic standpoint there are two important additional points to note about the threat of entry.

Exhibit 2

The experience curve as an entry barrier

In recent years, the experience curve has become widely discussed as a key element of industry structure. According to this concept, unit costs in many manufacturing industries (some dogmatic adherents say in all manufacturing industries) as well as in some service industries decline with "experience," or a particular company's cumulative volume of production. (The experience curve, which encompasses many factors, is a broader concept than the better-known learning curve, which refers to the efficiency achieved over a period of time by workers through much repetition.)

The causes of the decline in unit costs are a combination of elements, including economies of scale, the learning curve for labor, and capital-labor substitution. The cost decline creates a barrier to entry because new competitors with no "experience" face higher costs than established ones, particularly the producer with the largest market share, and have difficulty catching up with the entrenched competitors.

Adherents of the experience curve concept stress the importance of achieving market leadership to maximize this barrier to entry, and they recommend aggressive action to achieve it, such as price cutting in anticipation of falling costs in order to build volume. For the combatant that cannot achieve a healthy market share, the prescription is usually, "Get out."

Is the experience curve an entry barrier on which strategies should be built? The answer is: not in every industry. In fact, in some industries, building a strategy on the experience curve can be potentially disastrous. That costs decline with experience in some industries is not news to corporate executives. The significance of the experience curve for strategy depends on what factors are causing the decline.

A new entrant may well be more efficient than the more experienced competitors; if it has built the newest plant, it will face no disadvantage in having to catch up. The strategic prescription, "You must have the largest, most efficient plant," is a lot different from "You must produce the greatest cumulative output of the item to get your costs down."

Whether a drop in costs with cumulative (not absolute) volume erects an entry barrier also depends on the sources of the decline. If costs go down because of technical advances known generally in the industry or because of the development of improved equipment that can be copied or purchases from equipment suppliers, the experience curve is not entry barrier at all—in fact, new or less experienced competitors may actually enjoy a cost advantage over the leaders. Free of the legacy of heavy past investments, the newcomer or less-experienced competitor can purchase or copy the newest and lowest-cost equipment and technology.

If, however, experience can be kept proprietary, the leaders will maintain a cost advantage. But new entrants may require less experience to reduce their costs than the leaders needed. All this suggests that the experience curve can be a shaky entry barrier on which to build a strategy.

While space does not permit a complete treatment here, I want to mention a few other crucial elements in determining the appropriateness of a strategy built on the entry barrier provided by the experience curve:

> The height of the barrier depends on how important costs are to competition compared with other areas like marketing, selling, and innovation.

> The barrier can be nullified by product or process innovations leading to a substantially new technology and thereby creating an entirely new experience curve. New entrants can leapfrog the industry leaders and alight on the new experience curve, to which those leaders may be poorly positioned to jump.

> If more than one strong company is building its strategy on the experience curve, the consequences can be nearly fatal. By the time only one rival is left pursuing such a strategy, industry growth may have stopped and the prospects of reaping the spoils of victory long since evaporated.

First, it changes, of course, as these conditions change. The expiration of Polaroid's basic patents on instant photography, for instance, greatly reduced its absolute cost entry barrier built by proprietary technology. It is not surprising that Kodak plunged into the market. Product differentiation in printing has all but disappeared. Conversely, in the auto industry economies of scale increased enormously with post– World War II automation and vertical integration—virtually stopping successful new entry.

Second, strategic decisions involving a large segment of an industry can have a major impact on the conditions determining the threat of entry. For example, the actions of many U.S. wine producers in the 1960s to step up product introductions, raise advertising levels, and expand distribution nationally surely strengthened the entry roadblocks by raising economies of scale and making access to distribution channels more difficult. Similarly, decisions by members of the recreational vehicle industry to integrate vertically in order to lower costs have greatly increased the economies of scale and raised the capital costs barriers.

Powerful Suppliers and Buyers

Suppliers can exert bargaining power on participants in an industry by raising prices or reducing the quality of purchased goods and services. Powerful suppliers can thereby squeeze profitability out of an industry unable to recover cost increases in its own prices. By raising their prices, soft-drink concentrate producers have contributed to the erosion of profitability of bottling companies because the bottlers, facing intense competition from powdered mixes, fruit drinks, and other beverages, have limited freedom to raise their prices accordingly. Customers likewise can force down prices, demand higher quality or more service, and play competitors off against each other—all at the expense of industry profits.

The power of each important supplier or buyer group depends on a number of characteristics of its market situation and on the relative importance of its sales or purchases to the industry compared with its overall business.

A *supplier* group is powerful if:

It is dominated by a few companies and is more concentrated than the industry it sells to.

Its product is unique or at least differentiated, or if it has built up switching costs. Switching costs are fixed costs buyers face in changing suppliers. These arise because, among other things, a buyer's product specifications tie it to particular suppliers, because it has invested heavily in specialized ancillary equipment or in learning how to operate a supplier's equipment (as in computer software), or because its production lines are connected to the supplier's manufacturing facilities (as in some manufacture of beverage containers.)

It is not obliged to contend with other products for sale to the industry. For instance, the competition between the steel companies and the aluminum companies to sell to the can industry checks the power of each supplier.

It poses a credible threat of integrating forward into the industry's business. This provides a check against the industry's ability to improve the terms on which it purchases.

The industry is not an important customer of the supplier group. If the industry is an important customer, suppliers' fortunes will be closely tied to the industry, and they will want to protect the industry through reasonable pricing and assistance in activities like R&D and lobbying.

A *buyer* group is powerful if:

It is concentrated or purchases in large volumes. Large-volume buyers are particularly potent forces if heavy fixed costs characterize the industry—as they do in metal containers, corn refining, and bulk chemicals, for example—which raise the stakes to keep capacity filled.

The products it purchases from the industry are standard or undifferentiated. The buyers, sure that they can always find alternative supplers, may play one company against another, as they do in aluminum extrusion.

The products it purchases from the industry form a component of its product and represent a significant fraction of its cost. The buyers are likely to shop for a favorable price and purchase selectively. Where the product sold by the industry in question is a small fraction of buyers' costs, buyers are usually much less price sensitive.

It earns low profits, which create great incentive to lower its purchasing costs. Highly profitable buyers, however, are generally less price sensitive (that is, of course, if the item does not represent a large fraction of their costs).

The industry's product is unimportant to the quality of the buyers' products or services. Where the quality of the buyers' products is very much affected by the industry's product, buyers are generally less price sensitive. Industries in which this situation obtains include oil-field equipment, where a malfunction can lead to large losses; and enclosures for electronic medical and test instruments, where the quality of the enclosure can influence the user's impression about the quality of the equipment inside.

The industry's product does not save the buyer money. Where the industry's product or service can pay for itself many times over, the buyer is rarely price sensitive; rather he is interested in quality. This is true in services like investment banking and public accounting, where errors in judgment can be costly and embarrassing, and in businesses like the logging of oil wells, where an accurate survey can save thousands of dollars in drilling costs.

The buyers pose a credible threat of integrating backward to make the industry's product. The Big Three auto producers and major buyers of cars have often used the threat of self-manufacture as a bargaining lever. But sometimes an industry engenders a threat to buyers that its members may integrate forward.

Most of these sources of buyer power can be attributed to consumers as a group as well as to industrial and commercial buyers; only a modification of the frame of reference is necessary. Consumers tend to be more price sensitive if they are purchasing products that are undifferentiated, expensive relative to their incomes, and of a sort where quality is not particularly important.

The buying power of retailers is determined by the same rules, with one important addition. Retailers can gain significant bargaining power over manufacturers when they can influence consumers' purchasing decisions, as they do in audio components, jewelry, appliances, sporting goods, and other goods.

Strategic Action. A company's choice of suppliers to buy from or buyer groups to sell to should be viewed as a crucial strategic decision. A company can improve its strategic posture by finding suppliers or buyers who possess the least power to influence it adversely.

Most common is the situation of a company being able to choose whom it will sell to—in other words, buyer selection. Rarely do all the buyer groups a company sells to enjoy equal power. Even if a company sells to a single industry, segments usually exist within that industry that exercise less power (and that are therefore less price sensitive) than others. For example, the replacement market for most products is less price sensitive than the overall market.

A a rule, a company can sell to powerful buyers and still come away with above-average profitability only if it is a low-cost producer in its industry or if its product enjoys some unusual, if not unique, features. In supplying large customers with electric motors, Emerson Electric earns high returns because its low cost position permits the company to meet or undercut competitors prices.

If the company lacks a low cost position or a unique product, selling to everyone is self-defeating because the more sales it achieves, the more vulnerable it becomes. The company may have to muster the courage to turn away business and sell only to less potent customers.

Buyer selection has been a key to the success of National Can and Crown, Cork and Seal. They focus on the segments of the can industry where they can create product differentiation, minimize the threat of backward integration, and otherwise mitigate the awesome power of their customers. Of course, some industries do not enjoy the luxury of selecting "good" buyers.

As the factors creating supplier and buyer power change with time or as a result of a company's strategic decisions, naturally the power of these groups rises or declines. In the ready-to-wear clothing industry, as the buyers (department stores and clothing stores) have become more concentrated and control has passed to large chains, the industry has come under increasing pressure and suffered falling margins. The industry has been unable to differentiate its product or engender switching costs that lock in its buyers enough to neutralize these trends.

Substitute Products

By placing a ceiling on prices it can charge, substitute products or services limit the potential of an industry. Unless it can upgrade the quality of the product or differentiate it somehow (as via marketing), the industry will suffer in earnings and possibly in growth.

Manifestly, the more attractive the price-performance trade-off offered by substitute products, the firmer the lid placed on the industry's profit potential. Sugar producers confronted with the large-scale commercialization of high-fructose corn syrup, a sugar substitute, are learning this lesson today.

Substitutes not only limit profits in normal times, they also reduce the bonanza an industry can reap in boom times. In 1978 the producers of fiberglass insulation enjoyed unprecedented demand as a result of high energy costs and severe winter weather. But the industry's ability to raise prices was tempered by the plethora of insulation substitutes, including cellulose, rock wool, and styrofoam. These substitutes are bound to become an even stronger force once the current round of plant additions by fiberglass insulation producers has boosted capacity enough to meet demand (and then some).

Substitute products that deserve the most attention strategically are those that (a) are subject to trends improving their price-performance trade-off with the industry's product or (b) are produced by industries earning high profits. Substitutes often come rapidly into play if some development increases competition in their industries and causes price reduction or performance improvement.

Jockeying for Position

Rivalry among existing competitors takes the familiar form of jockeying for position—using tactics like price competition, product introduction, and advertising slugfests. Intense rivalry is related to the presence of a number of factors:

Competitors are numerous or are roughly equal in size and power. In many U.S. industries in recent years foreign contenders, of course, have become part of the competitive picture.

Industry growth is slow, precipitating fights for market share that involve expansion-minded members.

The product or service lacks differentiation or switching costs, which lock in buyers and protect one combatant from raids on its customers by another.

Fixed costs are high or the product is perishable, creating strong temptation to cut prices. Many basic materials businesses, like paper and aluminum, suffer from this problem when demand slackens.

Capacity is normally augmented in large increments. Such additions, as in the chlorine and vinyl chloride businesses, disrupt the industry's supply-demand balance and often lead to periods of overcapacity and price cutting.

Exit barriers are high. Exit barriers, like very specialized assets or management's loyalty to a particular business, keep companies competing even though they may be earning low or even negative returns on investment. Excess capacity remains functioning, and the profitability of the healthy competitors suffers as the sick ones hang on. If the industry suffers from overcapacity, it may seek government help, particularly if foreign competition is present.

The rivals are diverse in strategies, origins, and "personalities." They have different ideas about how to compete and continually run head-on into each other in the process.

As an industry matures, its growth rate changes, resulting in declining profits and (often) a shakeout. In the booming recreational vehicle industry of the early 1970s, nearly every producer did well; but slow growth since then has eliminated the high returns, except for the strongest members, not to mention many of the weaker companies. The same profit story has been played out in industry after industry—snowmobiles, aerosol packaging, and sports equipment are just a few examples.

An acquisition can introduce a very different personality to an industry, as has been the case with Black & Decker's takeover of McCullough, the producer of chain saws. Technological innovation can boost the level of fixed costs in the production process, as it did in the shift from batch to continuous-line photo finishing in the 1960s.

While a company must live with many of these factors—because they are built into industry economics—it may have some latitude for improving matters through strategic shifts. For example, it may try to raise buyer's switching costs or increase product differentiation. A focus on selling efforts in the fastest-growing segments of the industry or on market areas with the lowest fixed costs can reduce the impact of industry rivalry. If it is feasible, a company can try to avoid confrontation with competitors having high exit barriers and can thus sidestep involvement in bitter price cutting.

Formulation of Strategy

Once the corporate strategist has assessed the forces affecting competition in his industry and their underlying causes, he can identify his company's strengths and weaknesses. The crucial strengths and weaknesses from a strategic standpoint are the company's posture vis-à-vis the underlying causes of each force. Where does it stand against substitutes? Against the sources of entry barriers?

Then the strategist can devise a plan of action that may include (1) positioning the company so that its capabilities provide the best defense against the competitive force; and/or (2) influencing the balance of the forces through strategic moves, thereby improving the company's position; and/or (3) anticipating shifts in the factors underlying the forces and responding to them, with the hope of exploiting change by choosing a strategy appropriate for the new competitive balance before opponents recognize it. Each strategic approach will now be considered in turn.

Positioning the Company

The first approach takes the structure of the industry as given and matches the company's strengths and weaknesses to it. Strategy can be viewed as building defenses against the competitive forces or as finding positions in the industry where the forces are weakest.

Knowledge of the company's capabilities and of the causes of the competitive forces will highlight the areas where the company should confront competition and where to avoid it. If the company is a low-cost producer, it may choose to confront powerful buyers while it takes care to sell them only products not vulnerable to competition from substitutes.

The success of Dr Pepper in the soft-drink industry illustrates the coupling or realistic knowledge of corporate strengths with sound industry analysis to yield a superior strategy. Coca-Cola and Pepsi-Cola dominate Dr Pepper's industry, where many small concetrate producers compete for a piece of the action. Dr Pepper chose a strategy of avoiding the largest-selling drink segment, maintaining a narrow flavor line, forgoing the development of a captive bottler network, and marketing heavily. The company positioned itself so as to be least vulnerable to its competitive forces while it exploited its small size.

In the $11.5 billion soft-drink industry, barriers to entry in the form of brand identification, large-scale marketing, and access to a bottler network are enormous. Rather than accept the formidable costs and scale economies in having its own bottler network—that, following the lead of the Big Two and of 7UP—Dr Pepper took advantage of the different flavor of its drink to "piggyback" on Coke and Pepsi bottlers who wanted a full line to sell to customers. Dr Pepper coped with the power of these buyers through extraordinary service and other efforts to distinguish its treatment of them from that of Coke and Pepsi.

Many small companies in the soft-drink business offer cola drinks that thrust them into head-to-head competition against the majors. Dr Pepper, however, maximized product differentiation by maintaining a narrow line of beverages built around an unusual flavor.

Finally, Dr Pepper met coke and Pepsi with an advertising onslaught emphasizing the alleged uniqueness of its single flavor. This campaign built strong brand identification and great customer loyalty. Helping its efforts was the fact that Dr Pepper's formula involved lower raw-materials cost, which gave the company an absolute cost advantage over its major competitors.

There are no economies of scale in soft-drink concentrate production, so Dr Pepper could prosper despite its small share of the business (6 percent). Thus, Dr Pepper confronted competition in marketing but avoided it in product line and in distribution. This artful positioning combined with good implementation has led to an enviable record in earnings and in stock market.

Influencing the Balance

When dealing with the forces that drive industry competition, a company can devise a strategy that takes the offensive. This posture is designed to do more than merely cope with the forces themselves; it is meant to alter their causes.

Innovations in marketing can raise brand identification or otherwise differentiate the product. Capital investments in large-scale facilities or vertical integration affect entry barriers. The balance of forces is partly a result of external factors and partly in the company's control.

Exploiting Industry Change

Industry evolution is important strategically because evolution, of course, brings with it changes in the sources of competition. In the familiar product life-cycle pattern, for example, growth rates change, product differentiation is said to decline as the business becomes more mature, and the companies tend to integrate vertically.

These trends are not so important in themselves; what is critical is whether they affect the sources of competition. Consider vertical integration. In the maturing minicomputer industry, extensive vertical integration, both in manufacturing and in software development, is taking place. This very significant trend is greatly raising economies of scale as well as the amount of capital necessary to compete in the industry. This in turn is raising barriers to entry and may drive some smaller competitors out of the industry once growth levels off.

Obviously, the trends carrying the highest priority from a strategic standpoint are those that affect the most important sources of competition in the industry and those that elevate new causes to the forefront. In contract aerosol packaging, for example, the trend toward less product differentiation is now dominant. It has increased buyers' power, lowered the barriers to entry, and intensified competition.

The framework for analyzing competition can also be used to predict the eventual profitability of an industry. In long-range planning the task is to examine each competitive force, forecast the magnitude of each underlying cause, and then construct a composite picture of the likely profit potential of the industry.

The outcome of such an exercise may differ a great deal from the existing industry structure. Today, for example, the solar heating business is popu-lated by dozens and perhaps hundreds of companies, none with a major market position. Entry is easy, and competitors are battling to establish solar heating as a superior substitute for conventional methods.

The potential of this industry will depend largely on the shape of future barriers to entry, the improvement of the industry's position relative to substitues, the ultimate intensity of competition, and the power captured by buyers and suppliers. These characteristics will in turn, be influenced by such factors as the establishment of brand identities, significant econ-omies of scale or experience curves in equipment manufacture wrought by technological change, the ultimate capital costs to compete, and the extent of overhead in production facilities.

The framework for analyzing industry competition has direct benefits in setting diversification strategy. It provides a road map for answering the extremely difficult question inherent in diversification decisions: "What is the potential of this business?" Combining the framework with judgment in its application, a company may be able to spot an industry with a good future before this good future is reflected in the prices of acquisition candi-dates.

Multifaceted Rivalry

Corporate managers have directed a great deal of attention to defining their business as a crucial step in strategy formulation. Numerous authori-ties have stressed the need to look beyond product to function in defining a business, beyond national boundaries to potential international competi-tion, and beyond the ranks of one's competitors today to those that may become competitors tomorrow. As a result of these urgings, the proper definition of a company's industry or industries has become an endlessly debated subject.

One motive behind this debate is the desire to exploit new markets. Another, perhaps more important motive is the fear of overlooking latent sources of competition that someday may threaten the industry. Many managers concentrate so single-mindedly on their direct antagonists in the fight for market share that they fail to realize that they are also competing with their customers and their suppliers for bargaining power. Meanwhile, they also neglect to keep a wary eye out for new entrants to the contest or fail to recognize the subtle threat of substitute products.

The key to growth—even survival—is to stake out a position that is less vulnerable to attack from head-to-head opponents, whether established or new, and less vulnerable to erosion from the direction of buyers, suppliers, and substitute goods. Establishing such a position can take many forms— solidifying relationships with favorable customers, differentiating the product either substantively or psychologically through marketing, integrating forward or backward, or establishing technological leadership.

Bibliography

Caves, R. E., and M. E. Porter. "From Entry Barriers to Mobility Barriers: Conjectural Decisions and Contrived Deterrence to New Competition." *Quarterly Journal of Economics* 91 (1976): 421-34.

Elzinga, K. G. "The Restructuring of the U.S. Brewing Industry." *Industrial Organization Review* 1 (1973): 101-14.

Koch, J. V. "Industry Market Structure and Industry Price-Cost Margins." *Industrial Organization Review* 2 (1974): 186-93.

Porter, M. E. "The Structure within Industries' and Companies' Performance." *Review of Economics and Statistics* 61(1979): 214-27.

Scherer, F. M. *Industrial Market Structure and Economic Performance,* 2d ed. Skokie, Ill.: Rand McNally, 1980.

Weber, J. A. "Market Structure Profile Analysis and Strategic Growth Opportunities." *California Management Review* 20 (1977): 34-46.

appendix B Guide to Financial Analysis

One of the most important tools for assessing the strength of an organization within its industry is financial analysis. Managers, investors, and creditors all employ some form of this analysis as the beginning point for their financial decision making. Investors use financial analyses in making decisions about whether to buy or sell stock, and creditors use them in deciding whether or not to lend. They provide managers with a measurement of how the company is doing in comparison with its performance in past years and with the performance of competitors in the industry.

Although financial analysis is useful for decision making, there are some weaknesses that should be noted. Any picture that it provides of the company is based on past data. Although trends may be noteworthy, this picture should not automatically be assumed to be applicable to the future. In addition, the analysis is only as good as the accounting procedures that have provided the information. When making comparisons between companies, one should keep in mind the variability of accounting procedures from firm to firm. There are four basic groups of financial ratios: liquidity, leverage, activity, and profitability.

The specific ratios calculated for each of the basic groups are shown in Exhibit 1. Liquidity and leverage ratios represent an assessment of the risk of the firm. Activity and profitability ratios are measures of the return generated by the assets of the firm. The interaction between certain groups of ratios is indictated by arrows.

Typically two common financial statements are used in financial ana-

Prepared by Elizabeth Gatewood, University of Georgia.

Exhibit 1

Financial ratios

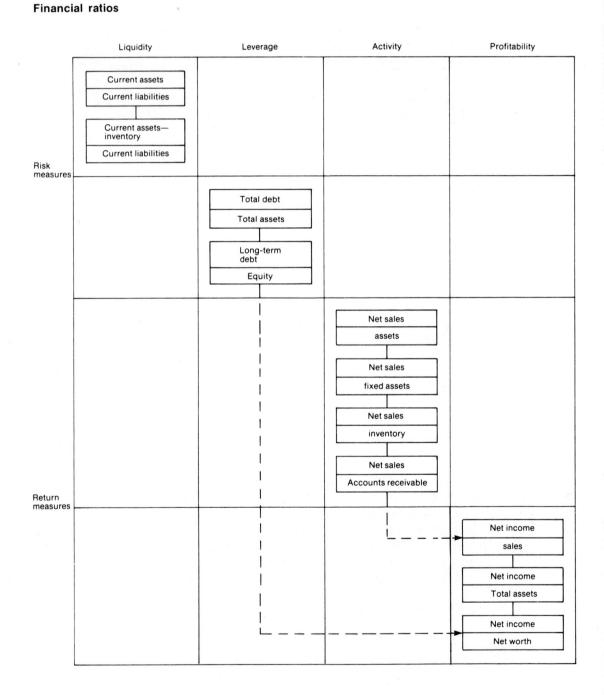

Exhibit 2

ABC Company balance sheet as of December 31

		1985		1984
Assets				
Current assets:				
Cash...		$ 140,000		$ 115,000
Accounts receivable		1,760,000		1,440,000
Inventory		2,175,000		2,000,000
Prepaid expenses..............................		50,000		63,000
Total current assets........................		4,125,000		3,618,000
Fixed assets:				
Long-term receivables		1,255,000		1,090,000
Property and plant............................	$2,037,000		$2,015,000	
Less: Accumulated depreciation	862,000		860,000	
Net property and plant		1,175,000		1,155,000
Other fixed assets.............................		550,000		530,000
Total fixed assets		2,980,000		2,775,000
Total assets		$7,105,000		$6,393,000
Liabilities and Stockholders' Equity				
Current liabilities:				
Accounts payable		$1,325,000		$1,225,000
Bank loans payable...........................		475,000		550,000
Accrued federal taxes		675,000		425,000
Current maturities (long-term debt)		17,500		26,000
Dividends payable		20,000		16,250
Total liabilities...........................		2,512,500		2,242,250
Long-term liabilities		1,350,000		1,425,000
Total liabilities..........................		3,862,500		3,667,250
Stockholders' equity:				
Common stock (104,046 shares outstanding				
in 1985; 101,204 shares outstanding in 1984) ..		44,500		43,300
Additional paid-in capital		568,000		372,450
Retained earnings.............................		2,630,000		2,310,000
Total stockholders' equity		3,242,500		2,725,750
Total liabilities and stockholders' equity.........		$7,105,000		$6,393,000

lyses: the balance sheet and the income statement. Exhibit 2 is a balance sheet and Exhibit 3 an income statement for the ABC Company. These statements will be used to illustrate the financial analyses.

Liquidity Ratios

Liquidity ratios are used as indicators of a firm's ability to meet its short-term obligations. These obligations include any current liabilities, including

Exhibit 3

ABC Company income statement for the years ending December 31

		1985		*1984*
Net sales		$8,250,000		$8,000,000
Less: Cost of goods sold	$5,100,000		$5,000,000	
Administrative expenses	1,750,000		1,680,000	
Other expenses............................	420,000		390,000	
Total.....................................		7,270,000		7,070,000
Earnings before interest and taxes		980,000		930,000
Less: Interest expense...........................		210,000		210,000
Earnings before taxes		770,000		720,000
Less: Federal income taxes......................		360,000		325,000
Earnings after taxes (net income)		$ 410,000		$ 395,000
Common-stock cash dividends		$ 90,000		$ 84,000
Addition to retained earnings....................		$ 320,000		$ 311,000
Earnings per common share......................		$ 3.940		$ 3.90
Dividends per common share		$ 0.865		$ 0.83

currently maturing long-term debt. Current assets move through a normal cash cycle of inventories—sales—account receivable—cash. The firm then uses cash to pay off or reduce its current liabilities. The best-known liquidity ratio is the current ratio: current assets divided by current liabilities. For the ABC Company the current ratio is calculated as follows:

$$\frac{\text{Current assets}}{\text{Current liabilities}} = \frac{\$4,125,000}{\$2,512,500} = 1.64 \ (1985)$$

$$= \frac{\$3,618,000}{\$2,242,250} = 1.61 \ (1984)$$

Most analysts suggest a current ratio of 2 to 3. A large current ratio is not necessarily a good sign; it may mean that an organization is not making the most efficient use of assets. The optimum current ratio will vary from industry to industry, the more volatile industries requiring higher ratios.

Since slow-moving or obsolescent inventories could overstate a firm's ability to meet short-term demands, the quick ratio is sometimes preferred to assess a firm's liquidity. The quick ratio is current assets minus inventories, divided by current liabilities. The quick ratio for the ABC Company is calculated as follows:

$$\frac{\text{Current assets} - \text{inventories}}{\text{Current liabilities}} = \frac{\$1,950,000}{\$2,512,500} = 0.78 \ (1985)$$

$$= \frac{\$1,618,000}{\$2,242,250} = 0.72 \ (1984)$$

A quick ratio of approximately 1 would be typical for American industries. Although there is less variability in the quick ratio than in the current ratio, stable industries would be able to operate safely with a lower ratio.

Leverage Ratios

Leverage ratios identify the source of a firm's capital—owners or outside creditors. The term "leverage" refers to the fact that using capital with a fixed interest charge will"amplify" either profits or losses in relation to the equity of holders of common stock. The most commonly used ratio is total debt divided by total assets. Total debt includes current liabilities and long-term liabilities. This ratio is a measure of the percentage of total funds provided by debt. A total debt-total assets ratio higher than 0.5 is usually considered safe only for firms in stable industries.

$$\frac{\text{Total debt}}{\text{Total assets}} = \frac{\$3,862,500}{\$7,105,000} = 0.54 \ (1985)$$

$$= \frac{\$3,667,250}{\$6,393,000} = 0.57 \ (1984)$$

The ratio of long-term debt to equity is a measure of the extent to which sources of long-term financing are provided by creditors. It is computed by dividing long-term debt by the stockholders' equity.

$$\frac{\text{Long-term debt}}{\text{Equity}} = \frac{\$1,350,000}{\$3,242,500} = 0.42 \ (1985)$$

$$= \frac{\$1,425,000}{\$2,725,750} = 0.52 \ (1984)$$

Activity Ratios

Activity ratios indicate how effectively a firm is using its resources. By comparing revenues with the resources used to generate them, it is possible to establish an efficiency of operation. The asset turnover ratio indicates how efficiently management is employing total assets. Asset turnover is calculated by dividing sales by total assets. For the ABC Company, asset turnover is calculated as follows:

$$\text{Asset turnover} = \frac{\text{Sales}}{\text{Total assets}} = \frac{\$8,250,000}{\$7,105,000} = 1.16 \, (1985)$$

$$= \frac{\$8,000,000}{\$6,393,000} = 1.25 \, (1984)$$

The ratio of sales to fixed assets is a measure of the turnover on plant and equipment. It is calculated by dividing sales by net fixed assets.

$$\text{Fixed asset turnover} = \frac{\text{Sales}}{\text{Net fixed assets}} = \frac{\$8,250,000}{\$2,980,000} = 2.77 \, (1985)$$

$$= \frac{\$8,000,000}{\$2,775,000} = 2.88 \, (1984)$$

Industry figures for asset turnover will vary with capital-intensive industries, and those requiring large inventories will have much smaller ratios.

Another activity ratio is inventory turnover, estimated by dividing sales by average inventory. The norm for American industries is 9, but whether the ratio for a particular firm is higher or lower normally depends upon the product sold. Small, inexpensive items usually turn over at a much higher rate than larger, expensive ones. Since inventories are normally carried at cost, it would be more accurate to use the cost of goods sold in place of sales in the numerator of this ratio. Established compilers of industry ratios such as Dun and Bradstreet, however, use the ratio of sales to inventory.

$$\text{Inventory turnover} = \frac{\text{Sales}}{\text{Inventory}} = \frac{\$8,250,000}{\$2,175,000} = 3.79 \, (1985)$$

$$= \frac{\$8,000,000}{\$2,000,000} = 4 \, (1984)$$

The accounts receivable turnover is a measure of the average collection period on sales. If the average number of days varies widely from the industry norm, it may be an indication of poor management. A too low ratio could indicate the loss of sales because of a too restrictive credit policy. If the ratio is too high, too much capital is being tied up in accounts receivable, and management may be increasing the chance of bad debts. Because of varying industry credit policies, a comparison for the firm over time or within an industry is the only useful analysis. Because information on credit sales for other firms is generally unavailable, total sales must be used. Since not all firms have the same percentage of credit sales, there is only approximate comparability among firms.

$$\begin{aligned}\text{Accounts receivable} \atop \text{turnover} = \frac{\text{Sales}}{\text{Accounts receivable}} = \frac{\$8,250,000}{\$1,760,000} = 4.69\,(1985)\end{aligned}$$

$$= \frac{\$8,000,000}{\$1,440,000} = 5.56\,(1984)$$

$$\text{Average collection period} = \frac{360}{\text{Accounts receivable turnover}}$$

$$= \frac{360}{4.69} = 77\,\text{days}\,(1985)$$

$$= \frac{360}{5.56} = 65\,\text{days}\,(1984)$$

Profitability Ratios

Profitability is the net result of a large number of policies and decisions chosen by an organization's management. Profitability ratios indicate how effectively the total firm is being managed. The profit margin for a firm is calculated by dividing net earnings by sales. This ratio is often called return on sales (ROS). There is wide variation among industries, but the average for American firms is approximately 5 percent.

$$\frac{\text{Net earnings}}{\text{Sales}} = \frac{\$410,000}{\$8,250,000} = 0.0497\,(1985)$$

$$= \frac{\$395,000}{\$8,000,000} = 0.0494\,(1984)$$

A second useful ratio for evaluating profitability is the return on investment—or ROI, as it is frequently called—found by dividing net earnings by total assets. The ABC Company's ROI is calculated as follows:

$$\frac{\text{Net earnings}}{\text{Total assets}} = \frac{\$410,000}{\$7,105,000} = 0.0577\,(1985)$$

$$= \frac{\$395,000}{\$6,393,000} = 0.0618\,(1984)$$

The ratio of net earnings to net worth is a measure of the rate of return or profitability of the stockholders' investment. It is calculated by dividing net earnings by net worth, the common-stock equity and retained-earnings account. ABC Company's return on net worth, also called ROE, is calculated as follows:

$$\frac{\text{Net earnings}}{\text{Net worth}} = \frac{\$410,000}{\$3,242,500} = 0.1264 \ (1985)$$

$$= \frac{\$395,000}{\$2,725,750} = 0.1449 \ (1984)$$

It is often difficult to determine causes for lack of profitability. The Du Pont system of financial analysis provides management with clues to the lack of success of a firm. This financial tool brings together activity, profitability, and leverage measures, and shows how these ratios interact to determine the overall profitability of the firm. A representation of the system is set forth in Exhibit 4.

The right side of the figure develops the turnover ratio. This section breaks down total assets into current assets (cash, marketable securities, accounts receivable, and inventories) and fixed assets. Sales divided by these total assets gives the turnover on assets.

The left side of the figure develops the profit margin on sales. The individual expense items plus income taxes are subtracted from sales to produce net profits after taxes. Net profits divided by sales gives the profit margin on sales. When the asset turnover ratio on the right side of Exhibit 4 is multiplied by the profit margin on sales developed on the left side of the figure, the product is the return on assets (ROI) for the firm. This can be shown by the following formula:

$$\frac{\text{Sales}}{\text{Total assets}} \times \frac{\text{Net earnings}}{\text{Sales}} = \frac{\text{Net earnings}}{\text{Total assets}} = \text{ROI}$$

The last step in the Du Pont analysis is to multiply the rate of return on assets (ROI) by the equity multiplier, which is the ratio of assets to common equity, to obtain the rate of return on equity (ROE). This percentage rate of return could, of course, be calculated directly by dividing net income by common equity. However, the Du Pont analysis demonstrates how the return on assets and the use of debt interact to determine the return on interact to determine the return on equity.

The Du Pont system can be used to analyze and improve the performance of a firm. On the left, or profit, side of the figure, attempts to increase profits and sales could be investigated. The possibilities of raising prices to improve profits (or lowering prices to improve volume) or seeking new products or markets, for example, could be studied. Cost accountants and production engineers could investigate ways to reduce costs. On the right, or turnover, side, financial officers could analyze the effect of reducing investment in various assets as well as the effect of alternative financial structures.

There are two basic approaches to using financial ratios. One approach is to evaluate the corporation's performance over several years. Financial

Exhibit 4

Du Pont's financial analysis

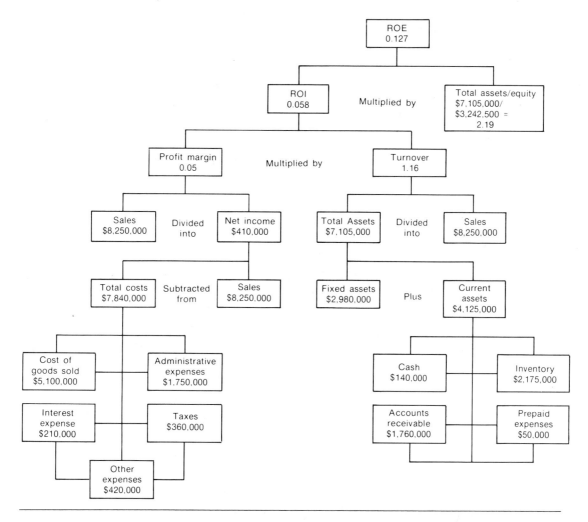

ratios are computed for different years, and then an assessment is made as to whether there has been an improvement or deterioration over time. Financial ratios can also be computed for projected, or pro forma, statements and compared with present and past ratios.

The other approach is to evaluate a firm's financial condition and compare it with the financial conditions of similar firms or with industry averages in the same period. Such a comparison gives insight into the firm's relative financial condition and performance. Financial ratios for industries are provided by Robert Morris Associates, Dun and Bradstreet, and various trade association publications. (Associations and their addresses are listed in the *Encyclopedia of Associations* or the *Directory of National Trade Associations.)* Information about individual firms is available through *Moody's Manual,* Standard and Poor's manuals and surveys, annual reports to stockholders, and the major brokerage houses.

As far as possible, accounting data from different companies must be standardized so that companies can be compared or so that a specific company can be compared with an industry average. It is important to read any footnotes of financial statements, since various accounting or management practices can have an effect on the financial picture of the company. For example, firms using sale-leaseback methods may have leverage pictures that are quite different from what is shown as debts or assets on the balance sheet.

Analysis of the Sources and Uses of Funds

The purpose of this analysis is to determine how the company is using its financial resources from year to year. By comparing balance sheets from one year to the next, one may determine how funds were obtained and the way in which these funds were employed during the year.

To prepare a statement of the sources and uses of funds it is necessary to (1) classify balance sheet changes that increase cash and changes that decrease cash, (2) classify from the income statement those factors that increase or decrease cash, and (3) consolidate this information on a sources and uses of funds statement form.

Sources of funds that increase cash are as follows:

1. A net decrease in any asset other than a depreciable fixed asset.
2. A gross decrease in a depreciable fixed asset.
3. A net increase in any liability.
4. Proceeds from the sale of stock.
5. The operation of the company (net income, and depreciation if the company is profitable).

Uses of funds include:

1. A net increase in any asset other than a depreciable fixed asset.
2. A gross increase in depreciable fixed assets.
3. A net decrease in any liability.
4. A retirement or purchase of stock.
5. Payment of cash dividends.

We compute gross changes to depreciable fixed assets by adding depreciation from the income statement for the period to net fixed assets at the end of the period and then subtracting from the total the net fixed assets at the beginning of the period. The residual represents the change in depreciable fixed assets for the period.

For the ABC Company the following change would be calculated:

Net property and plant (1985)	$1,175,000
Depreciation for 1985	+ 80,000
	$1,255,000
Net property and plant (1984)	−1,155,000
	$ 100,000

To avoid double counting, the change in retained earnings is not shown directly in the funds statement. When the funds statement is prepared, this account is replaced by the earnings after taxes, or net income, as a source of funds and dividends paid during the year as a use of funds. The difference between net income and the change in the retained-earnings account will equal the amount of dividends paid during the year. The accompanying sources and uses of funds statement was prepared for the ABC Company.

A funds analysis is useful for determining trends in working-capital positions and for demonstrating how the firm has acquired and employed its funds during some period.

ABC Company sources and uses of funds statement for 1985

Sources:	
Prepaid expenses	$ 13,000
Accounts payable	100,000
Accrued federal taxes	250,000
Dividends payable	3,750
Common stock	1,200
Additional paid-in capital	195,500
Earnings after taxes (net income)	410,000
Depreciation	80,000
Total sources	1,053,500
Uses:	
Cash	25,000
Accounts receivable	320,000
Inventory	175,000
Long-term receivables	165,000
Property and plant	100,000
Other fixed assets	20,000
Bank loans payable	75,000
Current maturities of long-term debt	8,500
Long-term liabilities	75,000
Dividends paid	90,000
Total uses	1,053,500

Conclusion

It is recommended that you prepare a chart such as Exhibit 5 so that you can develop a useful representation of these financial analyses. The chart allows a display of the ratios over time. The Trend column could be used to indicate your evaluation of the ratios over time (for example, "favorable," "neutral," or "unfavorable"). The Industry Average column could include recent industry averages on these ratios or those of key competitors. These would provide information to aid interpretation of the analyses. The Interpretation column can be used to describe your interpretation of the ratos for this firm. Overall, this chart gives a basic display of the ratios that provides a convenient format for examining the firm's financial condition.

Exhibit 5

A summary of the financial position of a firm

Ratios and working capital	1981	1982	1983	1984	1985	Trend	Industry average	Interpre- tation
Liquidity: Current								
Quick								
Leverage: Debt/Assets								
Debt/Equity								
Activity: Asset turnover								
Fixed asset ratio								
Inventory turnover								
Accounts receivable turnover								
Average collection period								
Profitability: ROS								
ROE								
ROE								
Working-capital position								

appendix C Guide to Information Sources for Use in Strategy and Policy Analysis

This basic guide is a timely and cost effective information resource for use by business executives, government officials, and academicians. In addition to classical sources of information, it includes the two newest, most popular sources: computerized on-line data bases and statistical sources.

Decisions are based on knowledge and information. The collection of relevant information is one of the most important steps in the decision-making process. Because knowledge is limited, relevant information is necessary to determine the scope of the problem and to select and implement the proper course of action. Gathering timely and precise information facilitates achievement of the desired result.

Information about the environment in which an organization operates is a vital asset and resource. Timely and reliable information about past and present conditions, constraints, and opportunities is a source of competitive power that will help an organization outperform its competitors with effective strategic decisions. Lack of information may result in great difficulties. Because decision makers operate with time and monetary constraints, there is a critical need for a selected list of available sources of information, properly annotated, which can be used in strategic decision making.

Data sources can be divided into four major categories:

Reprinted from Jugoslav S. Milutinovich, "Business Facts for Decision Makers: Where to Find Them," *Business Horizons,* March–April, 1985, pp. 63–80.

1. Government publications;
2. General reference sources of business information and ideas;
3. Specialized sources of specific data;
4. Statistical sources.

Exhibit 1 presents the organization of government publications and Exhibit 2 presents the organization of general reference sources. Each of those figures starts with an index that is followed by selected basic sources.

Well-organized decision makers must know how to search for relevant facts and information. They should have some strategy for library information research. A modified version of the Auraria library model for library research is presented in Exhibit 3. This model presents the basic steps one should follow in searching for relevant information.

Government Publications

No other entity collects more business information than the United States government. Huge quantities of primary data, most collected for governmental use, become sources of secondary data for the business community. The various departments, bureaus, agencies, and committees issue reports, statistical publications, bibliographies, and periodicals. The countless publications are excellent sources for authoritative studies and official information vitally important to business. While many works are available for a nominal charge, they are also accessible at the Department of Commerce field offices' reference libraries and Government Depository libraries.

Because of its scope, this section about Government Publications could stand alone as a source book of business information (refer to Exhibit 1). Citations are divided into four categories: Indexes; Census Data; Selected Sources of Data Generated by the Federal Government; and Selected Sources of Data Generated by the States.

Indexes

Adler, James B. *C/S/Index to Publications of U.S. Congress* (U.S. Government, Washington, DC). Published quarterly with annual cumulations, 1970 to present. Basic source for working papers of Congress. Information is in the form of abstracts of congressional documents (microfiche of actual documents available) covering the entire range of congressional publications. Two sections—indexes and abstracts. The subject title indexes use entry number referrals.

Andriot, John L., ed., *Guide to U.S. Government Publications* (U.S. Government, McLean, Va.: Documents Index). Published annually, 1973 to present. Annotated guide to publications of the various U.S. government agencies. Volume 1 contains a list of publications in existence as of

Exhibit 1

Government publications

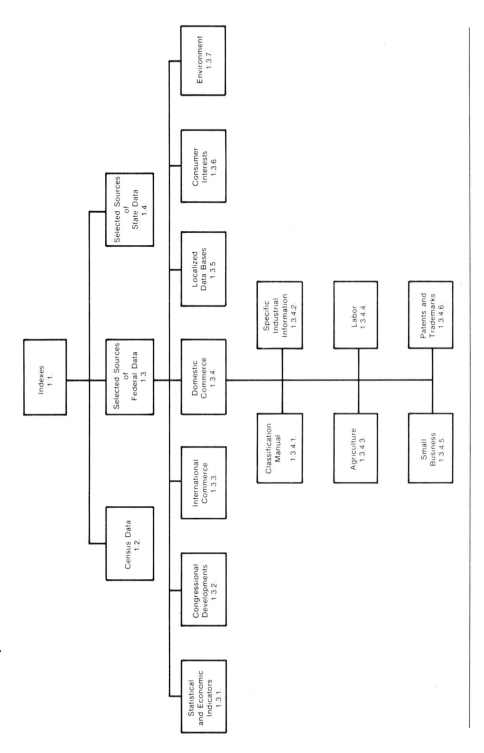

Exhibit 2

General business reference sources

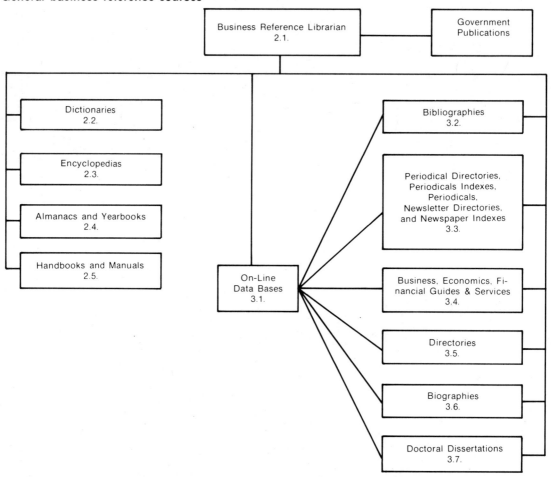

January 1973; Volume 2 covers publications of abolished agencies and discontinued publications; Volume 3 explains and outlines the Superintendent of Documents classification scheme, by which Volumes 1 and 2 are arranged. Agency and title index.

Business Service Checklist (Washington, DC: Department of Commerce). Published weekly. Serves as a guide to U.S. Department of Commerce publications and to key business indicators.

Business Services and Information: The Guide to the Federal Government (New York: Management Information Exchange, Wiley, 1978). Guide used for identifying U.S. government publications. Divided into four

Exhibit 3

Strategy for library information research

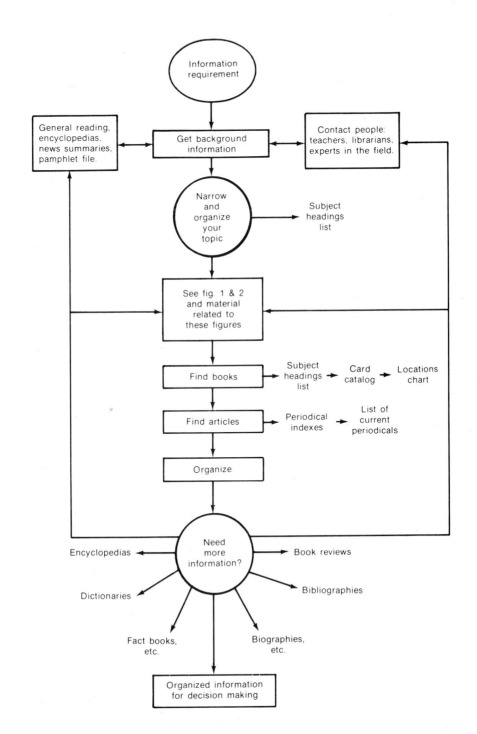

parts: Introduction; Text, which is an annotated list of publications arranged by subject; Appendix with phone numbers and agency addresses; Index.

The Federal Register (Washington, DC: Division of the Federal Register, National Archives). Published daily. Contains all regulatory matter issued by all national agencies and governmental bodies. These listings are both complete and official, and are indexed.

Code of Federal Regulations (Washington, DC: Division of the Federal Register, National Archives). Published quarterly, revised yearly. A compilation of regulations first published in *The Federal Register.*

Monthly Catalog of U.S. Government Publications (Washington, DC: U.S. Government Printing Office). Published monthly with annual cumulations. Most complete catalog available. Identifies and gives price and availability of federal documents in all subject areas. February issue includes "Directory of U.S. Government Periodicals and Subscription Publications." Includes subject, keyword, author/agency, title, and series report number indexes.

Monthly Checklist of State Publications (Washington, DC: Superintendent of Documents, GPO). Published monthly. A record of state documents and publications received by the Library of Congress.

Selected United States Government Publications (Washington, DC: Superintendent of Documents, GPO). Issued biweekly. Covers documents received by that office which are of some general interest and will be listed for sale. Each listing gives a short description of the contents of the publication, its price, and catalog number.

United States Code Congressional and Administrative News (St. Paul, Minn.: West Publishing Company). Published monthly with annual cumulations. Text of all Public Laws enacted by Congress, arranged by Public Law number, with a cumulative subject index. Includes legislative history, proclamations, executive orders, and an index of popular names of acts.

Census Data

The Bureau of the Census is by far the largest publisher of comprehensive statistical data. Its catalog, which is published monthly with annual cumulations, contains good, descriptive lists of all census publications.

The Census Bureau publishes only its most widely used censuses and surveys. Much more information is available, usually on computer tapes. This information provides limitless possibilities for subject cross-classifications or area tabulations.

The following sampling of information available through the census surveys is divided into three parts: Census Data Index; Census of Population Data; and Specific Census Data Sources.

Census Data Index

Bureau of the Census Catalog of Publications (Washington, DC: Department of Commerce, Bureau of the Census). Published quarterly with monthly supplements and annual cumulations. Complete index of Census Bureau data, including publications and unpublished materials. Main divisions are Publications, Data Files, and Special Tabulations.

Census of Population Data

Census of Population (Series PC) (Washington, DC: Department of Commerce, Bureau of the Census). Published every 10 years. Detailed characteristics of the population for states, counties, cities, and towns in a series of reports (PC(1)A-D) that give data on number of inhabitants, general population characteristics (age, sex, race, etc.), and general social and economic characteristics. Separate "Subject Reports," Series PC(2), cover statistics on ethnic groups, migration, fertility, marriage and living arrangements, education, employment, occupation and industry, and income.

Specific Census Data Sources

Produced and published to be used as major economic indicators.

Census of Agriculture (Washington, DC: Department of Commerce, Bureau of the Census). Published every five years. Reports data for all farms and for farms with sales of $2,500 or more by county and by state.

Census of Business (Washington, DC: Bureau of the Census). Published every five years. Multivolume. Tables. Contains statistical data on retail and wholesale trade and on selected service industries for the U.S., Guam, and the Virgin Islands. Arranged geographically and by Standard Industrial Classification (SIC) codes with subject reports. Issued for years ending in "2" and "7," the census is supplemented by "Monthly Retail Trade," "Selected Services Receipts," and the "Monthly Wholesale Trade" series.

Current Business Reports: Monthly Retail Trade and Accounts Receivable (Washington, DC: Bureau of the Census). Published monthly. Graphs, tables. Includes information on monthly sales for U.S. retail stores by kind of business, region, selected states, and Standard Metropolitan Statistical Areas (SMSAs). Also contains data on department stores and end-of-month accounts receivable. These reports are issued several weeks after the end of the month reported; a companion series, *Current Business Reports: Advance Monthly Retail Sales,* providing preliminary data, is issued one week after the month reported. These cumulate into an *Annual Retail Trade* series and finally into the quinquennial *Census of Business.*

Current Business Reports: Monthly Wholesale Trade (Washington, DC: Bureau of the Census). Published monthly. Graphs, tables. Contains monthly figures for wholesale inventories and sales arranged by kinds of business and geographic divisions. The reports are issued several weeks after the end of the month reported and cumulate into the quinquennial *Census of Business.*

Census of Construction Industries (Washington, DC: Bureau of the Census). Published every five years. Several volumes, maps, tables. Compiled using data from government and private organizations and reports from construction firms. Contains detailed data on construction establishments: number employed; payroll; payments and expenditures; assets; depreciation; and income. A comprehensive source of statistical data on the construction industry.

Census of Governments (Washington, DC: Bureau of the Census). Published every five years. Multivolume. Charts, graphs, tables. Important source for detailed statistics on governmental finance. Compiled using data from the Census Bureau, Census Advisory Committee on State and Local Government Statistics, and other federal agencies. Issued for years ending in "2" and "7." The following major subjects are included: governmental organization; taxable property values; public employment; governmental finance; local government; tax revenues; holdings of selected public-employment retirement systems; construction expenditures; and topical studies.

Census of Housing (Washington, DC: Bureau of the Census). Published every ten years. Multivolume.

Volume I: States and Small Areas. A presentation of detailed occupancy characteristics, structural characteristics, equipment and facilities, and financial characteristics for each state and several possessions, as well as a U.S. summary. The depth of information varies by area.

Volume II: Metropolitan Housing. A collection of data on SMSAs having 100,000 or more inhabitants, with cross-classifications of housing and household characteristics for analytical use.

Volume III: City Blocks. A collection of data that includes descriptions of conditions and plumbing facilities, average number of rooms, average contract monthly rents, average valuations, total population, number of housing units occupied by nonwhites, and number of persons per room.

Volume IV: Components of Inventory Change. A description of the physical changes that have taken place since the last census for the SMSAs with more than one million inhabitants.

Volume V: Residential Financing. Gives ownership and financial information.

Census of Manufacturers (Washington, DC: Bureau of the Census). Published every five years. Supplies data on U.S. manufacturing firms categorized under the headings of Final Area Reports and Final Industry Reports:

Final Area Reports presents statistics on value added by manufacturing, employment, payrolls, new capital expenditures, and number of establishments.

Final Industry Reports includes a series of separate reports on value of shipments, capital expenditures, value added by manufacturing, cost materials and employment for approximately 450 manufacturing industries. The data are classified by geographic region and state, employment size, class of establishment, and degree of primary products specialization.

Census of Mineral Industries (Washington, DC: Bureau of the Census). Published every five years. Tables. Compiled using data from surveys of establishments engaged in the extraction of minerals. Provides detailed data on the number of mineral industry establishments with data on employment, payrolls, assets, expenditures, consumption, costs, shipments, and receipts. This information is presented by industry, geographic area, and subject. Volume 5 of the 1972 *Census of Manufacturers* includes indexes of production for individual mineral industry groups. This data is not issued in any other form.

Census of Retail Trade (Washington, DC: Bureau of the Census). Published every five years. Compiles data for states, SMSAs and counties, and cities with populations of 2,500 or more by type of business. Data include number of establishments, sales, payroll, and personnel.

Census of Selected Services (Washington, DC: Bureau of the Census). Published every five years. Includes data on hotels, motels, beauty parlors, barber shops, and other retail service organizations. Survey also includes information on number of establishments, receipts, payrolls for states, SMSAs, counties, and cities.

Census of Transportation (Washington, DC: Bureau of the Census). Published every five years. Tables. Compiled using data from mail survey of carriers and Census of Population data. Issued for years ending in "2" and "7." Provides travel data on the civilian populations, truck inventory and use, and shipment of commodities by manufacturers. Most of this data is not publicly available elsewhere. This work is the most important cumulative general source for U.S. transportation data.

Census of Wholesale Trade (Washington, DC: Bureau of the Census). Published every five years. Presents statistics for states, SMSAs, and counties on number of establishments, sales, payroll, and personnel for kind of business.

Census Tract Reports (Washington, DC: Bureau of the Census). Published every ten years. Detailed report on population and housing.

Construction Reports (Washington, DC: Bureau of the Census). Tables. Each of the ten subseries in this series provides current statistical data on some specific aspect of the housing industry. Six of the most important periodicals: Vacant Housing Units in the U.S. (quarterly), Housing Starts (monthly), Housing Authorized by Building Permits and Public Contracts (monthly), Building Permits, Sales of New One-Family Homes (monthly), and Construction Expenditure of State and Local Tax Revenue (quarterly).

Highlights of U.S. Export and Import Trade (Washington, DC: Bureau of the Census). Published monthly. Tables. Compiled using data from the Bureau of Customs. Reports unadjusted and seasonally adjusted data on trade by commodity group, country and world area, U.S. customs regions and districts, method of shipment, and end use category. Issued two months after month of coverage. The most comprehensive of several regular trade statistical series.

Selected Sources of Data Generated by the Federal Government

Categories include statistical and national economic indicators, congressional developments, international commerce, domestic commerce, localized data bases, consumer interests, and the environment. Pertinent publications for specific industries and activities are listed under "domestic commerce."

Statistical and Economic Indicators

American Statistical Index (Washington, DC: Congressional Information Service). Published monthly with annual cumulations, 1970 to present. Important source for identifying statistical publications published by the U.S. government. Indexes and abstracts statistics on numerous topics from the publications of many government agencies. Index volume contains four separate indexes that list publications by subject and name; by geographic, economic, and demographic categories; by title; and by agency report numbers. Abstract volume gives brief descriptions of the publications and their content.

Business Conditions Digest (Washington, DC: Department of Commerce, Bureau of Economic Analysis). Published monthly. Supplemented weekly by *Advance Business Conditions Digest*. Provides a look at many of the economic time series found most useful by business analysts and forecasters. Presents approximately 600 economic time series in charts and tables. Appendixes provide historical data, series descriptions, seasonal adjustment factors, and measures of variability. Economic measures listed include: selected components of the national income and national product; measures of prices, wages, and productivity; measures of the labor force, employment, and unemployment; data on federal, state, and local government activities; measures of U.S. international transactions; and selected economic comparisons with major foreign countries. An essential economics reference tool.

Economic Report of the President (together with the Annual Report of the Council of Economic Advisors) (Washington, DC: Government Printing Office). Published annually. The annual report of the CEA comprises the major portion of this publication. Discusses economic policy and outlook and economic trends of the year. Includes statistical tables relating to income, employment, and publication.

Economic Indicators (Washington, DC: Superintendent of Documents, GPO). Published monthly. Charts, tables. A digest of current information on economic conditions of prices, wages, production, business activity, purchasing power, credit, money, and federal finance. Gives monthly figures for the past two years; frequently goes back as far as 1939.

Measuring Markets: A Guide to the Use of Federal & State Statistical Data (Washington, DC: Department of Commerce, GPO, 1974). Materials published by state and federal governments, which are useful in marketing research. Sources for population, income, employment, sales statistics, and some state taxes are included. Examples demonstrate the use of federal statistics in market analysis.

Statistical Abstract of the United States (Washington, DC: Department of Commerce, Bureau of the Census, GPO). Published annually, 1879 to present. Tables. Arranged in 34 categories, it is a reliable source for statistical summaries of the economy, business, population, and politics. Emphasis is on information of national scope, plus tables for regions, states, and some local areas. Table of contents, introductory text to each section, source notes for each table, and bibliography of sources are extremely useful guides to additional material. Subject index.

Historical Statistics of the U.S.: Colonial Times to 1970 (Washington, DC: Department of Commerce). 2 volumes. A supplement to the *Statistical Abstract of the United States,* it correlates data.

Survey of Current Business (Washington, DC: Department of Commerce, Bureau of Economic Analysis, GPO). Published monthly, 1921 to present. Official source of Gross National Product, National Income, and International Balance of Payments. Important reference for business statistics, including general economic and industrial statistics for specific products plus articles analyzing current business situations. Subject index. Statistics are indexed in *American Statistical Index* (see above). Companion publication: *Business Statistics,* weekly and biennial volumes that provide historical data for statistical series in surveys of current business.

Congressional Developments

These entries focus on activities of Congress and the federal government.

Commerce Business Daily (Washington, DC: Department of Commerce, Office of Field Operations). Published daily. Lists U.S. government procurement invitations, contract awards, subcontracting leads, sales of surplus property, and foreign business opportunities. Addresses are included. A code indicates which notices are intended wholly or in part for small businesses. The organization, by general subject categories, is not immediately apparent but can be grasped quickly by those searching regularly for particular kinds of contracts.

Congressional Quarterly (Washington, DC: Congressional Quarterly, Inc.). Published weekly, with quarterly cumulated index and an annual *CQ Almanac,* a compendium of legislation for one session of Congress. An excellent weekly service for up-to-date news on all activities of Congress and the federal government. Each issue includes the status of legislation and congressional voting charts. A record of the government for one presidential term is published every four years as *Congress and the Nation.*

U.S. Government Manual (Washington, DC: GPO). Published annually. An indispensable official handbook of the federal government. Describes personnel, purposes, and programs of most government agencies.

International Commerce

Commerce Today (Washington, DC: Department of Commerce). Published biweekly. Gives current information on commodities and foreign countries, especially those of interest to the foreign trader. Other phases covered include industrial developments, laws, and regulations of foreign countries.

Foreign Commerce Handbook: Basic Information and Guide to Sources (Washington, DC: U.S. Chamber of Commerce). Published every five years. Useful guide to foreign commerce sources.

Foreign Economic Trends and Their Implications for the United States (Washington, DC: Bureau of International Commerce). Pamphlets issued semiannually or annually for each country. Prepared by the U.S. Foreign Service/Embassies. Contains one summary table, a narrative of economic trends, and an analysis of possible implications of these trends for U.S. foreign trade.

International Economic Indicators and Competitive Trends (Washington, DC: Bureau of International Economic Policy and Research). Published quarterly. Graphs, tables. Compiled using data from the International Trade Analysis staff. Presents a variety of comparative economic statistics for the U.S. and seven major competitor nations, with an analysis of the economic outlook.

Overseas Business Reports (Washington, DC: Bureau of International Commerce). Published annually. Compiled using data from the Office of International Marketing. Each report deals with a group of countries' basic economic structure, trade regulations, practices and policies, market potential, and investment laws. Designed to aid business in gaining access to, and increasing its share of, foreign markets.

Domestic Commerce

Classification Manual

Standard Industrial Classification Manual (Washington, DC: U.S. Government Printing Office, 1973). Classifies establishments by type of activity in which engaged, to facilitate the collection, tabulation, presentation, and analysis of data, and to promote uniformity and comparability in presenting statistical data collected by various agencies of the U.S. government, state agencies, trade associations, and private research organizations. Covers entire range of economic activities.

Specific Industrial Information

This section is a sampling of reports on industrial information by many governmental departments, bureaus, agencies, and committees.

Airlines

Handbook of Airline Statistics (Washington, DC: Civil Aeronautics Board). Published annually. Data updated monthly by *Air Carrier Traffic Statistics* and quarterly by *Air Carrier Financial Statistics*. Maps, tables. Compiled using data from the Bureau of Accounts and Statistics and the U.S. Civil Aeronautics Board. Includes airline statistics for trends in passenger, freight, express, and mail revenues and traffic; flying operation expenses; aircraft expenses and depreciation; promotion, sales, and administrative expenses; and data on capital gains, interest expenses, income taxes, subsidies, dividends, investments, long-term debts, and rates of return on stockholders' equity. An essential source for background information and statistical data on the status of commercial air transportation in the U.S.

FAA Statistical Handbook of Aviation (Washington, DC: Federal Aviation Administration). Published annually. Maps, tables. Compiled using data from federal government agencies and industry organizations. Statistical data on civil aviation activity such as airports, scheduled air carrier operations, and accidents. A convenient reference for current and retrospective statistics on the aviation industry.

Banking and Finance

Corporation Income Tax Returns (Washington, DC: Internal Revenue Service). Published annually. Charts, graphs, tables. Compiled using data from estimates based on a sample of all tax returns filed during a specified period. Serves as a detailed report on corporate sources of income, assets, dividends, deductions, credits, income tax, and tax payments. Statistics are conveniently classed by industry, size of total assets, and size of business.

Federal Reserve Bulletin (Washington, DC: Board of Governors of the Federal Reserve System). Published monthly. A source of statistics on banking, deposits, loans and investments, money market rates, securities prices, industrial production, flow of funds, and various other areas of finance in relation to government, business, real estate, and consumer affairs.

Statistical Bulletin (Washington, DC: Securities and Exchange Commission). Published monthly. Charts, tables. Compiled using data from the NY and American Stock Exchanges, other registered U.S. exchanges, and periodic surveys by the SEC. Summarizes new securities offerings, trading, stock price indexes, and round-lot and odd-lot trading. Valuable to those interested in the operation and regulation of security exchange activities.

Broadcasting

Statistics of Communications Common Carriers (Washington, DC: Federal Communications Commission). Published annually. Graphs, tables. Compiled using data from monthly and annual reports filed with the FCC. Contains detailed financial and operating data, by company, for all telephone and telegraph companies and communications holding companies engaged in interstate and foreign communication service, and for the U.S. Communications Satellite Corporation. Invaluable for information about specific utilities and the communications industry in general.

Construction

Construction Review (Washington, DC: Bureau of Domestic Commerce). Published monthly. Tables. Compiled using data from federal, state, and local government agencies and trade associations. Provides current and retrospective statistical data on all aspects of the construction industry, by geographic area. Brings together virtually all current government statistics pertaining to the industry. Issues also include brief articles.

Highways

Highway Statistics (Washington, DC: Federal Highway Administration). Published annually. Data pertinent to motor fuel, motor vehicles, driver licensing, highway-user taxation, state highway financing, highway mileage, and federal aid for highways. An important source for highway transportation data.

Highway Transportation Research and Development Studies (Washington, DC: Federal Highway Administration). Published annually. A compendium describing current highway research and development activities at the federal, state, industry, and university level.

Highway Safety Literature (Washington, DC: National Highway Traffic Safety Administration). Published semimonthly; no charge. Abstracts recent literature on highway safety. International coverage. Arranged topically.

Marketing

Marketing Information Guide (Washington, DC: Department of Commerce). Published monthly. Annotations of selected current publications and reports, with basic information and statistics on marketing and distribution.

Mining and Petroleum

Minerals Yearbook (Washington, DC: Bureau of the Mines). Published annually. Three volumes. Statistics on metals, minerals, and mineral products, along with economic and technical developments and trends in the U.S. and foreign countries. Volume 1: *Metals, Minerals, and Fuels;* Volume 2: *Domestic Reports;* Volume 3: *International Reports.* Data usually apply to information gathered two to three years before data of publication.

Sales by Producers of Natural Gas to Interstate Pipeline Companies (Washington, DC: Department of Energy). Published annually. Gives sales by size groups, states, and pricing areas; sales to individual purchasers; and pipeline companies' purchases from producers, as well as their own production.

Statistics of Interstate Natural Gas Pipeline Companies (Washington, DC: Department of Energy). Published annually. Statistical compendium of financial and operating information. Includes income and earned surplus, gas operating revenues, customers and sales, capital stock and long-term debt, gas utility plant, gas accounts, physical property, and number of employees for specific companies, with industry compilations.

Mineral Industry Surveys (Washington, DC: Bureau of the Mines). Published irregularly. Charts, graphs, maps, tables. Statistical data on metals, nonmetals, and fuels, regarding production, consumption, shipments. Information also provided on fatal and non-fatal injuries, hours worked, and reports on developments in industrial safety and health programs.

Printing and Publishing

Printing and Publishing (Washington, DC: Bureau of Domestic Commerce). Published quarterly. Tables. Compiled using data from the Departments of Commerce and Labor. Statistical report on printing, publishing, and allied industries, issued four months after the month for which data is reported. Covers foreign trade by country and product, sales and profits, employment, and earnings by industry.

Railroads

Rail Carload Cost Sales by Territories (Washington, DC: Interstate Commerce Commission, Bureau of Accounts). Published annually. Includes data for rail carload mileage cost scales by district, region, and type of car, and unit costs for various weight loads by type of equipment, adjusted and unadjusted. Data grouped into seven regions of the U.S. by carriers with revenues of $5 million or more. An invaluable source of cost breakdowns for rail operations.

Transportation

Transport Economics (Washington, DC: Interstate Commerce Commission). Published quarterly. Tables. Provides analysis and summary of operating statistics, finances, equipment, and employment for carriers in interstate commerce (such as rail, motor, water, air, and pipeline). Supplements and cumulates into *Transport Statistics in the United States.*

Transport Statistics in the United States (Washington, DC: Interstate Commerce Commission). Published annually. Six parts issued separately. Maps, tables. Transport statistics on traffic operations, equipment, finances, and employment as they relate to railroads, water carriers, pipelines, motor carriers, freight forwarders, and private car lines.

Utilities

Electric Power Monthly (Washington, DC: Department of Energy). Tables. Statistics on production, fuel consumption, capacity, sales, and operating revenues and income. December issue includes data on peak loads, energy requirements, and system capacities for the previous ten years and estimates for the following ten years. Supplemented by and cumulated from *National Electric Power Generation and Energy Use Trends,* which is published quarterly.

Agriculture

Agriculture Statistics (Washington, DC: Department of Agriculture). Published annually. Tables. Compiled using data from USDA counts and estimates, census statistics, the Department of Labor, the Foreign Service, and other federal agencies. The annual agriculture reference book. Includes statistical data on acreage, yield and production of crops, commercial crops, prices paid and received by farmers, livestock production, market supplies and prices, imports and exports, farm resources, income and expenses, consumption and family living, and agricultural programs. Historical series limited to the last ten years. An indispensable tool for agribusiness. Well-indexed for quick access to specific information.

Statistical Summary (Washington, DC: Department of Agriculture, Statistical Reporting Service). Published monthly. Designed for ready reference, this report summarizes statistical data estimated for or collected on prices, sales, stocks, and production of agricultural products, such as fibers, grains, vegetables, nuts, fruits, seeds, livestock, milk, and dairy products.

Labor

Area Trends in Employment and Unemployment (Washington, DC: Manpower Administration). Published monthly. Describes area labor market developments and outlooks for 150 major employment centers, with separate brief summaries for selected areas, including those with concentrated persistent unemployment and underemployment.

Area Wage Surveys (Washington, DC: Bureau of Labor Statistics). Published annually. Tables. Issued as a subseries of the *BLS Bulletin* series. Provides occupational earnings data for nearly 100 SMSAs, published separately for each SMSA. Useful information for wage and salary administration, collective bargaining, and for determining plant location.

Directory of National Unions and Employee Associations (Washington, DC: Bureau of Labor Statistics). Published biennially. Issued as a subseries of the *BLS Bulletin* series. Includes a listing of national and international unions, summary of significant labor developments, and appendixes.

Employment and Earnings (Washington, DC: Bureau of Labor Statistics). Published monthly. Charts and tables giving data on employment, hours, earnings, and labor turnover for states, metropolitan areas, and industries.

Personnel Literature (Washington, DC: Civil Service Commission, Library). Published monthly. Lists selected books, pamphlets, government documents, unpublished dissertations, microforms, and the contents of periodicals received in the CSC Library. Because the CSC Library comprehensively collects personnel literature, this is an exceedingly useful index-bibliography for research, but it is not cumulative.

Handbook of Labor Statistics (Washington, DC: Bureau of Labor Statistics). Published annually. Tables. The basic statistical reference book on U.S. labor characteristics and conditions. Includes retrospective data and assembles in one volume the major BLS labor statistical series. Ceased publication with 1981 annual.

Labor Relations Reporter (Washington, DC: Bureau of National Affairs, Inc.). Loose-leaf books with weekly updates. Covers labor laws, fair employment practices, wages and hours, arbitration and court decisions.

Employment and Training Report of the President (Washington, DC: Manpower Administration). Published annually since 1963. Charts, graphs, and tables reporting the employment, earnings, size, and demographic characteristics of the labor force and Department of Labor manpower programs. Historical data and projections are included.

Monthly Labor Review (Washington, DC: Bureau of Labor Statistics). Published monthly. Reviews labor issues, including employment, wages, collective bargaining, industrial relations, labor law, and foreign developments. Contains statistics and book reviews.

Small Business

Small Business Bibliographies (Washington, DC: Small Business Administration). Published irregularly. Briefly describes particular business activities. Substantial bibliography includes federal, state, and nongovernmental publications. Preface to each issue may be helpful to those seeking career information.

Patents and Trademarks

Index of Patents Issued from the U.S. Patent Office (Washington, DC: Patent Office). Published annually. Two volumes. Volume 1 indexes patents listed in the year's issues of the *Official Gazette* by name of patentee. Entries include a general designation of the invention, patent number, date of issue, and classification code. Volume 2 indexes patents by subject of invention as indicated by the classification code number identified in the *Manual of Classification.* A convenient appendix is a list of libraries receiving current issues of U.S. patents and of depository libraries receiving the *Official Gazette.*

Index of Trademarks Issued from the U.S. Patent Office (Washington, DC: Patent Office). Published annually. Alphabetically indexes registrants of trademarks issued and/or published in the *Official Gazette* during the calendar year.

Localized Data Bases

Congressional District Data Book (Washington, DC: Department of Commerce, Bureau of the Census). Published irregularly. Various data from the census and election statistics for districts of the Congress. Includes maps of states with counties, congressional districts, and selected places.

County and City Data Book (Washington, DC: Department of Commerce, Bureau of the Census). Published irregularly. Various statistical information for counties, cities, SMSAs, unincorporated towns, and urbanized areas. For each county or county equivalent, 196 statistical items are given. Provides information supplemental to the *Statistical Abstract* (refer to Statistical and Economic Indicators).

County Business Patterns (Washington, DC: Department of Commerce, Bureau of the Census). Published annually. Contains county, state, and U.S. summary statistics on employment, number and employment size of reporting business units, and taxable payrolls for approximately 15 industry categories. Statistics are particularly suited to analyzing market potential, establishing sales quotas, and locating facilities.

Consumer Interests

Consumer Legislative Monthly Report (Washington, DC: Department of Health and Human Services, Office of Consumer Affairs). Published monthly when Congress is in session. Lists and briefly describes consumer-related bills introduced into the current Congress. Though summaries of bills are very brief, inclusion of bill sponsors and committees referred to gives access to further information. Topical arrangement and index are convenient to use.

Environment

102 Monitor, Environmental Impact Statements (Washington, DC: Council on Environmental Quality). Published monthly. Tables. Provides abstracts of environmental impact statements concerning proposed projects of federal agencies, as well as legislation relating to environmental impact statements.

Selected Sources of Data Generated by State Governments

This list categorizes sources of economic data. Much of the information generated at the state level is prepared by agricultural and/or business colleges of state universities.

Department of Geology or Conservation. Monographs are available from this department in most states, describing the geology of various geographic areas within the state in question. Water supply, fish and game conservation, and mineral resources of the state are also described.

Department of Health. Public health statistics are available on state births and deaths. Usually published monthly. Some states publish tracts on various diseases such as arthritis or skin infections; other publications may be available on such topics as disinfection of drinking water.

Department of Highways. Statistics, planning, and highway descriptions are available as maps and pamphlets. Data of this department will include road clearances of highway structures, public safety programs, and accident prevention projects.

Division of Insurance. Annual reports are based on the compilations of annual statements by insurance companies doing business in the state.

Division of Statistics. This division prepares monthly publications on labor statistics, such as employment, earnings, and labor supply of wage earners. Some assemble wholesale and retail trade information.

Industrial Commission. In most states, this commission puts out monthly bulletins on industrial safety and hygiene. Sometimes responsible for publicity to attract new industry to the states.

Public Utilities Commission. Statistical reports on railroads, express companies, and steam heat and telephone utilities. In many cases, annual reports provide excellent overviews of commission activities.

Statistical Reference Index (Washington, DC: Congressional Information Service). Published annually, 1980 to present. Indexes and abstracts statistical publications of state governments, associations, business organizations, commercial publishers, independent research organizations, and university research bureaus.

General Reference Sources of Business Information and Ideas

Business Reference Librarian

The business reference librarian should be consulted as a time-saving first step in gathering business facts. This specialist has the best sources at his or her fingertips and can give expert guidance. He or she compiles book-lists concerning specific areas, identifies special library collections, and is aware of books scheduled for publication. The business reference librarian is a member of the Special Libraries Association, a formal group of librarians who meet monthly, keeping abreast of the best reference material available. Through networking, the librarian is aware of the holdings in all business reference libraries in the general area and in university, public, and corporate libraries open to the public.

The business reference librarian can also tap into the interlibrary loan system—a free, cooperative exchange system of books and periodicals from member libraries across the country.

Dictionaries

Dictionaries are useful to the business manager or student wanting to check the meaning, spelling, or pronunciation of words, terms, and phrases.

Crowley, Ellen T., ed., *Acronyms, Initialisms, & Abbreviations Dictionary,* 9th ed. (Detroit: Gale Research Co., 1985). A guide to alphabetical designations, contractions, acronyms, initialisms, abbreviations. Supplemented by *New Acronyms, Initialisms, & Abbreviations.*

Filkins, James F. and Donald L. Caruth, *Lexicon of American Business Terms* (New York: Simon & Schuster, 1973). Brief dictionary containing 3,000 of the most common business terms.

French, Derek and Heather Saward, *Dictionary of Management* (New York: International Publications Service, 1975). Defines about 4,000 management and economic terms and techniques used by managers and writers about management. Includes abbreviations and brief descriptions of major associations and organizations.

Johannsen, Hano and G. Terry Pag, *International Dictionary of Management: A Practical Guide* (Boston: Houghton Mifflin, 1975). Covers the entire area of business and management. Contains 5,000 entries defining terms, concepts, initials, and acronyms in international usage, plus short descriptions on associations and organizations. Cross references.

Nemmers, E.E., *Dictionary of Economics and Business,* 4th ed. (Totowa, N.J.: Rowman & Littlefield, 1978). Paperback giving brief definitions for commonly used business terms.

Wood, Donna, ed., *Trade Names Dictionary,* 4th ed. (Detroit: Gale Research Co., 1985). Two volumes. A guide to trade names, brand names, product names, with addresses of their manufacturers, importers, marketers, or distributors. Supplemented periodically by *New Trade Names.*

Encyclopedias

Encyclopedias compile information on a wide range of topics and answer the need for basic, concise data. Entries are signed articles with frequent illustrations, plates, diagrams, maps, bibliographies, and indexes.

Akey, Denise, ed., *Encyclopedia of Associations* (Detroit: Gale Research Co.). Published annually. In-depth guide to associations. Four volumes: Vol. 1. National Organizations of the U.S.; Vol. 2. Geographic and Executive Index; Vol. 3. New Associations and Projects; Vol. 4. International Organizations.

Exporters' Encyclopedia (New York: Dun & Bradstreet). Published annually. Detailed facts on shipments to every country in the world. Covers regulations, types of communication and transportation available, foreign trade organizations, general export information, general reference tables, and listings of ports.

Schmittroth, John Jr., ed., *Encyclopedia of Information Systems and Services,* 6th ed. (Detroit: Gale Research Co., 1985). Two volumes: Vol. 1. International (excluding U.S.); Vol. 2. U.S. Describes approximately 1,500 data bases. Describes more than 2,000 organizations in U.S. and 60 other countries that produce, process, store, and use bibliographic and non-bibliographic information. Supplemented periodically by *New Information Systems and Services.*

Sullivan, Linda E., ed., *Encyclopedia of Governmental Advisory Organizations,* 3rd ed. (Detroit: Gale Research Co., 1980). Reference guide to presidential advisory committees, public advisory committees, and other government related boards, panels, task forces, commissions, and conferences that serve in a consulting, coordinating, advisory, research, or investigative capacity.

Wasserman, Paul, C. Georgi, and J. Woy, *Encyclopedia of Business Information Sources,* 5th ed. (Detroit: Gale Research Co., 1983). Quick survey of basic information sources covering 1,215 subjects. Provides specific citations, dealing with a single point, with the business manager in mind. Includes reference works, periodicals, trade associations, statistical sources, and on-line data bases.

Almanacs and Yearbooks

Almanacs are collections of current factual information covering a broad range of topics.

World Almanac and Book of Facts (New York: Newspaper Enterprise Association). Published annually. Facts on many diverse subjects.

Yearbooks are factbooks providing current information. They usually give more information than almanacs.

Commodity Year Book (New York: Commodity Research Bureau). Published annually. Statistical yearbook with data on production, prices, stocks, exports, and imports for more than 100 commodities. Editorial comments on new developments affecting commodities.

Statesman's Year Book (New York: St. Martin's Press). Published annually. First three sections are factual data about international organizations, U.S. & Commonwealth countries. Final section provides descriptive data and statistics on other countries, including history, government, population, and commerce.

Handbooks and Manuals

Business handbooks and manuals are excellent reference tools that present concise introductions to the concepts, procedures, and techniques for specific managerial functions. These compendiums are well organized and indexed, providing easy access to the precise information needed.

Albert, Kenneth J., ed., *The Strategic Management Handbook* (New York: McGraw, 1983). Discusses concepts, principles, and practices of strategic management. Contains how-to material, highlighted with real-life cases and examples. Written by experts from management consulting firms, Fortune 500 companies, and top business schools.

Davidson, Sidney and Roman Weil, eds., *Handbook of Modern Accounting*, 3rd ed. (New York: McGraw, 1983). Illustrated. Defines important terms and procedures. Covers recent developments, their implications and applications.

Fettridge, Clark and Robert S. Minor, eds., *Office Administration Handbook* (Chicago: Dartnell Corp., 1981). Discusses methods of handling office, personnel, and administrative problems.

Grikscheit, Gary M., Harold C. Cash, and W.J.E. Crissy, *Handbook of Selling: Psychological, Managerial, and Marketing Bases* (New York: Wiley, 1981). Discusses selling strategy and tactics. Deals with how to organize information about a customer and answer customer objections.

Makridakis, Spyros and Steven C. Wheelwright, eds., *The Handbook of Forecasting: A Manager's Guide* (New York: Wiley-Interscience, 1983). Explains which forecasting methods work and which do not. Divided into four sections: role and application of forecasting in organizations; approaches to forecasting; methods and forecasting challenges for the 1980s; and managing the forecasting function.

Scheer, Wilbert E., *Personnel Administration Handbook* (Chicago: Dartnell Corp., 1979). Reference book for personnel managers or administrators. Covers wage and salary administration, labor relations, interviewing, recruiting, hiring, measuring work performance, merit increases, and terminations.

Stansfield, Richard H., *Advertising Manager's Handbook* (Chicago: Dartnell Corp., 1982). Reference book on advertising strategies. Case studies included. Covers such topics as the campaign concept, copy, art, budgeting, and media selection.

Walmsley, Julian, *The Foreign Exchange Handbook: A User's Guide* (New

York: Wiley-Interscience, 1983). Provides an in-depth coverage of major currency markets. Discusses some of the economic and technical influences on currency and money markets. Other topics covered include financial futures and gold markets, payment systems, and exposure management and control. Provides standard foreign exchange calculations and money market formulas.

Specialized Sources of Specific Data

On-Line Data Bases

The information explosion can be attributed to computer technology, which has revolutionized the search for business facts. By using a data base, which is an organized collection of information in a particular subject area, decision makers benefit from the accessibility and adaptability of massive resources now available. This tool is an expensive one, but is certainly cost-effective when measured by time savings. Total cost depends on the data bases selected for the search, the amount of time used, and the number of references retrieved.

The actual process of a computer search is a simple one. A questionnaire is completed, specifically describing the problem and indicating important authors, journals, or key facts useful in retrieving references. While the search is being completed, computer, librarian, and researcher interact in redirecting and redefining. Citations can be printed immediately or mailed within five business days.

Three major vendors offer on-line interactive search access to hundreds of data bases. Bibliographic Retrieval Services (BRS), Scotia, N.Y., and DIALOG/Lockheed Informations Services in Palo Alto, Cal., store general bibliographic data; some of their data bases overlap. The third, SDC Search Service, System Development Corporation, Santa Monica, Cal., emphasizes technical and statistical information.

Listings of computer based services can be found in the following directories.

Directory of Computer Based Services (Washington, DC: Telenet Communications Corp.). Published annually. Lists data banks, commercial service bureaus, educational institutions, and companies that offer interactive computer based services to the public through the nationwide Telenet network. Lists data bases that may be accessed, a brief description of the contents, and identifies those offering the data base.

Directory of On-line Information Resources (Rockville, Md.: CSG Press, 1980). Easy-to-use guide to selected, publicly accessible bibliographic and non-bibliographic on-line data bases. 225 data bases available, file descriptions, coverage, and size. Subject and source index; phone and address list of data base suppliers.

The business data bases are divided into three areas: bibliographies, statistics, and directories.

Bibliographies: On-line interactive search access to various bibliographic data bases.

ABI/INFORM. August 1971 to present. 134,636 records. All phases of business management and administration. Stresses general decision sciences information that is widely applicable. Includes specific product and industry information. Scans 400 primary publications in business and related fields.

Management Contents (Skokie, Ill.: Management Contents, Inc.). 1974 to present, with monthly updates. Current information on a variety of business and management related topics for use in decision making and forecasting. Articles for 200 U.S. and foreign journals, proceedings, and transactions are fully indexed and abstracted to provide up-to-date information in areas of accounting, design sciences, marketing, operations research, organizational behavior, and public administration.

Monthly Catalog of U.S. Government Publications (Washington, DC: U.S. Government Printing Office). Published monthly with annual cumulations (see entry under Government Publications Indexes). 101,401 records of reports, studies, fact sheets, maps, handbooks, and conferences.

New York Times Information Bank (see entry under Periodicals).

PAIS International Bulletin (New York: Public Affairs Information Service). Published monthly, 1976 to present. Worldwide coverage of more than 800 English-language journals and 6,000 non-serial publications. 136,653 citations.

Predicasts Terminal System (Cleveland: Predicasts, Inc.). Bibliographic and statistical data base providing instant access to many business journals and other special reports for searches of current articles, statistics, geographic location of companies. Abstracts a wide range of periodical abstracts and indexes.

Statistics: In-depth statistics easily adapted for a wide variety of manipulations.

Economic Time Series:

Business International/Data Time Series (Business International Corp.).
PTS/U.S. Time Series (Predicasts, Inc.).

Marketing Statistics:

BLS Consumer Price Index (Department of Labor, Bureau of Labor Statistics).
BLS Producer Price Index (Department of Labor, Bureau of Labor Statistics).

Financial Statistics:

Disclosure II (Washington, DC: Disclosure, Inc.). 1977 to present. Updated weekly. Extracts of reports filed with the U.S. Securities and Exchange Commission by publicly owned companies. 11,000 company reports provide a reliable and detailed source of public financial and administrative data. Source of information for marketing intelligence, corporate planning and development, portfolio analysis, legal and accounting research.

Directories: Arranged by subject, title, geographic location, and code numbers.

CATFAX: Directory of Mail Order Catalogs.
EIS Industrial Plants (Economic Information Systems, Inc.).
Foreign Traders Index (Department of Commerce).
Trade Opportunities (Department of Commerce).

Bibliographies

Bibliographies, lists of printed sources of information on a topic, are the most important starting point for business facts. They can quickly lead the business executive or student to original available sources of information on a specific topic.

Bibliographic Index: A Cumulative Bibliography of Bibliographies (Bronx, N.Y.: H.W. Wilson Co.). Published three times annually. Lists, by subject, sources of bibliographies containing 50 or more citations of books, pamphlets, and periodicals.

Bibliography of Publications of University Bureaus of Business and Economic Research: The AUBER Bibliography (Boulder, Col.: Association for University Business and Economic Research). Published annually. Bibliography of publications that do not appear in other indexes. Written by bureaus of business and economic research and members of the American Association of Collegiate Schools of Business. Includes books, series, working papers, and articles published by each business school. Divided into two parts: subject and institution. Author index.

Brownstone, David M. and Gorton Carruth, *Where to Find Business Information: A Worldwide Guide for Everyone Who Needs the Answers to Business Questions,* 2nd ed. (New York: John Wiley & Sons, 1982). List of 5,000 current foreign and domestic, private and public business information sources.

Business Books in Print (New York: R.R. Bowker). Published irregularly. (Note: same information available in the "Business" portion of the Subject Index of *Books in Print,* which is published annually.) Presents finding, ordering, and bibliographic data for more than 31,500 books and periodicals from U.S. publishers and university presses on business, finance, and economics. Indexed by author, title, and business subjects. Directory of publishers.

Business Literature (Newark, N.J.: Public Library of Newark, Business Library). Published ten times each year. Annotated lists of current business topics.

Business and Technology Sources (Cleveland: Cleveland Public Library). Published quarterly. Bulletin developed to cover one subject per issue; lists numerous other publications concerning the topic.

Core Collection: An Author and Subject Guide (Boston: Harvard University Baker Library). 1971 to present. Revised annually. Selective listing of more than 4,000 English-language business books in the Harvard Business School Library. Lists books by author and subject.

Daniells, Lorna M., comp., *Business Reference Sources: An Annotated Guide for Harvard Business School Students,* revised edition (Boston: Harvard University Baker Library, 1979). Comprehensive annotated bibliography of entire field of business covering selected books and reference sources.

Figueroa, Oscar and Charles Winkler, *A Business Information Guidebook* (New York: AMACAM, 1980). Useful first point of reference for locating sources of business and economic information.

Management Information Guides (Detroit: Gale Research Co.). A group of bibliographic references to business information sources in many fields. Each volume includes general reference works, film strips, government and institutional reports. Two examples of this source are:

Norton, Alice, *Public Relations Information Sources* [Management Information Service Guide No. 22] (Detroit: Gale Research Co., 1970). Annotated bibliography of general sources, public relation tools, and international public relations.

Service to Business and Industry (New York: Brooklyn Public Library, Business Library). Published ten times each year. Annotated bibliographies covering current business topics.

Subject Catalogue: A Cumulative List of Works Represented by Library of Congress Printed Cards (Washington, DC: U.S. Library of Congress). Published quarterly, with yearly and five-year cumulated editions, 1950 to present. Comprehensive current annotated bibliography on every subject from all parts of the world. Cross reference of subject headings is an important guide suggesting many different, appropriate headings on subjects in several standard sources, opening up new resources. A good starting point in an information search.

Tega, Vasie G., *Management and Economics Journals: A Guide to Information Sources* (Detroit: Gale Research Co., 1977). Bibliography of periodicals in the fields of management and economics.

Vernon, K.D.C., ed., *Use of Management and Business Literature* (Woburn, Mass.: Butterworths, 1975). Bibliography of information published in the English language on business and management. Includes a description of British publications and library practices, forms of business information, and surveys of literature in corporate finance, management, accounting, organizational behavior, manpower management and industrial relations, marketing, computers, and quantitative methods and production.

Wasserman, Paul, C. Georgi, and J. Woy, *Encyclopedia of Business Reference Sources,* 5th ed. (Detroit: Gale Research Co., 1983). Survey of basic information tolls covering 1,215 subject sources (see Encyclopedias). Includes reference works, periodicals, trade associations, statistical sources, and on-line data bases.

Periodical Directories, Periodical Indexes, Periodicals, Newsletter Directories, and Newspaper Indexes

Periodical directories are helpful reference tools for finding major industry publications relevant to a specific area.

Business Publication Rates and Data (Skokie, Ill.: Standard Rate and Data Service, Inc.). Published monthly. Index to business, trade, and technical publications arranged by "market served" classifications.

Ulrich's International Periodicals Directory (New York: R.R. Bowker Co.). Published annually. Subject index of more than 55,000 entries for in-print periodicals published worldwide. Contains "Abstracting and Indexing Services" chapter.

Periodical indexes are valuable sources of current information for a broad scope of subjects. Abstracts provide the added feature of descriptive notation.

Accountants Index (New York: American Institute of Certified Public Accountants). Published quarterly with annual cumulations. Comprehensive index of English-language books, pamphlets, government documents, and articles on accounting and related fields. Author, title, and subject listing.

Business Periodicals Index (New York: Wilson Company). Published monthly with quarterly and annual cumulations, 1958 to present. Cumulative subject index covering 270 business periodicals in the English language. Subject categories are very specific. Separate book review index follows subject index in the annual volume.

Cumulative Index (New York: Conference Board). Published annually. Useful subject index for wide range of studies, pamphlets, and articles that the Conference Board research firm has published in the areas of business economics, corporate administration, finance, marketing, personnel, international operations, and public affairs. Covers material published during the past 20 years, with emphasis on the most recent 10 years.

Current Contents: Social and Behavioral Sciences (Philadelphia: Institute for Scientific Information). Published weekly, 1961 to present. Reproduces the tables of contents of journals in business, management, economics, computer applications, and other disciplines in social and behavioral sciences. Worldwide coverage of 1,330 journals. Subject, author, and publishers' address indexes.

Predicasts' F&S Index United States (Cleveland: Predicasts, Inc.). Published weekly, with monthly, quarterly, and annual cumulations, 1960 to present. Index covering company, industry, and product information from business-oriented periodicals and brokerage house reports in the U.S. Information arranged by company name, SIC number, and company according to SIC groups.

Predicasts' F&S Index International. Same as above, except that it gives information about the rest of the world, excluding Europe.

Predicasts' F&S Index Europe. Same as *F&S International,* but with coverage of European continent only.

Index of Economic Articles (Homewood, Ill.: Richard D. Irwin, Inc.). Published annually. Bibliographies from 200 English-language journals on articles, communications, papers, and proceedings discussions. Classified index and author index.

Management Contents (Skokie, Ill.: G.D. Searle & Co.). Published biweekly. Reproduction of the tables of contents of a selection of 150 of the best business/management journals. Each issue can be scanned for significant articles. Now available as on-line data base.

Public Affairs Information Service Bulletin (PAIS) (New York: Public Affairs Information Service). Published weekly, 1915 to present. Cumulations five times each year and annually. Selective subject index of current books, yearbooks, directories, government documents, pamphlets plus 1,000 periodicals relating to national and international economic and public affairs. Factual and statistical information. Brief annotations of entries. Now available as on-line data base.

Work Related Abstracts (Detroit: Information Coordinators). Published monthly with annual indexes, 1972 to present. Abstract of articles, dissertations, and books concerning labor, personnel, and organizational behavior. Loose-leaf format. Arranged by subject in 20 categories. Subject index. Subject headings list published annually.

Business periodicals feature articles of use and interest to business managers and students. Specialized journals report new research findings and developments. Two examples of general business periodicals are:

Business Week (New York: McGraw-Hill). Published weekly. Business news magazine with concise articles on new business trends and developments. Special issues: Survey of Corporate Performance and Investment Outlook. Indexed in BPI, F&S, PAIS (see indexes).

Fortune (New York: Time, Inc.). Published monthly. Topics of general interest cover new products and industries, politics and world affairs, biographical information. May issue: Fortune 500/500 largest U.S. industrial corporations. Indexed in BPI, F&S, and PAIS (see indexes).

Other general business periodicals include: *Across the Board; Barron's National Business and Financial Weekly; Business Briefs; Boardroom Reports; Columbia Journal of World Business; Commerce Business Daily; Commercial and Financial Chronicle; Dun's; Forbes; Nation's Business;* and *Supervisory Management.*

Academic journals are also important periodicals. Three examples are:

Business Horizons (Bloomington: Indiana University Graduate School of Business). Published bimonthly. Readable articles, balanced between practice and theory, of interest to management and academicians. Indexed in BPI, F&S, and PAIS.

Harvard Business Review (Boston: Harvard University Graduate School of Business Administration). Published bimonthly. Professional management journal featuring practical articles on all aspects of general management and policy. Indexed in BPI, F&S, and PAIS.

Journal of Business (Chicago: University of Chicago Business School). Published quarterly. Scholarly journal geared to professional and academic business and economic theory and methodology. Includes short subject list of books. Indexed in BPI, F&S, and PAIS.

Each major industry issues publications containing specific information concerning their field. Some examples are:

Advertising Age (Chicago: Crain Communications, Inc.). Published weekly. February issue, "Agency Billings," provides data on advertising agencies ranked by billings for the year. August issue, "Marketing Profiles of the 100 Largest National Advertisers," provides data on leading product lines, profits, advertising expenditures, and names of marketing personnel.

Sales Management (New York: Bill Communications, Inc.). Published semimonthly. "Survey of Buying Power," published in July and October issues, is a prime authority on U.S. and Canadian buying income, buying power index, cash income, households, merchandise line sales, population, and retail sales information. National and regional summaries, market ratings, and metro-market and county-city market data by states.

Some important management journals are: *The Journal of Creative Behavior; California Management Review; Human Relations; Administrative Science Quarterly; Academy of Management Review; Sloan Management Review; Academy of Management Journal; Organizational Behavior and Human Performance; Industrial and Labor Relations Review; Personnel Psychology.*

Newsletters of trade associations and professional societies can provide valuable business facts and services. The following directories are useful in finding the appropriate newsletter:

National Directory of Newsletters and Reporting Services (Detroit: Gale Research Co., 1981). Lists and provides information on newsletters and publications closely akin to newsletters issued regularly by business, associations, societies, clubs, and government agencies. Features reference guide to national and international services, financial services, association bulletins, and training and educational services. Cumulative subject, publisher, and title indexes.

Oxbridge Directory of Newsletters (New York: Oxbridge Communications, Inc.). Published annually. Lists 5,000 U.S. and Canadian newsletters in 145 subject areas along with advertising and subscription rates, description of contents, names of key personnel, and names, addresses, and telephone numbers of the publishers.

Newspaper indexes are helpful sources of information about current events and newsworthy materials not appearing in other types of periodicals.

New York Times Index (New York: The New York Times Co.). Published every two weeks with annual cumulations. Dates back to 1851. Detailed index summarizing and classifying news alphabetically by subject, persons, and organizations. Cross references. Also on-line data base from January 1969.

Wall Street Journal Index (New York: Dow Jones Company, Inc.). Published monthly with annual cumulations, 1958 to present. Complete report on current business. Subject index of all articles that have appeared in the *Journal,* grouped in two sections: Corporate News and General News.

Business, Economics, and Financial Guides and Services

Business services are information agencies that compile, interpret, and distribute data on specific subjects. These guides are kept up to date by revised and supplemental data issued on various schedules.

Babson's Business Service (Babson Park, Mass.: Business Statistics Organization, Inc.). Issued in three bulletins:

Business Inventory-Commodity Price Forecasts. Published monthly. Pertinent discussions on business topics as well as short sketches of supply, demand, price, and buying advice of major commodities.

Business Management-Sales and Wage Forecasts. Published monthly. Covers current problems on labor and wages; keeps abreast of current developments in sales and buying power. *Babson's Washington Service* is published by the same organization.

Babson Weekly Staff Letter covers current trends and business problems.

Business and Investment Service (New York: International Statistical

Bureau, Inc.). Published weekly. Analyses of production in basic industries. Includes political analyses of interest. Section entitled "Selected Securities Guide" presents stock market trends and indexes, as well as earnings and prices of stocks in selected industries. Additional services available are a quarterly security list; a monthly trend of distribution; a foreign newsletter; and postwar reports.

Chase Manhattan Foreign Trade Service (New York: Chase Manhattan Bank). Published annually with additional supplements. Service for Chase Manhattan Bank customers gives foreign exchange and export trade information for many countries.

Dun and Bradstreet Credit Service (New York: Dun and Bradstreet). Published every two months. Collects, analyzes, and distributes credit information on manufacturers, wholesalers, and retailers. Includes general information on the character, experience, and ability of the enterprise, plus a highly detailed statement covering the antecedents, methods of operation, financial statement analysis, management progress, and payment record for each entry. Also operates a foreign division.

Grant, Mary M. and Norma Cote, eds., *Directory of Business and Financial Services,* 7th ed. (New York: Special Libraries Association, 1976). (Note: new edition planned for 1985.) Guide to existing national and international business, economic, and financial services describing 1,051 publications issued by 421 publishers. Each listing includes coverage, frequency, price, and addresses. Arranged alphabetically by title; publisher and subject index use referral numbers.

John Herling's Labor Letter (Washington, DC: John Herling's Labor Letter). Published weekly. Gives current information on labor topics, legislation, and opinions in Washington.

The Kiplinger Washington Letter (Washington, DC: Kiplinger Washington Agency). This is a condensed and confidential letter to subscribers. It analyzes economic and political events and attempts some forecasting. The news service features continuous events and reports from the "grass roots" membership. Additional publications include: *Kiplinger Tax Letter,* published biweekly, which reviews federal tax legislation, and *Kiplinger Agricultural Letter,* published biweekly, which gives pertinent developments affecting agriculture.

Moody's Bond Record (New York: Moody's Investors Service). Published weekly. Provides statistics, prices, and other information for bonds of all types, including municipals.

Moody's Dividend Record (New York: Moody's Investors Service). Published weekly. Gives current information on dividend declarations, payment dates, exdividend dates, dividend dates, income bond interest payments, payments on bond and default, stock split-ups, stock subscription rights, and preferred stocks called.

Moody's Handbook of Common Stocks (New York: Moody's Investors Service). Published quarterly. Covers more than 1,000 selected common stocks listed alphabetically. Each company page has a 10-year statistical history, a 15-year price chart, the company's background, recent developments, and investment quality. Industry cross-index.

Moody's Manuals (New York: Moody's Investors Service). Published semi-weekly with annual cumulations, 1900 to present. Major investment service composed of seven financial manuals: *Moody's Transportation Manual; Moody's Public Utilities Manual; Moody's Bank and Finance Manual; Moody's Industrial Manual; Moody's OTC Industrial Manual; Moody's International Manual; Moody's Municipal and Government Manual.* Provides corporate news and financial information on American, Canadian, and foreign companies listed on U.S. stock exchanges. Loose-leaf news reports, covering corporate news releases, are issued twice each week. Annual volumes include brief company history, subsidiaries, plants, officers and directors, products, and financial data. Special features pertinent to subject area. All titles indexed in *Moody's Complete Corporate Index* (pamphlet).

Moody's Stock Survey (New York: Moody's Investors Service). Published weekly. Presents data on stocks including recommendations for purchase, sale, or exchange of individual stocks. Discussions on industry trends and developments.

Standard and Poor's Corporation Services (New York). Offer comprehensive investment data weekly, with annual cumulations. Their publications include: *American Exchange Stock Reports; Bond Outlook; Called Bond Record; Convertible Bond Reports; Daily Dividend Record; Facts and Forecast Service* (daily); *Industry Issues; The Outlook; Stock Reports: Over-the-Counter and Regional Exchanges; Standard NYSE Stock Reports.*

Standard Rate and Data Service (Wilmette, Ill.). Issues 12 volumes of publishing rates and data on the following areas: Business Publications (monthly); Canadian Advertising (monthly); Consumer Magazine and Farm Publications (monthly); Direct Mail Lists (semiannually); Networks (bimonthly); Newspapers (monthly); Print Media Production Data (semiannually); Spot Radio (monthly); Spot Television (monthly); Transit Advertising (quarterly); Weekly Newspaper (semiannually); plus a Newspaper Circulation Analysis.

Trading Areas and Population Data in Eastern United States (New York: Hagstrom). Issues a number of maps of the metropolitan New York, Philadelphia, and adjacent areas. These are city, county, and special area maps giving detailed information useful to marketing and forecasting.

United Business and Investment Report (Boston). Published weekly. This investment service offers a commentary on the current situation with a forecast of business, financial, and economic conditions.

Loose-leaf services offer efficient, up-to-date information, especially for business law topics and taxes. Laws, regulations, rules, orders, and decisions, along with explanations and interpretations, are set up in loose-leaf volumes. Weekly or biweekly packets include new revisions in an effort to keep the business community current with frequent changes in the federal and state laws.

The following are the major loose-leaf services.

Bureau of National Affairs, Inc., Washington, DC. Issues reports on government actions which affect labor, management, and legal professions. Some of its reports are:

Daily Report for Executives. Overnight service. Discusses such topics as legislation in Congress, tax rulings and decisions, transportation rulings, and price and cost trends.

Daily Labor Report. Overnight service. Discusses important labor-management agreements, major NLRB and court decisions.

Business International Corporation, New York. Publishes information about worldwide business problems and opportunities, emphasizes international management, laws, regulations and business forecasts. Its loose-leaf services are:

Financing Foreign Operations (New York: Business International). Published weekly. Eight-page weekly report for managers of worldwide operations.

Investing, Licensing and Trading Operations Abroad (New York: Business International). Published monthly. Current information for each country on foreign investment, competition, and price.

Commerce Clearing House Services, Chicago. Publishes more than 100 loose-leaf reports, covering various topics in the fields of tax and business regulatory law. Publications include *Federal Banking Law Reports, Government Contracts Reports, Contract Appeals Decisions, Insurance Law Reports.*

Prentice-Hall Services, Englewood Cliffs, N.J. Publishes loose-leaf reports covering the latest laws and regulations. Gives comments and interpretations of the laws. Publications include: *American Federal Tax Reports, Tax Court Service, Tax Ideas, Prentice-Hall Management Letter.*

Directories

Directories provide brief data on companies, organizations, or individuals. They are used for a variety of purposes: to determine the manufacturer of a specific product; to check companies located in a particular area; to verify company names, addresses, and telephone numbers; and to identify company officers.

Benjamin, William A., ed., *Directory of Industry Data Sources: U.S. and Canada,* 2nd ed. (Cambridge, Mass.: HARFAX, 1982). Three volumes. Includes more than 15,000 annotated entries describing a wide range of information sources on 60 industries. Arranged in 5 parts: general reference sources; industry data sources; directory of all publishers mentioned in part 2; extensive subject and title indexes.

Consultants and Consulting Organizations Directory, 6th ed. (Detroit: Gale Research Co., 1984). Indexes over 8,000 firms, people, and organizations involved in consulting. Main arrangement is geographic, with subject, personal name, and organization name indexes.

Corporate 500: The Directory of Corporate Philanthropy, 2nd ed. (Detroit: Public Management Institute, 1982). Data about corporate philanthropy of the nation's 500 largest corporations. Lists eligible activities, corporate headquarters, board and committee members, contact people, and grant recipients.

Darnay, Brigitte T., ed., *Directory of Special Libraries and Information Centers,* 8th ed. (Detroit: Gale Research Co., 1983). Three volumes: Special Libraries and Information Centers in the United States and Canada; Geographic and Personnel Indexes; New Special Libraries. Provides information about holdings, services, and personnel of more than 16,000 special libraries, information centers, documentation centers.

Directory of Corporate Affiliations (Skokie, Ill.: National Register Publishing Co., Inc.). Published annually with quarterly updates titles *Corporate Action.* Lists 3,000 American parent companies with their 16,000 divisions, subsidiaries, and affiliates.

Ethridge, James M., ed., *The Directory of Directories,* 3rd ed. (Detroit: Gale Research Co., 1985). Nearly 7,000 informative, up-to-date listings of current directories. 2,100 subject headings and cross references.

Kruzas, Anthony T. and Robert C. Thomas, eds., *Business Organizations & Agencies Directory,* 2nd ed. (Detroit: Gale Research Co., 1984). Supplies exact names to write, phone, or visit for current facts, figures, rulings, verifications, and opinions on business matters. Names agencies, associations, groups, federations, organizations, and, whenever possible, authorized contact people.

Kruzas, Anthony T. and Kay Gill, eds., *Government Research Centers Directory,* 2nd ed. (Detroit: Gale Research Co., 1982). Identifies research and development facilities funded by the government. Describes research centers, bureaus and institutes, testing and experiment stations, statistical laboratories.

Kruzas, Anthony T. and Kay Gill, eds., *International Research Centers Directory,* 2nd ed. (Detroit: Gale Research Co., 1984). Identifies and describes research and development facilities throughout the world (excluding the U.S.). Includes government, university, and private installations.

Million Dollar Directory (New York: Dun and Bradstreet). Published annually in three volumes. Lists 39,000 U.S. companies worth $1 million or more. Gives officers and directors, products or services, SIC number, sales, and number of employees. Division, geographic, location indexes. Also available as on-line data base.

National Trade and Professional Associations of the U.S. and Canada and Labor Unions (Washington, DC: Columbia Books, Inc.). Published annually. Listing of trade and professional organizations and labor unions with national memberships. Key word, geographic, and budget size indexes.

Rand McNally International Banker's Directory. Published semiannually. Multi-volume. Referred to as the "Blue Book." Contains names of officers and directors of all banks in the world. Details include basic principles and practices of banking, with the latest information on all domestic and foreign banks, statements, personnel, U.S. banking, and commercial laws. Also includes the most accessible banking points for 75,000 nonbanking towns and Federal Reserve Districts and banks.

Reference Book (New York: Dun and Bradstreet Marketing Services Division). Published every two months. Available only to customers of D&B Business Information Reports. Detailed lists of names and addresses of U.S. firms by state, city, SIC code, line of business, estimated financial strength, and credit appraisal. Information can be retrieved in any desired sequence.

Research Centers Directory, 9th ed. (Detroit: Gale Research Co., 1984-85). Listings include research institutes, centers, foundations, laboratories, bureaus, experiment stations, and similar nonprofit research facilities, activities, and organizations in the U.S. and Canada. Identifies special research facilities and their availability for use by outsiders. Contains sections on business, economic, and multidisciplinary programs. Subject research center and institutional indexes.

Research Services Directory, 2nd ed. (Detroit: Gale Research Co., 1982). Lists for-profit organizations providing research services on a contract or fee-for-service basis to clients. Covered research activities include business, education, energy and the environment, agriculture, government, public affairs, social sciences, art and the humanities, physical and earth sciences, life sciences, and engineering and technology.

Schmittroth, John, Jr., ed., *Telecommunications Systems and Services Directory* (Detroit: Gale Research Co., 1983). 3 parts. Four indexes, cumulative in each part. Provides descriptions of communications systems serving the need for rapid and accurate transmission of data, voice, text, and images. Covers voice and data communications networks, teleconferencing, videotex and teletext, electronic funds transfer, telex, facsimile, and two-way cable television.

Standard and Poor's Corporation Records (New York: Standard and Poor's Corp.). Published semimonthly in loose-leaf format, 1925 to present. Corporate news and financial information on American, Canadian, and foreign companies. Provides company history, officers, and product data. *Daily News* covers current corporate developments. Indexes to main entry and subsidiaries.

Standard and Poor's Register of Corporations, Directors and Executives

(New York: Standard and Poor's Corp.). Published annually, 1928 to present. Vol. 1: Alphabetical list of U.S. and Canadian corporations includes product or line of business, SIC code, and number of employees. Vol. 2: Alphabetical list and brief biography of executives in U.S. and Canada. Vol. 3: Indexes corporations by SIC code, geographic area, new individuals, obituaries, and new companies.

Surveys, Polls, Censuses, and Forecasts Directory (Detroit: Gale Research Co., 1983). Describes studies conducted in many areas including economics, business, science, technology.

Thomas Register of American Manufacturers (New York: Thomas Publishing Co.). Published annually. Comprehensive U.S. directory restricted to manufacturing firms. Vols. 1-7 are indexes to manufacturers by product; Vol. 7 includes a list of trade names. Vol. 8 lists manufacturers by company name, including information similar to Standard & Poor's *Register.* Vols. 9-12 are compilations of manufacturers' catalogues.

Wasserman, Paul and Marek Kaszubski, eds., *Law and Legal Information Directory,* 2nd ed. (Detroit: Gale Research Co., 1982). Guide to national and international organizations, bar associations, the federal court system, federal regulatory agencies, law schools, continuing legal education, paralegal education, scholarships and grants, awards, prizes, special libraries, information systems and services, research centers, legal periodical publications, book and media publishers.

Wasserman, Paul and Janice McLean, eds., *Training & Development Organizations Directory,* 3rd ed. (Detroit: Gale Research Co., 1983). Contains profiles on 1,967 individuals and organizations that conduct training and development programs for business, industry, and governments.

Biographies

Biographical reference books are useful sources of information regarding people, living or deceased. They provide dates of birth and death, nationality, and information about occupations.

Dun and Bradstreet's Reference Book of Corporate Management (New York: Dun and Bradstreet). Published annually. Directory of top executives arranged by company, birthdate, college, and employment history.

Who's Who in America (Chicago: Marquis Who's Who, Inc.). Published every two years. Biographies of prominent living Americans.

Who's Who in Consulting (Detroit: Gale Research Co., 1983). Reference guide to professional personnel engaged in consultation for business, industry, and government.

Who's Who in Finance and Industry (Chicago: Marquis Who's Who, Inc.). Published every two years. Contains brief biographies of financial and industrial, national and international leaders.

Marquis Who's Who Publications/Index to All Books (Chicago: Marquis

Who's Who, Inc.). Published annually. An index to 250,000+ biographical sketches currently contained in Marquis' *Who's Who* volumes.

Doctoral Dissertations

Somewhat obscure sources of research are the unpublished doctoral dissertations required in university PhD programs. These are clearly indexed and available on photocopies or microfilm:

American Doctoral Dissertations (Ann Arbor, Mich.: University Microfilms International). Published annually. A complete listing of all doctoral dissertations accepted at American and Canadian universities. Arranged by broad subject classification, and, under each heading, alphabetically by name of university. Author index. Publication is slow.

Dissertation Abstracts International (Ann Arbor, Mich.: University Microfilms International). Published monthly. Section A: The Humanities and Social Sciences; Section B: The Sciences; Section C: European Dissertations. Informative abstracts of dissertations submitted by more than 345 cooperating institutions. Arranged in same categories as *American Doctoral Dissertations;* each issue is a detailed "Keyword Title Index." *DATRIXII* offers a personalized search service for all past and current dissertations.

Statistical Sources

Statistics are an absolute necessity to decision makers. They are becoming increasingly valuable and available through computer on-line data bases. The most comprehensive compilations are provided by governmental agencies, universities, and trade associations. These statistics determine U.S. and regional business trends. Data are also gathered for specific industries. Examples are banking and monetary statistics; labor and marketing statistics; and plant and equipment expenditures studies. Other sources concentrate on important international statistics and foreign economic trends.

Statistical sources are divided into two major sections: indexes and selected statistical sources for general information, and international and industrial marketing statistics.

Indexes

Predicasts, Inc., *Predicasts Forecasts* (Cleveland: University Circle Research Center). Published quarterly, cumulated annually. Abstracts business and financial forecasts for specific U.S. industrial products and the general economy. Presents composite data for economic, construction, energy, and other indicators.

Standard and Poor's Trade and Securities Statistics (New York: Standard and Poor's Corp.). Loose-leaf, with monthly supplements. Current and basic statistics in the following areas: banking and finance; production and labor; price; indexes (commodities); income and trade; building and building materials; transportation and communications; electric power and fuels; metals; auto, rubber and tires; textiles, chemicals, paper; agricultural products; security price index record.

Wasserman, P., J. O'Brien, and K. Clansky, *Statistics Sources: A Subject Guide to Data on Industrial, Business, Social, Educational, Financial and Other Topics for the U.S. and Internationally,* 9th ed. (Detroit: Gale Research Co., 1984). Finding guide to statistics indexes information from domestic and international sources. Arranged dictionary style; includes selected bibliography of key statistical sources.

Selected Statistical Sources

General

Levine, Sumner N., ed., *The Dow Jones-Irwin Business and Investment Almanac* (Homewood, Ill.: Dow Jones-Irwin). Published annually. Tables and graphs. Most basic, comprehensive statistical information on various aspects of business, finance, investments, and economics for recent trends. Includes articles on tax, accounting, and labor developments. Subject index.

Industry

Many business projects involve gathering statistical and/or investment data on a particular industry. The following sources provide useful statistics on leading industries and analyze current trends and future projections.

Balachandran, M., *A Guide to Trade and Securities Statistics* (Ann Arbor, Mich.: Pierian Printing, 1977). Specialized guide of composite statistical data available in 30 of the most widely used loose-leaf services and statistical yearbooks. Analyzed on an item-by-item basis, using a subject/keyword approach. Sources are listed and described at the front of the volume.

Real Estate Analyst Reports (St. Louis: Wenzlick Research Co.). Published monthly. Loose-leaf real estate analyses include: *The Agricultural Bulletin; As I See* (commentary); *Construction Bulletin; Mortgage Bulletin; Real Estate Analyst.*

Yearbook of Industrial Statistics (New York: United Nations). Published annually. Supplemented monthly in *Monthly Bulletin of Statistics.* Vol 1: General Industrial Statistics. A body of international statistics on population, agriculture, mining, manufacturing, finance, trade, and education. Vol. 2: Supplies internationally comparable data on the production of industrial commodities internationally.

Marketing

Access to current statistical data is essential to those engaged in market research. Marketing departments attempting to determine sales potential, set sales quotas, or establish effective sales territories are interested in details such as population, number of households, age, sex, marital status, occupation, education level, income, and purchasing power. Much of this information is available from U.S. government sources. Individual states also publish statistical series, often on a more timely basis than the federal government. Private companies also generate data applicable to marketing functions.

Commercial Atlas and Marketing Guide (Chicago: Rand McNally Services). Published annually, 1884 to present. Includes maps for each state in the U.S. and a section of maps of foreign countries. Marketing statistics for states and some worldwide data, such as airline and steamship distances, are provided. Also included are population statistics and figures for retail sales, bank deposits, auto registrations, etc., for principal cities.

Editor and Publisher Market Guide (New York: Editor and Publisher). Published annually, 1884 to present. Market data are provided for more than 1,500 U.S. and Canadian cities in which newspapers are published. Included are figures for population, households, principal industries, and retail outlets. Estimates are given by county and newspaper city, and strategic market segment analysis is performed for such items as population and personal income. Total retail sales are arranged by state.

Survey of Business Power Data Service (New York: Sales and Marketing Management). Published annually, 1977 to present. A spin-off of the July and October statistical issues of *Sales and Marketing Management* magazine. Arranged in three volumes: Volume 1, county and city population characteristics, such as household distribution, effective buying income, total retail store sales, and various buying power indexes; Volume 2, retail sales by individual store groups and merchandise line. Volume 2 includes retail sales by individual store groups and merchandise line categories for the current year; Volume 3, TV market data, metro area and county projections for population, effective buying income, and retail sales.

International

International Marketing Handbook (Detroit: Gale Research Co., 1981). Provides a marketing profile of 138 nations. Data regarding transportation and utilities, credit, foreign trade outlook, investment, industry trends, distribution sales, advertising and research, trade regulations, and market profile. 1983 supplement.

Consumer Europe 1982, 4th ed. (Detroit: Gale Research Co., 1982). Provides data on the production, sales, and distribution of more than 150 consumer product categories. Focuses on Western Europe.

European Marketing Data and Statistics (London: Euromonitor Publications Ltd.). Published annually. The volume's 70,000 statistics provide current marketing data on the population, employment, production, trade, economy, consumer expenditures, market sizes, retailing, housing, health and education, culture and mass media, and communications of Europe's 26 major countries.

Handbook of the Nations, 3rd ed. (Detroit: Gale Research Co., 1983). Provides political and economic data for 190 countries. Economic data includes statistics on the GNP, agriculture, major industries, electric power, exports, imports, major trade partners, and the budget.

Index to International Statistics (Washington, DC: Congressional Information Service). Published monthly, with quarterly and annual cumulations. Indexes publications of international intergovernmental organizations, such as the U.N., the Common Market, and the World Bank. Geographic index is included.

International Marketing Data and Statistics (London: Euromonitor Publications Ltd.). Published annually. Handbook that supplies statistical tables and latest data for 45 countries in the Americas, Africa, Asia, and Australia. Information is geared toward marketing use.

Japan Trade Directory (Tokyo: Japan External Trade Organization, 1984–85). Provides information about 1,700 Japanese companies and their 8,500 products and services. Three sections: products and services, prefectures and companies, advertising.

Stopford, John M., ed., *World Directory of Multinational Enterprises,* 2nd ed. (Detroit: Gale Research Co., 1982). Two volumes. Provides information on 550 multinational corporations, with five-year financial summaries. Ranks corporations according to sales, diversification, and other criteria.

Wasserman, Paul and Jacqueline O'Brien, *Statistics Sources,* 9th ed. (Detroit: Gale Research Co., 1984). Facts and figures on 12,000 subjects for nearly every country in the world. Arranged in dictionary style with cross-references, it cites annuals, yearbooks, directories, and other publications.

World Bank Annual Report (Washington, DC: World Bank). Published annually. Tables. Summarizes the activities of the World Bank and International Development Association. Reviews economic trends in developing countries, capital flow, and external public department.

World Business Cycles (London: The Economist Newspapers Ltd., 1982). Provides business and economic data for three decades (1950 to 1980) for many countries worldwide. Also provides longer term data for Great Britain and the United States.

World Trade Annual (New York: Walker & Co.). Published annually. Five volumes offering statistics and detailed information on various aspects of the world trade situations.

Sources from which this article was compiled:

Bernard Bernier, Katherine Gould, and Humphrey Porter. *Popular Names of U.S. Government Reports* (Washington, DC: Library of Congress, 1976).

David M. Brownstone and Gorton Carruth. *Where to Find Business Information. A Worldwide Guide for Everyone Who Needs the Answers to Business Questions* (New York: John Wiley and Sons, 1979).

Lorna M. Daniells. *Business Information Sources* (Berkeley, Calif.: University of California Press, 1976).

Oscar Figueroa and Charles Winkler. *A Business Information Guidebook* (New York: AMACOM, 1980).

C.R. Goeldner and Laura M. Dirks. "Business Facts: Where to Find Them," *MSU Business Topics,* Summer 1976, pp. 23–36.

Andrew S. Grove. *High Output Management* (New York: Random House, 1983).

Richard L. King, ed. *Business Serials of the U.S. Government* (Chicago: American Library Association, 1978).

Linda J. Piele, John C. Tyson, and Michael B. Sheffey. *Materials and Methods for Business Research,* Library ed. (New York: The Libraryworks, 1980).

Paul Wasserman, C.C. Georgi, and J. Woy. *Encyclopedia of Business Information Sources,* 4th ed. (Detroit: Gale Research Co., 1980).